Standard Catalog of®

MILITARY FIREARMS

The Collector's Price and Reference Guide

3RD EDITION

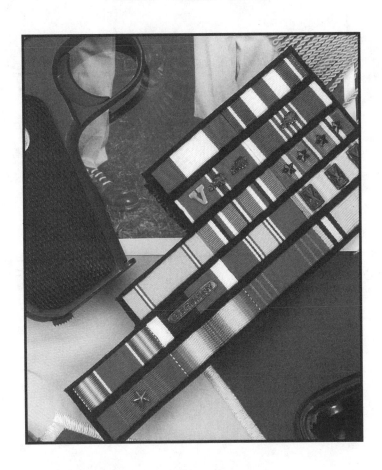

NED SCHWING

Published by

Gun Digest®Books

An imprint of F+W Publications

700 East State Street • Iola, WI 54990-0001
715-445-2214 • 888-457-2873

Please call or write for our free catalog of publications.
Our toll-free number to place an order or obtain a free catalog is 800-258-0929
or please use our regular business telephone 715-445-2214.

Library of Congress Catalog Number: 2005906841

ISBN: 0-87349-902-6

Printed in the United States of America

Designed by Patsy Howell
Edited by Kevin Michalowski

Cover photos by Paul Goodwin

The morale and matériel are interdependent.
Weapons without courage are ineffective, but so are
the bravest troops without sufficient weapons to protect
them and their morale. Courage soon oozes when
soldiers lose confidence in their weapons

Captain Sir Basil Lindell Hart, 1944

In Flanders Fields

In Flanders fields the poppies grow
Between the crosses, row on row,
That mark our place; and in the sky
The larks, still bravely singing, fly
Scarce heard amid the guns below

We are the Dead. Short days ago
We lived, felt dawn, saw sunset glow,
Loved, and were loved, and now we lie
In Flanders fields

Take our quarrel with the foe:
To you from failing hands we throw
The torch: be yours to hold it high.
If ye break faith with us who die
We shall not sleep, though poppies grow

In Flanders fields

John McCrae

CONTENTS

DIRECTORY

ACKNOWLEDGMENTS

Orvel Reichert is a collector of World War II-era semi-automatic pistols, especially the P38, and has been an invaluable help in sorting out a sometimes confusing array of pistol variations. He can be reached at P.O. Box 67, Vader, WA 98593, 360-245-3492, e-mail address: mr.p38@localaccess.com

Joe Gaddini, of SWR, has provided invaluable technical assistance on Class III firearms and suppressors. He can be reached at 119 Davis Road, Suite G-1, Martinez, GA 30907, 706-481-9403.

Thanks to Eric M. Larson for his knowledgeable information on Federal gun laws.

A special thanks to Simeon Stoddard, former curator of the Cody Firearms Museum, for his research and contribution on the M1 Garand rifle.

Nick Tilotta is an expert on Thompson submachine guns. He helped to explain all of the subtle differences between models and variations. He can be reached at P.O. Box 451, Grapevine, TX 76099, 817-481-6616.

Don Westmoreland is a serious student of Japanese and German World War II automatic weapons. His knowledge was extremely valuable.

Stan Andrewski, a crackerjack gunsmith, can be reached at 603-746-4387 for those who desire nothing but the best in the way of repair and refinishing work on their Class III firearms.

Dan Shea, editor and publisher of the *Small Arms Review*, lent his mastery of Class III firearms.

Ted Dawidowicz of Dalvar, USA made photos available of currently imported Polish military firearms. He may be reached at 740 E. Warm Springs Rd. Ste. #122, Henderson, NV 89015, 702-558-6707.

I want to thank Jim Alley of I.D.S.A. Books for his expert advice concerning the scope of this book based on his encyclopedic knowledge of military books. He was also generous with the use of his extensive personal library. Jim can be reached at P.O. Box 1457-G, Piqua, OH 45356, 937-773-4203.

Blake Stevens, Collector Grade Publications, shared his vast knowledge of military firearms as well as photos from his first-class publications. Blake can be reached at P.O. Box 1046, Cobourg, Ontario, Canada K9 4W5, 905-342-3434.

A special thanks to all the manufacturers and importers who supplied us with information and photographs on their products.

Ted Willems and Bruce Wolberg of *Gun List* have been most helpful with information and locating hard-to-find firearms.

Many thanks to J.B. Wood for taking the time to point out, "a few discrepancies" in the 1st edition.

Ricky Kumor Sr. spent much of his valuable time making constructive suggestions and sharing his bottomless expertise of military firearms.

James Rankin gave freely of his vast experience as an author and small arms expert to steer this book in the right direction. His assistance is gratefully acknowledged.

Mark Keefe, editor of the *American Rifleman*, is a keen student of military firearms. He was particularly helpful on Lee-Enfield rifles with small but important details that are so useful to the collector.

A special note of appreciation to Chuck Karwan, one of the contributing editors of this book, who gave unselfishly of his enormous store of knowledge of military firearms.

Richard R. Wray, one of the deans of the Class III community with 50 years of experience, and Ken Keilholtz with over 30 years of experience, both extremely knowledgeable Class III collectors, gave generously of their time and expertise to make this a more useful and more accurate publication. Photos of their comprehensive collections are seen throughout this book.

J.R. Moody willingly gave of his time and expertise based on his years of practical hands-on experience with Class III weapons and sniper rifles.

Many thanks to Pedro Bello for sharing his extensive experience and knowledge of machine pistols.

Charlie Cutshaw provided valuable assistance on hard-to-find information about rarely encountered weapons.

Paul Miller shared with us his deep knowledge of military firearms.

John M. Miller's, CWO, U.S. Army (Ret), assistance was invaluable from his vast knowledge of firearms built on his extensive collection and practical experience.

Bob Naess is a wealth of information on a wide variety of machine guns and their values as well as their availability. Bob can be reached at 802-226-7204.

Mike LaPlante went out of his way to straighten out the maze of variations that are to be found in the Colt M16 and AR-15 series of weapons.

I want to thank the contributing editors of this publication who have given of their time and knowledge to make this a better book. Any errors or omissions in this book are entirely the editor's responsibility.

PHOTO CREDITS

Many of the large-format photos in this book were taken by Paul Goodwin, a photographer of exceptional ability.

A special acknowledgment to Kris Leinicke, curator of the Rock Island Arsenal Museum, for allowing us full access to the museum's outstanding firearms collection.

Karl Karash supplied photos from his personal Colt 1911 collection.

Jim Rankin has an extensive library of photos he was kind enough to share with the readers.

Robert Fisch, curator of the museum at the United States Military Academy at West Point, was most helpful and cooperative in sharing that institution's wonderful treasure trove of historically important firearms.

Blake Stevens, Collector Grade Publications, furnished many outstanding photos from his comprehensive books.

Robert Segel lent photos of his superb collection of vintage machine guns, beautifully photographed and displayed.

Many thanks to Charles Kenyon for the use of photos for his forthcoming book on Luger pistols.

Chuck Karwan shared many photos from his extensive photo archives of military firearms.

Ricky Kumor Sr. photographed many of the rare and high quality military weapons that flow through his shop.

Tom Nelson of Ironside International Publishers kindly permitted us to reprint some of his photos of rare weapons from his outstanding series of books on automatic firearms.

John M. Miller helped with photos of early military firearms.

Paul Scarlata was generous not only with photos from his outstanding military rifle books, but with historical photos as well.

Ryerson Knight was most helpful with photos of pocket pistols.

My thanks to Dr. Leonardo M. Antaris for the use of the outstanding photos from his book, *Star Firearms*.

INTRODUCTION

The 3rd edition of the *Standard Catalog of Military Firearms* features improved and expanded sections of the popular M1 Garand and M1 Carbine. These rifles are readily available to the collector, and supplies, for the most common examples, are affordable. Variations have been defined more sharply due to valuations of the more rare examples. The collector should pay close attention to the originality of each rifle as this determines value. Many M1 Garand and M1 carbines have been refinished therefore losing their collectable value. This advice applies to all military collectables as well.

The number of photos has been increased to 1,750 to give the collector a better idea of what he may encounter, and what to look for in the way of features and markings. More photos mean more information to the collector.

We have also added more auction results of rare and seldom encountered firearms. This auction feature is not necessarily important for pricing information, as one sale does not make a value, but rather as a chance for the reader to see what has come on the market. This is an opportunity for us to observe weapons that we would not normally encounter, and in some cases it may be the only glimpse of a really rare firearm.

The "Snap Shot" feature continues to be popular with readers. It offers the opportunity for readers to have a vicarious look and feel of firearms we may never be able to handle, much less shoot. In this edition our writers continue to give their knowledgeable opinions on a wide variety of weapons.

Good luck with your collecting and be safe in your shooting.

Ned Schwing
Editor

GRADING SYSTEM

In the opinion of the editor all grading systems are subjective. It is our task to offer the collector and dealer a measurement that most closely reflects a general consensus on condition. The system we present seems to come closest to describing a firearm in universal terms. We strongly recommend that the reader acquaint himself with this grading system before attempting to determine the correct price for a particular firearm's condition. Remember, in most cases, condition determines price.

NIB—New in Box
This category can sometimes be misleading. It means that the firearm is in its original factory carton with all of the appropriate papers. It also means the firearm is new; that it has not been fired and has no wear. This classification brings a substantial premium for both the collector and shooter.

Excellent
Collector quality firearms in this condition are highly desirable. The firearm must be in at least 98 percent condition with respect to blue wear, stock or grip finish, and bore. The firearm must also be in 100 percent original factory condition without refinishing, repair, alterations, or additions of any kind. Sights must be factory original as well. This grading classification includes both modern and antique (manufactured prior to 1898) firearms.

Very Good
Firearms in this category are also sought after both by the collector and shooter. Firearms must be in working order and retain approximately 92 percent metal and wood finish. It must be 100 percent factory original, but may have some small repairs, alterations, or non-factory additions. No refinishing is permitted in this category. Both modern and antique firearms are included in this classification.

Good
Modern firearms in this category may not be considered to be as collectable as the previous grades, but antique firearms are considered desirable. Modern firearms must retain at least 80 percent metal and wood finish, but may display evidence of old refinishing. Small repairs, alterations, or non-factory additions are sometimes encountered in this class. Factory replacement parts are permitted. The overall working condition of the firearm must be good as well as safe. The bore may exhibit wear or some corrosion, especially in antique arms. Antique firearms may be included in this category if their metal and wood finish is at least 50 percent original factory finish.

Fair
Firearms in this category should be in satisfactory working order and safe to shoot. The overall metal and wood finish on the modern firearm must be at least 30 percent and antique firearms must have at least some original finish or old re-finish remaining. Repairs, alterations, nonfactory additions, and recent refinishing would all place a firearm in this classification. However, the modern firearm must be in working condition, while the antique firearm may not function. In either case, the firearm must be considered safe to fire if in a working state.

Poor
Neither collectors nor shooters are likely to exhibit much interest in firearms in this condition. Modern firearms are likely to retain little metal or wood finish. Pitting and rust will be seen in firearms in this category. Modern firearms may not be in working order and may not be safe to shoot. Repairs and refinishing would be necessary to restore the firearm to safe working order. Antique firearms will have no finish and will not function. In the case of modern firearms, their principal value lies in spare parts. On the other hand, antique firearms in this condition may be used as "wall hangers" or as an example of an extremely rare variation or have some kind of historical significance.

Pricing Sample Format

NIB	Exc.	V.G.	Good	Fair	Poor
550	450	400	350	300	200

PRICING

The prices given in this book are __RETAIL__ prices.

Unfortunately for shooters and collectors, there is no central clearinghouse for firearms prices. The prices given in this book are designed as a guide, not as a quote. This is an important distinction because prices for firearms vary with the time of the year and geographical location. For example, interest in firearms is at its lowest point in the summer. People are not as interested in shooting and collecting at this time of the year as they are in playing golf or taking a vacation.

It is not practical to list prices in this book with regard to time of year or location. What is given is a reasonable price based on sales at gun shows, auction houses, *Gun List* prices, and information obtained from knowledgeable collectors and dealers. The firearms prices listed in this book are **RETAIL PRICES** and may bring more or less depending on the variables discussed above. If you choose to sell your gun to a dealer, you will not receive the retail price but instead a wholesale price based on the markup that particular dealer needs to operate.

Also, in certain cases there will be no price indicated under a particular condition but rather the notation "**N/A**" or the symbol "—". This indicates that there is no known price available for that gun in that condition or the sales for that particular model are so few that a reliable price cannot be given. This will usually be encountered only with very rare guns, with newly introduced firearms, or more likely with antique firearms in those conditions. Most antique firearms will be seen in the good, fair, and poor categories.

One final note. The prices listed here come from a variety of sources: retail stores, gun shows, individual collectors, and auction houses. Due to the nature of business, one will usually pay higher prices at a retail store than at a gun show. In some cases, auctions will produce excellent buys or extravagant prices, depending on any given situation. Collectors will sometimes pay higher prices for a firearm that they need to fill out their collection, when in other circumstances they will not be willing to pay market price if they don't have to have the gun. The point here is that prices paid for firearms is an ever-changing affair based on a large number of variables. The prices in this book are a **GENERAL GUIDE** as to what a willing buyer and willing seller might agree on. You may find the item for less, and then again you may have to pay more depending on the variables of your particular situation.

Sometimes we lose sight of our collecting or shooting goals and focus only on price. Two thoughts come to mind. First, one long time collector told me once that, "you can never pay too much for a good gun." Second, Benjamin Franklin once said, "the bitterness of poor quality lingers long after the sweetness of a low price."

In the final analysis, the prices listed here are given to assist the shooter and collector in pursuing their hobby with a better understanding of what is going on in the marketplace. If this book can expand one's knowledge, then it will have fulfilled its purpose.

There is one pricing comment that should be made about military firearms in particular. The prices given in this book for foreign firearms are for guns that do not have an importer's stamp affixed to them. This stamping became a federal requirement in 1968. The importer's stamp was required to be placed on the receiver or frame of the firearm in a conspicuous location. To many collectors this makes little difference in their collecting. To others it makes a significant difference and this group will pay more for firearms without an importer's stamp.

Note also that the prices listed below for Class III weapons reflect the gun only with one magazine and no accessories. The prices for medium and heavy machine guns do not include bipods or tripods. These necessary items are extra. Buyer and seller should note that machine gun mounts come in various configurations. Mounts may range in price from several hundred dollars to several thousand dollars depending on type.

A further caution regarding the buying and selling of Class III firearms. These weapons are highly restricted by federal law. Some states do not allow its citizens to own these firearms. Because the value of these Class III firearms lies not only in the historical and technical significance of the weapon, it also lies in the grandfathered paper that accompanied each gun. The values sited in this publication can change overnight if federal or state law changes. Be aware. Be cautious.

EDITOR'S REQUEST: Guns that are rare, scarce, obscure, or seldom traded are difficult if not impossible to price. We have provided prices as an estimate only. The editor welcomes any information that would improve pricing for these uncommon items.

ADDITIONAL CONSIDERATIONS

Perhaps the best advice is for the collector to take his time. Do not be in a hurry and do not allow yourself to be rushed into making a decision. Learn as much as possible about the firearms you are interested in collecting or shooting. Try to keep current with prices through *Gun List* and this publication. Go to gun shows, not just to buy or sell but to observe and learn. It is also helpful to join a firearms club or association. These groups have older, experienced collectors who are glad to help the beginner or veteran. One of the best starting points in firearms collecting is to read as much as possible. There are many first-rate publications available to the beginner and veteran collector alike that will not only broaden his knowledge of a particular collecting field, but also entertain and enlighten as well.

In the preparation of this book, I have encountered a vast number of models, variations, and subvariations. It is not possible to cover these in the kind of detail necessary to account for every possible deviation in every model produced. The collector needs to read in-depth studies of models and manufacturers to accomplish this task. Knowledge and experience together fashion the foundation for successful collecting.

Firearms collecting is a rewarding hobby. Firearms are part of our nation's history and represent an opportunity to learn more about their role in that American experience. If done skillfully, firearms collecting can be a profitable hobby as well.

AUCTION HOUSE CREDITS

The following auction houses were kind enough to allow the Catalog to report unusual firearms from their sales. The directors of these auction concerns are acknowledged for their assistance and support.

Amoskeag Auction Company, Inc.
   250 Commercial Street, Unit #3011
   Manchester, NH 03101
   Attention: Jason or Melissa Devine
   603-627-7383
   603-627-7384 FAX

Bonhams & Butterfield
   220 San Bruno Avenue
   San Francisco, CA 94103
   Attention: James Ferrell
   415-861-7500 ext. 3332
   415-861-8951 FAX

Old Town Station Ltd.
   P.O. Box 15351
   Lenexa, KS 66285
   Attention: Jim Supica
   913-492-3000
   913-492-3022 FAX

Rock Island Auction Company
   1050 36th Avenue
   Moline, IL 61265
   Attention: Patrick Hogan
   800-238-8022
   309-797-1655 FAX

Greg Martin Auctions
   660 Third Street, Suite 100
   San Francisco, CA 94107
   800-509-1988
   415-522-5706 FAX

Little John's Auction Service, Inc.
   1740 W. La Veta
   Orange, CA 92868
   Attention: Carol Watson
   714-939-1170
   714-939-7955 FAX

THE EDITOR

Ned Schwing is the author of:

Five books on Winchester and Browning firearms. His latest book is *The Winchester Collector's Pocket Guide.* His articles have appeared in the *American Rifleman, Guns Illustrated, Shooting Sportsman, Waffen Digest, Double Gun Journal,* and other firearm publications.

CONTRIBUTING EDITORS

Bob Ball
   Springfield Armory & Mauser rifles
   P.O. Box 562
   Unionville, CT 06085

Bailey Brower
   Savage military pistols
   P.O. Box 111
   Madison, NJ 07940

Jim Cate
   J.P. Sauer pistols
   406 Pine Bluff Dr.
   Chattanooga, TN 37412
   423-892-6320

Jason Devine
   Winchester lever actions
   250 Commercial Street, Unit #3011
   Manchester, NH 03101
   603-627-7383
   603-627-7384 FAX

Gene Guilaroff
   Modern military firearms
   P.O. Box 173
   Alvaton, KY 42122
   270-622-7309
   e-mail: arclight@nctc.com

Karl Karash
   Colt Model 1911 & 1911A1
   288 Randall Road
   Berlin, MA 01503
   978-838-9401
   987-589-2060 FAX

Chuck Karwan
   Colt New Service, Browning High-Power,
   Lee-Enfield, Webley revolvers
   958 Cougar Creek Road
   Oakland, OR 97462
   541-459-4134

Richard M. Kumor Sr.
   c/o Ricky's Gun Room
   WWII era military firearms
   P.O. Box 286
   Chicopee, MA 01021
   413-592-5000
   413-594-5700 FAX
   e-mail: Rickysinc@aol.com
   Web site: rickysinc.com

CWO John M. Miller (U.S. Army, Ret.)
   19th and 20th century military small arms
   c/o Ned Schwing
   Krause Publications
   700 E. State St.
   Iola, WI 54990

Gale Morgan
   Luger and Mauser pistols
   Pre-World War I pistols
   P.O. Box 72
   Lincoln, CA 95648
   916-645-1720

Robert E. Naess
   Class III guns of all types
   P.O. Box 471
   Cavendish, VT 05142
   802-226-7204
   e-mail: margoc@mail.tds.net

Jerry Prasser
   Recon Ordnance Company
   Class III & military weapons
   P.O. Box 829
   Fond du Lac, WI 54936
   920-922-1515
   920-922-0737 FAX

Jim Rankin
   Walther pistols & pre-war auto pistols
   3615 Anderson Road
   Coral Gables, FL 33134
   305-446-1792

Orvel Reichert
   World War II-era semiautomatic
   pistols
   P.O. Box 67
   Vader, WA 98593
   360-245-3492
   e-mail: mr.p38@localaccess.com

Joe Schroeder
   Steye/Mannlicher pistols
   P.O. Box 406
   Glenview, IL 60025
   847-724-8816
   847-657-6500
   847-724-8831 FAX

John Stimson Jr.
   High Standard pistols
   540 W. 92nd St.
   Indianapolis, IN 46260
   317-831-2990

Simeon Stoddard
   Swiss, Swedish, and Finnish rifles
   P.O. Box 2283
   Cody, WY 82414

Jim Supica
   Smith & Wesson
   P.O. Box 15351
   Lenexa, KS 66285
   913-492-3000

Nick Tilotta
   Western Firearms Co.
   Thompson submachine guns
   P.O. Box 451
   Grapevine, TX 76099
   817-481-6616
   817-251-5136 FAX
   www.westernfirearms.com

Denis Todd
   M16s
   239 Baltimore Pike
   Springfield, PA 19064
   610-543-7300
   dtoddmg@aol.com

Michael Wamsher
   World War I & II Weapons
   17732 West 67th Street
   Shawnee, KS 66217
   913-631-0686

BIBLIOGRAPHICAL NOTES

There are a number of excellent comprehensive books on military history for the period that this volume covers. Perhaps the best, at least in my opinion, are two outstanding studies by Edward Ezell. They are: *Small Arms of the World,* 12th edition, Stackpole Books, 1983, and *Handguns of the World,* Stackpole Books, 1981.

For early military revolvers, the two-volume work by Rolf H. Muller, *Geschichte und Technik der Europaischen Militarrevolver,* Journal-Verlag Schwend, 1982, is excellent.

For modern military weapons, *Jane's Infantry Weapons* gives a broad overview, with technical data, of just about any modern military weapon in use in recent times.

Donald Webster's book, *Military Bolt Action Rifles, 1841-1918,* Museum Restoration Service, 1993, filled some important gaps in information on early bolt action rifles.

There are additional titles that are of interest and offer beneficial information: *Pistols of the World,* 3rd ed., Hogg and Weeks, DBI Books, 1992. *Rifles of the World,* John Walter, DBI Books, 1993. *Military Small Arms of the 20th Century,* 7th ed., Hogg and Weeks, Krause Publications, 1999. *Small Arms Today,* 2nd ed., Edward Ezell, Stackpole Books, 1988. *The Greenhill Military Small Arms Data Book,* Ian Hogg, Greenhill Books, 1999. *Modern Machine Guns,* John Walter, Greenhill Books, 2000. *The Encyclopedia of Modern Military Weapons,* Chris Bishop, ed., Barnes & Noble, 1999. *The World's Submachine Guns,* Vol. I, Thomas B. Nelson, 1964. *The World's Assault Rifles,* Vol. II, Musgrave and Nelson, 1967. *The World's Fighting Shotguns,* Vol. IV, Thomas F. Swearengen, Ironside, 1978. *Flayderman's Guide to Antique American Firearms...and Their Values,* 7th edition, Krause Publications, 1998. Paul S. Scarlata's *Collecting Classic Bolt Action Military Rifles,* Andrew Mobray Publishers, 2001, gives a good overview of this field for the collector. I have endeavored to give the reader a listing of helpful books of specific weapons at the beginning of each section, where applicable, so that he may easily pursue additional information that is outside the scope of this book.

SNAP SHOTS

This is a feature for the Military Catalog that intends to give the reader a firsthand look at selected firearms, both old and new, from the writer's individual perspective. Due to space limitations, these reviews are kept to a 300-word maximum. Despite this restriction, we think these commentaries are valuable to the reader. We hope that this will personalize and bring to life what otherwise might be a dispassionate rendition of technical facts and descriptions. We all have our likes and dislikes when it comes to firearms. I hope our readers enjoy our contributors' personal opinions and insights.

CONTRIBUTORS

Charles Cutshaw:

Charles Cutshaw is a decorated veteran of the U.S. Army with service in Vietnam. Mr. Cutshaw also served as a civilian technical intelligence officer for 17 years. He is a recognized authority on small arms and ammunition. He is also the editor of *Jane's Ammunition Handbook,* co-editor of *Jane's Infantry Weapons,* small arms editor of *Jane's International Defense Review Magazine,* and contributing editor to numerous firearms publications. He is also the author of *The New World of Russian Small Arms and Ammo* as well as co-author (with Valery Shilin) of *Legends and Reality of the AK* and (with Dianne Cutshaw) a comprehensive major study of firearms, law enforcement, and crime in the United States. He has published numerous articles in monthly domestic and international periodicals.

Robert Segel:

Robert has had a lifelong passion for automatic weapons. At the age of nine, he got the opportunity to shoot an uncle's M3A1 Grease Gun. Immediately after that, he went to a gun show with his father and bought a DEWAT Sten MKII and has been collecting machine guns ever since. He bought his first live gun in 1979; a 21/28 Navy Thompson. Since then, he has been adding to his collection of pre 1945 machine guns specializing in the World War I era weapons – particularly water-cooled guns. His extensive collection of classic machine guns is known worldwide and also has the world's largest collection of machine gun memorabilia.

Robert began writing about machine guns in 1990 for the old *Machine Gun News* and was a contributing editor for that publication. He then began writing for *Small Arms Review* magazine and was a contributing editor for that magazine for four years and, in 2004, was made the senior editor. He has had over 50 articles published on machine guns and is an acknowledged contributor to nine books.

Kenny Durham:

Kenny Durham has over 35 years of experience with black powder firearms of all types. As a competitor, he has won numerous awards at state and national levels in muzzle loading and black powder cartridge rifle competitions. His main interests are muzzle loading, single shot, and lever action rifles. But he also has an affinity for single-action sixguns and 19th century U.S. military arms. For the past five years, Kenny has served as an associate editor and staff writer for *Shoot! Magazine,* wherein his articles regularly appear. Articles by Kenny have also appeared in *Black Powder Guns & Hunting, The Australian Shooter* and *The ABCs of Reloading (Krause).* Additionally, Kenny authored much of the book *Black Powder And The Old West (Shoot! Magazine).*

Chuck Karwan:

Chuck attended and graduated from the U.S. Military Academy where he spent a tremendous amount of time in the West Point Museum firearms study collection learning everything he could about firearms. He eventually graduated from Airborne, Jump Master, Jungle School, Ranger School (Honor Graduate), and the Special Forces Officers Course, among others, and was five-time heavyweight wrestling champion of all the military services. He served a combat tour in Vietnam with the 1st Cavalry Division where he acquired a substantial collection of captured weapons that were donated to the West Point Museum. His gun collecting interests and knowledge are broad, covering everything from muzzle loaders to machine guns. He left the military in 1978 to start a career in writing and has written hundreds of articles in a wide variety of firearms-related magazines including a recent article in the *American Rifleman.* He has authored two books on combat handgunnery and has contributed chapters and articles to several dozen other books. He is an avid hunter and also frequently serves as a legal expert on firearms.

Frank James:

Frank W. James has been writing firearms-related articles and commentaries for over 17 years. Currently he is a projects editor for *Guns & Ammo Handguns* and a contributing editor to *Combat Handguns.* He has published over 900 articles in seven countries during his career. He is the IDPA Area Coordinator for the states of Indiana and Michigan. He is also a Special Deputy with the White County Sheriff's Department, Monticello, Indiana, as well as that agency's firearms instructor. He is certified by the Indiana Law Enforcement Academy to teach police handgun, shotgun, and patrol carbine. He is an active shooting competitor, primarily in IDPA handgun competition, but he has participated over many years in IPSC (USPSA), NRA Small Bore rifle, NRA Bullseye pistol, and the Masters International Tournament. He has completed training in several of the Heckler & Koch International Training Division courses, as well as Thunder Ranch, the SIGARMS Academy, and the Yavapi Firearms Academy. In 1995, he was named the OUTSTANDING WRITER OF THE YEAR by Anchutz-Precision Sales, Inc. He is the author of the *MP5 Submachine Gun Story,* available from Krause Publications.

Paul Scarlata:

Paul is a resident of North Carolina and has been involved in gun collecting and the shooting sports longer then he would care to admit on these pages. For the last 14 years he has been a full time writer and contributes to the *Shotgun News, Shooting Times, American Rifleman, G&A Handguns, Man at Arms, Military History, SWAT, Front Sight, Women & Guns,* a number of Krause annuals and – in his spare time – writes for gun and military history magazines in eight foreign countries. Paul bought his first military surplus rifle at the tender age of 17 and has amassed – and disposed of – several rather extensive collections since then. Presently he is accumulating Krag-Jorgensens.

While his writing covers all aspects of the shooting sports, his primary interest lies in military small arms from the 1875-1945 period. His first book, *Collecting Classic Bolt Action Military Rifles,* was published in 2000 and his second, *Mannlicher Military Rifles,* was released in 2004.

James Rankin:

James Rankin has been an avid collector of weapons throughout his life with his main interest centering on firearms produced in Germany, especially those produced by the Walther Company. He has authored five books on Walther firearms, three in English and two in German along with a number of nationally published firearms magazine articles.

He received a commission in the United States Army upon graduation from college. While in the Army he was an instructor in small arms and a graduate of the Army's Airborne and Ranger schools.

His scope of knowledge includes most projectile fired firearms from the flintlock and percussion era to today's modern weapons. He does expertise work with the courts, police departments, and insurance companies. At present he is working on a three-volume set of books covering all semi-automatic pistols.

Bob Hausman:

Bob is the publisher of the firearms industry's two most widely read professional trade publications, *The New Firearms Business* and *The International Firearms Trade.* For subscription information, send an e-mail to: FirearmsB@aol.com

CLASS III FIREARMS

In order to better understand the pricing structure of NFA weapons, it is necessary to understand the different chronological sequences of NFA weapons.

PRE-1968: The Gun Control Act of 1968 was one of the most crucial. Pursuant to NFA weapons, the 1968 Act stipulated that no more imported machine guns could be brought into the system. As a result, pre-1968 imported guns command a premium because of their original manufacture. During 1968, the NFA branch of the ATF allowed a one-month amnesty period so that returning servicemen from Vietnam could register their war trophies. It was during this period that many AK47s, PPSH41s, and MP40 machine guns were put into the system. Many more U.S. and foreign manufactured guns were also registered at this time as well. All of these guns command a premium because of their originality and registration.

NOTE: This group of guns is often referred to as fully transferable weapons.

PRE-1986 CONVERSIONS: Domestic production of NFA weapons continued until 1986, when the 1986 Gun Control Act prohibited the registration of domestic machine guns. Thus the door was closed to any further production of machine guns available to individuals. NFA weapons already registered could remain in the system and be transferred to qualified individuals. This situation drove prices higher and continues to do so. This group of weapons consists of many desirable semi-automatics that were legally converted into fully automatic weapons. These include the HK94s converted to the MP5, the HK91s converted to the G3, and the HK93 converted to the HK33. There were many Browning .30 and .50 caliber machine guns manufactured during this time frame as well. But remember, pedigree determines price. An original pre-1968 Israeli-manufactured UZI will fetch over $9,000 whereas a U.S. manufactured UZI built during the same time period will only bring $3,000.

NOTE: The reader needs to be aware that there are different classifications of Class 3 guns that are not original guns but are instead referred to as "sideplate guns." These are principally Browning Model 1917s, 1919s, Vickers, and a few others. These are guns with non-original side-plates. There are also re-welds or rewats. These are guns that were deactivated and then reactivated. Pricing for these categories can be confusing, and it is suggested that the collector or shooter seek expert advice before a sale.

PRE-1986 DEALER SAMPLES: Those individuals who wish to be Class 3 dealers in machine guns have many more NFA weapons to choose from, especially the newer, more contemporary designs. Pre-1986 dealer samples, imported before 1986, can be transferred between dealers only and retained personally by them after they surrender their Class 3 licenses. Only people who wish to engage in active business of buying and selling machine guns should do this as it entails much more paperwork and responsibility. These dealer samples can only be transferred to other dealers. Some of these contemporary guns are very rare and desirable. For example, a pre-1986 dealer sample FN MAG machine gun in excellent condition will bring upwards of $60,000 because only about six of these guns were imported into the country before 1986. Supply and demand rule here.

Post-1986 dealer samples are even more restrictive. Only dealers who can produce a law enforcement letter wishing to demonstrate these weapons can obtain them. Unlike the pre-1986 samples, these post-1986 samples cannot be retained after their license is surrendered. It is for this reason that post-1986 dealer sample prices are not given.

Always follow NFA rules. When in doubt, call or write the ATF for clarification.

ADVISORY: For those readers who are interested in advancing their knowledge and understanding of Class III firearms, it is recommended that they subscribe to *Small Arms Review*, a first rate publication that has many informative and useful features. There are sections on the law, new products, and illuminating articles on all aspects of NFA weapons and their history. *Small Arms Review* may be contacted at Moose Lake Publishing, 223 Sugar Hill Rd., Harmony, ME 04942. Telephone 207-683-2959 or FAX 203-683-2172. E-mail SARreview@aol.com. Web site: http://www.smallarmsreview.com.

NOTE: *The prices listed for Class III firearms reflect the most current information as of publication date. Class III firearms are very volatile with rapid and sudden price changes. It is highly recommended that the latest market prices be verified in a particular market prior to a sale.*

DEWAT (Deactivated War Trophy) MACHINE GUNS

Mention should be made that these guns, which have been rendered inactive according to BATF regulations, have a general value that is a rough percentage of its active counterpart: that percentage is approximately 85%. This percentage is only an approximation because of a wide range of factors ranging from who performed the deactivation, the extent of the work, how difficult it would be to reactivate the gun, and whether or not the work could be done without altering the basic look and function of the original. The collector should note that very rare machine guns, DEWAT or not, will bring the same price.

It should be noted also that reactivated machine guns are priced as conversions, because they are no longer in original condition.

Thompson Model 1921A DEWAT • Courtesy Amoskeag Auction Company

An M-3 submachine gun registered as a DEWAT • Courtesy Amoskeag Auction Company

WHAT IS A MILITARY FIREARM?

Some examples that might surprise

Ned Schwing

At a recent Greg Martin auction I noticed several Winchester .22 caliber rifles marked with the "U.S." stamp and "flaming bomb" used to denote military-purchased firearms. Military collectors know, of course, that all kinds of firearms were used in armed conflicts, from .22 caliber revolvers to double barrel shotguns. Combatants used whatever firearm was available to them in combat. However, the accepted military firearms are ones that were purchased and issued to troops by governments. Rifles such as the M1 Garand, the Model 1903 Springfield, various British Enfields, Russian Mosin-Nagants, and so on are some examples of well-known military firearms. These are what we might refer to as conventional military firearms. But there are other types of military firearms that were not used in combat, purchased by governments for military uses such as training arms, guard weapons, or other purposes.

The Greg Martin auction included a Winchester Model 1903 .22 caliber semi-automatic rifle marked with U.S. over Ordnance bomb stamped on top of the frame at the rear. My research at the Cody Firearms Museum indicates that the U.S. Army purchased a number of these rifles during World War I for the express purpose of using them as sniper rifles in the close confines of trench warfare. Some of the Model 03s were fitted with a threaded barrel for a Maxim suppressor. How successful these rifles were at that assigned task is unknown, but the concept is certainly an interesting one.

The auction also included a Winchester Model 1890 .22 caliber slide-action rifle. This too was marked with U.S. over the Ordnance bomb. Research shows that these rifles were purchased by the U.S. Navy and Coast Guard for predator control around military facilities. Research also confirms that the Winchester Model 1906 was used for the same purpose. The U.S. Navy purchased Harrington & Richardson Model 65 .22 caliber semi-automatic rifles most likely for training purposes. Another .22 caliber rifle that sold at auction was a Winchester Model 52B competition target rifle marked "US PROPERTY".

The U.S. military did not confine itself to just .22 caliber rifles. The famous Winchester Model 70 was used by the military not only as a target rifle for competitive purpose, but as a military sniper rifle as well, in conflicts such as

A Winchester Saddle ring Carbine U.S. marked with close-up of receiver markings. Circa 1920. Courtesy Greg Martin Auctions

A Winchester Model 1903 U.S. stamped with Ordnance bomb. Rear tang sight. Close-up of martial markings on top of receiver. Courtesy Greg Martin Auctions

This Rock Island Arsenal marked Winchester Model 70 is fitted with a Lyman Alaskan All-Weather scope. Circa 1941. Courtesy Greg Martin Auctions

This Harrington & Richardson Model 65 is marked with the Ordnance bomb and "PROPERTY U.S. NAVY". Courtesy Greg Martin Auctions

World War II, Korea, and Vietnam. Many of these Model 70s were chambered for the .30-06 cartridge but some were chambered for the .300 Winchester Magnum in the Vietnam era. During World War I the U.S. military purchased many Winchester Model 94 saddle ring carbines in .30-30 caliber for guarding defense plants, and U.S. borders. A few of these carbines were used in France by military personnel.

Military purchases were not confined to rifles. The U.S. military also bought .22 caliber semi-automatic pistols. A number of contracts for Colt Woodsman Match Target were let by the U.S. Army and U.S. Marine Corp for these pistols before and during WWII. High Standard sold its Model B-US and Model HD during World War II as well, and its famous Model HD-MS suppressed pistol for the OSS. During the 1950s and 60s High Standard sold its Supermatic S-101 and Citation Model 102 & 103, as well as its Supermatic Tournament 102 & 103 to the U.S. military. Colt sold its

Service Model ACE to the U.S. Army. This .22 caliber target pistol was mostly likely a training arm.

Other unusual and surprising handguns in this auction to have the U.S. ordnance stamp is the Smith & Wesson Model 56 .38 caliber revolver. The Model 56, with a 1970 factory letter, sold for $3,375, and is in about 95 percent condition. A Colt Detective Special also sold at auction for $956.25. It was shipped to an Army facility in Pennsylvania in 1970 when the Army purchased 1,000 Detective Specials in this one order. Another unusual military purchase was for a Sturm Ruger Model GS32N 357 Magnum revolver with 2.54-inch barrel. Stamped "US" on the left side of the frame, it sold for $787.50 and is in excellent overall condition.

Another Ruger revolver the Speed Six, military designation "SS84-L, sold for $787.50. This revolver was fitted with a lanyard ring and stamped "US" on the right side of the frame. Condition is mint. I can think of several uses for

A Winchester Model 52B marked "US PROPERTY". Circa 1953. Courtesy Greg Martin Auctions

This Winchester Model 1890 is in a standard configuration except for its martial markings. Courtesy Greg Martin Auctions

A U.S. marked Remington Model 40-X in .22 caliber with 28-inch barrel with target sights. Courtesy Greg Martin Auctions

these revolvers; from recreational shooting to concealed carry for personal protection. I would strongly recommend Charles W. Pate's book on *U.S. Handguns of World War II; the Secondary Pistols and Revolvers*, as an important source of information for these types of handguns.

Military collectors are well aware of the military use of shotguns from World War I through the present conflicts. The United States seems to be the leading advocate for this weapon of choice in close quarters combat. From the trenches of France in the first World War to the deserts of the Middle East the shotgun has proved its value. The U.S. military relied on commercial shotguns from the Winchester Model 1897 to the Mossberg RI 96. Shotguns purchased by the military will have the U.S. and flaming bomb stamped on them. Some models were specially modified with heat shields and bayonet lugs. Military shotguns are a recognized military collectable, and have been for some time.

So the questions is: Are the above mentioned firearms military firearms or commercial? The answer, in my opinion, is that, of course, they are military firearms in the true sense of the word since the military purchased them for military use, perhaps not combat use, but certainly for a wide variety of military purposes. They are outside the traditional view of what a military firearm perhaps should be, but nevertheless add an interesting an unusual aspect to any military forearms collection.

Colt Detective Special shipped to Letterkenny Army Depot in 1970. Backstrap stamped "US".
Courtesy Greg Martin Auctions

A Ruger Model GS32N in .357 Magnum caliber with 2.45-inch barrel. Right side of frame stamped "US" and left side stamped "NIS".
Courtesy Greg Martin Auctions

Buying Military Surplus Bolt Action Rifles

Paul Scarlata

I have been collecting bolt-action military rifles for.....well, let's just say an extended period of time, and I have found it the most fascinating – and rewarding – of the many firearms-related activities I take part in. Whether you collect them for historical reasons, are intrigued by their technical/mechanical aspects, or simply enjoy shooting them, bolt-action military rifles are fun. And, compared to other types of gun collecting, they are still – so far – affordable fun.

But would-be collectors need to be careful. In fact, in a book I wrote on this branch of gun collecting (*Collecting Classic Bolt Action Military Rifles*), the very first section was entitled "Caveat Emptor – Let the Buyer Beware!"

An all too common opinion you will hear voiced concerning surplus military rifles is that they are "...old pieces of junk" that are (a) cheaply made, (b) dangerous to shoot, and/or (c) inaccurate. Let me assure you right now that this is a gross misconception that, unfortunately, is repeated by those who should know better. It doesn't take a Ph.D. to realize that mass-produced military rifles were not intended to be used for bench rest shooting or deer hunting. This is not to say that many of them are not capable of extraordinary accuracy, because they are. While the accuracy requirements for bolt-action military rifles varied greatly from army to army and generation to generation, generally a rifle was considered acceptable if it could put five rounds into a 3-inch group at 100 yards/meters. Such accuracy would be considered acceptable from a modern, iron-sighted sporting rifle.

It goes without saying that – except under the most dire conditions – no army would be so foolish as to send their troops in harm's way with unsafe weapons or ones that were likely to malfunction. The bolt-action rifle was the predominant military long arm from the 1880s through the early 1950. These rifles – and the ammunition they fired – represent the apex of their respective development and should be considered trend setters. Extensive research and development using the most advanced technologies of the time were used in their development and most were produced from quality materials by skilled workers, using the finest manufacturing methods of the era.

But this being said, those of us who purchase military bolt-action rifles should be cognizant of the fact that the **newest** one we are likely to encounter on today's market is at least 50 years old, while some of them passed their 100th birthday a long time ago. Time tends to have a deleterious effect on wood and steel and regardless of the quality of the original materials and the skill of manufacture, the safety of any rifle this long in the tooth should be looked upon with a healthy dose of skepticism.

A number of years ago I purchased a surplus Swedish m/1896 Mauser rifle in "rough" condition. It had all matching serial numbers and the receiver bore markings showing it had been manufactured at the Carl Gustaf Gevarsfactori in Eskilstuna, Sweden in 1912. It was also marked with the Finnish army's "SA" acceptance stamp showing it was one of the 77,000 Mausers provided to Finland during the Russo-Finnish War of 1939-40. Further examination showed it was equipped with the post-WWII style front and rear sights indicating this particular rifle was one of the Mausers the Finns returned to Sweden when it looked as if their Nordic neighbor might have to fight off a German invasion.

Thus I had an 88-year-old rifle (composed of all original components!) that had been used by two different armies and under the harshest Arctic conditions imaginable. It had been cared for – with varying degrees of enthusiasm – by innumerable soldiers, volunteers, conscripts and reservists. While it had obviously seen some rough service, mechanically it appeared sound and the bore, while quite worn, still displayed a decent amount of rifling.

My gunsmith checked the head space which, he assured me, was within specs. I test fired the Swede with some recent production mil-spec commercial 6.5x55 ammunition, and it proved to be a very good shooter. So what at first might appear to have been a "...piece of junk" turned out to be an interesting, and most shootable, classic military rifle.

With the lifting of the import ban imposed by the Gun Control Act of 1966, military surplus bolt-action rifles are again available to American collectors. With the collapse of the Evil Empire (a.k.a. Soviet Union), the newly free nations of Eastern Europe decided to empty their warehouses of WWII (and older) surplus weaponry in hopes of exchanging it for good old hard currency. All of a sudden the market was awash with a new wave of former German, Soviet, Austrian, Yugoslavian, Japanese, Chinese, and diverse other nationalities, rifles left over from the Second Great Unpleasantness.

And while I'm not trying to rain on anyone's parade, we should all keep in mind that there are several big differences between today and the "Golden Age of Surplus Firearms" in the 1950s and '60s.

First off, the rifles under discussion are now going on 40 years older. During that time most of them were kept in storage under conditions ranging from excellent to unspeakable. In the last half decade I have seen Swiss Kar. 31 Schmidt-Rubins in like new condition while at the same time the market was flooded with Mausers from Eastern Europe and South America whose condition was so poor that it too painful to bear commenting upon.

When buying a surplus bolt-action rifle the wise purchaser will take certain precautions. In the interests of the public good, I will list several of them here:

1. Verify that the serials numbers on the major components match. The majority of rifles on today's market have been rebuilt several times and/or assembled from parts. If you intend to shoot your rifle

be certain that, at the least, the receiver and bolt numbers match. If they don't, one can assume the rifle was assembled from parts by unknown persons of varying skill and abilities. Such rifles are fine for display but, as with all surplus rifles, **should not be fired** unless they are checked by a competent gunsmith.

2. Check for hairline cracks on the receiver and bolt, in addition to cracks or bulges on barrels. The latter are often hidden by the stock or forearm but can often be detected by careful examination of the inside of the barrel with a bore light. Rifles with badly damaged muzzle crowns should be avoided if you are looking for a shooter, although minor dents and dings in this area can often be polished out. The condition of the bore may or may not effect shootability. I have seen many rifles whose bores display a fair amount of wear and pitting but were still capable or more then acceptable accuracy.

3. Small cracks in the stocks are not an indication of misuse – wood is a fragile material and age, moisture, solvents and lubricants can all have a negative effect on it, although these will not always influence performance. Large cracks in the stock, especially near recoil bolts, stock wrists and the thin sections along the magazine well or receiver, could grow when the rifle is fired. Some arsenals, and surplus dealers, repair stocks with countersunk screws and bolts, often covering these restorations with wood filler. I would shy away from rifles whose stocks have been scraped down to remove dents, dings, grease and finish. Indications of this mistreatment is wood bulged up around barrel bands, screw heads, and other metal fittings. Besides destroying interesting markings (which could increase the value of your rifle), such treatment can destroy the integrity of the stock.

4. After purchasing your rifle detail strip it, clean it thoroughly and reexamine it for all of the above. You **should not** attempt to fire any military surplus rifle until you have had its headspace and general condition checked over by a competent gunsmith.

5. Be certain that you are firing the correct ammunition in your rifle. There are any number of cartridges that can be chambered in rifles not intended for them and it should be remembered, that over their long service lives, many bolt-action military rifles were converted to fire different cartridges. Once you have determined the correct cartridge for your rifle, use nothing but quality surplus or – if available – commercial ammunition for shooting.

Regarding surplus ammunition: Quality of materials and manufacture, age, storage conditions and the naturally occurring breakdown of chemical components will all adversely effect ammunition. Military surplus cartridges, especially those that were produced during war time, are often fabricated by manufacturers that have little or no prior experience in manufacturing small arms cartridges. Much of the surplus ammunition on today's market originates in technologically backward countries, which assures little in the way of quality. And unlike the rifle you intend to fire it out of, visual inspection gives few hints as to a cartridge's actual quality or condition.

I have fired surplus cartridge that were three quarters of a century old that performed perfectly, while experiencing duds and hangfires with ammunition less then a third of that age. The most common problem encountered – duds – is the most harmless – if proper precautions are followed!

If the cartridge does not produce a satisfying "bang" when the trigger is pulled, keep the rifle on your shoulder and pointed in a safe direction. DO NOT open the bolt until you have counted to 30! Hangfires are common with older or poor quality ammunition and having a cartridge case burst apart as you pull the bolt to the rear is something you want to avoid at all costs! Any ammunition that malfunctions should be disposed of immediately – and properly.

And I want to add one last bit of advice regarding ammunition. Working in a sporting goods store does not make the average clerk an "expert." Many of these persons have limited knowledge of modern sporting firearms and often know little, if anything at all, about military surplus rifles and their ammunition. It is a sad fact that too many of them are loathe to admit their shortcomings in this area and would rather give you the wrong advice or sell you the wrong ammunition then admit their ignorance.

Another subject that I feel should be broached has to do with money (a.k.a. cash, legal tender, dinero, filthy lucre). The supply of military bolt-action rifles is rapidly shrinking, especially those that, because of scarcity or condition, are especially desirable. Because of the immutable laws of supply and demand the result has been a steady increase in prices. While during the aforementioned "Golden Age" one could pick up an excellent condition Krag-Jorgensen for $39.95. I'm afraid those halcyon days are long past. In fact, the last M1898 Krag I added to my personal collection cost me closer to $1,000 than not.

Because of ignorance, or too often avarice, some persons selling these rifles put a high tariff on them. Often the seller will regale the prospective buyer with tales and legends regarding the rifle's (take your choice) rarity, historical importance, use by a famous person or military unit or that "...it'll make a great deer hunting rifle." The result being that too many newbies end up paying exorbitant prices for what is in fact a fairly common, and inexpensive, rifle.

It would behoove those of you considering the purchase of a bolt-action military rifle to do a bit of homework before you sally forth to the next gun show. If possible, decide beforehand what type of rifle you want. Then study the available reference books – of which the one you're holding right now happens to be an excellent example – and inform yourself as to the scarcity, desirability and going price for said rifle. Another source of information are the many gun collectors' forums on the Internet. Posting a question on one of these forums often results in obtaining a plethora of good information. Inquiries can also be made to various gun magazines.

Lastly, one of the most time honored traditions among gun collectors is dickering. It has been my experience that the amount listed on the price tag of a surplus rifle at a gun show is the seller's opening figure. Don't be afraid to make a lower offer, most sellers expect it and I know several who will be downright disappointed if you don't haggle over each and every rifle on their table! It's all part of the tradition – and fun – of the gun show scene.

ARGENTINA

Argentine Military Conflicts, 1870-Present

During the latter part of the 19th century Argentina suffered from political instability and military coups. This instability continued into the 20th century. Argentina adopted a pre-Axis neutrality during World War II and finally entered the war on the Allied side in 1945. With a military coup in 1944 Colonel Juan Peron rose to power and implemented a popular dictatorship. The subsequent 30 years saw Peron and his wives come and go in power with the eventual coup in 1976 that led to a repressive military junta led by General Galteri. In 1982, Argentina occupied the Falkland Islands and was defeated by the British in the war that followed. The balance of its 20th century history is marked by economic difficulties and austerity measures.

NOTE: Argentina manufactures most of its small arms in government factories located in different locations around the country. This factory is known as the *Fabrica Militar de Armas Portatiles "Domingo Matheu"* (FMAP "DM"). It is located in Rosario.

HANDGUNS

Argentina also used a small number of Star Select fire pistols for its special forces. See *Spain, Handguns, Star Model M.*

FN Model 1935 GP

Designated by the Argentine military as the "Browning Pistol PD." Licensed from FN and manufactured by FMAP "DM." Since 1969, Argentina has built about 185,000 of these pistols some of which have been sold commercially. This 9x19 caliber pistol is marked on the left side of the slide, "FABRICA MILITAR DE ARMAS PORTATILES "D.M." ROSARIO, D.G.F.M., LICENCIA F N BROWNING, INDUSTRAI ARGENTINA."

Exc.	V.G.	Good	Fair	Poor
600	400	300	225	150

Argentine D.G.F.M.

(Direccion General de Fabricaciones Militares) made at the F.M.A.P. (Fabrica Militar de Arms Portatiles (Military Factory of Small Arms)) Licensed copies SN 24,000 to 112,494 (Parts are generally interchangeable with Colt. Most pistols were marked "D.G.F.M. - (F.M.A.P.)." Late pistols were marked FM within a cartouche on the right side of the slide. These pistols are found both with and without import markings, often in excellent condition, currently more often in refinished condition, and with a seemingly endless variety of slide markings. None of these variations have yet achieved any particular collector status or distinction, unless "New In Box." A "New In The Box" DGFM recently sold at auction for $1200. In fact, many of these fine pistols have and continue to be used as the platforms for the highly customized competition and target pistols that are currently popular.

Courtesy Karl Karash collection

Exc.	V.G.	Good	Fair	Poor
550	425	350	275	225

Argentine Hi-Power • Courtesy Blake Stevens, from
The Browning High-Power Automatic Pistol, Stevens

Argentine Made Ballester Molina

Un-licensed, Argentine re-designed versions (parts are NOT interchangeable with Colt except for the barrel and magazine). These pistols are found both with and without import markings. Pistols without import markings usually have a B prefix number stamped on the left rear part of the mainspring housing and are often in excellent to New original condition. The vast majority of currently available pistols are found in excellent but refinished condition. Only the pistols with no import markings that are in excellent to New original condition have achieved any particular collector status. Most of these pistols that are being sold today are being carried and shot, rather than being collected. 99-100 percent = Exc + 40 percent; Refinished = Fair/Poor.

Courtesy Karl Karash collection

Exc.	V.G.	Good	Fair	Poor
425	300	250	185	135

SUBMACHINE GUNS

Shortly after World War II, Argentina purchased a number of Beretta Model 38A2 directly from Beretta. The Argentine military also used the Sterling Mark 4 and the Sterling Mark 5 (silenced version) purchased directly from Sterling against British forces during the Falkland War. The Argentine Coast Guard purchased HK MP5A2 and MP5A3 guns from Germany.

The Argentines have also produced a number of submachine guns of its own design and manufacture. The PAM 1, PAM 2, the FMK series, and the Mems series were, or are, all Argentine submachine guns. It is doubtful if any of these guns were imported into the U.S. prior to 1968 and are therefore not transferable.

RIFLES

In 1879, the Argentine army adopted the Remington Rolling rifle in .43 caliber as its standard issue rifle. This was followed by the Mauser Model 1891 rifle.

The Model 1909 was replaced by the FN FAL series of rifles. This was the standard rifle of the Argentine armed forces. About 150,000 of these rifles have been issued in various configurations and the majority of these were manufactured in Argentina at FMAP "DM" Rosario.

Argentina has also used the U.S. M1 carbine, the Beretta BM59 rifle, and the Steyr SSG sniper rifle.

MAUSER

M1891 Rifle

This rifle was made in Germany with a 29.1" barrel and 5-round magazine. Full stock with straight grip with half-length upper handguard. Rear sight V-notch. Chambered for the 7.65x53mm cartridge. Weight is about 8.8 lbs. Marked with Argentine crest on receiver ring.

Courtesy Rock Island Auction Company

Exc.	V.G.	Good	Fair	Poor
450	350	300	150	90

Argentine Model 1891 rifle • Courtesy Paul S. Scarlata

M1891 Carbine

Full stock with straight grip. Front sight protectors and sling loops attached to bottom of stock behind the triggerguard. Turned down bolt. Barrel length is 17.6". Caliber is 7.65x53mm. Weight is about 7.2 lbs.

Exc.	V.G.	Good	Fair	Poor
500	400	300	200	150

M1909 Rifle

Based on the Gew design and fitted with a 29" barrel and tangent rear sight graduated to 2000 meters. Almost full stock with pistol grip. The 5-round magazine fits in a flush box magazine with hinged floor plate. Chambered for the 7.65x53mm cartridge. Some of these rifles were made in Germany and about 85,000 were built in Argentina. Argentine crest on receiver ring. Weight is about 9 lbs.

Cleaning and maintenance of the Argentine Model 1909 • Courtesy Paul S. Scarlata

Courtesy Rock Island Auction Company

Model 1909 with close-up of receiver ring showing Argentine crest • Courtesy Stoddard Martial collection, Paul Goodwin photo

Exc.	V.G.	Good	Fair	Poor
550	425	375	250	175

M1909 Sniper Rifle w/o scope

Same as above but for bent bolt and scope. Some telescopes were German-made for the Argentine army.

Exc.	V.G.	Good	Fair	Poor
1750	1100	750	600	400

M1909 Cavalry Carbine

Built by the German company DWM and Argentine companies as well. This 7.65x53mm rifle has a full-length stock with straight grip and 21.5" barrel. Upper handguard is 2/3 length. Bayonet fittings. Weight is about 8.5 lbs. About 19,000 of these carbines were produced in Argentina between 1947 and 1959.

Exc.	V.G.	Good	Fair	Poor
500	400	300	225	150

M1909 Mountain Carbine

Sometimes referred to as the Engineers model. This is a cut down Model 1909 rifle with 21.25" barrel with bayonet lug. Rear sight graduated to 1400 meters. Weight is about 8.5 lbs.

Exc.	V.G.	Good	Fair	Poor
500	400	300	225	150

FN FAL (Argentine Manufacture)

A number of these have been imported into the U.S. in semi-automatic configuration. Marked, "FABRICA MILITAR DE ARMAS PORTATILES-ROSARIO, INDUSTRAI ARGENTINA."

Exc.	V.G.	Good	Fair	Poor
3250	2500	1500	900	450

FN Model 49

This semi-automatic rifle in 7.62x51 NATO caliber was sold to Argentina after WWII. Barrel length is 22" and magazine capacity was 10 or 20 rounds. Weight is about 9.5 lbs. Used primarily by the Argentine Navy.

Exc.	V.G.	Good	Fair	Poor
850	650	500	—	—

SHOTGUNS

Mossberg Model 500

In 1976, the Argentine navy acquired the Mossberg Model 500 in 12 gauge.

Exc.	V.G.	Good	Fair	Poor
600	500	400	200	100

MACHINE GUNS

The Argentine military has used a wide variety of machine guns from various sources. Obsolete guns include the Browning Model 1917 water-cooled gun. More current machine guns are the Browning .50 caliber M2 HB, the FN MAG, the French AAT-52, and the MG3.

Argentine Maxim Model 1895

This gun was sold to Argentina from both British and German sources. Standard pattern early Maxim gun with smooth brass water jacket and brass feed plates. Most likely chambered for the 7.65x53mm Mauser cartridge. Rate of fire was about 400 rounds per minute. Weight of the gun was approximately 60

Model 49 built for Argentina • Courtesy Stoddard Martial collection, Paul Goodwin phot

lbs. Marked in Spanish on the receiver as well as the country of manufacture.

NOTE: According to Dolf Goldsmith, author of *The Devil's Paintbrush,* some 55 of these guns are in private hands in the U.S.

Pre-1968 (Rare)

Exc.	V.G.	Fair
35000	32500	30000

Pre-1986 conversions

Exc.	V.G.	Fair
25000	22000	20000

Pre-1986 dealer samples

Exc.	V.G.	Fair
N/A	N/A	N/A

British Maxim Nordenfelt M1895 in 7.65mm • Courtesy private NFA collection, Paul Goodwin photo

AUSTRALIA

Australian Military Conflicts, 1870-Present

The period of the last quarter of the 19th century was marked by colonization and westward expansion similar to that in the U.S. In 1901 the various colonies were federated as states into a Commonwealth of Australia. Australia fought on the side of Great Britain in both world wars. Australia sent troops to Vietnam in the 1960s and 1970s.

HANDGUNS

The Australian military currently uses the Browning Model 1935 designated the L9A1. These guns were manufactured by Inglis during World War II and since by FN. Chambered for 9mm cartridge. The first FN built pistols were purchased in 1963.

Australian Model L9A1 Pistol

This model is the standard British issue 9mm Model 1935 pistol built by FN under contract. Marked, "PISTOL, SELF-LOADING" instead of "PISTOL, AUTOMATIC." First ordered in June of 1963.

Exc.	V.G.	Good	Fair	Poor
700	550	400	200	150

SUBMACHINE GUNS

Australian military forces currently use its own designed and produced F1 submachine gun as well as the HK MP5 and MP5SD. The Sterling L34A1 silenced version is also used by special operations units.

Owen

This Australian submachine gun is chambered for the 9mm cartridge. It features a top mounted 33-round magazine and quick release barrel attachment. The barrel is 9.75" long and the rate of fire is 700 rounds per minute. Weight is about 9.25 lbs. It was produced from 1941 to 1944. Marked "OWEN 9MM MKI LYSAGHT PK AUSTRALIA PATENTED 22/7/41" on the right side of the frame.

Pre-1968
Exc.	V.G.	Fair
14500	13000	12000

Pre-1986 conversions (reweld)
Exc.	V.G.	Fair
10000	9000	8000

Pre-1986 dealer samples
Exc.	V.G.	Fair
9000	3500	3000

Austen Mark I

Introduced in 1943 this gun is a take-off on the British Sten with a folding butt similar to the MP40. Chambered for the 9mm cartridge and fitted with an 8" barrel with forward grip. Uses a 28-round box magazine. Rate of fire is approximately 500 rounds per minute. Weight is about 9 lbs. About 20,000 were produced between 1943 and 1945 by Diecasters and Carmichael in Australia.

Austen Submachine Gun • Courtesy Thomas Nelson, from *The World's Submachine Guns, Vol. 1*

Pre-1968
Exc.	V.G.	Fair
14500	13000	12000

Pre-1986 conversions
Exc.	V.G.	Fair
N/A	N/A	N/A

Pre-1986 dealer samples
Exc.	V.G.	Fair
9000	2500	2000

F-1

First introduced in 1962, this submachine gun was built by the Australian arsenal at Lithgow. Chambered for the 9mm cartridge and fitted with an 8" barrel, this gun has a round receiver with a wooden buttstock with pistol grip and perforated barrel jacket. The 34-round magazine is top mounted. Weight is about 7 lbs. Rate of fire is approximately 600 rounds per minute.

NOTE: It is not known how many, if any, of these guns are in the U.S. and are transferable. Prices listed below are estimates only.

Pre-1968
Exc.	V.G.	Fair
15000	13500	12000

Pre-1986 conversions
Exc.	V.G.	Fair
N/A	N/A	N/A

Pre-1986 dealer samples
Exc.	V.G.	Fair
N/A	N/A	N/A

Owen • Paul Goodwin photo

RIFLES

In 1985 the Australian Defense Ministry adopted the Steyr AUG 5.56mm F8 rifle as its service rifle. Australia also uses the British Parker Hale M82 Sniper Rifle, as well as the U.S. M16A1 rifle.

L1A1 Rifle

This is the British version of the FN-FAL in the "inch" or Imperial pattern. Most of these rifles were semiautomatic only. This rifle was the standard service rifle for the British Army from about 1954 to 1988. The rifle was made in Lithgow, Australia, under license from FN. The configurations for the L1A1 rifle are the same as the standard FN-FAL Belgium rifle. Only a few of these rifles were imported into the U.S. They are very rare. This "inch" pattern British gun will also be found in other Commonwealth countries such as Australia, New Zealand, Canada, and India.

Australian L1A1 Rifle • Courtesy Blake Stevens, *The FAL Rifle*

NOTE: Only about 180 Australian L1A1s were imported into the U.S. prior to 1989. These are rare and in great demand.

Exc.	V.G.	Good	Fair	Poor
6000	4500	—	—	—

MACHINE GUNS

Between 1925 and 1930 the Australian firm of Lithgow built the Vickers machine gun. Later, between 1938 and 1940, the same company built the Bren gun in .303 caliber. Approximately 12,000 Vickers and 17,000 Bren guns were built in Australia during this period. After World War II the Australian military adopted the U.S. M60 machine gun, the Browning 1919A4, and the .50 caliber Browning M2HB. More recently, that country's military uses the Belgian FN MAG, and the German MG3.

Australian Bren

This is a slightly modified version of the MK I built by the Small Arms Factory, Lithgow, beginning in 1940. Marked "MA" and "LITHGOW" on the right side of the receiver. A total of 17,429 guns were produced when production stopped August 13, 1945.

Pre-1968 (Extremely Rare)

Exc.	V.G.	Fair
35000	—	—

Pre-1986 conversions

Exc.	V.G.	Fair
N/A	N/A	N/A

Pre-1986 dealer samples

Exc.	V.G.	Fair
N/A	N/A	N/A

Australian Vickers

Manufactured by the Small Arms Factory in Lithgow beginning in 1929. The gun was last built in 1945. Serial numbers began with the number 1 and went to 9,999. From then on the prefix "B" was added. Highest serial number recorded is B2344.

Pre-1968

Exc.	V.G.	Fair
N/A	—	—

Pre-1986 conversions (side-plate using Colt 1915 or 1918 plates)

Exc.	V.G.	Fair
10500	9500	9000

Pre-1986 dealer samples

Exc.	V.G.	Fair
9000	8500	8000

AUSTRIA-HUNGARY AUSTRIA

Austrian/Hungarian Military Conflicts, 1870-Present

In 1867 the Austro-Hungarian monarchy ruled this important and critical part of Europe. Germany and Austria-Hungary entered into an alliance called the Dual Alliance and later, in 1882 when Italy joined, the Triple Alliance. In the same year Serbia and Romania joined this group as well. Eventually this partnership between Germany and Austria-Hungary pitted them against England and France for control of Europe. With the advent of World War I and the defeat of the Dual Alliance, the Austrian-Hungarian rule came to an end. Between 1914 and 1918 Austria-Hungary had a total of 7,800,000 serving in its armed forces. By the end of the war 2,482,870 had been killed or wounded, about 1/3 of total military personnel. In 1918 German Austria became a republic. The small nation was beset by social, economic, and political unrest throughout the 1920s and in 1934 a totalitarian regime was established. Austria became part of the German Third Reich in 1938. After the end of World War II, Austria was restored to a republic and occupied by the allies until 1955 when it became a sovereign nation. Austria joined the European Union in 1995.

HANDGUNS

Model 1870

This revolver is built on a Lefaucheux-Francotte double action solid frame with fixed cylinder with mechanical rod ejection. It is chambered for the 11.3mm cartridge and fitted with a 7.3" round barrel. The non-fluted cylinder holds 6 rounds. The frame and barrel were iron, not steel. Checkered wooden grips with lanyard loop. Built by the Austrian firm of Leopold Gasser, and marked "L.GASSER, WIEN, PATENT, OTTAKRING." Weight is about 53 oz., or 3.3 lbs., making it one of the heaviest military service revolvers of its time. When the Model 1878 was introduced and adopted by the Austro-Hungarian army, the Model 1870 was sold to the Balkan States and was sometimes referred to as the "Montenegrin" revolver.

Military Unit Marked

Exc.	V.G.	Good	Fair	Poor
1250	750	400	250	150

Non-Unit Marked

Exc.	V.G.	Good	Fair	Poor
900	600	350	225	150

Model 1870/74 Gasser Trooper's Model

Similar to the above model but built with cast steel instead of iron. It was issued from 1874 to 1919. Built by the Austrian firm of Leopold Gasser. Weight is still about 53 oz.

Military Unit Marked

Exc.	V.G.	Good	Fair	Poor
1250	750	400	250	150

Non-Unit Marked

Exc.	V.G.	Good	Fair	Poor
900	600	350	225	150

Model 1878 Officer's Model

Because the Model 1870 revolver was so heavy and large, Johann Gasser, Leopold's younger brother, designed a smaller version chambered for the 9mm (9x26) cartridge. The barrel length was 4.8" and the overall length was reduced as well. The weight of this revolver was about 27 oz.

Exc.	V.G.	Good	Fair	Poor
850	600	350	200	150

Model 1898 Rast & Gasser

This model was built on the Schmidt-Galand double action solid frame with 8-round cylinder with loading gate and mechanical ejection rod. Chambered for the 8mm cartridge and fitted with a 4.5" round barrel. The caliber was too light to be effective as a military sidearm. The firing pin was a spring-loaded frame-mounted plunger instead of the more common hammer mounted type. Checkered wooden grips with lanyard loop. In service from 1898 to 1938. Weight is about 33 oz.

Model 1870 • Courtesy J. B. Wood

Courtesy Geschichte und Technik der europaischen Militarrevolver, Journal-Verlag Schwend GmbH with permission

Model 1898 • Paul Goodwin photo

Short Grip

Exc.	V.G.	Good	Fair	Poor
650	400	200	150	90

Short Barrel

Exc.	V.G.	Good	Fair	Poor
3500	2000	1200	400	200

STEYR
Osterreichische Waffenfabrik Gesellschaft GmbH, Steyr (1869-1919)
Steyr-Werke AG (1919-1934)
Steyr-Daimler-Puch, Steyr (1934-1990)
Steyr-Mannlicher GmbH, Steyr (1990-)

Steyr Model 1893 Gas Seal Test Revolver

Chambered for the 8mm cartridge this 7-shot 5.5" barrel revolver was built by Steyr as a prototype for the Austrian army. Fewer than 100 were built. Several different variations. It is recommended that an expert be consulted prior to a sale.

Courtesy Geschichte und Technik der europaischen Militarrevolver, Journal-Verlag Schwend GmbH with permission

Exc.	V.G.	Good	Fair	Poor
15000	9000	5000	2000	—

Roth Steyr Model 1907

Based on the patents granted to Karel Krnka and Georg Roth, the 8mm Model 1907 had a rotating barrel locking system and was the first self-loading pistol adopted by the Austro-Hungarian army. It was also the first successful double action automatic pistol. Add 20 percent for early Steyr examples without a large pin visible on right side of frame, or for those made in Budapest instead of Steyr.

An Austrian Model 1898 Service revolver sold at auction for $632.50. Barrel length is 4.5". Condition is Arsenal refinished. Grips are excellent.
Rock Island Auction Company, August 2004

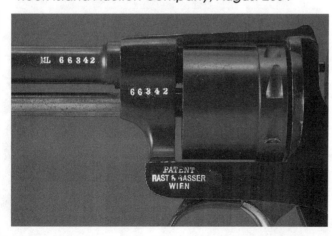

Courtesy Joseph Schroeder

Exc.	V.G.	Good	Fair	Poor
750	600	500	350	250

Steyr Hahn Model 1911

The Steyr Hahn was originally introduced as a commercial pistol but was quickly adopted by the Austro-Hungarian, Chilean, and Romanian militaries. Magazine capacity is 8 rounds. Weight is about 30 oz. Commercial examples were marked "Osterreichische Waffenfabrik Steyr M1911 9m/m" on the slide, have a laterally adjustable rear sight, and are rare. Austrian militaries are marked simply "STEYR" and the date of manufacture, while those made for Chile and Romania bear their respective crests. During WWII the Germans rebarreled a number of Steyr Hahns to 9mm Parabellum for police use, adding "P.08" to the slide along with appropriate Waffenamt markings. The German army designation for this pistol was "Pistole Mod 12(o)."

Courtesy Orvel Reichert

Commercially Marked

Exc.	V.G.	Good	Fair	Poor
1350	1000	750	500	350

P.08 Marked Slides

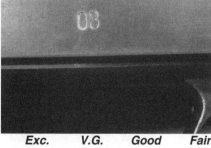

Close-up of slide showing conversion number "08" for 9x19 caliber • Courtesy Orvel Reichert

Exc.	V.G.	Good	Fair	Poor
800	500	350	200	125

SNAP SHOT
WHAT'S IT LIKE - STEYR'S REPETIERPISTOLE M.12

Austria-Hungarian pistols featured unique operating, trigger and magazine systems to say nothing of one-of-a-kind cartridges. Most were produced by the Osterreichische Waffenfabrik Gesellschaft of Steyr, the Dual Monarchy's premier arms maker.

Adopted in 1914, Steyr's Repetierpistole M.12 used a rotating barrel locking system developed by Karel Krnka. The barrel is held in the frame by a helical lug that engages a groove cut into the frame. As the slide recoils the lug moves in the groove, rotating the barrel and unlocking dual lugs from the slide, permitting the slide to continue to the rear, ejecting the spent cartridge. The bullet's twisting in the rifling grooves exerted a force in the opposite direction to the barrel's direction of rotation which kept the barrel and slide locked for the necessary distance.

It was chambered for the 9mm scharfe Pistolepatrone M.12 which consisted of a straight-walled, rimless case 23mm long topped with a 116 gr. FMJ bullet at a velocity of 1125 fps. * The M.12 had a non-removable magazine in the grip that was loaded with eight-round charger clips. Besides being adopted by Austria-Hungary, before 1918 the M.12 was purchased by Chile, Romania, Bulgaria, the German State of Bavaria and after WWI also saw service with Yugoslavia, Greece, Italy, Poland and Czechoslovakia.

The M.12 I test fired was manufactured in 1915 and was in excellent condition. The owner even supplied me with a charger to facilitate loading the magazine. As luck would have it, Hornady recently began offering the 9mm Bergmann cartridge, which is dimensionally and ballistically identical to the 9mm Steyr. Firing from a rest I was able to put eight rounds into a nice 1 7/8" group. Hmmm....an extremely accurate pistol? Shooting offhand at a combat target at 7 yards, it proved easy to keep 16 rounds inside of the A zone.

M.12 pistols were rugged, no frills handguns designed to stand up to the rigors of combat. And unlike many European military handguns of its time, they were chambered for a serious combat cartridge.

* – During WW2 the Germans rebarreled many M.12s for the 9mm Luger cartridge.

Paul Scarlata

Austrian Military

Exc.	V.G.	Good	Fair	Poor
500	350	200	150	100

FEG (Frommer) Stop Model 19

Introduced in 1912 and took a whole new approach compared to any of the pistols this company had produced to that point. It is still unconventional as it uses two recoil springs in a tube above the barrel and resembles an air pistol in this way. It is chambered for 7.65mm or 9mm short and has a 3.75" barrel. The detachable magazine holds 7 rounds, and the sights are fixed. This locked-breech action, semiautomatic pistol was a commercial success. It was used widely by the Austro-Hungarian military during WWI. It was manufactured between 1912 and 1920.

Courtesy James Rankin

Exc.	V.G.	Good	Fair	Poor
400	250	200	150	100

Glock 17

Adopted by the Austrian military in 1983. This model is chambered for the 9mm Parabellum cartridge. It is a double action only semiautomatic that has a 4.49" barrel and a 17-shot detachable magazine. The empty weight of this pistol is 21.91 oz. This pistol is offered with either fixed or adjustable sights at the same retail price. The finish is black with black plastic grips. It is furnished in a plastic case with an extra magazine. This pistol was introduced in the U.S. in 1985 and is still currently produced.

NIB	Exc.	V.G.	Good	Fair	Poor
600	450	325	300	275	175

Note: Add $70 if equipped with Meprolight night sights. Add $90 if equipped with Trijicon night sights. Add $30 if equipped with adjustable sights.

SUBMACHINE GUNS

Steyr-Solothurn MP 30

Introduced in 1930 and built at the Steyr plant under license from the Swiss firm, Solothurn. It was adopted by the Austrian police. Chambered for the 9x23 Steyr cartridge and fitted with a 7.8" jacketed barrel. It is fed by a 32-round magazine and has a rate of fire of about 500 rounds per minute. Wood buttstock with unusual upswept appearance. It is select fire. Weight is about 9.5 lbs. Produced from 1930 to 1935 with approximately 6,000 manufactured.

Steyr Model 1930 • Courtesy Thomas Nelson, from *World's Submachine Guns, Vol. I*

Pre-1968

Exc.	V.G.	Fair
9000	8500	7500

Pre-1986 conversions (reweld)

Exc.	V.G.	Fair
7000	6500	5500

Pre-1986 dealer samples

Exc.	V.G.	Fair
5000	4500	3500

Steyr-Solothurn S1-100 (MP 34(o))

This gun machine was designed in Germany, perfected in Switzerland, and built in Austria. Steyr-Solothurn was a shell company established to enable the German company Rheinmetall to evade the restrictions of the Versailles Treaty that prevented them from producing military small arms. The gun was used by the Austrian army as well as the German army. It is chambered for the 9x23 Steyr cartridge as well as others. The German army used them in 9mm Parabellum while Austrian troops used the gun chambered for the 9mm Mauser cartridge. The gun was also sold to Portugal where it was designated the Model 42. Barrel length is almost 7.8". Magazine capacity is 32 rounds. Rate of fire is about 500 rounds per minute. Fixed wooden butt and forearm. Weight is approximately 9.5 lbs. Produced from 1934 to 1939. On this gun, a magazine loading device is built into the magazine housing.

Pre-1968

Exc.	V.G.	Fair
9500	8000	7500

Pre-1986 conversions (reweld)

Exc.	V.G.	Fair
6500	6000	5500

Pre-1986 dealer samples

Exc.	V.G.	Fair
4500	4000	3500

MP 34 • Paul Goodwin photo

Model 1886 • Courtesy West Point Museum, Paul Goodwin photo

Steyr Mpi69

Built in Austria, this submachine gun is chambered for the 9mm cartridge. It was adopted by the Austrian army in 1969. The gun features a 10" barrel and 25- or 32-round magazine. It has a rate of fire of 550 rounds per minute. It is marked "STEYR-DAIMLER-PUCH AG MADE IN AUSTRIA" on top of the receiver. The folding stock is metal. The gun weighs about 7 lbs. Production stopped in 1990.

Photo courtesy private NFA collection

Pre-1968 (Rare)

Exc.	V.G.	Fair
8000	6500	6000

Pre-1986 conversions

Exc.	V.G.	Fair
N/A	N/A	N/A

Pre-1986 dealer samples

Exc.	V.G.	Fair
4500	4000	3500

RIFLES

MANNLICHER
Built by Steyr & Fegyvergyar

Model 1885

This was the first magazine rifle used by Austria-Hungary and the first straight-pull rifle used as a general issue shoulder arm. This model required that a clip be used to load the box magazine, loose cartridges could not be loaded. Like the U.S. M1 Garand, clips were ejected up from the receiver when empty. Chambered for the 11.15mmx58R black powder cartridge. Barrel length is 31" with two barrel bands. Box magazine held 5 clip loaded rounds. Weight was about 10 lbs. Only about 1500 of these rifles were built.

Exc.	V.G.	Good	Fair	Poor
1200	900	700	500	300

Model 1886

This rifle was produced in large numbers and adopted for general service use. This model is similar to the Model 1885 but unlike the M85, the clip of this rifle ejected out of the bottom of the magazine. Still chambered for the 11.15mmx58R black powder cartridge. Barrel length was 30". After 1888 most of these rifles were converted to 8x50R smokeless powder. Two barrel bands with pistol grip stock. This rifle was made at Steyr. Weight was slightly under 10 lbs.

Exc.	V.G.	Good	Fair	Poor
450	300	200	100	75

Model 1888

This model is the same as the Model 1886 except chambered for the 8x50R black powder cartridge.

Exc.	V.G.	Good	Fair	Poor
550	400	250	150	100

Model 1888/1890

This variation is the result of the change-over from black powder to smokeless. This model was chambered for the 8x50R smokeless powder cartridge with a stronger bolt locking wedge. Barrel length was 30". New sights were added to accommodate the new cartridge. These sights were graduated. This model was also made at Steyr. A number of these were sold to Bulgaria, Greece, and Chile. A number of these rifles were used during WWI and some were found in irregular units during WWII.

Exc.	V.G.	Good	Fair	Poor
500	350	200	150	75

Model 1888/1890 • Courtesy West Point Museum, Paul Goodwin photo

Austrian infantryman with Model 1886 rifle with bayonet • Courtesy Paul S. Scarlata from *Mannlicher Military Rifles*, Andrew Mobray Publishers

Austrian soldiers with Model 95 rifles • Courtesy Paul S. Scarlata from *Mannlicher Military Rifles*, Andrew Mobray Publishers

Model 1890 Carbine

This model represented a departure from previous models, not only in design, but incorporated a stronger action to better handle the 8x50R smokeless cartridge. On this model the bolt head contained the extractor. The result of this new design was that the trigger was behind the end of the bolt handle. Barrel length was 19.5" with a single barrel band and no handguard. There is no bayonet lug on this rifle. The box magazine capacity was 5 rounds of clip loaded ammunition. Weight is about 7 lbs.

Exc.	V.G.	Good	Fair	Poor
750	500	350	200	100

Model 1895 Infantry Rifle

Chambered for the 8x50R cartridge, this straight pull bolt action rifle was fitted with a 30" barrel with an integral clip loaded magazine and wooden handguard. This model has essentially the same action as the Model 1890 Carbine. Fitted with leaf sights. Weight is about 8 lbs. Produced from 1895 to about 1918 both at Steyr and Budapest. The rifle was marked with either of these two locations on top of the receiver ring along with "M95."

This was the primary shoulder arm of the Austro-Hungarian army during WWI and was made in huge quantities. The rifle was also used by Bulgaria and Greece. Many of these models were used in Italy during WWII, as well as the Balkans during that same period of time.

NOTE: In the 1930s, both Austria and Hungary converted large numbers of these rifles to 8x56Rmm. Many of these rifles were converted to carbines at the same time. Converted rifles will have an "S" or "H" stamped over the chamber.

- -

Close-up of receiver ring of Model 1895 Steyr Rifle

Model 1895 Steyr Rifle • Courtesy West Point Museum, Paul Goodwin photo

Between the two world wars, many Model 95s were converted to 8x57mm short rifles and fitted with 24" barrels. These rifles used the standard Mauser stripper clip instead of the Mannlicher system. Receivers were marked "M95M" and "M95/24". Yugoslavia was the main user of these rifles.

Exc.	V.G.	Good	Fair	Poor
300	200	125	75	50

Model 1895 Sharpshooter's Rifle
Same configuration as the Infantry rifle except for the addition of double set triggers. Rare.

Exc.	V.G.	Good	Fair	Poor
850	600	500	400	200

Model 1895 Sniper Rifle
Same as the Sharpshooter's rifle but fitted with a telescope sight. Extremely rare.

Exc.	V.G.	Good	Fair	Poor
3000	2500	2000	—	—

Model 1895 Cavalry Carbine
Essentially the same as the Infantry rifle with a shorter barrel. Barrel length is 19.5". The sling swivels are located on the side on the stock and there is no bayonet lug or stacking hook. Weight is about 7 lbs. Produced until 1918.

Exc.	V.G.	Good	Fair	Poor
450	350	275	—	—

Model 1895 Short Rifle (Stuzen M95)
This model was designed for non-cavalry use as it was fitted with a bayonet lug and sling swivels on the underside of the rifle. It was also fitted with a stacking hook attached to the barrel band. When the bayonet is attached, a blade sight is integral with the bayonet barrel ring for sighting purposes. Weight is about 7.5 lbs.

Exc.	V.G.	Good	Fair	Poor
450	300	250	125	75

FEGYVERGYAR
Fegyver es Gepgyar Resvenytarsasag, Budapest, (1880-1945)
Femaru es Szersazamgepgyar NV (1945-1985)
FEG Arms & Gas Appliances Factory (1985-)

Model 35 Rifle
This turn-bolt rifle is based on the Romanian Model 1893 Mannlicher turn bolt but chambered for the 8x56Rmm cartridge. It is clip loaded with a full-length stock (two-piece around receiver) and full upper handguard. Barrel length is 23.5". Magazine capacity is 5 rounds. Weight is about 9 lbs.

Model 35 with close-up of receiver ring • Private collection, Paul Goodwin photo

Exc.	V.G.	Good	Fair	Poor
450	300	200	125	75

STEYR
Osterreichische Waffenfabrik Gesellschaft GmbH, Steyr (1869-1919)
Steyr-Werke AG (1919-1934)
Steyr-Daimler-Puch, Steyr (1934-1990)
Steyr-Mannlicher GmbH, Steyr (1990-)

Werndl Model 1867 Infantry Rifle
This is a single shot rotary breech block action with external side hammer. It is full stocked with exposed muzzle and bayonet fitting. Chambered for the 11.15x58R Werndl cartridge. Barrel length is 33.6". Weight is about 9.75 lbs. About 600,000 Model 1867 rifles were built.

Exc.	V.G.	Good	Fair	Poor
450	400	300	200	100

SNAP SHOT
WHAT'S IT LIKE - THE M.1866/77 WERNDL

While it has often been overlooked in the gun press, one of the most prolific arms manufacturers of all time was the Osterreichische Waffenfabriks Gesellschaft of Steyr, Austria. Under the direction of Josef Werndl, during the late 19th and early 20th centuries, Steyr annually produced more military rifles than any other private company or state arsenal in the world. And this success began with one of the most unique breech-loading, blackpowder military rifles of all time, the Infanterie-Gewehr M.1867.

Better known as the "Werndl," this rifle used a one-of-a-kind rotating drum breech designed by Karl Holub. To load the rifle the external hammer is placed at half cock and the breech drum rotated 1/3 of a turn to the right aligning a cut in the drum with the chamber, exposing it for loading. As the breech opens a stud on the extractor shaft moves in a groove on the drum, pulling it rearward and extracting the spent case. A new cartridge was inserted, the breech rotated back to the left, the hammer cocked and the rifle fired. Infantry rifles were originally chambered for the 11mm scharfe Patrone M.66 (11x42R) cartridge while later models used the improved 11mm scharfe Patrone M.77 (11x58R). Carbines were chambered for special reduced-power cartridges.

While simple in operation and well made, the Werndl suffered from poor extraction and fouling. Despite these problems, various Werndl rifles and carbines were used by the Austro-Hungarian empire from 1867 to 1890 when they were replaced by Mannlichers. But many remained in use with rear echelon units until 1918.

I test fired a Werndl Jager-Gewehr M.1867/77 made in 1872 with custom reloaded ammunition on my club's 100-yard range. Loading was simple and straightforward and the trigger featured a crisp let off. With the rear sight on its lowest setting of 200 schritt ("paces") it printed about a foot high but was accurate with my best group measuring a pleasing 3.25 inches. Not too bad for a 130-year-old fraulein, eh?

Paul Scarlata

Werndl Model 1867 Carbine

Similar to the rifle above but with a 22.4" barrel. Chambered for the 11x36R Werndl cartridge. Weight is approximately 7 lbs. About 11,000 carbines were produced.

Exc.	V.G.	Good	Fair	Poor
750	600	400	250	100

Werndl Model 1873 Infantry Rifle

This model is an improved version of the Model 1867 with central exposed hammer. Caliber is 11x41RM Werndl. Barrel length is 33.2". Weight is about 9.25 lbs. Total production was about 400,000.

Exc.	V.G.	Good	Fair	Poor
450	400	300	200	100

Werndl Model 1873 Carbine

Similar to the M1873 rifle but with a 22.8" barrel. Chambered for the 11x36R Werndl cartridge. Weight is about 7 lbs. Total production for this model was about 100,000 carbines.

Exc.	V.G.	Good	Fair	Poor
600	500	400	250	100

Werndl Model 1867/77 Rifles and Carbines

This model was the Model 1873 but redesigned for the 11x58R cartridge with a modified rear sight graduated from 200 to 2100 steps.

Exc.	V.G.	Good	Fair	Poor
500	400	300	200	100

Model 95 Rifle (Model 31)

A number of Model 95 rifles and short rifles were modified to accept the 8x56Rmm cartridge after World War I. The letter "H" is stamped on the barrel or the receiver. This is a straight pull rifle with 19.6" barrel and a 5-round fixed magazine. Weight is approximately 7.5 lbs.

Exc.	V.G.	Good	Fair	Poor
150	100	75	50	25

Model 1903

Built for Greece in 6.5x54mm.

Exc.	V.G.	Good	Fair	Poor
400	275	200	125	75

NOTE: For Carbine version add a 50 percent premium.

Model 1904

Similar to the Dutch Model 1895 but chambered for 8x57mm rimless cartridge. Many of these rifles were sold to China and about 11,000 were sold to the Irish Ulster Volunteer Force.

Courtesy Paul S. Scarlata from *Mannlicher Military Rifles*, Andrew Mobray Publishers

Exc.	V.G.	Good	Fair	Poor
350	200	125	75	50

NOTE: For Irish Ulster marked versions add a 30 percent premium.

Model SSG-PI

This model features a black synthetic stock originally designed as a military sniper rifle. Fitted with a cocking indicator, single or double set trigger, 5-round rotary magazine or 10-round magazine. Receiver is milled to NATO specifications for Steyr ring mounts. Barrel length is 26". Rifle weighs about 9 lbs. Offered in .308 Win.

NOTE: This model was originally called the SSG 69.

NIB	Exc.	V.G.	Good	Fair	Poor
1700	1300	1000	—	—	—

Steyr AUG (Armee Universal Gewehr)

Produced by Steyr-Mannlicher beginning in 1978, this rifle is chambered for the 5.56x45mm cartridge. It is a bullpup design with a number of different configurations. Barrel lengths are 13.6" in submachine gun configuration, 16.3" in carbine, 19.8" in rifle, and 24.2" in a heavy barrel sniper configuration. Magazine is 30 or 42 rounds. Carry handle is an optic sight of 1.5 power. Adopted by Austrian army and still in production. Weight is 7.7 lbs. in rifle configuration. Rate of fire is about 650 rounds per minute.

Photo courtesy private NFA collection

Pre-1968

Exc.	V.G.	Fair
N/A	N/A	N/A

Pre-1986 conversions

Exc.	V.G.	Fair
8000	7500	7000

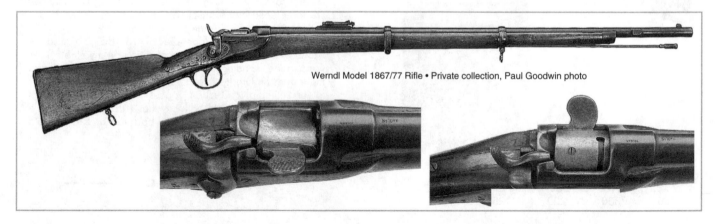

Werndl Model 1867/77 Rifle • Private collection, Paul Goodwin photo

Pre-1986 dealer samples

Exc.	V.G.	Fair
7500	7300	7000

Steyr AUG (Semiautomatic Version)

As above but in semiautomatic only. Two versions. The first with green furniture and fitted with a 20" barrel. The second with black furniture and fitted with a 16" barrel.

First Model

NIB	Exc.	V.G.	Good	Fair	Poor
3900	3250	2250	—	—	—

Second Model

NIB	Exc.	V.G.	Good	Fair	Poor
4200	3700	2750	—	—	—

MAUSER

M1914 Rifle

This rifle is identical to the Model 1912. Austrian rifles are fitted with large sling swivels in order to accommodate the Austrian sling. Some of these rifles are unit marked on the buttplate or buttplate tang.

Exc.	V.G.	Good	Fair	Poor
700	500	425	225	100

MACHINE GUNS

Austrian Hungary also used the Maxim, having purchased some in 1889. These guns were designated the Model 89/1, then with modifications called the M89/04. Austrian Hungary used their own design, the Skoda M1893, but this gun was never considered successful.

Model 07/12 Schwarzlose

The gun was designed by Andreas Wilhelm Schwarzlose and built in Austria by Steyr. First model was the 1905 chambered for the standard military 8x50Rmm cartridge. Successor was the Model 1907/12 which was marked as the M07/12. The gun was built until 1918 in 8x50R. The Czechs built a version called the M7/24 chambered for the 7.92 cartridge. The Romanians converted Steyr M07/12s to 7.92 with lengthened water jackets. The gun was also manufactured by the Dutch, Swedish, and Hungarians. It was adopted by Austria-Hungary in 1905. It was also sold to the Dutch, Greeks, and Germans as well. It saw use in WWI. Barrel length was 24.4" and rate of fire was about 500 rounds per minute. Fed by a 250-round cloth belt. The gun was produced until 1918. Marked "MG SCHWARZLOSE M7/12" on the rear of the receiver. Weight is about 44 lbs. Italy used this gun, as part of World War I reparations, through World War II.

Aircraft versions with modified internals to increase the rate of fire were marked M7/12 (16/A) and M7/12 (16/R), and these have no jackets on the barrel. Note that the gun marked "MG SCHWARZLOSE M7/12," which is correct, but the other side is marked "WAFFENFABRIK STEYR" with the date of manufacture underneath.

No factory Schwarzlose were built with ventilated shrouds. They were either fitted with water-jackets or had bare exposed barrels for aircraft use. No doubt there were field expedients of various sorts, but there is no evidence of any factory ventilated shrouds.

NOTE: The predecessor to this gun was the Model 1905. Its rate of fire was about 350 rounds per minute, and it was fitted with a smaller oil reservoir. An aircraft version of the Model 07/12 was the Model 07/16, which had a rate of fire of about 600 rounds per minute. Early versions were water-cooled, later versions were air-cooled. Last version had no jacket.

Model 07/12 Schwarzlose • Private NFA collection, Paul Goodwin photo

An unusual machine gun placement; a Schwarlose in a tree •
Courtesy Paul S. Scarlata

Pre-1968

Exc.	V.G.	Fair
30000	27500	25000

Pre-1986 conversions (reweld)

Exc.	V.G.	Fair
22000	20000	18000

Pre-1986 dealer samples

Exc.	V.G.	Fair
N/A	N/A	N/A

SNAP SHOT
SCHWARZLOSE M07/12

The Austrian Schwarzlose M07/12 water-cooled machine gun reminds me of a pair of old army boots. It is big, heavy, clunky and lacks sexy styling, but is smooth, reliable and dependable and the right tool for the job. The Schwarzlose saw service from World War I through World War II, and was made by several different manufacturers in a variety of calibers. It is unique in that the bolt does not lock as it is a blowback weapon. Uncommon in rifle caliber machine guns, the bolt is at a mechanical disadvantage before moving rearward thus, combined with a short barrel, the high peak of dangerous expanding gas pressure levels pass before the bolt moves rearward out of battery.

Shooting the Schwarzlose is a different kind of experience due to the oddities of a number of components. There is a perceived slight delay, almost a hesitation, when a shot is fired for the recoiling parts to overcome the mechanical disadvantage of the bolt. Feeding of the 250-round cloth belt is accomplished with a wheel sprocket that feeds from underneath the gun and spent cartridge cases are expelled forcefully out the left side ejection port. Additionally, there is a cartridge oiler reservoir in the top cover that squirts oil on the cartridge cases as it is fed into the chamber and the folding grip handles are horizontal. Nevertheless, it is exactly the combination of these operational peculiarities that make shooting the Schwarzlose so enjoyable. The internal parts are big and heavy giving this gun a robust, solid feeling during firing and the stubby but heavy tripod provides a solid shooting platform. Shooting antique machine guns is more than just putting lead downrange. It is the acknowledgement of early designs, manufacturing techniques, operating and feed systems that, in some cases, are almost 100 years old. Satisfaction is derived from the entire historical and operational experience.

Robert G. Segel

BELGIUM

Belgian Military Conflicts, 1870 – Present

Throughout the last quarter of the 19th century, Belgium experienced rapid economic growth that led to colonization, mainly in the Belgian Congo. Germany occupied Belgium in both World War I and World War II. During World War I, Belgium had 270,000 men under arms. A total of almost 83,000 were killed or wounded during the war. In World War II, Belgium had 650,000 military personnel of which 23,000 were killed or wounded. Belgium became a member of NATO in 1949 where that organization's headquarters are located in Brussels.

Bibliographical Notes

The best overview of Belgian military firearms are two books by Claude Gaier; *FN 100 Years, The Story of the Great Liege Company, 1889-1989*, 1989, and *Four Centuries of Liege Gunmaking*, 1985.

HANDGUNS

E. & L. NAGANT

Model 1878 Officer's (Fluted Cylinder)

This 6-shot double action centerfire revolver is chambered for the 9mm cartridge. Solid frame with fixed cylinder sliding rod ejection. Octagon barrel is 5.5". Issued to Belgian officers, it is marked with the Nagant address and logo. Wooden checkered grips with lanyard loop. Weight is about 33 oz. Produced from 1878 to 1886.

Courtesy Geschichte und Technik der europaischen Militarrevolver, Journal-Verlag Schwend GmbH with permission

Exc.	V.G.	Good	Fair	Poor
1750	900	500	300	200

Model 1883 (Non-Fluted Cylinder)

This model was also chambered for the 9mm centerfire cartridge. Fitted with a 5.5" octagon barrel. Wooden checkered grips with lanyard loop. A simplified version of the Model 1878 Officer's revolver. This model was used by NCOs, artillery, and troops in the Belgian army from 1883 to 1940.

Courtesy Geschichte und Technik der europaischen Militarrevolver, Journal-Verlag Schwend GmbH with permission

Exc.	V.G.	Good	Fair	Poor
1250	750	400	275	150

Model 1878/86 Officer's (Fluted Cylinder)

This 6-shot revolver was issued to officers in the Belgian army. Chambered for the 9mm cartridge and fitted with a 5.5" octagon barrel. Checkered wooden grips with lanyard loop. Produced from 1886 to 1940.

Courtesy Geschichte und Technik der europaischen Militarrevolver, Journal-Verlag Schwend GmbH with permission

Exc.	V.G.	Good	Fair	Poor
1500	850	450	300	175

Model 1883/86

Similar to the Model 1878/86 Officer's but issued to NCOs as a regular sidearm. Cylinder is non-fluted. The hammer rebounds slightly after the revolver has been fired.

Courtesy Geschichte und Technik der europaischen Militarrevolver, Journal-Verlag Schwend GmbH with permission

Exc.	V.G.	Good	Fair	Poor
1250	750	400	275	150

GAVAGE, ARMAND

A 7.65mm caliber semiautomatic pistol with a fixed barrel and a concealed hammer. Similar in appearance to the Clement. Markings with "AG" molded into the grips. Some (1,500 est.) have been found bearing German Waffenamts. Manufactured from 1930s to 1940s.

Exc.	V.G.	Good	Fair	Poor
550	350	250	150	100

FABRIQUE NATIONALE

NOTE: For historical and technical information, see Blake Stevens, *The Browning High Power Automatic Pistol*, Collector Grade Publications, 1990.

Model 1903

A considerable improvement over the Model 1900. It is also a blowback-operated semiautomatic; but the recoil spring is located under the barrel, and the firing pin travels through the slide after being struck by a hidden hammer. The barrel is held in place by five locking lugs that fit into five grooves in the frame. This pistol is chambered for the 9mm Browning long cartridge and has a 5" barrel. The finish is blued with molded plastic grips, and the detachable magazine holds 7 rounds. There is a detachable shoulder stock/holster along with a 10-round magazine that was available for this model. These accessories are extremely rare and if present would make the package worth approximately five times that of the pistol alone. There were approximately 58,000 manufactured between 1903 and 1939. This model was one of the Browning patents that the Eibar Spanish gunmakers did so love to copy because of the simplicity of the design.

It should be noted that during World War I the Spanish supplied almost one million Model 1903 copies for the French army.

Production Note: FN had a number of contract sales to foreign countries from 1907 to about 1928. These countries are:
Sweden: 1907-190810,000
Russia: 1908-19108,200
Ottoman Empire: 1908-19238,000
England: 1914100
Holland: 192280
Estonia: 1922-19284616
El Salvador: 1927-?
Paraguay: 1927324

Courtesy Richard M. Kumor Sr.

Exc.	V.G.	Good	Fair	Poor
650	450	375	275	175

Model 1910 "New Model"

Chambered for 7.65mm and 9mm short. It has a 3.5" barrel, is blued, and has molded plastic grips. The principal difference between this model and its predecessors is that the recoil spring on the Model 1910 is wrapped around the barrel. This gives the slide a more graceful tubular appearance instead of the old slab-sided look. This model has the triple safety features of the 1906 Model 2nd variation and is blued with molded plastic grips. This model was adopted by police forces around the world. It was manufactured between 1912 and 1954.

Courtesy Orvel Reichert

Exc.	V.G.	Good	Fair	Poor
500	300	250	175	125

Model 1922

Similar to the Model 1910, with a longer 4.5" barrel and correspondingly longer slide. This model was a military success, and approximately 200,000 were produced during the WWII German occupation of Belgium in 1940-1944. These pistols that bear the Waffenamt acceptance marks are known as the "Pistole Modell 626(b)," and are chambered for 7.65mm only. The Germans also had a 9mm version designated the "Pistole Modell 641(b)." These pistols would bring a 10 percent premium. There were approximately 360,000 of these pistols produced during the German occupation. There are a number of subvariations that may effect value. There were also contracts from France, Yugoslavia, and Holland, as well as Belgian military versions. They were manufactured between 1912 and 1959.

Model 1922 • Paul Goodwin photo

Exc.	V.G.	Good	Fair	Poor
450	250	175	125	100

Model 1935

The last design from John Browning and was developed between 1925 and 1935. This pistol is known as the Model 1935, the P-35, High-Power or HP, and also as the GP (which stood for "Grand Puissance") and was referred to by all those names at one time or another. The HP is essentially an improved version of the Colt 1911 design. The swinging link was replaced with a fixed cam, which was less prone to wear. It is chambered for the 9mm Parabellum and has a 13-round detachable magazine. The only drawback to the design is that the trigger pull is not as fine as that of the 1911, as there is a transfer bar instead of a stirrup arrangement. This is necessary due to the increased magazine capacity resulting in a thicker grip. The barrel is 4.75" in length. It has an external hammer with a manual and a magazine safety, was available with various finishes and sight options, and was furnished with a shoulder stock. The Model 1935 was used by many countries as their service pistol; as such there are many variations. We list these versions and their approximate values. There are books available specializing in this model, and it would be beneficial to gain as much knowledge as possible if one contemplates acquisition of this fine and highly collectible pistol.

Prewar Commercial Model

Found with either a fixed sight or a sliding tangent rear sight and is slotted for a detachable shoulder stock. It was manufactured from 1935 until 1940. Wood holster stock, add 50 percent.

Fixed Sight Version
Exc.	V.G.	Good	Fair	Poor
650	525	475	375	275

Tangent Sight Version
Exc.	V.G.	Good	Fair	Poor
1000	850	675	550	400

Prewar & WWII Military Contract

The Model 1935 was adopted by many countries as a service pistol, and some of them are as follows:

Belgium

Exc.	V.G.	Good	Fair	Poor
1200	1050	900	600	375

Canada and China (See *John Inglis & Company*)

Denmark (See *Denmark*)

Great Britain

Exc.	V.G.	Good	Fair	Poor
1150	1000	850	550	325

Estonia

Exc.	V.G.	Good	Fair	Poor
1200	1050	900	600	375

Holland

Exc.	V.G.	Good	Fair	Poor
1250	1100	950	650	400

Latvia

Exc.	V.G.	Good	Fair	Poor
1500	1350	1050	775	500

Lithuania

Exc.	V.G.	Good	Fair	Poor
1250	1100	950	650	400

Romania

Exc.	V.G.	Good	Fair	Poor
1500	1350	1050	775	500

German Military Pistole Modell 640(b)

In 1940 Germany occupied Belgium and took over the FN plant. The production of the Model 1935 continued, with Germany taking the output. The FN plant was assigned the production code "ch," and many thousands were produced. The finish on these Nazi guns runs from as fine, as the Prewar Commercial series, to downright crude, and it is possible to see how the war was progressing for Germany by the finish on their weapons. One must be cautious with some of these guns, as there have been fakes noted with their backstraps cut for shoulder stocks, producing what would appear to be a more expensive variation. Individual appraisal should be secured if any doubt exists.

Fixed Sight Model

Paul Goodwin photo

Exc.	V.G.	Good	Fair	Poor
600	450	400	300	250

Tangent Sight Model

50,000 manufactured.

Courtesy Orvel Reichert

Exc.	V.G.	Good	Fair	Poor
850	750	700	550	400

Captured Prewar Commercial Model

These pistols were taken over when the plant was occupied. They are slotted for stocks and have tangent sights. There were few produced between serial number 48,000 and 52,000. All noted have the "WaA613" Nazi proof mark. Beware of fakes!

Exc.	V.G.	Good	Fair	Poor
1500	1400	1150	750	500

Postwar Military Contract

Manufactured from 1946, and they embody some design changes—such as improved heat treating and barrel locking. Pistols produced after 1950 do not have barrels that can interchange with the earlier model pistols. The earliest models have an "A" prefix on the serial number and do not have the magazine safety. These pistols were produced for many countries, and there were many thousands manufactured.

Fixed Sight

Exc.	V.G.	Good	Fair	Poor
550	450	375	300	250

Tangent Sight

Exc.	V.G.	Good	Fair	Poor
750	675	575	400	300

Slotted and Tangent Sight

Exc.	V.G.	Good	Fair	Poor
1500	1250	750	500	400

Sultan of Oman

This is the only post war Hi-Power that is designated a Curio and Relic pistol. It has a tangent sight. The grip is slotted to accept a shoulder stock which is a legal accessory to this model. Less than 50 of these pistols were brought into the U.S. Canceled contract military sidearm for Oman. Very rare.

NIB	Exc.	V.G.	Good	Fair	Poor
6000	5750	4500	—	—	—

NOTE: For pistols with no shoulder stock deduct $1,000.

SUBMACHINE GUNS

Prior to 1940, Belgium used the MP28 (Model 34) as its standard military submachine gun.

FN also manufactured, under license from Israeli Military Industries (IMI), a copy of the UZI submachine gun.

Vigneron M2

This sub gun was issued to the Belgian army in 1953. It was also used by those same forces in the Belgian Congo. Many of these guns were taken by Congo forces after independence. A number of Vigneron guns may be found over much of Central Africa. The gun is chambered for the 9mm cartridge and has a wire folding stock. Barrel length is 11.75" with the rear portion of the barrel finned. A muzzle compensator is also standard. Magazine capacity is 32 rounds. Rate of fire is about 600 rounds per minute. Capable of select fire. Markings are found on the right side of the magazine housing and read, "ABL52 VIG M1." Also on the right side of the receiver is stamped "LICENCE VIGNERON." Weight is about 7.25 lbs. The gun was in production from 1952 to 1962.

Pre-1968

Exc.	V.G.	Fair
12500	11000	10000

Pre-1986 conversions

Exc.	V.G.	Fair
N/A	N/A	N/A

Pre-1986 dealer samples

Exc.	V.G.	Fair
6000	5500	5000

RIFLES

NOTE: For historical information, technical data, and photos on the FN-FAL rifle, see Blake Stevens', *The FAL Rifle, Classic Edition*, Collector Grade Publications, 1993.

MAUSER (FN)

Model 1889 Rifle

The Mauser rifle that Fabrique Nationale was incorporated to manufacture. It is chambered for 7.65mm and has a 30.5" barrel. The magazine holds 5 rounds. The unique feature that sets the Belgian rifle apart from the Mausers made by other countries is the thin steel tube that encases the barrel. This was the first Mauser to use a charger loaded detachable box magazine. The sights are of the military type. The finish is blued, with a walnut stock. This rifle was also made by the American firm of Hopkins and Allen, and is considered rare.

Model 1889 Rifle • Courtesy Paul S. Scarlata

Exc.	V.G.	Good	Fair	Poor
400	300	225	150	100

NOTE: For rare Hopkins and Allen examples, add a premium of 150 percent.

M1889 Carbine with Bayonet

Barrel length is 21". Fitted for a bayonet. Weight is about 7.5 lbs.

Exc.	V.G.	Good	Fair	Poor
450	350	235	160	100

M1889 Carbine with Yataghan

Barrel length is 21". Fitted for a unique bayonet. Weight is about 7.5 lbs.

Exc.	V.G.	Good	Fair	Poor
450	350	250	200	150

Mauser/FN Model 1889 Rifle • Paul Goodwin photo

Model 1889 Carbine • Paul Goodwin photo

M1889 Carbine Lightened

Fitted with a 15.75" barrel and turned down bolt. A slotted sling bracket mounted on left side of buttstock.

Exc.	V.G.	Good	Fair	Poor
450	350	250	175	100

M1889 Carbine Lightened with Yataghan

Same as above but with longer stock. A unique bayonet, handle has no guard and frequently having a double curved blade, was also issued with this carbine.

Exc.	V.G.	Good	Fair	Poor
450	350	250	175	100

M1890 Turkish Rifle

Captured Turkish Model 1890 rifles with Belgian rear sight similar to the Model 1889 rifle. No handguard. Original Turkish markings remain. Belgian proofs.

Exc.	V.G.	Good	Fair	Poor
400	300	250	200	100

M1916 Carbine

Similar to the Model 1889 with Yataghan bayonet but with different bracket on buttstock.

Exc.	V.G.	Good	Fair	Poor
400	300	250	200	100

M1935 Short Rifle

This model is very similar to the German 7.92 Kar 98k and uses the M98 bolt system. It is fitted with a 5-round flush magazine. Barrel length is 23.5". Weight is about 9 lbs.

Exc.	V.G.	Good	Fair	Poor
450	350	300	225	125

M50 Short Rifle

Post war surplus rifle converted to .30-06 caliber. Barrel length is 23.2". Tangent leaf rear sight graduated to 2000 meters. Marked "B/ABL/DATE." Weight is approximately 9 lbs.

Exc.	V.G.	Good	Fair	Poor
450	300	250	200	100

M1889/36 Short Rifle

This model is a converted Model 1889 with a 23.5" barrel with wooden handguard. The upper barrel band and front sight are of the Model 1935 type. The bolt system appears similar to the Model 98. Chambered for the 7.65mm Mauser cartridge. Weight is about 9 lbs.

Exc.	V.G.	Good	Fair	Poor
300	200	150	90	60

M35/46 Short Rifle

Similar to the M50 short rifle.

Exc.	V.G.	Good	Fair	Poor
450	300	250	200	100

M24/30 .22 Caliber Training Rifle–Army

This is a military training rifle in .22 caliber built for the Belgian army after World War II.

Exc.	V.G.	Good	Fair	Poor
450	350	250	175	125

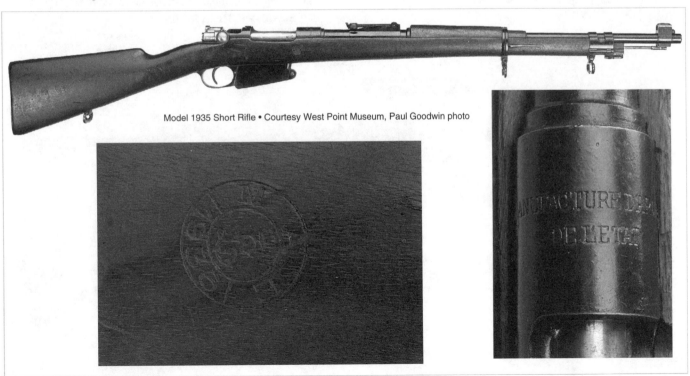

Model 1935 Short Rifle • Courtesy West Point Museum, Paul Goodwin photo

M24/30 .22 Caliber Training Rifle–Navy

Same as above but for the Belgian navy.

Exc.	V.G.	Good	Fair	Poor
450	350	250	175	125

FN M30 Postwar Short Rifle (M24/30, M35/46)

Built after WWII for the Belgian army. It uses the standard M98 action. Converted from Model 1935 rifle to .30-06 caliber. Barrel length is 23.3". Weight is about 9 lbs. Magazine capacity is 5-round in an integral box.

Model 30 post-war short rifle • Courtesy Daniel Rewers Collection, Paul Goodwin photo

Exc.	V.G.	Good	Fair	Poor
400	300	250	200	135

FABRIQUE NATIONALE

Model 1949 or SAFN 49

A gas-operated semiautomatic rifle chambered for 7x57, 7.92mm, and .30-06. It has a 23" barrel and military-type sights. The integral magazine holds 10 rounds. The finish is blued, and the stock is walnut. This is a well-made gun that was actually designed before WWII. When the Germans were in the process of taking over Belgium, a group of FN engineers fled to England and took the plans for this rifle with them, preventing the German military from acquiring a very fine weapon. This model was introduced in 1949, after hostilities had ceased. This model was sold on contract to Egypt, chambered for 7.92mm; to Venezuela, chambered for 7x57; and to Argentina, Colombia, Indonesia, Belgium, and Luxembourg chambered for the .30-06. Argentina models were chambered for the 7.65x53mm as well as the Argentina navy which had its rifles chambered for their 7.62 NATO cartridge.

Courtesy Richard M. Kumor Sr.

Exc.	V.G.	Good	Fair	Poor
575	475	325	225	150

NOTE: The Egyptian model has recently been imported in large numbers and is worth approximately 25 percent less. For .30-06 caliber add 20 percent. For Argentina navy 7.62 NATO examples add 50 percent.

Model 30-11 Sniper Rifle

Chambered for the 7.62 NATO cartridge. It has a 20" heavy barrel and Anschutz sights. There is a flash suppressor mounted on the muzzle. It is built on a highly precision-made Mauser bolt action fed by a 9-round, detachable box magazine. The walnut stock is rather unique in that the butt is made up of two parts, with the rear half being replaceable to suit the needs of different-sized shooters. It is issued with a shooting sling, bipod, and a foam-lined carrying case. This is a rare firearm on the commercial market as it was designed and sold to the military and police markets.

Courtesy Jim Supica, Old Town Station

Exc.	V.G.	Good	Fair	Poor
5000	4500	3500	2750	2000

FN-FAL

A gas-operated, semiautomatic version of the famous FN battle rifle. This weapon has been adopted by more free world countries than any other rifle. It is chambered for the 7.62 NATO or .308 and has a 21" barrel with an integral flash suppressor. The sights are adjustable with an aperture rear, and the detachable box magazine holds 20 rounds. The stock and forearm are made of wood or a black synthetic. This model has been discontinued by the company and is no longer manufactured.

The models listed below are for the metric pattern Type 2 and Type 3 receivers, those marked "FN MATCH." The models below are for semiautomatic rifles only. FN-FAL rifles in the "inch" pattern are found in the British Commonwealth countries of Australia, India, Canada, and of course, Great Britain. These rifles are covered separately under their own country headings.

50.00–21" Rifle Model

NIB	Exc.	V.G.	Good	Fair	Poor
3000	2750	2250	2000	1850	1000

18" Para Model • Courtesy Blake Stevens from *The FAL Rifle*

21" Para Model • Courtesy Blake Stevens, from *The FAL Rifle*

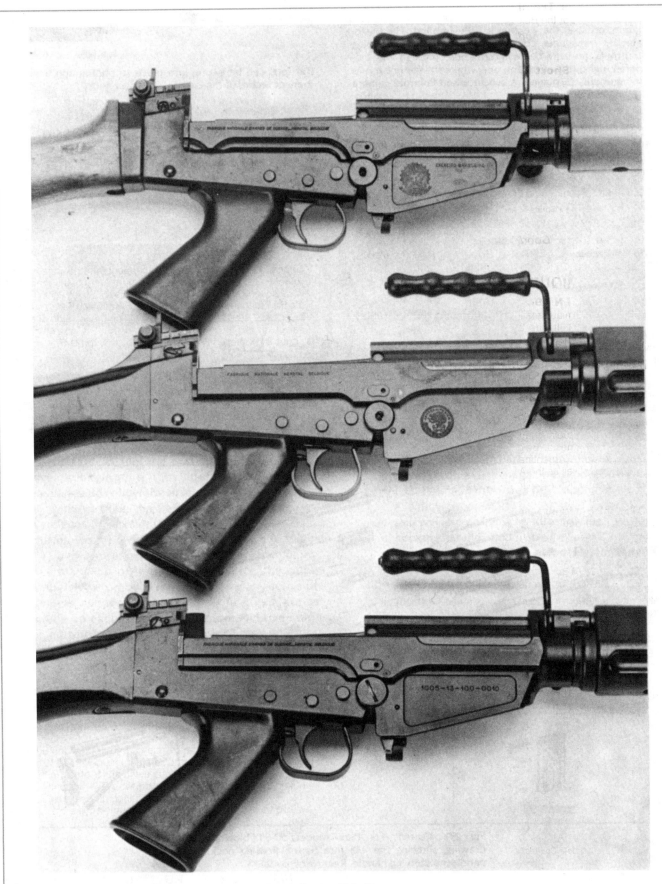

FAL Receivers: Top - Type 2; Middle - Type 3; Bottom - Type 1 • Courtesy Blake Stevens

FN Heavy Barrel Model • Courtesy
Blake Stevens, from *The FAL Rifle*

50.63–18" Paratrooper Model

NIB	Exc.	V.G.	Good	Fair	Poor
3800	3350	2950	2750	2450	1100

50.64–21" Paratrooper Model

NIB	Exc.	V.G.	Good	Fair	Poor
3300	3000	2700	2200	1900	1000

50.41–Synthetic Butt H-Bar

NIB	Exc.	V.G.	Good	Fair	Poor
2800	2400	2000	1800	1200	1000

50.42–Wood Butt H-Bar

NIB	Exc.	V.G.	Good	Fair	Poor
2800	2400	2000	1800	1200	1000

FN FAL "G" Series (Type 1 Receiver)

Converted semiautomatic FAL. These rifles are subject to interpretation by the BATF as to their legal status. A list of BATF legal serial numbers is available. This information should be utilized prior to a sale in order to avoid the possibility of the sale of an illegal rifle. There was a total of 1,848 legal "G" Series FN FAL rifles imported into this country.

Standard

NIB	Exc.	V.G.	Good	Fair	Poor
7000	5500	4000	3000	2000	1000

Lightweight

NIB	Exc.	V.G.	Good	Fair	Poor
7000	5500	4000	3000	2000	1000

NOTE: There are a number of U.S. companies that built FN-FAL receivers and use military surplus parts. These rifles have no collector value as of yet.

FN FAL–Select Fire Assault Rifle

First produced in 1953, this 7.62x51mm select fire rifle has been used worldwide. It is fitted with a 20.8" barrel and a magazine that holds 20 rounds. It is available in several different configurations. Weight is about 9.8 lbs. Marked "FABRIQUE NATIONALE HERSTAL." Markings will also indicate many other countries made this rifle under license from FN.

Pre-1968 (Rare)

Exc.	V.G.	Fair
12500	10500	9000

Photo courtesy FN

Pre-1986 conversions

Exc.	V.G.	Fair
6500	5500	4500

Pre-1986 dealer samples

Exc.	V.G.	Fair
6000	5000	4500

FN CAL

Chambered for the 5.56x45mm cartridge and designed with a rotary bolt. It is fitted with an 18.2" barrel and has a magazine capacity of 20 or 30 rounds. Weight is about 6 lbs. With folding stock. Produced from 1966 to 1975 and is marked "FABRIQUE NATIONALE HERSTAL MOD CAL 5.56MM" on the left side of the receiver. This rifle was not widely adopted. A rare rifle. Only about 20 of these rifles were imported into the U.S.

NIB	Exc.	V.G.	Good	Fair	Poor
7000	6500	5000	3000	—	—

FN CAL-Select Fire Assault Rifle

Chambered for the 5.56x45mm cartridge and designed with a rotary bolt. It is fitted with an 18.2" barrel and has a magazine capacity of 20 or 30 rounds. Its rate of fire is 650 rounds per minute. Weight is about 6 lbs. With folding stock. Produced from 1966 to 1975 and is marked "FABRIQUE NATIONALE HERSTAL MOD CAL 5.56MM" on the left side of the receiver. This rifle was not widely adopted.

Photo courtesy private NFA collection

Pre-1968 (Rare)

Exc.	V.G.	Fair
12500	10500	9500

Pre-1986 conversions

Exc.	V.G.	Fair
7500	7000	6800

Pre-1986 dealer samples

Exc.	V.G.	Fair
6500	5500	4500

FNC

A lighter-weight assault-type rifle chambered for the 5.56mm cartridge. It is a gas-operated semiautomatic with an 18" or 21" barrel. It has a 30-round box magazine and is black, with either a fixed or folding stock. This model was also discontinued by FN. The same problem with fluctuating values applies to this weapon as to the L.A.R., and we strongly advise that one research the market in a particular geographic location as prices can fluctuate radically.

Standard

Fixed stock, 16" or 18" barrel.

NIB	Exc.	V.G.	Good	Fair	Poor
3000	2800	2500	2000	1500	1000

Paratrooper Model

Folding stock, 16" or 18" barrel.

NIB	Exc.	V.G.	Good	Fair	Poor
3000	2800	2500	2000	1500	1000

NOTE: The above prices are for Belgian-made guns only.

FN FNC–Select Fire Assault Rifle

This model, introduced in 1979, took the place of the CAL. Chambered for the 5.56x45mm cartridge and fitted with a 17.5" barrel, it weighs about 8.4 lbs. It has a 30-round magazine capacity. Rate of fire is 700 rounds per minute. Fitted with a metal folding stock. This model will accept M16 magazines. Marked "FNC 5.56" on left side of receiver. This rifle was adopted by the Belgian, Indonesian, and Swedish militaries.

Pre-1968

Exc.	V.G.	Fair
N/A	N/A	N/A

Pre-1986 conversions

Exc.	V.G.	Fair
5500	4500	4000

Pre-1986 dealer samples

Exc.	V.G.	Fair
4000	3800	3500

FN BAR Model D (Demontable)

Photo courtesy Jim Thompson

This was the FN version of the Browning automatic rifle. It is fitted with a quick change barrel and pistol grip. It was offered in a variety of calibers from 6.5 Swedish Mauser to the 7.92x57mm Mauser. It is fitted with a 19.5" barrel and has a rate of fire of either 450 or 650 rounds per minute. Weight is about 20 lbs. Marked "FABRIQUE NATIONALE D'ARMES DE GUERRE HERSTAL-BELGIQUE" on left side of receiver.

FN sold about 700 Model Ds to Finland in 1940 which the Finns used during their "Winter War" with the Russians. These Finnish BARs were chambered for the 7.63x54R cartridge. Also a small number of FN guns were sold to China (2,000) and Ethiopia in the 1930s. These BARs were chambered for the 7.92x57mm Mauser cartridge. After World War II FN sold its Model 30 BAR to a number of countries around the world.

Pre-1968 (Very Rare)

Exc.	V.G.	Fair
35500	30000	27500

Pre-1986 conversions

Exc.	V.G.	Fair
22000	20000	18000

Pre-1986 dealer samples

Exc.	V.G.	Fair
17500	16000	15000

MACHINE GUNS

Fabrique Nationale has a long history of manufacturing John M. Browning's firearms. These firearms include the Browning Model 1917, M1919, and .50 caliber heavy gun. The light machine guns were chambered in a variety of calibers and sold around the world by FN. During World War II the FN factory was occupied by German troops, but after the war in 1945 when production finally returned to normal levels, the Belgians produced the air-cooled Browning guns in 7.62x63mm (.30-06) for the Belgian army. When NATO adopted the 7.62x51mm cartridge, FN designed and built the FN MAG machine gun.

FN MAG (Mitrailleuse d'Appui Generale) (M240)

First produced in Belgium in 1955, this machine gun is chambered for the 7.62x51mm cartridge. It is fitted with a 21.3" quick change barrel and has an adjustable rate of fire of 700 to 1000 rounds per minute. It is belt-fed with metal links. The basic configuration uses a wooden buttstock, smooth barrel with bipod attached to gas cylinder, pistol grip, and slotted flash hider. The gun can also be attached to a tripod as well as used with an anti-aircraft mount. Weight is about 22 lbs. Marked "FABRIQUE NATIONALE D'ARMES DE GUERRE HERSTAL BELGIUM" on the right side of the receiver. This gun is still in production and is in use by over 80 countries worldwide.

There is an aircraft version of this gun designated as Model 60-30 (single mount) or 60-40 (twin mount). The gun can also be mounted in a coaxial configuration such as a tank or armored vehicle.

Pre-1968 (Very Rare)

Exc.	V.G.	Fair
125000+	—	—

Pre-1986 conversions

Side-plates, 65 registered.

Exc.	V.G.	Fair
75000	70000	67500

Pre-1986 dealer samples

Exc.	V.G.	Fair
85000	—	—

NOTE: This is an extremely rare machine gun with prices based on scarcity and demand. It is possible for prices to exceed $125,000 under certain conditions.

FN Minimi (M249)

Designed as a squad automatic weapon (SAW) and chambered for the 5.56x45mm cartridge, this machine gun has a rate of fire of 700 to 1,000 rounds per minute and is equipped with a 30-round box magazine or 100 to 200-round boxed belts. Rate of fire with box magazine is higher than when using belt. The quick change barrel length is 18" and weight is about

15 lbs. Marked "FN MINIMI 5.56" on the left side of the receiver. First produced in 1982, this gun is called the M249 machine gun in the U.S. Army. It is also in service in a number of other countries such as Canada, Australia, and Italy.

Photo courtesy private NFA collection

Pre-1968
Extremely rare, 1 known.

Exc.	V.G.	Fair
100000	—	—

Pre-1986 conversions
Exc.	V.G.	Fair
N/A	N/A	N/A

Pre-1986 dealer samples
Extremely rare, only 6 known.

Exc.	V.G.	Fair
50000	—	—

A U.S. M240 sold at auction for $97,750. Fully transferable. Barrel length is 24.5 inches. Condition is 98 percent original overall finish. Bore excellent.
Amoskeag Auction Company, November 2004

BRAZIL

Brazilian Military Conflicts, 1870–Present

Pedro II was the ruler of Brazil from 1840 until 1889. During this period the country grew and prospered, while at the same time overthrowing several neighboring dictatorships. In 1889 a military revolt overthrew Pedro II and Brazil was proclaimed a republic. In 1891 the country was officially named the United States of Brazil with a constitution similar to that of the U.S. During World War I, Brazil contributed ships and supplies to the Allied forces. After the war, economic difficulties created a series of crises and unrest which led to widespread revolt. Finally, in 1930 a military coup brought relative stability to the country for the next 15 years. Brazil was on the Allied side during World War II and it contributed important military support such as military bases and supplies to the Allied effort. After the end of the war, Brazil suffered through four decades of unstable governments. In 2001, Brazil had a total military force of 287,600, of which 189,000 were in the army. First line reserves number 1,115,000. These include 385,600 para-military forces.

HANDGUNS

NOTE: Brazil used a number of Colt Model 1911A1 pistols (Pst M1911A1). These pistols are still in service in second line units. Mauser shipped a few hundred Model 1912/14 pistols to Brazil. In the 1930s about 500 Mauser Schnellfeuer pistols were purchased and a few are still in service. Brazil has also purchased the Beretta Model 92 from Italy.

In the 1980s Brazil began to produce its own version of the Colt 1911A1 known as the Imbel M973. Other variations of this pistol have been produced in 9x19, 9x17, and .38 Super. No examples of these pistols are known in the U.S.

A number of Smith & Wesson Model 1917s were used by Brazil and many have found their way into the U.S.

SUBMACHINE GUNS

Brazil has used or is using in second line units the U.S. M3 gun, the Beretta Model 12, the H&K MP5 and MP5SD. Brazil has additionally issued the Walther MPK. A few Thompson M1s and U.S. Reisings are used as well.

URU Model 2

Chambered for the 9mm parabellum cartridge and fitted with a 7" barrel with slotted barrel jacket. Made of stampings with round receiver. Forward magazine acts as a handgrip. Magazine capacity is 30 rounds. Detachable wooden butt or steel single strut stock. Rate of fire is about 750 rounds per minute. Weight is about 6.5 lbs. Produced in Brazil at Bilbao SA in Sao Paulo.

Pre-1968

Exc.	V.G.	Fair
N/A	N/A	N/A

Pre-1986 conversions

Exc.	V.G.	Fair
N/A	N/A	N/A

Pre-1986 dealer samples

Exc.	V.G.	Fair
3000	2500	2250

RIFLES

Brazil uses the HK 33E, the M16 (Model 614), the M16A2, and the FN FAL and variations, built under license from FN. The Brazilian military also uses the U.S. M1 rifle converted to 7.62 NATO caliber.

MAUSER

M1894 Rifle

Similar to the Spanish Model 1893 but with a cylindrical bolt head. Barrel length is 29". Chambered for the 7x57 cartridge. Magazine is flush mounted and has a 5-round capacity. Adjustable rear sight from 400 to 2,000 meters. Brazilian crest on receiver ring. Produced by DWM and FN.

Exc.	V.G.	Good	Fair	Poor
300	225	125	100	75

M1894 Carbine

As above but with 18" barrel and adjustable rear sight to 1,400 meters. No bayonet lug.

Exc.	V.G.	Good	Fair	Poor
350	250	150	100	75

M1904 Mauser-Verueiro Rifle

Chambered for the 6.5x58Pmm cartridge, this model was fitted with a 29" barrel. Tangent sight graduated to 2,000 meters. Brazilian crest on receiver ring. Produced by DWM.

Exc.	V.G.	Good	Fair	Poor
325	250	200	150	100

M1907 Rifle

Built by DWM from 1904 to 1906. Sold to Brazil in 1907. Chambered for the 7x57mm cartridge. Pistol grip stock. Fitted with a 29" barrel. Tangent rear sight graduated to 2,000 meters. Built by DWM. Brazilian crest on receiver ring.

Exc.	V.G.	Good	Fair	Poor
325	250	200	150	100

M1907 Carbine

As above with shorter barrel. Produced from 1907 to 1912 by DWM.

Exc.	V.G.	Good	Fair	Poor
400	300	250	175	100

M1908 Rifle

Similar in appearance to the Gew 98. Chambered for the 7x57mm cartridge. Built by DWM between 1908 and 1914. Fitted with a 29.25" barrel. Magazine capacity is 5 rounds. Tangent rear sight graduated to 2,000 meters. Brazilian crest on receiver ring.

Courtesy Rock Island Auction Company

Exc.	V.G.	Good	Fair	Poor
325	225	125	100	75

M1908 Short Rifle

Same as the Model 1908 rifle but with a 22" barrel.

Exc.	V.G.	Good	Fair	Poor
300	200	150	100	70

M1922 Carbine

Chambered for the 7x57mm cartridge and fitted with a 19.5" barrel. Magazine capacity is 5 rounds. Tangent rear sight graduated to 1,400 meters. Built by FN. Weight is about 6.5 lbs.

Exc.	V.G.	Good	Fair	Poor
275	175	130	90	60

VZ 24 Short Rifle

This rifle was built in Czechoslovakia and sold to Brazil in 1932. Bent bolt handle with flat bolt knob. Finger grooves in forend. Czech markings (BRNO). About 15,000 sold to Brazil.

Exc.	V.G.	Good	Fair	Poor
300	200	125	90	75

M1935 Mauser Banner Rifle

Chambered for the 7x57mm cartridge. Fitted with a 28.75" barrel. Magazine capacity is 5 rounds. Tangent rear sight graduated to 2,000 meters. Brazilian crest on receiver ring. Finger grooves in forend. Weight is about 10 lbs.

Exc.	V.G.	Good	Fair	Poor
400	300	240	195	120

M1935 Mauser Banner Carbine

As above but with 21.5" barrel. Rear sight graduated to 1,400 meters. Bent bolt handle. Stock cut to accommodate the downturn of the bolt handle. Mauser banner logo on the receiver ring. Brazilian crest on receiver ring. Weight is about 9 lbs.

Exc.	V.G.	Good	Fair	Poor
600	450	300	200	150

M1908/34 Short Rifle

Built in Brazil at Itajuba. The stock for this model used local wood and not European walnut. Chambered for the .30-06 cartridge. Fitted with a 23.5" barrel. Tangent rear sight graduated to 2,000 meters. Weight is about 9.75 lbs. Brazilian crest on receiver ring. Manufacturer's markings on side rail.

Exc.	V.G.	Good	Fair	Poor
350	250	195	150	90

M1954 Caliber .30-06 Short Rifle

This model was also built in Brazil and chambered for the .30-06 cartridge. Fitted with a 23.25" barrel. Tangent rear sight graduated to 2,000 meters. Pistol grip stock with finger grooves. Nose cap fitted with a bayonet lug. Weight is about 8.75 lbs. Brazilian crest on receiver ring.

Exc.	V.G.	Good	Fair	Poor
350	250	180	125	90

MACHINE GUNS

The Brazilian military uses a wide variety of machine guns. They are: the FN MAG, Browning M1919A4, the Browning .50 M2 HB, the Danish Madsen converted to .30 caliber, and even the Hotchkiss LMG in 7mm. The Brazilian military has also developed, in the 1990s, its own design called the Uirapuru GPMG in 7.62x51mm.

A Brazilian Mauser Model 1935 rifle sold at auction for $3,450. Condition was Near Mint. Supplied with leather case, matching bayonet with scabbard, and test target.
Rock Island Auction Company, December 2001

CANADA

Canadian Military Conflicts, 1870–Present

In 1867, under the British North America Act, the Dominion of Canada was created. In 1982 the British Parliament in London gave Canada's constitution full self control. Because Canada has such close ties to Great Britain, much of Canada's military history closely follows Great Britain, especially during both World Wars and Vietnam.

HANDGUNS

INGLIS, JOHN & COMPANY

Introduction by Clive M. Law

This firm manufactured Browning Pattern .35 semiautomatic pistols for the Canadian, Chinese, and British governments. Pistols are parkerized dark gray and include black plastic grips and a lanyard ring. Premium paid for pistols which still display the Canadian "Lend-Lease" decal on the front grip strap. Fewer than 160,000 pistols were manufactured between 1943 and 1945. Add $350 for original Canadian-produced wood stocks. Prices shown here are for original finish unaltered pistols, prices lower for recent Chinese and British imports.

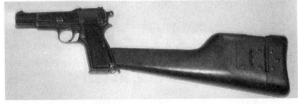

Courtesy Richard M. Kumor Sr.

Mk. 1 No. 1 (Chinese Marked)

The first 4,000 pistols destined for the Chinese government included a six character Chinese marking on the slide, as well as a serial number which incorporated the letters "CH." Includes a tangent rear sight and a stock slot.

Exc.	V.G.	Good	Fair	Poor
2000	1650	1400	950	800

Mk. 1 No. 1

Identical to the Chinese-marked model but without the Chinese characters.

Exc.	V.G.	Good	Fair	Poor
1250	1000	925	825	750

Mk. 1 No. 1*

Externally identical to the No. 1 Mk. 1 but the slide includes the marking Mk. 1*. This mark may be factory applied, or applied in the field after conversion.

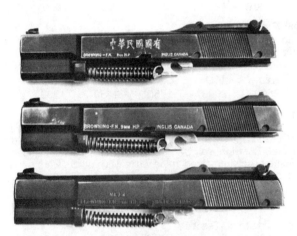

Inglis slides from top to bottom: Chinese pattern No. 1 Mk.1, Canadian forces No. 2 Mk.1, later Chinese-type No. 1 Mk. 1* • Courtesy Blake Stevens, *The Browning High-Power*, Stevens

Exc.	V.G.	Good	Fair	Poor
750	600	475	425	375

No. 2 Mk. 1

The first 10,000 pistols made for Canada/Britain display the standard slide legend, fixed rear sight in the distinctive Inglis "hump," and no stock slot. All No. 2 type pistols will incorporate the letter "T" within the serial number.

Exc.	V.G.	Good	Fair	Poor
1000	925	850	775	675

No. 2 Mk. 1*

Identical to the No. 2 Mk. 1 externally but the slide includes the marking Mk. 1*. This mark may be factory applied, or applied in the field after conversion. Some examples imported from England or New Zealand may include the "No. 2" stamped or engraved on the slide.

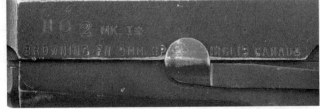

Paul Goodwin photo

Exc.	V.G.	Good	Fair	Poor
750	600	500	425	375

No. 2 Mk. 1* Slotted

A small quantity of pistols, mostly in the 3Txxx range, were made up from Chinese frames and includes the stock slot. Beware of fakes.

Exc.	V.G.	Good	Fair	Poor
1500	1250	925	625	500

DP Pistols

Approximately 150 No. 1 type pistols, some with the Chinese inscription, were made up as display and presentation pistols. Serial numbers will range from approximately DP1 to DP150.

Exc.	V.G.	Good	Fair	Poor
2500	2000	1750	1450	1200

Inglis Diamond

In the last week of production, Inglis marked a small quantity of pistols with their trademark, the word Inglis within a diamond. Both the No. 1 and No. 2-style pistols were affected. Some pistols remained in the white while others were parkerized. It is believed that fewer than 50 pistols were marked.

Exc.	V.G.	Good	Fair	Poor
2500	2250	1900	1650	1200

New Zealand Issue

Only 500 pistols were acquired by New Zealand in the 1960s. A serial number list will soon be published which will identify 400 of these pistols. A small quantity was modified, and marked, by the NZ Special Air Service.

Exc.	V.G.	Good	Fair	Poor
1250	950	700	575	525

British Issue

A large quantity of pistols have been imported from the British Ministry of Defense over the past several years. These pistols often display a black "paint" finish and may be marked "FTR" (Factory Thorough Repair) or "AF" (meaning unknown).

Exc.	V.G.	Good	Fair	Poor
600	525	500	475	425

Dutch Issue

The Netherlands used over 10,000 Inglis pistols. Early versions display a small crown over W mark on the rear sight while later models will have Dutch serial numbers, Belgian proofs, and Belgian barrels.

Exc.	V.G.	Good	Fair	Poor
2500	2300	2100	1800	1600

Belgian Issue

Belgium received 1,578 pistols as aid from Canada in the 1950s. These remained in use with the Gendarmerie until recently. Some pistols will display a grey "paint" finish and have numbered magazines. These have been wrongly identified as Danish navy in the past.

Exc.	V.G.	Good	Fair	Poor
3000	2500	2300	2100	1700

SAVAGE

Savage Model 1907

Canada purchased 500 Model 1907 pistols sometime during World War I. Chambered for 7.65mm. These pistols were later redirected to England but most will have the Canadian Broad Arrow stamped on the frame near the safety.

Exc.	V.G.	Good	Fair	Poor
750	600	400	200	150

SUBMACHINE GUNS

Canadian Sten MK II

These are Canadian built Sten MK II guns built at Long Branch between February 1942 and September 1945. A total of 133,497 guns were produced in this interval. Canadian built Stens are marked "LONG BRANCH" on the magazine housing with the date of manufacture.

NOTE: Canadian Stens do not bring a premium over British-made Stens.

Pre-1968

Exc.	V.G.	Fair
6500	5000	4000

Pre-1986 conversions (or U.S.-manufactured receivers)

Exc.	V.G.	Fair
3500	3000	2500

Pre-1986 dealer samples

Exc.	V.G.	Fair
3500	3000	2000

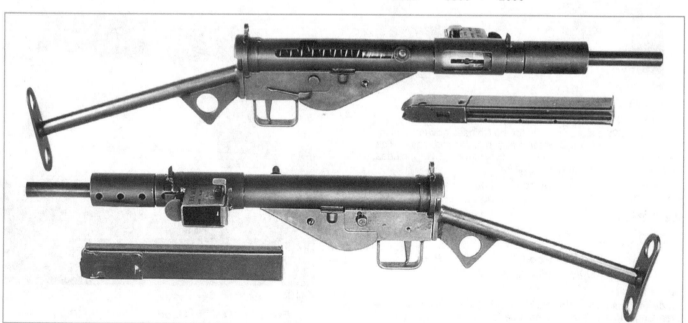

Canadian Sten Mark II • Courtesy Robert G. Segel

Sterling-Canadian C1

Chambered for the 9mm cartridge, this submachine gun features a 7.75" barrel and collapsible metal stock. The rate of fire is 550 rounds per minute. Weight is about 6 lbs. Produced from 1953 to 1988. Still made in India under license. Marked "SMG 9MM C1" on the magazine housing.

The Canadian version of the Sterling is much like the British except for a 30-round magazine without rollers as followers, a different type bayonet (FAL), and internal modifications. A 10-round magazine is also available. Designated the "C1" by the Canadian military. It was first produced in Canada in the late 1950s.

Courtesy private NFA collection

Pre-1968 (Very Rare)

Exc.	V.G.	Fair
12000	10000	9000

Pre-1986 conversions

Exc.	V.G.	Fair
7000	6000	5500

Pre-1986 dealer samples

Exc.	V.G.	Fair
6000	5500	5000

RIFLES

PEABODY

Canadian Rifle Musket (1867)

Chambered for the .50-60 Peabody rimfire cartridge and fitted with a 36" barrel. Blued barrel with case hardened furniture. "CM" marked on right side of buttstock and "DWB" on left wrist. Canada purchased 3,000 of these rifles but a total of 5,000 were produced.

Exc.	V.G.	Good	Fair	Poor
—	1250	800	500	200

ROSS RIFLE CO.

Designed in 1896 by Sir Charles Ross, this straight pull rifle was manufactured in a variety of styles. Due to problems with the bolt design, it never proved popular and was discontinued in 1915.

Mark I

This rifle was adopted by the Canadian military in 1903. Barrel length is 28". Chambered for .303 caliber with a "Harris Controlled Platform Magazine" that can be depressed by an external lever to facilitate loading. Magazine capacity is 5 rounds. Marked "ROSS RIFLE COM. QUEBEC CANADA" on left side of receiver. About 5,000 of these rifles were built.

Courtesy Buffalo Bill Historical Center, Cody, Wyoming

Exc.	V.G.	Good	Fair	Poor
550	425	300	150	100

Mark I Carbine

As above, with a 26" barrel without bayonet lug.

Exc.	V.G.	Good	Fair	Poor
450	300	250	200	150

Mark II

Introduced in 1905 with a modified rear sight, longer handguard, no receiver bridge. Marked "ROSS RIFLE CO. QUEBEC CANADA 1905."

Courtesy Paul S. Scarlata from *Mannlicher Military Rifles*, Andrew Mobray Publishers

Exc.	V.G.	Good	Fair	Poor
550	425	300	150	100

Mark III

Built between 1910 and 1916 with improved lockwork and stripper clip guides. Extended single column 5-round box magazine. Barrel length is 30". Marked "ROSS RIFLE CO." over "CANADA" over "M10" on receiver ring. About 400,000 of these rifles were produced with about 67,000 sent to the British Army.

Courtesy Buffalo Bill Historical Center, Cody, Wyoming

Mark III Ross rifle • Courtesy Paul S. Scarlata

Exc.	V.G.	Good	Fair	Poor
500	350	275	175	125

Mark III*

As above, with a magazine cutoff.

Exc.	V.G.	Good	Fair	Poor
450	300	250	200	150

Ross Military Match Rifle

A .280 Ross or .303 caliber straight pull military-style rifle with a 30" barrel having peep sights. Blued with a walnut stock. Similar in appearance to the Mark III except for flush magazine with .280 version.

Exc.	V.G.	Good	Fair	Poor
825	600	400	250	125

Ross .22 single-shot rifle. Close-up of "broad arrow" on buttstock and receiver markings • Courtesy Stoddard Martial collection, Paul Goodwin photo

Canadian No. 4 Mk1 T "Long Branch" with original Lyman Alaskan scope set. Scope is mounted on a Griffin & Howe type base and mount. All numbers match on this rifle. Notice the broad arrow mark on the base of the top turret • Courtesy Michael Wamsher, Paul Goodwin photo

Canadian No. 4 Mk1 T "Long Branch" Sniper with original matching Canadian "R.E.L." scope set (No. 32 Mk3). All numbers match on this rifle. Notice the broad arrow on the left side of the scope • Courtesy Michael Wamsher, Paul Goodwin photo

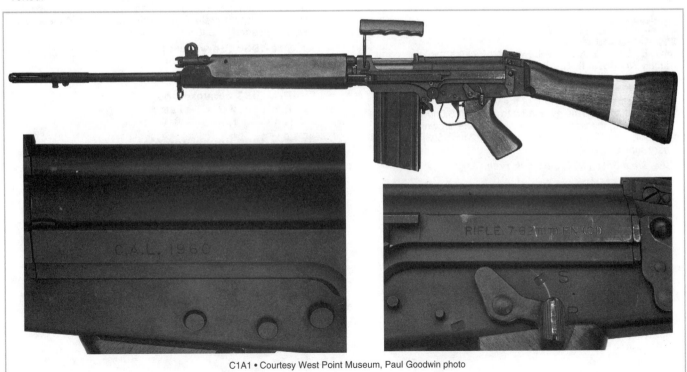

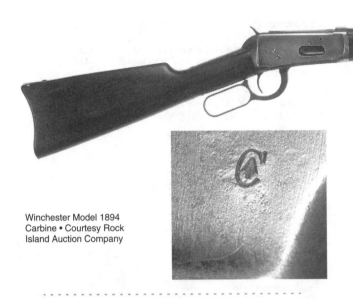

Winchester Model 1894
Carbine • Courtesy Rock
Island Auction Company

- -

Ross Military Training Rifle

Chambered for the .22 caliber cartridge this straight pull rifle is single shot only.

Exc.	V.G.	Good	Fair	Poor
N/A	—	—	—	—

LEE ENFIELD
Long Branch

Rifle No. 4 Mark I (T) & Mark I* (T)

These are sniper versions of the No. 4 Mark I and the Mark I*. Fitted with scope mounts on the left side of the receiver and a wooden cheekpiece screwed to the buttstock. A No. 32 or a No. 67 (Canadian) telescope was issued with these rifles. A few, estimated to be about 100, were fitted with U.S. Lyman scopes. Many of these rifles were converted by Holland & Holland. About 25,000 rifles using various telescopes were converted.

Exc.	V.G.	Good	Fair	Poor
1500	1150	700	500	350

NOTE: Prices above are for rifles in original wood case and scope numbered to the rifle. For rifles without case deduct 10 percent. A subvariation of this model has no scope fitted to the rifle and is not stamped with a "T" on the butt.

WINCHESTER

Model 1894 Carbine

This is the Canadian military version of the Winchester saddle ring carbine. Fitted with a 20" barrel and chambered for the .30-30 cartridge. Extra set of sling swivels added to left side of buttstock and forearm. Stamped with the Canadian "Broad Arrow" (an arrow inside the letter C).

Exc.	V.G.	Good	Fair	Poor
1750	1500	950	450	250

FABRIQUE NATIONALE

C1/C1A1 (FN FAL)

Canada was one of the first countries to adopt the FN-FAL rifle. This is a semiautomatic version with 21" barrel. Twenty-round box magazine. The rear sight on the C1 is a revolving disk with five different sized openings. Ranges calibrated from 200 to 600 yards; numbered 2 to 6 on the sight. The sight may be folded when not in use. Weight is about 9.5 lbs. About 1959 the C1 was modified to use a 2-piece firing pin and a plastic carry handle replaced the wooden type. Both types of rifles utilize the long prong flash hider on the muzzle.

Exc.	V.G.	Good	Fair	Poor
2500	2000	1500	1000	500

NOTE: For C1/C1A1 registered as NFA firearms see prices listed.

C1A1 • Courtesy West Point Museum, Paul Goodwin photo

Pre-1968 (Rare)

Exc.	V.G.	Fair
9000	8500	8000

Pre-1986 conversions

Exc.	V.G.	Fair
5500	5000	4500

Pre-1986 dealer samples

Exc.	V.G.	Fair
4000	3500	3000

C2/C2A1

This is Canada's version of the FN heavy barrel Squad Light Automatic Rifle. Select fire with a rate of fire of about 700 rounds per minute. Barrel length is 21". Magazine capacity is 30 rounds. Weight is approximately 15 lbs. Built by Long Branch Arsenal, Ontario.

Pre-1968 (Rare)

Exc.	V.G.	Fair
10000	9000	8000

Pre-1986 conversions

Exc.	V.G.	Fair
6000	5500	5000

Pre-1986 dealer samples

Exc.	V.G.	Fair
5000	4500	4000

C7/C8 (M16A2)

In 1985 the Canadian firm of Diemaco began producing a Canadian version of the Colt M16A2 rifle. There are differences between the Colt-built M16 and the Diemaco version. However, due to import restrictions on Class 3 weapons, no Diemaco M16s were imported into the U.S. for transferable civilian sale. Therefore, no Diemaco lowers are available to the civilian collector. There are Diemaco uppers in the U.S. that will fit on Colt lowers. The 20" rifle version is designated the C7 while the 16" carbine version is called the C8. There are a number of other Diemaco Canadian uppers that may be seen in the U.S., such as the LMG and 24" barreled versions. Prices should be comparable with Colt uppers.

MACHINE GUNS

NOTE: Canada used the Lewis and Vickers machine guns during World War II. The Toronto firm of John Inglis produced Mark I and Mark II Bren guns in .303 caliber in large quantities for British and Canadian troops. Beginning in 1943 Canada produced almost 60 percent of the total Bren gun production for World War II. This amounted to about 186,000 guns produced during the war. Canada also uses the Browning Model 1919A4, called the C1 machine gun in 7.62mm (.308) as its primary light machine gun.

See *Great Britain Machine Guns, Bren*.

Canadian Bren Mk I and Mk II

The first examples of the Canadian Bren were built in 1940 by the Inglis Company. A total of 186,000 Brens were built in Canada with 56,000 going to the Canadian army. Marked with the date and manufacturer (Inglis) on the right side of the receiver.

Pre-1968

Exc.	V.G.	Fair
45000	42500	40000

Pre-1986 conversions

Exc.	V.G.	Fair
25000	22500	20000

Pre-1986 dealer samples

Exc.	V.G.	Fair
17500	15000	13000

Inglis Bren Mk I • Courtesy Blake Stevens, *The Bren Gun Saga*, Dugelby

Canadian Chinese Bren Mk II

Full production of Mk II Bren guns in 7.62x57mm began in January of 1944 and ended in 1945. These guns were produced under a Chinese contract. About 39,300 of these guns are marked with Chinese characters and Inglis with the date of manufacture. Some 3,700 guns were sent to resistance groups in Europe. These were not marked in Chinese, but marked with "ch" prefix serial numbers. A few of these guns were converted to .308 for Canadian use.

Pre-1968 (Very Rare)

Exc.	V.G.	Fair
45000	42500	40000

Pre-1986 conversions

Exc.	V.G.	Fair
N/A	N/A	N/A

Pre-1986 dealer samples

Exc.	V.G.	Fair
N/A	N/A	N/A

CHINA & PEOPLE'S REPUBLIC OF CHINA

Chinese Military Conflicts, 1870–2000

By 1870 China was affected by foreign influence from Great Britain, France, Germany, and Russia. The central government in China was further weakened by its defeat in the Sino-Japanese War of 1894-1895. The decade of the 1890s ended with China's fierce attempt to overthrow foreign influence by means of the Boxer Rebellion, 1898 to 1900. The period of the early 20th century was marked by internal strife which eventually led to Chinese warlords gaining control of the government in 1916. These warlords were eventually ousted in 1927 by the Nationalist leader Chiang Kai-shek in alliance with the Communists. The year 1927 marked the beginning of a long Chinese civil war between the Nationalist and the Communists ending with the Communists' Long March of 1934-35 and their exile. In 1931 Japan occupied Manchuria, and in 1937 the Japanese mounted a full-scale invasion of China. Both the Nationalists and the Communists fought in an uneasy alliance against the Japanese. By the end of World War II, the civil war again ignited and the Communists became victorious in 1949 when the People's Republic of China was proclaimed. China entered the Korean War on the side of the North Koreans in 1950. In the last 50 years China has been occupied with intellectual turmoil (Cultural Revolution) and other domestic ferment.

HANDGUNS

MAUSER

Between the two world wars, the Chinese military purchased a number of Mauser 1896 pistols directly from Mauser and other commercial sources. These purchases consisted mainly of Bolos and Model 1930s. In addition to these purchases, China made its own copies of the Mauser broomhandle as well as the Astra. *See Germany, Handguns, Mauser for more detailed descriptions and prices.*

CHINESE MAUSERS

The Chinese government purchased a large quantity of Mauser pistols directly from Mauser and continued to do so until they began purchasing Browning Hi-Power pistols from FN in the mid 1930s. The Chinese bought many Bolos and Model 1930 pistols. Some of these pistols are marked with Chinese characters, many are not. The Chinese also made their own copies of Mauser broomhandles as well as Spanish copies. Some of the more commonly encountered varieties are listed here.

Chinese Marked, Handmade Copies

Crude copies of the Model 96; unsafe to fire.

Exc.	V.G.	Good	Fair	Poor
500	400	350	250	175

Taku-Naval Dockyard Model

Approximately 6,000 copies of the Model 96 were made at the Taku-Naval Dockyard. Values listed below include a correct shoulder stock/holder.

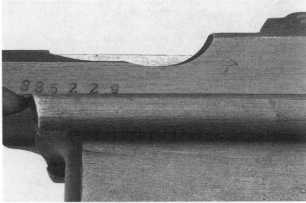

Taku Naval Dockyard Model • Private collection, Paul Goodwin photo

Exc.	V.G.	Good	Fair	Poor
2500	1500	1000	500	400

Shansei Arsenal Model

Approximately 8,000 Model 96 pistols were manufactured in .45 ACP caliber at the Shansei Province Arsenal in 1929. Magazine capacity is 10 rounds.

NOTE: Within the past several years, a large quantity of Model 96 pistols exported to or made in China have been imported into the United States. It has been reported that some *newly* made copies of the Shansei .45 were recently exported from China. **Proceed with caution**.

NOTE: Copies of the Model 96 were made by Unceta (Astra), Eulogio Arostegui (Azul), and Zulaica y Cia (Royal) and marketed by the firm of Beistegui Hermanos. These copies are covered in their own sections of this text.

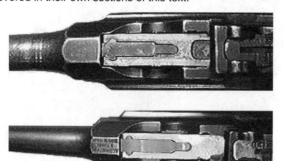

Courtesy Gale Morgan

Shansei Panel Marking

Courtesy Gale Morgan

Exc.	V.G.	Good	Fair	Poor
5000	3500	2250	1500	1300

CHINA STATE ARSENALS

Type 51/54 Pistol (TT33)

A 7.62mm semiautomatic pistol with a 4.5" barrel and 8-shot magazine. This model was produced in a number of communist countries. It is essentially a Soviet Tokarev TT-33.

Exc.	V.G.	Good	Fair	Poor
500	450	375	225	100

NOTE: For cut-aways add 200 percent.

From top to bottom: M20 export model, K54, K51 • Courtesy Chuck Karwan

Type 59 Makarov

This semiautomatic pistol is similar in appearance to the Walther PP pistol and is chambered for the 9mm Makarov (9x18mm) cartridge. It has a double-action trigger and is fitted with fixed sights. Barrel length is 3.6" and overall length is 6.4". Weight is approximately 25 oz. Magazine capacity is 8 rounds.

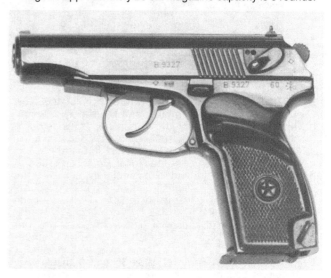

Exc.	V.G.	Good	Fair	Poor
150	100	80	60	50

Type 80

A Chinese version of the Mauser 96 pistol chambered for the 7.63x25mm cartridge. Fitted with a 7" barrel and detachable 10- or 20-round magazine, this pistol is capable of select fire. Weight is approximately 40 oz. *See Mauser Schnellfeuer.*

SUBMACHINE GUNS

Type 43/53

This is a Chinese copy of a Soviet PPS 43 built during the Korean War.

Pre-1968

Exc.	V.G.	Fair
16000	15000	14000

Pre-1986 conversions

Exc.	V.G.	Fair
N/A	N/A	N/A

Pre-1986 dealer samples

Exc.	V.G.	Fair
N/A	N/A	N/A

Type 50

This model is a Chinese copy of the Soviet PPSh-41 submachine gun. It is chambered for the 7.62 Soviet pistol cartridge. Barrel is 10.5" and magazine capacity is 25, 32, or 40 rounds. Rate of fire is 600 rounds per minute. Weight is approximately 7.5 lbs. Markings are located on top of the receiver.

Pre-1968

Exc.	V.G.	Fair
15000	13500	12000

Pre-1986 conversions

Exc.	V.G.	Fair
N/A	N/A	N/A

Pre-1986 dealer samples

Exc.	V.G.	Fair
N/A	N/A	N/A

North Vietnamese Type 50 M • Paul Goodwin photo

North Vietnamese K-50M
Similar to the Type 50 but unlike the Soviet model, this gun features a telescoping metal stock and no muzzle compensator.

Pre-1968

Exc.	V.G.	Fair
16500	15000	13000

Pre-1986 conversions

Exc.	V.G.	Fair
N/A	N/A	N/A

Pre-1986 dealer samples

Exc.	V.G.	Fair
N/A	N/A	N/A

RIFLES

MAUSER

Mauser Rifles
The Chinese used a wide variety of Mauser rifles from the Gew 71 to the Chinese Model 1924. Some of these are marked with Chinese characters and others are not.

For in-depth information on Chinese Mausers, see Robert W.D. Ball's, *Mauser Military Rifles of the World*, 3rd Edition, Krause Publications, 2003.

G71 Rifle
This rifle is identical to the German model of the same designation.

Exc.	V.G.	Good	Fair	Poor
450	325	250	190	120

K71 Carbine
This carbine is identical to the German model of the same designation.

Exc.	V.G.	Good	Fair	Poor
450	350	225	200	150

M1895 Rifle
This model is identical to the Chilean Model 1895 rifle.

Exc.	V.G.	Good	Fair	Poor
250	200	175	130	90

Hunyaug Rifle

Exc.	V.G.	Good	Fair	Poor
250	200	175	130	90

M1907 Rifle
This model is based on the German Model 1904. Chambered for the 7.92x57mm cartridge. Fitted with a 29" barrel and 5-round magazine. Tangent rear sight to 2,000 meters. Made with a pistol grip stock and upper handguard. On the receiver ring two superposed diamonds are marked with the Chinese date for rifles made in China. German built rifles will have Mauser or DWM stamped on them. Weight is about 8.25 lbs.

Exc.	V.G.	Good	Fair	Poor
300	200	175	125	90

M1907 Carbine
As above but with 21.75" barrel and tangent sight to 1,400 meters. Turned down bolt handle and full stock. No bayonet. Weight is about 8 lbs.

Exc.	V.G.	Good	Fair	Poor
300	200	150	90	60

M1912 Steyr Rifle
Chambered for the 7x57mm cartridge and fitted with a 28.75" barrel. Weight is about 9 lbs. Built in Austria.

Exc.	V.G.	Good	Fair	Poor
350	225	175	120	90

M98/22 Rifle
Manufactured by CZ in BRNO, this rifle is based on the Mexican Model 1912 with a Model 98 action. It is half cocked with a full-length upper handguard with pistol grip. Chambered for the 7.92x57mm Mauser cartridge. Barrel length is 29" with a 5-round integral magazine. Weight is about 9.5 lbs. China purchased about 70,000 of these rifles.

Exc.	V.G.	Good	Fair	Poor
300	200	160	110	90

FN M24 and 30 Short Rifles

Exc.	V.G.	Good	Fair	Poor
175	120	90	60	40

M21 Short Rifle
A Chinese copy of the FN Model 30 Short Rifle. Pistol grip stock with upper handguard from receiver to upper band. Chambered for the 7.92x57mm cartridge and fitted with a 23.6" barrel. Tangent rear sight to 2,000 meters. Weight is about 8.5 lbs. Chinese characters marked on the receiver ring.

Exc.	V.G.	Good	Fair	Poor
200	150	120	90	50

Chiang Kai-shek Short Rifle
Chambered for the 7.92x57mm cartridge. Fitted with a 23.6" barrel. Tangent rear sight to 2,000 meters. Magazine capacity is 5 rounds in a flush mounted box magazine. Weight is approximately 8.75 lbs. Chinese markings on the receiver ring. Manufactured between 1936 and 1949, this rifle became the standard issue for Chinese troops.

Exc.	V.G.	Good	Fair	Poor
200	150	120	90	50

VZ24 Short Rifle
This is the Czech Model 24 short rifle purchased from Czechoslovakia in the mid-1930s. Approximately 100,000 were purchased and all have a "P" prefix in the serial number. All are

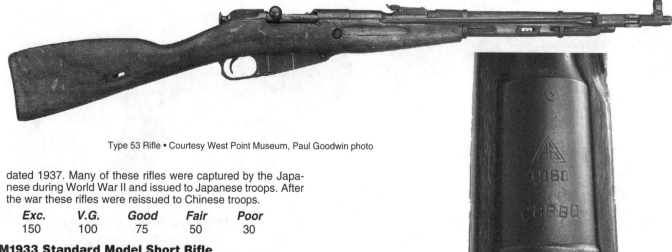

Type 53 Rifle • Courtesy West Point Museum, Paul Goodwin photo

dated 1937. Many of these rifles were captured by the Japanese during World War II and issued to Japanese troops. After the war these rifles were reissued to Chinese troops.

Exc.	V.G.	Good	Fair	Poor
150	100	75	50	30

M1933 Standard Model Short Rifle

Chambered for the 7.92x57mm cartridge and fitted with a 23.6" barrel. Magazine capacity is 5 rounds in a flush-mounted box magazine. Tangent rear sight to 2,000 meters. Mauser banner trademark is marked on the receiver ring. Weight is about 8.75 lbs. Stock has a pistol grip and upper handguard. Straight bolt handle.

Exc.	V.G.	Good	Fair	Poor
225	170	140	110	90

M1933 Standard Model Carbine

As above but with turned down bolt handle and sling swivels mounted on left side of stock. Chambered for the 7.92x57mm cartridge but also offered in 7.65x53mm and 7x57mm. Mauser trademark on receiver ring. Weight is about 8.5 lbs.

Exc.	V.G.	Good	Fair	Poor
225	170	140	110	90

VZ24 with Japanese Folding Bayonet (Chinese copy)

A copy of the VZ24 and fitted with a Japanese Model 44 folding bayonet. Pistol grip stock and straight bolt handle. Barrel length is 23". Chambered for the 7.92x57mm cartridge. Rear tangent sight to 2,000 meters. Chinese markings on the receiver. Weight is about 9 lbs.

Exc.	V.G.	Good	Fair	Poor
275	175	150	120	100

Manchurian Mauser Rifle (Mukden Arsenal)

See *Japan, Rifles*.

ARISAKA

In 1946 the Chinese had large numbers of Japanese Type 99 rifles. These rifles were altered to 7.92x57mm, 8x57mm, or 7.62x39mm calibers. Original Type 99 barrels were cut and rechambered. Most parts were refinished. Prices are in the $200 to $300 range for very good examples.

Type 53

This is a Chinese copy of the Soviet Model 1944 Mosin-Nagant carbine. Production began in 1953. Early models up to 1959 have Chinese characters for the model designation stamped on the receiver. Rifles made after 1959 do not have these characters. Chinese rifles have the bolt, magazine, floorplate, and buttplate serial-numbered to the rifle. Production ended sometime in the early 1960s.

Exc.	V.G.	Good	Fair	Poor
250	150	125	75	50

Type 56 Carbine (SKS)

A 7.62x39mm semiautomatic rifle with a 20.5" barrel and 10-shot fixed magazine. Blued with oil finished stock. This rifle was a standard service arm for most Eastern Bloc countries prior to the adoption of the AK-47.

Pre-Ban Rifles

Exc.	V.G.	Good	Fair	Poor
400	300	—	—	—

NOTE: The importation of post-ban SKS rifles has resulted in an oversupply of these rifles with the result that prices are less than $100 for guns in excellent condition. However, this situation may change and if that occurs the price will adjust accordingly. Study local conditions before purchase or sale of this firearm.

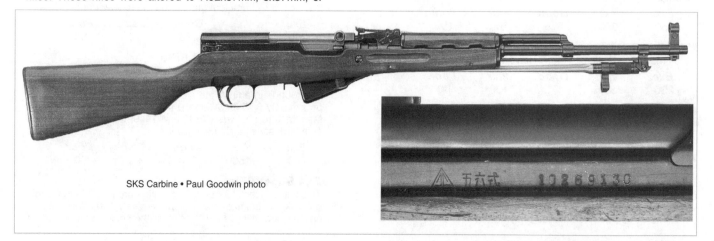

SKS Carbine • Paul Goodwin photo

Chinese Type 56-1 • Paul Goodwin photo

North Korean Type 56 Carbine (SKS)

Same overall design as the Chinese version but with high quality fit and finish. Reddish-brown laminated stock. Rare.

Pre-Ban Rifles

Exc.	V.G.	Good	Fair	Poor
1400	1000	800	600	300

Chinese Type 56 Rifle

A close copy of the AK-47 and first produced in 1958, this select fire rifle is chambered for the 7.62x39mm cartridge. It is fitted with a 16" barrel and has a magazine capacity of 30 rounds. This model has a folding bayonet hinged below the muzzle. Weight is about 8.4 lbs. Rate of fire is 600 rounds per minute. Markings on left side of receiver. Still in production. This rifle was adopted by Chinese forces and was seen in Cambodia as well.

There are a number of subvariations of the Type 56. Early guns had machined receivers with Chinese characters for selector markings, some of which are marked "M22" to designate export sales. Another style is fitted with a folding spike bayonet as well as a machined receiver. Still another style has a stamped receiver, Chinese characters for selector markings, and a folding spike bayonet. All are direct copies of the Soviet model AK-47.

Another variation of the Type 56 was the Type 56-1, which featured prominent rivets on a folding metal butt. No bayonet. Other variants of the Type 56-1 are fitted with a folding spike bayonet and folding metal buttstock. The Type 56-2 has a skeleton tubular stock which folds to the right side of the receiver with no bayonet. There is also the Type 56-C with plastic furniture, side folding butt with cheekpiece, and improved sights with no bayonet.

NOTE: Type 56 rifles manufactured by China North Industries (NORINCO) will have stamped on the left side of the receiver the number "66" in a triangle.

Pre-1968

Exc.	V.G.	Fair
32500	30000	28000

Pre-1986 conversions

Exc.	V.G.	Fair
15000	14000	13000

Pre-1986 dealer samples

Exc.	V.G.	Fair
15000	14000	13000

NOTE: Add about 25 percent for Type 56-1 examples.

Type 56 (AK Clone semiautomatic versions)

Imported from China in semiautomatic versions and built by Poly Tech and Norinco in different styles and configurations, some of which are listed below.

Milled Receiver—Poly Tech

Exc.	V.G.	Good	Fair	Poor
1500	1200	800	500	250

Stamped Receiver—Poly Tech

Exc.	V.G.	Good	Fair	Poor
1100	800	500	300	150

Stamped Receiver—Norinco

Exc.	V.G.	Good	Fair	Poor
950	700	450	250	150

NOTE: For folding stock version add 20 percent.

Type 79

A Chinese copy of the Soviet Dragunov SVD sniper rifle.

Exc.	V.G.	Good	Fair	Poor
3000	2500	1500	1000	750

MACHINE GUNS

NOTE: See also *Great Britain, Machine Guns, Bren MK2.*

Type 24

The Chinese copy of the German Model 1909 commercial Maxim built under the supervision of German engineers.

Pre-1968

Exc.	V.G.	Fair
20000	18000	17000

Pre-1986 conversions

Exc.	V.G.	Fair
12500	11000	10000

Pre-1986 dealer samples

Exc.	V.G.	Fair
N/A	N/A	N/A

Type 26

This is the Czech VZ26 purchased in the 1930s.

Type 53 • Courtesy West Point Museum, Paul Goodwin photo

Pre-1968
Exc.	*V.G.*	*Fair*
28000	26000	24000

Pre-1986 conversions
Exc.	*V.G.*	*Fair*
18000	16000	15000

Pre-1986 dealer samples (Rare)
Exc.	*V.G.*	*Fair*
N/A	N/A	N/A

Type 53

This is a Chinese copy of the Soviet DPM machine gun.

Pre-1968
Exc.	*V.G.*	*Fair*
20000	18000	16000

Pre-1986 conversions
Exc.	*V.G.*	*Fair*
10000	9000	8000

Pre-1986 dealer samples
Exc.	*V.G.*	*Fair*
N/A	N/A	N/A

Type 54

The Chinese made a variation of the Soviet DShK 38/46 gun.

Pre-1968
Exc.	*V.G.*	*Fair*
—	35000	30000

Type 57 with mount • Courtesy West Point Museum, Paul Goodwin photo

Pre-1986 conversions

Exc.	V.G.	Fair
—	27000	—

Pre-1986 dealer samples (Rare)

Exc.	V.G.	Fair
—	20000	20000

Type 56

This is a Chinese copy of the Soviet Model RPD light machine gun.

Pre-1968 (Very Rare)

Exc.	V.G.	Fair
40000	37500	35000

Pre-1986 conversions (rewelds)

Exc.	V.G.	Fair
33000	27500	25000

Pre-1986 dealer samples (Rare)

Exc.	V.G.	Fair
25000	23000	20000

Type 57

This is a Chinese copy of the Soviet SG-43.

Pre-1968

Exc.	V.G.	Fair
30000	28000	25000

Pre-1986 conversions

Exc.	V.G.	Fair
25000	23000	20000

Pre-1986 dealer samples (Rare)

Exc.	V.G.	Fair
N/A	N/A	N/A

Type 58

This is a licensed Chinese-made copy of the Soviet RP-46.

Pre-1968

Exc.	V.G.	Fair
25000	23000	21000

Pre-1986 conversions

Exc.	V.G.	Fair
10000	9000	8000

Pre-1986 dealer samples (Rare)

Exc.	V.G.	Fair
N/A	N/A	N/A

Type 58 • Courtesy West Point Museum,
Paul Goodwin photo

CZECHOSLOVAKIA

Czechoslovakian Military Conflicts, 1918–1993

Czechoslovakia, as an independent nation, was established at the end of World War I from the ruins of the Austro-Hungarian Empire. In 1939 the country was invaded and occupied by Germany. After the war ended in 1945, Czechoslovakia was re-established under Communist rule. Czechoslovakia was split in 1993 into the Czech Republic and Slovakia, both independent states.

Bibliographical Notes:

Perhaps the best general work on Czech firearms is *Czech Firearms and Ammunition*, by Dolinek, Karlicky, and Vacha, Prague, 1995. Jan Still, *Axis Pistols*, 1986.

NOTE: The term "VZ" stands for model (*Vzor*) in Czech. This abbreviation is used in place of the English word Model. The author has sometimes used both terms but never together.

HANDGUNS

Most Czech handguns are of domestic design and manufacture. See below.

Army Pistole 1922

Semiautomatic pistol chambered for the .380 ACP (9x17mm short) cartridge. Barrel length is 3.5". Magazine capacity is 8 rounds. Weight is approximately 22 oz. Adopted by the Czech army in 1922 and called the M22. This was the first Czech designed and manufactured service semiautomatic pistol. It was based on a German locked breech design and made under license from Mauser. Blued with checkered plastic grips. Manufactured between 1921 and 1923. Because of production difficulties, only about 22,000 were built.

Exc.	V.G.	Good	Fair	Poor
650	500	350	200	150

CZ 1924

The first large production military pistol produced by CZ. It is a locked-breech pistol with a 3.5" rotating barrel chambered for the 9mm short cartridge, external hammer, and a magazine safety. It features a rounded slide and is blued with a wrap-around walnut grip. Magazine capacity is 8 rounds. The slide is marked "Ceska Zbrojovka A.S. v Praze." Weight is approximately 24 oz. About 170,000 of these pistols were produced between 1922 and 1938.

NOTE: A limited number of pistols have been noted marked "CZ 1925" and "CZ 1926." There are various minor design changes on each model, and it is conjectured that they were prototypes that were manufactured on the road to the production of the less complicated, blowback-operated CZ 1927 pistol.

Exc.	V.G.	Good	Fair	Poor
500	375	300	200	100

NOTE: For Nazi-proofed add 50 percent.

CZ 1927

A semiautomatic pistol chambered for the 7.65mm cartridge (.32 ACP), marked the same as the CZ 1924, but the cocking grooves on the slide are cut vertically instead of sloped as on the earlier model. This model was blued with checkered, wrap-around, plastic grips. These early guns were beautifully made and marked "Ceska Zbrojovka AS v Praze."

This version remained in production during the German occupation of Czechoslovakia between 1939 and 1945. Occupation pistols are marked, "Bohmische Waffenfabrik im Prag." The Germans used the code "fnh" on these wartime pistols and designated the model the "Pistole Mod 27(t)." The finish declined as the war progressed, with the very late guns rough but functional. There are several subvariations of this pistol that may affect value (see Still). A total of about 450,000 were produced during the German occupation. After the war, these pistols continued in production until 1951. There were almost 700,000 manufactured.

Early CZ 27 with Nazi production markings • Courtesy Orvel Reichert

CZ 1924 • Courtesy Orvel Reichert

Early CZ 27 with Nazi production markings • Courtesy Orvel Reichert

Exc.	V.G.	Good	Fair	Poor
500	400	300	200	165

NOTE: For Nazi-proofed add 50 percent.

CZ27 with silencer • Courtesy Orvel Reichert

NOTE: Some of these pistols were made with an extended barrel for the use of a silencer. This variation brings a large premium. Less than 10 CZ 27s were made in .22 caliber. An expert opinion is suggested if a sale is contemplated.

CZ 1938

It is chambered for the 9mm short cartridge (.380 Auto) and has a 4.65" barrel. Except for a few examples with a conventional sear and slide safety, it is double action-only with exposed hammer, and difficult to fire accurately. It utilizes a 9-round, detachable box magazine; and the slide is hinged at the muzzle to pivot upward for ease of cleaning and disassem-

bly. It is well made and well finished, but is as large in size as most 9mm Parabellum pistols. Production began in 1938, and the Germans adopted it as the "Pistole Mod 39" on paper; but it is doubtful that any were actually used by the German army. It now appears that the P39(t), which is the Nazi designation, were all sent to Finland and a large number with "SA" (Finnish) markings have recently been surplussed along with their holsters. A few SA marked guns have been modified by the Finnish army to function single or double action. About 40,000 of these pistols were manufactured.

Exc.	V.G.	Good	Fair	Poor
500	400	350	250	175

A CA 27 sold at auction for $3,737.50. Chambered for the 7.65mm cartridge and fitted with a 5-inch barrel. Barrel extended for silencer, "fnh" code. German Army acceptance stamps. Condition is 95 percent original finish.
Rock Island Auction Company, August 2004

CZ 1938 Nazi-Proofed (P39[t])

Fewer than 1,000 of these pistols were Nazi-proofed late in the war. E/WaA76 acceptance stamp on left frame and barrel.

Exc.	V.G.	Good	Fair	Poor
—	1500	1250	600	300

CZ 1950

This is a blowback-operated, semiautomatic, double action pistol chambered for the 7.65mm cartridge with a 3.75" barrel. Magazine capacity is 8 rounds. Weight is about 23 oz. It is patterned after the Walther Model PP with a few differences. The safety catch is located on the frame instead of the slide; and the triggerguard is not hinged, as on the Walther. It is dismantled by means of a catch on the side of the frame. Although intended to be a military pistol designed by the Kratochvil brothers, it proved to be under-powered and was adopted by the police. There were few released on the commercial market.

CZ 1950 • Courtesy Chuck Karwan

Exc.	V.G.	Good	Fair	Poor
300	200	150	100	75

Model 1970

This model was an attempt to correct dependability problems with the Model 50. There is little difference to see externally between the two except for markings and the grip pattern. Markings are "VZOR 70 CAL 7.65." Production began during the 1960s and ended in 1983.

Courtesy Rock Island Auction Company

Exc.	V.G.	Good	Fair	Poor
300	200	150	100	75

CZ 1952

Since the Czechoslovakian army was not happy with the under-powered CZ 1950 pistol, they began using Soviet weapons until 1952, when this model was designed. It was designed for a new cartridge known as the 7.62mm M48. It was similar to the Soviet cartridge but loaded to a higher velocity. This is a single action, semiautomatic pistol with a 4.5" barrel. It has a locked breech that utilizes two roller cams. Magazine capacity is 8 rounds.

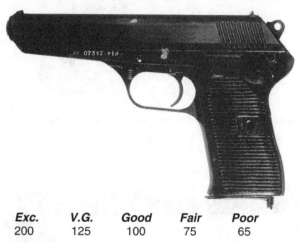

Exc.	V.G.	Good	Fair	Poor
200	125	100	75	65

CZ 75 B

Introduced in 1994, this CZ model is an updated version of the original CZ 75. It features a pinned front sight, a commander hammer, non-glare ribbed barrel, and a squared triggerguard. Also offered in .40 S&W chamber. Offered in both commercial and military versions the CZ 75 B is used by more than 60 countries around the world in 9mm. Approximately 1,250,000 military pistols are in service. The Czechs use the pistol in their Special Forces units.

NIB	Exc.	V.G.	Good	Fair	Poor
450	350	300	250	175	125

NOTE: For .40 S&W add $30. For glossy blue add $20, for dual tone finish add $25, and for nickel add $25. For tritium night sights add $80.

CZ 82/83

This is a fixed barrel .380 caliber pistol. It features an ambidextrous safety and magazine catch behind the triggerguard. The pistol is stripped by means of a hinged triggerguard. Barrel length is 3.8", overall length is 6.8", and weight is about 23 oz.

The Model 82 designation is the military model, while the Model 83 is the commercial version. The Model 83 is offered in 3 calibers: the 9x18, .380, and 9mm. The military Model 82 is offered in only 1 caliber, the 9mm Makarov. The Model 82 is the side arm of the Czech army. The Model 82 is no longer in production, but the Model 83 is currently manufactured.

NIB	Exc.	V.G.	Good	Fair	Poor
350	250	200	175	150	125

SUBMACHINE GUNS

The Czechs built the CZ 247 and the CZ 47 after World War II, but did not adopt these guns for their own military use. Instead they were exported to South America and other countries. These submachine guns are chambered for the 9mm Parabellum cartridge and are similar in appearance to the CZ 1938 gun but with a 40-round magazine.

CZ 23/25

The Model 23 has a wooden stock while the Model 25 has a folding metal stock; otherwise all other dimensions are the same. Introduced in 1948, this submachine gun is chambered for the 9mm cartridge. Magazine capacity is 25- or 40-round box type. Rate of fire is about 600 rounds per minute. Weight is approximately 8 to 8.5 lbs., depending on model. This gun introduced the hollow bolt that allows for the short length of the gun (17.5" with butt folded, 27" with butt extended) and was copied in the UZI. The magazine well is located in the pistol grip, another feature copied by the UZI. The trigger mechanism is designed so that light pressure gives semiautomatic fire while full trigger pressure gives full automatic fire. Weight of the gun is about 7 lbs. A variation of this model is called the Model 24/26 and is the same except for the caliber: 7.62mm.

NOTE: Prices listed are estimates only.

Courtesy Thomas Nelson, *The World's Submachine Guns, Vol. 1*

Pre-1968
Exc.	V.G.	Fair
12500	11000	10000

Pre-1986 conversions
Exc.	V.G.	Fair
N/A	N/A	N/A

Pre-1986 dealer samples
Exc.	V.G.	Fair
6000	5500	5000

ZK 383

This submachine gun was first introduced in 1933. It is chambered for the 9mm Parabellum cartridge and fitted with a 12.8" quick change barrel with jacket. Adjustable rate of fire from 500 to 700 rounds per minute by means of a removable insert in the bolt. This model fitted with a bipod. Rear sight is a V-notch tangent graduated to 800 meters. Weight is about 9.5 lbs. This gun was sold to Bulgaria, some South American countries, and was used by the German army from 1938 to 1945.

A variation of this model called the ZK 383P was used by police units and does not have a bipod or quick change barrel. The ZK 383H was a limited production version with a folding magazine housing fitted to the bottom of the gun rather than the side.

Pre-1968
Exc.	V.G.	Fair
14000	13000	12000

Pre-1986 conversions
Exc.	V.G.	Fair
N/A	N/A	N/A

Pre-1986 dealer samples
Exc.	V.G.	Fair
N/A	N/A	N/A

ZK 383 • Courtesy Thomas Nelson, *The World's Submachine Guns, Vol. 1*

Skorpion Samopal VZ61

Introduced in 1960 this weapon is sometimes referred to as a machine pistol because of its size. Chambered for the 7.65x17SR Browning (.32 ACP) cartridge. Export models of this gun are chambered for the 9x17mm (.380 ACP[VZ63]), 9x18mm Makarov (VZ64), and the 9x19mm Parabellum (VZ68). The gun has a 4.5" barrel and is fitted with a wooden pistol grip. Overall length with butt folded in 10.5", with butt extended the length is 20.5". Weight is approximately 3 lbs. Rate of fire is about 700 rounds per minute. A licensed copy is made in Yugoslavia called the Model 84.

Pre-1968
Exc.	V.G.	Fair
N/A	N/A	N/A

Pre-1986 conversions
Exc.	V.G.	Fair
N/A	N/A	N/A

Pre-1986 dealer samples (Rare)
Exc.	V.G.	Fair
9500	9000	8500

RIFLES

Immediately after World War I the Czechs continued to use the Mannlicher Model 1895 rifle until 1924 when they began production of their own Mauser action rifles.

Skorpion • Courtesy West Point Museum, Paul Goodwin photo

MAUSER
Ceskoslovensha Zbrojovaka (ZB), Brno

NOTE: In 1924 the Czechs began to manufacture a number of Mauser-designed rifles for export, and for its own military use. Czech Mausers were based on the Model 98 action. Many of these rifles were sold to other countries and will be found under *Germany, Mauser, Rifles.*

M1898/22 Rifle

Manufactured by CZ in Brno this rifle is based on the Mexican Model 1912 with a Model 98 action. It is half cocked with a full-length upper handguard with pistol grip. Chambered for the 7.92x57mm Mauser cartridge. Barrel length is 29" with a 5-round integral magazine. Weight is about 9.5 lbs. This rifle was used by Turkey as well as other countries.

Courtesy Rock Island Auction Company

Exc.	V.G.	Good	Fair	Poor
200	100	75	50	35

VZ23 Short Rifle

Used by the Czech army this 7.92x57mm rifle was fitted with a 21.5" barrel and 5-round magazine. Tangent leaf rear sight graduated to 2,000 meters. Most were marked, "CZECHOSLO-VAKIAN FACTORY FOR ARMS MANUFACTURE, BRNO" on the receiver ring. Weight is about 9 lbs.

Exc.	V.G.	Good	Fair	Poor
200	100	75	50	35

VZ12/33 Carbine

This rifle was produced primarily for export. It has a pistol grip stock with 3/4 length upper handguard and two barrel bands fairly close together. Bolt handle is bent down. Barrel length is 21.5" with 5-round magazine. Rear leaf sight is graduated to 1,400 meters. Weight is about 8 lbs. Country crest stamped on receiver.

Exc.	V.G.	Good	Fair	Poor
175	100	75	50	35

VZ16/33 Carbine

Designed for paramilitary units this rifle has a 19.25" barrel. Chambered for the 7.92x57mm cartridge as well as other calibers depending on country. Magazine capacity is 5 rounds. Tangent rear leaf sight graduated to 1,000 meters. Czech crest stamped on receiver ring. This rifle formed the basis on the German Model 33/40 paratroop carbine used during WWII.

Courtesy Cherry's Fine Guns

Exc.	V.G.	Good	Fair	Poor
450	300	220	160	120

Czech VZ24 with receiver markings and crest • Paul Goodwin photo

CZECH STATE

Ceskoslovenska Zbrojovka Brno (BRNO) was established in 1919 as the state arms factory. It was originally state owned but later, in 1924, was reorganized as a limited liability company.

M1895

The Czechs built about 5,000 of these Mannlicher rifles.

Exc.	V.G.	Good	Fair	Poor
500	350	250	150	100

Model 24 (VZ24)

This rifle marks the first Czech produced military rifle for the Czech army. It was based on the Mauser 98 action. The rifle was in wide use by other countries such as Germany prior to WWII. Chambered for the 7.92mm cartridge and fitted with a 23" barrel, this model had a 5-round non-detachable box magazine. The rear sight was graduated from 300 to 2,000 meters in 100 meter increments. Weight is about 9 lbs.

Exc.	V.G.	Good	Fair	Poor
450	300	200	100	75

NOTE: Prices are for rifles with matching numbers and original markings.

Model ZH29

Introduced in 1929, this semiautomatic rifle was designed by Emmanuel Holek of CZ at Brno. It is chambered for the 7.92x57mm cartridge and is fitted with a 21.5" barrel with aluminum cooling jacket over the barrel. Fitted with a bayonet lug. The detachable box magazine has a 10- or 25-round capacity.

Weight is about 10 lbs. Exported to Thailand and Ethiopia. Very rare.

Courtesy Thomas Nelson, *The World's Submachine Guns, Vol. 1*

Exc.	V.G.	Good	Fair	Poor
13500	10500	7500	—	—

Model ZK420S

Chambered for the 7.92x57mm cartridge this rifle was first introduced in 1942 but did not appear in its final form until 1946. It was also offered in 7mm, .30-06, and 7.5mm Swiss. This was a gas operated semiautomatic rifle with 21" barrel and upper handguard. The detachable magazine has a 10-round capacity. Front sight is hooded. Rear sight is notched tangent with ramp. Weight is about 10 lbs. Not adopted by Czech military but tested by many countries. Built by CZ Brno in limited numbers. Very rare.

Exc.	V.G.	Good	Fair	Poor
10500	9000	8000	—	—

Model 52

Chambered for 7.62x45 caliber, this gas operated semiautomatic rifle is fitted with a 20.5" barrel. This model has a full stock with pistol grip. Folding non-detachable bayonet. Hood-

A ZH29 sold at auction for $10,925. Sold to the Chinese in the 1920s and captured by the Japanese during its invasion of that country. Condition is 90 percent original blue.
Rock Island Auction Company, December 2004

ed front sight and notched tangent rear sight with ramp. Detachable box magazine with 10-round capacity. Weight is about 9.7 lbs. First produced in 1952.

Exc.	V.G.	Good	Fair	Poor
500	300	250	—	—

Model 52/57

Similar to the Model 52 except chambered for the 7.62x39 cartridge.

Courtesy Richard M. Kumor Sr.

Exc.	V.G.	Good	Fair	Poor
650	500	400	300	150

Model 1957 Sniper Rifle

This rifle, introduced in 1954, is built on a Mosin Nagant 1891/30 action and fitted with a 28.7" barrel chambered for the 7.62x54mmR cartridge. Magazine capacity is 5 rounds. Half stock with pistol grip and handguard. Rifle is supplied with a 2.5x telescope. Weight is approximately 9.5 lbs. Built by CZ in Brno. Production ended in 1957.

Exc.	V.G.	Good	Fair	Poor
900	750	500	400	200

VZ58

First produced in 1959, this select fire assault rifle is chambered for the 7.62x39mm Soviet cartridge. Its appearance is similar to an AK-47 but it is an entirely different design. It is gas operated but the bolt is locked to the receiver by a vertically moving block similar to the Walther P-38 pistol. Early rifles were fitted with a plastic fixed stock while later rifles used a folding metal stock. Barrel length is 16". Rate of fire is about 800 rounds per minute. Weight is approximately 7 lbs. Production ceased in 1980. Made at CZ Brno and Povaske Strojarne. The two versions of this gun are designated the VZ58P with fixed stock and the VZ58V for metal folding stock.

Pre-1968

Exc.	V.G.	Fair
9500	8500	8000

Pre-1986 conversions

Exc.	V.G.	Fair
N/A	N/A	N/A

Pre-1986 dealer samples

Exc.	V.G.	Fair
7000	6500	6000

MACHINE GUNS

The Czechs used the Steyr-built Schwarzlose Model 7/24 adopted to 7.92mm immediately after World War I. Czechoslovakia has also used the Soviet SG43 and the Soviet DT. Today the Czech army uses the ZB 59 as its primary machine gun. The ZB 59 is called a universal machine gun when mounted on a bipod. It is also used by the Czech military with a light barrel.

ZB VZ26

Manufactured by CZ Brno, this weapon is a light air-cooled gas-operated select-fire machine gun chambered for the 7.92x57mm Mauser cartridge. Fitted with a 23.7" finned barrel, it has a rate of fire of 500 rounds per minute. It is fed by a 20- or 30-round box magazine. Bipod and carry handle standard. Wooden butt with pistol grip. Quick change barrel. It was adopted by over two dozen countries around the world. It was the forerunner of the famous British Bren gun (model designation ZGB33). Produced from 1925 to 1945. On left side of receiver marked "BRNO," and on right side marked "LEHKY KULOMET ZB VZ26." Weight is about 21 lbs. This gun was, and still is, used in large numbers throughout the world.

ZB made small improvements to the VZ26 along with the date of the improvements. These guns are essentially the same as the ZB 26, but are known as the ZB VZ27 and VZ28.

Pre-1968

Exc.	V.G.	Fair
35000	32500	30000

Pre-1986 conversions

Exc.	V.G.	Fair
25000	23000	20000

Pre-1986 dealer samples

Exc.	V.G.	Fair
N/A	N/A	N/A

ZB VZ30

This weapon has an outward appearance almost identical to that of the VZ26 but with the exception of a new bolt movement

VZ57 Sniper • Private collection, Paul Goodwin photo

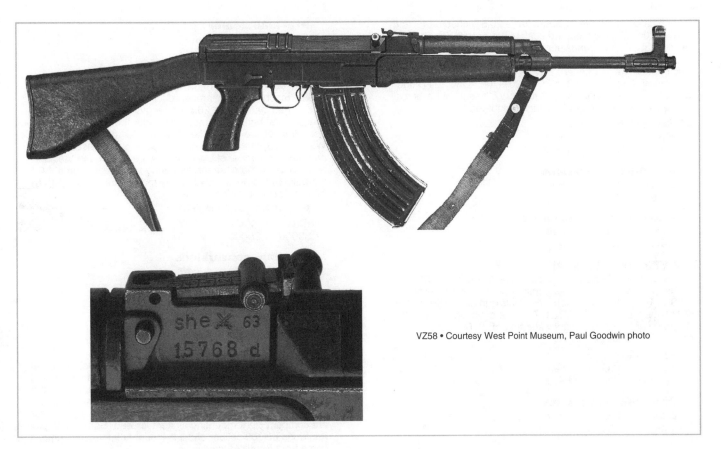

VZ58 • Courtesy West Point Museum, Paul Goodwin photo

ZB VZ26 with both left and right side receiver markings • Paul Goodwin photo

design different from the VZ26. It has a 26.5" finned barrel and uses a 30-round top mounted straight box magazine. The rate of fire is about 600 rounds per minute. Weight of the gun is approximately 21 lbs. This model was adopted by China, Spain, and Iran. Between 1939 and 1945 it was also used by the German army. A variation of the ZB VZ30 is the ZB VZ30J (Yugoslavian or Venezuelan) similar to the VZ30 but with a heavy knurled portion of the barrel at the breech end.

Pre-1968

Exc.	V.G.	Fair
20000	18500	17000

Pre-1986 conversions

Exc.	V.G.	Fair
14000	13500	13000

Pre-1986 dealer samples

Exc.	V.G.	Fair
N/A	N/A	N/A

ZGB VZ30 (VZ32/33/34)

Same as the VZ30 but modified to fire the British .303 cartridge. Uses a curved 20-round magazine to accommodate the .303 cartridge. Improved versions of this gun are known as the VZ32, the VZ33, and the VZ34. These later versions use a 30-round magazine and a slightly shorter barrel. Reduced rate of fire to 500 rounds per minute.

Pre-1968

Exc.	V.G.	Fair
18500	17000	16000

Pre-1986 conversions

Exc.	V.G.	Fair
14000	13500	13000

Pre-1986 dealer samples

Exc.	V.G.	Fair
N/A	N/A	N/A

ZB VZ37 (Model 53 for export)

Introduced in 1937 this gun was designed as a medium air-cooled machine gun chambered for the 7.92x57mm cartridge. The finned barrel was 26.5" in length. Uses a 100- or 200-round metal belt. Grips mounted under the receiver with trigger. Rate of fire was either 500 or 700 rounds per minute. Weight is approximately 40 lbs. This gun is usually tripod mounted. A number of these guns were supplied to Viet Cong and North Vietnamese forces during the 1960s. Some 4,000 were sold to Israel in 1949. Many more were exported to the Middle East and Africa.

Pre-1968 (Very Rare)

Exc.	V.G.	Fair
30000	25000	22000

Pre-1986 conversions

Exc.	V.G.	Fair
N/A	N/A	N/A

Pre-1986 dealer samples

Exc.	V.G.	Fair
N/A	N/A	N/A

ZB 39

In 1939 the Czechs exported a small number (est. less than 100) of this gun to Bulgaria in 8x56R Austrian Mannlicher caliber. This gun is stamped with the Bulgarian crest and other markings. The gun is fitted with a forward sling swivel, a ring-mounted extension around the wrist of the stock, and a different compact sight mounting system is used. Some examples are found in .303 caliber and it is thought that these examples come from South Africa.

ZB53 (VZ37) with both left and right side receiver markings • Paul Goodwin photo

VZ39 Export Gun • Courtesy Robert E. Naess

Pre-1968
Extremely rare, only 1 transferable example known.

Exc.	V.G.	Fair
Too Rare To Price		

Pre-1986 conversions
Exc.	V.G.	Fair
N/A	N/A	N/A

Pre-1986 dealer samples
Exc.	V.G.	Fair
N/A	N/A	N/A

VZ52/57
This gun is based on the ZB VZ30. It is chambered for the 7.62x39 rimless cartridge (Warsaw Pact). The gun was originally chambered for the 7.62x45 rimless cartridge (VZ52). Barrel length is 27" and is quick change. It is fed by a 100-round belt or 25-round detachable box magazine. Rate of fire is 900 rounds per minute with box magazine and about 1,100 rounds per minute with belt. Weight is about 17.5 lbs. with bipod. This is a select fire weapon with the finger pressure on the trigger determining full auto or single-round fire. The gun was introduced in 1952. This gun is often seen in Central America.

VZ52/57 • Courtesy Blake Stevens, *The Bren Gun Saga*

Pre-1968 (Very Rare)
Exc.	V.G.	Fair
25000	22500	20000

Pre-1986 conversions
Exc.	V.G.	Fair
N/A	N/A	N/A

Pre-1986 dealer samples
Exc.	V.G.	Fair
N/A	N/A	N/A

Model 07/24 Schwarzlose
This is a Czech-built Schwarzlose chambered for the 7.92 cartridge.

Pre-1968
Extremely rare, 1 transferable example known.

Exc.	V.G.	Fair
25000	—	—

Pre-1986 conversions
Exc.	V.G.	Fair
N/A	N/A	N/A

Pre-1986 dealer samples
Exc.	V.G.	Fair
N/A	N/A	N/A

DENMARK

Danish Military Conflicts, 1870–Present

After losing part of its territory to Prussia and Austria in 1862, Denmark concentrated its energies on improving its domestic, economic, and social conditions. Denmark maintained a peaceful coexistence with its European neighbors until it was occupied in 1940 by the German army. Following the end of the war, Denmark joined NATO in 1949, and in 1973 joined the European Union.

HANDGUNS

In addition to the handguns listed below, the Danes used the Browning Hi-Power 9mm pistol designated the Model 46. They also used the Swedish Model 40 Lahti, called the Model 40S by the Danes. In the late 1940s the Danes adopted the SIG 9mm Model 47/8 pistol (P-210-2).

Model 1871

This 6-shot revolver was built on a Lefaucheux-Francotte solid frame fixed cylinder with non-mechanical ejection. This is an 11mm pinfire revolver. Octagon barrel length is 5". Weight is about 34 oz. Smooth wooden grips with lanyard loop. Built by the Belgian firm of Auguste Francotte. Issued to the Danish navy from 1871 to 1882.

Courtesy Geschichte und Technik der europaischen Militarrevolver, Journal-Verlag Schwend GmbH with permission

Exc.	V.G.	Good	Fair	Poor
850	600	400	200	125

Model 1871/81

This model is a converted centerfire 11mm Model 1871. The conversion was done at the Danish navy yard in Copenhagen in 1881. All other specifications are the same as the Model 1871.

Courtesy Geschichte und Technik der europaischen Militarrevolver, Journal-Verlag Schwend GmbH with permission

Exc.	V.G.	Good	Fair	Poor
750	500	300	150	75

Model 1865/97

This revolver is built on the Chamelot-Delvigne solid-frame, fixed-cylinder action with non-mechanical ejection. It was originally issued to the Danish navy in 1865 as an 11mm pinfire sidearm and was later converted in Kronberg to 11.45mm centerfire revolver. The revolver is fitted with a lever-type safety that blocks the hammer from the cylinder when engaged. Barrel length is 5". Checkered wood grips with lanyard loop located behind the hammer. Weight is about 30 oz. Issued to the Danish navy from 1897 to 1919.

Courtesy Geschichte und Technik der europaischen Militarrevolver, Journal-Verlag Schwend GmbH with permission

Exc.	V.G.	Good	Fair	Poor
1750	1000	600	350	200

Model 1882

This revolver was built on the Lefaucheux-Francotte solid-frame fixed cylinder with non-mechanical ejection. Capacity was 6 rounds and the gun was chambered for the 9mm cartridge. The half-round half-octagon barrel was 5.5". This revolver was issued to Danish NCOs from 1888 to 1919.

Courtesy Geschichte und Technik der europaischen Militarrevolver, Journal-Verlag Schwend GmbH with permission

Exc.	V.G.	Good	Fair	Poor
1200	650	400	200	125

Model 1886

This revolver was chambered for the 9.5mm cartridge and fitted with a 3" barrel. Built by Auguste Francotte in Liege, Belgium, and issued to military police units in the Danish army beginning in 1886.

Courtesy Geschichte und Technik der europaischen Militarrevolver, Journal-Verlag Schwend GmbH with permission

Exc.	V.G.	Good	Fair	Poor
750	500	300	200	75

Model 1891

This revolver employed top-break, hinged frame with latch. This model was chambered for the 9mm cartridge and fitted with a 6.3" half-round half-octagon barrel. Checkered wooden grips with lanyard loop. Built by J.B. Ronge in Liege, Belgium. Weight is about 33 oz. Issued to Danish navy units from 1891 to 1941.

NOTE: A training version of this revolver was also used by the Danish navy and was chambered for the 5.1mm cartridge. All other specifications are the same.

Standard Model

Courtesy Geschichte und Technik der europaischen Militarrevolver, Journal-Verlag Schwend GmbH with permission

Exc.	V.G.	Good	Fair	Poor
1200	650	400	250	150

Model 1891/96 Training Version

Courtesy Geschichte und Technik der europaischen Militarrevolver, Journal-Verlag Schwend GmbH with permission

Exc.	V.G.	Good	Fair	Poor
3500	1750	800	500	300

Bergmann-Bayard Model 1908

Built by the Belgium firm of Pieper SA from 1908 to about 1914. Caliber is 9x23mm Bergman-Bayard with 4" barrel. Many foreign contracts were built in this model.

Courtesy Rock Island Auction Company

Exc.	V.G.	Good	Fair	Poor
1250	950	700	400	200

Bergmann-Bayard Model 1910-21

After WWI Pieper could no longer supply Bergmann-Bayard pistols to the Danish army, so Denmark made their own at their two national arsenals, Haerens Rustkammer and Haerens Tojus as the Model 1910-21. Most pre-war Pieper-made pistols were modified to 1910-21 configuration during the post-war years.

Courtesy Rock Island Auction Company

Exc.	V.G.	Good	Fair	Poor
1500	1100	850	700	300

Model 46

This is the Danish designation for the post-war Browning Hi-Power. Marked "M 1946 HV" on the left side of the frame. Fixed sights.

Courtesy Orvel Reichert

Courtesy Orvel Reichert

Exc.	V.G.	Good	Fair	Poor
1350	1100	950	650	400

P210 (Model 49)

See *Switzerland, Handguns, SIG*

SUBMACHINE GUNS

The Danish military has also used the Finnish Suomi MP41, the Swedish Model 37/39, and the HK MP5A2 and MP5A3 submachine guns.

Danish Hovea M49

Introduced in 1949 this submachine gun is chambered for the 9mm Parabellum cartridge and fitted with an 8.5" barrel. Folding metal butt. Magazine capacity is 35 rounds. Rate of fire is about 600 rounds per minute. Weight is approximately 7.5 lbs. This gun was originally developed by Husqvarna for the Swedish army. Denmark purchased the rights and built the gun for its own forces.

Courtesy private NFA collection

Pre-1968

Exc.	V.G.	Fair
20000	18000	16000

Pre-1986 conversions

Exc.	V.G.	Fair
N/A	N/A	N/A

Pre-1986 dealer samples

Exc.	V.G.	Fair
9500	8500	7500

Madsen M50

This submachine gun was produced from 1945 to 1953 by the Danes. It is chambered for the 9mm cartridge and is fitted with a 7.8" barrel. Its rate of fire is about 500 rounds per minute. Marked "MADSEN" on the right side of receiver. Weight is approximately 7 lbs.

This gun has some unusual features, such as a flat receiver with barrel attached with locking nut that when unscrewed allows the left side of the receiver to fold back to expose the right side, which contains all the moving parts. Fitted with a quick change barrel. Very simple design allows for fast and economical construction.

Photo courtesy private NFA collection

Pre-1968

Exc.	V.G.	Fair
8000	7000	6000

Pre-1986 conversions

Exc.	V.G.	Fair
4000	3500	3000

Pre-1986 dealer samples

Exc.	V.G.	Fair
4000	3000	2000

RIFLES

More recently Danish military forces have used the U.S. M16A1 rifle, the HK G3, the M1 Garand , and the Enfield Model 1917 rifle.

REMINGTON ROLLING BLOCK

Bibliographical Note: For detailed information, photos and technical data see *The Military Remington Rolling Block Rifle*, George Layman, 4th ed., 1999.

Model 1867 Rifle

This rifle was modified from rimfire to centerfire. Chambered for the 11.7x42R Danish/Remington cartridge. Fitted with a 35.7" barrel. Weight is approximately 9.25 lbs. Full stocked with exposed muzzle and bayonet bar with lug on right side. Three barrel bands. On the left side of the receiver is marked "M.1867" with the Danish Crown. The upper tang is marked with either "REMINGTON" or "KJOBENHAVN" with the year of manufacture.

Exc.	V.G.	Good	Fair	Poor
—	600	450	300	125

Model 1867 Carbine

Similar to the rifle but with half length walnut stock with one barrel band and 21" barrel. Three variations were produced: Artillery, Engineer, and Cavalry. Weight is approximately 7 lbs.

Exc.	V.G.	Good	Fair	Poor
—	750	600	400	200

Model 1867/93 Marine Rifle

This rifle was built in Denmark at Kjobenhavn Arsenal. It was essentially a Model 1867 rifle rebuilt to fire the 8x58R Danish Krag cartridge. Barrel length is 21" and weight is about 7 lbs. Nose-cap has bayonet fittings.

Exc.	V.G.	Good	Fair	Poor
—	600	450	300	125

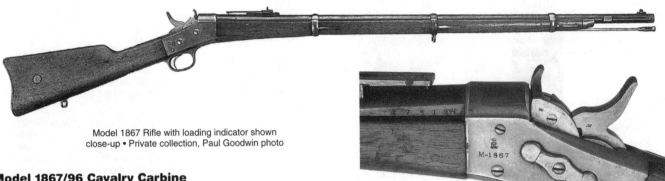

Model 1867 Rifle with loading indicator shown
close-up • Private collection, Paul Goodwin photo

Model 1867/96 Cavalry Carbine

This model was also built in Denmark and was a Model 1867 carbine re-chambered for the 11.7x51R Danish cartridge.

Exc.	V.G.	Good	Fair	Poor
—	750	600	400	200

MAUSER

The rifles listed below represent war surplus captured from the Germans at the end of World War II. These rifles were converted by the Danes to military target rifles.

G98 Action Military Target Rifle (Model 52)

Exc.	V.G.	Good	Fair	Poor
500	300	200	150	100

K98k Action Military Target Rifle (Model 58)

Exc.	V.G.	Good	Fair	Poor
500	300	200	150	100

KRAG JORGENSEN

The Krag rifle was developed in Norway and first adopted by Denmark. It was standard issue in some form through World War II. For a list of U.S. models and prices see *United States, Rifles, Krag Jorgensen*. For those collectors who are interested in the Danish Krags, the only major difference, other than caliber, lies in the operation of the loading gate. Prices listed below are for unaltered Danish Krags. The forerunner of the U.S. Krags was the Model 1889 rifle.

NOTE: All Danish Krags are chambered for the 8x58Rmm cartridge.

Danish Model 1889

This rifle was developed by Ole Krag and Eric Jorgensen. It used a single forward bolt locking lug plus a bolt guide rib. Chambered for the 8x58Rmm cartridge, the rifle was fitted with a 33" barrel with full stock and no pistol grip. The barrel is fitted with a full-length metal handguard. A flush loose-loaded box

magazine was used. The bolt handle was straight. There were a number of different carbine versions but all of these were full stocked and fitted with 23.5" barrel with bayonet lugs on all but one variation: the artillery carbine (see below). These guns are marked prior to 1910 "GEVAERFABRIKEN KJOBENHAVN" [date] over "M89" on the left side of the receiver. Approximately 140,000 of these rifles and carbines were manufactured prior to 1930. During the German occupation in WWII, the Germans reintroduced the rifle for its own use.

Exc.	V.G.	Good	Fair	Poor
600	400	250	150	100

Danish troops with their Krags • Courtesy Paul S. Scarlata

Model 1889 Infantry Carbine

Introduced in 1924, this model is a converted Model 1889 rifle with metal barrel jacket and bayonet stud. Barrel length is 24". Tangent rear sight. Magazine capacity is 5 rounds. Weight is about 8.5 lbs. Marked "F" before the serial number.

Exc.	V.G.	Good	Fair	Poor
750	500	300	200	100

Model 1889 Artillery Carbine

Similar to the Infantry carbine and also introduced in 1924, this model features a turn down bolt handle, a triangle shaped upper sling swivel, and a hanger stud on the left side of the stock.

Exc.	V.G.	Good	Fair	Poor
750	500	300	200	100

Danish Model 1889 Rifle • Courtesy West Point Museum, Paul Goodwin photo

Model 1889 Engineer Carbine
This model was introduced in 1917. It is fitted with a wooden handguard and a slightly shorter barrel, about 1/2". Marked with "I" before the serial number.

Exc.	V.G.	Good	Fair	Poor
750	500	300	200	100

Model 1889 Cavalry Rifle
Introduced in 1914, this model is fitted for a bayonet. Straight bolt handle. Marked with "R" before the serial number.

Exc.	V.G.	Good	Fair	Poor
600	400	250	150	100

Model 1928 Sniper Rifle
This model is based on the Model 1889 with half stock but fitted with a 26" heavy barrel, micrometer rear sight, and hooded front sight. Wooden handguard. Turned down bolt. Similar in appearance to the U.S. 30 caliber-style "T" rifle. Weight is approximately 11.5 lbs.

Exc.	V.G.	Good	Fair	Poor
1250	950	700	500	200

MADSEN

Model 47
Sometimes referred to as the Madsen light military rifle, this post-WWII bolt-action rifle was sold to Colombia in limited quantities of 5,000 guns. Fitted with a rubber buttplate. Chambered in a number of calibers including the .30-06. Barrel length was 23" with a magazine capacity of 5 rounds. Weight was about 8 lbs.

Courtesy Richard M. Kumor Sr.

Exc.	V.G.	Good	Fair	Poor
750	500	350	—	—

NOTE: Add $75 for rifles with numbered matching bayonet.

MACHINE GUNS

After World War II Denmark used the British Bren gun chambered for the .303 caliber, the Swedish Model 37 6.5mm gun, the U.S. Model 1919A4 and A5 versions, and the .50 M2 Browning. More recently the Danes use the German MG 42/59.

Madsen
This was the first practical light machine gun. It was produced from 1897 to 1955. It is chambered for several calibers from 6mm to 8mm. It is fitted with a 22.7" barrel and a top feeding 25-, 30-, or 40-round magazine. Rate of fire is 450 rounds per minute. Its weight is approximately 20 lbs. Marked "MADSEN MODEL" on the right side of the receiver. Found all over the world during a 50-year period.

Pre-1968

Exc.	V.G.	Fair
12000	11000	10000

Pre-1986 conversions

Exc.	V.G.	Fair
N/A	N/A	N/A

Pre-1986 dealer samples

Exc.	V.G.	Fair
6000	5000	4000

Madsen-Satter
First produced in 1952, this belt-fed machine gun is chambered for the 7.62x51mm NATO cartridge. Designed to be used on a tripod for sustained fire, it had a rate of fire of 650 to 1000 rounds per minute (adjustable). Fitted with a 22" barrel. Weight is approximately 23.4 lbs. Marked "MADSEN-SETTER" on left front side of receiver. Many South American countries used this gun as do many other countries around the world. Production stopped on this gun in 1960 in Denmark but continued under license to Indonesia until the 1970s.

Photo courtesy private NFA collection

Pre-1968 (Very Rare)

Exc.	V.G.	Fair
25000	23000	22000

Pre-1986 conversions

Exc.	V.G.	Fair
N/A	N/A	N/A

Pre-1986 dealer samples (Rare)

Exc.	V.G.	Fair
20000	18000	17000

Chilean Madsen Model 1950 with receiver markings and crest • Paul Goodwin photo

FINLAND

Finnish Military Conflicts, 1870-Present

Finland was annexed by Russia in 1809 but was allowed considerable independence throughout the 19th century. Finnish nationalism began to grow during the latter part of the 19th century, and, by the early 20th century, Finland established its own parliament in 1906. Finnish independence was declared in 1917. Beginning in 1918, a civil war erupted in which the White Guard aided by German troops defeated the leftist Red Guard supported by the Soviet Union. As a result of this conflict a republic was established in 1919. In 1939 Soviet troops invaded Finland, and by 1940 Finnish forces were defeated, despite a heavy cost to the Soviet troops. Finland joined the German attack on the Soviet Union in 1941. Finland was again defeated by Soviet forces by 1944. Finland was then forced to expel the Germans which resulted in a massive loss of life and property to the Finnish people. A 1947 treaty between Finland and the Soviet Union ceded some Finnish territory to the Soviets, and in 1948 the Finns signed a mutual defense pact with the Soviets. During the post-war period, Finland attempted to stay neutral and preserve its independence. By 1990, with the collapse of the Soviet Union, the 1948 treaty was moot and in 1995 the Finns joined the European Union.

NOTE: The Finns established their own arms factory soon after independence. It was called *Souojeluskuntain Ase-ja Konepaja Oy* (SAKO). In 1926 the Finns constructed a state rifle factory called the *Valtion Kivaaritehdas* (VKT, later Valmet). Also in the 1920s another state arms plant was built called *Tikkakoski* (TIKKA).

HANDGUNS

NOTE: During the 1920s and 1930s the Finnish army relied primarily on the Model 1895 Russian Nagant revolver and the Spanish 7.65mm self-loading pistols, the Ruby (Model 19). During World War I the Finns were supplied with the Mauser M1896 Broomhandle in a late wartime commercial configuration. In the early 1920s the Finns adopted a commercial model of the DWM Luger, called by the Finns the Model 23. By the late 1920s the Finnish military decided to adopt and domesticly produce a 9mm self-loading pistol of their own. It was called the Lahti.

The Finns, more recently, have used the FN M1935 in 9mm and the French MAB PA-15 pistol in 9mm.

M35 Lahti

This 9x19mm semiautomatic pistol was adopted in 1935 and built at VKT. This pistol is a locked-breech semiautomatic that features a bolt accelerator that does much to make this a reliable firearm. This pistol is the same as the Swedish Model 40 Lahti, 4.7" barrel and 8-round magazine, except that it has a loaded chamber indicator on top of the pistol, a different assembled recoil spring, and the Finnish pistol's grips are marked "VKT." Finnish army markings on top of slide. This pistol was designed to function in extreme cold and has a reputation for reliability. About 5,700 wartime Lahti pistols were produced.

Exc.	V.G.	Good	Fair	Poor
1250	1000	800	550	300

SUBMACHINE GUNS

The first Finnish submachine gun was developed by Aimo Lahti in 1922. This gun later became the Model 1926 with only about 200 built in 7.65mm caliber. A perfected design was later built called the Model 1931 Suomi. Since the end of World War II the Finns have used the Sten Mark II and Mark III guns.

Suomi Model 1931

First produced in Finland in 1931, this submachine gun is chambered for the 9mm cartridge. It was widely used by Scandinavian armies as well as several countries in South America. It features a 12.25" barrel with wooden stock and 71-round drum magazine. Box magazine capacity is 20 or 50 rounds. Rate of fire is 900 rounds per minute. Weight is about 10 lbs. Marked on the end cap and left side of the receiver. Production stopped in 1944. A total of about 80,000 were produced by TIKKA.

This gun was also made in Sweden where it was designated the Model 37-39. In Switzerland it was called the Model 43/44. In Denmark it was made by Madsen.

Pre-1968

Exc.	V.G.	Fair
16000	14500	13000

Pre-1986 conversions

Exc.	V.G.	Fair
N/A	N/A	N/A

Pre-1986 dealer samples

Exc.	V.G.	Fair
7500	6500	5500

Suomi Model 1944

This Finnish gun is based on the Russian Model PPS-43, but the Model 1944 fires the 9mm cartridge. It is fitted with a 9.66" barrel and accepts a 36-round box magazine or 71-round drum

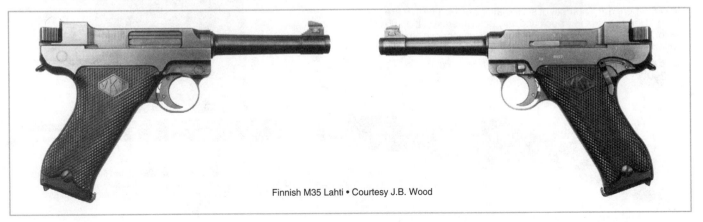

Finnish M35 Lahti • Courtesy J.B. Wood

Model 1931 • Paul Goodwin photo

magazine. Rate of fire is 650 rounds per minute. Weight is about 6.35 lbs. Production stopped in 1945. Marked on left side of receiver. TIKKA built about 10,000 of these guns.

Pre-1968

Exc.	V.G.	Fair
16000	14500	13000

Pre-1986 conversions

Exc.	V.G.	Fair
N/A	N/A	N/A

Pre-1986 dealer samples

Exc.	V.G.	Fair
7500	6500	5500

RIFLES

NOTE: Prior to 1917 Finland was part of Russia. All Finnish military rifles are built on Russian Model 1891 Mosin Nagant actions.

For technical data and photos, see Terence Lapin's, *The Mosin-Nagant Rifle,* and Doug Bowser's *Rifles of the White Death*.

Model 1891 (Finnish Army Variation)

Basically a Russian Model 1891 but with a Finnish two-piece stock, sights calibrated to meters, trigger modified to two stage pull, and frequently with the addition of sling swivels. Large numbers of captured Russian Model 1891s were reconfigured this way as late as 1944. Many, but not all, have Finnish-made barrels with a length of 31.6".

NOTE: There are a number of subvariations of this rifle that are beyond the scope of this book and may be of interest to the collector. It is suggested that the Lapin and Bowser books be consulted.

Exc.	V.G.	Good	Fair	Poor
250	150	100	75	60

Finnish irregulars with their Model 1891 rifles • Courtesy Paul S. Scarlata

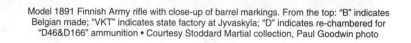

Model 1891 Finnish Army rifle with close-up of barrel markings. From the top: "B" indicates Belgian made; "VKT" indicates state factory at Jyvaskyla; "D" indicates re-chambered for "D46&D166" ammunition • Courtesy Stoddard Martial collection, Paul Goodwin photo

Model 1891 Dragoon (Finnish Army Variation)

Basically a Russian Model 1891 Dragoon rifle modified as above with a side mounted Mauser Kar 98-type sling. Barrel length is 28.8". About 19,000 of these rifles were produced. Rare.

Exc.	V.G.	Good	Fair	Poor
400	250	150	100	75

Model 91 Dragoon and close-up of rear sight of Model 91 Dragoon • Private collection, Paul Goodwin photo

Model 91/24 with SIG heavy stepped barrel for bayonet attachment. Close-up of barrel markings indicate armor's notation that barrel has been shortened and re-chambered • Courtesy Stoddard Martial collection, Paul Goodwin photo

Model 91/24 Civil Guard Infantry Rifle

This model built by SAKO and consisted of new heavy Swiss or German barrels fitted to reworked Model 1891 Russian actions. Due to the larger diameter barrel, some barrels were turned down at the muzzle end so it would be the same diameter as the Russian barrel and accept the Russian bayonet. In other cases the larger barrel diameter was left and the bayonets modified instead. Chambered for 7.62x54R cartridge and fitted with 32" barrel. Box magazine capacity was 5 rounds. Weight is about 9.4 lbs.

Exc.	V.G.	Good	Fair	Poor
300	200	125	75	50

Model 91/24 Civil Guard Carbine

As above but with 24" barrel. It is estimated that 650 of these carbines were produced. Very Rare.

Exc.	V.G.	Good	Fair	Poor
800	600	400	300	150

Model 1927 Army Short Rifle

This rifle was made by Valmet, is a shorter version of the Model 1924, and fitted with a 27" barrel instead of 31". It has a full stock with bayonet lug with a ramp and leaf rear sight, graduated to 800 meters, and front sight guards for the blade front sight. Early stocks were modified from the Model 1891 stocks, and this made for a very weak forend, which was prone to breakage with the bayonet installed. The fore cap was a hinged, two-piece affair. Weight is about 9 lbs.

Exc.	V.G.	Good	Fair	Poor
350	250	150	75	50

Model 1927 rifle with 1st style barrel band. This band was modified in 1937 • Courtesy Simeon Stoddard, Paul Goodwin photo

Model 1927 Short Rifle with close-up of receiver, notice reinforcing in forearm near muzzle, notice that this is the 2nd style front barrel band • Private collection, Paul Goodwin photo

Model 1927 Rifle with Modified Front Barrel Band (2nd style)

The front band on these rifles was reinforced with two extensions along the forend to help with the split stock problem on the first type Model 1927 rifles. Many were also fitted with new stocks that were larger in diameter at the front of the fore stock to add strength as well. These rifles have a higher survival rate because many early rifles were modified with this type of front barrel band.

Exc.	V.G.	Good	Fair	Poor
300	200	125	75	50

Model 1927/91-30 Modified Rifle

During the Winter War with Russia, any rifle that could shoot was needed by the Finnish army. Many Model 1927 rifles were restocked with Model 91-30 stocks to make them useable.

Exc.	V.G.	Good	Fair	Poor
350	250	150	75	50

Model 1927 Cavalry Carbine

Similar to the Model 1927 rifle but fitted with a 24" barrel and turned down bolt. Side mounted sling. Weight is approximately 8.75 lbs. About 2,500 were produced with serial numbers between 72,800 and 74,900. Very rare as most were converted to rifles. Some of these were imported into the U.S. in the 1960s and modified into inexpensive hunting rifles.

M27 Rifle on top and M27 Carbine at bottom • Courtesy Chuck Karwan

M27 Carbine action • Courtesy Chuck Karwan

Exc.	V.G.	Good	Fair	Poor
750	500	350	225	150

Model 1928 Civil Guard Short Rifle

Similar to the Model 1927 except with minor differences such as a non-hinged front barrel band that was stronger and a fore stock enlarged in diameter to help prevent splitting. It weighs about 9.2 lbs. The letters "SY" are stamped on the receiver ring. Built by SAKO.

Exc.	V.G.	Good	Fair	Poor
350	250	175	75	50

Model 1928/30 Civil Guard Short Rifle

This is the same as the Model 1928 Short Rifle but with an improved magazine and different rear sight graduated to 2,000

Model 1928 Civil Guard rifle close-up of "SY" stamping indicating High Command of the Civil Guard • Courtesy Simeon Stoddard, Paul Goodwin photo

Model 1928 Civil Guard rifle • Courtesy Simeon Stoddard, Paul Goodwin photo

Model 28/30 showing rear sight and receiver markings • Private collection, Paul Goodwin photo

meters. It weighs about 9.6 lbs. On the receiver is stamped with an "S" topped with three fir sprigs in a gear wheel. Built by SAKO.

Exc.	V.G.	Good	Fair	Poor
300	200	150	75	50

Model 91/30 rifle with close-up of barrel markings indicating Tikka manufacture • Courtesy Stoddard Martial collection, Paul Goodwin photo

Finnish Model 91/30

This was a Finnish manufactured rifle produced by Tikka in 1943 and 1944. About 24,000 were built. Most of these rifles were not used in WWII but kept in storage until 1986 when sold as surplus. Barrel length is 28.7', caliber is 7.62x53R and sights are calibrated from 100 to 2,000 meters. Weight is about 8.75 lbs.

Exc.	V.G.	Good	Fair	Poor
175	100	70	40	25

Model 1939 Short Rifle (Army and Civil Guard)

Similar to the Model 1928/30 but with larger diameter bore to accommodate a heavier bullet (201 grains). One-piece stock with pistol grip and new rear sight fitted to this model. Barrel length is 27" but lighter in weight than the Model 28/30. Weight is about 10 lbs. Produced by SAKO, TIKKA, and VKT. The rifle was produced until 1944 but a few examples were produced in 1945. Approximately 5,000 to 6,000 of these rifles had barrels made in Belgium. These are marked with a "B" on the barrel.

Exc.	V.G.	Good	Fair	Poor
250	175	125	75	50

NOTE: Add a 25 percent premium for SAKO-built rifles. Rifles marked "Sk.Y" (Civil Guard) will command a 100 percent premium.

Finnish army ownership marking on a Swedish Model 1896 • Courtesy Stoddard Martial collection, Paul Goodwin photo

Swedish Model 1896 Rifle

Used by the Finns without modifications, these rifles have "SA" Finnish army property markings on the receiver. Some of these rifles were lent to the Finnish government, some were sold to them.

Exc.	V.G.	Good	Fair	Poor
250	175	100	75	50

Model 1939 with close-up of rear sight • Private collection, Paul Goodwin photo

Italian Carcanco

Marked with the "SA" property marking on the rear left side of the barrel.

Exc.	V.G.	Good	Fair	Poor
150	100	50	30	15

FINNISH SNIPER RIFLES

Beginning in 1937 the Finns began to develop a sniper rifle built around the Mosin-Nagant rifle. Approximately 400 M39 sniper rifles were built with a 3X Physica telescope. These scopes were a prismatic box design for use, not only on rifles, but on machine guns and mortars as well. During World War II the Finns used the Model 39 rifle with German Ajacks scope. About 500 of these rifles were built, and were known as the Model 39/43. Finland also used Soviet scopes on its rifles with Ajacks mounts. These Soviet scopes were designated the PE and PEM. The only difference was that the PEM scope has no focusing ring on the eyepiece.

NOTE: There are no known examples of Finnish sniper rifles in the U.S.

TRG-21

The receiver is similar to the TRG-S, but the polyurethane stock features a unique design. The trigger is adjustable for length and two-stage pull and also for horizontal or vertical pitch. This model also has several options that would affect the price: muzzle brake, one-piece scope mount, bipod, quick detachable sling swivels, and military nylon sling. The rifle is offered in .308 Win. only. It is fitted with a 25.75" barrel and weighs 10.5 lbs.

NIB	Exc.	V.G.	Good	Fair	Poor
3500	2750	1850	—	—	—

TRG-22

This model is similar to the TRG-21 but meets the exact specifications to comply with the Finnish military requirements. Introduced in 2000.

NIB	Exc.	V.G.	Good	Fair	Poor
2700	2000	—	—	—	—

TRG-41

Exactly the same as the TRG-21 except chambered for the .338 Lapua Magnum cartridge.

NIB	Exc.	V.G.	Good	Fair	Poor
4350	3500	2500	1500	—	—

TRG-42

This model is similar to the TRG-41 but meets the exact specifications to comply with the Finnish military requirements. Introduced in 2000.

NIB	Exc.	V.G.	Good	Fair	Poor
3100	2300	—	—	—	—

Valmet M62

Based on the third model AK-47 but with internal differences built by Valmet. SAKO also built many of these rifles. Machined receiver. Perforated plastic forend and handguard. Tube butt. Barrel length is 16.5". Magazine is 30 rounds. Rate of fire is about 650 rounds per minute. Weight is about 9 lbs. Production in Finland began in 1965. Rifles produced from 1965 to 1969 were designated "M 62 PT." PT stands for day sight. In 1969 Model 62s were produced with folding night sights. Beginning in 1972 these night sights were fitted with tritium inserts.

NOTE: There are a number of different versions of this rifle: the M62-76–a Finnish AKM; the M62-76M plastic stock; M62-76P wood stock; M62-76T tubular steel folding stock.

Pre-1968

Exc.	V.G.	Fair
N/A	N/A	N/A

Pre-1986 conversions

Exc.	V.G.	Fair
7500	6500	5500

Right and left side of M62 • Courtesy Blake Stevens, *Kalashnikov, The Arms and the Man*, Collector Grade Publications

Pre-1986 dealer samples

Exc.	V.G.	Fair
6000	5000	4000

Valmet M62S

A semiautomatic version of the M62 imported for sale in the U.S. by Interarms. Offered in both 7.62x39mm and 5.56x45mm calibers.

NIB	Exc.	V.G.	Good	Fair	Poor
3000	2800	2300	900	750	300

Valmet M71

A different version of the M62 with solid plastic butt and rear sight in front of chamber. Sheet metal receiver. Chambered for the 7.62x39mm and the 5.56x45mm cartridges. Weight reduced to 8 lbs.

Pre-1968

Exc.	V.G.	Fair
N/A	N/A	N/A

Pre-1986 conversions

Exc.	V.G.	Fair
7500	6500	5500

Pre-1986 dealer samples

Exc.	V.G.	Fair
6000	5000	4000

Valmet M71S

A semiautomatic version of the M71 imported for sale in the U.S. by Interarms.

Model 71S • Courtesy Blake Stevens, *Kalashnikov: Arms and the Man*, Ezell

NIB	Exc.	V.G.	Good	Fair	Poor
1350	1000	850	650	450	300

Valmet M76

This model has a number of fixed or folding stock options. It is fitted with a 16.3" barrel and has a magazine capacity of 15, 20, or 30 rounds. Its rate of fire is 700 rounds per minute. It is chambered for the 7.62x39mm Soviet cartridge or the 5.56x45mm cartridge. Weight is approximately 8 lbs. Marked "VALMET JYVAKYLA m78" on the right side of the receiver. Produced from 1978 to 1986.

There are a total of 10 variants of this model.

Model 76 (stamped receiver) • Courtesy Blake Stevens, *Kalashnikov: Arms and the Man*, Ezell

Pre-1968

Exc.	V.G.	Fair
N/A	N/A	N/A

Pre-1986 conversions

Exc.	V.G.	Fair
8000	7000	6500

Pre-1986 dealer samples

Exc.	V.G.	Fair
6000	5000	4000

NOTE: For rifles in 7.62x39mm caliber add a 20 percent premium. For rifles chambered for .308 caliber deduct $2,500.

Model 78 (Semiautomatic)

As above, in 7.62x51mm, 7.62x39mm, or .223 with a 24.5" heavy barrel, wood stock, and integral bipod. Semiautomatic-only version.

NIB	Exc.	V.G.	Good	Fair	Poor
1750	1350	1000	850	600	300

MACHINE GUNS

During the early years the Finns used the Maxim Model 09, Maxim Model 21, and the Maxim Model 09-32, all chambered for the 7.62mm cartridge.

Lahti Saloranta Model 26

Designed and built as a light machine gun this model was chambered for the 7.62mm rimmed cartridge. Fitted with a 20-round box magazine or a 75-round drum magazine. The rate of fire was about 500 rounds per minute. Weight is approxi-

Valmet Model 78 • Courtesy Chuck Karwan

mately 23 lbs. This gun was also chambered for the 7.92mm cartridge for sale to the Chinese prior to World War II.

Pre-1968

Exc.	V.G.	Fair
Too Rare To Price		

Pre-1986 conversions

Exc.	V.G.	Fair
N/A	N/A	N/A

Pre-1986 dealer samples

Exc.	V.G.	Fair
N/A	N/A	N/A

Valmet M62 (AK)

First introduced in 1962, this assault rifle is chambered for the 7.62x39mm cartridge. Fitted with a 16.5" barrel. Plastic forend with single strut butt. Thirty-round magazine. Rate of fire is about 650 rounds per minute. Weight is about 9 lbs.

Model 62 • Courtesy Blake Stevens, *Kalashnikov: Arms and the Man*, Ezell

Pre-1968

Exc.	V.G.	Fair
N/A	N/A	N/A

Pre-1986 conversions

Exc.	V.G.	Fair
10000	8500	7500

Pre-1986 dealer samples

Exc.	V.G.	Fair
6000	5000	4000

Valmet M78

This model is a heavy-barrel version of the Valmet M76. Barrel length is 18.75". It is offered in 7.62x39mm and 5.56x45mm calibers as well as few in 7.62 NATO. Marked "VALMET Jyvaskyla M78" on the right side of the receiver. Rate of fire is about 650 rounds per minute and magazine capacity is 15 or 30 rounds. Weight is about 10.3 lbs. Produced from 1978 to 1986.

Photo courtesy private NFA collection

Pre-1968

Exc.	V.G.	Fair
N/A	N/A	N/A

Pre-1986 conversions

Exc.	V.G.	Fair
10000	9000	8000

Pre-1986 dealer samples

Exc.	V.G.	Fair
6000	5000	4000

NOTE: For guns chambered for 7.62x39 add 20 percent.

FRANCE

French Military Conflicts, 1870-Present

With the French defeat in the Franco-Prussian War, 1870-1871, Napoleon III was ousted and the Third Republic established. France was involved in overseas colonial expansion in North Africa and Indochina. The French army bore the brunt of heavy fighting during World War I. During the war, France had 8,600,000 men under arms, of which 5,714,000 were killed or wounded, a casualty rate of 66 percent. France surrendered to Germany in 1940 and was occupied by German troops. In unoccupied France the Vichy government was headed by Marshall Petain. General Charles de Gaulle led the Free French government in exile. In the summer of 1944 the allied armies drove the German troops out of France, and when the end of the war came in 1945 a Fourth Republic was formed in 1946. The French Army received a stunning defeat in Indochina at Dien Bien Phu (1954) and other elements of the French military were busy in Algeria in that country's war for independence against France. In 1958 Charles de Gaulle returned to power to lead the Fifth Republic and attempted to restore French world prestige. France was involved with the U.S. in Desert Storm in Kuwait as well as a NATO member in various "peacekeeping" ventures.

HANDGUNS

NOTE: At the outbreak of the Franco-Prussian War the French military purchased a large number of revolvers from Colt, Remington, and Starr. These revolvers were percussion arms.

Bibliographical Note: For additional historical information, technical data, and photos, see Eugene Medlin and Jean Huon, *Military Handguns of France, 1858-1958*, Excalibur Publications, 1993.

Model 1870 Navy (Navy Contract)

This 6-shot solid-frame fixed-cylinder revolver uses a mechanical ejection system. Chambered for the 11mm cartridge and fitted with a 4.7" round barrel. Smooth wooden grips with lanyard loop. Adopted by the French navy in 1870 and remained in service until 1900. Built by the French firm "LEFAUCHEUX" in Paris. Marked "E LEFAUCHEUX" on the top of the frame, and on the right side "BVT. S.G.D.G. PARIS" with a naval anchor on the butt cap of the grip. This revolver was the first centerfire handgun to be adopted by any nation's military. About 6,000 revolvers were built under contract.

A modified version of this pistol was built by the French arsenal at St. Etienne (MAS) designated the Model 1870N. About 4,000 of these revolvers were produced and are marked, "MODEL 1870" on the top strap and "MODIFIE N" on the right side of the sighting groove. The military arsenal proof of MAS is on the cylinder and the underside of the barrel.

Revolvers fitted with military extractors have the extractor located along the barrel while civilian revolvers have the extractor located offset from the barrel.

Military Extractor

Courtesy Geschichte und Technik der europaischen Militarrevolver, Journal-Verlag Schwend GmbH with permission

Exc.	V.G.	Good	Fair	Poor
5000	3500	2000	1000	500

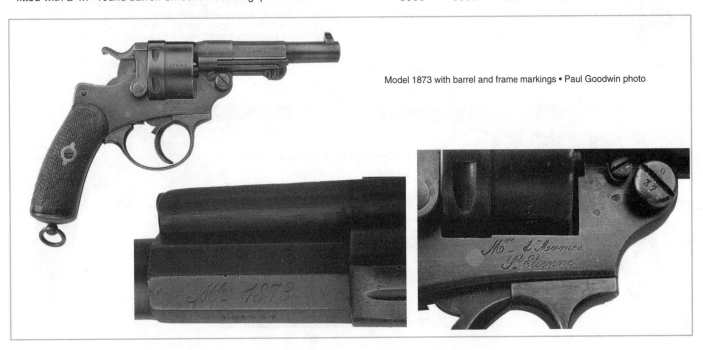

Model 1873 with barrel and frame markings • Paul Goodwin photo

Civilian Extractor

Exc.	V.G.	Good	Fair	Poor
3000	2000	1500	600	300

Model 1873 Navy

Built on a Chamelot-Delvigne type locking system with a solid frame, fixed cylinder, and mechanical rod ejection. Chambered for the 11mm cartridge and fitted with a 4.7" half-round half-octagon barrel. Non-fluted cylinder. It is both a single- and double-action revolver. Finish was left in the white. Marked " MRE D'ARMES ST. ETIENNE" on the right side of the frame. On top of the barrel marked "MLE 1873 M" or "NAVY." There are many other small markings on the revolver as well. Weight is approximately 36 oz. Used by the French navy for its NCOs from 1874 to 1945. Built by French military armory at St. Etienne. Between 1873 and 1886 approximately 350,000 of these revolvers were produced.

Navy

Exc.	V.G.	Good	Fair	Poor
950	600	500	300	175

"Mle 1873"

Exc.	V.G.	Good	Fair	Poor
600	400	250	100	75

Army

Exc.	V.G.	Good	Fair	Poor
500	375	200	150	100

Model 1874

The Model 1874 was essentially the same as the Model 1873 but with a fluted cylinder. Used by French naval officers from 1878 to 1945. Between 1874 and 1886 approximately 36,000 of these revolvers were produced.

A Model 1874 Army revolver sold at auction for $805. Condition is 90 percent original blue.
Amoskeag Auction Company, Sept. 2003

Army

Exc.	V.G.	Good	Fair	Poor
800	600	400	300	175

Navy

Exc.	V.G.	Good	Fair	Poor
2500	1500	750	350	200

Model 1892

Close-up of the barrel marking indicating year of manufacture on Model 1892 • Courtesy Stoddard Martial collection, Paul Goodwin photo

Chambered for an 8mm centerfire cartridge and has a 4.6" barrel with a 6-shot cylinder. Weight is about 30 oz. It is erroneously referred to as a "Lebel," but there is no certainty that Nicolas Lebel had anything to do with its design or production, but was the chairman of the selection board that chose the design. This revolver is a simple double action, with a swing-out

Model 1892 with frame markings • Paul Goodwin photo

cylinder that swings to the right side for loading. The design of this weapon is similar to the Italian Model 1889. There is one redeeming feature on this revolver, and that is a hinged side plate on the left side of the frame that could be swung away after unlocking so that repairs or cleaning of the lockwork could be performed with relative simplicity. The cartridge for which this weapon was chambered was woefully inadequate. This revolver remained in use from its introduction in 1893 until the end of WWII in 1945, mainly because the French never got around to designing a replacement.

NOTE: There are a number of commercial variations of this revolver, some of which are Spanish-made copies and others are St. Etienne commercial examples.

Navy (anchor on butt)

Exc.	V.G.	Good	Fair	Poor
750	550	300	150	100

Army

Exc.	V.G.	Good	Fair	Poor
550	350	200	125	75

Model 1892 "A Pompe"

As above, except that the cylinder latch is a sleeve around the ejector rod that can be moved forward to release the cylinder.

Exc.	V.G.	Good	Fair	Poor
750	550	300	150	100

Le Francais Model 28 Type Armee

A unique pistol chambered for the 9mm Browning cartridge. It is a large pistol with a 5" barrel that was hinged with a tip-up breech. This is a blowback-operated semiautomatic pistol that has no extractor. The empty cases are blown out of the breech by gas pressure. The one feature about this pistol that is desirable is that it is possible to tip the barrel breech forward like a shotgun and load cartridges singly, while holding the contents of the magazine in reserve. This weapon has fixed sights and a blued finish, with checkered walnut grips. It was manufactured in 1928 and built by Manufrance. This pistol was submitted to the French government for military issue but was not accepted. Only a few pistols were purchased by the French government for trials.

Courtesy James Rankin

Exc.	V.G.	Good	Fair	Poor
1250	950	750	500	200

Model 1935A

A 7.65mm French Long caliber semiautomatic pistol with a 4.3" barrel. Magazine capacity is 8 rounds. Fixed sights. Weight is about 26 oz. Eventually became known as the Model 1935A. This pistol was designed and built for the French military and about 10,000 were produced up to June 20, 1940, when the factory, SACM (Societe Alsacienne des Constructions Mecaniques, Cholet, France), was occupied by German troops. About 24,000 were built and used by the German army during World War II.

Model 1935A • Courtesy private collection

German Waffenamt Model (7.65mm Pistole 625f)

Exc.	V.G.	Good	Fair	Poor
550	450	250	125	100

Standard Model

Exc.	V.G.	Good	Fair	Poor
425	300	150	100	75

Model 1935S

As above, with an enlarged chamber area that locked into the ejection port and a 4.3" barrel. Built by MAC Chatellerault, MAS, SAGEM, and MF (Manufrance). About 85,000 pistols were produced between 1939 and 1953. The French Foreign Legion used this pistol in fighting in Indo-China in 1953 and 1954. It was also used by French forces during the Algerian Rebellion between 1954 and 1962.

Model 1935S • Courtesy Richard M. Kumor Sr.

Exc.	V.G.	Good	Fair	Poor
300	200	150	100	75

MAB Model D

This semiautomatic pistol is built along the lines of the FN Model 1910. Built in Bayonne, France (MAB). Chambered for the 7.65mm cartridge. Early examples had a steel frame and later ones had an alloy frame. German army test and acceptance marks stamped on pistol. About 50,000 were produced during World War II.

Exc.	V.G.	Good	Fair	Poor
550	450	350	300	150

MAC/MAS Model 1950

A 9mm Parabellum caliber semiautomatic pistol with a 9-shot magazine. Barrel length is 4.4". Weight is about 34 oz. Blued, with ribbed plastic grips. The pistol's design was strongly influenced by the Model 1935S. The Model 1950 was used by all of the French military forces as the standard issue sidearm, including nations that were former French colonies. Approximately less than 350,000 Model 1950s were produced.

MAS Model 1950 • Private collection, Paul Goodwin photo

Exc.	V.G.	Good	Fair	Poor
650	450	350	275	200

MAS G1

This is a Beretta 92G, which is a double action 9mm pistol with decocking lever. Barrel length is 4.9". Magazine capacity is 15 rounds. Weight is about 34 oz. Military marked.

Exc.	V.G.	Good	Fair	Poor
N/A	—	—	—	—

MAB PA-15

This pistol is a French military version of the commercial Unique Model R Para. Chambered for the 9mm Parabellum cartridge and fitted with a 4.5" barrel. Magazine capacity is 15 rounds. Weight is about 38 oz. This pistol was officially adopted by the French military. A target version of this pistol, the F1 Target, was adopted by the French air force and army.

Exc.	V.G.	Good	Fair	Poor
550	450	300	200	100

UNIQUE

When the French Vichy government signed an armistice with Germany in 1940, the Germans occupied Handaye in France, the site of Manufacture D'Armes Des Pyrenees. This factory then produced for the German army the Model 16 and Model 17.

Model 16

Chambered for the 7.65mm cartridge this pistol was fitted with a 7-round magazine. German army proof test and acceptance stamp. Hard rubber grips. About 2,000 were built under German supervision.

Courtesy Orvel Reichert

Exc.	V.G.	Good	Fair	Poor
300	200	150	100	75

Model 17

Similar to the above but with a 9-shot magazine. About 30,000 of these pistols were built under German control.

Exc.	V.G.	Good	Fair	Poor
350	250	200	150	100

Unique Model 17 with Nazi markings • Courtesy Orvel Reichert

Unique Kriegsmodell

This is an improved Model 17 with exposed hammer. Approximately 18,000 were manufactured under German occupation.

Exc.	V.G.	Good	Fair	Poor
600	450	300	200	100

SAVAGE

Model 1907 (French Model 1907-13)

A .32 or .380 semiautomatic pistol with a 3.75" or 4.25" barrel, depending upon caliber, and a 9- or 10-shot magazine. Blued with hard rubber grips. The .380 caliber model is worth approximately 30 percent more than the values listed below. This pistol was sold to the French government during World War I and used by the French military. These guns were not stamped with French acceptance marks. The first shipment was made in 1914. Most of these pistols were fitted with a lanyard ring. French contract Model 1907 pistols were chambered for the 7.65mm cartridge and are fitted with a chamber indicator. Most French pistols will have the caliber designation in both ".32 CAL" and "7.65MM" stamped on the slide. Approximately 30,000 to 40,000 of these pistols were sold to France. Serial number ranges for these pistols are 105,000 to 130,000 and 136,000 to 167,000. There are a few in the 80,000 to 90,000 serial number range. There were less than 50 experimental Savage pistols numbered 000xx-A. These rare pistols will bring a substantial premium.

Courtesy Orvel Reichert

Exc.	V.G.	Good	Fair	Poor
850	600	450	300	150

NOTE: It is very rare to find a military Savage in very good or better condition. Be aware of refinished pistols.

SUBMACHINE GUNS

The French used the German 9mm Erma submachine gun prior to World War II. The first French designed and built submachine gun was the MAS 35, designated the SE-MAS Type L, chambered for the 7.65 long pistol cartridge and built at Manufacture d'Armes de St. Etienne, St. Etienne, France. This gun was quickly superseded by the more common MAS 38.

MAS 35 SE

This model is the forerunner of the MAS 38. Chambered for the 7.65mm long cartridge. Barrel length is 8.8". Rate of fire is approximately 600 rounds per minute. Full auto fire only. Fed by a 32-round box magazine. Rear sight has 100 and 200 meter settings. Weight is about 6.25 lbs.

Pre-1968

Exc.	V.G.	Fair
7500	6500	5500

Pre-1986 conversions

Exc.	V.G.	Fair
N/A	N/A	N/A

Pre-1986 dealer samples

Exc.	V.G.	Fair
N/A	N/A	N/A

MAS 38

Built in France and chambered for the 7.65mm French Long cartridge. Fitted with an 8.75" barrel and a magazine capacity of 32 rounds. Fitted with a fixed wooden butt. Rate of fire is about 650 rounds per minute. Uses a folding trigger for safety. Weight is approximately 6.5 lbs. On the left side of the receiver marked "CAL 7.65 L MAS 1938." Produced from 1938 to 1946.

Private NFA collection • Gary Gelson photo

Pre-1968

Exc.	V.G.	Fair
7000	6000	5500

MAS 35 SE • Private NFA collection, Paul Goodwin photo

MAS 38 • Courtesy West Point Museum, Paul Goodwin photo

Pre-1986 conversions

Exc.	V.G.	Fair
N/A	N/A	N/A

Pre-1986 dealer samples

Exc.	V.G.	Fair
N/A	N/A	N/A

MAS 49 with receiver markings • Paul Goodwin photo

MAT 49

This French submachine gun was first produced in 1949 and is no longer in production. Built at the French arsenal at Tulle using a stamped steel frame and receiver. It is chambered for the 9mm cartridge and fitted with a 9" barrel. The magazine housing acts as a forward grip and folds forward under the barrel. Fitted with an ejection port cover. It was used by French forces and is still found in former French colonies. The magazine capacity is 32 rounds and the weight is about 8 lbs. Rate of fire is 600 rounds per minute. Markings are "M.A.T. MLE 49 9M/M" on the left side of the receiver.

Pre-1968

Exc.	V.G.	Fair
16000	14000	12000

Pre-1986 conversions (reweld)

Exc.	V.G.	Fair
14000	12000	10000

Pre-1986 dealer samples

Exc.	V.G.	Fair
N/A	N/A	N/A

Hotchkiss Type Universal

Introduced in 1949 and intended as a police weapon. Select fire. It is a basic blowback design and chambered for the 9mm Parabellum cartridge. Fitted with a 10.8" barrel. Magazine capacity is 32 rounds. Rate of fire is about 650 rounds per minute.

The gun is made so that it can be folded to a very compact size. The stock, magazine, and barrel collapse to make the overall length of the gun only 17.2". Weight is approximately 7.5 lbs. This submachine gun saw limited use in Indo-China and a small number of guns were sold to Venezuela in the early 1950s.

Courtesy Robert E. Naess

Pre-1968

(Extremely Rare, 1 transferable sample known)

Exc.	V.G.	Fair
20000	—	—

Pre-1986 conversions

Exc.	V.G.	Fair
N/A	N/A	N/A

Pre-1986 dealer samples

Exc.	V.G.	Fair
N/A	N/A	N/A

RIFLES

CHASSEPOT

Model 1866 Rifle

This needle gun, bolt-action, single-shot model was an improvement over the German Dreyse. Chambered for the 11mm nitrated paper or cloth cartridge with an internal priming pellet. Barrel length is 32.5" with full stock with two barrel bands. These rifles were adopted by the French military in 1866. The rifle was made by a number of different French arsenals as well as contractors in England, Belgium, Spain, and Austria. About 600,000 of these rifles were captured by the Germans during the Franco-Prussian War in 1870-71. Some of these were converted to 11x50.2R Bavarian Werder cartridge, and stamped with German acceptance marks. Some rifles were then later converted to the 11.15x60R Mauser cartridge. A total of 1,000,000 rifles were built by 1870.

Exc.	V.G.	Good	Fair	Poor
550	450	300	200	100

Model 1866 Carbines

Several different variations of carbines were built on the Chassepot action. Some were half stocked and others had full stocks. Some were fitted with brass buttplates, triggerguards, and barrel bands.

Exc.	V.G.	Good	Fair	Poor
1250	1000	850	700	300

PEABODY

Spanish Rifle (1869)

Identical to the Spanish Rifle. Chambered for the .43 Spanish centerfire cartridge and fitted with a 33" barrel. Full stock with two barrel bands. Blued barrel and case hardened furniture. About 33,000 rifles were produced for the French government.

Exc.	V.G.	Good	Fair	Poor
—	750	600	350	150

GRAS

Model 1874 & M1874/M14 & M80

An 11x59Rmm caliber bolt action single shot rifle with a 32" barrel with a walnut stock, two iron barrel bands, and a metal tip. The bayonet is a spike blade with a wood handle and a brass butt cap. Many of these rifles were converted early in WWI to 8x50.5Rmm Lebel caliber by sleeving the barrel and re-chambering. This converted rifle was designated the 1874/M14. Many of the conversions were fitted with wooden handguards. The rifle was built at Chatellerault, Mutzig, Tulle and so marked.

There was a Musketoon version, model designation M1874, with 27" barrel and 3 brass barrel bands. The Musketoon did not have a bayonet lug. It was made at St. Chatellerault and so marked.

A Carbine version was also built at St. Etienne and so marked. It was designated the M80 and was fitted with a 20" barrel with two brass barrel bands.

Rifle

Exc.	V.G.	Good	Fair	Poor
1250	850	650	450	150

Model 1866 Rifle • Courtesy Rock Island Auction Company

Model 1874 Rifle (ramrod is missing) • Courtesy Rock Island Auction Company

Musketoon

Exc.	V.G.	Good	Fair	Poor
1500	1150	800	550	200

Carbine

Exc.	V.G.	Good	Fair	Poor
1500	1150	800	550	200

Model 1878 & 1878/M84 Navy

This rifle was produced at Steyr on contract with the French navy and marines. It was fitted with a 29" barrel and chambered for the 11x59R Gras cartridge. It has a 6-round magazine tube in the forend. The rifle was loaded through the action with the bolt open. These rifles will probably be marked "STEYR MLE. 1878 MARINE" on the left side of the receiver.

The 1878/M84 variation had the magazine extending slightly beyond the forend cap. The 1878/84 was produced at Chatellerault and St. Etienne. It was not made by Steyr.

Exc.	V.G.	Good	Fair	Poor
650	500	300	100	50

LEBEL

The Lebel system was invented by Nicolas Lebel in 1886. The French replaced the single shot Gras Model 1874 rifle with this weapon. This was the first successful smallbore rifle and sent the rest of the European continent into a dash to emulate it. The Lebel was chambered for the 8mm Lebel cartridge with smokeless powder. The Lebel system was used until World War I when it was supplemented by the Berthier rifle.

Model 1886 "Lebel"

Chambered for the 8mm Lebel cartridge. While the cartridge was the first to use smokeless powder, the rifle was based on the old Gras Model 1874. It has a 31" barrel and holds 8 shots in a tubular magazine that runs beneath the barrel. This design is long and heavy and was not in use for long before being replaced by the more efficient box magazine weapons, such as those from Mauser. This rifle has a two-piece stock with no upper handguard. It is held on by two barrel bands, and a cruciform bayonet could be fixed under the muzzle. Weight of the rifle was about 9.5 lbs. Although this rifle was made obsolete rather quickly, it did have the distinction of being the first successful smokeless powder smallbore rifle; there were shortened examples in use until the end of WWII. This rifle was made at Chatellerault, St. Etienne, and Tulle arsenals and so marked.

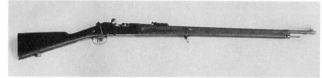

Courtesy Richard M. Kumor Sr.

Exc.	V.G.	Good	Fair	Poor
650	450	200	100	50

Model 1886/M93/R35

A shorter version of the above. Fitted with a 17.7" barrel and a 3-round tubular magazine. Weight was about 7.8 lbs. Issued in 1935.

Courtesy Richard M. Kumor Sr.

Exc.	V.G.	Good	Fair	Poor
550	400	250	150	75

NOTE: Add 50 percent for Nazi marked models.

BERTHIER-MANNLICHER

Adolph Berthier was a French army officer. He developed his new design to accommodate the new, more modern 8mm cartridge. His bolt action rifles employed Mannlicher-style clips which were used to form part of the box magazine design. These clips fell out of the bottom of the action when the last round was chambered. Most of the Berthier rifles used 3-round clips.

Model 1890 Cavalry Carbine

This bolt action model has sling swivels mounted on the left side of the stock. The carbines did not have a bayonet lug. One-piece stock had a straight grip without a handguard. The stock just forward of the triggerguard was swelled giving a pot-belly appearance. This swell contained the magazine. Stock had two cross bolts. Bolt handle was extra long. Barrel length was 17.7". Weight was approximately 6.8 lbs. These carbines were built at Chatellerault and St. Etienne arsenals and so marked in script on the left side of the receiver.

Exc.	V.G.	Good	Fair	Poor
450	325	250	150	75

Courtesy Paul S. Scarlata, *Collecting Classic Bolt Action Military Rifles, French troops and their M1892s.*

Model 1892 Artillery

This model was similar in appearance to the Model 1890 carbine with the exception that it was fitted with a bayonet lug and bottom sling swivels. No handguard.

Courtesy Paul S. Scarlata, *Collecting Classic Bolt Action Military Rifles*

Exc.	V.G.	Good	Fair	Poor
450	325	250	150	75

Model 1892 Carbine

Chambered for the 8x50.5Rmm Lebel cartridge and fitted with a 17.5" barrel. One-piece stock bellied forward to fully enclose a box magazine with a 5-round capacity. Original Model 1892 carbine were not fitted with upper handguards, but conversions were so fitted. Turned down bolt handle. Marked "MLE. 1892" on the left side of the receiver.

Exc.	V.G.	Good	Fair	Poor
650	500	400	200	150

Model 1892/M16

This is a conversion of the Model 1892 with the addition of a 5-round extended magazine and upper handguard. Conversion was done during WWI, hence the 1916 designation.

Exc.	V.G.	Good	Fair	Poor
350	200	125	90	70

NOTE: For rifles originally chambered for .22 rimfire add 100 percent.

Model 1902

This model was based on the Model 1890 and 1892 carbines. It was designed for use by colonial troops in Indo-China. It was fitted with a 25" barrel with no upper handguard. One piece stock with straight grip with swell for magazine in front of triggerguard. Long bolt handle. Two cross bolts. These rifles were built at Chatellerault, St. Etienne, and Tulle arsenals, and so marked on the left side of the receiver. Weight was about 8 lbs.

Model 1902 • Courtesy West Point Museum, Paul Goodwin photo

Exc.	V.G.	Good	Fair	Poor
300	175	100	75	50

Model 1907

Similar to the Model 1902 but with a 31.5" barrel. No upper handguard. Other specifications the same as the Model 1902 except weight was about 8.5 lbs.

Exc.	V.G.	Good	Fair	Poor
350	200	150	100	75

Serbian soldier with Model 1907 Berthier, Courtesy Paul S. Scarlata

Model 1907/15

Similar to the Model 1907 except for a straight bolt design. Barrel length was 31.5" with upper handguard. Besides being built at the three French arsenals, this rifle was also made by Remington-UMC on contract in 1914 and 1915. These examples are so marked on the left side of the receiver. Weight is about 8.25 lbs.

Exc.	V.G.	Good	Fair	Poor
350	200	150	100	75

NOTE: Add 300 percent for Remington-built rifles.

Model 1916 Rifle

Similar to the Model 1907/15 except fitted with a 5-round extended magazine.

Courtesy Paul S. Scarlata, *Collecting Classic Bolt Action Military Rifles*

Exc.	V.G.	Good	Fair	Poor
350	200	150	100	75

Model 1916 Carbine

This is a Model 1916 rifle with a 17.7" barrel and 5-round magazine. Weight is about 7 lbs.

Exc.	V.G.	Good	Fair	Poor
400	275	200	150	100

Model 1907/15 • Courtesy West Point Museum, Paul Goodwin photo

MAS Model 1917 • Courtesy West Point Museum, Paul Goodwin photo

Model 1907/15-M34

This model was fitted with a 23" barrel and a new Mauser-type 5-round staggered column magazine. Clips were no longer needed in this design. It was chambered for the 7.5x54 rimless cartridge. Weight is about 8 lbs. Some of these rifles were used during WWII.

Exc.	V.G.	Good	Fair	Poor
650	500	350	250	100

Model 1886/74/1917 Signal Rifle

A scarce variation of the military issue rifle.

Courtesy Richard M. Kumor Sr.

Exc.	V.G.	Good	Fair	Poor
950	700	400	200	100

MAUSER

Post-WWII Modified K98k Carbine

Exc.	V.G.	Good	Fair	Poor
550	450	350	175	100

DAUDETEAU
St. Chamond

Model 1896

Chambered for the 6.5x53.5SRmm Daudeteau No. 12 cartridge. Fitted with a 32.5" barrel. Fixed box charger-loaded magazine with 5-round capacity as part of triggerguard. Full stock with half length upper handguard. Weight is approximately 8.5 lbs. Several thousand rifles were made for military trials. All of these rifles were produced between 1896 and 1897.

Courtesy Rock Island Auction Company

Exc.	V.G.	Good	Fair	Poor
700	550	350	250	150

FRENCH STATE ARSENALS
MAS, MAT

Model 1917

An 8x50mm Lebel caliber semiautomatic gas operated rifle with a 31.4" barrel, 5-shot half-oval charger loaded magazine, and full-length walnut stock with cleaning rod. Weight is about 11.5 lbs. Produced by MAT.

Exc.	V.G.	Good	Fair	Poor
1500	1200	800	—	—

Model 1918

As above in an improved version, with a 23.1" barrel. Uses a standard cartridge charger. Weight is about 10.5 lbs.

Exc.	V.G.	Good	Fair	Poor
1700	1400	800	—	—

NOTE: This note applies to both the Models 1917 and 1918. Many of these rifles had their gas systems deactivated and were issued to colonial troops as straight pull rifles. Deduct 50 percent for these examples.

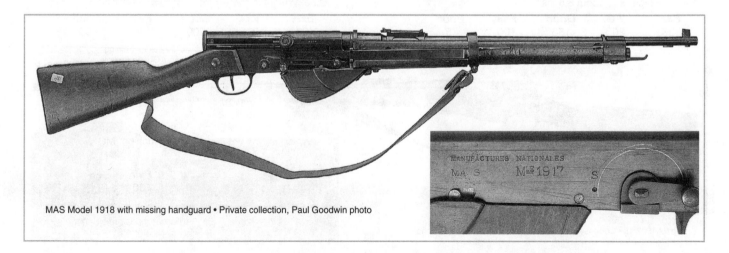

MAS Model 1918 with missing handguard • Private collection, Paul Goodwin photo

MAS 36 LG48 with grenade launcher built into barrel • Courtesy private collection, Paul Goodwin photo

MAS 36

A 7.5x54mm caliber bolt action rifle with a 22.6" barrel and 5-shot magazine. Bolt handle slants forward. Blued with a 2-piece walnut stock. Weight is about 8.25 lbs. The standard French service rifle from 1936 to 1949. The postwar version of this rifle has a grenade launcher built into the end of the barrel (see right). This was the last bolt action general service rifle to be adopted by a major military power.

Courtesy Rock Island Auction Company

Exc.	V.G.	Good	Fair	Poor
300	175	150	100	75

MAS 36 LG48

This is a MAS 36 rifle with a grenade launcher built into the barrel of the rifle. A folding sight arm was located on the left side of the barrel. Grenade range was varied by rotating the collar around the muzzle. Produced from about 1948 to 1951 and used extensively by the French army in Indo-China.

Exc.	V.G.	Good	Fair	Poor
550	400	300	200	100

MAS 36 CR39

As above, with an aluminum folding stock and 17.7" barrel. Weight is about 8 lbs. Designed for parachute and mountain troops. This is a rare variation.

Courtesy Richard M. Kumor Sr.

MAS 36 Para rifle in arsenal refinish with wooden stock • Courtesy Richard M. Kumor Sr.

Exc.	V.G.	Good	Fair	Poor
1500	1150	750	350	150

Close-up of the MAS 36 .22 caliber training rifle • Private collection, Paul Goodwin photo

MAS 36 Sub-Caliber

This variation is a MAS 36 but with a special cartridge case designed for .22 caliber long rifle ammunition. Marked "5.5 REDUCED CALIBER" on the receiver.

Exc.	V.G.	Good	Fair	Poor
700	600	500	400	300

MAS 44

This model was the first semiautomatic adopted by the French military. It later developed into the Model 49.

MAS 45 with close-up of receiver marking •
Courtesy Daniel Rewers, Paul Goodwin photo

Courtesy Richard M. Kumor Sr.

Exc.	V.G.	Good	Fair	Poor
650	500	400	250	100

MAS 45
This is a bolt action military training rifle chambered for the .22 caliber cartridge.

Exc.	V.G.	Good	Fair	Poor
500	400	—	—	—

MAS 49
Introduced in 1949, this model is a 7.5x54mm gas-operated semiautomatic rifle with a 22.6" barrel and full-length walnut stock. It has a grenade launcher built into the front sight. Fitted with a 10-round magazine. No bayonet fittings. Weight is about 9 lbs.

Courtesy Richard M. Kumor Sr.

Exc.	V.G.	Good	Fair	Poor
500	400	300	275	100

MAS 49/56
This model is a modification of the Model 49. It is fitted with a 20.7" barrel. Principal modification is with NATO standard grenade launcher. A special grenade sight is also fitted. This model has provisions to fit a bayonet. Weight is about 8.5 lbs.

Courtesy Richard M. Kumor Sr.

Exc.	V.G.	Good	Fair	Poor
400	300	250	175	100

Model FR-F 1 Sniper Rifle
Introduced in 1964, this 7.5x54mm rifle is based on the MAS 36 and uses the same style two-piece stock with pistol grip. Barrel length is 22" with bipod attached to forend. Barrel is fitted with a muzzle brake. Fitted with open sights but 3.8 power telescope often used. Magazine capacity is 10 rounds. Many of these rifles were converted to 7.62mm caliber.

Exc.	V.G.	Good	Fair	Poor
5500	4500	4000	—	—

Model FR-F 2 Sniper Rifle
A 1984 improved version of the F 1 rifle. The forearm has a plastic covering. The bipod is now attached to a yoke around the barrel, and the barrel is covered with a thermal sleeve to reduce heat. The features and dimensions the same as the F 1.

Exc.	V.G.	Good	Fair	Poor
6500	5500	5000	—	—

FAMAS F 1 Assault Rifle
Introduced in 1980, this bullpup design rifle is chambered for the 5.56x45mm cartridge and fitted with a 19.2" barrel with fluted chamber. Select fire with 3-shot burst. Muzzle is designed for grenade launcher and fitted with flash hider. This model is also fitted for a bayonet and a bipod. Magazine capacity is 25 rounds. Rate of fire is about 950 rounds per minute. Weight is approximately 8 lbs.

Pre-1968
Exc.	V.G.	Fair
N/A	N/A	N/A

Pre-1986 conversions
Exc.	V.G.	Fair
N/A	N/A	N/A

Pre-1986 dealer samples
Exc.	V.G.	Fair
8000	7500	7000

FAMAS F 1 Rifle
Same as above but in semiautomatic version only. Scarce.

FAMAS Rifle • Courtesy Chuck Karwan

Exc.	V.G.	Good	Fair	Poor
8000	6000	—	—	—

MACHINE GUNS

Model 1907 St. Etienne

Built by the French arsenal MAS, this is a reversed gas-action gun chambered for the 8x50R Lebel cartridge. It was an unsuccessful attempt to improve on the Hotchkiss gun. The rate of fire is between 400 and 500 rounds per minute and is regulated by changing the gas cylinder volume. Barrel jacket is half-length over a 28" barrel. Fitted with spade grips with trigger. Fed by 24 or 30 metal strips. Weight is approximately 57 lbs. with tripod. This gun was not able to withstand the rigors of trench warfare and was withdrawn from combat in Europe.

Model 1907 St. Etienne blow forward mechanism • Robert G. Segel collection

Model 1907 St. Etienne • Robert G. Segel collection

Pre-1968 (Rare)

Exc.	V.G.	Fair
75000	—	—

Pre-1986 conversions

Exc.	V.G.	Fair
N/A	N/A	N/A

Pre-1986 dealer samples

Exc.	V.G.	Fair
N/A	N/A	N/A

Model 52 (AAT Mle. 52)

Introduced in 1952 as a general purpose machine gun with light 19" quick-change barrel with flash hider and bipod. This gun employs a blowback operation with two-piece bolt and fluted chamber. Chambered for the 7.62mm cartridge. The buttstock is a single-piece metal folding type. Rate of fire is about 700 rounds per minute and is belt-fed from the left side. Weight is about 21 lbs.

A heavy barrel version of this gun is built around a 23.5" barrel. Weight is about 24 lbs. Gun is usually placed on a U.S. M2 tripod. All other specifications same as light barrel version.

Pre-1968

Exc.	V.G.	Fair
25000	23000	20000

Pre-1986 conversions

Exc.	V.G.	Fair
N/A	N/A	N/A

Pre-1986 dealer samples

Exc.	V.G.	Fair
N/A	N/A	N/A

Hotchkiss Model 1914

This model is an improvement over the original Model 1897 gun but with steel cooling fins instead of brass. Otherwise it remains an air-cooled gun chambered for the 8x50R Lebel cartridge. It is fed by a 24- or 30-round metal strip or by a 250-

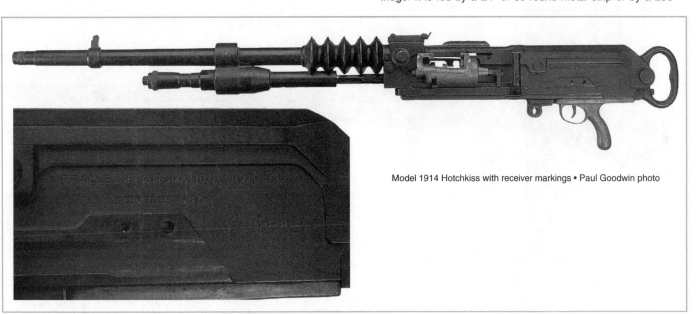

Model 1914 Hotchkiss with receiver markings • Paul Goodwin photo

round belt. Its rate of fire is about 500 rounds per minute. Barrel length is 31" and weight is about 55 lbs. The tripod for the Hotchkiss weighed another 55 lbs. by itself. In production from 1914 to 1930. Marked "MILTRAILLEUSE AUTOMATIQUE HOTCHKISS M1914 SDGD CALIBERE ——" on left side of receiver. The gun was used by the French army in both WWI and WWII. During WWI it was used by a number of Allied forces as well. As a matter of fact, American forces used the Hotchkiss more widely than any other machine gun. After World War II the gun appeared with French forces in Indo-China where the Viet Minh and later the Viet Cong used the gun.

NOTE: An earlier version of this gun, the Model 1909, was fitted with brass cooling fins instead of steel. The original design of the Hotchkiss was the Model 1897. This gun was fed by 30 round metal strips and had a rate of fire of about 600 rounds per minute. Similar in appearance to the Model 1909. This gun was very popular with the Japanese who used it during the Russo-Japanese War of 1904-1905. This led the Japanese to develop the Type 92 for Japan's use during World War II.

Model 1914 Hotchkiss • Robert G. Segel collection

Pre-1968

Exc.	V.G.	Fair
12000	10000	9000

Pre-1986 conversions

Exc.	V.G.	Fair
10000	8500	8000

Pre-1986 dealer samples

Exc.	V.G.	Fair
8000	7000	6000

A Von Karner modified Model 1914 rechambered for the 7.62x54Rmm Russian cartridge. Modified for the Dutch government prior to World War II for use in the East Indies against Japanese forces. Most were sunk by Japanese subs before reaching their destination. Courtesy John M. Miller

Chauchat Model 1915 (C.S.R.G.)

This model is a light air-cooled machine gun using a long recoil operation with a rotating bolt. It is chambered for the 8x50R Lebel and features an 18.5" barrel with barrel jacket. The 20-round magazine is a semi-circular type located under the receiver. Wooden buttstock and bipod. Rate of fire is about 250 rounds per minute. Used during WWI. The gun was inexpensively built and was not considered combat reliable.

A U.S. version firing the .30-06 cartridge was designed and built by the French and called the Model 1918. This version was not used by U.S. forces during WWI because it would not function properly. The M1918 has a 16-round magazine and a rate of fire of about 300 rounds per minute. U.S. military purchased about 19,000 of these guns chambered for the .30-06 cartridge.

After World War I Belgium used the M1918 chambered for the 7.65mm cartridge and by Greece (Gladiator) chambered for the 8mm Lebel.

Pre-1968

Exc.	V.G.	Fair
4500	4000	3500

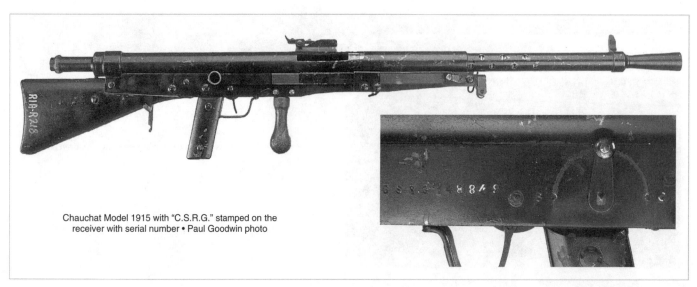

Chauchat Model 1915 with "C.S.R.G." stamped on the receiver with serial number • Paul Goodwin photo

Chatelerault M24/29 • Courtesy private NFA collection, Paul Goodwin photo

Pre-1986 conversions (Rewat)

Exc.	V.G.	Fair
4000	3000	2500

Pre-1986 dealer samples

Exc.	V.G.	Fair
N/A	N/A	N/A

NOTE: For U.S. versions add 100 percent.

Chatellerault M1924/M29

This is an air-cooled light gas piston machine gun that the French referred to as an automatic rifle. It is chambered for the 7.5x54mm French cartridge. Fitted with a 19.7" barrel with flash hider and bipod. Wooden butt and forearm. Select fire with two triggers. Fed by a 25-round detachable top-mounted box magazine. Rate of fire is about 500 rounds per minute. Weight is approximately 24 lbs. with bipod. Introduced in 1929, the gun was used extensively in combat by French troops.

Another version of this model is known as the M1931A introduced in 1931. It is essentially an M1924/29 for use on a tank as a fixed place machine gun with tripod. Fitted with a 23" heavy barrel. The gun can use a 36-round box magazine or 150-round drum, both of which attach to the right side of the gun. Its rate of fire is 750 rounds per minute.

Pre-1968

Exc.	V.G.	Fair
17000	16000	15000

Pre-1986 conversions

Exc.	V.G.	Fair
15000	14000	13000

Pre-1986 dealer samples

Exc.	V.G.	Fair
N/A	N/A	N/A

GERMANY

German Military Conflicts, 1870–Present

Prussia, under Otto von Bismark, achieved unification of the German states with victories in the Austro-Prussian War of 1866 and the Franco-Prussian War of 1870-1871. In 1871 William I of Prussia was named emperor of Germany and the nation's economic and military power began to grow and spread throughout the world. The outbreak of World War I was in part due to German expansion, threatening British and French interests. German military strength totaled 13,400,000. By war's end the total of killed and wounded was 6,400,000. With the end of World War I, and Germany's defeat, came a period of political and economic instability that led to the rise of the Nazi party. In 1933 Adolf Hitler was named Chancellor of Germany. With the invasion of Poland on September 1, 1939, World War II began. A total of 17,900,000 served in the German armed forces during World War II, and of those 7,856,600 were killed or wounded. After the war ended, parts of eastern Germany were absorbed by Poland and Russia. In 1949 West and East Germany were formed. The military weapons in this section cover Germany up to the formation of both East and West Germany with the postwar period only concerned with firearms produced in West Germany. East German military firearms are covered under the Russian, U.S.S.R. section. Both East and West Germany were reunited in 1990.

HANDGUNS

Bibliographical Note: For information on a wide variety of German military handguns see Jan Still, *Axis Pistols*, 1986.

REICHS REVOLVER
Germany

There are two basic versions of the German Standard Service Revolver designed by the Small Arms Commission of the Prussian army in the 1870s. Revolvers of this type were produced by the Erfurt Royal Arsenal, F. Dreyse of Sommerda, Sauer & Sohn, Spangenberg & Sauer, and C.H. Haenel of Suhl. Normally, the maker's initials are to be found on an oval above the triggerguard.

Model 1879

A 10.55mm caliber revolver with a 7.2" stepped octagon barrel, 6-shot cylinder and fixed sights. Standard finish is browned with smooth walnut grips having a lanyard ring at the base. Weight is about 36 oz. Regimental markings are on the butt crown plate. These revolvers are fitted with a safety catch. There is no provision for cartridge ejection. Each empty shell is removed with the cylinder axis pin. In use from 1882 until 1919.

Exc.	V.G.	Good	Fair	Poor
1200	850	500	300	200

NOTE: Add 20 percent for Mauser-built revolvers.

Model 1883

As above with a 5" stepped octagon barrel and round bottom grips with lanyard loop. Weight is about 32 oz. The finish on early production guns was browned, and on the balance of production the finish was blued. Regimental markings are located on the backstrap. In use from 1885 until 1919. Mauser-built M1883s are rare.

SNAP SHOT
WHAT'S IT LIKE - THE GERMAN M.1879 REICHS REVOLVER

While the German Army of the 1870s was the best trained and equipped Continental military force, there was one area where they were sadly lacking – they did not have a standard-issue handgun. The Gewehr-Prufungs-Kommission (Rifle Testing Commission) was ordered to rectify the situation but, after examining what was available, they designed their own – the Modell 1879 Deutsche Armeerevolver.

This massive revolver (length: 13.4"; weight: 2.5 lbs.) contained several features that commission members obviously felt were important – even if no one else did! The most glaring is the inclusion of a safety lever on the left sideplate. The hammer was placed on half-cock and the lever was rotated downward, interposing a solid steel shaft behind the hammer preventing backward movement while a heavy duty sear prevented forward movement. Another unique (stupid?) feature was the lack of an ejection system! Unloading was accomplished by pushing spent cases out of the cylinder one at a time with a rod that was attached by a cord to the ammunition pouch. The M.1879 used a simple (primitive?) single-action lock work. It appears to be a case of over engineering in an attempt to produce an extremely rugged handgun that would last forever. Apparently many did, as they remained in service until 1918.

M.1879, and the later M.1884, revolvers fired the 10.6mm scharfe Revolver-Patrone M.79 loaded with 20 gr. of black powder which propelled its 262 gr. lead bullet to 700 fps.

I obtained a M.1879 from a fellow collector that was manufactured by the Mauser Waffenfabrik in 1880. While it was in excellent condition the trigger pull was extremely heavy and rough. When test firing at 15 yards with custom reloaded ammo, a poor set of sights and the "trigger pull from hell" resulted in five-round groups in the 4-inch-plus range. Well, if you didn't shoot the enemy with the M.1879 – it would have made one heck of a club!

Paul Scarlata

Exc.	V.G.	Good	Fair	Poor
850	600	400	250	175

NOTE: For Mauser-built revolvers add 250 percent.

STEYR

Steyr Hahn Model 1911

The Steyr Hahn was originally introduced as a commercial pistol but was quickly adopted by the Austro-Hungarian, Chilean, and Romanian militaries. Commercial examples were marked "Osterreichische Waffenfabrik Steyr M1911 9m/m" on the slide, have a laterally adjustable rear sight, and are rare. Austrian militaries are marked simply "STEYR" and the date of manufacture, while those made for Chile and Romania bear their respective crests. During WWII the Germans rebarreled a number of Steyr Hahns to 9mm Parabellum for police use, adding "P.08" to the slide along with appropriate Waffenamt markings.

Courtesy Orvel Reichert

Commercially marked

Exc.	V.G.	Good	Fair	Poor
1350	1000	750	500	350

German WWII Issue (P.08 marked)

Exc.	V.G.	Good	Fair	Poor
800	500	350	200	125

DREYSE

Dreyse 7.65mm

Chambered for the 7.65mm cartridge, with a 3.6" barrel and a 7-shot magazine. Blowback and striker fired. The slide marked "Dreyse Rheinmetall Abt. Sommerda." Blued with plastic grips. Weight is about 25 oz. Originally intended for commercial sales this model was issued to staff officers and rear area troops in 1917.

Courtesy Orvel Reichert

Exc.	V.G.	Good	Fair	Poor
400	250	175	100	75

Dreyse 9mm

As above, but chambered for the 9mm cartridge with a 5" barrel and an 8-shot magazine. The slide marked "Rheinische Mettellwaaren Und Maschinenfabrik, Sommerda." Blued with plastic grips. Weight is about 37 oz. Used by troops in World War I but not officially adopted by the German military.

Courtesy James Rankin

Exc.	V.G.	Good	Fair	Poor
3000	2000	800	450	300

BERGMANN, THEODOR
Gaggenau, Germany

Bergmann Model 1910-21
See Denmark

MAUSER

Model 1896 "Broomhandle Mauser Pistol"

Manufactured from 1896 to 1939, the Model 1896 Pistol was produced in a wide variety of styles as listed below. It is recommended that those considering the purchase of any of the following models should consult Breathed & Schroeder's System Mauser, Chicago, 1967, as it provides detailed descriptions and photographs of the various models. See also Wayne Erickson and Charles Pate, The Broomhandle Pistol, 1896-1936, 1985.

NOTE: A correct, matching stock/holster will add approximately 40 percent to value of each category.

"BUYER BEWARE" ALERT by Gale Morgan: Over the past several years large quantities of "Broomhandle" Mausers and Astra "copies" have been imported into the United States. Generally these are in poor or fair condition and have been offered for sale in the $125 to $300 price range, primarily as shooters or parts guns. Over the past year or so, a cottage industry has sprung up where these very common pistols have been "converted" to "rare, exotic, near mint, original" specimens selling well into the four figure price range. I have personally seen English Crest, the U.S. Great Seal, unheard-of European dealers, aristocratic Coats-of-Arms, and Middle East Medallions beautifully photo-etched into the magazine wells and rear panels of some really common wartime commercials with price tags that have been elevated to $2,500 plus. They are quite eye-catching and if they are sold as customized/modified Mausers, the seller can price the piece at whatever the market will bear. However, if sold as a factory original–BUYER BEWARE.

Courtesy Wallis & Wallis, Lewes, Sussex, England

Turkish Contract Cone Hammer

Chambered for 7.63mm Mauser cartridge and fitted with a 5.5" barrel. Rear sight is marked in Farsi characters. Grips are grooved walnut with 21 grooves. Proof mark is a 6-pointed star on both sides of the chamber. Marked in Turkish script and bearing the crest of Sultan Abdul-Hamid II on the frame. Approximately 1,000 were sold to Turkey.

Courtesy Joe Schroeder

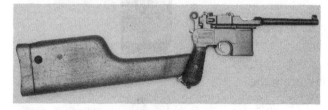

Courtesy Gale Morgan

Exc.	V.G.	Good	Fair	Poor
12000	8000	6500	3000	2000

Contract Transitional Large Ring Hammer

This variation has the same characteristics of the "Standard Cone Hammer" except the hammer has a larger, open ring. It is fitted with a 5.5" barrel and an adjustable sight marked from 50 to 500 meters. Grips are walnut with 23 grooves. Some of these pistols were issued to the German army for field testing.

Courtesy Gale Morgan

Exc.	V.G.	Good	Fair	Poor
3500	2800	2500	1150	800

Model 1899 Flat Side–Italian Contract

Similar to the above, with a 5.5" barrel, adjustable rear sight, and the frame sides milled flat. Left flat of chamber marked with "DV" proof. A "crown over AV" is stamped on the bottom of the barrel. All parts are serial numbered. Approximately 5,000 were manufactured in 1899.

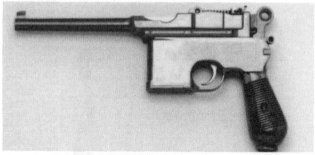

Courtesy Butterfield & Butterfield, San Francisco, California

Exc.	V.G.	Good	Fair	Poor
4300	3000	1500	1200	900

Contract Flat Side

Fitted with a 5.5" barrel with adjustable rear sight marked 50 to 500 meters. Grips are walnut with 23 grooves. The proof mark is the German military acceptance proofs. This model was used for field testing by the German army in 1899 or 1900. Number of pistols is unknown but most likely very small.

Exc.	V.G.	Good	Fair	Poor
2700	2200	1500	1000	750

Persian Contract

Persian rising sun on left rear barrel extension. Persian Lion crest in center of rear frame panel. Barrel length is 5.5" and grips are walnut with 34 grooves. Adjustable rear sight marked from 50 to 1,000 meters. Prospective purchasers should secure a qualified appraisal prior to acquisition. Serial numbers in the 154000 range.

Exc.	V.G.	Good	Fair	Poor
4200	3500	2250	1400	1000

Standard Wartime Commercial

Identical to the prewar Commercial Model 96, except that it has 30-groove walnut grips and the rear of the hammer is stamped "NS" for new safety. A number of these have the Austrian military acceptance marks in addition to the German commercial proofs. These pistols were also used by the German army as well.

Courtesy Gale Morgan

Exc.	V.G.	Good	Fair	Poor
1700	1100	800	500	350

9mm Parabellum Military Contract

As above, in 9mm Parabellum caliber with 24-groove grips, stamped with a large "9" filled with red paint. Rear sights are adjustable with 50 to 500 meter markings. This model has German military acceptance marks on the right side of the chamber. Fit and finish on these pistols are poor. Some examples have the Imperial German Eagle on the front of the magazine well. About 150,000 of these pistols were built for the German government.

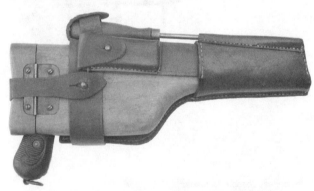

Mauser 9mm military contract "red nine" rig • Courtesy Gale Morgan

Exc.	V.G.	Good	Fair	Poor
2300	1500	1000	700	450

1920 Rework

A Model 96 modified to a barrel length of 3.9" and in 7.63mm Mauser or 9mm Parabellum caliber. Rear sight on this model is fixed. German military acceptance marks are located on the right side of the chamber. Often encountered with police markings.

Courtesy Gale Morgan

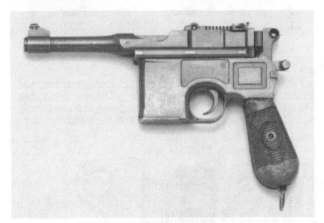

Courtesy Butterfield & Butterfield, San Francisco, California

Exc.	V.G.	Good	Fair	Poor
1200	1000	500	400	350

Late Postwar Bolo Model

Chambered for the 7.63mm Mauser cartridge and fitted with a 3.9" barrel. Rear sight marked for 50 to 500 meters or 50 to 1,000 meters. Grips are walnut with 22 grooves. Some of these pistols will bear Chinese characters. The Mauser banner trademark is stamped on the left rear panel.

Courtesy Gale Morgan

Courtesy Gale Morgan

Exc.	V.G.	Good	Fair	Poor
2200	1200	700	400	200

Early Model 1930

A 7.63mm caliber Model 96 with a 5.2" stepped barrel, 12-groove walnut grips and late style safety. The rear adjustable sight is marked in 50 to 1,000 meters. Some of these pistols have Chinese characters on the left side of the magazine well.

Courtesy Gale Morgan

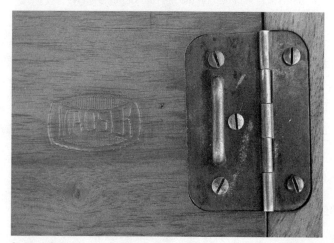

Courtesy Gale Morgan

Exc.	V.G.	Good	Fair	Poor
2000	1600	1200	800	500

Late Model 1930

Identical to the above, except for solid receiver rails.

Exc.	V.G.	Good	Fair	Poor
2500	1750	1200	800	400

Model 1930 Removable Magazine

Similar to the above, but with a detachable magazine. Prospective purchasers should secure a qualified appraisal prior to acquisition. Too rare to price.

Mauser Schnellfeuer (Model 712 or Model 32)

This is not a submachine gun but rather a machine pistol. Chambered for 7.63mm Mauser cartridge. Barrel length is 5.5" and rear sight is adjustable from 50 meters to 1,000 meters. Walnut grips with 12 grooves. Magazine capacity is 10 or 20 rounds with a detachable magazine. This pistol is often encountered with Chinese markings as it was very popular in the Orient. Approximately 100,000 were produced. Rate of fire is between 900 and 1,100 rounds per minute. It should be noted that the Model 712 was used to some limited extent by the Waffen SS during World War II as well as the German Luftwaffe. Stamped with army test proof.

NOTE: The prices listed below are for guns with commercial markings and correct Mauser Schnellfeuer stock. Schnellfeuer stocks are cut larger inside to accommodate selector switch. For German army acceptance stamped pistols add 5-10 percent depending on condition. For pistols without stock or incorrect stock deduct $750 to $1,000.

Photo courtesy Joseph Schroeder

Pre-1968

Exc.	V.G.	Fair
9500	8000	7500

Pre-1986 conversions

Exc.	V.G.	Fair
N/A	N/A	N/A

Pre-1986 dealer samples

Exc.	V.G.	Fair
4500	4000	3000

LUGER

Bibliographical Note: See Charles Kenyon's, *Lugers at Random*, Handgun Press, 1969, for historical information, technical data, and photos. See also Jan Still, *Axis Pistols*, 1986.

Just before the turn of the 20th century, Georg Luger (1849-1923) redesigned the Borchardt semiautomatic pistol so that its mainspring was housed in the rear of the grip. The resulting pistol, the German army's Pistole '08, was to prove extremely successful and his name has become synonymous with the pistol, despite the fact his name never appeared on it.

The following companies manufactured Luger pattern pistols at various times:

1. DWM – Deutsch Waffen und Munitions – Karlsruhe, Germany
2. The Royal Arsenal of Erfurt, Germany
3. Simson & Company – Suhl, Germany
4. Mauser – Oberndorf, Germany
5. Vickers Ltd. – England
6. Waffenfabrik Bern – Bern, Switzerland, see *Switzerland, Handguns, Luger.*
7. Heinrich Krieghoff – Suhl, Germany

NOTE: The model listings below contain the commonly accepted Lugers that are considered military issue. It should be pointed out that in wartime commercial pistols were often diverted to military use if necessary.

DEUTSCHE WAFFEN UND MUNITIONS

1900 Swiss Contract

4.75" barrel, 7.65mm caliber. The Swiss Cross in Sunburst is stamped over the chamber. The military serial number range is 2001-5000; the commercial range, 01-21250. There were approximately 2,000 commercial and 3,000 military models manufactured.

Paul Goodwin photo

Swiss Cross & Sunburst •
Courtesy Gale Morgan

Exc.	V.G.	Good	Fair	Poor
5500	4000	2000	1500	1000

NOTE: Wide trigger add 20 percent.

1900 American Eagle

4.75" barrel, 7.65mm caliber. The American Eagle crest is stamped over the chamber. The serial range is between 2000-200000, and there were approximately 11,000-12,000 commercial models marked "Germany" and 1,000 military test models without the commercial import stamp. The serial numbers of this military lot have been estimated at between 6100-7100.

Paul Goodwin photo

Exc.	V.G.	Good	Fair	Poor
4500	3200	1500	850	600

1900 Bulgarian Contract

An old model, 1900 Type, with no stock lug. It has a 4.75" barrel and is chambered for the 7.65mm cartridge. The Bulgarian crest is stamped over the chamber, and the safety is marked in Bulgarian letters. The serial range is 20000-21000, with 1,000 manufactured. This is a military test model and is quite rare as most were rebarreled to 9mm during the time they were used. Even with the 9mm versions, approximately 10 are known to exist. It was the only variation to feature a marked safety before 1904.

A U.S. Army Model 1900 test pistol with holster, roll press stamp, M1910 garrison belt, and magazine pouch was sold at auction for $18,400. Condition is 96 percent original blue. Bore is fair. Holster is excellent. Roll press is excellent.
Rock Island Auction Company, August 2004

Exc.	V.G.	Good	Fair	Poor
12000	8000	4000	2500	1800

1902 American Eagle Cartridge Counter

As above, with a "Powell Indicating Device" added to the left grip. A slotted magazine with a numbered window that allows visual access to the number of cartridges remaining. There were 50 Lugers altered in this way at the request of the U.S. Board of Ordnance, for U.S. army evaluation. The serial numbers are 22401-22450. Be especially wary of fakes!

Exc.	V.G.	Good	Fair	Poor
30000	25000	16000	6000	3500

1904 Navy

6" thick barrel, 9mm caliber. The chamber area is blank, and the extractor is marked "Geladen." The safety is marked "Gesichert." There were approximately 1,500 manufactured in the one- to four-digit serial range, for military sales to the German navy. The toggle has a "lock" comparable to 1900 types.

Exc.	V.G.	Good	Fair	Poor
40000	30000	16000	6000	4500

1906 U.S. Army Test Luger .45 Caliber

5" barrel, .45 ACP caliber. Sent to the United States for testing in 1907. The chamber is blank; the extractor is marked "Loaded," and the frame is polished under the safety lever. The trigger on this model has an odd hook at the bottom. Only five of these pistols were manufactured.

Exc.	V.G.	Good	Fair	Poor

Too Rare To Price

1906 Swiss Military

Same as the Swiss Commercial, with the Geneva Cross in shield appearing on the chamber.

Exc.	V.G.	Good	Fair	Poor
4500	3100	2000	900	700

1906 Swiss Police Cross in Shield

As above, with a shield replacing the sunburst on the chamber marking. There were 10,215 of both models combined. They are in the 5000-15215 serial number range.

1906 Swiss Police Cross in Shield • Courtesy Gale Morgan

Paul Goodwin photo

Exc.	V.G.	Good	Fair	Poor
4700	3700	2000	1000	700

1906 Dutch Contract

4" barrel, 9mm caliber. It has no stock lug, and the chamber is blank. The extractor is marked "Geleden" on both sides, and the safety is marked "RUST" with a curved upward pointing arrow. This pistol was manufactured for military sales to the Netherlands, and a date will be found on the barrel of most examples encountered. The Dutch refinished their pistols on a regular basis and marked the date on the barrels. There were approximately 4,000 manufactured, serial numbered between 1 and 4000.

Courtesy Gale Morgan

Paul Goodwin photo

Exc.	V.G.	Good	Fair	Poor
4200	3000	1500	800	600

1906 Royal Portuguese Navy

4" barrel, 9mm caliber, and has no stock lug. The Royal Portuguese naval crest, an anchor under a crown, is stamped above the chamber. The extractor is marked "CARREGADA" on the left side. The frame under the safety is polished. There were approximately 1,000 manufactured with one- to four-digit serial numbers.

Exc.	V.G.	Good	Fair	Poor
12000	9000	6500	4000	2500

1906 Royal Portuguese Army (M2)

4.75" barrel, 7.65mm caliber. It has no stock lug. The chamber area has the Royal Portuguese crest of Manuel II stamped upon it. The extractor is marked "CARREGADA." There were approximately 5,000 manufactured, with one- to four-digit serial numbers.

Portuguese Army "M2" • Courtesy Gale Morgan

Exc.	V.G.	Good	Fair	Poor
3500	2700	1200	600	500

1906 Republic of Portugal Navy

4" barrel, 9mm caliber. It has no stock lug, and the extractor was marked "CARREGADA." This model was made after 1910, when Portugal had become a republic. The anchor on the chamber is under the letters "R.P." There were approximately 1,000 manufactured, with one- to four-digit serial numbers.

Exc.	V.G.	Good	Fair	Poor
11000	9000	5500	3500	2500

1906 Brazilian Contract

4.75" barrel, 7.65mm caliber. It has no stock lug, and chamber area is blank. The extractor is marked "CARREGADA," and the frame under the safety is polished. There were approximately 5,000 manufactured for military sales to Brazil.

Paul Goodwin photo

Exc.	V.G.	Good	Fair	Poor
3000	2400	1100	750	450

1906 Bulgarian Contract

4.75" barrel, 7.65mm caliber. It has no stock lug, and the extractor and safety are marked in cyrillic letters. The Bulgarian crest is stamped above the chamber. Nearly all of the examples located have the barrels replaced with 4" 9mm units. This was done after the later 1908 model was adopted. Some were refurbished during the Nazi era, and these pistols bear Waffenamts and usually mismatched parts. There were approximately 1,500 manufactured, with serial numbers of one to four digits.

Courtesy Rock Island Auction Company

Exc.	V.G.	Good	Fair	Poor
9500	7000	5000	3500	1500

1906 Russian Contract

4" barrel, 9mm caliber. It has no stock lug, and the extractor and safety are marked with cyrillic letters. Crossed Nagant rifles are stamped over the chamber. There were approximately 1,000 manufactured, with one- to four-digit serial numbers; but few survive. This is an extremely rare variation, and caution should be exercised if purchase is contemplated.

Paul Goodwin photo

Close-up of 1906 Russian Contract • Courtesy Gale Morgan

Exc.	V.G.	Good	Fair	Poor
14000	12000	6500	4000	2500

1906 Navy 1st Issue

6" barrel, 9mm caliber. The safety and extractor are both marked in German, and the chamber area is blank. There is a stock lug, and the unique two-position sliding navy sight is mounted on the rear toggle link. There were approximately 12,000 manufactured for the German navy, with serial numbers of one to five digits. The wooden magazine bottom features concentric rings.

NOTE: Many of these pistols had their safety changed so that they were "safe" in the lower position. Known as "1st issue altered." Value at approximately 20 percent less.

Paul Goodwin photo

Paul Goodwin photo

Close-up of 1906 Navy 1st Issue • Courtesy Gale Morgan

Exc.	V.G.	Good	Fair	Poor
8000	6000	3000	1300	950

1906 Navy 2nd Issue

As above, but manufactured to be safe in the lower position. Approximately 11,000 2nd Issue Navies manufactured, with one- to five-digit serial numbers—some with an "a" or "b" suffix. They were produced for sale to the German navy.

Paul Goodwin photo

Exc.	V.G.	Good	Fair	Poor
5500	3500	1500	950	700

1908 Navy

As above, with the "Crown M" military proof. They may or may not have the concentric rings on the magazine bottom. There were approximately 40,000 manufactured, with one- to five-digit serial numbers with an "a" or "b" suffix. These Lugers are quite scarce as many were destroyed during and after WWI.

Exc.	V.G.	Good	Fair	Poor
4500	3200	2000	1100	800

A DWM 1906 Navy 1st Issue was sold at auction for $18,400. Complete with holster and board stock. Early production model with original safety lever. Condition is 98 percent with mint bore. All serial numbers are matching.
Rock Island Auction Company, August 2004

A Model 1908 Navy sold at auction for $6,900. All matching numbers. Condition is 96 percent with bright straw.
Rock Island Auction Company, Dec. 2004

1914 Navy

Similar to the above, but stamped with the dates from 1914-1918 above the chamber. Most noted are dated 1916-1918. There were approximately 30,000 manufactured, with one- to five-digit serial numbers with an "a" or "b" suffix. They are scarce as many were destroyed or altered as a result of WWI, even though about 40,000 were built.

Paul Goodwin photo

Exc.	V.G.	Good	Fair	Poor
4500	3000	1500	950	700

1908 Military 1st Issue

4" barrel, 9mm caliber. This was the first Luger adopted by the German army. It has no stock lug, and the extractor and safety are both marked in German. The chamber is blank. There were approximately 20,000 manufactured, with one- to five-digit serial numbers—some with an "a" suffix.

Exc.	V.G.	Good	Fair	Poor
1800	1200	600	500	350

1908 Military Dated Chamber (1910-1913)

As above, with the date of manufacture stamped on the chamber.

Exc.	V.G.	Good	Fair	Poor
1500	1000	600	500	350

1914 Military

As above, with a stock lug.

Exc.	V.G.	Good	Fair	Poor
1150	900	650	500	350

1914 Artillery

Fitted with an 8" barrel and chambered for the 9mm Parabellum cartridge, it features a nine-position adjustable sight that has a base that is an integral part of the barrel. This model has a stock lug and was furnished with a military-style flat board stock and holster rig (see Accessories). The chamber is dated from 1914-1918, and the safety and extractor are both marked. This model was developed for artillery and machine gun crews; and many thousands were manufactured, with one- to five-digit serial numbers—some have letter suffixes. This model is quite desirable from a collector's standpoint and is rarer than its production figures would indicate. After the war many were destroyed as the allies deemed them more insidious than other models for some reason.

A 1914 DWM Artillery Model, dated 1915, sold at auction for $8,625. Also includes holster and board stock with loading tools and cleaning rod. Condition of pistol is 98 percent. Holster and stock are also excellent. *Rock Island Auction Company, August 2004*

Courtesy Rock Island Auction Company

Close-up of rear sight on 1914 Artillery • Courtesy Gale Morgan

Exc.	V.G.	Good	Fair	Poor
3000	2000	1300	900	600

NOTE: For models stamped with 1914 date add 50 percent.

DWM Double Dated

Has a 4" barrel, 9mm cartridge. The date 1920 or 1921 is stamped over the original chamber date of 1910-1918, creating the double-date nomenclature. These are arsenal-reworked WWI military pistols and were then issued to the

German military and/or police units within the provisions of the Treaty of Versailles. Many thousands of these Lugers were produced.

Courtesy Rock Island Auction Company

Courtesy Rock Island Auction Company

Exc.	V.G.	Good	Fair	Poor
1300	800	550	400	300

1920 Police/Military Rework
As above, except that the original manufacture date was removed before the rework date was stamped. There were many thousands of these produced.

Exc.	V.G.	Good	Fair	Poor
800	650	500	350	300

1920 Navy Carbine
Assembled from surplus navy parts with the distinctive two position, sliding navy sight on the rear toggle link. Most are marked with the export stamp (GERMANY) and have the naval military proofmarks still in evidence. The safety and extractor are marked, and rarely one is found chambered for the 9mm cartridge. Few were manufactured.

1920 Navy Carbine • Paul Goodwin photo

Exc.	V.G.	Good	Fair	Poor
6250	5000	3000	1800	900

1923 Dutch Commercial & Military
Fitted with a 4" barrel, 9mm caliber. It has a stock lug, and the chamber area is blank. The extractor is marked in German, and the safety is marked "RUST" with a downward pointing arrow. This model was sold commercially and to the military in the Netherlands. There were approximately 1,000 manufactured in the one- to three-digit serial range, with no letter suffix.

Exc.	V.G.	Good	Fair	Poor
3500	2400	1000	850	550

Royal Dutch Air Force
Fitted with a 4" barrel, 9mm caliber. Marked with the Mauser Oberndorf proofmark and serial numbered in the 10000 to 14000 range. The safety marked "RUST."

Exc.	V.G.	Good	Fair	Poor
4000	2500	1000	800	550

VICKERS LTD.

1906 Vickers Dutch
Has a 4" barrel, 9mm caliber. There is no stock lug, and it uses a grip safety. The chamber is blank, and the extractor is marked "Geleden." "Vickers Ltd." is stamped on the front toggle link. The safety is marked "RUST" with an upward pointing arrow. Examples have been found with an additional date as late as 1933 stamped on the barrel. These dates indicate arsenal refinishing and in no way detract from the value of this variation. Arsenal reworks are matte finished, and the originals are a higher polished rust blue. There were approximately 10,000 manufactured in the 1-10100 serial number range.

Paul Goodwin photo

Exc.	V.G.	Good	Fair	Poor
3500	2800	1800	1200	750

ERFURT ROYAL ARSENAL

1908 Erfurt
Has a 4" barrel, 9mm caliber. It has no stock lug, and the year of manufacture, from 1910-1913, is stamped above the chamber. The extractor and safety are both marked in German, and "ERFURT" under a crown is stamped on the front toggle link. There were many thousands produced as Germany was involved in WWI. They are found in the one- to five-digit serial number range, sometimes with a letter suffix.

Exc.	V.G.	Good	Fair	Poor
1400	950	600	400	350

1914 Erfurt Military

Has a 4" barrel, 9mm caliber. It has a stock lug and the date of manufacture over the chamber, 1914-1918. The extractor and safety are both marked in German, and the front link is marked "ERFURT" under a crown. The finish on this model is rough; and as the war progressed in 1917 and 1918, the finish got worse. There were many thousands produced with one- to five-digit serial numbers, some with letter suffixes.

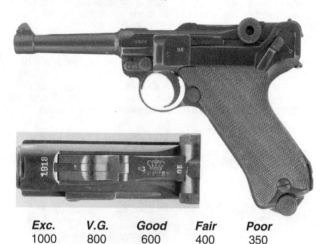

Courtesy Rock Island Auction Company

Exc.	V.G.	Good	Fair	Poor
1000	800	600	400	350

1914 Erfurt Artillery

Fitted with an 8" barrel, 9mm caliber. It has a stock lug and was issued with a flat board-type stock and other accessories, which will be covered in the section of this book dealing with same. The sight is a nine-position adjustable model. The chamber is dated 1914-1918, and the extractor and safety are both marked in German. "ERFURT" under a crown is stamped on the front toggle link. There were a great many manufactured with one- to five-digit serial numbers, some with a letter suffix. This model is similar to the DWM Artillery except that the finish is not as fine.

Paul Goodwin photo

Exc.	V.G.	Good	Fair	Poor
2900	1700	1100	800	600

Double Date Erfurt

Has a 4" barrel, 9mm caliber. The area above the chamber has two dates: the original 1910-1918, and the date of rework, 1920 or 1921. The extractor and safety are both marked in German, and this model can be found with or without a stock lug. "ERFURT" under a crown is stamped on the front toggle link. Police or military unit markings are found on the front of the grip straps more often than not. There were thousands of these produced by DWM as well as Erfurt.

Exc.	V.G.	Good	Fair	Poor
750	600	500	400	350

WAFFENFABRIK BERN

See *Swiss, Handguns, Bern*

SIMSON & CO.
SUHL, GERMANY

Simson & Co. Rework

Fitted with a 4" barrel, and chambered for either the 7.65 or 9mm caliber. The chamber is blank, but some examples are dated 1917 or 1918. The forward toggle link is stamped "SIMSON & CO. Suhl." The extractor and safety are marked in German. Most examples have stock lugs; some have been noted without them. The only difference between military models and commercial models is the proofmarks.

Exc.	V.G.	Good	Fair	Poor
2000	1300	900	600	500

Simson Dated Military

Has 4" barrel, 9mm caliber. There is a stock lug, and the year of manufacture from 1925-1928 is stamped above the chamber. The extractor and the safety are both marked in German. The checkered walnut grips of Simson-made Lugers are noticeably thicker than others. This is an extremely rare variation. Approximately 2,000 were manufactured with one- to three-digit serial numbers, and few seem to have survived.

Paul Goodwin photo

Exc.	V.G.	Good	Fair	Poor
3000	2200	1500	850	550

Simson S Code

Has a 4" barrel, 9mm caliber. The forward toggle link is stamped with a Gothic "S". It has a stock lug, and the area above the chamber is blank. The extractor and the safety are both marked. The grips are also thicker. There were approximately 12,000 manufactured with one- to five-digit serial numbers—some with the letter "a" suffix. This pistol is quite rare on today's market.

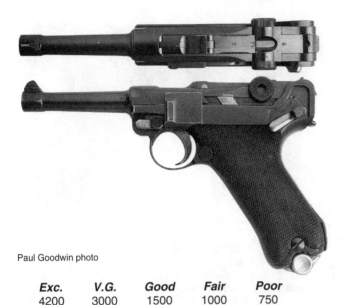

Paul Goodwin photo

Exc.	V.G.	Good	Fair	Poor
4200	3000	1500	1000	750

EARLY NAZI ERA REWORKS MAUSER

Produced between 1930 and 1933, and normally marked with Waffenamt markings.

Death's Head Rework

Has a 4" barrel, 9mm caliber. It has a stock lug, and a skull and crossbones are stamped, in addition to the date of manufacture, on the chamber area. This date was from 1914-1918. The extractor and safety are both marked. The Waffenamt proof is present. It is thought that this variation was produced for the 1930-1933 era "SS" division of the Nazi Party. Mixed serial numbers are encountered on this model and do not lower the value. This is a rare Luger on today's market, and caution should be exercised if purchase is contemplated.

Exc.	V.G.	Good	Fair	Poor
2500	1500	950	600	450

Kadetten Institute Rework

4" barrel, 9mm caliber. It has a stock lug, and the chamber area is stamped "K.I." above the 1933 date. This stood for Cadets Institute, an early "SA" and "SS" officers' training school. The extractor and safety are both marked, and the Waffenamt is present. There were only a few hundred reworked, and the variation is quite scarce. Be wary of fakes.

Exc.	V.G.	Good	Fair	Poor
3200	2500	1100	800	600

Mauser Unmarked Rework

4" barrel, 9mm caliber. The entire weapon is void of identifying markings. There is extensive refurbishing, removal of all markings, rebarreling, etc. The stock lug is present, and the extractor and safety are marked. The Waffenamt proofmark is on the right side of the receiver. The number manufactured is not known.

Exc.	V.G.	Good	Fair	Poor
1450	1000	850	600	450

MAUSER MANUFACTURED LUGERS 1930-1942 DWM

Mauser Oberndorf

4" barrel, 9mm caliber. It has a stock lug, blank chamber area, and a marked extractor and safety. This is an early example of Mauser Luger, and the front toggle link is still marked "DWM" as leftover parts were intermixed with new Mauser parts in the production of this pistol. This is one of the first Lugers to be finished with the "Salt" blue process. There were approximately 500 manufactured with one- to four-digit serial numbers with the letter "v" suffix. This is a rare variation.

Exc.	V.G.	Good	Fair	Poor
5000	3200	2000	1500	900

1935/06 Portuguese "GNR"

4.75" barrel, 7.65mm caliber. It has no stock lug but has a grip safety. The chamber is marked "GNR," representing the Republic National Guard. The extractor is marked "Carregada"; and the safety, "Seguranca." The Mauser banner is stamped on the front toggle link. There were exactly 564 manufactured according to the original contract records that the Portuguese government made public. They all have four-digit serial numbers with a "v" suffix.

Paul Goodwin photo

Exc.	V.G.	Good	Fair	Poor
3700	2700	1600	900	750

S/42 K Date

4" barrel, 9mm caliber. It has a stock lug, and the extractor and safety are marked. This was the first Luger that utilized codes to represent maker and date of manufacture. The front toggle link is marked "S/42" in either Gothic or script; this was the code for Mauser. The chamber area is stamped with the letter "K," the code for 1934, the year of manufacture. Approximately 10,500 were manufactured with one- to five-digit serial numbers—some with letter suffixes.

Courtesy Richard M. Kumor Sr.

Exc.	V.G.	Good	Fair	Poor
6000	4000	2200	1200	1000

S/42 G Date

As above, with the chamber stamped "G," the code for the year 1935. The Gothic lettering was eliminated, and there were many thousands of this model produced.

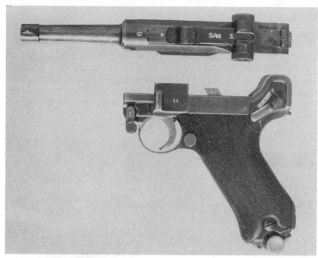

Courtesy Orvel Reichert

Exc.	V.G.	Good	Fair	Poor
2800	2000	1000	650	450

Dated Chamber S/42

4" barrel, 9mm caliber. The chamber area is dated 1936-1940, and there is a stock lug. The extractor and safety are marked. In 1937 the rust blue process was eliminated entirely, and all subsequent pistols were salt blued. There were many thousands manufactured with one- to five-digit serial numbers—some with a letter suffix.

Paul Goodwin photo

Paul Goodwin photo

Exc.	V.G.	Good	Fair	Poor
1600	1100	750	500	400

NOTE: Rarest variation is early 1937 with rust blued and strawed parts, add 20 percent.

Code 42 Dated Chamber

4" barrel, 9mm caliber. The new German code for Mauser, the number 42, is stamped on the front toggle link. There is a stock lug. The chamber area is dated 1939 or 1940. There were at least 50,000 manufactured with one- to five-digit serial numbers—some have letter suffixes.

Exc.	V.G.	Good	Fair	Poor
1500	850	650	400	350

41/42 Code

As above, except that the date of manufacture is represented by the final two digits (e.g. 41 for 1941). There were approximately 20,000 manufactured with the one- to five-digit serial number range.

Exc.	V.G.	Good	Fair	Poor
1600	1350	900	700	500

byf Code

As above, with the "byf" code stamp on the toggle link. The year of manufacture, either 41 or 42, is stamped on the chamber. This model was also made with black plastic, as well as walnut grips. There were many thousands produced with the one- to five-digit serial numbers—some with a letter suffix.

A byf 41 Luger property of adjutant to General Fretter Pico sold at auction for $9,200. Complete with Type I holster. Matching serial numbers. Condition is 98 percent.
Rock Island Auction Company, August 2004

Paul Goodwin photo

Exc.	V.G.	Good	Fair	Poor
1300	950	750	450	350

Persian Contract 4"

4" barrel, 9mm caliber. It has a stock lug, and the Persian crest is stamped over the chamber. All identifying markings on this variation—including extractor, safety, and toggle—are marked in Farsi, the Persian alphabet. There were 1,000 manufactured. The serial numbers are also in Farsi.

Persian Contract 4" • Paul Goodwin photo

Exc.	V.G.	Good	Fair	Poor
6500	5000	3500	2500	2000

Persian Contract Artillery

As above, with an 8" barrel and nine-position adjustable sight on the barrel. This model is supplied with a flat board stock. There were 1,000 manufactured and sold to Persia.

Courtesy Rock Island Auction Company

Exc.	V.G.	Good	Fair	Poor
3500	2850	1800	1300	1000

1934 Mauser Dutch Contract

4" barrel, 9mm caliber. The year of manufacture, 1936-1939, is stamped above the chamber. The extractor is marked "Geladen," and the safety is marked "RUST" with a downward pointing arrow. The Mauser banner is stamped on the front toggle link. Checkered walnut grips. This was a military contract sale, and approximately 1,000 were manufactured with four-digit serial numbers with a letter "v" suffix.

Paul Goodwin photo

Exc.	V.G.	Good	Fair	Poor
3500	3000	2000	1100	850

1934 Mauser Swedish Contract

4.75" barrel, 9mm or 7.65mm caliber. The chamber is dated 1938 or 1939. The extractor and safety are both marked in German, and there is a stock lug. The front toggle link is stamped with the Mauser banner. There were only 275 dated 1938 and 25 dated 1939 in 9mm. There were only 30 chambered for 7.65mm dated 1939. The serial number range is four digits with the letter "v" suffix.

Exc.	V.G.	Good	Fair	Poor
4300	3000	2000	1500	700

1934 Mauser German Contract

4" barrel, 9mm caliber. The chamber is dated 1939-1942, and the front toggle link is stamped with the Mauser banner. There is a stock lug, and the extractor and safety are both marked. The grips are either walnut or black plastic. There were several thousand manufactured with one- to five-digit serial numbers—some with letter suffixes. They were purchased for issue to police or paramilitary units.

Exc.	V.G.	Good	Fair	Poor
2800	2300	1500	800	550

Austrian Bundes Heer (Federal Army)

4" barrel, 9mm caliber. The chamber is blank, and there is a stock lug. The extractor and safety are marked in German, and the Austrian federal army proof is stamped on the left side of the frame above the triggerguard. There were approximately 200 manufactured with four-digit serial numbers and no letter suffix.

Exc.	V.G.	Good	Fair	Poor
2500	1850	1200	700	500

Mauser 2-Digit Date

4" barrel, 9mm caliber. The last two digits of the year of manufacture—41 or 42—are stamped over the chamber. There is a stock lug, and the Mauser banner is on the front toggle link. The extractor and safety are both marked, and the proofmarks were commercial. Grips are either walnut or black plastic. There were approximately 2,000 manufactured for sale to Nazi political groups. They have one- to five-digit serial numbers—some have the letter suffix.

Mauser 2-Digit Date • Courtesy Gale Morgan

Exc.	V.G.	Good	Fair	Poor
2800	2200	1500	900	650

KRIEGHOFF MANUFACTURED LUGERS

S Code Krieghoff

4" barrel, 9mm caliber. The Krieghoff trademark is stamped on the front toggle link, and the letter "S" is stamped over the chamber. There is a stock lug, and the extractor and safety are both marked. The grips are brown checkered plastic. There were approximately 4,500 manufactured for the Luftwaffe with one- to four-digit serial numbers.

Courtesy Rock Island Auction Company

Exc.	V.G.	Good	Fair	Poor
5000	3200	1800	950	750

Grip Safety Krieghoff

4" barrel, 9mm caliber. The chamber area is blank, and the front toggle link is stamped with the Krieghoff trademark. There is a stock lug and a grip safety. The extractor is marked "Geleden," and the safety is marked "FEUER" (fire) in the lower position. The grips are checkered brown plastic. This is a rare Luger, and the number produced is not known.

Exc.	V.G.	Good	Fair	Poor
6000	4000	2800	1400	900

36 Date Krieghoff

4" barrel, 9mm caliber. It has a stock lug and the Krieghoff trademark on the front toggle link. The safety and extractor are marked, and the grips are brown plastic. The two-digit year of manufacture, 36, is stamped over the chamber. There were approximately 700 produced in the 3800-4500 serial number range.

Paul Goodwin photo

Exc.	V.G.	Good	Fair	Poor
4500	3850	2200	1200	950

4-Digit Dated Krieghoff

As above, with the date of production, 1936-1945, stamped above the chamber. There were approximately 9,000 manufactured within the 4500-14000 serial number range.

Courtesy Gale Morgan

Exc.	V.G.	Good	Fair	Poor
4000	3000	1850	950	750

LUGER ACCESSORIES

Detachable Carbine Stocks

Approximately 13" in length, with a sling swivel and horn buttplate.

Exc.	V.G.	Good	Fair	Poor
4500	3500	1500	700	500

Artillery Stock with Holster

The artillery stock is of a flat board style approximately 13.75" in length. There is a holster and magazine pouches with straps attached. This is a desirable addition to the Artillery Luger.

Exc.	V.G.	Good	Fair	Poor
1500	1000	500	400	300

Navy Stock without Holster

As above, but 12.75" in length with a metal disc inlaid on the left side.

Exc.	V.G.	Good	Fair	Poor
3000	1500	1000	500	400

NOTE: With holster add 100 percent.

Ideal Stock/Holster with Grips

A telescoping metal tube stock with an attached leather holster. It is used in conjunction with a metal-backed set of plain grips that correspond to the metal hooks on the stock and allow attachment. This Ideal Stock is U.S. patented and is so marked.

Exc.	V.G.	Good	Fair	Poor
2000	1400	1000	700	450

Drum Magazine 1st Issue

A 32-round, snail-like affair that is used with the Artillery Luger. It is also used with an adapter in the German 9mm submachine gun. The 1st Issue has a telescoping tube that is used to wind the spring. There is a dust cover that protects the interior from dirt.

Exc.	V.G.	Good	Fair	Poor
1500	800	600	350	300

Drum Magazine 2nd Issue

As above, with a folding spring winding lever.

Exc.	V.G.	Good	Fair	Poor
1300	700	500	350	300

Drum Magazine Loading Tool

This tool is slipped over the magazine and allows the spring to be compressed so that cartridges could be inserted.

Exc.	V.G.	Good	Fair	Poor
800	550	500	300	200

Drum Magazine Unloading Tool

The origin of this tool is unknown and caution should be exercised prior to purchase.

Drum Carrying Case

The same caveat as above applies.

Exc.	V.G.	Good	Fair	Poor
250	200	125	100	50

Holsters

Produced in a wide variety of styles.

Exc.	V.G.	Good	Fair	Poor
450	30033	150	60	50

LANGENHAN, FRIEDRICH

Langenhan Army Model

A blowback-operated semiautomatic pistol chambered for the 7.65mm Auto Pistol cartridge. It has a 4" barrel and a detachable magazine that holds 8 rounds. Weight is about 24 oz. The pistol was made with a separate breechblock that is held into the slide by a screw. This feature doomed this pistol to eventual failure as when this screw became worn, it could loosen when firing and allow the breechblock to pivot upwards—and the slide would then be propelled rearward and into the face of the shooter. This is not a comforting thought. This pistol was produced and used in WWI only and was never offered commercially. It is marked "F.L. Selbstlade DRGM." The finish is blued, and the grips are molded rubber, with "F.L." at the top.

CAUTION: This is an unsafe weapon to fire.

Courtesy James Rankin

Exc.	V.G.	Good	Fair	Poor
300	225	200	150	100

P.38

THE GERMAN WWII SERVICE PISTOL

Walther developed its German military service pistol, the P.38 or Model HP (Heerespistole), in 1937. It was adopted by the German military as its primary handgun in 1938. The background behind this adoption by the German military is an interesting one. In the 1930s, the German Army High Command wanted German arms manufacturers to develop a large-caliber semiautomatic pistol to replace the Luger, which was difficult and costly to manufacture. The army wanted a pistol that was easy to manufacture as well as simple to assemble and disassemble. It also required a pistol that could be produced by several manufacturers if necessary and one whose parts would be interchangeable among manufacturers. Walther had just completed its Model HP for worldwide distribution and had the advantage over the other German companies. The German High Command approved Walther's design with only a few mechanical changes. This designation, the P.38, was not used by Walther on its commercial guns. Production began in late 1939 for both civilian and military use. Both military and commercial versions were produced throughout the war years. The civilian pistol was referred to as the MOD HP until late in the war, when a few were marked "MOD P.38" to take advantage of the identity of the military pistol. In late 1942, Mauser and Spreewerke began production of the P.38. Mauser was assigned the code "BYF" and in 1945 the code was changed to "SVW." Spreewerke's code was "CYQ." Late in the war the die stamp broke and the code appears as "CVQ."

The P.38 is a double-action semiautomatic pistol that is short-recoil operated and fires from a locked breech by means of an external hammer. It is chambered for the 9mm Parabellum and has a 5" barrel. The detachable magazine holds 8 cartridges and the front sight is adjustable for windage. Initially the finish was a high quality blue, but when the war effort increased, less time was spent on the finish. The P.38 was equipped with two styles of plastic grips. Early pistols have a checkered grip and later grips are the military ribbed variety; the later style is much more common. The P.38 was produced by three companies and each had its own distinct markings and variations as outlined below. Despite the large number of variations that the P.38 collector will encounter, it is important for him to be aware that there are no known documented examples of P.38s that are factory engraved, nickel-plated, have barrels that are longer or shorter than standard, or built as military presentation pistols.

Collectors should be made aware of a final note. The P.38 pistol was first adopted more than 50 years ago. During that period of time the pistol has seen use all over the world. After the end of WWII several governments came into possession of fairly large quantities of P.38s and used them in their own military and police agencies. Many countries have reworked these older P.38s with both original and new component parts. The former U.S.S.R. is the primary source of reworked P.38s. Many of these pistols have been completely refinished and re-proofed by a number of countries. The collector should be aware of the existence of reworked P.38s and examine any P.38 carefully to determine if the pistol is original German military issue. These reworked pistols bring substantially lower prices than original P.38s.

NOTE: As of 1997 the Ukraine is now the primary source of pistols. Almost all are importer marked and have been cold dipped blued. Some are reworked and others are original except for the finish.

SNAP SHOT
WHAT'S IT LIKE - WALTHER'S PISTOLE 38

In 1929 the German firm of Karl Walther Waffenfabrik took the handgun world by storm by introducing the first successful double action/single action (DA/SA) semiauto pistol – the Polizei Pistole, or simply PP. While widely popular with Continental police forces, when Hitler's Wehrmacht began their rearmament in the early 1930s they asked for DA/SA handgun, but one that fired the full power 9mm Patrone 08 (9mm Luger) cartridge.

Walther's engineers came up with a completely new DA/SA, locked breech pistol to meet the army's requirements. It was adopted in 1938 as the Pistole 38 ("P38") and, the rest is history. Lightweight with good ergonomics and firing a powerful cartridge, many consider the P38 as the best combat handgun of WWII. Production continued after the war and the P38 was adopted by dozens of armies and police forces around the world. It has been said that the P38 was the first of that breed of pistols that later became known as the "Wondernines."

A friend supplied a P38 that his father "liberated" in Germany in 1945. It bore the "byf" code of the Mauser Werke and the date "44" and the frame, slide, barrel and magazine all had matching serial numbers and Waffenamt acceptance marks. Overall condition was VG+ with a bright, shiny bore but, probably as a result of war time production, the DA trigger pull was quite gritty and heavy. While the rear sight was too wide – or the front sight too narrow? – they were better than those on many pistols of that era. It had a comfortable, hand-filling grip and despite being a bit muzzle light, pointed well. The controls were well located and it boasted fairly good SA trigger pull.

I ran 100 rounds through the Walther on a combat target at a distance of 7 yards and, despite preconceptions to the contrary, was able to place all of my shots in the higher scoring zones. Aside from a DA trigger pull that might make Arnold Swartzenegger grunt, I found little about the P38 to criticize. In fact, I sort of liked it.

Paul Scarlata

WALTHER COMMERCIAL

The Commercial version of the P.38 is identified by commercial proofmarks of a crown over N or an eagle over N. Production started at around serial number 1000 and went through serial number 26659. This was the first of the commercial pistols and was a high-quality, well-made gun with a complete inscription on the left slide. A few of these early pistols were equipped with checkered wooden grips. The quality decreased as the war progressed. There are many variations of these commercial models and values can vary from $1,000 to $16,000. It is suggested that these pistols be appraised and evaluated by an expert. For postwar Walther P.38 pistols see the Walther section.

A few of the Walther commercial model variations follow:

MOD HP-Early w/High Gloss Blue

Courtesy Orvel Reichert

Exc.	V.G.	Good	Fair	Poor
3000	1750	750	600	400

MOD HP-Early w/High Gloss Blue & Alloy Frame

Courtesy Orvel Reichert

Exc.	V.G.	Good	Fair	Poor
10000	6500	3500	2000	1000

MOD HP-Late w/Military Blue Finish

Courtesy Orvel Reichert

Exc.	V.G.	Good	Fair	Poor
2000	1400	750	550	350

NOTE: Add $500 for "Eagle/359" on right side.

Selected P.38 Stampings

Late Mauser 44-45 right slide

Late war cog hammer

fnh barrel code

Reject mark * (asterisk)

Walther right slide

cyq right slide

Postwar East German military

Early 42-43 right slide

All photos courtesy Orvel Reichert

A Walther single-action Model HP 7.65mm pistol sold at auction for $23,000. Only seven single-action Model HP pistols have been identified. Barrel length is 4.9 inches. Condition is 98 percent original blue with mint bore.
Rock Island Auction Company, August 2004

A commercial HP pistol with high polish sold at auction for $8,050. All features are correct. Condition is 99 percent.
Rock Island Auction Company, Dec. 2004

A MOD HP in 9mm used for Luftwaffe trials was sold at auction for $3,450. Stamped with Eagle/359. Condition is 95 percent high polish blue.

Rock Island Auction Company, August 2004

MOD P38–Late with Military Blue

1,800 produced.

Courtesy Orvel Reichert

Exc.	V.G.	Good	Fair	Poor
2700	1400	750	600	400

A Walther commercial Mod P3B sold at auction for $7,475. Complete with holster and spare magazine. It was the property of the mayor of Leipzig and was taken from him in April 1945.

Rock Island Auction Company, August 2004

WALTHER MILITARY

Courtesy Orvel Reichert

Courtesy Orvel Reichert

ZERO SERIES

This was the first of the military P.38s and they are well made with a high polish finish. These pistols have the Walther banner and the designation P.38. The serial number began with 01 and went through about 013714. The First Zero Series has a concealed extractor and rectangular firing pin. About 1,000 First Zero Series were built. The Second Zero Series has a rectangular firing pin and standard extractor, with a production of about 2,300. The Third Zero Series has a standard firing pin and standard extractor and has the highest production with 10,000 built.

First Issue Zero Series

Courtesy Orvel Reichert

Exc.	V.G.	Good	Fair	Poor
8500	5500	3500	2500	1500

A first development letter suffix zero series pistol sold at auction for $21,850. Two-digit serial number with an "a" suffix. Condition is 98 percent overall.

Rock Island Auction Company, Dec. 2004

Second Issue Zero Series

Exc.	V.G.	Good	Fair	Poor
7000	4500	3250	2000	1000

Third Issue Zero Series

Exc.	V.G.	Good	Fair	Poor
3500	2200	1250	800	500

480 CODE

This code was utilized by Walther in late 1940 and represents the first true military contract pistols. There were approximately 7,250 guns produced under this code. There are two subvariations: one with a round lanyard loop and the other with a rectangular lanyard loop.

Exc.	V.G.	Good	Fair	Poor
8500	5500	3000	1750	1000

"AC" CODES

This variation follows the 480 code.

"ac" (no date)

This variation has on the slide "P.38ac" then the serial number only. This is the first use of the "ac" code by Walther. There were approximately 2,700 pistols produced with this code and this is the rarest of all military P.38s.

A P.38 "ac (no date)" sold at auction for $5,462.50. Condition is 90 percent original blue. Grips are excellent.

Rock Island Auction Company, August 2004

Courtesy Orvel Reichert

Exc.	V.G.	Good	Fair	Poor
9500	6000	4250	2800	2000

"ac40"

There are two types of "ac40s." The first variation is the ac with the 40 added, that is the "40" was hand stamped below the "ac". There are about 6,000 of these produced. The second variation is the "ac40" rolled on together. There are also about 14,000 of these produced as well. The "ac" 40 added is more valuable than the standard "ac40."

"ac40" (added)

Courtesy Orvel Reichert

Exc.	V.G.	Good	Fair	Poor
3800	2500	1750	1000	600

"ac40" (standard)

Courtesy Orvel Reichert

Exc.	V.G.	Good	Fair	Poor
2500	1200	950	700	500

"ac41"

There are three variations of the "ac41." The first variation has "ac" on left triggerguard and features a high gloss blue. About 25,000 of this variation were made. The second variation, about 70,000 were produced, also has a high gloss blue but does not have "ac" on the triggerguard. The third variation features a military blue rather than a high gloss blue and had a production run of about 15,000 pistols.

"ac41" (1st variation)

Courtesy Orvel Reichert

Exc.	V.G.	Good	Fair	Poor
2200	1100	700	500	350

"ac41" (2nd variation)

Courtesy Orvel Reichert

Exc.	V.G.	Good	Fair	Poor
1500	750	600	450	300

"ac41" (3rd variation)

Courtesy Orvel Reichert

Exc.	V.G.	Good	Fair	Poor
1300	600	475	400	300

"ac42"

There are two variations of the "ac42" code. The first has an eagle over 359 stamped on all small parts as do all preceding variations and a production of 21,000 pistols. The second variation does not have the eagle over 359 stamped on small parts. This second variation has a large production run of 100,000 pistols.

"ac42" (1st variation)

Courtesy Orvel Reichert

Exc.	V.G.	Good	Fair	Poor
1300	550	400	350	275

"ac42" (2nd variation)

Exc.	V.G.	Good	Fair	Poor
1100	500	400	300	250

"ac43"

This code has three variations. The first is a standard date with "ac" over "43". It has an early frame and extractor cut. The second variation has the late frame and extractor cut. Both variations are frequently encountered because approximately 130,000 were built.

"ac43" (1st variation)

Courtesy Orvel Reichert

Exc.	V.G.	Good	Fair	Poor
900	450	300	250	200

"ac43" (2nd variation)

Exc.	V.G.	Good	Fair	Poor
550	350	300	250	200

"ac43" single line slide

This variation represents the beginning of the placement of the date on the same line with the production code. There were approximately 20,000 built in this variation.

Courtesy Orvel Reichert

Exc.	V.G.	Good	Fair	Poor
1200	550	450	350	250

"ac44"

This variation also has the date stamped beside "ac" and is fairly common. About 120,000 were produced.

Courtesy Orvel Reichert

ac44 FN Slide left and right sides • Courtesy Orvel Reichert

Exc.	V.G.	Good	Fair	Poor
800	450	300	250	200

Note: Add $300 for FN frame (Eagle/140).

"ac45"

This code has three variations. The first has all matching numbers on a plum colored frame. About 32,000 of this first variation were produced. The second variation has a capital "A" in place of the lowercase "a." The third variation has all major parts with factory mismatched numbers, with a single eagle over 359 on the slide. The first variation is the most common of this code.

"ac45" (1st variation)

Courtesy Orvel Reichert

Exc.	V.G.	Good	Fair	Poor
800	450	300	250	200

"ac45" (2nd variation)

Courtesy Orvel Reichert

Exc.	V.G.	Good	Fair	Poor
950	500	325	300	250

"ac45" (3rd variation)

Courtesy Orvel Reichert

Exc.	V.G.	Good	Fair	Poor
750	400	300	250	200

Note: Add $200 for pistols with Czech barrels; barrel code "fnh."

"ac45" Zero Series

This is a continuation of the commercial pistols with a military marked slide. This series has "ac45" plus the 0 prefix serial number on the left side as well as the usual P.38 roll stamp. It may or may not have commercial proofmarks. A total of 1,200 of these "ac45" Zero Series guns were produced in 1945. They are often seen with a plum colored slide.

Exc.	V.G.	Good	Fair	Poor
2800	1750	750	600	400

MAUSER MILITARY

The following P.38s were produced by Mauser and are identified by various Mauser codes.

Courtesy Orvel Reichert

"byf42"

Approximately 19,000 P.38s were manufactured in this variation. Some of these pistols will have a flat blue finish.

Courtesy Orvel Reichert

Exc.	V.G.	Good	Fair	Poor
2200	1200	700	500	300

"byf43"

A common variation of the P.38 with approximately 140,000 produced.

Courtesy Orvel Reichert

Exc.	V.G.	Good	Fair	Poor
950	550	300	250	200

"byf44"

Another common variation with a total production of about 150,000 guns.

Courtesy Orvel Reichert

Exc.	V.G.	Good	Fair	Poor
950	550	300	250	200

Note: Add $100 for dual tone finish that is a combination of blue and gray components.

AC43/44-FN slide

Courtesy Orvel Reichert

Exc.	V.G.	Good	Fair	Poor
2200	1200	725	600	450

"svw45"

The Mauser code is changed from "byf" to "svw." This variation was produced until the end of the war when France took over production and continued through 1946. French-produced guns will have a 5-point star on the right side of the slide. A large number of these French pistols have been imported thereby depressing values.

"svw45"-German Proofed

Courtesy Orvel Reichert

Exc.	V.G.	Good	Fair	Poor
2200	1200	725	550	400

"svw45"-French Proofed

Courtesy Orvel Reichert

Exc.	V.G.	Good	Fair	Poor
650	400	300	250	200

"svw46"-French Proofed

Courtesy Orvel Reichert

Exc.	V.G.	Good	Fair	Poor
800	500	400	350	300

MAUSER "POLICE" P.38

Mauser produced the only Nazi era Police P.38 during the 1943 to 1945 period. It is generally believed that only 8,000 guns were serially produced, although a few "oddballs" show up beyond that range.

Police guns are easily recognized by the appearance of a commercial proof (eagle over N) instead of the Military proof (eagle over swastika). They also have a civilian (Police) acceptance stamp (either an Eagle L or Eagle F).

The guns will have a stacked code with date below the code. Earliest guns were coded "byf" over "43" and later, "byf" over "44". In the late 1944 production, a group of slides manufactured for Walther at the FN plant in Belgium were received and used. These slides all have the "ac" over "43" or "ac" over "44" code. Finally, in 1945, a few "svw" over "45" coded guns were made. These Walther coded slides are hard to find .... the 1945 guns are *quite* rare.

Because of the increased value of these guns, it is wise to have them examined by an expert before purchasing.

"byf/43"

Exc.	V.G.	Good	Fair	Poor
2500	1700	1200	800	500

"byf/44"

Exc.	V.G.	Good	Fair	Poor
2500	1700	1200	800	500

"ac/43"

Exc.	V.G.	Good	Fair	Poor
5000	3500	2000	1250	800

"ac/44"

Exc.	V.G.	Good	Fair	Poor
5000	3500	2000	1250	800

"svw/45"

Exc.	V.G.	Good	Fair	Poor
6000	4500	2500	1600	1000

SPREEWERKE MILITARY

Production of the P.38 began at Spreewerk in late 1942 and Spreewerke used the code "cyq" that had been assigned to it at the beginning of the war.

"cyq"

Eagle/211 on frame, 2 known.

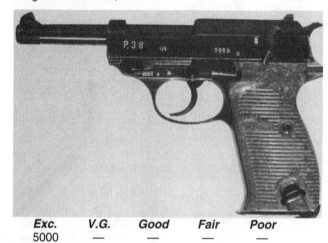

Exc.	V.G.	Good	Fair	Poor
5000	—	—	—	—

"cyq" (1st variation)

The first 500 of these guns have the eagle over 359 on some small parts and command a premium. Value depends on markings and an expert should be consulted for values.

A Police "ac43" code P38 was sold at auction for $6,900. Stamped Eagle/F on left side of slide. Gray slide and frame. Condition is 98 percent original finish. Excellent bore.
Rock Island Auction Company, August 2004

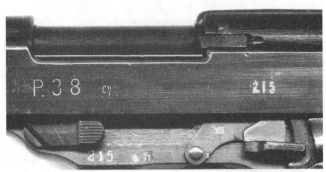

Courtesy Orvel Reichert

Exc.	V.G.	Good	Fair	Poor
1400	1000	750	600	500

"cyq" (standard variation)
There were approximately 300,000 of these pistols produced in this variation which makes them the most common of all P.38 variations.

Courtesy Orvel Reichert

Exc.	V.G.	Good	Fair	Poor
800	400	275	250	200

Note: If "A" or "B" prefix add $250.

A "cyq" series with an "A" prefix serial number • Courtesy Orvel Reichert

"cyq" Zero Series
This variation features a Zero ahead of the serial number and only about 5,000 of these guns were produced.

Courtesy Orvel Reichert

Exc.	V.G.	Good	Fair	Poor
1250	550	400	350	275

NOTE: Add $250 for AC43 or AC44 marked "FN" slide.

Walther Model P-1
This is a postwar P.38. This model was adopted by the German army as the standard sidearm in 1957, and remained in service until 1980.

Exc.	V.G.	Good	Fair	Poor
600	350	275	250	200

MAUSER POCKET PISTOLS
Bibliographical Note: For historical information, technical data, and photos see Roy Pender III, *Mauser Pocket Pistols, 1910-1946*, Houston, 1971.

Model 1914
A 7.65mm caliber semiautomatic pistol with a 3.5" barrel, fixed sights, and wrap-around walnut grips. The slide marked "Waffenfabrik Mauser A.G. Oberndorf A.N. Mauser's Patent." The frame has the Mauser banner stamped on its left side. Manufactured between 1914 and 1934. Almost all model 1914 pistols built between serial numbers 40,000 and 180,000 will be seen with German military acceptance stamps. A few will have the Prussian Eagle stamped on the front of the triggerguard.

Courtesy Butterfield & Butterfield, San Francisco, California

Courtesy Ryerson Knight

Exc.	V.G.	Good	Fair	Poor
450	300	225	150	100

Model 1934
Similar to the Model 1910 and Model 1914, with the slide marked "Mauser-Werke A.G. Oberndorf A. N." It has the Mauser banner stamped on the frame. The reverse side is marked with the caliber and "D.R.P. u A.P." Manufactured between 1934 and 1939. Those with Nazi Waffenamt markings are worth approximately 20 percent more than the values listed

below. Those marked with an eagle over the letter "M" (navy marked) are worth approximately 100 percent more than the values listed below.

Courtesy Gale Morgan

Courtesy Ryerson Knight

Exc.	V.G.	Good	Fair	Poor
525	400	300	150	100

Model HSC

A 7.65mm or 9mm short caliber double action semiautomatic pistol with a 3.4" barrel, 7- or 8-shot magazine and fixed sights. Introduced in 1938 and produced in the variations listed below.

Courtesy Ryerson Knight

Courtesy Orvel Reichert

A Mauser/Nickel 9mm Luger experimental pistol was sold at auction for $51,750. This pistol might have been the successor to the Luger pistol. Fitted with a 3.44 inch barrel. Blued finish with walnut grips. Condition is 98 percent rust blue.
Rock Island Auction Company, August 2004

A Mauser Model HSC prototype pistol in 9mm sold at auction for $69,000. Fitted with a 5.25 inch barrel. Walnut grips. Double action trigger with 8-round magazine. Condiition is 95 percent blue.
Rock Island Auction Company, April 2004

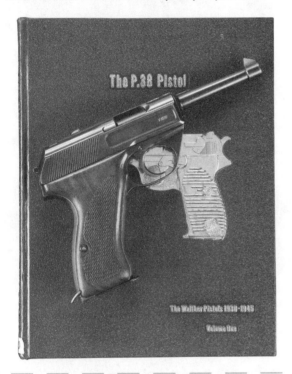

Low Grip Screw Model
As above, with screws that attach the grip located near the bottom of the grip. Highly polished blue, checkered walnut grips, and the early address without the lines and has the Eagle N proof. Some have been observed with Nazi Kreigsmarine markings. Approximately 2,000 were manufactured.

Exc.	V.G.	Good	Fair	Poor
3500	2500	1400	750	650

Early Commercial Model
A highly-polished blued finish, checkered walnut grips, the standard Mauser address on the slide, and the Eagle N proofmark. The floorplate of the magazine stamped with the Mauser banner.

Early Commercial model with magazine stamping • Courtesy Ryerson Knight

Exc.	V.G.	Good	Fair	Poor
650	500	350	175	125

Transition Model
As above, but not as highly finished.

Exc.	V.G.	Good	Fair	Poor
525	400	300	150	100

Early Nazi Army Model
Highly polished with Waffenamt No. 135 or 655 markings. Checkered walnut grips. Acceptance marks are located on the left side of the triggerguard.

Courtesy Orvel Reichert • Close-up courtesy Ryerson Knight

Exc.	V.G.	Good	Fair	Poor
650	550	400	200	125

Late Nazi Army Model
Blued or parkerized, with walnut or plastic grips, and the 135 acceptance mark only. It also has the Eagle N proof.

Exc.	V.G.	Good	Fair	Poor
450	375	250	150	100

Early Nazi Navy Model
Highly polished with checkered walnut grips and the eagle over "M" marking on the front grip strap.

Courtesy Ryerson Knight

Exc.	V.G.	Good	Fair	Poor
1000	800	550	400	300

Wartime Nazi Navy Model
Similar to the above, with the navy acceptance mark on the side of the triggerguard. Blued, with either checkered walnut or plastic grips. It has the standard Mauser address and banner and also the Eagle N proof.

Exc.	V.G.	Good	Fair	Poor
700	600	500	400	200

Early Nazi Police Model

Identical to the Early Commercial Model with an eagle over "L" mark on the left side of the triggerguard.

Courtesy Orvel Reichert

Exc.	V.G.	Good	Fair	Poor
600	500	425	250	175

Wartime Nazi Police Model

As above, with a three-line Mauser address.

Exc.	V.G.	Good	Fair	Poor
500	400	350	250	175

Wartime Commercial Model

As above, without acceptance markings on the triggerguard.

Exc.	V.G.	Good	Fair	Poor
425	350	300	200	125

French Manufactured Model

Blued or parkerized with walnut or plastic grips and the triggerguard marked on the left side with the monogram "MR."

Exc.	V.G.	Good	Fair	Poor
325	275	225	150	100

SAUER, J. P. & SON

Bibliographical Note: For historical information, technical data, and photos see Jim Cate's text.

Text and prices by Jim Cate

SAUER MODEL 1913

FIRST SERIES, which incorporates an extra safety button on the left side of the frame near the trigger and the rear sight, is simply a milled recess in the cocking knob itself. The serial number range runs from 1 to approximately 4750 and this first series is found only in 7.65mm caliber. All were for commercial sales as far as can be determined. Some were tested by various militaries, no doubt.

A. European variation—all slide legends are in the German language.

B. English Export variation—slide legends are marked J.P. Sauer & Son, Suhl - Prussia, "Sauer's Patent" Pat'd May 20 1912.

Both were sold in thick paper cartons or boxes with the color being a reddish purple with gold colored letters, etc. Examples of the very early European variation are found with the English language brochure or manual as well as an extra magazine, cleaning brush, and grease container. These were shipped to England or the U.S. prior to Sauer producing the English Export variation.

A. European variation

Exc.	V.G.	Good	Fair	Poor
1100	900	650	400	250

B. English Export variation

Exc.	V.G.	Good	Fair	Poor
1450	1150	800	500	300

Original box with accessories and manual: Add $500 if complete and in very good to excellent condition.

SECOND SERIES, extra safety button eliminated, rear sight acts as cocking knob retainer.

A. Commercial variation

Normal European/German slide markings are normally found; however, it has been called to my attention that there are English Export pistols in this **SECOND SERIES** which have the English markings on the slide which are similar to those found on the **FIRST SERIES** of the Model 1913. This is applicable to both the 7.65mm and 6.35mm model pistols. These are exceptionally scarce pistols and should command at least a 50 percent premium, perhaps more due to their rarity. This commercial variation had factory manuals printed in English, Spanish, and German which came with the cardboard boxed pistols. With the original Sauer box accessories and manual: Add $300 if in very good to excellent condition.

Caliber 7.65mm variation

Exc.	V.G.	Good	Fair	Poor
450	375	300	250	100

Caliber 7.65mm variation with all words in English (i.e. Son, Prussia, etc.)

Exc.	V.G.	Good	Fair	Poor
700	575	450	300	200

Caliber 6.35mm variation

This particular pistol must be divided into three (3) subvariations.

This variation appears to be in a serial number range of its own. The first subvariation appears to run from 1 to 40,000. It is highly doubtful if this quantity was manufactured. The second subvariation incorporates a Zusatzsicherung or Additional Safety which can be seen between the normal safety lever and the top of the left grip. It locked the trigger bar when in use. This second range appears to run from approximately serial number 40,000 to 51,000, which probably was continuous in the number produced. Lastly, the third subvariation examples were manufactured during or after 1926. The triggerguard has a different shape; the slide has a greater area of vertical milled finger grooves; the added Additional Safety (Zusatzsicherung) now acts as the hold open device as well. These are found up to approximately 57,000. Then a few examples of the first subvariation are found from 57,000 up to about 62,500. This was, no doubt, usage of remaining parts.

Caliber 6.35mm first subvariation

Exc.	V.G.	Good	Fair	Poor
350	300	250	150	75

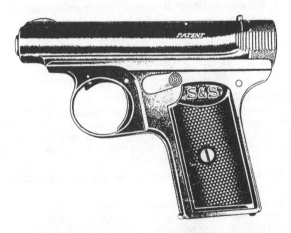

Caliber 6.35mm second subvariation

Exc.	V.G.	Good	Fair	Poor
350	300	250	150	75

Caliber 6.35mm third subvariation

Exc.	V.G.	Good	Fair	Poor
450	375	300	200	100

Caliber 6.35mm English export variation (all words in English; i.e. Son, Prussia, etc.)

Very rare, only one example known.

Exc.	V.G.	Good	Fair	Poor
850	700	500	300	200

Please note that any commercial pistol could be special ordered with a factory nickel finish, special grip material (pearl, wood, etc.), as well as different types of engraving. It would be in your best interest to have these pistols examined by an expert.

B. Police variations

These will be of the standard German Commercial configuration but nearly always having the Zusatzsicherung (Additional Safety) added to the pistol. This safety is found between the regular safety lever and the top of the left grip. Police used both calibers, 7.65mm and 6.35mm, but the 7.65 was predominant. After the early part of the 1930s the 6.35 was not available to police departments. Thus the 6.35mm police marked Sauer is rather scarce in relation to the 7.65mm caliber. A few in 7.65mm are dated 1920 on the left side of the frame and were used by auxiliary policemen in Bavaria. Normal police property markings are on the front or rear grip-straps. Most were originally issued with at least two magazines and a police accepted holster. The magazines were usually numbered and the holsters are found with and without pistol numbers.

Caliber 6.35mm police marked but without Zusatzsicherung

Exc.	V.G.	Good	Fair	Poor
400	350	275	200	75

Caliber 6.35mm police marked with Zusatzsicherung

Exc.	V.G.	Good	Fair	Poor
450	375	275	200	75

Caliber 7.65mm police marked without Zusatzsicherung

Exc.	V.G.	Good	Fair	Poor
375	325	275	175	125

Caliber 7.65mm police marked with Zusatzsicherung

Exc.	V.G.	Good	Fair	Poor
400	350	275	175	125

NOTE: Add 10 percent for one correctly numbered magazine, or 20 percent if found with both correctly numbered magazines. Add 30 percent if found with correct holster and magazines.

C. R.F.V. (Reich Finanz Verwaltung)

This Sauer variation is rarely found in any condition. The R.F.V. markings and property number could be 1 to 4 digits. This variation is found in both calibers and was used by the Reich's Customs and Finance Department personnel.

Caliber 6.35mm R.F.V. marked pistols

Exc.	V.G.	Good	Fair	Poor
800	650	500	350	250

Caliber 7.65mm R.F.V. marked pistols

Exc.	V.G.	Good	Fair	Poor
750	600	400	300	200

D. Imperial Military variations

These were normal German commercial variations of the time period having either the Imperial Eagle acceptance marking applied on the front of the triggerguard and having the small Imperial Army inspector's acceptance marking (crown over a scriptic letter) on the right side of the frame close to the Nitro proof; or having just the Imperial Army inspector's marking alone. Usually these pistols are found in the 40,000 to 85,000 range. However, the quantity actually Imperial Military accepted is quite low even though thousands were privately purchased by the officer corps. There are examples in 6.35mm which are Imperial Military accepted but these are very scarce.

Caliber 7.65mm Imperial Military accepted pistols

Exc.	V.G.	Good	Fair	Poor
550	450	350	275	150

Caliber 6.35mm Imperial Military accepted pistols

Exc.	V.G.	Good	Fair	Poor
700	500	375	300	150

E. Paramilitary marked Sauer pistols, of the 1925-35 period

A very few of the Model 1913 pistols will have been marked by paramilitary groups or organizations of this period. Usually this marking is no more than a series of numbers above another series of numbers, such as 23 over 12. These are found usually on the left side of the frame next to the left grip. Most of these numbers are indicative of property numbers assigned to a particular pistol's belonging to a particular SA Group, Stahlhelm, or a right-wing organization such as the Red Front (early communist). Any pistol of this type should be examined by an expert to determine if it is an original example.

Exc.	V.G.	Good	Fair	Poor
350	300	275	200	100

F. Norwegian police usage, post World War II

After the war was over many surplus German weapons were put back into use by the government of Norway. The Germans had occupied this country and large numbers of weapons remained when the fighting ended. This included a large number of surplus Sauer pistols being utilized by the police (POLITI) forces. Most of the Sauers that were used by the Politi which have been imported into the U.S. have been the Model 1913; however, there were a number of the Model 1930 pistols which reached our country as well. All examples, regardless of the model, have the word POLITI stamped on the slide as well as a rampant lion on a shield under a crown marking. Following this is the property number and this number is also stamped into the left side of the frame. Most saw much usage during the postwar period. All are in 7.65mm caliber.

Exc.	V.G.	Good	Fair	Poor
350	300	200	150	100

MODEL 38 AND 38-H (H MODEL) VARIATIONS

A. MODEL 38

This pistol started at 260,000. It is Crown N Nitro proofed, has a cocking/decocking lever, and a loaded indicator pin, and is double action. It has a high polish blue; is in 7.65mm (the standard production pistol); is found without the thumbsafety on the slide; with a pinned mag release. VERY RARE.

1. One Line Slide Legend variation

About 250 produced.

Exc.	V.G.	Good	Fair	Poor
2500	1600	1200	600	300

2. Two Line Slide Legend variation C/N proofs

Blued, with pinned magazine release (about 850 produced). VERY RARE.

Exc.	V.G.	Good	Fair	Poor
1850	1400	1000	500	275

3. Two Line Slide Legend variation C/N proofs

Blued, magazine release button retained by a screw. RARE.

Exc.	V.G.	Good	Fair	Poor
1000	850	600	400	275

NOTE: Add $250 for factory nickel; $350 for factory chrome; $1000 for engraving; $500 for NIROSTA marked barrel.

4. SA der NSDAP Gruppe Thuringen marked variation

Blued, C/N proofs, with mag release button held by a screw. VERY RARE.

Exc.	V.G.	Good	Fair	Poor
3000	2000	1000	500	275

B. MODEL 38-H or H MODEL

This model has a thumbsafety on the slide, Crown N Nitro proof, high polish blued finish, a cocking/decocking lever, double action, and is found in 7.65mm caliber as the standard production pistol. This model is found only with the two line slide legend or logo. Type 1, variation 2.

1. Standard Commercial variation as described above

Exc.	V.G.	Good	Fair	Poor
850	700	475	300	175

NOTE: Add $100 for factory nickel (factory chromed has not been identified); $1000 for factory engraving; $250 for exotic grip material; $500 for NIROSTA marked stainless barrel.

2. SA der NSDAP Gruppe Thuringia variation

Same as 1 above except having SA markings on slide, with blued finish. VERY RARE.

Exc.	V.G.	Good	Fair	Poor
2500	1800	600	350	200

NOTE: Add $700 for SA marked ankle holster in excellent condition.

3. L.M. MODEL

(Leicht Model–lightweight model); frame and slide made of DURAL (Duraluminum), in the 264800 range, with thumb safety, and regular black bakelite grips. EXTREMELY RARE.

Exc.	V.G.	Good	Fair	Poor
3850	3250	2500	1500	850

4. Police accepted variation

Found with Police Eagle C acceptance on left triggerguard and having Crown N proofs. RARE.

Exc.	V.G.	Good	Fair	Poor
850	700	500	300	175

TYPE TWO MODEL 38-H (H MODEL)

There are no Model 38 pistols in the Type Two description, only the H Model with thumbsafety. These begin at serial number 269100 and have the Eagle N Nitro proofs, with a blued high polish finish and black bakelite grips. The normal caliber is 7.65mm.

A. H Model

1. Standard Commercial

Exc.	V.G.	Good	Fair	Poor
750	550	475	300	200

NOTE: Add $1500 for boxed examples complete with factory manual, clean ring rod, all accessories, extra magazine, etc. $250 for factory nickel, $350 for factory chrome, $1000 for factory engraving.

2. .22 Caliber variation, found in 269900 range

Slide and magazines are marked CAL. .22 LANG. (Some with steel frame and slides; some with Dural frames and slides.) VERY RARE.

Exc.	V.G.	Good	Fair	Poor
2500	1800	1000	400	250

3. Jager Model

A special order pistol in .22 caliber which is similar in appearance to Walther's 1936 Jagerschafts pistol. VERY RARE, and watch for fakes.

Exc.	V.G.	Good	Fair	Poor
2500	1850	1200	600	250

4. Police Eagle C and Eagle F acceptance variations

These are the first Eagle N (post January 1940) police accepted pistols and are found in the 270000 to 276000 ranges.

Exc.	V.G.	Good	Fair	Poor
650	500	400	325	200

NOTE: Add 25 percent for E/F.

5. German Military variation

This is the first official military accepted range of 2000 pistols. It is in a TEST range found between 271000 and 273000. Two Eagle 37 military acceptance marks are found on the triggerguard.

Exc.	V.G.	Good	Fair	Poor
1200	900	675	475	300

6. Second Military variation

These pistols are found with the high polish finish but have only one Eagle 37 acceptance mark. The letter H is found on all small parts.

Exc.	V.G.	Good	Fair	Poor
600	425	350	275	175

7. Police Eagle C acceptance variation

This variation includes the remainder of the high polish blued police accepted pistols.

Exc.	V.G.	Good	Fair	Poor
575	425	350	275	175

NOTE: Add $50 for matching magazine, $200 for both matching magazines and correct police holster; $300 for both matching mags and correct matching numbered, police accepted & dated holster.

TYPE THREE 38-H MODEL (H MODEL)

This terminology is used because of the change of the exterior finish of the Sauer pistols. Due to the urgency of the war, the order was received to not polish the exterior surfaces of the pistols as had been done previously. There was also a change in the formulation of the grip's material. Later in this range there will be found stamped parts, zinc triggers and magazine bottoms, etc. used to increase the pistol's production. Type Three has a full slide legend.

A. H Model

1. Military accepted with one Eagle 37 Waffenamt mark

Exc.	V.G.	Good	Fair	Poor
500	450	350	275	150

2. Commercial, with only Eagle N Nitro proofmarks

Exc.	V.G.	Good	Fair	Poor
450	400	350	250	150

NOTE: See Type Two Commercial info, prices apply here also.

3. Police accepted with the Police Eagle C acceptance

Exc.	V.G.	Good	Fair	Poor
500	425	350	250	150

NOTE: See Type Two Police info, prices apply here also.

A Model 38-H Sauer pistol in 7.65mm caliber was sold at auction for $43,125. Engraved with silver finish and ivory grips. Property of Colonel-General Joseph Dietrich, an imporant German Nazi general. Condition is 97 percent original finish.
Rock Island Auction Company, August 2004

TYPE FOUR 38-H MODEL (H MODEL)

This is a continuation of the pistol as described in Type Three except the J.P. Sauer & Sohn, Suhl legend is dropped from the slide and only CAL. 7.65 is found on the left side. The word PATENT may or may not appear on the right side. Many are found with a zinc trigger.

A. H Model

1. Military accepted with one Eagle 37 Waffenamt mark

Exc.	V.G.	Good	Fair	Poor
500	450	350	275	150

2. Commercial, having only the Eagle N Nitro proofs

Exc.	V.G.	Good	Fair	Poor
450	400	350	250	150

NOTE: See Type Two Commercial info, prices apply here also.

3. Police accepted with the Police Eagle C acceptance

Exc.	V.G.	Good	Fair	Poor
500	450	350	275	150

NOTE: See Type Two price info, prices apply here also.

4. Eigentum NSDAP SA Gruppe Alpenland slide marked pistols

These unique pistols are found in the 456000 and 457000 serial number ranges. They have thumb safety levers on the slides.

Exc.	V.G.	Good	Fair	Poor
2800	1800	1000	450	250

5. NSDAP SA Gruppe Alpenland slide marked pistols

These unique pistols are found in the 465000 serial number range. They have thumb safety levers on the slide.

Exc.	V.G.	Good	Fair	Poor
2800	1800	1000	450	250

6. H. Himmler Presentation Pistols

These desirable pistols have a high polish finish with DEM SCHARFSCHUTZEN - H. HIMMLER on the left side of the slide (with no other markings), and J.P. SAUER & SOHN over CAL.7.65 on the right side (opposite of normal). These pistols came in imitation leather cover metal cases with cloth interiors having a cleaning brush, extra magazine and cartridges.

Exc.	V.G.	Good	Fair	Poor
15000	12000	8500	3500	1000

B. MODEL 38

To speed up production even more, the thumb safety (Hand-sicherung-Hammer safety) was eliminated. The side continues to be marked only with CAL. 7.65. The frame's serial number changes from the right side to the left side at 472000 with overlaps up to 489000.

1. Military accepted with one Eagle 37 Waffenamt mark

Exc.	V.G.	Good	Fair	Poor
450	400	350	250	175

2. Commercial, having only the Eagle N Nitro proofs

Exc.	V.G.	Good	Fair	Poor
450	400	350	250	175

NOTE: See Type Two Commercial info, prices apply here also.

3. Police accepted with the Police Eagle C acceptance

Exc.	V.G.	Good	Fair	Poor
575	450	400	300	200

4. Police accepted with the Police Eagle F acceptance

Exc.	V.G.	Good	Fair	Poor
475	400	350	250	175

NOTE: (3&4) See Type Two Police info above, prices apply here also.

TYPE FIVE MODEL 38 & H MODEL PISTOLS

There are two different basic variations of the Type Five Sauer pistols. Either may or may not have a thumbsafety lever on the slide. The main criteria is whether the frame is factory numbered as per normal and follows the chronological sequence of those pistols in the preceding model. After the frames were used, which were already numbered and finished upon the arrival of the U.S. army, the last variation came about. Neither variation has any Nitro proofmarks.

A. First variation

Factory numbered sequential frames starting on or near serial number 506800. Slides and breech blocks may or may not match.

Exc.	V.G.	Good	Fair	Poor
475	350	275	225	100

B. Second variation

Started with serial number 1; made from mostly rejected parts, generally have notched triggerguards, may or may not be blued, no Nitro proofs, slides may or may not have factory legends, etc. Approximately 300 assembled.

Exc.	V.G.	Good	Fair	Poor
750	500	300	200	100

NOTE: There are some pistols which have postwar Russian Crown N Nitro proofs. The Russians may have assembled a very few pistols after the U.S. army left this section after the war. Several have been found with newly made barrels in 7.65mm with a C/N proof.

A cased Sauer Model 38-H sold at auction for $31,625. Stamped with Eagle/N proof. Engraved on left side of slide with S.S. Chief Henrich Himmler signature. Condition is near mint.
Rock Island Auction Company, August 2004

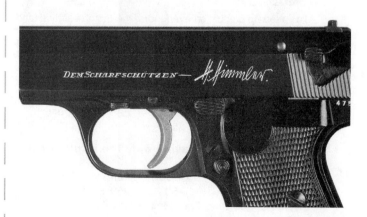

WALTHER

Bibliographical Note: For technical details, historical information, and photos see James Rankin, *Walther*, Volumes I, II, and III, 1974-1981.

Model 6

A 9mm semiautomatic pistol. The largest of the Walther numbered pistols. Approximately 1,500 manufactured. Blued with checkered hard rubber grips with the Walther logo on each grip. Sometimes seen with plain checkered wood grips. Introduced 1915.

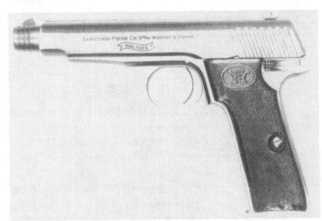

Courtesy James Rankin

Exc.	V.G.	Good	Fair	Poor
7000	5000	3000	1500	700

Model PP

Courtesy James Rankin

A semiautomatic pistol in .22, .25, .32, and .380 caliber. Introduced in 1928. It was the first successful commercial double action pistol. It was manufactured in finishes of blue, silver, and gold, and with three different types of engraving. Grips were generally two-piece black or white plastic with the Walther banner on each grip. Grips in wood or ivory are seen, but usually on engraved guns. There are many variations of the Model PP and numerous NSDAP markings seen on the pre-1946 models that were produced during the Nazi regime. All reflect various prices.

Model PP .22 Caliber

Exc.	V.G.	Good	Fair	Poor
800	600	350	250	150

Model PP .25 Caliber

Exc.	V.G.	Good	Fair	Poor
5800	4000	2500	1500	600

Model PP .32 Caliber High Polished Finish

Exc.	V.G.	Good	Fair	Poor
450	325	275	225	175

Model PP .32 Caliber Milled Finish

Exc.	V.G.	Good	Fair	Poor
425	325	250	200	125

Model PP .380 Caliber

Exc.	V.G.	Good	Fair	Poor
950	750	550	475	350

Model PP .32 Caliber with Duraluminum Frame

Exc.	V.G.	Good	Fair	Poor
800	675	550	400	200

Model PP .32 Caliber with Bottom Magazine Release

Exc.	V.G.	Good	Fair	Poor
1100	800	600	400	200

Model PP .32 Caliber with Verchromt Finish

Exc.	V.G.	Good	Fair	Poor
2000	1450	1000	700	400

A Walther prototype "Hi-Power" 9mm pistol sold at auction for $48,875. Fitted with a 4.75-inch barrel and walnut grips. Double action trigger. Possible replacement for P-38 pistol. No serial number. Condition is 95 percent blue.
Rock Island Auction Company, April 2004

WALTHERS

Collecting the Military Model's PP and PPK and their earlier cousins

James Rankin

If you are a firearms collector or entertain the idea of becoming one, the collecting of Walther manufactured firearms is a very exciting and rewarding one. With Walthers you have a wide range of firearms that the Walther Company manufactured or is manufacturing from which to choose. There are rifles, shotguns, pistols and flare and air guns. All have different models, variations of the models, calibers and gauges. Second, if you become knowledgeable in the field your purchases should increase in value not only allowing you to have the excitement of collecting, but the accumulation of equity in your collection.

The Walther Company, led by its family members, have been manufacturing, firearms since 1886 when Carl Walther founded a gun shop in the town of Zella, which was later incorporated into the town of Zella-Mehlis, Germany. At first, Walther produced shotguns and rifles, Later, Fritz Walther, Carl's oldest son, joined the firm and brought his genius for design to the company and it expanded its production into pistols.

Although the Walther Company has produced many types of pistols from the early 1900s, the Models PP and PPK were latecomers on the automatic pistol scene when compared to such pistol manufacturers such as Mauser, Luger and Colt as they did not make their appearance till 1929. However, shortly thereafter they were being sold in all parts of the world. These beautifully made pistols were the first of the original double-action blowback semi-automatic pistols. They had a successful commercial design with a high polished blue finish that was second to none.

A few years after the Models PP and PPK appearance on the world's firearm market, Adolf Hitler and the National Socialist German Workers Party took over the reigns of the German government, the military and the police. It was then that a majority of the Walther production was contracted for by the NSDAP, German army and the national police.

With the emergence of the NSDAP as the power in Germany, the increase in military power was ordered, and the Army High Command-OKH-Heereswaffenamt began placing contracts with the Walther Company for both the Walther Models PP and PPK. Most of the models were contracted for in caliber 7.65mm. There were contracts for a smaller amount in the Model PP in caliber 9mm Kurz and even less in the Model PPK in the same caliber. Depending on their serial number range these pistols showed Crown over N. or Eagle over N. nitro proofing on the right side of the pistol's slide, barrel and chamber. The military acceptance proofs, Eagle over 359 and Eagle over WaA359 were placed on the left side of the pistol's slide and frame to the rear of the model designation and the to the rear of the trigger on the frame.

The Models PP and PPK with the Waffenamt proofs began with a high polished blue finish on each pistol. But as the years progressed toward the end of World War II and the labor diminished these models showed a milled finish. The following is a short description of the Models PP and PPK bearing the Waffenamt proofs.

The first of the Models PP and PPK with the high polished blue finish had the Eagle over 359 proof on the left side of the slide and frame with an

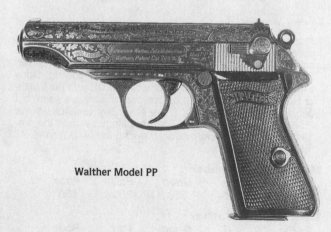

Walther Model PP

Walther Model PPK
with Party Leader Grips

occasional proof on the left rear of the slide at the tang. Grips were black on the Model PP and brown on the Model PPK.

The second series of proofs was the Eagle over WaA359. These too were found on high polished Models PP and PPK except there was no proof on the rear of the slide at the tang. Grips were black and brown respectively.

The third series was the Eagle over WaA359 found on the milled finish models till the end of World War II. On these later pistols the proofs remained in the same location on the pistols with some changes in the pistols themselves. On the Model PP you will find the standard two-piece black grips as well as reddish colored grips. Near the end of World War II there pressed wood grips with the Walther Banner. On some of the late PP models there will be an AC proof on the right side of the slide in conjunction with the serial number. Some of the late Waffenamt Model PPs will have no legends or inscriptions on the left side of the slide. These models have flat frames with no step at the trigger guard hinge, and some have no indicator pin. On the Model PPK the pistol will have the standard brown one piece wrap around Walther grips and will be found with grayish grips as well as black ones.

The Model PP and PPK in 9mm Kurz are both fairly rare pistols. With Waffenamt proofs they are even rarer. These pistols usually have bottom magazine releases. Their magazines will have the Walther Banner and Cal. 9mm on the left side of the magazine. Many of the 9mm Kurz models had the magazines numbered to the serial number on the pistol. These 9mm Kurz models all had a high polished finish.

There were earlier manufactured Walthers that were used by the military. Walther began to manufacture pistols in 1908 with their production of

the Model 1. The Model 4 produced in 1910 was their first really successful pistol. This semi-automatic was the approximate size of the Model PPK saw use in World War I although there are no records showing that the German military placed a contract with the Walther Company. Most were carried as side arms by officers of the German Imperial Army. The Model 6 was basically a large Model 4 in caliber 9mm Parabellum. It was designed for the German Imperial Army in 1915. It was the first pistol that Walther designed and produced for the military and the first Walther in 9mm parabellum. It was produced for a period of two years and there were probably less than 1500 manufactured. After the war some Model 6s remained at the factory. They were proofed "Made in Germany" and exported, some to the United States. In the United States the Model 6 is quite rare and commands a high price.

The Model 7 was a small version of the Model 6 in 6.35mm. Walther produced these pistols for the military for about six months. They were carried by many German officers. Although in 6.35mm it was the largest 6.35mm pistol produced by Walther at the time.

In 1920 and 1921 Walther produce both the Models 8 and 9 for commercial sales. They were the first of the modern Walthers with many features seen later in the Models PP and PPK. Both these pistols were favorites of German officers in World War II as hide out pistols. However, the Model 8 was carried by many officers in a holster on their belt.

The military Model PPK is more difficult to find than the Model PP. The high polished pistols in both models are both fairly rare. It will take sometime for a collector to put a collection of Waffenamt Models PP and PPK together, but with perseverance one should be quite pleased with his or her collection. One should remember in the collecting of firearms, Walthers or any other maker, condition is everything.

Walther Model 6

Courtesy Orvel Reichert

Model PP .32 Caliber in Blue, Silver, or Gold Finish and Full Coverage Engraving

Blue

Exc.	V.G.	Good	Fair	Poor
5000	3500	3000	1200	700

Silver

Exc.	V.G.	Good	Fair	Poor
6000	4000	3000	1200	700

Gold

Exc.	V.G.	Good	Fair	Poor
6500	4500	3500	1500	700

NOTE: Add $250 for ivory grips with any of the three above. Add $700 for leather presentation cases. Add $500 for .22 caliber. Add $1000 for .380 caliber.

Model PP .32 Caliber, Allemagne Marked

Exc.	V.G.	Good	Fair	Poor
850	700	550	325	250

Model PP .32 Caliber, A.F. Stoeger Contract

Exc.	V.G.	Good	Fair	Poor
2500	1750	1050	700	400

Model PP .32 Caliber with Waffenamt Proofs, High Polished Finish

The Waffenamt proofs were the military eagle over 359 on the early models. Military eagle over WaA359 on later models. The Waffenamt proof was on the left side of the frame to the rear of the trigger and on the left side of the slide in front of the slide serrations. The 9mmk models have a bottom magazine release. Rare in both .22 LR and 9mmk calibers.

Model PP Waffenamt • Courtesy James Rankin

Exc.	V.G.	Good	Fair	Poor
1200	800	375	275	150

Model PP .32 Caliber with Waffenamt Proofs Milled Finish

Exc.	V.G.	Good	Fair	Poor
450	375	325	250	150

A cased Model PP engraved with ivory grips and gold plated finish sold at auction for $40,250. Believed to be property of a senior party official. Condition is 92 percent gold plated finish. Grips are excellent.
Rock Island Auction Company, April 2004

Model PP .32 Caliber, Police Eagle/C Proofed, High Polished Finish

The police proofs were the police eagle over the swastika with the letter "C" to the right of the swastika. Later models have the eagle over the swastika with the letter "F" (*see below*). The police proof was on the left side of the frame to the rear of the trigger.

Model PP Police • Courtesy James Rankin

Exc.	V.G.	Good	Fair	Poor
1200	800	375	250	150

Model PP .32 Caliber, Police Eagle/C and Police Eagle/F Proofed, Milled Finish

Exc.	V.G.	Good	Fair	Poor
900	600	375	275	150

Model PP .32 Caliber, NSKK Marked On The Slide

The NSKK, National Sozialistisches Kraftfahr Korps, Transport Corps. These pistols were issued to officers in the corps. The NSKK emblem is on the left side of the frame in front of the slide serrations.

Model PP NSKK Marked • Courtesy James Rankin

Exc.	V.G.	Good	Fair	Poor
2500	2000	850	550	300

NOTE: Add $700 with proper NSKK DRGM AKAH holster.

Model PP .32 Caliber, NSDAP Gruppe Markings

The SA, Sturm Abteilung, was comprised of various districts throughout Germany and each was separately named. The proof was SA der NSDAP on the top line with the name of the district below. These proofs were found on the front grip strap. Some later models had the SA proof on the rear grip strap. A few SA models had a two-digit number following the district name. The .22 LR model is rare.

Listed below are the SA districts:

Alpenland, Berlin-Brandenburg, Bayerische Ostmark, Bayer-wald, Donau, Eibe, Franken, Hansa, Hessen, Hochland, Kurp-flaz, Mitte, Mittelrhein, Neckar, Nordsee, Neiderrhein, Neidersachsen, Nilfswerk, Nordwest, Oder, Ostmark, Osterre-ich, Oberrhein, Ostland, Pommern, Schlesien, Sachsen, Sud-mark, Sudeten, Sudwest, Tannengberg, Thuringen, Standarte Feldherrnhalle, Weichsel, Westfalen, Westmark.

Model PP NSPAD Marked • Courtesy James Rankin

Exc.	V.G.	Good	Fair	Poor
2000	1500	1000	500	300

NOTE: Add $600 with proper SA DRGM AKAH holster.

A Walther PP NSDAP/Grupper Hessen 7.65mm sold at auction for $5,462.50. Condition is 97 percent original blue.
Rock Island Auction Company, August 2004

Model PP .32 Caliber PDM Marked with Bottom Magazine Release

The PDM, Polizei Direktion Munchen, Police Department Munich. The PDM mark was placed on equipment belonging to the Munich police. It can be found on the left side of the frame behind the trigger and is followed by one to four numbers. The PDM pistol has a bottom magazine release.

Model PP PDM marked • Courtesy James Rankin

Exc.	V.G.	Good	Fair	Poor
850	700	550	475	300

Model PP .32 Caliber RJ Marked

The RJ, Reich Jugend, Hitler Youth Organization. The RJ proof is on front grip strap. Some models are in .22 caliber.

Model PP RJ marked • Courtesy James Rankin

Exc.	V.G.	Good	Fair	Poor
750	600	475	400	150

Model PP .32 Caliber. RFV Marked. High Polished or Milled Finish

Model PP RFV marked • Courtesy James Rankin

Exc.	V.G.	Good	Fair	Poor
700	600	475	400	150

Model PP .32 Caliber RBD Munster Marked

The RBD Munster, State Railway Directorate Munster in Westfalen. The RBD Munster is on the front grip strap followed by (Westf.).

A Walther Model PP "RFV" was sold at auction for $6,900. Property of SS General Karl Wolff. Wolff was the overall German commander in Italy in 1944-1945. Pistol comes with a Type III Mod PP holster. Condition is 95 percent original blue. Holster is in very good condition.

Rock Island Auction Company, August 2004

Model PP RBD • Courtesy James Rankin

Exc.	V.G.	Good	Fair	Poor
2200	1750	1200	650	400

Model PP .32 Caliber RpLt Marked

The RpLt, Rigspoliti, Danish State Police, is on the left side of the frame directly above the forward part of the triggerguard. The RpLt is followed by "Nr". The number is from one to four digits, and is an inventory number within the police department.

Model PP RpLt marked • Courtesy James Rankin

Exc.	V.G.	Good	Fair	Poor
950	750	475	375	200

Model PP .32 Caliber RZM Marked

The RZM, Reichs Zueg Meisterei, was the equipment office of the NSDAP, and the RZM model of the PP was carried by an NSDAP member who was awarded the use of the pistol. The RZM emblem is on the left side of the slide in front of the slide serrations. Rare.

Exc.	V.G.	Good	Fair	Poor
2500	2000	1250	600	300

Model PP .32 Caliber Statens Vattenfallsverk Marked

The Statens Vattenfallsverk was contracted by Sweden for use in hydro-electric plant security. The Staten Vattenfallsverk is on the right side of the slide to the front of the slide serrations. There is an "Nr" above each inscription for inventory control. Some of these pistols have Duraluminum frames.

Model PP Statens Vattenfallsverk • Courtesy James Rankin

Exc.	V.G.	Good	Fair	Poor
1000	800	550	375	200

Model PP .32 Caliber AC Marked

The Model AC was a late wartime pistol with a milled finish. The AC proofmark was usually found on either side of the slide. These pistols sometimes did not have the Walther inscription or trademark. Wood grips replaced the plastic.

Model PP AC marked • Courtesy James Rankin

Exc.	V.G.	Good	Fair	Poor
450	375	300	250	150

Model PP .32 Caliber, Duraluminum Frame

Exc.	V.G.	Good	Fair	Poor
750	600	500	400	150

Model PP .380 Caliber, Bottom Magazine Release and Waffenamt Proofs

Exc.	V.G.	Good	Fair	Poor
2000	1500	700	500	300

Model PP Persian Contract

This model was contracted by Persia for its police units. It is a bottom magazine release model with the Persian Royal Crest and Farsi inscription on the left side of the slide, and the Walther Banner and inscription on the right side of the slide.

Model PP Persian Contract • Courtesy James Rankin

Exc.	V.G.	Good	Fair	Poor
3500	2950	2250	1000	500

Model PPK

A semiautomatic pistol in .22, .25, .32, and .380 caliber. Introduced six months after the Model PP in 1929. A more compact version of the Model PP with one less round in the magazine and one-piece wrap-around checkered plastic grips in brown, black, and white with the Walther banner on each side of the grips. The Model PPK will be found with the same types of finishes as the Model PP as well as the same styles of engraving. Grips in wood or ivory are seen with some of the engraved models. As with the Model PP there are many variations of the Model PPK and numerous NSDAP markings seen on the pre-1946 models that were produced during the Nazi regime. All reflect various prices.

Courtesy Orvel Reichert

Courtesy James Rankin

Model PPK .22 Caliber

Exc.	V.G.	Good	Fair	Poor
1200	700	475	325	175

Model PPK .25 Caliber

Exc.	V.G.	Good	Fair	Poor
6000	4000	1850	1000	500

Model PPK .32 Caliber, High Polished Finish

Exc.	V.G.	Good	Fair	Poor
550	450	325	250	150

Model PPK .32 Caliber, Milled Finish

Exc.	V.G.	Good	Fair	Poor
500	400	325	250	150

Model PPK .380 Caliber

Courtesy Orvel Reichert

Exc.	V.G.	Good	Fair	Poor
2200	1750	1300	750	375

Model PPK .32 Caliber with Duraluminum Frame

Exc.	V.G.	Good	Fair	Poor
950	800	600	400	200

Model PPK .32 Caliber with Verchromt Finish

Exc.	V.G.	Good	Fair	Poor
2500	1800	1200	700	350

Model PPK .32 Caliber in Blue, Silver, or Gold Finish and Full Coverage Engraving

Blue
Exc.	V.G.	Good	Fair	Poor
5000	3500	2500	1200	700

Silver
Exc.	V.G.	Good	Fair	Poor
6000	4000	3000	1200	700

Gold
Exc.	V.G.	Good	Fair	Poor
6500	4500	3500	1500	700

NOTE: Add $750 for ivory grips with any of the three above. Add $700 for leather presentation cases. Add $500 for .22 caliber. Add $1000 for .380 caliber.

Model PPK .32 Caliber Marked Mod. PP on Slide
Exc.	V.G.	Good	Fair	Poor
5000	4000	2500	1500	1000

Model PPK .32 Caliber with Panagraphed Slide
Exc.	V.G.	Good	Fair	Poor
650	550	450	300	200

Model PPK .32 Caliber, Czechoslovakian Contract
Exc.	V.G.	Good	Fair	Poor
1850	1500	1000	550	300

Model PPK .32 Caliber. Allemagne Marked
Exc.	V.G.	Good	Fair	Poor
800	700	600	400	250

Model PPK .32 Caliber with Waffenamt Proofs and a High Polished Finish

The Waffenamt proofs were the military eagle over 359 on the early models. Military eagle over WaA359 on later models. The Waffenamt proof was on the left side of the frame to the rear of the trigger and on the left side of the slide in front of the slide serrations. The 9mmk models have a bottom magazine release. Rare in both .22 LR and 9mmk calibers.

Exc.	V.G.	Good	Fair	Poor
1200	800	550	400	250

Model PPK .32 Caliber with Waffenamt Proofs and a Milled Finish
Exc.	V.G.	Good	Fair	Poor
800	600	375	300	175

Model PPK .32 Caliber. Police Eagle/C Proofed, High Polished Finish
Exc.	V.G.	Good	Fair	Poor
675	575	450	300	175

Model PPK .32 Caliber. Police Eagle/C Proofed, Milled Finish

The police proofs were the police eagle over the swastika with the letter "C" to the right of the swastika. Later models have the eagle over the swastika with the letter "F" (*see below*). The police proof was on the left side of the frame to the rear of the trigger.

Exc.	V.G.	Good	Fair	Poor
650	500	375	275	175

Model PPK .32 Caliber. Police Eagle/F Proofed, Duraluminum Frame. Milled Finish
Exc.	V.G.	Good	Fair	Poor
900	700	550	350	225

Model PPK .22 Caliber. Late War, Black Grips
Exc.	V.G.	Good	Fair	Poor
1200	750	600	450	300

Model PPK .32 Caliber, Party Leader Grips, Brown

The Party Leader-gripped PPK was the honor weapon of the NSDAP and was given to political leaders from the Fuhrer. The

A cased engraved SA presentation PPK pistol was sold at auction for $46,000. Blued finish. Grips have silver NSDAP Eagle/Swastika inset in right side. Gold monogram. Condition is 98 percent original finish. Excellent bore. Grips have small crack.
Rock Island Auction Company, August 2004

Party Leader grip is usually mottled brown plastic with the NS-DAP eagle holding a swastika circled by a wreath on each side of the grip. Near the end of WWII a small number of Party Leader grips were black (*see below*).

Courtesy Rock Island Auction Company

Exc.	V.G.	Good	Fair	Poor
2750	2550	2350	2250	2000

Model PPK .32 Caliber, Party Leader Grips, Black

Exc.	V.G.	Good	Fair	Poor
3250	3000	2750	2550	2500

NOTE: If grips are badly cracked or damaged on the two Party Leaders above, reduce $2000 each valuation.
Add $500 with proper Party Leader DRGM AKAH holster.

Model PPK .32 Caliber RZM Marked

Courtesy Rock Island Auction Company

Exc.	V.G.	Good	Fair	Poor
900	700	500	400	300

A Party Leader PPK pistol was sold at auction for $10,350. Complete with holster and extra magazine. Magazines numbered 1 and 2. Condition is 99 percent.
Rock Island Auction Company, August 2004

Model PPK .32 Caliber PDM Marked with Duraluminum Frame and Bottom Magazine Release

The PDM, Polizei Direktion Munchen, Police Department Munich. The PDM mark was placed on equipment belonging to the Munich police. It can be found on the left side of the frame behind the trigger and is followed by one to four numbers. The PDM pistol has a bottom magazine release. This model is much rarer than the PP version.

Exc.	V.G.	Good	Fair	Poor
2500	1800	1150	750	450

Model PPK .32 Caliber. RFV Marked

Exc.	V.G.	Good	Fair	Poor
2000	1750	1150	650	400

Model PPK .32 Caliber. DRP Marked

The DRP, Deutsche Reichs Post, German Postal Service. The DRP is found on the left side of the frame behind the trigger.

Model PPK DRP marked • Courtesy James Rankin

Exc.	V.G.	Good	Fair	Poor
800	650	550	450	275

Model PPK .32 Caliber. Statens Vattenfallsverk

The Statens Vattenfallsverk was contracted by Sweden for use in hydro-electric plant security. The Staten Vattenfallsverk is on the right side of the slide to the front of the slide serrations. There is an "Nr" above each inscription for inventory control. Some of these pistols have Duraluminum frames.

Exc.	V.G.	Good	Fair	Poor
1400	1200	700	450	300

Model P99 Military

Similar to the P99 but with military finish.

NIB	Exc.	V.G.	Good	Fair	Poor
625	475	375	—	—	—

HECKLER & KOCH

VP 70Z

This is a blowback-operated semiautomatic chambered for the 9mm Parabellum cartridge. It is striker-fired and double action only. The barrel is 4.5" long, and the double-column magazine holds 18 rounds. The finish is blued, and the receiver and grips are molded from plastic. This model was discontinued in 1986.

NIB	Exc.	V.G.	Good	Fair	Poor
550	450	350	300	250	200

VP 70M

This is similar to the VP 70Z except for a very important feature: When a shoulder stock is added, the internal mechanism is altered to fire full automatic 3-round burst. When the shoulder stock is removed, the pistol reverts back to semiautomatic. The rate of fire is a very high 2,200 rounds per minute. This version has no safety devices. First produced in 1972 and discontinued in 1986.

H&K VP 70M • Courtesy Thomas Nelson, *World's Machine Pistols, Vol. II*

Pre-1968

Exc.	V.G.	Fair
N/A	N/A	N/A

Pre-1986 conversions

Exc.	V.G.	Fair
15000	—	—

Pre-1986 dealer samples

Exc.	V.G.	Fair
N/A	N/A	N/A

P9

This is a single action, delayed-blowback semiautomatic pistol chambered for 9mm or 7.65mm Parabellum. The action is based on the G-3 rifle mechanism and is single action only. The barrel is 4" in length, and the pistol has an internal hammer and a thumb-operated hammer drop and decocking lever. There is also a manual safety and a loaded-chamber indicator. The finish is parkerized, and the grips are molded plastic and well contoured. It has fixed sights. This model was manufactured between 1977 and 1984. This model is rarer than the P9S model. This was H&K's first military pistol.

NIB	Exc.	V.G.	Good	Fair	Poor
1500	1200	850	500	400	300

SUBMACHINE GUNS

MP18/1 (WWI)

This was the first German submachine gun and it was designed by Hugo Schmeisser in 1916. It was used by German military forces in WWI. The gun was chambered for the 9mm Parabellum cartridge. The barrel length is 7.5" and the snail magazine holds 32 rounds. The rate of fire is about 450 rounds per minute. Markings are "MP 18 L" above the chamber and "C.G HANEL WAFFENFABRIK SUHL" on the left side of the receiver. Not produced after 1945. Weight is about 9 lbs.

Pre-1968

Exc.	V.G.	Fair
12500	11000	10000

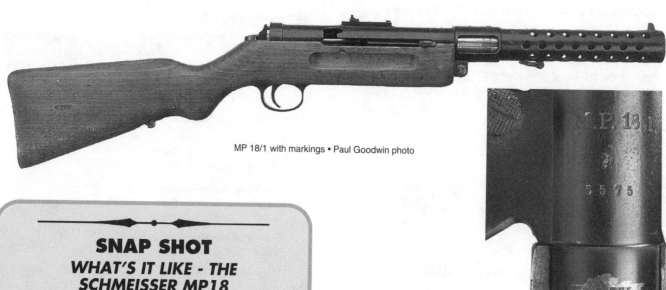

MP 18/1 with markings • Paul Goodwin photo

SNAP SHOT
WHAT'S IT LIKE - THE SCHMEISSER MP18

The first *"true"* submachine gun was the German produced MP18. All the history books list the Italian Villar Perosa, but the Villar Perosa was really a pistol-caliber squad-type weapon that involved two barrels and a mounting system which precluded individual shoulder fire. The MP18 by contrast was fitted with a wood stock and fits the perfectly the modern definition of a submachine gun.

It was designed by Hugo Schmeisser at the Bergmann factory beginning in 1916. The German army had over 35,000 of these guns on hand and deployed by November of 1918, but by then the tide of events had overwhelmed them.

The MP18 was a first generation submachine gun in that it used a heavy machined receiver as well as a substantial number of machined parts. The first magazine used with the MP18 was the 32 round 'snail' magazine borrowed from the German Luger. The magazine housing was located on the left side of the receiver and turned rearward at a 45-degree angle to better accept the Luger enhanced-capacity magazine. The cocking handle was located on the right side of the receiver and the gun featured a full-auto only mechanism.

Following World War I, a quantity of MP18s were returned to the C.G. Haenel firm of Suhl, Germany to have the magazine housing replaced with a more conventional design which employed a straight 'stick' magazine using a double column of ammunition but a single feed position at its reinforced lips. The Treat of Versailles limited the German Army to only 100,000 men and prohibited the possession of submachine guns so all of these modified MP18s were assigned to the German civil police.

There are a few examples of the later police modified MP18s in this country which are legally registered and owned by private collectors. All of them exhibit robust construction and a dependable performance when tested on a square range. In contrast to more modern designs, the MP18 is heavy, fires with a rather slow rate of fire and features a design that involves far too much complicated machining, but it was the first of its kind and, more importantly, it was a good design.

Frank James

Pre-1986 conversions

Exc.	V.G.	Fair
12500	11000	10000

Pre-1986 dealer samples

Exc.	V.G.	Fair
6000	5500	5000

MP18/1 (Postwar)

Introduced into combat by German troops in 1918. Designed by Hugo Schmeisser and built by Bergmann. Chambered for 9mm cartridge. In place of the 32-round snail drum, a box magazine holds 20 or 32 rounds. The magazine is essentially the only difference between the WWI guns and the postwar examples. Barrel length is 8". Rate of fire is about 400 rounds per minute. Was in use from 1918 to 1930s. Weight is about 9 lbs.

Private NFA collection • Gary Gelson photo

Pre-1968

Exc.	V.G.	Fair
12500	11000	10000

Pre-1986 conversions

Exc.	V.G.	Fair
12500	11000	10000

Pre-1986 dealer samples

Exc.	V.G.	Fair
6000	5500	5000

Bergman MP28

This model is an improved version of the MP18. It is fitted with a tangent sight and straight magazine. It also has a selector switch to allow for semi-auto fire. Rate of fire is approximately 500 rounds per minute. Chambered for a variety of calibers including 9mm Parabellum, 9mm Bergmann, 7.65mm Parabellum, 7.63mm, and .45 ACP. Magazine capacity is 20, 32, or 50 rounds with special 25-round magazine for .45 ACP models. Built in Belgium by Pieper. Many of these guns were sold to South American countries. They were also used by German Police units including SS units. It was never adopted by the German army. Markings over the chamber are "MP 28 II SYSTEM SCHMEISSER PATENT." Weight is 8.8 lbs.

Courtesy Richard M. Kumor Sr.

Pre-1968

Exc.	V.G.	Fair
12500	11000	1000

Pre-1986 conversions

Exc.	V.G.	Fair
8500	7500	6500

Pre-1986 dealer samples

Exc.	V.G.	Fair
6000	5500	5000

Erma EMP

First developed in Germany in 1934, this submachine gun was chambered for the 9mm cartridge. It was fitted with a wooden vertical fore-grip. The gun was fitted with a 9.75" barrel with a 20- or 32-round magazine. The rate of fire was 500 rounds per minute. The weight was about 8.25 lbs. Marked "EMP" on rear receiver cap. Production ceased in 1945. This gun was used extensively in the Spanish Civil War.

Pre-1968

Exc.	V.G.	Fair
9500	8000	7000

Pre-1986 conversions

Exc.	V.G.	Fair
6500	5500	4500

Pre-1986 dealer samples

Exc.	V.G.	Fair
4500	3500	3000

HK MP5

First produced in 1965, this submachine gun is quite popular worldwide, being in service in a number of countries. It is produced in 9mm, .40 S&W, and 10mm. It is offered in a number of variations. The basic model is fitted with an 8.75" barrel with retractable stock. Magazine capacity is 15 or 30 rounds. Rate of fire is 800 rounds per minute. Weight is approximately 5.5 lbs. Marked "MP5 KAL 9MMX19" on top rib of receiver.

Courtesy Richard M. Kumor Sr.

Pre-1968 (Rare)

Exc.	V.G.	Fair
19500	17500	16000

Erma EMP • Paul Goodwin photo

Pre-1986 conversions

Exc.	V.G.	Fair
14500	13000	12000

NOTE: Add 15 percent for registered receiver using OEM parts.

Pre-1986 dealer samples

Exc.	V.G.	Fair
9500	8500	8000

HK MP5 K

This model is essentially the same as the MP5 with the exception of a 4.5" barrel. Weight is about 4.4 lbs.

Photo courtesy Heckler & Koch

Pre-1968 (Rare)

Exc.	V.G.	Fair
N/A	N/A	N/A

Pre-1986 conversions

Exc.	V.G.	Fair
8500	8000	7500

NOTE: Add 15 percent for registered receiver using OEM parts.

Pre-1986 dealer samples

Exc.	V.G.	Fair
4500	4000	3500

HK MP5 SD

This variation of the MP5 uses a suppressor, making it one of the quietest submachine guns ever. The barrel is ported so that supersonic 9mm ammunition can be used at subsonic levels. Rate of fire is 800 rounds per minute. Magazine capacity is 15 or 30 round magazines. Barrel length is 7.7" and weight is approximately 7 lbs. This model comes in six different configurations that may affect price.

Courtesy Heckler & Koch

Pre-1968

Exc.	V.G.	Fair
N/A	N/A	N/A

Pre-1986 conversions

Exc.	V.G.	Fair
15500	14000	13000

NOTE: Add 15 percent for registered receiver using OEM parts.

Pre-1986 dealer samples

Exc.	V.G.	Fair
7500	7000	6500

HK 53

This submachine gun fires the 5.56x45mm cartridge. It is fitted with an 8.25" barrel and retractable stock. Magazine capacity is 25 rounds. Rate of fire is about 700 rounds per minute. Weight is approximately 6.7 lbs. Marked "MP53 KAL 5.56X45" on top rib of receiver. The gun is in service in several military and police units around the world.

Courtesy Heckler & Koch

HK 53 in firing port configuration • Paul Goodwin photo

MP38 • Paul Goodwin photo

Pre-1968

Exc.	V.G.	Fair
N/A	N/A	N/A

Pre-1986 conversions

Exc.	V.G.	Fair
12500	11000	9500

Pre-1986 dealer samples

Exc.	V.G.	Fair
6000	5500	4500

Steyr-Solothurn (Solothurn SI-100 or MP34[o])
See *Austria, Submachine Guns, Steyr.*

MP34/I & MP35/I
Similar in appearance to the MP28, and produced in Germany by Walther in Zella Mehlis. Chambered for the 9mm cartridge and fitted with a 7.8" or 12.6" barrel. Other calibers were offered such as the 9mm Bergmann, 9mm Mauser, .45 ACP, and 7.63 Mauser. Rear sight had a V-notch tangent graduated to 1,000 meters. The gun had a cocking handle much like a rifle located at the rear of the receiver. Fitted with two triggers, the outer one fired semiautomatic and the inner one fired full automatic. The 24- or 32-round magazine fed from the right side. Rate of fire was about 650 rounds per minute and weight is approximately 9 lbs. The MP35/I was a modified MP34/I and was used by the German SS. Built by Junker & Ruh. Many more MP35/I guns were built than MP34/I.

Private NFA collection, Gary Gelson photo

Pre-1968

Exc.	V.G.	Fair
9500	8500	7500

Pre-1986 conversions

Exc.	V.G.	Fair
—	—	—

Pre-1986 dealer samples

Exc.	V.G.	Fair
4500	4000	3500

NOTE: For "SS" marked MP35 guns add $3,000.

MP38
This German submachine gun was first produced in 1938. It is often called the Schmeisser but that is incorrect. It was designed by Vollmer and built by the Erma company. It is chambered for the 9mm cartridge and is fitted with a 9.75" barrel. It has a folding stock and a magazine capacity of 32 rounds. Its rate of fire is 500 rounds per minute. Full automatic fire only. Weight is approximately 9 lbs. Marked "MP38" on the rear receiver cap. Production ceased in 1940. Produced by Erma. This was the standard submachine gun of the German army during World War II. Over 1,000,000 were produced.

NOTE: In 1940 and 1941 some Model 38s were modified to prevent accidental discharges, by replacing the one-piece retracting handle with a two-piece one that incorporated a cutout which could be locked to prevent firing. This modified Model 38 is designated the Model 38/40.

Pre-1968 (Rare)

Exc.	V.G.	Fair
22500	20000	17500

Pre-1986 conversions (or U.S. manufactured parts)

Exc.	V.G.	Fair
8500	7500	6500

Pre-1986 dealer samples

Exc.	V.G.	Fair
N/A	N/A	N/A

German Manufacturing Codes for the MP38 & MP40

Erma	1938 to 1940	"27"
Erma	1940 to 1944	"afy"
Haenal	1938 to 1940	"122"
Haenal	1940 to 1944	"fxo"
Steyr	1939 to 1940	"660"
Steyr	1940 to 1944	"bnz"

MP40
This model was the successor to the MP38 with faster manufacturing components. The steel receivers pressed with a corrugated magazine housing. The grip frame is pressed steel as well. Weight and barrel length are the same as the MP38 as is magazine capacity and rate of fire. This model was produced from 1940 to 1945 by Erma. Marked "MP40" on the rear receiver cap. Approximately 1,000,000 of these guns were produced.

MP40 • Paul Goodwin photo

NOTE: There is a rare modification of this submachine gun designated the MP40/II, which is fitted with a magazine housing that holds two magazines. These magazines fit in an oversized sliding housing that moves laterally, allowing a full magazine to be moved into place when the first magazine becomes empty. Not developed until late 1943. Not considered a successful attempt to increase ammunition capacity.

Pre-1968

Exc.	V.G.	Fair
14000	12500	11500

Pre-1986 conversions (or U.S. manufactured receivers)

Exc.	V.G.	Fair
8500	7500	7000

Pre-1986 dealer samples

Exc.	V.G.	Fair
7000	6500	5500

MP41

This model was built by Schmeisser to compete with the official adopted military MP40. The gun was not adopted by the German army. The result is that very few of these guns exist. The MP40-style receiver and barrel were fitted to a wooden buttstock and a select fire mechanism was added. Weight is about 8 lbs. Marked "MP41 PATENT SCHMEISSER C.G.HAENEL SUHL" on the top of the receiver. About 27,500 of these guns were built between 1941 and 1945.

MP41 • Private NFA collection, Gary Gelson photo

Pre-1968 (Rare)

Exc.	V.G.	Fair
16500	14000	12000

Pre-1986 conversions

Exc.	V.G.	Fair
8500	7500	6500

A DEWAT MP40 sold at auction for $10,925. Date stamped 1940 coded "660." Condition is 30 percent original blue. One 30-round magazine.
Amoskeag Auction Company, May 2004

Pre-1986 dealer samples

Exc.	V.G.	Fair
8000	7000	6000

Walther MPK and MPL

This German submachine gun was first produced in 1963. The MPK is a short barrel (6.7") version and the MPL is the long barrel (10.14") version. Magazine capacity is 32 rounds of 9mm. Rate of fire is 55 rounds per minute. Weight empty is 6.1 lbs. Markings are on the left side of the receiver. Production of this model ceased in 1985.

Photo courtesy private NFA collection

Pre-1968 (Rare)

Exc.	V.G.	Fair
10000	9000	8500

M1935 Carabineros Carbine • Courtesy Rock Island Auction Company

Pre-1986 conversions

Exc.	V.G.	Fair
N/A	N/A	N/A

Pre-1986 dealer samples

Exc.	V.G.	Fair
5000	4000	3500

RIFLES

Mauser Military Bolt Action Rifles For Countries Not Listed Under Separate Heading

Argentina
See *Argentina, Rifles, Mauser.*

Austria
See *Austria, Rifles, Mauser.*

Belgium
See *Belgium, Rifles, Mauser.*

Bolivia

M1895 Rifle

Exc.	V.G.	Good	Fair	Poor
200	165	120	100	70

M1907 Rifle

Exc.	V.G.	Good	Fair	Poor
325	275	225	150	100

M1907 Short Rifle

Exc.	V.G.	Good	Fair	Poor
325	275	225	150	100

VZ24 Short Rifle

Exc.	V.G.	Good	Fair	Poor
400	350	275	225	125

M1933 Standard Model Export Model Short Rifle

Exc.	V.G.	Good	Fair	Poor
325	275	225	150	100

M1950 Series B-50 Rifle

Exc.	V.G.	Good	Fair	Poor
400	350	275	225	125

Brazil
See *Brazil, Rifles, Mauser.*

Chile

Courtesy Rock Island Auction Company

M1893 Rifle

Exc.	V.G.	Good	Fair	Poor
250	200	150	100	60

M1895 Rifle

Courtesy Rock Island Auction Company

Exc.	V.G.	Good	Fair	Poor
750	500	400	300	150

M1895/61 7.62 NATO Conversion

Exc.	V.G.	Good	Fair	Poor
350	300	240	195	120

M1895 Short Rifle

Exc.	V.G.	Good	Fair	Poor
225	190	150	90	60

M1896 Carbine

Exc.	V.G.	Good	Fair	Poor
225	190	150	90	60

M1912 Steyr Rifle

Courtesy Rock Island Auction Company

Exc.	V.G.	Good	Fair	Poor
250	190	140	100	70

M1912 Steyr Short Rifle

Exc.	V.G.	Good	Fair	Poor
250	190	140	100	70

M1912/61 7.62 NATO Conversion

Exc.	V.G.	Good	Fair	Poor
350	300	250	200	125

M1935 Carabineros Carbine

Exc.	V.G.	Good	Fair	Poor
800	650	450	300	150

China
See *China, Rifles, Mauser.*

Colombia

M1891 Rifle (Argentine Pattern)

Exc.	V.G.	Good	Fair	Poor
120	90	75	55	35

M1904 Rifle

Exc.	V.G.	Good	Fair	Poor
190	160	130	100	75

M1912 Steyr Rifle

Exc.	V.G.	Good	Fair	Poor
170	130	110	90	55

VZ23 Short Rifle

Exc.	V.G.	Good	Fair	Poor
170	130	110	90	55

Steyr-Solothurn A-G M1929 Short Rifle

Exc.	V.G.	Good	Fair	Poor
190	160	130	100	75

FN M24 and 30 Short Rifles

Exc.	V.G.	Good	Fair	Poor
150	120	100	75	45

VZ12/33 Carbine

Exc.	V.G.	Good	Fair	Poor
170	130	110	90	55

FN M1950 Short Rifle

Exc.	V.G.	Good	Fair	Poor
170	130	110	90	55

Costa Rica

M1895 Rifle

Exc.	V.G.	Good	Fair	Poor
120	100	80	60	35

M1910 Rifle

Exc.	V.G.	Good	Fair	Poor
140	110	90	70	40

FN M24 Short Rifle

Exc.	V.G.	Good	Fair	Poor
130	110	90	70	40

Czechoslovakia

See *Czechoslovakia, Rifles, Mauser.*

Denmark

See *Denmark, Rifles, Mauser.*

Dominican Republic

M1953 Rifle

Exc.	V.G.	Good	Fair	Poor
325	290	275	175	90

M1953 Short Rifle

Exc.	V.G.	Good	Fair	Poor
325	290	250	160	90

Ecuador

M71/84 Rifle

Exc.	V.G.	Good	Fair	Poor
175	150	100	80	50

M1891 Rifle (Argentine Pattern)

Exc.	V.G.	Good	Fair	Poor
125	90	70	50	30

M1907 Rifle

Exc.	V.G.	Good	Fair	Poor
150	120	90	70	45

M1910 Rifle

Exc.	V.G.	Good	Fair	Poor
150	110	80	60	50

VZ24 Short Rifle

Exc.	V.G.	Good	Fair	Poor
80	60	50	30	20

VZ12/33 Carbine

Exc.	V.G.	Good	Fair	Poor
125	110	90	70	40

FN M30 Short Rifle

Exc.	V.G.	Good	Fair	Poor
110	90	70	60	40

El Salvador

M1895 Rifle

Exc.	V.G.	Good	Fair	Poor
125	90	80	60	40

VZ12/33 Carbine

Exc.	V.G.	Good	Fair	Poor
125	110	90	70	40

Estonia

Czech Model L Short Rifle

Exc.	V.G.	Good	Fair	Poor
400	350	300	250	200

Ethiopia

FN M24 Carbine

Exc.	V.G.	Good	Fair	Poor
400	375	325	275	225

M1933 Standard Model Short Rifle

Exc.	V.G.	Good	Fair	Poor
450	375	350	300	250

M1933 Standard Model Carbine

Exc.	V.G.	Good	Fair	Poor
450	375	350	300	250

France

See *France, Rifles, Mauser.*

Greece

M1930 Short Rifle

Exc.	V.G.	Good	Fair	Poor
350	300	220	120	60

M1930 Carbine

Exc.	V.G.	Good	Fair	Poor
N/A	—	—	—	—

Guatemala

M1910 Rifle

Exc.	V.G.	Good	Fair	Poor
150	120	80	60	40

VZ25 Short Rifle (Model 24)

Exc.	V.G.	Good	Fair	Poor
175	130	90	70	40

VZ33 Carbine

Exc.	V.G.	Good	Fair	Poor
190	160	120	90	60

Haiti

FN M24/30 Short Rifle

Exc.	V.G.	Good	Fair	Poor
175	140	90	60	30

Honduras

G 71 Rifle

Exc.	V.G.	Good	Fair	Poor
300	250	200	130	90

M1895 Rifle (Chilean Pattern)

Exc.	V.G.	Good	Fair	Poor
150	110	90	60	25

M1933 Standard Model Short Rifle

Exc.	V.G.	Good	Fair	Poor
350	280	230	175	120

Iraq

Post-WWII-style Carbine

Exc.	V.G.	Good	Fair	Poor
200	160	120	80	40

Ireland

G 71 Rifle

Exc.	V.G.	Good	Fair	Poor
400	325	250	200	150

Israel

See *Israel, Rifles, Mauser.*

Japan

See *Japan, Rifles, Mauser.*

Latvia

VZ24 Short Rifle

Exc.	V.G.	Good	Fair	Poor
190	150	110	80	60

Liberia

FN M24 Short Rifle

Exc.	V.G.	Good	Fair	Poor
200	160	80	75	40

Lithuania

FN M30 Short Rifle

Exc.	V.G.	Good	Fair	Poor
225	190	160	110	80

FN M246 Short Rifle

Exc.	V.G.	Good	Fair	Poor
275	250	200	130	100

Luxembourg

M1900 Rifle

Exc.	V.G.	Good	Fair	Poor
500	400	300	190	110

FN M24/30 Short Rifle

Exc.	V.G.	Good	Fair	Poor
175	140	90	60	30

Manchuria

See *Japan, Rifles.*

Mexico

See *Mexico, Rifles, Mauser.*

Morocco

Post-WWII FN Carbine

Exc.	V.G.	Good	Fair	Poor
225	190	150	110	80

Netherlands

See *Netherlands, Rifles, Mauser.*

Nicaragua

VZ23 Short Rifle

Exc.	V.G.	Good	Fair	Poor
300	250	200	125	90

VZ12/33 Carbine

Exc.	V.G.	Good	Fair	Poor
350	300	225	140	100

Norway

See *Norway, Rifles, Mauser.*

Orange Free State

M1895 Rifle

Exc.	V.G.	Good	Fair	Poor
325	275	225	150	100

M1895 Chilean-marked Rifle

Exc.	V.G.	Good	Fair	Poor
325	275	225	150	100

M1896 Loewe & Co. Rifle

Exc.	V.G.	Good	Fair	Poor
350	275	225	175	100

M1897 DWM Rifle

Exc.	V.G.	Good	Fair	Poor
400	350	275	225	125

Paraguay

M1895 Rifle (Chilean Pattern)

Exc.	V.G.	Good	Fair	Poor
150	110	80	40	20

M1907 Rifle

Exc.	V.G.	Good	Fair	Poor
225	200	160	100	80

M1907 Carbine

Exc.	V.G.	Good	Fair	Poor
225	190	160	110	80

M1909 Haenel Export Model Rifle

Exc.	V.G.	Good	Fair	Poor
300	240	190	120	90

M1927 Rifle

Exc.	V.G.	Good	Fair	Poor
180	130	90	60	30

M1927 Short Rifle

Exc.	V.G.	Good	Fair	Poor
180	130	90	50	30

FN M24/30 Short Rifle

Exc.	V.G.	Good	Fair	Poor
225	190	150	100	80

M1933 Standard Model Short Rifle

Exc.	V.G.	Good	Fair	Poor
300	250	200	150	90

M1933 Standard Model Carbine

Exc.	V.G.	Good	Fair	Poor
300	250	200	150	90

Persia/Iran

M1895 Rifle

Exc.	V.G.	Good	Fair	Poor
200	150	120	90	70

Persian M98/29 Long Rifle • Courtesy Rock Island Auction Company

FN M24/30 Short Rifle

Exc.	V.G.	Good	Fair	Poor
275	225	175	100	70

M98/29 Long Rifle

Exc.	V.G.	Good	Fair	Poor
750	500	400	300	150

VZ24 Short Rifle

Exc.	V.G.	Good	Fair	Poor
350	300	250	200	100

M30 Carbine

Exc.	V.G.	Good	Fair	Poor
500	400	300	175	100

M49 Carbine

Exc.	V.G.	Good	Fair	Poor
550	450	300	175	100

Peru

M1891 Rifle M1891 Carbine

Exc.	V.G.	Good	Fair	Poor
175	140	100	75	35

M1895 Rifle

Exc.	V.G.	Good	Fair	Poor
190	150	100	75	35

M1909 Rifle

Exc.	V.G.	Good	Fair	Poor
425	350	275	225	100

VZ24 Short Rifle

Exc.	V.G.	Good	Fair	Poor
325	275	225	150	100

VZ32 Carbine

Exc.	V.G.	Good	Fair	Poor
275	225	150	100	65

M1935 Short Rifle (converted to .30-06)

Exc.	V.G.	Good	Fair	Poor
225	225	175	125	90

M1935 Short Rifle

Courtesy Rock Island Auction Company

Exc.	V.G.	Good	Fair	Poor
425	350	275	225	100

Poland

See *Poland, Rifles, Mauser.*

Portugal

See *Portugal, Rifles, Mauser.*

Romania

See *Romania, Rifles.*

Saudi Arabia

FN M30 Short Rifle

Exc.	V.G.	Good	Fair	Poor
250	190	120	80	40

Serbia/Yugoslavia

See *Yugoslavia, Rifles, Mauser.*

Slovak Republic

VZ24 Short Rifle

Exc.	V.G.	Good	Fair	Poor
375	300	225	150	90

South Africa

M1896 ZAR Rifle

Exc.	V.G.	Good	Fair	Poor
395	300	250	180	100

ZAE M1896 B Series Rifle

Exc.	V.G.	Good	Fair	Poor
395	300	230	160	100

M1896 ZAR Loewe Long Rifle

Exc.	V.G.	Good	Fair	Poor
375	290	200	150	90

M1895/1896 C Series

Exc.	V.G.	Good	Fair	Poor
375	300	225	160	90

Spain

See *Spain, Rifles, Mauser.*

Sweden

See *Sweden, Rifles, Mauser.*

Syria

M1948 Short Rifle

Courtesy Rock Island Auction Company

Exc.	V.G.	Good	Fair	Poor
150	125	100	80	40

Thailand/Siam

G 71 Rifle
Exc.	V.G.	Good	Fair	Poor
350	300	200	150	110

M1903 (Type 45) Rifle
Exc.	V.G.	Good	Fair	Poor
225	175	140	110	90

M1904 Rifle
Exc.	V.G.	Good	Fair	Poor
325	290	260	190	150

M1923 (Type 66) Short Rifle
Exc.	V.G.	Good	Fair	Poor
225	175	150	120	90

Transvaal

G 71 Rifle
Exc.	V.G.	Good	Fair	Poor
450	400	300	200	150

Turkey
See *Turkey, Rifles, Mauser.*

Uruguay

G 71 Rifle
Exc.	V.G.	Good	Fair	Poor
350	300	200	150	110

M1895 Rifle
Exc.	V.G.	Good	Fair	Poor
175	140	90	60	30

M1908 Rifle
Exc.	V.G.	Good	Fair	Poor
190	160	130	100	70

M1908 Short Rifle
Exc.	V.G.	Good	Fair	Poor
190	160	160	100	70

FN M24 Short Rifle
Exc.	V.G.	Good	Fair	Poor
225	190	170	110	70

VZ37 (937) Short Rifle
Exc.	V.G.	Good	Fair	Poor
400	300	200	120	80

VZ37 (937) Carbine
Exc.	V.G.	Good	Fair	Poor
400	300	200	120	80

Venezuela

G 71/84 Rifle
Exc.	V.G.	Good	Fair	Poor
290	200	150	100	70

M1910 Rifle
Exc.	V.G.	Good	Fair	Poor
200	160	140	100	80

VZ24 Short Rifle

Courtesy Stoddard Martial collection, Paul Goodwin photo

Exc.	V.G.	Good	Fair	Poor
250	200	150	100	70

FN M24/30 Short Rifle

Courtesy Cherry's Fine Guns

Exc.	V.G.	Good	Fair	Poor
400	300	200	120	80

FN M24/30 Carbine

Courtesy Rock Island Auction Company

Exc.	V.G.	Good	Fair	Poor
400	300	200	100	70

FN M24/30 Military Target Rifle
Exc.	V.G.	Good	Fair	Poor
350	300	200	125	90

Yemen

FN M30 Short Rifle
Exc.	V.G.	Good	Fair	Poor
300	220	175	110	80

For historical information, technical data, and photos see Hans Dieter Gotz, *German Military Rifles and Machine Pistols, 1871-1945*, Schiffer Publishing 1990.

MAUSER

Established in 1869 by Peter and Wilhelm Mauser, this company came under the effective control of Ludwig Loewe and Company of Berlin in 1887. In 1896 the latter company was reorganized under the name *Deutsches Waffen und Munition* or, as it is better known, DWM.

For history and technical details, see Robert W.D. Ball's, *Mauser Military Rifles of the World*, 3rd edition, Krause Publications, 2003.

NOTE: There are a number of variations to the Mauser rifle listed below that are found in various countries, approximately 54, throughout the world. These can be identified by the country crest stamped most likely on the receiver ring of the rifle. The rifles listed form the basis of whatever variations may be encountered elsewhere.

Model 1871

This was the first German metallic cartridge rifle. It was a 11x60Rmm caliber single shot bolt action rifle with a 33.5" barrel with bayonet lug, full-length stock secured by two barrel bands, and a cleaning rod. There is no upper handguard on this model. This model did not have an ejector so empty shells had to be removed manually. The rear sight was a leaf type with graduations out to 1,600 meters. Weight was about 10 lbs. The barrel marked "Mod. 71" together with the year of production and the manufacturer's name, of which there were several. First produced in 1875. Blued with a walnut stock.

Courtesy Milwaukee Public Museum, Milwaukee, Wisconsin

Exc.	V.G.	Good	Fair	Poor
750	500	400	300	150

SNAP SHOT
WHAT'S IT LIKE - THE MODEL 1891 ARGENTINE MAUSER

The case can be made that, since 1898, no improvements of any note have been made – or have proven necessary – to bolt-action rifle technology. But while Paul Mauser's Gewehr 98 has garnered the fame, his first small-bore, smokeless powder rifle – developed in 1888 – pioneered several of the most revolutionary features that were to ensure the Mauser's popularity:

1. A one-piece bolt with dual frontal lugs that locked directly into the receiver ring. The firing mechanism is inserted into the rear of the tubular bolt body for greater rigidity and strength.
2. A charger (stripper clip) – a stamped steel or brass strip with a flat spring retaining five cartridges – was inserted into guides on the receiver and the rounds pushed down into the magazine.
3. A fully enclosed box magazine with no cutoff. The weapon was to always be used as a charger-loaded, repeater.

Adopted by Belgium (Fusil Mle. 1889) and Turkey (Tufek 1890), this rifle went on to achieve its greatest success in Latin America. In 1891 the Argentine army placed orders for 210,000 Mauser Modelo Argentino 1891 rifles and carbines. This was quickly followed by similar orders from Bolivia, Columbia, Ecuador, and Peru. All Model 1889/90/91-type Mausers were chambered for the 7.65x53 Mauser cartridge with a bottle necked, rimless case 53mm long topped with a 211 gr. round-nosed, FMJ bullet moving at approximately 2132 fps.

I recently had a chance to test fire an Argentine Model 1891 Carbine. Considering its 17.6" barrel and attenuated sighting radius I placed my targets at 75 yards. Loading the magazine was fast and fumble free and rounds were chambered and ejected easily and, while the small sights left much to be desired, they were counterbalanced by a rather decent trigger. With a lowest sight setting of 300 meters, my first shots were high but once I estimated where to hold I was able to shoot groups in the 3-inch range. But with its short barrel and light weight, recoil and muzzle blast were "impressive!"

My opinion of the Model 1891-type Mauser? Not too bad for a first try!

Paul Scarlata

Model 1871 Jaeger Rifle

As above, with a 29.4" barrel and finger grip extension behind the triggerguard. Weight is about 10 lbs.

Courtesy Bob Ball

Exc.	V.G.	Good	Fair	Poor
800	650	550	450	300

Model 1871 Carbine

As above, with a 20" barrel and no bayonet lug. It was full stocked to the muzzle. Weight is about 7.5 lbs.

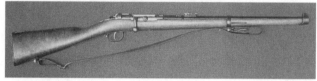

Courtesy Bob Ball

Exc.	V.G.	Good	Fair	Poor
1500	750	500	350	225

Model 71 Mauser • Courtesy Paul S. Scarlata

Model 71/84 Rifle • Courtesy Rock Island Auction Company

Model 1871 Short Rifle

As above, but with upper and lower barrel bands and bayonet lug.

Exc.	V.G.	Good	Fair	Poor
950	600	475	350	225

Model 79 G.A.G. Rifle (Grenz-Aufsichts-Gewehr)

Fitted with a 25" barrel and built by Haenel in Suhl and so marked. It is also marked "G.A.G." Used by German border guards. It is full stock almost to the muzzle. It is chambered for the 11x37.5mm cartridge. Weight is about 7 lbs. Single shot.

Exc.	V.G.	Good	Fair	Poor
600	500	400	250	100

Model 71/84 Rifle

The Model 71 modified by the addition of a tubular 8-round magazine. This model was fitted with an ejector. Barrel length 31.5". Weight is approximately 10 lbs. Issued in 1886. About 900,000 were produced. Marked "I.G.MOD.71/84" on the left side of the receiver.

Exc.	V.G.	Good	Fair	Poor
800	600	500	350	275

Model 88 commission rifle • Courtesy Paul S. Scarlata

Model 88 Commission Rifle

A 7.92x57mm caliber bolt action rifle with a 29" barrel, 5-shot magazine, full-length stock, bayonet lug, and cleaning rod. Marked "GEW. 88" together with the year of manufacture and the maker's name. This was the first military rifle to take a rimless cartridge. Weight is about 9 lbs. About 1,000,000 of these rifles were produced. Many of these rifles were later modified to charger loading, therefore original Model 88 rifles are uncommon. These rifles were used in World War I by German, Austro-Hungarian, Bulgarian, and Turkish armies.

Exc.	V.G.	Good	Fair	Poor
300	250	200	150	90

Model 98 Rifle (Gewehr 98)

The best known of all Mauser rifles. A 7.92mm bolt action rifle with a 29" barrel, 5-shot flush fitting magazine, full-length stock, half-length handguard, cleaning rod, and bayonet lug. Pre-1915 versions had a steel grommet through the buttstock and finger grooves on the forend. These early guns also were fitted with a V-notch rear sight adjustable from 400 to 2,000 meters. Rifles built after World War I were fitted with tangent rear sights graduated from 100 to 2,000 meters. Marked "GEW. 98" together with the date of manufacture and maker's name. Weight is about 9 lbs. About 3,500,000 of these rifles were built from its introduction in 1898 to 1918.

This rifle was built by the following government arsenals and commercial firms: Amberg, Danzig, Erfurt, Spandau, Mauser, DWM, J.P. Sauer & Sohn, V. Chr. Schilling, C.G. Haenel, Simson & Co., and Waffenwerke Oberspree Kornbusch & Co.

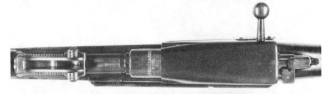

Mauser GEW 98 with trench cover • Courtesy John M. Miller

Exc.	V.G.	Good	Fair	Poor
500	400	300	150	80

Model 98 Carbine

As above, with 17" barrel and full stock to the muzzle without handguard. Not fitted for a bayonet. Produced at the Erfurt arsenal from 1900 to 1902. About 3,000 were produced. In 1902 the Model 98A, with bayonet bar and cleaning rod, was also produced at Erfurt until 1905. Weight was about 7.5 lbs.

Exc.	V.G.	Good	Fair	Poor
800	650	400	250	150

World War I GEW 98 Sniper with offset claw
mount • Private collection, Paul Goodwin photo

Mauser 98 AZ • Courtesy Paul S. Scarlata

Model 98 AZ Carbine/Model 98a

This model has the same stock as the Model GEW 98 but with
a slot through the buttstock. Barrel length was 24". Bolt handle
was turn down type and the full stock went to the muzzle with
full upper handguard. Fitted with a bayonet stud and curved
stacking bar on the forearm cap. Magazine capacity is 5
rounds. Weight is about 8 lbs. Introduced in 1908 with about
1,500,000 total production. Stamped "KAR 98" on the left side
of the receiver. After WW I these rifles were renamed the Model 98a. Fitted with a small ring receiver.

Exc.	V.G.	Good	Fair	Poor
500	300	225	150	100

Model 98 Transitional Rifle

As a result of the armistice, Model 98 rifles were modified with
a simple tangent rear sight, the markings were ground off, and
they were arsenal refinished.

Exc.	V.G.	Good	Fair	Poor
500	300	225	150	100

Model 98/98a Carbine

Model 98 KAR 98b Rifle

Also a product of the armistice the Model 98 rifle was altered with the addition of a flat tangent rear sight, removed stacking hook, and a slot was cut for a sling in the buttstock. The bolt handle was bent. Otherwise this is a Model 98 rifle.

Exc.	V.G.	Good	Fair	Poor
500	300	275	200	150

Model 98k Carbine (Short Rifle)

This was the standard shoulder arm of the German military during World War II. Introduced in 1935 about 11,000,000 were produced. Barrel length is 23.6". Magazine capacity is 5 rounds of 7.92mm. Rear sight was a tangent leaf graduated to 2,000 meters. Weight is about 8.5 lbs. Produced by a number of German arsenals using a variety of different identifying codes. Date of production is found on the receiver ring.

Courtesy Buffalo Bill Historical Center, Cody, Wyoming

Exc.	V.G.	Good	Fair	Poor
750	450	300	175	90

Model 98k Carbine (Short Rifle with extended magazine)

This model is a 98k with a non-removable 25-round magazine. It was an attempt to solve the problem of the limited magazine capacity of the standard 98k. This magazine could be filled singly or with 5-round clips.

NOTE: Beware of after-factory add-ons. Prices listed below are for verifiable samples.

Courtesy Amoskeag Auction Company

Exc.	V.G.	Good	Fair	Poor
4000	3000	2500	1500	750

Model 1916 Self-Loading Flyer's Rifle

First built in 1916 by Mauser at Oberndorf this is a semiautomatic recoil operated rifle chambered for the 7.92x57mm cartridge. Fitted with a 26" barrel. Some sources list the magazine capacity at 25 rounds, others at 20 rounds. The magazine is slightly curved. Weight of rifle is about 10.5 lbs. The rifle was issued with 10 magazines. It is estimated that somewhere between 1,000 and 2,000 were produced. The rifle was designed to be used by airborne gunners during WWI. Very Rare.

Exc.	V.G.	Good	Fair	Poor
15000	12500	10000	5000	—

Model 98 Training Rifle

This is a single shot paramilitary rfile built in the 1930s and used as a training rifle for members of the Nazi party. Fitted with a 26" barrel. Tangent rear sight from 25 to 200 meters. Weight is about 8.5 lbs.

Courtesy Rock Island Auction Company

Exc.	V.G.	Good	Fair	Poor
4500	3250	1500	750	500

German Sniper Rifles

The German sniper rifle used the K98k rifle as its foundation from 1914 to the end of WWII, although other models such as the G41 and G43 were as employed in that role later in World War II. To simplify a somewhat complex subject, German Sniper rifles are separated into five distinct types. These varieties are based on the type of telescope sight used on the rifle.

- The 1st Type is the short rail system.
- The 2nd type is the ZF41 and ZF41/1 scopes.
- The 3rd type is the turret mount system in both low and high variations.
- The 4th type is the long rail system.
- The 5th type is the claw mount system.

Different systems were used at different times and often overlap each other. Each system has its own varieties of telescopes made by different manufacturers. Some scopes are numbered to the rifle while others are not. Some rifles and scopes bear the markings of the Waffen-SS, and these will bring a premium.

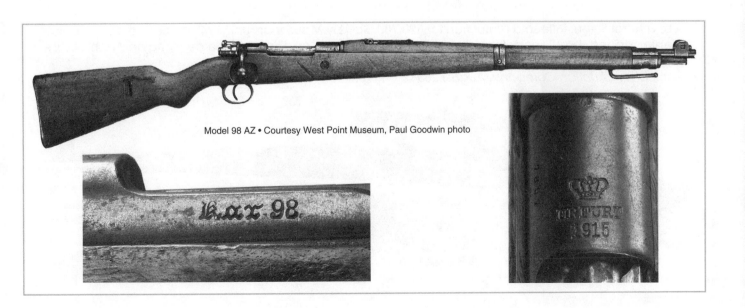

Model 98 AZ • Courtesy West Point Museum, Paul Goodwin photo

A KKW .22 caliber rifle with ZF41 scope was sold at auction for $4,887.50. German acceptance stamps. Condition is 90 percent with cloudy optics.
Rock Island Auction Company, August 2004

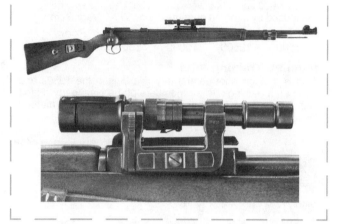

There were a number of different manufacturers of sniper scopes during the period between 1914 and 1945, and each of these manufacturers was assigned a production code. For example, Schneider & Co. was "dkl". These codes and other pertinent information, including historical information, data, and photos, can be seen in *The German Sniper, 1914-1945*, Peter R. Senich, Paladin Press, 1982.

NOTE: Prices listed below are for the rifle and the correct scope and base, i.e. verifiable examples. Sometimes the scope and base are not numbered. It is recommended that an expert opinion be sought prior to a sale. It should be further noted that the prices for German sniper rifles are subject to variations with different scope and mount combinations. Proceed with caution.

Model 98k Sniper Rifle (High Turret Model)

A sniper version of the 98K with different manufactured scopes. This variation has a 6.35mm recess depth greater in the front base cone than the low turret mount. Thus the distinguishing feature in these sniper rifles is the mount, although high-quality German-made scopes will bring a premium.

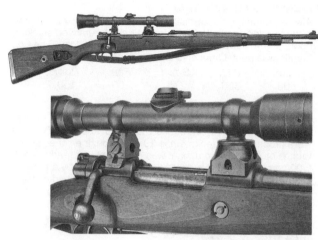

Mauser 98k with high turret scope • Courtesy private collection, Paul Goodwin photo

Exc.	V.G.	Good	Fair	Poor
12500	7500	5000	2000	1000

Model 98k Sniper Rifle (Low Turret Model)

As above but with a lower front base cone than the high turret mount.

Exc.	V.G.	Good	Fair	Poor
12500	7500	5000	2000	1000

A K-98 High Turret Sniper Rifle sold at auction for $12,650. Late 1944 production. Kahles scope coded "CAD." Scope has sun shade, Arctic lens cap, and black lens cover. All matching numbers including scope. Condition is 98 percent original finish.
Rock Island Auction Company, April 2004

A Low Turret Sniper Rifle sold at auction for $20,700. Built by Mauser around 1942-43. Scope is a Hensoldt-Wetzlar, coded "bmj." Scope has blue "t" for cold weather. Condition is 95 percent original finish. Scope is 80 percent with clear optics.
Rock Island Auction Company, August 2004

Model 98k Short Rail Sniper Rifle •
Courtesy Amoskeag Auction Company

A K-98k Type 2 Short Rail Sniper Rifle sold at auction for $5,060. Rifle date 1938 with S/243 manufacturer's code (Mauser-Berlin-Borsigwalde). Scope is Zeiss Zielveir 4x. Condition is 90 percent blue with clear optics.
Amoskeag Auction Company, March 2004

Model K98k Sniper Rifle (Short Rail System)

This mounting system was originally intended for police use during the mid-1930s. Beginning in 1941 this mounting was adopted for general combat use with 98k rifles. Ajack, Zeiss, Hensoldt, and Kahles in 4x are the often-encountered scopes on these mounts. Some of these short rail models were produced specifically for the Waffen-SS and these will command a considerable premium for correctly marked rifles and scopes.

Exc.	V.G.	Good	Fair	Poor
8000	5000	3000	2000	1000

Model K98k Sniper Rifle (Long Rail System)

This mounting system was not utilized in the German military until 1944. This system required that the 98k rifle be modified by having an enlarged receiver flat machined to accommodate the mounting base. This receiver flat has three large tapped screw holes and two smaller holes for tapered pins. It should be noted that these are very valuable and collectable rifles that are subject to fakes. Consult an expert prior to a sale.

Exc.	V.G.	Good	Fair	Poor
12500	7500	5000	2000	1000

Model K98k Sniper Rifle (Claw Mount System)

According to Senich about 10,000 "bnz" code 98k rifles were produced with claw mounts from late in 1943 to 1944. Various 4x scopes were used on these mounts but the most often encountered is the Hensoldt, Wetzlar (code "bmj"). Original issue rifles will have the rifle, base, and scope with matching numbers.

Exc.	V.G.	Good	Fair	Poor
12500	7500	5000	2000	1000

German "bcd 4" Long Rail Sniper. This is the blued variation with flat ground safety • Courtesy Michael Wamsher, Paul Goodwin photo

A late war K98 Side Rail Sniper Rifle sold at auction for $12,650. Fitted with a Hensoldtwerk model marked "DIALYTAN 4x 79211" over a blue "t". Condition is 99 percent original finish with clear optics. All matching numbers except mount.
Rock Island Auction Company, April 2004

A German "bnz" Single Claw Sniper Rifle sold at auction for $13,800. Produced late 1943-1944. Correct numbers. Hensoldt-Wetzar coded "bmj" scope with winter "t". Condition is 97 percent original blue.
Rock Island Auction Company, December 2004

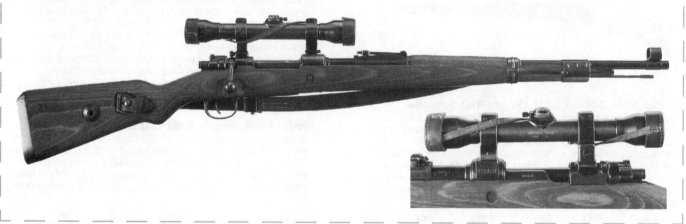

A K98k Sniper rifle with ZF41 scope sold at auction for $4,312.50. Condition is 90 to 95 percent original finish. Scope is cloudy.
Rock Island Auction Company, August 2004

German "bcd4" Long Rail Sniper with later phosphate finish with "key" safety. Note the original checkered butt plate • Courtesy Michael Wamsher, Paul Goodwin photo

Model K98k Sniper Rifle (ZF41)

This version of the 98k is fitted with a ZF41 scope (1.5x). It is not, in the true sense of the word, a sniper rifle but rather the scope is fitted as an aid to marksmanship. More than 300,000 were produced in this configuration between 1941 and 1945.

Exc.	V.G.	Good	Fair	Poor
3500	2500	1250	750	400

Model K98k Sniper Rifle (Dual Rail)

This sniper version is fitted with a dual rail scope mount. It is estimated that only about 25 of these rifles were built using this sight system.

Exc.	V.G.	Good	Fair	Poor
Too Rare To Price				

Model 1933 Standard Model Short Rifle

Introduced in 1933 and fitted with a 23.6" barrel full stock with pistol grip and finger grooves in forend. Short upper handguard. Weight is about 8.75 lbs. Used extensively by the German Condor Legion in the Spanish Civil War, 1936 to 1939. Stamped with Mauser banner on receiver ring with date of manufacture.

Exc.	V.G.	Good	Fair	Poor
350	275	225	150	100

K98k Dual Rail Sniper Rifle • Courtesy Richard M. Kumor Sr.

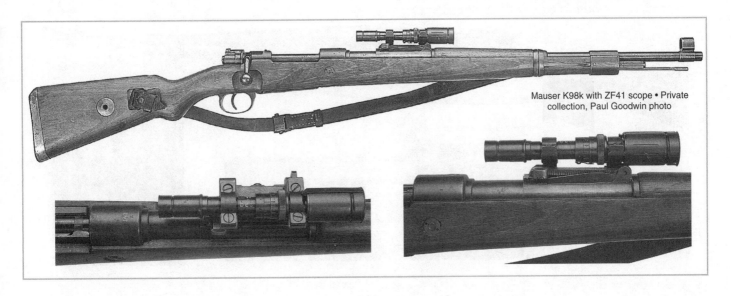

Mauser K98k with ZF41 scope • Private collection, Paul Goodwin photo

Model 33/40 • Courtesy West Point Museum, Paul Goodwin photo

Model 1933 Standard Model Carbine

Similar to the Model 98k but forearm has finger grooves. Mauser banner stamped on top of receiver ring with date of manufacture. Weight is about 8.5 lbs.

Exc.	V.G.	Good	Fair	Poor
600	500	375	200	125

Model 33/40 Carbine

This carbine was made in Brno in Czechoslovakia during World War II after it was occupied by the German army. This model featured a laminated stock with full upper handguard. Fitted with a 19.2" barrel and marked "G. 33/40" together with the year of production and the maker's code. Marked "dot" over the date or "945" over the date. Weight is about 8 lbs.

Exc.	V.G.	Good	Fair	Poor
1200	800	500	300	200

Waffen SS and their Gew 33/40 rifles • Courtesy Paul S. Scarlata

Model 29/40 Rifle (G29o)

This rifle was built by Steyr for the German Luftwaffe. It has a bent bolt and an "L" marked stock. There is some confusion over the origins of this model and its correct designations and configurations. Consult an expert prior to a sale to avoid vexation.

Exc.	V.G.	Good	Fair	Poor
1000	800	500	300	200

Model 24 (t) Rifle

This is the German version of the Czech VZ24 rifle built during the German occupation of that country during WWII.

Courtesy Rock Island Auction Company

Exc.	V.G.	Good	Fair	Poor
650	500	300	150	100

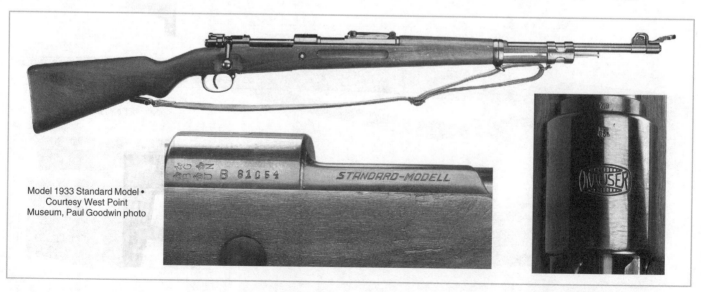

Model 1933 Standard Model •
Courtesy West Point
Museum, Paul Goodwin photo

VG-1 Rifle • Courtesy West Point Museum, Paul Goodwin photo

Model VG-98

These are crude half-stocked 7.92mm weapons produced near the end of the war to arm the German population. Barrel length is about 21" and some use a 10-round magazine while other examples are single shot. Weight is about 7 lbs. It is made from parts of older, often unserviceable Mausers. Will command premium prices.

Exc.	V.G.	Good	Fair	Poor
3500	2700	2200	1200	600

Model VG-1 (Volksturm Gewehr)

This rifle was made in the last days of WWII and is crudely made. It used the magazine of a semiautomatic Model 43 rifle. Beware of firing this weapon. It is roughly made but because of historical interest and high demand, prices command a premium.

Exc.	V.G.	Good	Fair	Poor
5750	4500	3200	—	—

Model VG-2

Chambered for the 7.9mm cartridge and fitted with a 10-round G43 magazine. This bolt action rifle has a 21" barrel with no bayonet lug. Cheaply built. Receiver is a "U" shaped stamping. Rare.

Exc.	V.G.	Good	Fair	Poor
5500	5000	4000	—	—

Model VG-5

Another last-ditch, locally produced rifle made at the very end of World War II. Chambered for the 7.92x33mm Kertz cartridge. Stamped receiver. Magazine is MP44 type. Simply and roughly made.

Exc.	V.G.	Good	Fair	Poor
6000	5000	4000	—	—

A Model VG-1 sold at auction for $7,475. Chambered for 8mm cartridge and fitted with a 20.5-inch barrel. Produced in late war period. Ten-round K-43 magazine.
Rock Island Auction Company, Dec. 2004

A VG-5 sold at auction for $17,250. Fitted with a 14.5-inch barrel and chambered for the 7.92x32 cartridge. Complete with canvas sling and STG-44 30-round magazine. Condition is good, but crudely made as it should be. Bright bore.
Amoskeag Auction Company, March 2004

Model 1918 Anti-Tank Rifle

Chambered for the 13x92SR cartridge, this was the first Mauser anti-tank rifle. Barrel length is 39" and weight is about 37 lbs. The Mauser banner is stamped on the upper receiver over the date "1918." Used successfully by the Germans against Allied tanks during WWI.

Courtesy Amoskeag Auction Co., Inc.

Exc.	V.G.	Good	Fair	Poor
4000	3000	2700	2200	1800

GERMAN WWII MILITARY RIFLES

Model G 41 Rifle(M)

First produced in 1941. Built by Mauser (code S42). Not a successful design and very few of these rifles were produced. These are extremely rare rifles today. Chambered for the 7.92mm Mauser cartridge. Semiautomatic gas operated with rotating bolt. It was full stocked with a 10-round box magazine. Barrel length is 21.5" and weight is about 11 lbs. The total produced of this model is estimated at 20,000 rifles.

Courtesy Richard M. Kumor Sr.

Exc.	V.G.	Good	Fair	Poor
9500	8000	—	—	—

Model G 41(W)

Similar to the above model but designed by Walther and produced by "duv" (Berlin-Lubeck Machine Factory) in 1941. This rifle was contracted for 70,000 units in 1942 and 1943. Correct examples will command a premium price.

Courtesy Richard M. Kumor Sr.

Exc.	V.G.	Good	Fair	Poor
5000	3000	1500	—	—

Model G 43(W) (K43)

An improved version of the G 41(W), introduced in 1943, with a modified gas system that was the more typical gas and piston design. Built by Carl Walther (code "ac"). Full stocked with full-length handguard. Wood or plastic stock. Receiver has a dovetail for telescope sight (#43@4 power). Barrel length is 22" and magazine capacity is 10 rounds. Weight is approximately 9.5 lbs. It is estimated that some 500,000 of these rifles were produced. On the right side of the breech housing, machined into it, there is a telescope rail about .28" in length. Used by German sharpshooters during World War II and also by the Czech army after WWII.

Exc.	V.G.	Good	Fair	Poor
6000	3500	2000	—	—

NOTE: Add 150 percent for original scope.

Courtesy Rock Island Auction Company

G 43 left side with receiver markings, note rough finish • Paul Goodwin photo

Exc.	V.G.	Good	Fair	Poor
1250	1000	750	250	100

A Walther G 43 Sniper rifle was sold at auction for $5,750. Receiver is machined with forged bolt. Late production. Condition is 98 percent. Scope marked GW ZF4. Scope is excellent. All serial numbers match but scope and mount do not match rifle.
Rock Island Auction Company, August 2004

A Mauser G 41 rifle sold at auction for $16,100. Early production model. Condition is 95 percent original blue.
Rock Island Auction Company, April 2004

A Walther G 41 sold at auction for $6,900. Condition is 96 percent. All matching numbers.
Rock Island Auction Company, August 2004

A rare Walther G 41 rifle with push-button bolt release mechanism sold at auction for $13,800. Condition is 95 percent original finish. Only about 7,500 rifles with this bolt release were built.
Rock Island Auction Company, August 2004

A K43 Sniper rifle sold at auction for $12,650. All matching numbers including mount. Condition is 98 percent overall original finish.
Rock Island Auction Company, April 2004

Model FG 42 (Fallschirmjager Gewehr)

This select fire 7.92x57mm rifle was adopted by the Luftwaffe for its airborne troops. It was designed to replace the rifle, light machine gun, and submachine gun. It incorporates a number of features including: straight line stock and muzzle brake, reduced recoil mechanism, closed-bolt semiautomatic fire, and open-bolt full-auto fire. Rate of fire is about 750 rounds per minute. It had a mid-barrel bipod on early (1st Models, Type "E") models and front mounted barrel bipod on later (2nd Models, Type "G") models. Barrel attachment for pike-style bayonet. First Models were fitted with steel buttstocks, sharply raked pistol grips, and 2nd Models with wooden stocks and more vertical pistol grips. The 20-round magazine is left side mounted. Fitted with a 21.5" barrel, the rifle weighs about 9.5 lbs. This breech mechanism was to be used years later by the U.S. in its M60 machine gun.

FG 42 with original German FG 42 ZF 4 scope and without scope and wooden buttstock • Courtesy private NFA collection, Paul Goodwin photo

FG 42 with original German ZFG 42 scope and without scope and steel buttstock • Courtesy private NFA collection, Paul Goodwin photo

Pre-1968

Exc.	V.G.	Fair
45000	35000	25000

Pre-1986 conversions

Exc.	V.G.	Fair
N/A	N/A	N/A

Pre-1986 dealer samples

Exc.	V.G.	Fair
N/A	N/A	N/A

NOTE: For rifles fitted with original German FG 42 scopes add between $5,000 and $10,000 depending on model. Consult an expert prior to a sale.

A German ZF 4 Sniper Scope sold at auction for $3,565. Condition is mint with original wooden case. Complete with leather sling and sun shade.
Amoskeag Auction Company Inc., Jan. 2003

MKb42(W) • Courtesy West Point Museum, Paul Goodwin photo

the front sight was too wide, and covered the target at 300m. The construction was too complex which resulted in lack of reliability. Trigger pull was excessive for accurate fire.

Pre-1968 (Very Rare)

Exc.	V.G.	Fair
18000	16500	15000

Pre-1986 conversions

Exc.	V.G.	Fair
N/A	N/A	N/A

Pre-1986 dealer samples

Exc.	V.G.	Fair
N/A	N/A	N/A

STURMGEWEHR GROUP

Because the German military thought the 7.92x57mm cartridge too powerful for its needs, a new cartridge was developed to provide less recoil, lighter weight, and less expensive production. This new cartridge, developed in the mid 1930s by Gustav Genschow, Polte, and others, was called the 7.92x33mm Kurtz (Short) cartridge. The entire cartridge was 1.89" in length and had a bullet weight of 125 grains. This new cartridge was introduced in 1943 and spawned a new series of firearms designed for that cartridge.

Bibliographical Note: For a complete and exhaustive account of the sturmgewehr rifles see Hans-Dieter Handrich's, *Sturmgewehr: From Firepower to Striking Power*, Collector Grade Publications, 2004.

MKb42(W)

This select fire open bolt machine carbine built by Walther was used on the Russian front. It was fitted with a 30-round box magazine and 16" barrel. Rate of fire was about 600 rounds per minute. It was fitted with a wooden stock and metal forearm. The rest of the weapon, with the exception of the barrel and bolt, was made from sheet metal to save cost and weight. Weight was about 9.75 lbs. A total of about 8,000 of these weapons were built by Walther. This model was not selected by the German Army because, according to Handrich's book,

MKb42(H) • Courtesy West Point Museum, Paul Goodwin photo

MKb42(H)

This was a similar design (open bolt) to the Walther version except for a 14.5" barrel and other internal differences. It was built by Haenel, and also saw extensive use on the Eastern Front. This version proved to be better than the Walther design. Its rate of fire was a somewhat slower 500 rounds per minute. Weight was approximately 11 lbs. Some 8,000 of these weapons were also produced. Handrich states that the advantages of the Haenel model were simple, reliable construction, greater sight radius for more accurate fire, good front sight, and uniform trigger pull.

NOTE: Some MKb42(H) rifles had bayonet lugs while others did not. All of these rifles were fitted with mounting rails for a telescope sight.

Pre-1968

Exc.	V.G.	Fair
14000	10000	8000

Pre-1986 conversions

Exc.	V.G.	Fair
N/A	N/A	N/A

Pre-1986 dealer samples

Exc.	V.G.	Fair
N/A	N/A	N/A

MP43, MP43/1

With some redesign this model was a newer MKb42(H). This weapon was adopted by the Waffenamt as standard issue in 1944. Originally built by Haenel, it was later produced by Mauser and Erma. This model was the forerunner of the MP44 and StG44. The MP43 had a stepped barrel while the MP43/1 had a straight barrel.

MP43 • Paul Goodwin photo

Pre-1968

Exc.	V.G.	Fair
8500	7500	7000

Pre-1986 conversions

Exc.	V.G.	Fair
6000	5500	5000

Pre-1986 dealer samples

Exc.	V.G.	Fair
N/A	N/A	N/A

A DEWAT MP44 was sold at auction for $9,200. Condition is 75 percent of non-original black paint. Missing bolt and operating nut.
Amoskeag Auction Company, May 2004

MP44

This German automatic rifle was first produced in 1943 and chambered for the 7.92x33 Kurz cartridge. Fitted with a solid stock and 16.3" barrel, it has a magazine capacity of 30 rounds. The rate of fire is 500 rounds per minute. Weight is about 11.5 lbs. Marked "MP44" on top of the receiver. Production ceased in 1945. This rifle was used extensively on the Eastern Front during World War II.

Pre-1968

Exc.	V.G.	Fair
15000	13500	13000

Pre-1986 conversions

Exc.	V.G.	Fair
7500	6500	5500

Pre-1986 dealer samples

Exc.	V.G.	Fair
N/A	N/A	N/A

StG44

This version of the MP43-MP44 series is nothing more than a name change from the MP44.

Pre-1968

Exc.	V.G.	Fair
12000	11000	10500

Pre-1986 conversions

Exc.	V.G.	Fair
6000	5500	5000

Pre-1986 dealer samples

Exc.	V.G.	Fair
N/A	N/A	N/A

Stg44 & G43 in combat, Courtesy Paul S. Scarlata

Model 86 SR

Introduced in 1993, this bolt action .308 is sometimes referred to as the Specialty Rifle. Fitted with a laminated wood and special match thumbhole stock or fiberglass stock with adjustable cheekpiece. Stock has rail in forearm and an adjustable recoil pad. Magazine capacity is 9 rounds. Finish is a non-glare blue. The barrel length with muzzle brake is 28.8". Many special features are found on this rifle, from adjustable trigger weight to silent safety. Mauser offers many options on this rifle as well that will affect the price. Weight is approximately 11 lbs.

NIB	Exc.	V.G.	Good	Fair	Poor
3300	2950	2500	1750	1250	750

Model 93 SR

Introduced in 1996, this is a tactical semiautomatic rifle chambered for the .300 Win. Mag. or the .338 Lapua cartridge. Barrel length is 25.5" with an overall length of 48.4". Barrel is fitted with a muzzle brake. Magazine capacity is 6 rounds for .300 and 5 rounds for .338 caliber. Weight is approximately 13 lbs.

NIB	Exc.	V.G.	Good	Fair	Poor
N/A	—	—	—	—	—

HECKLER & KOCH

Model 91

This rifle is recoil-operated, with a delayed-roller lock bolt. It is chambered for the .308 Winchester cartridge and has a 17.7" barrel with military-style aperture sights. It is furnished with a 20-round detachable magazine and is finished in matte black with a black plastic stock. This model is a semiautomatic version of the select fire G3 rifle. Some areas of the country have made its ownership illegal.

NIB	Exc.	V.G.	Good	Fair	Poor
3100	2750	2300	1550	1200	800

Model 91 A3

This model is simply the Model 91 with a retractable metal stock.

NIB	Exc.	V.G.	Good	Fair	Poor
3250	3000	2500	1600	1300	900

Model 93

This model is similar to the Model 91 except that it is chambered for the .223 cartridge and has a 16.4" barrel. The magazine holds 25 rounds, and the specifications are the same as for the Model 91. This is a semiautomatic version of the select fire HK33 rifle.

NIB	Exc.	V.G.	Good	Fair	Poor
3100	2750	2300	1500	1200	800

Model 93 A3

This is the Model 93 with the retractable metal stock.

NIB	Exc.	V.G.	Good	Fair	Poor
3250	3000	2500	1650	1300	900

Model 94

This is a carbine version chambered for the 9mm Parabellum cartridge, with a 16.5" barrel. It is a smaller-scaled weapon that has a 15-shot magazine.

NIB	Exc.	V.G.	Good	Fair	Poor
4200	3850	3300	2750	2200	1500

Model 94 A3

This model is a variation of the Model 94 with the addition of a retractable metal stock.

NIB	Exc.	V.G.	Good	Fair	Poor
4500	3900	3400	2900	2300	1500

HK G3

First adopted by the German army in 1959. Chambered for the 7.62x51mm cartridge and fitted with a 17.5" barrel. Solid wooden stock on early models and plastic stock on later models (A3). Folding stock (A2) also offered. Magazine capacity is 20 rounds with a rate of fire of 550 rounds per minute. Weight is about 9.7 lbs. Marked "G3 HK" on left side of magazine housing. This select fire rifle has seen service with as many as 60 military forces around the world. There are several variations of this model.

Photo courtesy Heckler & Koch

Pre-1968

Exc.	V.G.	Fair
11000	10000	9000

Pre-1986 conversions

Exc.	V.G.	Fair
8000	7500	7000

Pre-1986 dealer samples

Exc.	V.G.	Fair
5500	5000	4500

HK 33

This model is a reduced caliber version of the standard HK G3. First produced in 1968 this model is chambered for the 5.56x45mm NATO cartridge (.223 caliber). This rifle is available in several variants, namely a sniper version with set trigger, telescope sight and bipod; a retractable stock version (A3); and a carbine version (12.68"). The HK 33 features a 15.35" barrel without flash hider, and a magazine capacity of 25 or 40 rounds. The rate of fire is 750 rounds per minute. The rifle is marked "HK 33 5.56MM" with serial number on the left side of the magazine housing. The rifle is still in production and is in service in Chile, Brazil, various countries in southeast Asia, and Africa. Weight is approximately 8 lbs. for standard model.

HK 33 K • Photo courtesy Heckler & Koch

Pre-1968 (Very Rare)

Exc.	V.G.	Fair
15000	13500	12000

Pre-1986 conversions

Exc.	V.G.	Fair
8500	8000	7500

Pre-1986 dealer samples

Exc.	V.G.	Fair
7500	6500	6000

NOTE: The HK 33 K is the same as the HK 33 with the exception of a 13" barrel. Prices may differ slightly for the HK 33 K version.

HK G41

First produced in 1983, this 5.56x45mm chambered select fire rifle is fitted with a 17.5" barrel and has a magazine capacity of 30 rounds. Rate of fire is about 850 rounds per minute. Marked "HK G41 5.56MM" on the left side of the magazine housing. This model will accept M16 magazines. This model is also available with fixed or retractable stock. Weight is 9.7 lbs.

Pre-1968

HK G41 • Courtesy Heckler & Koch

Exc.	V.G.	Fair
N/A	N/A	N/A

Pre-1986 conversions

Exc.	V.G.	Fair
N/A	N/A	N/A

Pre-1986 dealer samples (Very Rare)

Exc.	V.G.	Fair
9000	8000	7500

PSG-1

This rifle is a high-precision sniping rifle that features the delayed-roller semiautomatic action. It is chambered for the .308 Winchester cartridge and has a 5-shot magazine. Barrel length is 25.6". It is furnished with a complete array of accessories including a 6x42-power illuminated Hensoldt scope. Rifle weighs 17.8 lbs.

NIB	Exc.	V.G.	Good	Fair	Poor
14500	12500	9000	7500	6000	4000

Model SL8-1

This is a new generation .223 rifle modeled after the military Model G36 (not available to civilians) and introduced in 2000. It is built of carbon fiber polymer and is gas operated. Thumbhole stock with cheekpiece. Barrel length is 20.8". Magazine capacity is 10 rounds. Adjustable sights. Weight is approximately 8.6 lbs.

NIB	Exc.	V.G.	Good	Fair	Poor
1600	1200	—	—	—	—

Model USC

Introduced in 2000, this semiautomatic blowback carbine is derived from HK's UMP submachine gun (not available to civilians). Chambered for the .45 ACP cartridge and fitted with a 16" barrel. Skeletonized stock. Accessory rail on top of receiver. Adjustable sights. Magazine capacity is 10 rounds. Weight is approximately 6 lbs.

NIB	Exc.	V.G.	Good	Fair	Poor
1200	900	—	—	—	—

SHOTGUNS

SAUER, J.P. & SON

Luftwaffe Survival Drilling

A double barrel 12 gauge by 9.3x74R combination shotgun/rifle with 28" barrels. Blued with a checkered walnut stock and marked with Nazi inspection. Stampings on the stock and barrel breech. Normally furnished with an aluminum case.

Courtesy Richard M. Kumor Sr.

Exc.	V.G.	Good	Fair	Poor
6000	5500	3800	2500	—

NOTE: Add 50 percent to prices for case.

A Luftwaffe Survival Drilling by J.P. Sauer sold at auction for $10,925. Complete with sling and case. Condition is 99 percent original blue and case color. Case has 95 percent of original paint. *Amoskeag Auction Company Inc., Jan. 2004*

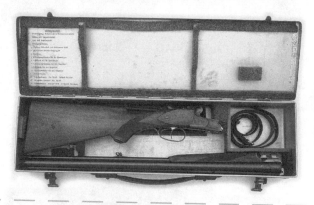

MACHINE GUNS

Germany adopted the Maxim gun and designated it the MG 01, which was built on the Belgian Maxim pattern Model 1900. It was not until 1908 that Germany produced its own version of the Maxim called the MG 08.

Bibliographical Note: For information on a wide variety of German machine guns, see Daniel D. Musgrave, *German Machineguns,* 2nd edition, Ironside International Publishers, 1992. Also Folke Myrvang, *MG 34-MG42, German Universal Machineguns*, Collector Grade Publications, 2002. Dolf L. Goldsmith, *The Devil's Paintbrush, (the Maxim Gun)* Collector Grade Publications, 2002

Maxim '08 • Courtesy private NFA collection,
Paul Goodwin photo

Maxim '08 (MG 08)

Germany adopted this gun at the turn of the 20th century. In 1908 they began to produce the gun themselves. This was the standard German heavy machine gun during WWI. Chambered for the 7.92x57mm cartridge this gun had a rate of fire of 400 to 500 rounds per minute from its 28" barrel. It was fed with a 100- or 250-round fabric belt. The gun weighed about 41 lbs. with a sled mount weighing about 83 pounds. The gun was marked "DEUTCHE WAFFEN UND MUNITIONSFABRIKEN BERLIN" with the year of production on the left side of the receiver. The serial number was located on the top of the receiver. The gun was produced from 1908 to about 1918.

Pre-1968

Exc.	V.G.	Fair
18000	16000	15000

Pre-1986 conversions

Exc.	V.G.	Fair
13000	11500	10500

Pre-1986 dealer samples

Exc.	V.G.	Fair
N/A	N/A	N/A

Maxim '08/15

A more movable version of the Maxim Model '08. Chambered for the 7.92x57mm Mauser cartridge and fitted with a 28" water-cooled barrel with bipod, it weighs about 31 lbs. It is fed by a 100-round cloth belt housed inside of a special drum with a rate of fire of 500 rounds per minute. Marked "LMG 09/15 SPANDAU" on top of the receiver. Spandau produced 50,000 guns.

Other manufacturers of the gun were:

- Erfurt–33,000
- Maschinen Fabrik Augsburg, Nurnburg (M.A.N.)–14,000
- Siemens & Halske (S&H)–13,000
- J.P. Sauer & Sohn, Suhl–11,000
- Rheinsche Maschinen & Metallwaren Fabrik
- (Rh.M. & M.F)–7,000
- Deutche Waffen und Munitions Fabriken
  D.W. & M.F.)–2,000

Another version of this gun with an air-cooled slotted barrel jacket was used in aircraft. Called the IMG 08/15.

Pre-1968

Exc.	V.G.	Fair
12000	10500	9500

Pre-1986 conversions

Exc.	V.G.	Fair
9000	8000	7000

Pre-1986 dealer samples

Exc.	V.G.	Fair
N/A	N/A	N/A

MG08/15 September 1939 in Poland • Courtesy Blake Stevens, *The Devil's Paintbrush*, Collector Grade Publications.

Model 1909

A DWM commercial version of the Model 1908 built for export. Fitted with a muzzle booster. Some were sent to Costa Rica as well as Brazil, Mexico, Romania, Switzerland, Belgium, China, and Persia. Some of these countries, like Switzerland and China, built their own military versions of the DWM 1909 commercial. A seldom-seen variation.

Maxim 1909 Commercial • Courtesy Blake Stevens, *The Devil's Paintbrush*, Goldsmith

Pre-1968

Exc.	V.G.	Fair
15000	13000	11500

Pre-1986 conversions (side-plate)

Exc.	V.G.	Fair
13000	11500	10500

Pre-1986 dealer samples

Exc.	V.G.	Fair
N/A	N/A	N/A

MG 08/15 • Courtesy West Point Museum, Paul Goodwin photo

Dreyse Model 1915 • Courtesy private NFA collection,
Paul Goodwin photo

Dreyse Model 1910/15

Chambered for the 7.92x57mm Mauser cartridge, this gun was based on the Louis Schmeisser patents of 1907. Built by Rheinmetall in Sommerda, Germany. Named in honor of Johann Niklaus von Dreyse who died in 1875. This is a water-cooled gun designed for sustained fire. Rate of fire is about 550 to 600 rounds a minute. Weight is approximately 37 lbs. Most of these guns were converted by Germany to MG 13s during the 1930s, so few original Dreyse models still survive. Very rare in unaltered condition.

Pre-1968

Exc.	V.G.	Fair
25000	23000	21000

Pre-1986 conversions

Exc.	V.G.	Fair
N/A	N/A	N/A

Pre-1986 dealer samples

Exc.	V.G.	Fair
N/A	N/A	N/A

Parabellum MG 14

Chambered for the 7.9mm cartridge, this was a water-cooled light machine gun. There was also an air-cooled version with a slotted water jacket. Barrel length is 27.75". Rate of fire is about 700 rounds per minute. Weight is about 21.5 lbs. This gun was derived from the Maxim but the main spring is located behind the receiver and is compressed during recoil. The gun was much lighter than the Maxim. Also, the Parabellum has no dead stop on the crank handle. The gun was the standard observer's machine gun in German two-seat aircraft during World War I. The gun was also used in Zeppelins as well as a ground gun. Built by DWM.

Pre-1968

Exc.	V.G.	Fair
Too Rare To Price		

Pre-1986 conversions

Exc.	V.G.	Fair
N/A	N/A	N/A

Pre-1986 dealer samples

Exc.	V.G.	Fair
N/A	N/A	N/A

MG 13

In 1932 the German army adopted the MG 13 as its standard machine gun. Chambered for the 7.92x57mm cartridge and fitted with a 28" air-cooled barrel, this gun is recoil operated. The butt is a single arm metal type with pistol grip. The bipod is attached close to the muzzle. A 25-round box magazine or a 75-round saddle drum magazine can be used. Weight is about 25 lbs. with bipod. Who manufactured the gun is unclear, but Simson of Suhl, Germany, is often reported to be the manufacturer, perhaps because the company was the only legal machine gun manufacturer under the Versailles Treaty. Evidence suggests that the gun was made at Sommerda by Rheinmetall.

NOTE: The 75-round drum for use with the MG 13 is rare because it uses an MG15 drum with a special magazine extension to fit into the side of the MG 13 magazine well.

Pre-1968

Exc.	V.G.	Fair
18000	16000	14000

Pre-1986 conversions

Exc.	V.G.	Fair
15000	13000	11000

Pre-1986 dealer samples

Exc.	V.G.	Fair
N/A	N/A	N/A

MG15 Aircraft Gun

Used by the German air force in its bombers, this air-cooled gun is chambered for the 7.92x57JS cartridge. Rate of fire is about 850 rounds per minute. Barrel length is 28". Saddle drum magazine with 75-round capacity was used. Weight is about 28 lbs. Built by Krieghoff. Made by Rheinmetall beginning in 1932.

Parabellum with original scope • Courtesy private NFA collection, Paul Goodwin photo

MG 13 • Courtesy West Point Museum, Paul Goodwin photo

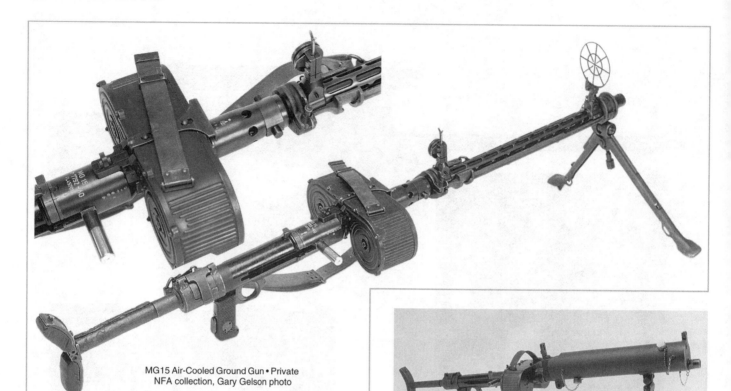

MG15 Air-Cooled Ground Gun • Private
NFA collection, Gary Gelson photo

Private NFA collection, Gary Gelson photo

Pre-1968

Exc.	V.G.	Fair
20000	18000	16500

Pre-1986 conversions

Exc.	V.G.	Fair
15000	13000	12000

Pre-1986 dealer samples

Exc.	V.G.	Fair
N/A	N/A	N/A

MG15 Water-Cooled Ground Gun

A converted aircraft machine gun, this water-cooled model was used by ground forces from 1944 to 1945. Barrel length was 30" and weight is about 33 lbs. Chambered for the 7.92x57JS cartridge. Rate of fire is about 750 rounds per minute. Ammunition capacity is a 75-round saddle drum magazine. Built by Krieghoff.

Pre-1968

Exc.	V.G.	Fair
18000	16000	14500

Pre-1986 conversions

Exc.	V.G.	Fair
15000	13000	12000

Private NFA collection, Gary Gelson photo

Pre-1986 dealer samples

Exc.	V.G.	Fair
N/A	N/A	N/A

MG15 Air-Cooled Ground Gun

Same as the aircraft gun but converted to ground use in 1944 and 1945 by attaching a bipod and single strut buttstock.

Pre-1968

Exc.	V.G.	Fair
25000	23000	21500

Pre-1986 conversions

Exc.	V.G.	Fair
22000	20000	18500

Pre-1986 dealer samples

Exc.	V.G.	Fair
N/A	N/A	N/A

MG34

Designed and built by Mauser, this was the first general purpose machine gun to be produced in large numbers. It was introduced into the German army in about 1936, and stayed in production until the end of the war in 1945. Chambered for the 7.92x57mm Mauser cartridge, this gun had a 25" barrel with a 50-round belt or 75-round saddle drum. Rate of fire was about 800 to 900 rounds per minute. Marked "MG34" with its serial number on top of the receiver. Weight was approximately 26.5 lbs. There were a number of different bipod and tripod mounts for this gun, as well as different gun configurations such as antiaircraft use, use in armored vehicles, and one configuration where only automatic fire was possible. After WWII the gun was used by the Czechs, French, and Israelis, as well as the Viet Cong. Superseded by the MG42.

SNAP SHOT
MG34

The German MG34 was a quantum leap in the advancement of the light machine gun. With a well made machined receiver, it incorporated a highly efficient feed mechanism and quick-change barrel. It is a select fire weapon with a rate of fire of 800-900 rounds per minute. To help prevent the barrel from overheating, ammunition was linked in 50-round sections of a non-disintegrating metallic belt often fed from an assault drum attached to the side. A mounted bipod allows proper use from the prone position. A Lafitte tripod was also employed that allowed rock steady use of the gun.

Because the MG34 is so light, and with its high rate of fire, firing with accuracy from the prone position or from an anti-aircraft mount can be a challenge. What it lacks in consistent controllability in full automatic fire is made up by the volume of lead sent downrange. While the 8mm Mauser round is adequate, and not known as a powerhouse, your shoulder will take a bit of a beating due to the light weight of the weapon. There is not a whole lot there to absorb recoil.

The MG34 can also be finicky. The trigger pack is a maze of springs, cams and buttons that must be properly maintained and constant lubrication is essential on all moving parts. Having said that, the MG34 is a blast to shoot. The high volume of lead, along with the recoil pounding your shoulder, makes you *know* that you have a tiger by the tail.

The MG34 is another one of those weapons that a thorough knowledge of its parts and operating system is mandatory. To keep the gun running you must know what is happening and what forces are at work inside the weapon. This will help alleviate operational problems and allow you to enjoy shooting the weapon with reasonable operational reliability.

Robert G. Segel

Pre-1968

Exc.	V.G.	Fair
35000	32500	30000

Pre-1986 conversions

Exc.	V.G.	Fair
25000	22500	20000

Pre-1986 dealer samples

Exc.	V.G.	Fair
N/A	N/A	N/A

MG34 with receiver markings • Paul Goodwin photo

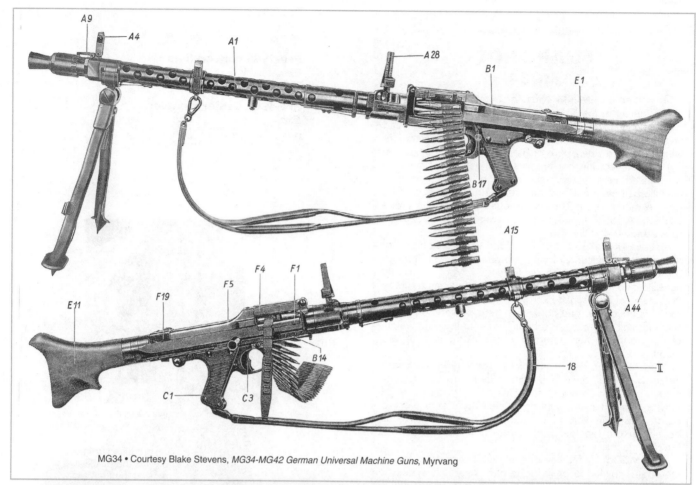

MG34 • Courtesy Blake Stevens, *MG34-MG42 German Universal Machine Guns*, Myrvang

MG34 in action • Courtesy Blake Stevens, *MG34-MG42 German Universal Machine Guns*, Collector Grade Publications

MG42 in action • Courtesy Blake Stevens, *MG34-MG42* German Universal Machine Guns, Collector Grade Publications

MG42-MG42/59-MG1-MG3

This gun replaced the MG34 and was chambered for the 7.92x57mm Mauser cartridge. It has a 20.8" quick change barrel and is fed by a 50-round belt. Its rate of fire is about 1,000 to 1,200 rounds per minute. The butt is synthetic with pistol grip. The gun weighs about 25 lbs. Marked "MG42" on the left side of the receiver. This gun was produced from 1938 until the end of the war in 1945. Its design was the result of wartime engineering which used roller locks – at the time a revolutionary design concept.

MG42 • Private NFA collection, Gary Gelson photo

Postwar models, the MG42/59 followed by the MG1 then the MG3, are still in use by the German army. These postwar guns are chambered for the 7.62x51mm cartridge. These models utilize many important improvements in manufacturing and design, and are in use by many countries throughout the world. There are a number of licensed versions of the MG42/59 made in Austria, Italy, Spain, Portugal, Turkey, Yugoslavia, and Switzerland.

MG3 • Photo courtesy private NFA collection

MG42

Pre-1968

Exc.	V.G.	Fair
37500	35000	32500

Pre-1986 conversions

Exc.	V.G.	Fair
32500	30000	28000

Pre-1986 dealer samples

Exc.	V.G.	Fair
17500	15000	13000

NOTE: For MG42/5 and MG42/59 add 75 percent premium (8 known). For MG3 add 125 percent (3 known).

HK11 (HK11A1-HK11E)

Designed as a light air-cooled machine gun chambered for the 7.62x51mm cartridge, this gun uses a roller-delayed bolt. The quick change barrel is 17.7" long. Fixed synthetic stock with pistol grip and bipod. Uses a 20-round box magazine or 80 dual drum. Rate of fire is about 850 rounds per minute. Weight is approximately 15 lbs.

NOTE: There is no drum magazine on the HK11A1.

Pre-1968

Exc.	V.G.	Fair
N/A	N/A	N/A

Pre-1986 conversions

Exc.	V.G.	Fair
16000	14000	12000

Pre-1986 dealer samples

Exc.	V.G.	Fair
13000	11000	9000

HK13 (HK13E)

This gun is similar to the HK11 but is chambered for the 5.56x45mm cartridge. Quick change 17.7" barrel. Fed by a 20-, 30-, or 40-round box magazine, or 100-round dual drum. Rate of fire is about 800 rounds per minute. Weight is approximately 12 lbs.

NOTE: There are a number of variants to this model. The HK13C has a baked-on forest camouflage finish. The HK13E is a modernized version with selective improvements, such as a 3-round burst capability. The rifling has been changed to stabilize 62 grain bullets. The HK13E1 is the same as the HK13E with rifling twist to accommodate 54 grain bullets. The HK13S has a baked-on desert camouflage scheme.

NOTE: There is a semiautomatic version of this gun. Value would be around $6,000 for one in excellent condition.

Pre-1968

Exc.	V.G.	Fair
N/A	N/A	N/A

Pre-1986 conversions

Exc.	V.G.	Fair
15000	13000	11000

Pre-1986 dealer samples

Exc.	V.G.	Fair
12000	11000	9000

HK21 (HK21E-HK23E)

These guns form a series of general purpose machine guns. The 21 series is chambered for the 7.62x51mm cartridge while the 23E is chambered for the 5.56x45mm cartridge. The HK21 is fitted with a 17.5" barrel and has a rate of fire of 900 rounds per minute. Its weight is about 17 lbs. Marked on the top of receiver. The HK21 was first produced in 1970 but is no longer in production, while the HK21E and 23E are still produced.

This series of guns has variations similar to the HK13 series of guns.

NOTE: The HK21E and HK23E will bring a premium of 75 percent over the older HK21/2.

HK23 • Courtesy Heckler & Koch

HK23E • Courtesy Heckler & Koch

Pre-1968 Model 21

Exc.	V.G.	Fair
20000	17500	16000

Pre-1986 conversions

Exc.	V.G.	Fair
20000	18000	17000

Pre-1986 dealer samples

Exc.	V.G.	Fair
20000	18000	17000

GREAT BRITAIN

British Military Conflicts, 1870-Present

The period from 1870 to 1901 marked the height of Britain's economic, political, commercial, and military influence. During this period, the far-flung British empire required the country to police its possessions frequently with force. The British army was involved in Africa, Asia, the Middle East, and even Ireland during this period. The Boer War in the last years of the 19th century, for example, required extensive military presence in South Africa. In 1914, Britain entered World War I. By the end of the war in 1918, the country had exhausted its wealth and manpower. During the war 5,700,000 served in the armed forces and of those 2,365,035 were killed or wounded, about 41 percent of those who served.

During the period between the two world wars, Britain tried to consolidate its remaining power which led to the appeasement of Nazi Germany and eventually World War II in 1939. At war's end, 5,896,000 had served. Of those, 582,900 were killed or wounded, about 10 percent. With the end of the war in 1945, Britain gave independence to many of its colonies and concentrated on domestic, economic, and social affairs. In 1982, the country was involved in a successful military engagement with Argentina over the Falkland Islands. As a member of NATO Britain continued to carry out its military responsibilities. As of 2001, the United Kingdom military forces had 211,430 personnel, of which 113,950 were in the army.

HANDGUNS

NOTE: During World War I, the British government contracted with two Spanish firms to build what was called the Old Pattern No.1 Mark I revolver by Garate y Compania and the Old Pattern No. 2 Mark I revolver by Trocaola, Aranzabal y Compania. Both companies were located in Eibar, Spain. These revolvers were chambered for the .455 caliber cartridge and were fitted with 5" barrels. Britain also acquired Colt New Service and Smith & Wesson First Model and Second Model Ejector .455 revolvers from the U.S. Approximately 75,000 of these S&W and Colt revolvers were sent to England between 1914 and 1916.

Adams Model 1872 Mark 2, 3, and 4

A .450 caliber double action revolver with a 6" octagonal barrel and 6-shot cylinder. Blued with walnut grips. Built by Adams Patent Small Arms Company. Weight was about 40 oz. This was the first breechloading revolver issued to the British mounted units. In service from 1872 to 1919.

Exc.	V.G.	Good	Fair	Poor
—	1250	600	400	200

WEBLEY & SCOTT, LTD.

Bibliographical Note: For historical information, technical data, and photos see William Dowell's, *The Webley Story*, Skyrac Press, 1987.

Mark I

A .455 caliber double action top break revolver with a 4" barrel and 6-shot cylinder. Blued with hard rubber grips. Manufactured from 1887 to 1894. Models issued to the Royal Navy have the letter "N" stamped on top of the frame behind the hammer.

NOTE: Military version chambered for .455 cartridge only while commercial versions were chambered for the .442 and .476 cartridges.

Courtesy Faintich Auction Services, Inc., Paul Goodwin photo

Exc.	V.G.	Good	Fair	Poor
450	250	175	125	100

Mark II

As above, with a larger hammer spur and improved barrel catch. Manufactured from 1894 to 1897.

Webley Mark II and its markings left side • Courtesy Rock Island Auction Company

Exc.	V.G.	Good	Fair	Poor
500	400	300	200	100

Mark III

As above, with internal improvements. Introduced in 1897.

Courtesy Rock Island Auction Company

Exc.	V.G.	Good	Fair	Poor
450	250	200	150	125

Mark IV

As above, with a .455 caliber and 4" or 6" barrel. Sometimes referred to as the "Boer War" model because it was supplied to British troops in South Africa between 1899 and 1902.

NOTE: This model was also commercially available in .22 caliber with 6" barrel, .32 caliber with 3" barrel, and .38 caliber with 3", 4", or 5" barrel.

Courtesy Faintich Auction Services, Inc., Paul Goodwin photo

Exc.	V.G.	Good	Fair	Poor
500	300	225	175	125

Mark V

As above, with a 4" (standard) or 6" barrel. Manufactured from 1913 to 1915.

Courtesy Faintich Auction Services, Inc., Paul Goodwin photo

Exc.	V.G.	Good	Fair	Poor
500	325	250	200	150

Mark IV .380 (.38S&W)

Webley produced a military version of its .38 revolver for military use during World War II. This model was intended to supplement the .38 Enfield revolvers.

Exc.	V.G.	Good	Fair	Poor
500	325	250	200	150

Mark VI

As above, with 6" barrel and square buttgrip. Introduced in 1915 and replaced in 1928.

SNAP SHOT
THE BIG BORE WEBLEY TOP BREAK REVOLVERS

In 1887 the British Government adopted the 4-inch barreled Webley Mark I .455 service revolver, the first of the series. Webley continued to refine their revolvers and in 1894 this resulted in the Mark II revolver. The most noticeable difference was the deletion of the hump at the top of the grip.

In 1897 the Mark III revolver was introduced that had a simpler cylinder retention system and other refinements. Two years later the Mark IV was adopted. Its barrel and cylinder were manufactured from a higher grade of steel.

In 1913 the Mark V with a slightly larger diameter cylinder was adopted. In 1915, the Mark VI, the last and best of the series was adopted. The Mark VI differed from the Mark V by having a more practical and controllable square butt grip and a 6-inch barrel with a replaceable front sight. Because of the demands of WWI, more Mark VI Webley revolvers were made than all other Marks combined. During and between the World Wars many earlier Marks of Webley revolvers were refurbished with Mark VI type 6-inch barrels and cylinders. The Mark VI was the primary British handgun in World War I and saw much service in WWII.

Military production of the Mark VI ceased in the 1920s when it began to be replaced by the similar but smaller Enfield No. 2 .380 revolver, though the .455 Webleys continued to serve honorably and well until the end of WWII.

Thousands of Webley .455 revolvers of all Marks were sold as surplus in the U. S. during the 1950s and '60s for as little as $15. To make them more salable, most had their cylinders and extractors faced off at the rear to allow firing .45 ACP ammunition in half moon clips. However, Webleys in their original configuration shoot better and are worth at least half again more than converted revolvers.

The Webley big-bore revolvers were probably the best combat revolvers of their day. Made from first class materials with impeccable fit and finish they were all, without exception, rugged, reliable, and fast to reload.

Charles Karwan

Courtesy Faintich Auction Services, Inc., Photo Paul Goodwin

Exc.	V.G.	Good	Fair	Poor
500	300	250	175	125

Model 1913-Semiautomatic Pistol

The Model 1913 was the result of years of development in conjunction with the British government and was finally adopted in 1913 as the Model 1913 MK1N for Royal Navy issue. It has the same breech-locking system as the Model 1910, but has an external hammer and is chambered for the .455 Webley self-loading cartridge. About 1,000 Model 1913s were sold commercially and serial numbered along with the smaller caliber pistols. In 1915, a variation of the Model 1913 with butt slotted for a shoulder stock, an adjustable rear sight, and a hammer safety was adopted for use by the Royal Horse Artillery. Shoulder stocks are very rare, and will double values shown for the RHA model. All militaries were numbered in their own series; about 10,000 made in both variations.

Model 1913

Exc.	V.G.	Good	Fair	Poor
1500	1200	800	500	300

Model 1913 (RHA model)

Courtesy Joseph Schroeder

Exc.	V.G.	Good	Fair	Poor
2500	2000	1500	850	600

Webley-Fosbery Model 1914

This is an automatic revolver that is recoil-operated by the barrel-cylinder group sliding across the frame to cock the hammer and revolve the cylinder using the zig-zag grooves in the cylinder. Chambered for the .455 cartridge. Cylinder has a 6-round capacity. Barrel length is 6". Weight is about 30 oz. This sidearm was not officially adopted by British forces but was widely used by them during World War I.

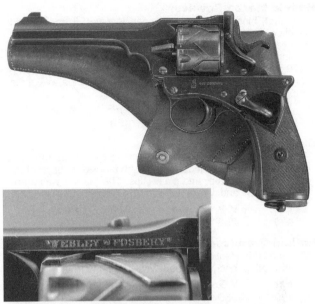

Webley-Fosbery Model 1914 • Courtesy Rock Island Auction Company

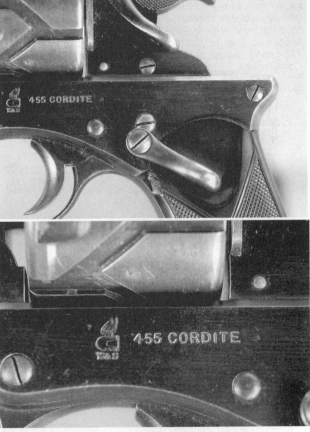

Webley-Fosbery Model 1914 • Courtesy Rock Island Auction Company

Exc.	V.G.	Good	Fair	Poor
4500	3750	2750	1750	1250

ENFIELD ROYAL SMALL ARMS FACTORY

In 1879, the British army needed revolvers, and the Royal Small Arms Factory was commissioned to produce them. The result was that on August 11, 1880, the Enfield Mark 1 was accepted for duty.

Enfield Mark 1 Revolver

A 6-shot, hinged-frame, break-open revolver. It has an odd ejection system—when the barrel is pulled down, the cylinder moves forward; and the extractor plate remains in place, retaining the spent cartridges. This revolver is chambered for the .476 cartridge and has a 6-shot cylinder. The barrel is 6" long, and the finish is blued with checkered walnut grips. Weight is about 40 oz.

Exc.	V.G.	Good	Fair	Poor
400	275	200	150	100

Enfield Mark 2

The Mark 2 is similar externally, with some design improvements—such as a rounded front sight, taper-bored cylinders, an integral top strap, and plain grips. The Mark 2 was introduced in 1881 and was replaced by the Webley Mark I in 1887.

Exc.	V.G.	Good	Fair	Poor
400	250	175	140	100

Enfield-Produced Webley Mark 6

This model is identical to the Webley-produced versions. It is of .455 caliber and is stamped "Enfield" on the frame.

Exc.	V.G.	Good	Fair	Poor
400	250	175	140	100

Enfield No. 2 Mark I/Mark 1*

Originally chambered for the .380 (.38 S&W). It is a 6-shot, break-open double action, with a 5" barrel. The finish is blued, with black plastic checkered grips. This model was actually a modified Webley design and was adopted in 1932. In 1938, the bullet was changed from a 200-grain lead "soft-nosed" to a 178-grain jacketed, in response to pressure from the Geneva Conference.

An Enfield No. 2 MK 1 sold at auction for $460. Condition is 95 percent dull blue.
Rock Island Auction Company, August 2004

Enfield No. 2 Mark 1* • Courtesy West Point Museum, Paul Goodwin photo

Exc.	V.G.	Good	Fair	Poor
350	200	150	125	100

Enfield No. 2 Mark I*

The same as the Mark I with the hammer spur and single action lockwork omitted in response to the Royal Tank Regiment's fear that the spur would catch on the tank as the crews were entering and exiting their confines.

NOTE: During WWII these pistols were also manufactured by Albion Motors Ltd. of Glasgow, Scotland. These pistols were produced between 1941 and 1943, and approximately 24,000 were made. They are marked "Albion" on the right side of the frame. These examples would not be valued differently than Enfield-made pistols. Enfield pistols with the marking "SM" or "SSM" will also be noted, and this refers to various parts produced by Singer Sewing Machine Company of England. These pistols were assembled at Enfield. Used until 1957, when the FN-Browning GP35 semiautomatic pistol replaced them.

Exc.	V.G.	Good	Fair	Poor
350	200	175	150	125

Enfield No. 2 Mark 1 • Paul Goodwin photo

SUBMACHINE GUNS

NOTE: For historical information and technical details see Laider and Howroyd, *The Guns of Dagenham; Lanchester, Patchett, Sterling*, Collector Grade Publications, 1999. Laider, *The Sten Machine Carbine*, Collector Grade Publications, 2000.

Lanchester Mk1/Mk1*

The British submachine gun was produced from 1940 to about 1942. It is chambered for the 9mm cartridge and is fitted with a 7.75" barrel. The magazine capacity is 50 rounds. Rate of fire is 600 rounds per minute. Weight is about 9.5 lbs. This British gun is almost an exact copy of the Bergmann MP28. The magazine housing is made of brass. The bayonet lug will accept a Model 1907 pattern bayonet. Most of these weapons were issued to the Royal Navy and stayed in service there until the 1960s. Markings are "LANCHESTER MARK I" on the magazine housing.

The Mk1* has had the fire selector switch in front of the triggerguard removed thus making the weapon capable of full automatic fire only.

Pre-1968

Exc.	V.G.	Fair
7000	6500	6000

Pre-1986 conversions

Exc.	V.G.	Fair
N/A	N/A	N/A

Pre-1986 dealer samples

Exc.	V.G.	Fair
3500	3000	2500

NOTE: Add a premium of 15 percent for the Mark 1 version.

Sten Mark II

The Mark II is the most common version of the Sten models. It is chambered for the 9mm cartridge and features a removable stock and barrel. The magazine capacity is 32 rounds. Barrel length is 7.66". The rate of fire is 550 rounds per minute. Markings are located on top of the magazine housing and are stamped "STEN MK II." Weight is approximately 6.6 lbs. Produced from 1942 to 1944 with about two million built in Britain, Canada, and New Zealand.

NOTE: The Mark II S is the silenced version of the Mark II. Fitted with a canvas foregrip. Weight is about 7.75 lbs. and rate of fire is about 450 rounds per minute.

Courtesy Richard M. Kumor Sr.

SNAP SHOT
BRITISH LANCHESTER MK1*

At the start of World War II, Great Britain had no submachine guns. An order was placed with the U.S. for 300,000 Thompsons and 249 million rounds of .45 ACP. (Ultimately, only 100,000 Thompsons ever reached England due to shipping losses.) England was in dire straights particularly after their significant equipment loss at Dunkirk. They needed "something" and quick. They had been evaluating the German MP28(II) and basically decided to copy it with a few minor changes. Thus was born the Lanchester Mk1 and the later modified Lanchester Mk1*. The British army grabbed all the Thompsons they could and the Lanchester was issued primarily to Royal Navy landing parties.

The Lanchester, being a copy of the German MP28(II), has all the looks, feel and operation of first-generation submachine guns; well made with full wooden furniture. The first model Mk1 was select fire but the modified Mk1* is full automatic only. Relatively heavy (weighing more than the British .303 service rifle) and bulky with the machined steel receiver, brass magazine housing and wood stock, it easily absorbed the recoil energy of the 9mm cartridge allowing for acceptable recoil control when firing full automatic bursts. A magazine loading tool was provided as magazine capacity is 50 rounds. This is one of the weaknesses of the weapon system. The base plate has a tendency to separate from the magazine body when trying to load all 50 rounds, resulting in the base plate, spring with follower, and rounds scattering in all directions at once. It should be noted that 32-round Sten magazines will also work in the Lanchester.

Firing from an open bolt, the heft and feel of shooting the Lanchester allows multiple shot placement on target with proper trigger control. The rate of fire is approximately 600 rounds per minute. It is a fun gun to shoot recalling the early days of submachine gun development.

Robert G. Segel

Lanchester Mark I* • Courtesy West Point Museum, Paul Goodwin photo

Pre-1968

Exc.	V.G.	Fair
5000	4500	4000

Pre-1986 conversions (or U.S.-manufactured receivers)

Exc.	V.G.	Fair
3000	2500	2500

Pre-1986 dealer samples

Exc.	V.G.	Fair
2500	2000	1000

Sten Mark III

This model was a expeditiously built version of the Marks 1 and 2, and featured a one-piece receiver and barrel jacket of welding tubing with a non-removable barrel. No flash hider. Built at Lines and Long Branch arsenals. All other specifications are the same as the Marks I and II.

Pre-1968

Exc.	V.G.	Fair
5000	4500	4000

Pre-1986 conversions (or U.S.-manufactured receivers)

Exc.	V.G.	Fair
3000	2500	2500

Pre-1986 dealer samples

Exc.	V.G.	Fair
2500	2000	1000

Sten Mark V

This version of the Sten was first produced in 1944. It featured a wooden stock and pistol grip. The barrel could accept a bayonet. Finish was better than standard service of the period. Barrel length was 7.75" and magazine capacity was 32 rounds. Rate of fire was 600 rounds per minute. Weight was increased to 8.6 lbs. over the Mark II. Marked "STEN M.C. MK V" on top of the magazine housing. Production ceased on this version in 1946.

NOTE: The Mark VI is the silenced version of the Mark V. Fitted with a long barrel and silencer assembly. Weight is about 9.8 lbs. and rate of fire is about 450 rounds per minute.

Sten Mark V • Photo courtesy Robert G. Segel

Pre-1968

Exc.	V.G.	Fair
5500	4500	4250

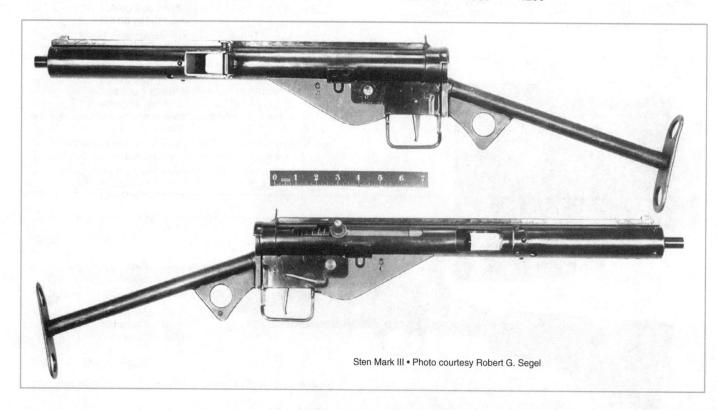

Sten Mark III • Photo courtesy Robert G. Segel

Pre-1986 conversions

Exc.	V.G.	Fair
3500	3000	2500

Pre-1986 dealer samples

Exc.	V.G.	Fair
2500	2000	1500

Sterling Mk 4 (L2A3)

Chambered for the 9mm cartridge this submachine gun features a 7.75" barrel, 34-round side mounted magazine, collapsible metal stock. The last version of the Sterling, the Mk 4, is a result of a long line of improvements to the gun beginning with the Pachett. The Pachett was originally developed during WWII and produced by the Sterling Co. in Dagenham, England and the Royal Ordnance Factory in Fazakerley, England. Next came the Mk 2 and the Mk 3 beginning in 1953 and the Mk 4 during the late 1950s.

It has seen wide use throughout the world having been adopted by the British army, New Zealand and approximately 40 other countries. The rate of fire is 550 rounds per minute. Weight is about 6 lbs. Produced from 1953 to 1988. Still made in India under license. Marked "STERLING SMG 9MM" on the magazine housing.

Photo courtesy private NFA collection

Pre-1968 (Rare)

Exc.	V.G.	Fair
15000	12500	11000

Pre-1986 conversions

Exc.	V.G.	Fair
8000	7000	6000

Pre-1986 dealer samples

Exc.	V.G.	Fair
7500	6000	5500

Sterling L34A1

This is a silenced version of the L2A3 Mark 4 gun. The silencer is fitted with a short wooden forearm. Barrel length is the same as the unlicensed version. Weight is about 8 lbs.

Pre-1968 (Rare)

Exc.	V.G.	Fair
15000	12500	11000

Pre-1986 conversions

Exc.	V.G.	Fair
10000	9000	8000

Pre-1986 dealer samples

Exc.	V.G.	Fair
7500	6000	5500

RIFLES

NOTE: For historical information and technical data see: Reynolds, E.G.B., *The Lee-Enfield Rifle*, Herbert Jenkins, Ltd., 1960. *The Lee-Enfield Story*, Ian Skennerton, 1993. Stevens,

Courtesy Blake Stevens, *The Guns of Dagenham*, Collector Grade Publications.

Blake, *UK and Commonwealth FALs*, Vol. 2, The FAL Series, Collector Grade Publications, 1980. Skennerton has also writen a number of monographs on other British rifles that are well worth study by the collector.

SNIDER

This design was the invention of Jacob Snider, an American from New York. The idea was to convert, in a simple way, muzzle-loading rifles to cartridge-firing-breech loaders. Snider cut away a rear section of the barrel and inserted a breech block with firing pin hinged at the side so that it could be opened and a cartridge inserted. The rifle was fired by an external hammer. Despite extraction problems, this design was used by the British Army, beginning in 1868 in the Ethiopian campaign, for six years and remained in service in second line units into the 1880s. It was the first general issue breech-loader in the British army, and perhaps more important was the parallel development of the Boxer cartridge for use in this rifle. The Boxer cartridge was a .577 caliber with steel rim and rolled heavy paper cartridge case (factory made, see photo below) that held the powder. The bullet was a soft lead.

NOTE: All Snider rifles and carbines are scarce. Examples in excellent condition are rarely encountered.

Bibliographical Note: It is strongly suggested that the reader interested in the myriad of details and variations of the Snider see Ian Skennerton's, *A Treatise On the Snider*, 1977.

Pattern 1 Rifled Musket

Converted Enfield muzzle-loading rifle. Barrel length is 36.5". Brass furniture with flat hammer face. Rear sight marked to 950 yards. Approved 1866.

Exc.	V.G.	Good	Fair	Poor
1500	1200	800	500	300

Pattern 1*

Similar to the Pattern 1 but with a countersunk barrel at the rear of the chamber to accommodate the cartridge rim. The asterisk (*) was marked on top of the receiver to indicate the conversion. Approved in May 1967.

Exc.	V.G.	Good	Fair	Poor
1500	1200	800	500	300

Pattern 2* • Courtesy Rock Island Auction Company

Pattern 2*

Similar to the Pattern I* but it is a direct conversion from the muzzle-loading Enfields and not the Pattern I*. The top of the receiver is marked "Mark II*". Also introduced in May 1867.

Exc.	V.G.	Good	Fair	Poor
1500	1200	800	500	300

Pattern 2**

This conversion is the most-often-encountered conversion. It has the cartridge recess like the earlier conversion, but also has a cupped hammer face, a better shaped extractor, and a larger breech block face. Introduced in May 1867.

Exc.	V.G.	Good	Fair	Poor
1250	1000	650	450	300

Pattern 3

Similar in outward appearance to the earlier conversions but with a flat hammer face and a spring-loaded locking latch on the left side of the breech block. The receiver is marked "III". Introduced in January 1869.

Exc.	V.G.	Good	Fair	Poor
1500	1200	800	500	300

Short Enfield Rifle P60 Mark II**

This conversion used an Enfield Pattern 1860 with the barrel cut to 30.5" from 33". Cupped hammer face. Two barrel bands, a sword bar, and case hardened furniture. Sling swivels on butt and upper barrel band. Sights marked to 400 yards on the rear sight and 1,000 yards on the leaf sight. Top of the receiver marked "II**". Introduced in March of 1867.

Exc.	V.G.	Good	Fair	Poor
1500	1200	800	500	300

Short Enfield Rifle P60 Mark II** Naval Rifle

Similar to the Mark II** army version except that brass furniture is used in place of iron. Some Naval rifles were not fitted with a butt sling swivel. Introduced in August of 1867.

Exc.	V.G.	Good	Fair	Poor
1500	1200	800	500	300

Short Enfield Rifle P60 Mark III

When this conversion was introduced in January of 1869, the steel barrel was also introduced, but a few early examples (about 1,200) were fitted with iron barrels. This rifle was actually a newly manufactured gun instead of a conversion of a muzzleloader. The top of the receiver is marked "III".

Exc.	V.G.	Good	Fair	Poor
1500	1200	800	500	300

Snider Pattern 2** showing views of breech and cartridge • Private collection, Paul Goodwin photo

Mark II** Engineers (Lancaster) Carbine

This is a converted Lancaster rifle with a 29" barrel length, brass furniture, and cupped hammer face. Two barrel bands with sling swivel on upper band. Butt-mounted rear swivel. "LANCASTER'S PATENT" stamped on the barrel. Rear leaf sight marked to 1,150 yards. Introduced in 1867 with about 5,000 rifles converted.

Exc.	V.G.	Good	Fair	Poor
1850	1450	950	600	350

Artillery Carbine P61 Mark II**

Introduced in May of 1867. It has 2 barrel bands, a sword bar, brass buttplate and trigger guard. The hammer face is cupped. The rear sight has a maximum range of 600 yards. Barrel length is 21.5". Receiver is marked "II**". About 60,000 were converted.

Exc.	V.G.	Good	Fair	Poor
1850	1450	950	600	350

Artillery Carbine P61 Mark III

This was a newly manufactured conversion with a spring loaded locking latch on the left side of the breech block. The barrel is steel and is 21.5" long. Brass furniture with flat hammer face. Marked "III" on the top of the action. Introduced in 1869.

Exc.	V.G.	Good	Fair	Poor
1850	1450	950	600	350

Artillery Carbine P61 Mark IV

This rifle uses the Mark III breech and is fitted with a 21.5" barrel. Rear sight graduated to 900 yards. Two barrel bands with the stock coming to within 1.125" of the muzzle. Brass furniture. Introduced in 1891.

Exc.	V.G.	Good	Fair	Poor
1850	1450	950	600	350

Cavalry Carbine P61 Mark II**

This carbine was fitted with a half stock. The butt was fitted with a trap for a 2-piece cleaning rod. Sling bar and ring on left side although some may not have the bar fitted. Brass furniture. Barrel length is 19.25" Rear sight is a ladder type to 600 yards fitted with a leather protector secured by a screw on each side of the stock. A snap cap is secured by a chain screwed into the triggerguard. No sling swivels. Introduced in May of 1867.

Exc.	V.G.	Good	Fair	Poor
1850	1450	950	600	350

Cavalry Carbine Mark III

This is a newly manufactured carbine using the Mark III breech. Only a few early examples used iron barrel, the rest used steel. Brass furniture. Flat hammer face. The stock was newly made. Introduced in January of 1869.

Exc.	V.G.	Good	Fair	Poor
1850	1450	950	600	350

Yeomanry Carbine Mark I

This carbine was converted from Snider long rifles and issued to volunteer cavalry forces. Fitted with a 19.2" barrel. Brass furniture. Flat hammer face. The side nail cups are from the long rifle and made of brass instead of steel. Introduced in July of 1880.

Exc.	V.G.	Good	Fair	Poor
1850	1450	950	600	350

Naval Rifle P58

Approved in August 1867 and fitted with a 30.5" barrel with brass furniture. Many were not fitted with a lower sling swivel. The receiver is marked, "II**" on the top near the barrel. Leaf sight is graduated to 1,000 yards with a ramp step from 100 to 400 yards. About 53,500 of these rifles were produced.

Exc.	V.G.	Good	Fair	Poor
1500	1200	800	500	300

Irish Constabulary Carbine Mark II** P56

This carbine is a conversion of the Enfield Pattern 1856 short rifle. Barrel length is 22.5". Iron furniture. Cupped hammer face. Sword bar. Two barrel bands. Stock stops 1.4" from muzzle. Sling swivels on upper barrel band and butt stock. Brass triggerguard. Stamped "II**" on receiver. Introduced in July of 1867.

Exc.	V.G.	Good	Fair	Poor
1850	1450	950	500	350

Irish Constabulary Carbine Mark III

Similar to the Mark II** but with flat hammer face and spring loaded locking latch on left side of breech block. Fitted with an iron barrel. Rear sight graduated to 900 yards. Introduced in January of 1869.

Exc.	V.G.	Good	Fair	Poor
1850	1450	950	500	300

Convict Civil Guard Carbine P53

This carbine was issued especially for penal service. Rounded forend, two barrel bands, no rear sight or sling swivels. Converted from Pattern 1853 rifle. Stamped II** on breech. Some of these carbines are rifled, while others are smoothbore with choked muzzle for shot cartridges. Introduced September of 1867.

Exc.	V.G.	Good	Fair	Poor
1850	1450	950	600	350

Martini-Henry

This single shot rolling block rifle was built on the Martini block action (a modification of the American Peabody action) and a rifled barrel by Alexander Henry. Early rifles built prior to 1885 used a fragile rolled cartridge case while later post 1885 versions used a solid case. The rifle was chambered for the .577-450 cartridge that used a paper patch bullet. The British army built these rifles with three different buttstock lengths and marked the 1/2" shorter than standard rifles with an "s" on the stock while longer stocks were marked with an "L." Standard length buttstocks were not marked. Martini-Henry rifles and carbines were used by British military forces all over the world during the latter quarter of the 19th century. Produced by Enfield, BSA, and LSA.

**When 'arf of your bullets fly wide in the ditch,
Don't call your Martini a cross-eyed old bitch;
She's human as you are - you treat her as sich,
An' she'll fight for the young British soldier.**

Rudyard Kipling

Martini in action • Courtesy Paul S. Scarlata

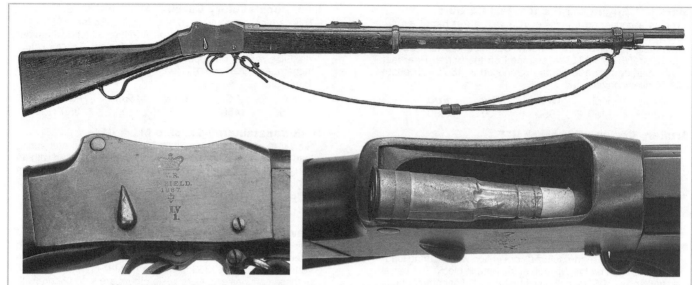

Martini-Henry Mark IV with close up of receiver and open breech with cartridge • Private collection, Paul Goodwin photo

Mark 1 Rifle

Chambered for the .577-450 Martini-Henry cartridge and fitted with a 33.2" barrel, this lever operated single shot rifle was fitted with a steel bayonet and was full stocked with no upper handguard. Weight is about 8.75 lbs. Introduced in 1874.

Courtesy Rock Island Auction Company

Exc.	V.G.	Good	Fair	Poor
1250	900	700	400	250

Mark 2 Rifle

Similar to the Mark 1 but with an improved trigger in 1877.

Exc.	V.G.	Good	Fair	Poor
1250	900	700	500	250

Mark 3 Rifle

An improved version introduced in 1879 of the Mark 2 with double lump barrel and wider breech block. Weight is slightly heavier than the Marks 1 and 2 at about 9 lbs.

Exc.	V.G.	Good	Fair	Poor
1250	900	700	500	250

Mark 4 Rifle

Introduced in 1887, this Mark was fitted with a longer lever, a thinner breech block with modified extractor, narrow buttstock with bayonet fitting to accommodate a P1887 sword bayonet. Weight is about 9.25 lbs.

Exc.	V.G.	Good	Fair	Poor
1250	900	700	500	250

Cavalry Carbine Mark 1

This configuration was introduced in 1877 and is a short version of the rifle with full stock, no handguard, front sight with protectors, and a reduced charge carbine cartridge; the .577-450 Martini-Henry Carbine cartridge. Barrel length is about 21.25". Weight is approximately 7.5 lbs.

Exc.	V.G.	Good	Fair	Poor
1500	1250	950	700	350

Artillery Carbine Mark 2

This model is similar to the Cavalry Carbine but with bayonet fittings. Introduced in 1879. Weight is about 7.7 lbs.

NOTE: Many Martini Henrys were converted to .303 British caliber. These conversions will command about the same price as unconverted rifles.

Exc.	V.G.	Good	Fair	Poor
1500	1250	950	700	350

LEE-METFORD

NOTE: The Lee-Metford rifles were produced at the Royal Small Arms Factory, Enfield; the Birmingham Small Arms Co.; Sparkbrook, Vickers, Birmingham, and the London Small Arms Co., and so marked on the right side under the bolt handle for rifles and on the left side for carbines.

The British used the MARK and * system to denote improvements. The "MARK" indicated a major design change or improvement. The "*" indicated a minor change.

TRIALS RIFLES

The first trials for magazine rifles for the British army began in 1880. There were a number of initial contenders which will not be covered here. By 1883, the number of serious competitors was reduced to those listed below.

Owen Jones

This model was an adaptation of the Martini action and fitted with a 33" barrel chambered for the .402 caliber Enfield-Martini cartridge. Five-round magazine. Folding rear sight graduated to 2,000 yards. Weight is about 10.5 lbs. An unknown number of these rifles were built with different type magazine feeds and styles.

Exc.	V.G.	Good	Fair	Poor
5500	4750	4000	2500	—

Lee-Burton

This rifle used the Lee action, the first British rifle to do so. Chambered for the .402 caliber Enfield-Martini cartridge and fitted with a 30.2" barrel. Built by Enfield. Magazine capacity is 5 rounds. Marked "ENFIELD 1886" of left side of the receiver. Weight is about 10 lbs. About 300 were produced.

Exc.	V.G.	Good	Fair	Poor
5500	4750	4000	2500	—

Improved Lee

These rifles were purchased directly from Remington in 1887. Chambered for the .43 caliber Spanish cartridge and fitted with a 32" barrel. Folding leaf rear sight was graduated to 1,200 yards. Magazine capacity was 5 rounds. Weighs approximate-

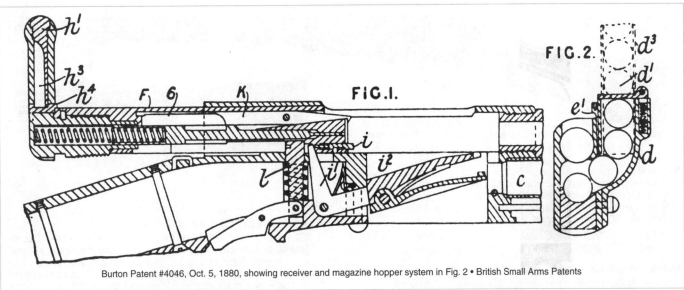

Burton Patent #4046, Oct. 5, 1880, showing receiver and magazine hopper system in Fig. 2 • British Small Arms Patents

ly 10 lbs. Marked with the Remington address on the receiver. About 300 were used in the trials. The only indication that this is a trials rifle is the marking "WD" on the right side of the butt.

Exc.	V.G.	Good	Fair	Poor
3750	3000	2500	1500	—

.303 Magazine Rifle-1888 Trials Model

Developed from the Improved Lee but chambered for the .303 cartridge and fitted with a 30.2" barrel. No upper handguard. Magazine capacity is 7 rounds. Marked, "ENFIELD 1888." Weight is about 9 lbs. Some 387 of these rifles were produced.

Exc.	V.G.	Good	Fair	Poor
4500	3750	3000	1750	—

Mark I

A bolt action service rifle chambered for the .303 black powder British cartridge. It was designed by James Paris Lee and incorporated rifling developed by William Metford. This rifling was specifically designed to alleviate the problem of black powder fouling. 30.2" barrel and an 8-round, detachable box magazine located in front of the triggerguard. Furnished with magazine cutoff, it features military-type sights and a cleaning rod mounted underneath the barrel and a trap in the steel buttplate to house cleaning tools. Finger grooves in forend. The finish is blued, with a full-length walnut stock held on by two barrel bands. Weight is about 10 lbs. It was introduced in 1888. Approximately 358,000 were produced.

Exc.	V.G.	Good	Fair	Poor
600	450	300	200	100

Mark I*

Similar to the Mark 1 except that the safety catch was removed from the cocking piece and a brass disc was inletted into the buttstock for regimental markings. There were a number of internal improvements, as well as the fitting of a different, blade-type front sight and V-notch rear sight graduated to 1,800 yards. This model was fitted with an 8-round magazine. It was introduced in 1892.

Exc.	V.G.	Good	Fair	Poor
600	450	300	200	100

Mark II

Has a modified magazine that holds 10 rounds in a double column. A half-length cleaning rod was located under the 30.2" barrel. No finger grooves in forend. Fitted with brass buttplate with long heel tang. Rear leaf sight graduated to 1,800 yards. No butt marking disk. It was introduced in 1892. Weight reduced to 9.25 lbs. About 250,000 were produced.

Exc.	V.G.	Good	Fair	Poor
600	450	300	200	100

Lee-Metford Mark 1* • Paul Goodwin photo

Mark 1 RIC Carbine with close-up of unique muzzle
modification • Private collection, Paul Goodwin photo

Mark II*

Has a lengthened bolt, with the addition of a safety catch. Barrel length is 30.2". No finger grooves in forend. All parts are interchangeable with the Mark II rifle. It was introduced in 1895. About 13,000 were produced.

Exc.	V.G.	Good	Fair	Poor
550	400	300	200	100

Mark I Carbine

Has a 20.75" barrel. Rear sight is graduated to 2,000 yards. Buttstock is fitted with a marking disk. No bayonet fittings. Weight was about 7.5 lbs. It was introduced in 1894. Approximately 18,000 were produced.

NOTE: Many Lee-Metford rifles were modified after 1902 to accept a stripper clip guide which required the removal of the dust cover. Such modification results in a deduction of 10 percent from original Lee-Metford rifles.

Exc.	V.G.	Good	Fair	Poor
850	700	500	300	150

ENFIELD ROYAL SMALL ARMS FACTORY

NOTE: This series of rifles is marked by the presence of deeper Enfield rifling rather than the shallow Metford rifling. The same manufacturers that built the Lee-Metford built the Lee-Enfield along with Ishapore, India, and Lithgow, Australia.

Lee-Enfield Rifle • Courtesy Paul S. Scarlata

Lee-Enfield Mark I Rifle

Chambered for the .303 cartridge and has a 30" barrel. The attached box magazine holds 10 rounds, and the sights are military-styled. Rear leaf sight graduated to 1,800 yards. The stock is full-length walnut, and there is a cleaning rod beneath it. There is a magazine cutoff located on the right side of the receiver. There are two barrel bands and a bayonet lug. The upper handguard extended from the receiver ring to the rear sight. The buttplate is brass with extended upper tang with trap for cleaning equipment. Weight is about 9.25 lbs. This model was manufactured between 1895 and 1899. Approximately 315,000 were manufactured.

Paul Goodwin photo

Exc.	V.G.	Good	Fair	Poor
900	750	600	400	200

Lee-Enfield Mark I* Rifle

No attached cleaning rod, otherwise the same as the Mark I rifle. It was introduced in 1899. Almost 600,000 of these rifles were produced.

Exc.	V.G.	Good	Fair	Poor
900	750	600	400	200

NOTE: Many long Lee-Enfield rifles were modified for charger loading (stripper clip). Prices are 10 percent less than unmodified rifles.

Lee-Enfield Mark I Carbine

This model is the same as the Lee-Metford except for the Enfield rifling and so marked. Slight different rear sight marked "EC" on bottom right hand corner of leaf. Introduced in 1896. Rear sight leather protector is standard on this carbine. Weight is about 7.5 lbs. Approximately 14,000 were produced.

Exc.	V.G.	Good	Fair	Poor
850	700	500	300	150

Lee-Enfield Mark I* Carbine

Same as the Mark I carbine but with no cleaning rod and no left side sling bar. Rear sight leather protector. Introduced in 1899. A little more than 26,000 were produced.

Exc.	V.G.	Good	Fair	Poor
850	700	500	300	150

Lee-Enfield Mark I RIC Carbine

This model was converted from Lee-Enfield carbines and was fitted with a bayonet lug for a Pattern 1888 bayonet. This required a collar to be added at the muzzle to increase the barrel diameter to accept the bayonet ring. It was first converted in 1905 for the Royal Irish Constabulary. About 11,000 were converted.

Exc.	V.G.	Good	Fair	Poor
500	400	250	100	75

Mark II • Courtesy West Point Museum, Paul Goodwin photo

No. 1 SMLE SERIES

The SMLEs were not designated No. 1s until the British changed their rifle nomenclature system in 1926. Guns made prior to that date were marked "SMLE," not No. 1.

SMLE Trials Rifle

About 1,000 of these rifles were built for trials in 1902. Fitted with a full-length handguard and a charger loading system. Barrel length is 25.2" with a .303 chamber. Sheet metal buttplate. Weight is about 8 lbs. A number of different features appeared on this rifle that were later incorporated into the regular production SMLE. Most of these rifles were converted to Aiming Tube Short Rifles in 1906 and are extremely rare.

Exc.	V.G.	Good	Fair	Poor
1500	1150	800	500	200

No. 1 SMLE Mark I

Introduced in 1902 this was the first of the "Short, Magazine Lee-Enfield" or No. 1 series of rifles. It was fitted with a full stock with pistol grip and a 25.2" barrel. It also had a full upper handguard. Rear sight is leaf-type graduated to 2,000 yards. The bayonet mountings are integral with the nosecap. Magazine capacity was 10 rounds. Magazine cutoff on right side of receiver. Weight was about 8 lbs. A little more than 360,000 of these rifles were produced.

Exc.	V.G.	Good	Fair	Poor
750	600	400	300	150

No. 1 SMLE Mark I*

A minor modification of the SMLE Mark I. Introduced in 1906. Fitted with a buttplate trap and a new style butt sling swivel. About 60,000 of these rifles were produced.

Exc.	V.G.	Good	Fair	Poor
650	550	400	250	100

No. 1 SMLE Mark II

The Mark I and II Long Lee converted by fitting a shorter and lighter barrel (25.2"), modifying the action to accept a stripper clip, and fitting new sights. It was introduced in 1903. Approximately 40,000 Mark IIs were manufactured.

Exc.	V.G.	Good	Fair	Poor
250	200	175	150	100

No. 1 SMLE Mark II*

A modification of the Mark II SMLE to add features from the SMLE Mark III so that it would correspond with that model. Introduced in 1908. About 22,000 were converted.

Exc.	V.G.	Good	Fair	Poor
250	200	175	150	100

No. 1 SMLE Mark III

Chambered for .303 British and has a 25.2" barrel with a 10-round magazine. The magazine has a cutoff, and the sights are military-styled with volley sights on the left side and open sights at top rear. The action is modified to accept a stripper clip and automatically eject it when the bolt is closed. Weight is approximately 8.5 lbs. This model was introduced in 1907. The Mark III was one of the more successful and famous British military rifles. It was used extensively in World War I and World War II. In many areas of the old British Commonwealth it is still used today. Almost 7,000,000 of these were produced.

Courtesy Richard M. Kumor Sr.

Exc.	V.G.	Good	Fair	Poor
200	150	100	60	30

NOTE: Add 30 percent for non-imported models.

No. 1 Mark III* • Courtesy West Point Museum, Paul Goodwin photo

No. 1 rifle (World War II version) with grenade launcher
• Courtesy private collection, Paul Goodwin photo

No. 1 Mark III and Mark III* Drill Rifles

These rifles were modified for drill use and stamped "DP." They feature a firing pin with no tip and on occasion a bolt head with the firing pin hole welded closed.

Exc.	V.G.	Good	Fair	Poor
100	50	40	30	15

No. 1 Mark III Single Shot Rifles

Converted to single shot at Ishapore, India, and have magazine well filled. Intended for use with "unreliable" Indian troops.

Exc.	V.G.	Good	Fair	Poor
150	100	85	60	30

No. 1 Mark III and Mark III* Grenade Launching Rifles

Built on the standard Mk III and Mk III* rifles with the addition of a wire wrapping on the front of the barrel. These rifles are usually marked "E.Y." to indicate only ball ammunition be used in an emergency. A cup-type grenade launcher was fitted.

Exc.	V.G.	Good	Fair	Poor
200	125	100	70	40

NOTE: For rifles without launcher deduct $50.

Lee-Enfield .410 Musket

Built around the No. 1 Mark III rifle and converted in Ishapore, India to a single shot .410 shotgun. Intended for guard duty. The rifle fired a special .303 case that was not necked down. This model, if in original configuration, will not accept a modern .410 shotshell. Those rifles that have been altered to accept modern .410 shells will be worth less.

.410 Musket with close-up of wood-filled magazine • Private collection, Paul Goodwin photo

Exc.	V.G.	Good	Fair	Poor
120	75	50	40	20

No. 1 SMLE Mark IV

This model was Lee-Metford and Lee-Enfield rifles converted to Mark III configuration. The receiver was modified for a charger bridge and safety catch. The dust cover lugs were also removed from the bolt. Adopted in 1907. Almost 100,000 of these rifles were converted.

Exc.	V.G.	Good	Fair	Poor
225	125	100	75	50

Rifle Charger Loading Long Lee-Enfield Mark I/I*

These are converted Lee-Enfield rifles adapted to charger loading. Many of these rifles were used in the early days of World War I by the British Royal Navy. Over 180,000 of these rifles were produced.

Exc.	V.G.	Good	Fair	Poor
800	700	550	300	150

No. 1 SMLE Mark III*

This variation does not have a magazine cutoff, the rear sight windage adjustment, left side auxiliary long range sights, a center swivel lug, or a brass buttstock marking disc. Over 2

No. 1 SMLE Mark I • Paul Goodwin photo

million of this model were made during World War I. It was last built in England in 1944 by B.S.A. This model was also manufactured in India at Ishapore until 1964, and in Australia at Lithgow through the 1950s, and are so marked. Weight is about 9 lbs.

Exc.	V.G.	Good	Fair	Poor
225	125	95	75	50

NOTE: For rifles built in Australia add 20 percent; for rifles built in India deduct 20 percent.

No. 1 SMLE Mark III* H

Built only at Lithgow arsenal in Australia and features a heavier barrel marked with an "H" near the receiver.

Exc.	V.G.	Good	Fair	Poor
400	300	200	150	100

No. 1 SMLE Mark V

Similar to the Mark III except for the use of a receiver mounted wide aperture rear sight. The folding sight is graduated from 200 yards to 1,400 yards with even number on the right side and odd on the left. Serial numbers range from 1 to 9999, then an "A" prefix was used. The standard pattern 1907 sword bayonet was issued with the rifle. Between 1922 and 1924 only 20,000 were produced. A scarce model.

Courtesy Richard M. Kumor Sr.

Close-up of Mark V rear sight • Courtesy Richard M. Kumor Sr.

Exc.	V.G.	Good	Fair	Poor
650	550	350	—	—

No. 1 SMLE Mark VI

This model had the rear sight located on the receiver bridge. It also used a heavier barrel, lighter nose cap, and smaller bolt head than previous models. It did have the magazine cutoff. Checkered forend. There were three variants of this rifle: Pattern A introduced in 1926, Pattern B introduced in 1929 to 1931 and Pattern C introduced in 1935. About 1,000 trials rifles were built in Pattern B.

Exc.	V.G.	Good	Fair	Poor
4000	2750	1750	—	—

NO. 4 SERIES

Rifle No. 4 Mark 1 Trials Model

Introduced in 1931 with about 2,500 being produced. This is a No. 1 Mark VI with the exception of the shape of the action, and designation markings. Some had no markings at all. Many were later converted to No. 4 Mark I (T) sniper rifles. Markings are commonly found on the right side of the butt socket.

Exc.	V.G.	Good	Fair	Poor
2500	1750	1100	—	—

Rifle No. 4 Mark I

An improved version of the No. 1 Mark VI that featured a stronger action with an aperture sight. It was issued in 1931. It was redesigned in 1939 for mass production with shortcuts taken for wartime production. Barrel length is 25.2" with 10-round magazine. The barrel diameter is larger than the SMLE series and extended almost 3" out of the forend. Weight is about 8.75 lbs. This model was used extensively during WWII. It is still in use today. About 2 million of these rifles were produced but none were built at Enfield. Instead they were built at Longbranch in Canada and Savage-Stevens.

No. 4 Mark 1 with U.S. property stamp, made by Stevens • Courtesy Rock Island Auction Company

Exc.	V.G.	Good	Fair	Poor
350	250	150	100	50

NOTE: Add 30 percent for non-imports.

Rifle No. 4 Mark I*

This model was almost identical to the No. 4 Mark I, but was produced in North America during WWII. The principal U.S. producer was Savage-Stevens (marked U.S. PROPERTY); in Canada marked "LONG BRANCH." The Savage-Stevens guns have a "C" in the serial number for Chicoppe Falls and guns with "L" serial numbers were produced at Longbranch. This model differed from the Mark 1 in that the bolt-head catch was eliminated and a cut-out on the bolt head track was used for its removal. Over 2 million were produced during the war.

Exc.	V.G.	Good	Fair	Poor
300	200	100	75	50

No. 4 Enfield in Korea • Courtesy Paul S. Scarlata

Rifle No. 4 Mark 2

This model was fitted with a trigger that was pinned to the receiver rather than the triggerguard. Introduced in 1949. This rifle had a higher quality finish than its wartime predecessors.

Courtesy Rock Island Auction Company

Exc.	V.G.	Good	Fair	Poor
300	175	125	80	50

Rifle No. 4 Mark 1/2 (converted No. 4 Mark I) & No. 4 Mark 1/3 (converted No. 4 Mark I*)

These models have new trigger mechanism installed to more closely emulate the Mark 2 and upgraded components. The conversion required altering the old markings. This was done with an electric pencil instead of a stamp. The result is quite obvious.

Exc.	V.G.	Good	Fair	Poor
250	150	100	75	50

JUNGLE CARBINES

No. 1 Shortened & Lightened Rifle

Fitted with a 20" barrel and a shortened forend. The rear aperture sight is mounted on the charger bridge and graduated for 200 and 500 yards. Fitted for a blade bayonet. Weight is about 8.75 lbs. About 32 of these rifles were built at Lithgow. The serial number has an "XP" prefix.

NOTE: Extremely rare. Beware of fakes. Seek expert advice prior to a sale.

Exc.	V.G.	Good	Fair	Poor
N/A	—	—	—	—

Rifle No. 6 Mark I & Mark I/I (AUST)

This model was essentially a trials rifle built in Australia at Lithgow. Similar to the No. 5 but with a No. 1 receiver. Metal components have been milled for lightening. Barrel length is 20.5" with flash hider. The Mark I differs from the Mark I/I in rear sight. Rear sight is open and graduated to 2,000 yards on the Mark I and the Mark I/I uses an aperture sight graduated from 200 to 800 yards. Both models have serial numbers with an "XP" prefix. Each model has two variations of buttplates: one standard brass and the other composition padded with hinges at bottom for trap access.

NOTE: Beware of fakes. Seek expert advice prior to a sale.

Exc.	V.G.	Good	Fair	Poor
2750	2000	1000	—	—

Rifle No. 5 Mark 1

Also known as the "Jungle Carbine." It is chambered for the .303 British cartridge and has a 20.5" barrel with an attached flash suppressor and a shorter forend and handguard. It is furnished with a rubber buttpad and modified rear sight graduated to 800 yards. This was not a popular weapon with the soldiers who carried it, as the recoil was excessive due to the lighter weight. Weight is approximately 7 lbs. About 250,000 were built. This model has its own distinctive knife bayonet.

Courtesy Richard M. Kumor Sr.

Exc.	V.G.	Good	Fair	Poor
500	400	300	175	125

SNIPER RIFLES

NOTE: For Canadian built No. 4 Mk1 T rifles see *Canada, Rifles.*

SMLE Sniper (Optical Sights)

These rifles are Mark III and Mark III* mounted with optical sights. These sights are comprised of a special front and rear sight that when used together form a telescope with a magnification of 2 to 3 power. About 13,000 of these rifles were fitted with these optical sights. Three different optical makers were used with Lattey being the largest. Conversions were performed by unit armorers beginning in 1915.

NOTE: Beware of fakes. Seek expert advice prior to a sale.

Exc.	V.G.	Good	Fair	Poor
3500	3000	2000	—	—

SMLE Sniper (Telescope Sights)

As above, but fitted with conventional telescope sights made by Periscope, Aldis, Winchester, and others. A total of about 9,700 of these rifles were fitted with telescope sights using Mark III and Mark III* rifles during World War I.

NOTE: Beware of fakes. Seek expert advice prior to a sale.

Exc.	V.G.	Good	Fair	Poor
3500	3000	2000	—	—

No. 1 Mark III* H.T. (Australian) Sniper

Introduced toward the end of World War II, this rifle used mostly rebuilt Mark III actions dating to between 1915 and 1918. Fitted with both high and low mounts. The standard bracket telescope tube is marked, "SIGHT TELESCOPE PATT 1918 (AUS)." These rifles are fitted with a heavy barrel. Only about 1,500 of these rifles were converted.

SCOPE NOTE: The No. 32 (Marks 1-3) scope was the most commonly used on British-made guns. The No. 32 and the Alaskan are not the same scope. About 100 Lyman Alaskan scopes were fitted to Longbranch No. 4 Mark 1*(T) rifles in 1944-1945. In addition to the British-made scopes, R.E.I. Ltd. in Canada made its own version of the No. 32 and these are usually found on Longbranch guns. The No. 67 scope, used on about 100 Longbranch (T)s was made by R.E.I. and differs from the design of the No. 32.

Exc.	V.G.	Good	Fair	Poor
3000	2500	1500	—	—

Rifle No. 4 Mark I (T) & Mark I* (T)

These are sniper versions of the No. 4 Mark I and the Mark1*. Fitted with scope mounts on the left side of the receiver and a wooden cheekpiece screwed to the buttstock. A No. 32 or a No. 67 (Canadian) telescope was issued with these rifles. Many of these rifles were converted by Holland & Holland. About 25,000 rifles using various telescopes were converted.

No. 4 Mark I (T) on top and Standard No. 4 Mark I at bottom • Courtesy Chuck Karwan

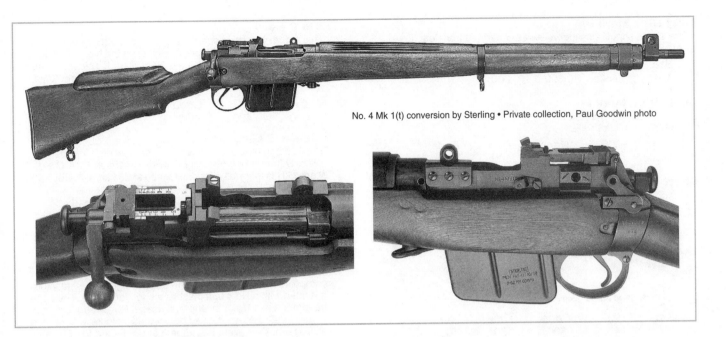

No. 4 Mk 1(t) conversion by Sterling • Private collection, Paul Goodwin photo

No.4 Mark I (T) close-up of action and scope • Courtesy Chuck Karwan

Exc.	V.G.	Good	Fair	Poor
1500	1150	700	500	350

NOTE: Prices listed are for rifles in original wood case and scope numbered to the rifle. For rifles without case deduct 10 percent. A subvariation of this model has no scope fitted to the rifle and is not stamped with a "T" on the butt.

L42A1

Introduced in 1970, this rifle is a converted No. 4 (T) chambered for the 7.62mm cartridge. Half stocked with upper handguard with 27.6" heavy barrel. A converted No. 32 Mark 3 scope is used marked, "TEL. STRT. STG. L1A1." Weight is about 12.5 lbs. Some 10,000 were converted at Enfield.

Exc.	V.G.	Good	Fair	Poor
2500	2000	1500	700	350

NOTE: Prices listed are for rifles with original wood case.

LEE-ENFIELD .22 CALIBER RIFLES

Short Rifle Mark I

This single shot .22 caliber model is converted from the Lee-Metford Mark I* rifle but with a 25" barrel. Introduced in 1907.

Exc.	V.G.	Good	Fair	Poor
650	450	300	200	100

- -

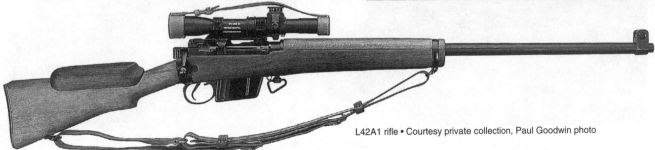

L42A1 rifle • Courtesy private collection, Paul Goodwin photo

Long Rifle Mark II

This single shot .22 caliber rifle was converted from long Lee-Enfield rifles. Adopted in 1912.

Exc.	V.G.	Good	Fair	Poor
650	450	300	200	100

Short Rifle Mark I*

This .22 caliber single shot conversion is modified from the Lee-Metford Mark I* rifle.

Exc.	V.G.	Good	Fair	Poor
1200	950	700	500	200

Short Rifle Mark III

This .22 caliber conversion is from the SMLE Mark II and Mark II*. Adopted in 1912.

Courtesy Rock Island Auction Company

Exc.	V.G.	Good	Fair	Poor
500	400	300	150	100

Rifle No. 2 Mark IV

This model uses converted SMLEs. Some of these conversions are fitted with new .22 caliber barrels and others use .303 barrels with .22 caliber bore liners. These rifles have special bolt heads. Weight is about 9 lbs.

Courtesy Rock Island Auction Company

Exc.	V.G.	Good	Fair	Poor
450	350	250	150	100

Rifle No. 2 Mark IV*

A subvariation of Rifle No. 2 Mark IV.

Exc.	V.G.	Good	Fair	Poor
450	350	250	150	100

Rifle C No. 7

This model was developed at the Long Branch Canadian arsenal. It is a single shot .22 caliber version of the No. 4. Canadian nomenclature is "Rifle C" No. 7 .22 in Mark I. This model was also made by B.S.A. with a 5-round magazine. About 20,000 were produced.

Exc.	V.G.	Good	Fair	Poor
500	400	300	175	125

Rifle No. 7 Mark 1

This is a conversion of the No. 4, not a new rifle. Introduced in 1948. Different bolt from the Canadian version Rifle C No. 7 Mark 1. This rifle was intended for use at 25 yards. About 2,500 were built at BSA.

Exc.	V.G.	Good	Fair	Poor
500	400	300	175	125

NOTE: Be aware that A.G. Parker built a commercial version of this rifle. For those models deduct $100.

No. 5 Trials Rifle

This rifle was the forerunner of the No. 8. It was designed as a competition small bore rifle with special sights and half stock. It is fitted with a No.4 butt that has a checkered grip. The upper handguard is a No. 5 in length. It uses a No. 1 magazine converted to .22 caliber. It could be used as a single shot or magazine feed. Rear sight is micrometer graduated to 100 yards. Target tunnel front sight. Barrel length is 19". Weight is about 8.5 lbs. About 100 of these rifles were built.

Exc.	V.G.	Good	Fair	Poor
1250	900	650	—	—

Rifle No. 8 Mark 1

This rifle was adopted in 1950. This is a single shot rifle with 24" barrel fitted with a rear peep sight. Half stocked with three sling swivels, the middle one is attached in front of the trigger-guard. Weight is 9 lbs. Approximately 17,000 of these rifles were produced.

No. 8 Mark 1 rifle • Private collection, Paul Goodwin photo

Exc.	V.G.	Good	Fair	Poor
700	550	300	200	100

No. 7 Mark 1 with close-up views of receiver • Private collection, Paul Goodwin photo

L39A1 rifle • Courtesy private collection, Paul Goodwin photo

Rifle No. 9 Mark 1

This .22 caliber single shot conversion was done by Parker Hale using No. 4 rifles. Main differences are the bolt, barrel, magazine, and rear sight. The magazine is an empty case without spring or follower. Weight is about 9.25 lbs. The conversion was done between 1956 and 1960. About 3,000 of these rifles were converted for the Royal Navy.

Exc.	V.G.	Good	Fair	Poor
700	550	300	200	100

7.62x51mm CONVERSIONS & MANUFACTURE

NOTE: The NATO cartridge 7.62x51mm was agreed upon by NATO in December of 1953. Conversions began soon after.

L8 Series

This series consists of converted No. 4 rifles from .303 to 7.62mm. Conversions involved a new barrel, and a new magazine stamped, "CR12A." The old receiver marks were eliminated and new ones using an electric pencil were substituted. Some rear sights graduated to 1,300 *meters*, and other graduated to 1,000 *meters*. Series conversions are as follows:

L8A1 converted from No. 4 MK 2
L8A2 converted from No. 4 MK 1/2
L8A3 converted from No. 4 MK 1/3
L8A4 converted from No. 4 MK I
L8A5 converted from No. 4 MK I*

Exc.	V.G.	Good	Fair	Poor
900	700	450	300	150

L39A1

This conversion uses a No. 4 Mark 2 action and is similar to a L42A1 sniper rifle without the scope. Fitted with target-type front and rear sights. Half stocked. Weight is about 10 lbs.

Exc.	V.G.	Good	Fair	Poor
1500	1100	750	400	200

NOTE: For 7.62 NATO magazine add $75. For English match sights by Parker Hale add $125.

L42A1

See *Sniper Rifles.*

Rifle 7.62mm 2A and 2A1 (India)

This rifle is based on a No. 1 Mark III* rifle utilizing newly made receivers of stronger steel to handle the higher .308 pressures. The Indians referred to it as "EN" steel. New rear sight graduated to 800 meters. New detachable box magazine with 10-

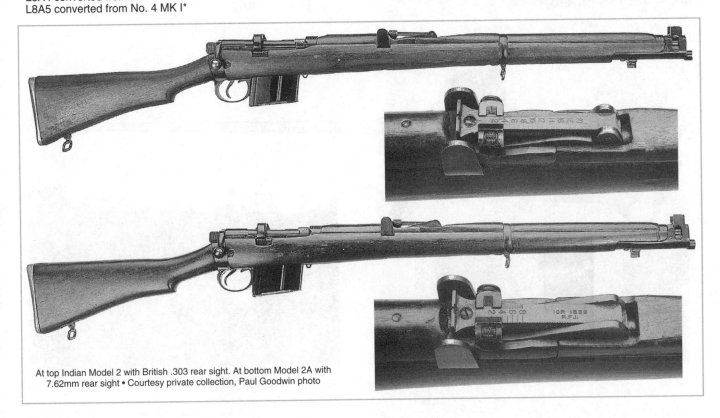

At top Indian Model 2 with British .303 rear sight. At bottom Model 2A with 7.62mm rear sight • Courtesy private collection, Paul Goodwin photo

round capacity. The buttplate is cast alloy. Manufactured in India at Ishapore. Weight is about 9.5 lbs. Most imported rifles are in the 2A1 configuration.

Exc.	V.G.	Good	Fair	Poor
250	125	50	30	15

ENFIELD FENCING MUSKETS

These are not firearms but rather fabricated or converted rifles made to look and feel like the real thing. They were used for bayonet practice and drilling practice. There are a large number of variations, at least 17, and to cover each is beyond the scope of this book. The prices listed below only represent a possible range of prices. Some rifles were later converted to fencing muskets.

Exc.	V.G.	Good	Fair	Poor
200	100	75	50	20

OTHER BRITISH RIFLES

Boys Anti-Tank Rifle

Developed in the 1930s, this rifle was chambered for the .55 caliber armor piercing cartridge. It was fitted with a 36" barrel with muzzle brake. It had a detachable 5-round box magazine. Weight was approximately 36 lbs. Available in two versions: a long barrel (36") and a short barrel airborne model. Not used much after 1940 due to inability to penetrate modern armor. Some of these rifles were used by the U.S. Marine Corp. in the Pacific during World War II.

NOTE: The Boys Rifle is listed as a destructive device by the ATF and is therefore subject to all NFA rules.

Exc.	V.G.	Good	Fair	Poor
4000	3000	2500	2000	1000

No. 3 Mark I (Pattern 14)

Built on a modified Mauser-type action and was chambered for the .303 British cartridge. It is fitted with a 26" barrel and 5-round magazine. It was a secondary-issue arm during WWI and was simpler to mass-produce than the SMLE. These rifles were produced in the U.S.A. by Remington and Winchester. There are a number of marks for this model divided between Remington, Eddystone, and Winchester.

The Mark IE was built at Remington Arms at Eddystone, Pennsylvania. The Mark IR were built at Remington Arms in Ilion, New York.

The Mark IW was built at Winchester Repeating Arms in New Haven, Connecticut.

Exc.	V.G.	Good	Fair	Poor
500	300	150	100	75

No. 3 Mark I* Pattern 14W(F) (T)

This is a No. 3 Mark I that has been converted to a sniper configuration. These rifles were built by Winchester during World War I. The (F) model has a long range aperture and dial sight along with the scope. On the (T) model the long range sights were removed. It is estimated that about 1,500 of these rifles were built. A rare rifle. Caution should be used prior to a sale.

Courtesy Richard M. Kumor Sr.

Close-up of sniper scope and mount • Courtesy Richard M. Kumor Sr.

Exc.	V.G.	Good	Fair	Poor
5000	4500	3500	—	—

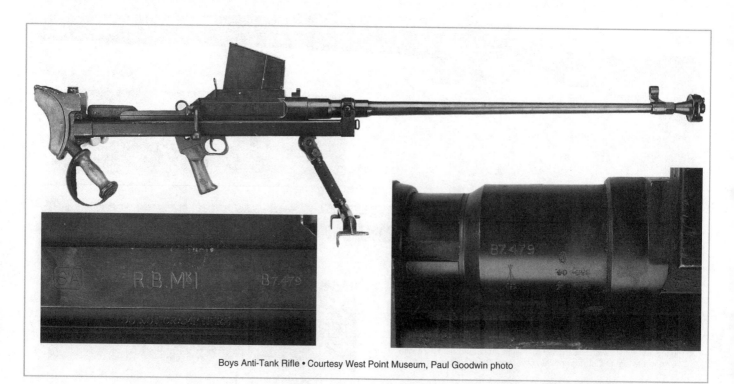

Boys Anti-Tank Rifle • Courtesy West Point Museum, Paul Goodwin photo

No. 3 Mark I • Courtesy West Point Museum, Paul Goodwin photo

STERLING

De Lisle Carbine

This rifle is built on a Lee-Enfield action with a .45 ACP caliber barrel fitted inside a large suppressor tube. Barrel length is 8.25". Magazine capacity is 8 rounds using a Colt Model 1911 magazine. Weight is about 7.5 lbs. About 100 to 150 of these rifles were built by Sterling during World War II for use in special operations. Most were destroyed after the war. All NFA rules apply to the purchase of these weapons. Rare.

Exc.	V.G.	Good	Fair	Poor
—	8000	6000	—	—

L1A1 Rifle

This is the British version of the FN-FAL in the "INCH" or Imperial pattern. Most of these rifles were semiautomatic only. This rifle was the standard service rifle for the British army from about 1954 to 1988. The rifle was made in Great Britain under license from FN. The configurations for the L1A1 rifle is the same as the standard FN-FAL Belgium rifle. Only a few of these rifles were imported into the U.S. They are very rare. This "inch" pattern British gun will also be found in other Commonwealth countries such as Australia, New Zealand, Canada, and India.

There are a number of U.S. companies that build or import L1A1 rifles, (imported rifles are in a sporter configuration) but these have no collector value. Rifles built with military surplus parts and U.S.-made receivers also have no collector value as of yet.

Exc.	V.G.	Good	Fair	Poor
—	6000	5000	—	—

NOTE: The only known pre-1986 L1A1 rifles imported into the U.S. are Australian and Canadian. See that country for prices. See also *Canada* for its C1 and C2 versions of the FN FAL.

ACCURACY INTERNATIONAL

Founded in 1980 by Malcom and Sarah Cooper, they designed sniper rifles which were later adopted by the British Army as the L96A1. This English company, located in Portsmouth, provides its rifles to military forces in over 43 countries, and these models have been used in Northern Ireland, Sri Lanka, Somalia, Bosnia, Rwanda, and in Desert Storm. Most of these rifles are currently NATO codified.

Model AE

Chambered for the 7.62x51 cartridge and fitted with a 24" heavy barrel. Stock is a black synthetic. Magazine capacity is 5 rounds. Weight is approximately 13.25 lbs.

Exc.	V.G.	Good	Fair	Poor
2500	—	—	—	—

Model AW

Chambered for the 5.56 NATO cartridge and the 7.62x51 NATO cartridge, this bolt action rifle is fitted with a 26" heavy match grade barrel with muzzle brake. Magazine capacity is 8 rounds for the 5.56 and 10 rounds for the 7.62x51. Olive green or black stock with adjustable buttstock. Optional bipod, scope, and other accessories can be included in a complete kit. Prices below are for rifle only. Weight is about 14.25 lbs.

FN-FAL L1A1 Rifle • Paul Goodwin photo

Exc.	V.G.	Good	Fair	Poor
4700	—	—	—	—

Model AWP

Similar to the Model AW but with black stock and metal and 24" barrel. Offered in .243 and .308 calibers. Weight is about 14 lbs.

Exc.	V.G.	Good	Fair	Poor
4400	—	—	—	—

Model AWS

A suppressed version of the AW model. Weight is about 13 lbs.

Exc.	V.G.	Good	Fair	Poor
N/A	—	—	—	—

Model AWM

Similar to the Model AW but chambered for the .300 Winchester Magnum or .338 Lapua Magnum cartridge. Fitted with a 26" barrel with muzzle brake. Magazine capacity is 5 rounds. Weight is about 15.5 lbs.

Exc.	V.G.	Good	Fair	Poor
5000	—	—	—	—

Model AW 50

Chambered for the .50 caliber Browning cartridge. Barrel length is 27" with muzzle brake. Magazine capacity is 5 rounds. Weight is about 33 lbs. Supplied with metal case, spare magazine, carry handle, sling, and tool kit.

Exc.	V.G.	Good	Fair	Poor
10925	—	—	—	—

PARKER-HALE

Founded in Birmingham, England in 1890, this firm converted Lee-Enfield rifles into sporting guns. During World War II it manufactured military ammunition and repaired service rifles. In 1992, the company was sold to Navy Arms who then established a subsidiary called Gibbs Rifle Co. to produce and sell the Parker-Hale line.

M82

This bolt action rifle uses a Mauser 98 action fitted to a heavy 26" barrel chambered for the 7.62x51mm cartridge. Magazine capacity is 4 rounds. Used as a sniper rifle by the Australian, New Zealand, and Canadian military. Marked "PARKER-HALE LTD BIRMINGHAM ENGLAND 7.62 NATO" on top of the barrel. Produced from 1982 to about 1984.

Exc.	V.G.	Good	Fair	Poor
2500	2000	1500	850	—

M85

This is an improved version of the M82 with a Mauser 98 type bolt action designed to compete for a British military contract against the Accuracy International rifle. It did not win the trials. It is fitted with a removable 10-round magazine, 27.5" heavy barrel with iron sights, and telescope mounts on the receiver. Rifle is half stocked with adjustable buttplate. Bipod is attached to forend rail. Weight is about 12.5 lbs. with scope. Chambered for the 7.62x51mm NATO round.

Exc.	V.G.	Good	Fair	Poor
3500	3000	2500	1500	—

MACHINE GUNS

NOTE: For historical information and technical details see: Dugelby, *The Bren Gun Saga*, Collector Grade Publications, 1999. Goldsmith, *The Grand Old Lady of No Man's Land, The Vickers Machinegun*, Collector Grade Publications, 1994.

Bren MK1

Introduced in 1938 and designed in Czechoslovakia as the ZB vz2,6 this British version is chambered for the .303 British cartridge during the early part of its service. After WWII it was adapted to the 7.62x51mm cartridge. It was fitted with a top mounted magazine of 30 rounds. Rate of fire is 500 rounds per minute. The gun was set up to fire selectively as well. The gun has a 24.8" barrel and an empty weight of 22 lbs. The rear sight

---

SNAP SHOT
THE BREN GUN

The Bren Gun was the best light machine gun of World War II. It was somewhat unorthodox in its appearance, but its beauty was found in its performance, often under extremely primitive conditions. The Bren Gun was developed from the Czech designed ZB26 and ZB27 light machine guns and adopted by the British military in 1938. Even its name reflects its heritage as the "Br" in Bren stands for Brno (as in Czechoslovakia) and the "en" for Enfield where it was originally produced.

It is a gas-operated design and features a quick-change barrel. The quick-change barrel contains the gas regulator with four different ports as well as a carrying handle. The ability to change barrels quickly and easily is an essential feature that was sadly missing on the American BAR and one of the reasons why the Bren Gun is universally praised.

Chambered for the British .303 service cartridge, the 30-round box magazine features a curved profile to accommodate this rimmed ammunition. The magazine fed through the top of the receiver and this helped the gun earn a sterling reputation for reliability because gravity helped the magazine spring feed the rounds into the gun. Naturally because of the top feed design the sights were off-set slightly. The gun earned accolades for its accuracy and dependability. During World War II Inglis in Canada produced a version chambered for the 7.92x57mm round for use in China. When Britain converted to the NATO standard 7.62x51 round in the late 1950's, the gun was converted to fire this ammo as well. After Argentina invaded the Falkland Islands, many of the responding British military forces were equipped with Bren Guns converted to 7.62 NATO caliber. While the Bren Gun is at nearly the end of its service life in front line military units it is sure to be found in reserve units and back-water countries formerly governed by the forces of the United Kingdom. It remains the best light machine gun of World War II.

Frank W. James

is an offset drum type. The buttstock has a hand grip and top strap. The bipod has fixed legs, and the cocking handle folds away. Marked "BREN MK" on the right side of the receiver.

The Bren MK2 (1941) has a leaf type rear sight and a simplified buttstock. The Bren MK3 (1944) is lighter (19 lbs) and fitted with a shorter barrel (22.2"). The Bren MK4 (1944) has minor differences in the buttstock. The L4A1 (1958) is a converted MK3 to 7.62mm caliber. The L4A2 (1958) is a converted MK3 with lighter bipod. The L4A3 is a converted MK2 to 7.62mm caliber: used by navy and RAF. The L4A4 (1960) is similar to the L4A2 except for a chrome lined barrel. The L4A6 is a converted L4A1 with chrome lined barrel.

In 1941, the MK2 was produced in Canada for the Chinese Nationalist army in 7.92x57mm caliber (see *Canada*). A .30-06 version was made in Taiwan.

Be aware that there are a number of different mounts for the Bren gun besides the traditional bipod. There is a tripod mount as well as an antiaircraft mount.

NOTE: The Vickers-Berthier gun is similar in external design, caliber, and general appearance as the Bren except it has a distinctive operating mechanism and other significant differences. This gun is made in India and that country used the gun in World War II. It is still in use in that country. This gun is extremely rare as only a few known transferable examples exist. For pre-1968 Vickers-Berthier guns a price of $35,000 in excellent condition would be a good starting place for value.

Bren MK I • Photo courtesy private NFA collection

Bren MK1

Pre-1968 (Rare)
Exc.	V.G.	Fair
45000	42000	40000

Pre-1986 conversions
Exc.	V.G.	Fair
35000	32000	30000

Pre-1986 dealer samples
Exc.	V.G.	Fair
22000	20000	18000

Bren MK2

Pre-1968 (Rare)
Exc.	V.G.	Fair
42000	40000	38000

Pre-1986 conversions
Exc.	V.G.	Fair
18000	17000	15000

Pre-1986 dealer samples
Exc.	V.G.	Fair
17500	15000	15000

Lewis 0.303in, Mark 1

This gas-operated machine gun is chambered for the .303 British cartridge. Though perfected by an American army officer, Colonel Isaac Lewis (1858-1931), it was first produced in Belgium in 1912 where it was used extensively by British forces during WWI. In fact, it was the principal British light machine gun used in WWI. It has a 26" barrel and a rate of fire of about 550 rounds per minute. Called by the Germans the "Belgian Rattlesnake." Magazine capacity is 47- or 97-round drum. Its weight is approximately 26 lbs. Marked "LEWIS AUTOMATIC MACHINE GUN/MODEL 1914 PATENTED" behind the magazine drum. The gun was produced by BSA and Savage Arms of the U.S. Production stopped in 1925. A number of other countries used the gun as well, such as France, Norway, Japan, Belgium, Honduras, and Nicaragua.

Lewis Mark 2 Aircraft Gun • Paul Goodwin photo

Vickers-Berthier • Courtesy private NFA collection, Paul Goodwin photo

The Lewis MK2 was introduced in 1915 which was a MK1 without the radiator and barrel jacket. The buttstock was removed and spade grips attached for aircraft use. The Lewis MK2* modified the gun to increase the rate of fire to about 800 rounds per minute. See also *United States, Machine Guns, Savage-Lewis M1917.*

Private NFA collection • Photo by Gary Gelson

Pre-1968
Exc.	V.G.	Fair
18000	16000	14000

Pre-1986 conversions
Exc.	V.G.	Fair
12000	10000	9000

Pre-1986 dealer samples
Exc.	V.G.	Fair
N/A	N/A	N/A

Vickers Mark 1

This British water-cooled machine gun was first produced in 1912 and chambered for the .303 British cartridge. In essence, an improved Maxim with the action inverted. It has a 28" barrel with corrugated water jacket and is fed by a 250 cloth belt. Its rate of fire is 450 rounds per minute. Its weight is approximately 40 lbs. It was also used in aircraft and stayed in service in various countries until the 1970s. Besides use in British forces, the gun was sold to South American countries between the two World Wars. Serial number is marked on top rear of water jacket. The Vickers gun was capable of sustained fire of 100,000 rounds without stopping.

British Vickers Mark IV • Courtesy Blake Stevens, *The Grand Old Lady of No Man's Land*

Variations of the Vickers Mark 1 are: the Mark 1*, which is an aircraft gun with a pierced and louvered barrel jacket for air-cooling. Some of these guns had a rate of fire of about 850 rounds per minute and marked "SU" for "speeded up." There were several other Vickers aircraft variations which incorporated minor modifications. The Vickers was also used on tanks. These variations were designated the Mark 4A, Mark 4B, Mark 6, Mark 6*, Mark 7. A .50 caliber Vickers was also produced for tank and naval use. These guns are designated the .5 inch Mark 3, and .5 inch Mark 4. These guns had a rate of fire of about 675 rounds per minute and weighed approximately 60 lbs.

NOTE: For the Colt produced version in .30-06 caliber see *United States, Machine Guns.*

Pre-1968
Exc.	V.G.	Fair
30000	28000	25000

SNAP SHOT
LEWIS GUN

The Lewis Gun is another one of those classic World War I guns that is just plain fun to shoot. At 27 pounds, it is almost impossible to control from a standing position unless you have a tremendous amount of upper body strength. It is designed to be fired from the hip in an advancing mode (as a trench broom) or from a prone position using a bipod.

Though the Lewis Gun has many excellent features and characteristics, (its portability, one-man operation, ease of changing pan magazines, resistance to environmental fouling, etc.), it is a complex weapon susceptible to a bewildering number of stoppages. The *British Small Arms Training Manual* of 1931 lists six "immediate action" stoppages and seven further possible stoppages for it. The detailing and explanation of the stoppages add up to 31 pages of small print. Nevertheless, when the stars and planets are properly aligned, and all the internal parts are in proper working order, the Lewis Gun is reliable and a formidable weapon.

Loading the pan magazine is a time-consuming process even when using the proper magazine pan loading tool. The 47-round rotating spiral pan magazine can be the source of many stoppages and it is crucial that the pans be in good working order and dent free. A feed jam can be an exasperating experience to clear.

The Lewis Gun is gas-operated and has a unique operating system employing a circular "watch spring" and rack and pinion system of op-rod and bolt movement. This is not conducive to a "smooth" operation but it is not detracting. Firing the Lewis gun produces a distinctive sound that easily identifies it on the firing line. The barrel is surrounded by a finned aluminum air cooling sleeve that is encased in a large housing. This housing extends a good 3 inches beyond the muzzle and results in a slightly "hollow" sound that is characteristic of the Lewis Gun. With a cyclic rate of fire of 550 rounds per minute, fire control is easily maintained though the gun is full automatic fire only. This is a gun that requires a thorough understanding of its parts and operation. But when mastered, it is pure joy to shoot.

Robert G. Segel

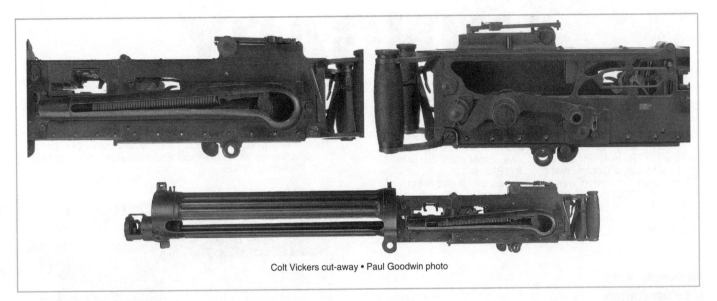

Colt Vickers cut-away • Paul Goodwin photo

Pre-1986 conversions
(Non-Martial current U.S. manufacture/side-plate)

Exc.	V.G.	Fair
15000	12500	11000

Pre-1986 dealer samples

Exc.	V.G.	Fair
10000	9000	8000

Hotchkiss Mark I

Although a French design, the British army purchased the rights to manufacture the Hotchkiss during World War I. These British guns were known as the Mark 1 and Mark 1* and were built in the Royal Small Arms factory in England. The British Hotchkiss was chambered for the .303 British cartridge. This version was fed by a 30-round metallic strip and had a rate of fire of about 500 rounds per minute. The gun weighed about 27 lbs. Barrel length was 23.5". The British Hotchkiss stayed in service in the British army until 1946. A belt-fed version (Mark I*) for use on tanks used a 250-round belt.

Courtesy Butterfield & Butterfield

Pre-1968

Exc.	V.G.	Fair
8500	8000	7500

Pre-1986 conversions

Exc.	V.G.	Fair
5000	4500	4000

Pre-1986 dealer samples

Exc.	V.G.	Fair
N/A	N/A	N/A

Besa

Introduced in 1939, this gun was a design bought from the Czech's ZB vz53 and produced in Britain by BSA in a slightly modified form. It was used primarily on tanks. It was an air-cooled gun chambered for the 7.92x57mm cartridge. It was gas operated but with a recoiling barrel. It has a rate of fire of approximately 500 or 800 rounds per minute using a selector switch for high or low rate. Weight of the gun is about 48 lbs. Feeds from a 250-round belt.

There are a number of variations of the initial model. The Mark 2 has some minor modifications. The Mark 3 has a single rate of fire of 800 rounds per minute. The Mark 3* has a single rate of fire of 500 rounds per minute.

Pre-1968

Exc.	V.G.	Fair
35000	32000	30000

Pre-1986 conversions

Exc.	V.G.	Fair
27000	25000	22500

Pre-1986 dealer samples

Exc.	V.G.	Fair
N/A	N/A	N/A

England also used the Maxim gun in this photo of Royal Navy • Courtesy Paul S. Scarlata

HUNGARY

Hungarian Military Conflicts, 1918-Present

Hungary followed a similar history to Austria following the break-up of the Austro-Hungarian Empire in 1918. In 1941, Hungary joined the Axis Alliance and in 1944 was invaded by the USSR. In 1946, a republic was established, but was overthrown by a Communist coup in 1948. In 1956, an anti-Communist revolution was suppressed by Soviet military forces. In 1990, democratic reform swept the country. In 1994, the Socialists won control of the government with the result that economic and social reforms are almost nonexistent.

HANDGUNS

STEYR
Osterreichische Waffenfabrik Gesellschaft GmbH, Steyr (1869-1919)
Steyr-Werke AG (1919-1934)
Steyr-Daimler-Puch, Steyr (1934-1990)
Steyr-Mannlicher GmbH, Steyr (1990-)

Model 1929

A blowback-operated semiautomatic chambered for the 9mm short cartridge. It has an external hammer, and the barrel was retained by four lugs. This was a simple and reliable pistol, and it was adopted by the military as a replacement for the Stop. This model was manufactured between 1929 and 1937. About 50,000 pistols were produced. It was also produced in a .22 Long Rifle.

Courtesy James Rankin

Exc.	V.G.	Good	Fair	Poor
500	300	200	175	125

Model 1937

An improved version of the Model 1929, with a grooved slide to make cocking easier. It was adopted as the M1937 by the Hungarian Military, and in 1941 the German government ordered 85,000 pistols chambered for 7.65mm to be used by the Luftwaffe. These pistols were designated the "P Mod 37

Kal 7.65." They were also marked "jhv," which was the German code for the Hungarian company. These German pistols also have a manual safety, which is not found on the Hungarian military version and bears the Waffenamt acceptance marks. This model was manufactured from 1937 until the end of WWII.

Courtesy James Rankin

Nazi Proofed 7.65mm Version (Pistole Modell 37[u])

Exc.	V.G.	Good	Fair	Poor
500	300	200	150	100

9mm Short Hungarian Military Version

Hungarian Military Model 37 • Courtesy Rock Island Auction Company

Exc.	V.G.	Good	Fair	Poor
450	300	175	125	75

Model 48 (7.62mm)

This is a Hungarian copy of the Soviet 7.62mm TT33 pistol. The pistol has molded plastic grips with the Hungarian coat of arms.

Hungarian M48 • Courtesy Chuck Karwan

Exc.	V.G.	Good	Fair	Poor
450	300	150	100	75

Tokagypt

A licensed copy of the TT33 pistol produced by Fegyvergar (FEG) of Hungary. Chambered for the 9mm cartridge, and intended for, but never issued to, the Egyptian army in the 1950s. Barrel length is 4.5" and magazine capacity is 7 rounds. Manual thumb safety. Weight is approximately 32 oz.

Hungarian Tokagypt • Courtesy Chuck Karwan

Exc.	V.G.	Good	Fair	Poor
750	650	500	350	150

NOTE: For pistols without markings deduct 25 percent. For pistols with importer stamps deduct 50 percent.

PA-63

An aluminum frame copy of the Walther PP in a slightly larger size. Chambered for the 9mm Makarov cartridge. This was the standard Hungarian service pistol until recently.

Exc.	V.G.	Good	Fair	Poor
250	150	120	90	75

R-61

This model is a smaller version of the PA-63. Chambered for the 9mm Makarov. This model is slightly longer than a Walther PPK and was intended for issue to high-ranking officers, CID, and police units.

Exc.	V.G.	Good	Fair	Poor
250	150	130	100	80

SUBMACHINE GUNS

Model 39

Produced by Danuvia in Budapest, this submachine gun is chambered for the 9x25mm Mauser Export cartridge. It is fitted with a 19.5" barrel and a full stocked rifle-style wooden stock. Magazine capacity is 40 rounds. The magazine folds into a recess in the forward part of the stock. Fitted with a bayonet lug. Gun features a two-part bolt design. Introduced in the late 1930s but not issued until 1941. Weight is about 8 lbs. Rate of fire is approximately 750 rounds per minute. About 8,000 were produced.

NOTE: It is not known how many, if any, of these guns are in the U.S. and are transferable. Prices listed are estimates only.

Model 39M • Courtesy Thomas Nelson, *The World's Submachine Guns, Vol. 1*

Pre-1968
Exc.	V.G.	Fair
15000	6500	6000

Pre-1986 conversions
Exc.	V.G.	Fair
4500	4000	3500

Pre-1986 dealer samples
Exc.	V.G.	Fair
N/A	N/A	N/A

Model 43

This model, introduced in 1942, is an improved version of the Model 39. It has a shorter barrel at 16.5", a folding stock, pistol grip, and an improved magazine. Weight is about 8 lbs. Rate of fire and caliber remains the same. Produced until 1945.

NOTE: It is not known how many, if any, of these guns are in the U.S. and are transferable. Prices listed below are estimates only.

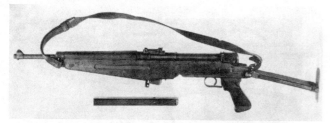

Model 43M • Courtesy Thomas Nelson, *The World's Submachine Guns, Vol. 1*

Pre-1968

Exc.	V.G.	Fair
12500	10500	9500

Pre-1986 conversions

Exc.	V.G.	Fair
6500	5500	4500

Pre-1986 dealer samples

Exc.	V.G.	Fair
N/A	N/A	N/A

Model 48

This is a Hungarian copy of the Soviet PPSh-41 submachine gun. See also *Russia, Submachine Guns*.

Pre-1968

Exc.	V.G.	Fair
12500	10500	9500

Pre-1986 conversions

Exc.	V.G.	Fair
6500	5500	4500

Pre-1986 dealer samples

Exc.	V.G.	Fair
6000	5000	4000

RIFLES

MANNLICHER
Built by Steyr & Fegyvergyar

Model 1935 Short Rifle

This model is based on the Romanian Model 1893. However, it is chambered for the 8x56R Hungarian Mannlicher cartridge. Barrel length is 23.6". Magazine capacity is 5 rounds in a clip loaded box magazine. Full stock with full-length handguard. Weight is approximately 9 lbs.

Exc.	V.G.	Good	Fair	Poor
350	200	150	100	75

FEGYVERGYAR
Fegyver es Gepgyar Resvenytarsasag, Budapest, (1880-1945)
Femaru es Szersazamgepgyar NV (1945-1985)
FEG Arms & Gas Appliances Factory (1985-)

Model Gewehr 98/40

Built by FEG but with many Mannlicher and Mauser components in its design. Based on Hungarian M1935 short rifle. Chambered for the 7.92x57mm cartridge and Mauser charger loaded. Two-piece stock. Barrel length is 23.6". Weight is about 9 lbs.

Model 98/40 • Private collection, Paul Goodwin photo

Exc.	V.G.	Good	Fair	Poor
200	125	100	50	—

Model 43 Rifle

This is a Model 35 redesigned on the German Model 98 and chambered for the 7.92mm cartridge. Barrel length is 23.75". Magazine capacity is 5-rounds fixed box. Rear sight is tangent with notch. Weight is approximately 8.5 lbs. Almost full stock with German bayonet fittings. Issued to the Hungarian army in 1943. Rare.

Model 43 rifle • Private collection, Paul Goodwin photo

Exc.	V.G.	Good	Fair	Poor
700	450	300	125	75

44.M (Mosin-Nagant)

This is the Hungarian copy of the Soviet 1944 Mosin-Nagant. Produced in 1952-1955 by FEG. This rifle can be identified by the Communist national crest (a star on top of a globe with a hammer but no sickle) on top of the receiver ring. Stocks are marked with a "B" in a circle and may have "02" on top of the receiver ring that is the code for Hungary.

Exc.	V.G.	Good	Fair	Poor
150	100	75	—	—

48.M (Mosin-Nagant)

This is a Hungarian copy of the M91/30 Mosin Nagant Soviet rifle chambered for the 7.62mm cartridge. Barrel length is 28.5". Five-round magazine. Weight about 8.5 lbs. Exported worldwide.

NOTE: Model 48 Sniper rifle was also made in Hungary and it is the same as the Soviet M91/30 Sniper rifle. See *Russia, Rifles.*

Exc.	V.G.	Good	Fair	Poor
150	100	50	—	—

STEYR
Osterreichische Waffenfabrik Gesellschaft GmbH, Steyr (1869-1919)
Steyr-Werke AG (1919-1934)
Steyr-Daimler-Puch, Steyr (1934-1990)
Steyr-Mannlicher GmbH, Steyr (1990-)

Model 95 Rifle (Model 31)

A number of Model 95 rifles and short rifles were modified to accept the 8x56mm cartridge after World War I. The letter "H" is stamped on the barrel or the receiver. This is a straight pull rifle with 19.6" barrel and a 5-round fixed magazine. Weight is approximately 7.5 lbs.

Exc.	V.G.	Good	Fair	Poor
200	100	65	40	25

HUNGARIAN AK CLONES

AKM-63

A close copy of the AKM but with plastic furniture. Fitted with a vertical grip under the forend. Weighs about 1/2 lb. less than the Russian AKM.

Pre-1968

Exc.	V.G.	Fair
18000	15000	13000

Pre-1986 conversions

Exc.	V.G.	Fair
8000	7000	6000

Pre-1986 dealer samples

Exc.	V.G.	Fair
9000	8000	7000

AKM-63 (Semiautomatic version)

This semiautomatic version of the AKM-63 is in a pre-ban (1994) configuration.

Exc.	V.G.	Good	Fair	Poor
1400	1100	800	—	—

NOTE: Add 20 percent for folding stock (AMD-65-style).

AMD-65

This model is an AKM-63 with a 12.5" barrel, two-port muzzle brake, and a side folding metal butt. Rate of fire is about 600 rounds per minute. Weight is approximately 7 lbs.

Pre-1968

Exc.	V.G.	Fair
25000	22500	20000

Pre-1986 conversions

Exc.	V.G.	Fair
15000	13000	11000

Pre-1986 dealer samples

Exc.	V.G.	Fair
12000	11000	10000

NGM

This assault rifle is the Hungarian version of the AK-74 chambered for the 5.56x45mm cartridge. Fitted with a 16.25" barrel. Magazine capacity is a 30-round box type. Rate of fire is about 600 rounds per minute. Weight is approximately 7 lbs.

Pre-1968

Exc.	V.G.	Fair
N/A	N/A	N/A

Pre-1986 conversions

Exc.	V.G.	Fair
15000	13000	11000

Pre-1986 dealer samples

Exc.	V.G.	Fair
N/A	N/A	N/A

MACHINE GUNS

Hungary was supplied with a wide variety of Soviet machine guns after World War II from the RPD to the DShK38. Many of these machine guns were later copied by the Hungarians while retaining the Soviet model designations.

ISRAEL

Israeli Military Conflicts, 1870-Present

In the late 19th century, the Zionist movement called for a Jewish homeland in Palestine. In World War I, Britain captured the area and appeared to support this purpose. In 1922, the League of Nations approved the British mandate of Palestine which resulted in a large Jewish immigration into the area. This influx was opposed by the Arabs, and with the end of World War II the U.N. divided Palestine into Jewish and Arab states. In 1948, the state of Israel was proclaimed. The Arabs rejected this proclamation and the result was the 1948-1949 war between Israel and Lebanon, Syria, Jordan, Egypt, and Iraq. Israel won the war and increased its territory by 50 percent. Arab opposition continued with subsequent conflicts: the Sinai campaign of 1956, the Six-Day War of 1967, and the Yom Kippur War of 1973. Israel won all of these conflicts. Israel and Egypt signed a peace treaty in 1979 with Israel withdrawing from the Sinai. The balance of the 1980s and 1990s is marked by fierce fighting in Lebanon and with the PLO. In 1993, Israel signed an accord with the PLO for self rule in Gaza and the West Bank. A peace treaty was signed with Jordan in 1994. The area remains highly volatile.

HANDGUNS

NOTE: Israel has used a number of different handguns during its early fight for independence and in the turbulent years after. These handguns included Enfield and Webley revolvers as well as Browning Hi-power, Lugers and P-38 pistols. They also built a modified copy of the Smith & Wesson Military & Police model chambered for the 9x19 cartridge which required the use of two three-round half-moon clips.

Beretta M1951

This 9mm semiautomatic pistol is the standard Israeli military sidearm. See *Italy, Handguns, Beretta.*

Jericho

A 9mm or .41 Action Express double action semiautomatic pistol with a 4.72" barrel, polygonal rifling, ambidextrous safety and fixed sights. Blued with plastic grips. Weight is approximately 36 oz. Magazine capacity is 16 rounds in 9mm. This pistol is primarily used by the Israeli police and other government agencies, generally in 9mm.

Exc.	V.G.	Good	Fair	Poor
600	400	350	300	200

SUBMACHINE GUNS

NOTE: Prior to the development of the UZI the Israelis used British Sten guns and other World War II submachine guns that were available for purchase on the arms market.

UZI

First produced in Israel in 1953, this submachine gun is chambered for the 9mm cartridge. It was designed by Uzi Gal and was based on the Czech designs that were used by Israeli forces in the 1947-48 conflicts. It is fitted with a 10.14" barrel and metal folding stock. It has a magazine capacity of 25, 32, or 40 rounds. Empty weight is about 7.7 lbs. Rate of fire is 600 rounds per minute. This gun enjoys widespread use and is found in military and police units all over the world. Marked "UZI SMG 9MM" on left side of receiver.

Pre-1968 (Very Rare)

Exc.	V.G.	Fair
15000	13000	11000

Pre-1986 conversions

Exc.	V.G.	Fair
5000	4000	3000

Pre-1986 dealer samples

Exc.	V.G.	Fair
4000	3000	2000

Vector UZI pre-1986 conversion

The receiver was produced, marked, and registered by Group Industries, Louisville, KY, prior to May 1986. Receiver fixed parts manufacturing and receiver assembly is done by Vector Arms, Inc. of North Salt Lake, UT. A total of 3,300 receivers built. All parts (South African) interchangeable with original IMI guns. Receiver parkerized. All other specifications same as original UZI.

Pre-1986 conversions

NIB/Exc.	V.G.	Fair
5000	4500	4000

Mini-UZI

First produced in 1987, this is a smaller version of the original UZI. It functions the same as its larger counterpart. Accepts 20-, 25-, and 32-round magazines. Rate of fire is about 900 to 1,100 rounds per minute. Weight is about 6 lbs. Overall length is about 14" with butt retracted and 23" with butt extended.

FN 98k Short Rifle • Private collection, Paul Goodwin photo

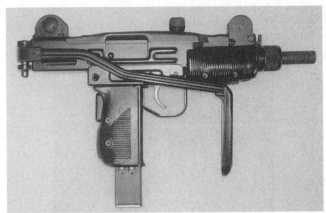

Photo courtesy private NFA collection

Pre-1968

Exc.	V.G.	Fair
N/A	N/A	N/A

Pre-1986 conversions

Exc.	V.G.	Fair
6500	5500	4500

Pre-1986 dealer samples

Exc.	V.G.	Fair
3500	2750	2500

RIFLES

NOTE: During the 1950s, Israel converted Mauser 98 rifles to 7.62mm caliber. Some of these were sold as surplus. The Israeli military employed a large number, about 150,000 Colt-built M16A1 rifles and M16A1 carbines during the 1970s. This weapon is still popular with the IDF today. They also have used FN-built and IMI-assembled FN-FAL rifles. Israeli military forces were even issued AKM rifles. In 1975 the U.S. government sold about 22,000 M14 rifles to the Israeli military.

Mauser

Czech Post-WWII 98k Short Rifle

This model is identical to the German Model K98k with the exception of an oversize triggerguard. Some have been converted to 7.62x51mm.

Exc.	V.G.	Good	Fair	Poor
350	225	190	125	80

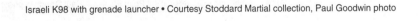

Israeli K98 with grenade launcher • Courtesy Stoddard Martial collection, Paul Goodwin photo

FN 98k-style Short Rifle (7.62 conversion)

This model was purchased directly from FN in the 1950s and is the same configuration as the German Model 98k carbine. It is marked with Israeli markings on the receiver ring.

Exc.	V.G.	Good	Fair	Poor
400	250	200	125	90

Galil ARM-Select Fire Assault Rifle

This automatic rifle is produced in Israel and is chambered for the 5.56x45mm cartridge. Similar in appearance to the AK-47 this rifle is fitted with an 18" barrel and folding stock. Magazine capacity is 35 or 50 rounds. Rate of fire is 550 rounds per minute. Model markings on the left side of the receiver are in Hebrew. Weight is approximately 8.7 lbs. First produced in 1971. Still in production.

Photo courtesy private NFA collection

Pre-1968
Exc.	V.G.	Fair
N/A	N/A	N/A

Pre-1986 conversions
Exc.	V.G.	Fair
12000	11000	10000

Pre-1986 dealer samples (Rare)
Exc.	V.G.	Fair
9000	9000	8500

Galil SAR-Select Fire Assault Rifle

Similar to the ARM but with a folding metal stock and a barrel length of 13". Weight of SAR is about 8.25 lbs.

Pre-1968
Exc.	V.G.	Fair
N/A	N/A	N/A

Pre-1986 conversions
Exc.	V.G.	Fair
12000	11000	10000

Galil SAR • Photo courtesy private NFA collection

Pre-1986 dealer samples
Exc.	V.G.	Fair
9000	9000	8500

Model AR

This rifle is an Israeli variant of the AK-47 based on the Valmet. It is also used by the South African military where it is called the R-4 rifle. It is a .223 or .308 caliber semiautomatic rifle with 16" or 19" barrels. Parkerized with the flip "Tritium" night sights and folding stock. The .308 version would bring about a 10 percent premium.

Model ARM Assault Rifle • Courtesy West Point Museum, Paul Goodwin photo

NIB	Exc.	V.G.	Good	Fair	Poor
2800	2400	2000	1500	900	700

Model ARM

As above, with a ventilated wood handguard and a folding bi-pod and carrying handle. The .308 will bring about a 10 percent premium.

NIB	Exc.	V.G.	Good	Fair	Poor
3000	2700	2000	1500	900	700

Galil Sniper Rifle

Introduced in 1983 and similar to the above rifle chambered for the 7.62x51 NATO caliber, with a 20" heavy barrel, adjustable wooden stock, and a 6/40 scope is furnished in addition to the Tritium night sights. Supplied to military in semiautomatic version only. Weight is about 14 lbs. Supplied with two 25-shot magazines and a fitted case.

NIB	Exc.	V.G.	Good	Fair	Poor
8500	7500	6000	4000	3000	2000

IDF Mauser Rifle Model 66SP

This is a bolt action rifle chambered for the .308 Win. cartridge. Adjustable trigger for pull and travel. Barrel length is 27". Specially designed stock has broad forend and a thumb hole pistol grip. Cheekpiece is adjustable as is the recoil pad. The rifle is fitted with an original Swarovsky 6x24 BDC Mil-Spec scope. Supplied with case. This rifle is military issue, built by Mauser for the Israel Defense Force in the early 1980s. Less than 100 imported into the U.S by Springfield Armory.

Exc.	V.G.	Good	Fair	Poor
3000	2500	—	—	—

MACHINE GUNS

Israel uses a variety of foreign-built machine guns from the FN MAG, Browning 1919 and Browning .50 caliber heavy machine gun. There are no known transferable Israel machine guns in the U.S.

ITALY

Italian Military Conflicts, 1870-Present

The period of the last quarter of the 19th century was one of the final nationalistic efforts at unification of the Italian states. By the end of the century this effort was achieved. In 1915 Italy entered World War I on the allied side, and by the end of the war in 1918 Italy was awarded additional territories, but social unrest and economic discord brought about the rise of fascism, and in 1922 Mussolini seized power. He created a totalitarian state and expanded Italian influence through armed aggression into Ethiopia in 1936, Albania in 1939, and entered World War II on the side of the Germans. In 1943 Italy surrendered to the Allies. In 1946, Italy became a republic. By 1947 Italy shed its colonies. The last 50 years has seen a rapid succession of governments trying to govern the country without much success.

HANDGUNS

Modello 1874

This was the first handgun adopted by the Kingdom of Italy's military forces. It was very similar to the French Model 1874 and is chambered for the 10.35mm cartridge. It is fitted with a 6.3" octagon barrel. Cylinder is fluted and grips are checkered wood with lanyard loop. Built by Siderugica Glisenti and others. Weight is about 40 oz. In use by the Italian military from 1872 to 1943.

Courtesy Supica's Old Town Station

Exc.	V.G.	Good	Fair	Poor
900	600	350	200	125

System Bodeo Modello 1889 (Enlisted Model)

A 10.4mm caliber revolver with a 4.5" octagonal barrel and 6-shot cylinder. Built on a Chamelot-Delvigne frame with loading gate on the right side. This revolver was adopted as the Italian service revolver in 1889 and was replaced by the Glisenti in 1910. Manufactured by various Italian arms companies. This revolver, in different configurations, remained in service until 1945.

Courtesy Rock Island Auction Company

Exc.	V.G.	Good	Fair	Poor
850	600	300	100	75

Modello 1889 (Officer's Model)

Essentially the same as the enlisted man's model with a round barrel, non-folding trigger, and conventional triggerguard.

Courtesy Richard M. Kumor Sr.

Exc.	V.G.	Good	Fair	Poor
850	600	300	100	75

Glisenti Model 1910

A 9mm Glisenti caliber semiautomatic pistol with a 3.9" barrel, fixed sights, and 7-shot magazine. Weight is about 30 oz. Manufactured from 1910 to 1915. As many as 100,000 of these pistols were produced and used during World War II.

WARNING: *Standard 9x19 ammo must not be shot in this gun.*

Courtesy Faintich Auction Service • Photo Paul Goodwin

Model 1910 with black plastic grips with crown • Courtesy Richard M. Kumor Sr.

Exc.	V.G.	Good	Fair	Poor
750	500	375	250	150

BERETTA, PIETRO

Model 1915

A 7.65mm caliber semiautomatic pistol with 3.5" barrel, fixed sights, and 7-shot magazine. Blued with walnut grips. Weight is about 20 oz. The slide is marked "PIETRO BERETTA BRESCIA CASA FONDATA NEL 1680 CAL. 7.65MM BREVETTO 1915." Manufactured between 1915 and 1922. Used by the Italian military during World War I and World War II. About 65,000 were produced, most of which were not martially marked.

Courtesy Rock Island Auction Company

Exc.	V.G.	Good	Fair	Poor
400	300	225	150	100

Model 1915 2nd Variation

As above, in 9mm Glisenti caliber with 3.75" barrel. Checkered wood grips. Weight is about 32 oz.

Exc.	V.G.	Good	Fair	Poor
450	350	275	200	125

Model 1915/1919

This model is an improved version of the above pistol but chambered for the 7.65mm cartridge. It also incorporates a new barrel-mounting method and a longer cutout in the top of the slide. Produced from 1922 to 1931 for the Italian military with about 50,000 manufactured, most without military markings.

Courtesy Orvel Reichert

Exc.	V.G.	Good	Fair	Poor
400	300	225	150	100

Model 1923

A 9mm caliber semiautomatic pistol with 4" barrel and 8-shot magazine. Blued with steel grips. The slide is marked "Brev 1915-1919 Mlo 1923." Exposed hammer. Italian army markings on left grip tang. Some pistols are cut for a shoulder stock. Manufactured from 1923 to 1935. Approximately 10,000 manufactured.

Exc.	V.G.	Good	Fair	Poor
650	500	350	225	150

Model 1931

A 7.65mm caliber semiautomatic pistol with 3.5" barrel and open-top slide. Blued with walnut grips and marked "RM" separated by an anchor. Issue limited to the Italian navy. Produced from 1931 to 1934 for the Italian navy. Approximately 8,000 manufactured.

Exc.	V.G.	Good	Fair	Poor
800	650	400	200	150

Model 1934

As above, with 9mm Corto (Kurz) caliber. The slide is marked, "P. Beretta Cal. 9 Corto-Mo 1934 Brevet Gardone VT." This inscription is followed by the date of manufacture that was given numerically, followed by a Roman numeral that denoted the year of manufacture on the Fascist calendar, which began in 1922. This model was the most common prewar Beretta pistol and was widely used by all branches of the Italian military. Examples are marked "RM" (navy), "RE" (army), "RA" (air force), and "PS" (police). Manufactured between 1934 and 1959.

Courtesy Orvel Reichert

Exc.	V.G.	Good	Fair	Poor
500	350	225	150	100

Air Force "RA" marked

Exc.	V.G.	Good	Fair	Poor
675	550	325	225	150

Navy "RM" marked

Exc.	V.G.	Good	Fair	Poor
750	650	400	250	175

Model 1934 Romanian Contract

See *Romania, Handguns.*

Model 1935

As above, in 7.65mm caliber. A number of these pistols were built and used by the German army during the occupation of Italy in World War II. Some of these pistols are marked with the German army acceptance stamp. Pistols produced in 1944 and 1945 were likely used by the German army without markings. Some of these wartime pistols are marked with Italian navy or air force markings. Production between 1934 and 1943 was about 200,000 pistols. Postwar versions are known. Manufactured from 1935 to 1959.

Courtesy Orvel Reichert

Exc.	V.G.	Good	Fair	Poor
450	325	225	150	100

Model 1951

Chambered for the 7.65 or 9mm cartridges, this model was fitted with a 4.5" barrel and had an 8-round magazine. Fixed sights. Weight was about 31 oz. This pistol was used by the Italian military as well as by Egypt (Helwan) and Israel. Sold commercially under the name "Brigadier."

Exc.	V.G.	Good	Fair	Poor
350	250	200	100	75

NOTE: For Egyptian copies deduct 50 percent.

Model 92

A 9mm caliber double action, semiautomatic pistol with a 5" barrel, fixed sights, and a 16-round, double-stack magazine.

Courtesy Orvel Reichert

Blued with plastic grips. Introduced in 1976 and is now discontinued. This model was used by the Italian State Police forces. The U.S. military version, the M9, is based on this series.

NOTE: There are a number of different versions of this pistol. The main differences lie in the safety type and magazine release, barrel length, and magazine capacity.

NIB	Exc.	V.G.	Good	Fair	Poor
500	400	375	300	250	200

BERNARDELLI, VINCENZO

Model PO 18

A 7.65mm or 9mm Parabellum caliber, double action, semi-automatic pistol with a 4.75" barrel and a 16-shot, double-stack, detachable magazine. All steel construction. Blued with plastic grips. Walnut grips are available for an additional $40. Introduced in 1985. The 7.65mm was designed for commercial sales while the 9mm was for military sales and should be so marked.

NIB	Exc.	V.G.	Good	Fair	Poor
650	550	400	275	200	100

Model PO 18 Compact

As above, with a 4" barrel and a shorter grip frame with a 14-shot, double-column magazine. Introduced in 1989.

NIB	Exc.	V.G.	Good	Fair	Poor
650	550	400	275	200	100

SUBMACHINE GUNS

Italy also uses the HK MP5A3 and MP5SD in its police and anti-terrorist units.

Villar Perosa Model 1915

This was the first submachine gun adopted by any military force. Chambered for the 9x19mm Glisenti cartridge. Barrel length is 12.5". Its rate of fire was about 1200 rounds per minute. Fed by a 25-round box top-mounted magazine. This gun was designed to be mounted in pairs on aircraft, various types of vehicles, and from fixed mounts with its spade grip. Weight of pair is about 14 lbs.

Pre-1968 (Very Rare)

Exc.	V.G.	Fair
25000	22500	20000

Pre-1986 conversions

Exc.	V.G.	Fair
N/A	N/A	N/A

Pre-1986 dealer samples

Exc.	V.G.	Fair
N/A	N/A	N/A

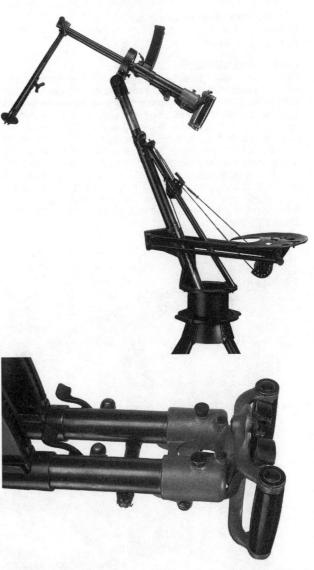

Twin Villar Perosa guns in simulated aircraft mount • Courtesy private NFA collection, Paul Goodwin photo

Villar Perosa Model 1918 (Beretta)

This gun is an adapted Villar Perosa fitted into a wooden stock with new trigger mechanism. Most of the original M1915 Villar Perosa's were converted to the Model 1918. Barrel length is 12.5". Magazine capacity is 25 rounds. Rate of fire is about 900 rounds per minute. Select fire. Weight is about 8 lbs. This gun was used by the Italian army from the end of WW I to WW II.

Beretta Model 1918 • Courtesy Thomas Nelson, *The World's Submachine Guns, Vol. 1*

Pre-1968 (Extremely Rare)

Exc.	V.G.	Fair
9500	9000	8000

Pre-1986 conversions

Exc.	V.G.	Fair
N/A	N/A	N/A

Pre-1986 dealer samples

Exc.	V.G.	Fair
N/A	N/A	N/A

Beretta Model 1938A

This Italian-made submachine gun is chambered for the 9mm Parabellum cartridge and was produced from 1938 to about 1950. It was in use by German, Italian, and Romanian armies in different eras. Argentina also purchased a number of Model 38As directly from Beretta. It is fitted with a 12.25" barrel, full rifle-style stock, and has a magazine capacity of 10, 20, 30, or 40 rounds. Its rate of fire is 600 rounds per minute. Markings on top of receiver are "MOSCHETTI AUT-BERETTA MOD 1938A BE-REVETTO NO 828 428 GARDONE V.T. ITALIA." This weapon was fitted with two triggers: The front trigger fires in the semiautomatic mode, and the rear trigger fires in the automatic mode. A few early models were fitted with a bayonet lug. Weight is about 9.25 lbs.

Private NFA collection • Photo by Gary Gelson

Pre-1968

Exc.	V.G.	Fair
11500	10500	9500

Pre-1986 conversions

Exc.	V.G.	Fair
N/A	N/A	N/A

Pre-1986 dealer samples

Exc.	V.G.	Fair
5500	4500	3500

Beretta Model 38/42

This is an improved wartime version of the Model 1938 without the barrel shroud. This was a less-well-finished model than the Model 1938A. Barrel length is a little over 8". Rate of fire is about 550 rounds per minute. Magazine capacity is 20 or 40 rounds. Produced from 1943 to about 1975. Weight is approximately 7 lbs. Marked "M.P. BERETTA MOD 38/42 CAL 9" on the top of the receiver. This model was used by Italian and German troops in Italy in the latter stages of World War II. Some of these guns were sold to Romania in 1944.

NOTE: A simplified version of the Model 38/42 is designated the Model 38/44 and features a lighter and more simple bolt design and main operating spring. This main spring is very similar to the one used in the British Sten gun. The Model 38/44 was sold to Syria, Pakistan, Iraq, and Costa Rica, among others, following World War II.

Pre-1968

Exc.	V.G.	Fair
10500	9000	8000

Pre-1986 conversions

Exc.	V.G.	Fair
N/A	N/A	N/A

Pre-1986 dealer samples

Exc.	V.G.	Fair
5000	4500	4000

F.N.A.-B Model 1943

This Italian submachine gun was built in 1943 and 1944. It is fitted with a 7.75" shrouded barrel. Chambered for the 9mm cartridge. Magazine capacity is 20 or 40 rounds with a machined magazine housing that folds forward when not in use. Rate of fire is 400 rounds per minute. The gun fires from the closed bolt position. It is made entirely of machined steel. It is estimated that some 7,000 of these guns were produced and were used by both Italian and German troops in WWII.

Pre-1968 (Rare)

Exc.	V.G.	Fair
12500	11000	10000

Pre-1986 conversions

Exc.	V.G.	Fair
N/A	N/A	N/A

Pre-1986 dealer samples

Exc.	V.G.	Fair
N/A	N/A	N/A

Beretta Model 38/42 • Private NFA collection, Paul Goodwin photo

An F.N.A.-B submachine gun was sold at auction for $12,650. Registered as a DEWAT. Condition is 90 percent blue with very good wooden grips.
Amoskeag Auction Company Inc., May 2004

Beretta Model 12

Chambered for the 9mm Parabellum cartridge, this sub gun was produced from 1959 to about 1978. It was manufactured basically from steel stampings. Fitted with a bolt that wraps around the barrel. Also fitted with a front vertical hand grip and either a folding metal stock or detachable wood stock. First used by Italian military in 1961. Also used in South America and Africa. Barrel is 7.75" long with a magazine capacity of 20, 30, or 40 rounds. Rate of fire is 500 rounds per minute. Marked "MOD12-CAL9/M PARABELLUM" on the top of the receiver. Weight is about 6.5 lbs.

Pre-1968 (Rare)

Exc.	V.G.	Fair
12500	11000	10000

Pre-1986 conversions

Exc.	V.G.	Fair
N/A	N/A	N/A

Pre-1986 dealer samples

Exc.	V.G.	Fair
6000	5500	5000

Beretta Model 12S

Similar to the Model 12 but with an improved safety system, sights, and folding stock fixture. Production began in 1978 when it replaced the Model 12.

Photo courtesy private NFA collection

Pre-1968

Exc.	V.G.	Fair
12500	11000	10000

Pre-1986 conversions

Exc.	V.G.	Fair
N/A	N/A	N/A

Pre-1986 dealer samples

Exc.	V.G.	Fair
6000	5500	5000

Franchi LF-57

First produced in Italy in 1960, this submachine gun is chambered for the 9mm cartridge. It was placed in service with the Italian navy. Produced until 1980. It is fitted with an 8" barrel and has a magazine capacity of 20 or 40 rounds. Equipped with a folding stock. Rate of fire is about 500 rounds per minute. Marked "S P A LUIGI FRANCHI-BRESCIA-CAL9P." Weight is 7 lbs.

Pre-1968

Exc.	V.G.	Fair
9500	8500	7500

Pre-1986 conversions

Exc.	V.G.	Fair
N/A	N/A	N/A

Pre-1986 dealer samples

Exc.	V.G.	Fair
4500	4000	3500

Beretta Model 93R

Built of the Beretta Model 92 frame and slide, this machine pistol is chambered for the 9mm Parabellum cartridge. It is fitted with a 6.1" barrel with muzzle brake and uses a 15- or 20-round magazine. Can be fitted with a shoulder stock. Rate of fire is about 1,100 rounds per minute. Has a 3-round burst mode, and a small swing-down metal foregrip mounted on the front of the triggerguard. Weight is about 2.5 lbs. Used by the Italian anti-terrorist units.

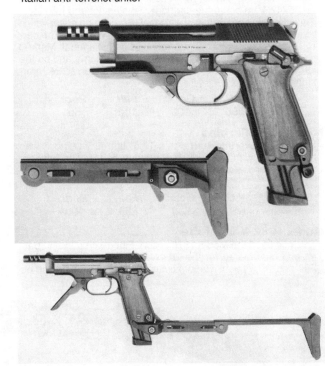

Beretta Model 93R • Courtesy Thomas Nelson, *The World's Machine Pistols, Vol. II*

Model 1870 Rifle • Private collection, Paul Goodwin photo

Pre-1968

Exc.	V.G.	Fair
N/A	N/A	N/A

Pre-1986 conversions

Exc.	V.G.	Fair
16000	15000	14000

Pre-1986 dealer samples

Exc.	V.G.	Fair
10500	4000	3500

RIFLES

Prior to 1965 Italy used the U.S. M1 carbine as well as the M1 Garand. Beretta manufactured a large number of these rifles and many are still in use by some military units. Also used by counter-terrorist units is the HK G3 SG1 sniper rifle and the Mauser Model 66 sniper rifle.

VETTERLI

NOTE: See also *Switzerland, Rifles, Vetterli.*

Model 1870 Rifle

This rifle was produced at Brescia and Torino arsenals under license from the Swiss firm Vetterli. It was chambered for the 10.35x47Rmm centerfire cartridge. Single shot and full stock. This rifle was fitted with a sheet steel bolt opening cover which rotates left to right to close over the receiver opening. The barrel was 34" in length with the rear portion hexagonal. Marked on the upper left barrel flat with the maker's name and on the left barrel flat, the date. There is also a short barrel (24") version of this rifle.

Exc.	V.G.	Good	Fair	Poor
550	350	200	100	50

Model 1870 Carbine

Same as above but fitted with a 17.5" barrel. The stock was half stocked with brass or steel forearm bands. The bayonet folded under the barrel with the blade tip inserted into the forearm.

Exc.	V.G.	Good	Fair	Poor
850	650	500	250	100

Model 1882 Naval Rifle

This rifle used the Model 1870 action. Fitted with a 28.75" barrel and chambered for the 10.4x47R Vetterli-Vitali cartridge. Full stocked. Weight is approximately 9 lbs. This model had no loading port but was charged by loading through the open action. The tube held 8 rounds. Made at Turni.

Exc.	V.G.	Good	Fair	Poor
850	650	500	250	100

Model 1870/87 Rifle/Carbine (Vetterli-Vitali)

This rifle was the same as the Model 1870 with the important exception of having been converted to magazine feed. The 4-round magazine was developed by Guiseppe Vitali. The magazine is unusual because the charger had to be fully inserted and then withdrawn with a string as the cartridge stripped away. Over 1,000,000 of these rifles were issued. A large number of these converted rifles and carbines were sold to Russia.

NOTE: Some of these rifles were converted to 6.5mm caliber and designated the Model 1870/87/15.

Exc.	V.G.	Good	Fair	Poor
850	650	500	250	100

Model 1870/87 Vetterli-Vitali rifle with close-up of stock cartouche • Courtesy Stoddard Martial collection, Paul Goodwin photo

Model 1891 Rifle • Courtesy West Point Museum, Paul Goodwin photo

CARCANO

NOTE: For drawings, data, and history see *The Carcano: Italy's Military Rifle* by Richard Hobbs, 1997.

Fucile Modello 1891 Rifle

Designed by Salvator Carcano, the Model 1891 was adopted as Italy's standard service rifle in 1892. A 6.5x52mm caliber bolt action rifle with a 30.6" barrel, 6-shot Mannlicher clip loading magazine, full-length stock, split bridge receiver, and a tangent rear sight with a wooden handguard and barrel bands retaining the stock. Fitted for a knife-type bayonet. On early versions the barrel behind the rear sights is octagonal. Weight is about 8.5 lbs. Produced at the Brescia and Terni arsenals. On post-1922 examples Roman numerals appear on the upper right barrel flat, denoting the year of the Mussolini rule. Many millions of this rifle were produced through World War II.

Exc.	V.G.	Good	Fair	Poor
350	200	125	75	40

Italian troops with their Carcano rifles, Courtesy Paul S. Scarlata

Model 1891 Carbine

Same as above but half stocked with an 18" barrel with folding bayonet attached to the muzzle. Weight is about 6.5 lbs.

Exc.	V.G.	Good	Fair	Poor
350	200	125	75	40

Model 1891 TS (Truppe Speciali)

Similar to the Carbine above but without permanently attached bayonet. The bayonet is attached to the fitting by rotating into position over the barrel.

Exc.	V.G.	Good	Fair	Poor
350	200	125	75	40

Model 1891/24 Carbine

Similar to the Model 1891 but with different rear sights and no folding bayonet.

Courtesy Richard M. Kumor Sr.

Exc.	V.G.	Good	Fair	Poor
350	200	125	75	40

Model 1891/28 Carbine

Chambered for the 6.5x52mm cartridge. Fitted with an 18" barrel. Otherwise similar in appearance to the Model 1891/24 carbine. This rifle was produced between 1928 and 1938 with

Model 91 TS Carbine showing bayonet fitting • Private collection, Paul Goodwin photo

barrel dates so stamped. Rear sight adjustable from 600 to 1,500 meters. Produced at a number of different Italian arsenals. Weight is about 6.75 lbs.

NOTE: The grenade launcher was called the "Tromboni Launchi Bombe."

M91/28 Carbine with grenade launcher • Courtesy Richard M. Kumor Sr.

NOTE: Model 91/28 Carbine is rare and will command a substantial premium. Models in excellent condition can sell as high as $5,000. This model is encountered so seldom that prices are not given. Consult an expert prior to a sale.

Model 1938 Short Rifle (Prototype)

This model is chambered for the 7.35x51mm cartridge and fitted with a 22" barrel. It has a 6-round detachable box magazine. Bent bolt handle. It is full stocked with one barrel band and exposed barrel and bayonet lug. Long handguard. Simple fixed rear sight. Weight is about 7.5 lbs. Produced at the Terni arsenal. Very rare.

Exc.	V.G.	Good	Fair	Poor
N/A	—	—	—	—

Model 1938 Short Rifle (Production version)

As above but with two barrel bands and half-length handguard. The left side of the butt stock is marked in large letters "cal. 7.35." Rear sight is fixed at 200 meters. Weight is about 6.5 lbs.

NOTE: This rifle marked the first new caliber for Italian military rifles, the 7.35mm. When World War II began, about 285,000 rifles had been built in 7.35mm. From then on all Model 1938 Short Rifles and their variants were produced in the older 6.5mm caliber.

Exc.	V.G.	Good	Fair	Poor
275	150	100	60	25

NOTE: For original 7.35mm rifles add a premium of 50 percent.

Model 1938 Cavalry Carbine

This model has a 17.75" barrel. It is fitted with a folding bayonet that fits under the barrel when not deployed. Chambered

for the 7.35x53mm or 6.5mm cartridge, this carbine was issued to Italian paratroopers in the late 1930s. Built by FNA in Brescia and other Italian firms. The rear sight is a fixed 200-meter sight for rifles chambered for the 7.35mm cartridge. About 100,000 were produced, but it is not often seen in North America. Weight is about 6.5 lbs.

NOTE: A very scarce carbine. No pricing information available.

Model 1938 Carbine • Courtesy West Point Museum, Paul Goodwin photo

Exc.	V.G.	Good	Fair	Poor
N/A	—	—	—	—

Model 1938 T.S. Carbine

Same as above but with bayonet not permanently attached. Weight is about 6.75 lbs. Approximately 200,000 of these rifles were built.

Courtesy Richard M. Kumor Sr.

Exc.	V.G.	Good	Fair	Poor
200	100	75	40	20

NOTE: For original 7.35mm rifles add a premium of 50 percent.

Model 1938 Rifle • Courtesy West Point Museum, Paul Goodwin photo

Model 1938/43 Cavalry & T.S. Carbine

Similar to the Model 1891 but with 5-round magazine. Also chambered for the 7.9mm German cartridge. "7.9" is marked behind the rear sight. Barrel length is 18". Rear sight is fixed at 200 meters. Made in small numbers during WWII during German occupation of Italy.

Exc.	V.G.	Good	Fair	Poor
400	300	200	100	75

Model 1941 Rifle

This is a 6.5mm rifle fitted with a 27.25" barrel and 6-round detachable box magazine. Very similar to the Model 1891 but for length and rear sight from 300 to 1,000 meters. Weight about 8.2 lbs.

NOTE: A few of these rifles were sold to Israel at the end of World War II and these are marked with the Star of David.

Courtesy Richard M. Kumor Sr.

Exc.	V.G.	Good	Fair	Poor
250	150	120	75	50

Italian Youth Rifle

Smaller version of full size military and chambered for 6.5mm cartridge. Barrel length is 14.4".

Courtesy Richard M. Kumor Sr.

Exc.	V.G.	Good	Fair	Poor
450	375	250	150	75

NOTE: Add $75 for dedication plaque.

Breda Model PG

Chambered for the 7x57mm rimless cartridge, this is a gas operated self-loading rifle with an 18" barrel and 20-round detachable box magazine. The particular rifle was made by Beretta for Costa Rica and is marked "GOBIERNO DE COSTA RICA," with the date 1935 and Roman numerals XIII. Weight was about 11.5 lbs. Fitted for a Costa Rican Mauser bayonet.

Exc.	V.G.	Good	Fair	Poor
750	600	450	250	150

Beretta Model BM59-Select Fire Assault Rifle

This select fire rifle closely resembles the U.S. M1 Garand rifle. Chambered for the 7.62x51mm cartridge, it is fitted with a 19" barrel and 20-round magazine. It has a rate of fire of 750 rounds per minute. Weight is about 10 lbs. Marked "P BERETTA BM59" on the top rear of the receiver. Produced from 1961 to 1966. This rifle did see service in the Italian army. There are a number of variations to this rifle, including the BM59 Alpini with folding stock short forearm and bipod for use by Alpine troops, and the BM59 Parachutist Rifle with 18" barrel, folding stock, and detachable muzzle brake (the Italians referred to it as a Tri-Comp).

Pre-1968

Exc.	V.G.	Fair
5500	5000	4500

Pre-1986 conversions

Exc.	V.G.	Fair
3500	3250	3000

Pre-1986 dealer samples

Exc.	V.G.	Fair
3000	2750	2500

Beretta AR70/.223 Select Fire Assault Rifle

Chambered for the 5.56x45mm cartridge, this select fire rifle was fitted with a 17.5" barrel and a 30-round magazine. Most were fitted with a solid buttstock while others were fitted with a folding stock. Weight was about 8.3 lbs. Marked "P BERETTA AR 70/223 MADE IN ITALY" on the left side of the receiver. This rifle was not widely adopted. Produced from 1972 to 1980.

Photo courtesy private NFA collection

Pre-1968 (Rare)

Exc.	V.G.	Fair
12000	8000	8000

Pre-1986 conversions

Exc.	V.G.	Fair
10000	7500	5000

Pre-1986 dealer samples

Exc.	V.G.	Fair
6500	5000	5000

- -

Breda Model PG • Paul Goodwin photo

Model BM59 • Courtesy West Point Museum, Paul Goodwin photo

Beretta SC 70 Select Fire Assault Rifle

Similar to the AR 70 and chambered for the 5.56x45mm cartridge. It feeds from a 30-round magazine. The SC 70 has a folding stock and is fitted with a 17.5" barrel. Weight is about 8.8 lbs. The SC 70 short carbine also has a folding stock and is fitted with a 13.7" barrel. Weight is about 8.3 lbs. Both of these rifles are still in production and used by the Italian army since approved for service in 1990.

SC 70 Carbine • Photo courtesy private NFA collection

SC 70 Short Carbine • Photo courtesy private NFA collection

Pre-1968

Exc.	V.G.	Fair
12000	9500	8500

Pre-1986 conversions

Exc.	V.G.	Fair
10000	8000	6500

Pre-1986 dealer samples

Exc.	V.G.	Fair
8000	6500	5500

AR-70

A .223 caliber, semiautomatic rifle with a 17.7" barrel, adjustable diopter sights, and an 8- or 30-shot magazine. Black epoxy finish with a synthetic stock. Weight is approximately 8.3 lbs.

NIB	Exc.	V.G.	Good	Fair	Poor
2500	2200	1900	1500	1000	—

BM-59 Standard Grade

A gas-operated semiautomatic rifle with detachable box magazine. Chambered for .308 cartridge. Walnut stock. Barrel length is 19.3" with muzzle brake. Magazine capacity is 5, 10, or 20 rounds. Weight is about 9.5 lbs.

NIB	Exc.	V.G.	Good	Fair	Poor
2200	1700	1200	700	400	—

SHOTGUNS

Franchi SPAS 12

A 12 gauge slide action or semiautomatic shotgun with a 21.5" barrel and 9-shot magazine. Anodized black finish with a composition folding or fixed stock. Weight is about 9.25 lbs.

NIB	Exc.	V.G.	Good	Fair	Poor
950	800	600	500	400	300

Franchi SPAS 15

Similar to the SPAS 12 but with a detachable 6-round box magazine. Tubular steel folding stock and 18" barrel or fixed stock with 21" barrel. Weight is about 8.5 lbs. Very few imported into the U.S.

NIB	Exc.	V.G.	Good	Fair	Poor
4500	4000	3500	2500	—	—

NOTE: For guns with folding stock and 18" barrel add $1,000.

MACHINE GUNS

Italy used the Maxim Model 1906 and Model 1911. Both of these models were chambered for the 6.5mm cartridge. During World War I, Italy purchased a number of Colt Model 1914 guns (Potato Diggers) chambered for the 6.5mm cartridge. When the war ended, Italy received a large number of Austrian Schwarzlose Model 1907/12 as war reparations. The first Italian light machine gun was the Breda Model 1924, the forerunner of the Breda Model 30.

After World War II, Italy adopted the U.S. Model 1919A4 and .50 NM2 HB guns, as well as the MG42/59, for which several Italian firms make the components under license.

Beretta M70/78

Similar to the Model 70/223 but fitted with a heavy 17.5" barrel. Magazine capacity is 30 or 40 rounds. Rate of fire is 700 rounds per minute. Marked "P BERETTA FM 70/78 MADE IN ITALY" on left side of the receiver. First produced in 1978 with production ending in 1983.

Revelli Model 1914 • Courtesy private NFA collection, Paul Goodwin photo

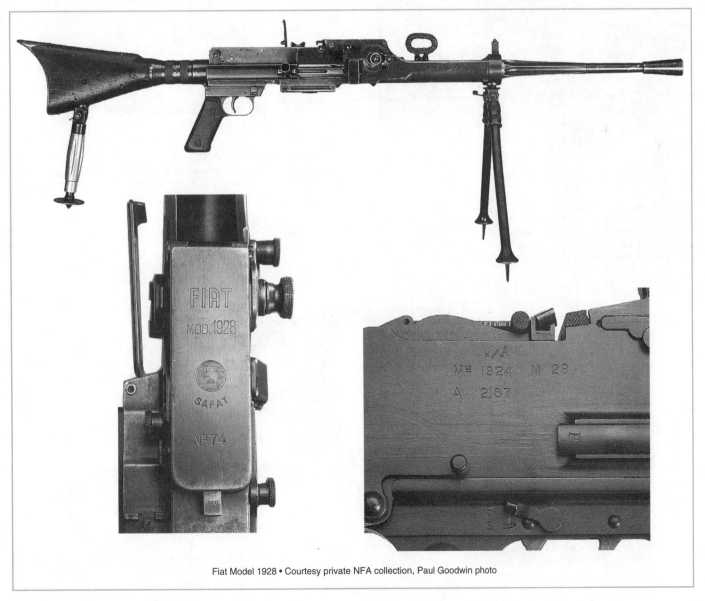

Fiat Model 1928 • Courtesy private NFA collection, Paul Goodwin photo

Pre-1968

Exc.	V.G.	Fair
N/A	N/A	N/A

Pre-1986 conversions

Exc.	V.G.	Fair
N/A	N/A	N/A

Pre-1986 dealer samples (Rare)

Exc.	V.G.	Fair
9000	9000	8500

World War I Italian machine gun team with Model 1914 Revelli • Robert G. Segel collection

Revelli Model 1914

This was the first Italian-designed medium machine gun to be made in quantity. It was chambered for the 6.5mm cartridge and fitted with a 26" barrel. It was fed by a unique 50-round magazine with 10 compartments holding 5 rounds each.

Because of its blowback system where the barrel moved a short distance rearward before the bolt moved away from the breech, there was no extraction system other than to oil the cartridges so that they did not rupture. Rate of fire was about 400 rounds per minute. Weight was 38 lbs. without tripod, 50 lbs. with tripod. The gun was manufactured by Fiat. Many of these guns were used by the Italians in World War II as well as in the first world war.

Pre-1968

Exc.	V.G.	Fair
7500	7000	6500

Pre-1986 conversions

Exc.	V.G.	Fair
N/A	N/A	N/A

Pre-1986 dealer samples (Rare)

Exc.	V.G.	Fair
N/A	N/A	N/A

Fiat Model 1928 (SAFAT)

This is a light version of the Revelli Model 1914. Chambered for the 6.5 Carcano cartridge. Magazine is a 20-round magazine. Rate of fire is about 500 rounds per minute. Weight is approximately 21 lbs. Only a few thousand were manufactured during its limited production. Very Rare.

Pre-1968

Exc.	V.G.	Fair
N/A	N/A	N/A

Pre-1986 conversions

Exc.	V.G.	Fair
N/A	N/A	N/A

Pre-1986 dealer samples (Rare)

Exc.	V.G.	Fair
N/A	N/A	N/A

Revelli/Fiat Model 35

This is a converted Revelli Model 1914 to 8mm. It is an air-cooled gun. It is fed by a 300-round belt. It's fired from a closed bolt. It was not a successful gun. Weight without tripod was 40 lbs.

Pre-1968

Exc.	V.G.	Fair
6000	5000	4500

Fiat Model 35 • Courtesy private NFA collection, Paul Goodwin photo

Breda Model 37 with receiver markings • Paul Goodwin photo

Breda Model 30

First produced in Italy in 1930, this machine gun was chambered for the 6.5x52mm cartridge. It is fitted with a 20.3" barrel. Magazine capacity is 20 rounds. Rate of fire is 475 rounds per minute. Marked "MTR LEGG MOD 30....BREDA ROMA" on top of receiver. Weight is about 22 lbs. Production on this model ceased in 1937. This was the primary Italian machine gun of World War II.

NOTE: A number of pre-1968 7mm Costa Rican contract guns are in the U.S. These are valued the same as the 6.5mm guns.

Pre-1968
Exc.	V.G.	Fair
9500	8500	8000

Pre-1986 conversions
Exc.	V.G.	Fair
N/A	N/A	N/A

Pre-1986 dealer samples (Rare)
Exc.	V.G.	Fair
5500	5000	4000

Breda Model 37

Chambered for the 8x59 Breda cartridge, this gas operated machine gun had a rate of fire of 450 rounds per minute. It was fitted with a 26.5" barrel and weighs approximately 43 lbs. It was fed with a 20-round strip. Marked "MITRAGLIATRICE BREDA MOD 37" on the left side of the receiver. Produced from 1936 to 1943, this was the standard heavy machine gun of the Italian army during World War II. The Model 37 was considered to be one of the best Italian machine guns used in World War II, mainly because of its reliability and accuracy.

Pre-1968
Exc.	V.G.	Fair
25000	22500	20000

Pre-1986 conversions
Exc.	V.G.	Fair
N/A	N/A	N/A

Pre-1986 dealer samples (12 known)
Exc.	V.G.	Fair
15000	14000	12000

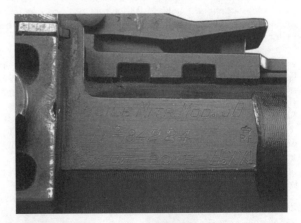

Breda Model 30 with receiver markings • Paul Goodwin photo

JAPAN

Japanese Military Conflicts, 1870-1945

The year 1868 marks the beginning of Japanese adoption of Western civilization and rapid modernization into an industrial and military power. The Japanese military was successful in the First Sino-Japanese War (1894-1895), as well as the Russo-Japanese War (1904-1905). In 1910, Japan annexed Korea and established a puppet-state in Manchuria in 1932. In 1937, the Japanese invaded northern China to begin the Sino-Japanese War (1937-1945). On December 7, 1941, the Japanese bombed Pearl Harbor, thus entering World War II. The war ended in August 1945. During World War II Japan had 9,100,000 men under arms. At the end of the war 1,834,000 had been killed or wounded. Since the end of World War II the Japanese military has operated on a very small scale, mostly for domestic defense.

Bibliographical Note: Little has been written about Japanese military weapons. For a good overview see A.J. Barker, *Japanese Army Handbook, 1939-1945*, 1979.

HANDGUNS

Bibliographical Note: For technical data, history, and photos see Fred Honeycutt, Jr., *Military Pistols of Japan*, 3rd Ed., Julian Books, 1994.

Type 26 Revolver

A 9mm caliber double action hinged-barrel revolver with a 6-shot cylinder. Because this pistol does not have a hammer spur, it only functions in double action. Fitted with a 4.75" barrel. Checkered beech grips. Grips from later examples have 19 serrations. Weight is about 31 oz. Manufactured from 1893 to 1924 in various government arsenals. Marked on right side of frame. This revolver was used by NCOs during WWII. Less than 60,000 of these revolvers were manufactured.

SNAP SHOT
WHAT'S IT LIKE - THE JAPANESE TYPE 26 REVOLVER

In the last third of the 19th century, the Japanese army changed from sword-wielding Samurai to a European-trained force armed with modern rifles of native design and manufacture. But because of the "cult of the sword" few Japanese officers carried handguns and it was not until 1893 that the Meiji 26 Nen Ken Ju * (Meiji Type 26) revolver was adopted for issue to enlisted personnel, non-commissioned officers and mounted troops.

The Type 26 was a six-shot design that combined features of the American S&W (top-break frame and extraction), French Mle. 1892 (removable sideplate) and Belgian Galand (trigger mechanism) revolvers. It featured a double-action-only lockwork and was chambered for the 9mm Type 26 cartridge which propelled a 150 gr. lead bullet to an unimpressive 660 fps. Manufactured at the Kokura arsenal for both military and civilian sales, production continued until 1923. While replaced in front line service by various Nambu pistols, the Type 26 remained in service until 1945.

I recently obtained a Type 26 to test fire. Mechanically it was perfect with a bright bore and the cylinder locked up tight with no play at all. The trigger pull was quite heavy, albeit consistent with no staging. Custom reloaded 9mm Type 26 ammunition was obtained from the Old Western Scrounger. Setting up a combat target at a 7 yards I sent 30 rounds of downrange and, despite less then optimal ergonomics provided by the small grips and small sights, and the heavy trigger pull, the revolver pointed quite naturally and I was able to put all of my rounds into a well centered group.

While the Type 26 seemed rugged and foolproof, it was not the most user friendly of handguns. I'd rather have a S&W Victory Model any day!

* - Japanese model numbers are the year of the reign of the current emperor the weapon was approved. The Type 26 Revolver was approved on the 26th year of the Meiji era (1893).

Paul Scarlata

A Type 26 revolver sold at auction for $1,495. Complete with T-26 holster. Condition is 99 percent.
Rock Island Auction Company, August 2004

Courtesy Amoskeag Auction Co., Inc.

Exc.	V.G.	Good	Fair	Poor
850	650	400	300	150

4th Year Type Nambu Pistol

This is a quality-built semiautomatic pistol chambered for the 8mm cartridge. It is fitted with a 4.7" barrel and has a magazine capacity of 8 rounds. It can be identified by the grip safety located on the front strap and tangent sights. The early models, known as "Grandpa" to collectors, can be identified by a wooden-bottom magazine and stock slot. Later pistols, known as "Papa" Nambu, have aluminum-bottom magazines and only a very few "Papas" were slotted for stocks. The values shown here are only approximate. Different variations may bring different prices and an appraisal is recommended. Pistols with original wooden stocks are worth considerably more.

It is estimated that approximately 8,500 of these pistols were produced.

Grandpa

Grandpa • Courtesy of James Rankin

Exc.	V.G.	Good	Fair	Poor
5000	3500	2000	1500	800

NOTE: Add $1,500 for original matching shoulder stock-holster.

Papa

Papa • Courtesy of James Rankin

Exc.	V.G.	Good	Fair	Poor
1500	900	650	450	300

Baby Nambu

As above, with a 3.5" barrel. 7mm cartridge is unique to the gun. A much smaller version of the Papa 8mm pistol. It is a well-made piece. Production ceased in 1927 with about 6,500 pistols produced.

Courtesy Rock Island Auction Company

Exc.	V.G.	Good	Fair	Poor
3500	2500	1500	1000	750

A Japanese Baby Nambu sold at auction for $5,175. Condition is 99 percent blue and 90 percent straw. *Rock Island Auction Company, December 2004*

14th Year Type Nambu Pistol/T-14

Similar to the 4th Year Type but without a grip safety and with grooved grips and a larger triggerguard. Manufactured until 1945. Early guns have a small triggerguard. Later models have a much larger triggerguard. Early guns will bring a premium of 20 percent. The month and year of production are indicated on the right side of the receiver, just below the serial numbers on both the Type 14 and Type 94 pistols. The guns are dated from the beginning of the reign of Hirohito (Sho-wa period), which started in 1925. Thus 3.12 means 1928-Dec. and 19.5 means 1944-May.

From 1926 to 1939 (small triggerguard) about 66,700 pistols were manufactured. From 1939 to 1945 (large triggerguard) approximately 73,000 pistols were produced.

Courtesy Orvel Reichert

An early Type 14 pistol with holster sold at auction for $7,475. Documentation from officer from USS Iowa. All numbers are matching. Condition is mint.
Rock Island Auction Company, December 2004

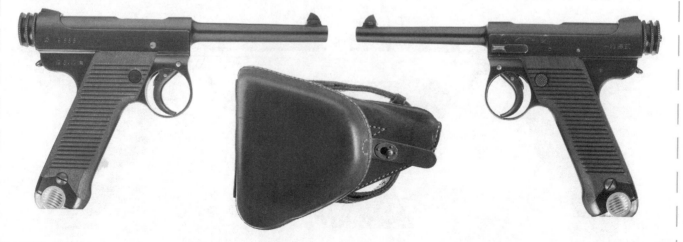

Type 94 Pistol/T-94

An 8mm caliber semiautomatic pistol with a 3.8" barrel and 6-shot magazine. Weight is about 27 oz. This was a secondary service pistol issued in WWII. Most late-war examples are poorly constructed and finished. Manufactured from 1935 to 1945. Approximately 70,000 of these pistols were produced.

Courtesy Rock Island Auction Company

Exc.	V.G.	Good	Fair	Poor
500	300	250	175	125

Hamada Skiki (Type) 2

Designed in 1942. There were several variations of this pistol chambered for both 7.65mm and 8mm Nambu. Production started in 1942 and ended in 1945. Probably less than 1,500 pistols were assembled. Rare. An expert opinion should be sought prior to a sale.

Courtesy James Rankin

Exc.	V.G.	Good	Fair	Poor
4500	3500	2500	2000	1500

T-14 pistol and rig with matching magazines. This example features the later large trigger guard • Courtesy Michael Wamsher, Paul Goodwin photo

Exc.	V.G.	Good	Fair	Poor
500	300	200	150	100

A Type 94 pistol dated Showah 12.8 sold at auction for $2,875. Conplete with two matching magazines and holster. Condition is mint. *Rock Island Auction Company, Dec. 2004*

SUBMACHINE GUNS

The Japanese military used Bergmann submachine guns built by SIG. These guns were similar to the MP 18 but chambered for the 7.63 Mauser cartridge and used a box magazine. These guns were fitted for a bayonet. It was not until the late 1930s that the Japanese began a development program to produce their own submachine gun; the first one was the Type 100/40.

Type 100/40

Adopted for use in 1940, this submachine gun is chambered for the 8x21mm Nambu cartridge and fitted with a 9" barrel with perforated jacket, fitted with a bayonet bar. It is mounted on a wooden half stock with tubular receiver made at the Kokura arsenal. These guns will also be seen with a folding stock made at the Nagoya arsenal. It is estimated that some 10,000 guns were built with fixed stocks and about 6,000 were built with folding stocks. Both types had 30-round box magazines. Rate of fire is approximately 450 rounds per minute. Weight was about 7.5 lbs. This model was issued primarily to paratroopers.

Japanese Type 100/40 • Courtesy Thomas Nelson, *World's Submachine Guns, Vol. I*

Pre-1968

Exc.	V.G.	Fair
13500	12000	11000

Pre-1986 conversions

Exc.	V.G.	Fair
N/A	N/A	N/A

Pre-1986 dealer samples

Exc.	V.G.	Fair
N/A	N/A	N/A

Type 100/44 • Courtesy West Point Museum, Paul Goodwin photo

Type 100/44

This model was first produced in Japan in 1944. It is chambered for the 8mm Nambu cartridge. The barrel is 9.2" long with a honeycombed barrel jacket without bayonet bar. The side-mounted magazine capacity is 30 rounds. Markings are in Japanese on the rear of the receiver. Produced until the end of the war. Weight is about 8.5 lbs. Rate of fire is 800 rounds per minute. Approximately 8,000 were produced at the Nagoya arsenal. This improved version was issued to the infantry.

Pre-1968

Exc.	V.G.	Fair
13500	12000	11000

SNAP SHOT
JAPANESE TYPE 100 (1944)

The 8mm Nambu Type 100 submachine gun was the only type of submachine gun produced by Japan in World War II. The first two versions of the Type 100 (1940) were well made with a cyclic rate of fire of 450 rounds per minute and came in two variations; a one-piece wood stock infantry version and a folding stock paratrooper version. The type 100 is a blowback operated, full automatic only submachine gun using a 30-round detachable two-position box magazine. The Kokura Arsenal produced approximately 7,000 of the infantry version and Nagoya produced approximately 3,000 of the paratroop version.

In mid 1944, the Atsuta Arsenal in Nagoya started producing the third and final variant of the Type 100 (1944). Simpler production methods were needed to mass produce the Type 100 to meet the increased demand. The Type 100 (1944) version used the same action and is constructed in similar ways as the Type 100 (1940) but manufacturing shortcuts were employed including the use of spot welding in construction. The main operating recoil spring was strengthened and elongated resulting in an increased rate of fire to 800 rounds per minute, almost doubling the earlier 1940 version. The 8mm Nambu pistol cartridge was so anemic that by increasing the rate of fire it would guarantee a higher number of hits, thereby producing the required mortal or debilitating wound effect. Approximately 7,000 to 8,000 were produced.

Loading and operating the Type 100 (1944) is similar to other blowback operated submachine guns. The magazine is hand loaded with 30 rounds and inserted into the magazine well. The bolt is retracted and the gun is ready to fire. The first impression on firing the Type 100 is the high rate of fire and is initially a bit surprising. Nevertheless, the operation is smooth and, with little perceived recoil, is easily controlled in long bursts. A muzzle compensator is attached to help prevent muzzle climb. Accuracy is adequate up to about 100 yards. The gun is well balanced and easy to handle. The only drawback is that a fully loaded magazine can be emptied in about 2.25 seconds.

The Type 100 is relatively rare in the U.S. collectors market as a small number were allowed to be brought home by G.I.s as war trophies, though they were generally not allowed to bring back magazines. Thus, an original Type 100 submachine gun magazine is far rarer than the gun itself.

Robert G. Segel

Pre-1986 conversions

Exc.	V.G.	Fair
N/A	N/A	N/A

Pre-1986 dealer samples

Exc.	V.G.	Fair
N/A	N/A	N/A

RIFLES

Bibliographical Note: For historical information, technical data and photos see *Military Rifles of Japan*, 4th edition. Fred Honeycutt Jr., 1993.

MARTINI

Model 1874 Peabody-Martini Rifle

Chambered for the .45 Turkish centerfire cartridge and fitted with a 32.5" barrel. Blued barrel and furniture with case hardened or blued receiver. Numbered in Arabic script. About 7,000 built for Japanese Navy.

Exc.	V.G.	Good	Fair	Poor
—	750	500	350	150

MURATA

This series of Japanese military rifles was designed by Major Tsuneyoshi, superintendent of Japanese small arms in the late 1870s. These first single-shot bolt action rifles were based on the French Gras design. Later, Murata was influenced by the French Lebel with its tubular magazine. These rifles were built at the Imperial arsenal in Tokyo.

Murata Type 13 (M.1880)

This was the first Japanese-designed bolt action rifle. This was a single-shot rifle with no extractor or safety. Chambered for the 11x60Rmm cartridge with a barrel length of 31.25". One piece full-length stock with two barrel bands. The machinery to build this rifle was purchased from Winchester. The rear barrel flat is stamped with the Imperial chrysanthemum. The left side of the receiver is stamped with Japanese characters.

Exc.	V.G.	Good	Fair	Poor
2000	1500	1000	600	400

Murata Type 16

Same as above but fitted with a 25" barrel for cavalry use.

Exc.	V.G.	Good	Fair	Poor
2500	1650	1200	700	500

Murata Type 18 (M.1885)

An 11mm caliber bolt-action rifle with a 31.25" barrel, and full-length stock secured by two barrel bands. This was an improved version of the Type 13, which added receiver gas escape ports, a flat-top receiver ring, and a safety. These rifles were used in the Sino-Japanese War of 1894 and the Russo-Japanese War as well.

Courtesy Rock Island Auction Company

Courtesy Buffalo Bill Historical Center, Cody, Wyoming

Exc.	V.G.	Good	Fair	Poor
1750	1200	800	200	100

Murata Type 22 (M.1889)

Produced circa 1889-1899 in caliber 8x53Rmm. Fitted with a 29.50" barrel with 8-round tubular magazine located in the forearm. This model was full stocked to the muzzle with straight grip. There were two variations of this rifle. The early version had a barrel band forward of the forend band. In the lat-

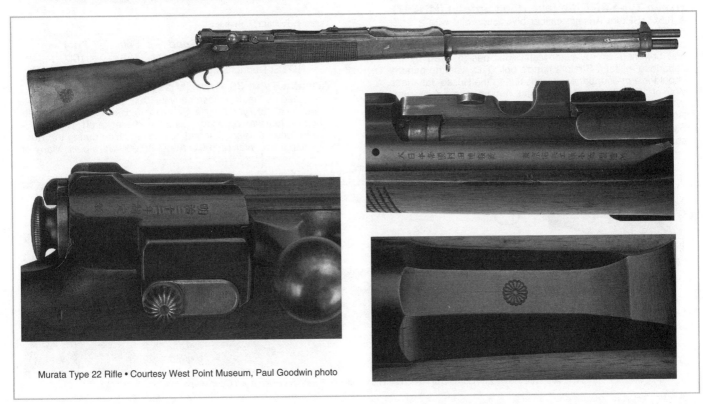

Murata Type 22 Rifle • Courtesy West Point Museum, Paul Goodwin photo

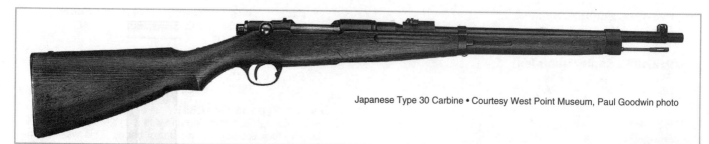

Japanese Type 30 Carbine • Courtesy West Point Museum, Paul Goodwin photo

er version, this extra band was eliminated. This was Japan's first smokeless powder military rifle and was the standard rifle issued to Japanese forces in the Sino-Japanese War of 1894. It remained in service until the Russo-Japanese War of 1904. Weight is about 8.7 lbs.

Rifle

Exc.	V.G.	Good	Fair	Poor
1850	1400	1000	300	200

Murata Type 22 Carbine
Introduced in 1894 and fitted with a 19.5" barrel and 5-round magazine. No bayonet fitting. A rare carbine.

Courtesy Richard M. Kumor Sr.

Exc.	V.G.	Good	Fair	Poor
2500	1900	1400	350	200

ARISAKA
This series of Japanese military rifles was developed by Colonel Nariake Arisaka, Superintendent of the Tokyo Arsenal. His task was to find a replacement for the Murata rifles that showed some defects during the Sino-Japanese War of 1894.

Arisaka Type 30 Rifle (aka Hook Safety) (M.1897)
A 6.5x51SRmm Arisaka caliber bolt action rifle with a 31.5" barrel, 5-shot magazine and full-length stock secured by two barrel bands and a wooden upper handguard. This was the first box-magazine Mauser-Mannlicher design used by the Japanese military. Straight handle bolt. This was the primary shoulder arm of Japanese troops during the Russo-Japanese War of 1904. Some of these rifles remained in service until WWII. A number of these rifles were sold to Great Britain and Russia during World War I. The Type 30 was also built for Siam (Thailand) and marked by that country's crest on the receiver bridge. It was designed by Nariaki Arisaka. Manufac-

tured from 1897 to 1905. The rifle gets its nickname, "hook-safety," from the prominent hook projecting from the left side of the rear of the bolt.

Exc.	V.G.	Good	Fair	Poor
600	500	375	125	75

Arisaka Type 30 Carbine (aka Hook Safety Carbine)
As above, with a 20" barrel and no upper handguard.

Courtesy Richard M. Kumor Sr.

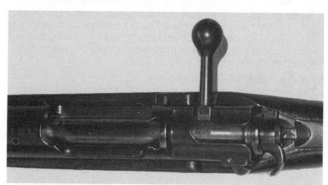

Courtesy Richard M. Kumor Sr.

Exc.	V.G.	Good	Fair	Poor
650	550	400	150	100

NOTE: Deduct 30 percent if mum stamping is ground off.

Arisaka Type 35 Navy (M.1902)
Adopted by the Japanese navy in 1902, this was an improved version of the Type 30 rifle. Some main differences are that the hook safety was reduced in length and checkered. The receiver included a spring-latched bolt cover. Used during the Russo-Japanese War of 1904. About 40,000 were built. Many of

Japanese Type 35 rifle with close up of breech and hook safety • Private collection, Paul Goodwin photo

Arisaka Type 38 Rifle • Courtesy West Point Museum, Paul Goodwin photo

these were sold to Great Britain and Russia during World War I. All dimensions are the same as the Type 30 rifle.

Exc.	V.G.	Good	Fair	Poor
450	350	250	150	100

SNAP SHOT
THE JAPANESE TYPE 38 ARISAKA RIFLE

The 6.5mm Type 38 (T38) Arisaka was introduced in 1905. Its name comes from COL Arisaka the Chief Superintendent of the Japanese arsenal where the rifle was developed.

Its action is a Mauser derivative, however, unlike most other Mauser derivatives the T38 action is arguably better than that of its daddy. The late gunsmith P. O. Ackley rated the Type 38 Arisaka as the strongest military rifle action he ever tested.

The bolt of the T38 is an absolute gem of simplicity. It has only six parts and that includes a very positive and easy-to-use manual safety mechanism. Takedown and reassembly of the T38 bolt can be done in seconds without tools.

In 1939 the Japanese began to replace the 6.5mm Type 38 Arisaka with the easier-to-make, shorter, lighter, and more powerful 7.7mm Type 99 Arisaka rifle but the latter never came close to replacing the Type 38.

It is not commonly known, but the Type 38 Arisaka was widely used in WWI by England and Russia. England purchased about 500,000 Arisaka rifles from Japan during WWI that were used to equip British naval and irregular forces, and used as training rifles. Russia purchased over 600,000 Arisakas from Japan between 1914 and 1916 arming entire divisions with these rifles.

The Type 38 Arisaka was made in 31.25-inch barreled rifle and 19-inch barreled carbine versions. In addition, a 25-inch barreled Cavalry rifle was made in small quantities. There was also a Type 44 cavalry carbine that used the same action as the Type 38 but had an integral folding bayonet and a Type 97 scoped sniper rifle version. The Type 38 family of rifles and carbines were made in huge numbers being in production from 1905 until the end of WWII and were still in wide use by the Chinese in Korea.

There is no question that the Type 38 family of Arisaka rifles and carbines were among the best and most historically significant bolt-action military rifles ever fielded.

Charles Karwan

Arisaka Type 38 Rifle (M.1905)

A 6.5mm Arisaka caliber bolt action rifle with a 31.5" barrel, 5-shot magazine and large bolt handle. Full-length stock secured by two barrel bands with finger grooves. Weight is about 9 lbs. It was based on the Model 1893 Spanish Mauser. This model was built with a separate sheet steel action cover sliding with the bolt action. This rifle saw extensive use as late as World War II. Some of these rifles were sold to England in 1914 and 1915 and about 600,000 were sold to Russia in 1915 and 1916 in 7mm Mauser caliber. These rifles were originally intended for Mexico and have the Mexican crest of the receiver. These Russian-purchased rifles ended up in Germany in 1917 and were used in the Russian Civil War of 1917. Manufactured from 1905 to 1945. Most production switched to the Type 99 in 7.7mm beginning in 1939. This model was built at a number of different locations from Tokyo, Korea, and China.

Exc.	V.G.	Good	Fair	Poor
200	150	125	90	65

Arisaka Type 38 Carbine

As above, with a 19" barrel and upper handguard. Equipped for a bayonet. Weight is about 7.25 lbs.

Courtesy Richard M. Kumor Sr.

Exc.	V.G.	Good	Fair	Poor
500	300	175	125	85

NOTE: Deduct 30 percent if mum stamping is ground off.

Thai Type 38 Conversions

Short Rifle—.30-06

Exc.	V.G.	Good	Fair	Poor
600	475	350	250	150

Half-Stock Carbine—6.5mm

Exc.	V.G.	Good	Fair	Poor
550	425	300	200	100

Mukden Arsenal Mauser • Private collection, Paul Goodwin photo

Manchurian Mauser Rifle (Mukden Arsenal)

This rifle has many features from both the Mauser 98 and the Arisaka. Barrel length is 29" and most rifles are chambered for the 7.92x57mm cartridge while some are chambered for the Japanese 6.5mm cartridge. Magazine capacity is 5 rounds. Bolt handle is pear shaped. Marked on top of receiver ring with Mukden arsenal symbol.

Exc.	V.G.	Good	Fair	Poor
750	600	450	250	100

Arisaka Type 44 Carbine

Similar to the Type 38 carbine but with an 18.5" barrel and folding bayonet that hinged into the forearm. Weight was about 9 lbs.

A Type 44 Carbine sold at auction for $1,265. Condition is 98 percent blue. Stock is in fine condition. Excellent bore.
Amoskeag Auction Company, Sept. 2003

Courtesy Rock Island Auction Company

Exc.	V.G.	Good	Fair	Poor
750	450	250	150	100

Arisaka Type 97 "Sniper's Rifle"

The Type 38 with a side-mounted 2.5-power telescope and a bipod. Introduced in 1937. The telescope mounted on each rifle was factory fitted and stamped with the serial number of the rifle. The rear sight was a peep with folding from 400 to 2,200 meters. Weight is approximately 11 lbs. with scope.

Exc.	V.G.	Good	Fair	Poor
4000	2500	1200	600	300

Japanese WWII Type 97 Sniper with close-up of scope and markings. All numbers match. Notice full "Mum"
• Courtesy Michael Wamsher, Paul Goodwin photo

A Type 97 Sniper rifle sold at auction for $8,050. Fitted with a 2.5x scope made by Tokyo Dai-Ich Rikugun Zoheisho factory. Condition is 95 percent original finish. Has Mum.
Rock Island Auction Company, December 2004

A Type 99 Sniper rifle with 4x scope sold at auction for $5,750. Mid-production. Scope built by Tokyo Shibaura Denki KK factory. Condition is 95 percent overall. No Mum.
Rock Island Auction Company, Dec. 2004

Courtesy Rock Island Auction Company

Exc.	V.G.	Good	Fair	Poor
500	400	300	100	50

NOTE: Add 30 percent for monopod and dust cover. Deduct 30 percent if mum stamping is ground off.

Arisaka Type 99 Short Rifle

This model is an improved version of the Type 38 rifle. A 7.7mm caliber bolt action rifle with a 26" barrel and full-length stock secured by two barrel bands. Non-detachable magazine capacity is 5 rounds. Fitted with a folding wire monopod. Weight is about 8.5 lbs. Adopted for military use in 1939. The rear sight on this rifle was a graduated leaf-type with folding arms to help aiming at aircraft. Parts such as floor plate, butt plate, bolt cover, and swivel bands were made from metal stampings.The monopod and anti-aircraft sight were phased out as the war progressed. The first use of this model in combat against U.S. forces was during the Battle of Guadalcanal beginning in August, 1942.

Arisaka Type 99 "Last Ditch" Rifle

This is a Type 99 simplified for easier production. Typical features include a cylindrical bolt knob, a fixed peep sight, no front sight guards and a wooden buttplate. Not all rifles have each of these features.

Exc.	V.G.	Good	Fair	Poor
300	200	150	125	100

Test Type 1 Paratroop Rifle

Bolt action rifle chambered for 6.5mm Japanese. Barrel length is 19". Cleaning rod is 17 3/16" long. The stock is a two-piece buttstock with full-length handguard and a hinge attached at the wrist. Metal finish is blued. Total number produced is approximately 200-300 rifles.

Exc.	V.G.	Good	Fair	Poor
1800	1500	1000	500	125

Type 100 Paratroop Rifle

Chambered for 7.7mm Japanese cartridge. Barrel length is 25-1/4" long. Blued cleaning rod 21-5/16" long. Rear sight is adjustable from 300 to 1500 meters. Two-piece buttstock with full handguard can be disassembled with an interrupted-thread connector. Bolt handle is detachable. Metal finish is blued. Total number produced is estimated at 500 rifles.

Exc.	V.G.	Good	Fair	Poor
250	150	100	80	60

NOTE: Add 15 percent for monopod.

Arisaka Type 99 Long Rifle

This variation is the same as the above model but fitted with a 31.4" barrel. Weight is about 9 lbs. This is a scarce variation.

A Type 99 Long Rifle with scope sold at auction for $2,587.50. Fitted with a 2.4x scope. Monopod. Mum ground off. Bolt and dust cover mismatched. Condition is 98 percent.
Rock Island Auction Company, August 2004

Courtesy Rock Island Auction Company

Exc.	V.G.	Good	Fair	Poor
4500	4000	3000	—	

Type 2 Paratroop Rifle

Similar to the model above but with a different style of take-down. This model uses a wedge and bail wire connector. This rifle production began in late 1943.

Courtesy Rock Island Auction Company

Exc.	V.G.	Good	Fair	Poor
2500	1850	1200	500	200

Type 99 "Sniper's Rifle"

The standard Type 99 with a 25.5" barrel and either a 2-1/2 power or 4-power telescope.

Exc.	V.G.	Good	Fair	Poor
2000	1700	1200	500	200

NOTE: The 4x scope is more rare than the 2-1/2 power scope. For 4x scope add $350.

Type 5 Semiautomatic Rifle

A 7.7mm semiautomatic rifle with a 10-round box magazine patterned after the U.S. M1. Made at the Kure Naval Arsenal in 1945. It is believed that approximately 20 were made. Prospective purchasers should secure a qualified appraisal prior to acquisition.

Courtesy Richard M. Kumor Sr.

Exc.	V.G.	Good	Fair	Poor
22000	19000	14000	—	—

MAUSER

G 71 Rifle

This is the same rifle as built for the German Empire. Chambered for the 11x60mm cartridge and fitted with a 33.5" barrel. Full stocked. Single shot. Weight is about 10 lbs.

Exc.	V.G.	Good	Fair	Poor
400	325	250	200	150

SNAP SHOT
ARISAKA TYPE 2 PARATROOPER RIFLE

The Type 2 Arisaka paratrooper rifle is one of only two military rifles to ever reach a significant level of production that had a barrel takedown feature. That is, the barrel can be quickly and easily removed to make a smaller package for parachuting or other purposes. The other was the M1941 Johnson semiautomatic rifle. Since I personally have several dozen parachute jumps with full size rifles, I am not quite sure why this was important.

The Type 2 was based on the excellent Japanese Type 99 7.7mm Arisaka rifle and has all the good features of that fine rifle such as a chrome-lined bore, a simple but extremely strong and reliable bolt that can be disassembled in seconds without tools, good sights, and a positive manual safety that is extremely convenient and fast to disengage.

The major difference is that the barrel and all the forward furniture is held to the receiver via a clever wedge system that is held firmly in place with a screw plug. Probably because of the elite nature of the units that the Type 2 was designed for, the Type 2 rifles were uniformly extremely well made. The Type 2 had a special shorter than normal bayonet. Total production, which began in 1943, was believed to be about 20,000.

However, as the war turned against the Japanese and they went on the defense, the importance of maintaining parachute units went away and further production of the Type 2 was discontinued. An exceptionally high percentage of the Type 2 rifles in circulation appear to have seen very little actual field use and were probably surrendered at the end of the war without seeing action.

Interestingly a scoped and sporterized Type 2 rifle has appeared in a wide range of movies including one of the Dirty Harry series. The evil bad guy typically takes the rifle out of a case and assembles it for dramatic effect.

The Type 2 Arisaka is rarely encountered and highly desirable because of its unique features and association with an elite enemy unit.

Charles Karwan

A Japanese Type 2 Paratroop rifle sold at auction for $1,995. Condition is 95 percent original blue with mint bore. Mum intact.
Amoskeag Auction Company, January 2003

Type 99 with 4x external scope • Courtesy private collection, Paul Goodwin photo

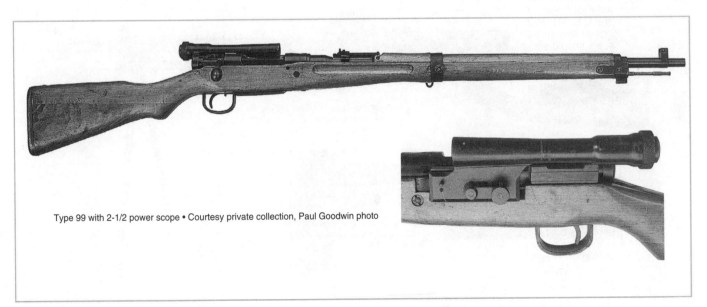

Type 99 with 2-1/2 power scope • Courtesy private collection, Paul Goodwin photo

MACHINE GUNS

The Japanese used the Hotchkiss gun during the Russo-Japanese War and later adopted the Model 1914 Hotchkiss. Both of these guns were chambered for the 6.5mm cartridge.

Japanese Type 1

Introduced in 1941 as an improvement over the Type 92. Barrel length is 23" with cooling fins the same diameter through its length. The muzzle is fitted with a flash hider. Fed by a 30-round metal strip and chambered for the 7.7mm cartridge. Rate of fire is approximately 550 rounds per minute. Weight is about 77 lbs. with tripod.

NOTE: Many of these guns were not stamped "Type 1" but instead "Type 92". The finned barrel is the key feature.

Pre-1968

Exc.	V.G.	Fair
14000	12500	11000

Pre-1986 conversions

Exc.	V.G.	Fair
N/A	N/A	N/A

Pre-1986 dealer samples

Exc.	V.G.	Fair
N/A	N/A	N/A

Japanese Type 3

Medium air-cooled gun chambered for 6.5x51SR Arisaka cartridge and introduced in 1914. The Hotchkiss Model 1897 influenced the design of this gun. Cooling fins on the barrel. Spade grips and tripod mount with sockets for carrying poles. Weight was about 63 lbs. Barrel length was 29.5". Fed from a metal 30-round strip. Rate of fire was about 400 rounds per minute. Introduced in 1914.

Pre-1968

Exc.	V.G.	Fair
12000	10000	9000

Pre-1986 conversions

Exc.	V.G.	Fair
N/A	N/A	N/A

Pre-1986 dealer samples

Exc.	V.G.	Fair
N/A	N/A	N/A

Japanese Type 11

First produced in 1922, this is a light air-cooled machine gun chambered for the 6.5x51SR Arisaka cartridge. The gun utilizes a 30-round hopper feed system. The 19" barrel is finned. Weight is about 22.5 lbs. Rate of fire is 500 rounds per minute. Fitted with a bipod. This was the most widely used machine gun by the Japanese military during combat in China between 1937 and 1939.

Pre-1968

Exc.	V.G.	Fair
9500	8000	7000

Pre-1986 conversions

Exc.	V.G.	Fair
N/A	N/A	N/A

Pre-1986 dealer samples

Exc.	V.G.	Fair
N/A	N/A	N/A

Japanese Type 89

This gun was produced in 1929 and is a copy of the British Vickers aircraft gun but chambered for the 7.7x56R (.303 British) cartridge. Weight is about 27 lbs.

Japanese Type 89 Vickers Aircraft • Courtesy Blake Stevens

Pre-1968

Exc.	V.G.	Fair
16500	15000	13000

Pre-1986 conversions

Exc.	V.G.	Fair
N/A	N/A	N/A

Pre-1986 dealer samples

Exc.	V.G.	Fair
N/A	N/A	N/A

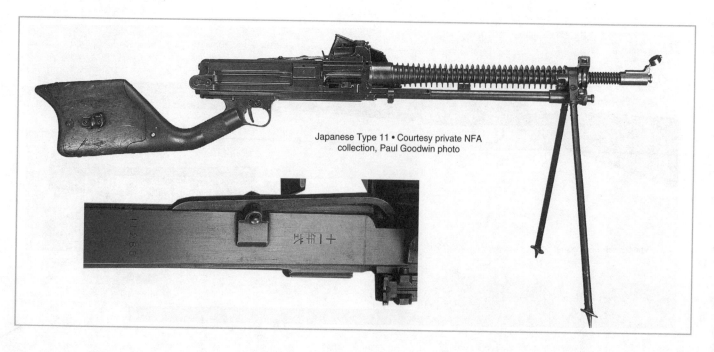

Japanese Type 11 • Courtesy private NFA collection, Paul Goodwin photo

Japanese Type 92

This is an improved version of the Type 3 gun introduced in 1932. Chambered for the 7.7x58SR cartridge. It was fitted with dropped grips behind and below the receiver instead of spade grips. Barrel length is 28". Fed by a metal 30-round strip. Rate of fire was about 450 rounds per minute. Weight is about 100 lbs. with tripod. Gun alone weighs approximately 60 lbs. The mount was designed so that two men could carry it by means of poles or pipes fitted into the legs of the mount. This was the most widely used Japanese machine gun of World War II.

NOTE: The Type 92 designation was also applied to the Japanese copy of the Lewis gun. See *Great Britain, Machine Guns, Lewis 0.303in, Mark 1.*

Type 92 • Private NFA collection, Gary Gelson photo

Type 92 on the only known privately held AA mount • Courtesy Robert E. Naess

Pre-1968

Exc.	V.G.	Fair
15000	14000	13000

Pre-1986 conversions

Exc.	V.G.	Fair
11000	10000	9000

Pre-1986 dealer samples

Exc.	V.G.	Fair
N/A	N/A	N/A

Japanese Type 92 Lewis

This is a licensed copy of the British Lewis gun. Caliber is .303. Built in both ground and aircraft configurations. There are some minor technical differences between the two. Spade grips. The Japanese tripod for this gun is unique to the gun.

NOTE: Prices listed below are for the gun *and* original Japanese tripod. Deduct $2,500 for no tripod or incorrect tripod.

Pre-1968

Exc.	V.G.	Fair
11000	10000	9000

Pre-1986 conversions

Exc.	V.G.	Fair
N/A	N/A	N/A

Pre-1986 dealer samples

Exc.	V.G.	Fair
N/A	N/A	N/A

Japanese Type 96

Designed by General Kijiro Nambu and introduced in 1936, this light, air-cooled machine gun is chambered for the 6.5mm cartridge. It was considered an improvement over the Model 11. This model has a top-mounted box magazine with a 30-round capacity. The cartridges are oiled when loaded into the magazine by an oiler built into the magazine loader. Barrel length is a finned 22" quick-change affair with carrying handle. The wood buttstock has a pistol grip. Rate of fire is about 550 rounds per minute. Weight is approximately 20 lbs. These guns are sometimes seen with a 2.5 power scope fitted on the receiver. This was the standard light machine gun of the Japanese military from 1936 to 1939.

NOTE: Ammo and magazines are scarce.

Pre-1968

Exc.	V.G.	Fair
6500	5000	4500

Pre-1986 conversions

Exc.	V.G.	Fair
4000	3000	2500

Pre-1986 dealer samples

Exc.	V.G.	Fair
N/A	N/A	N/A

Japanese Type 97

This model was designed in 1937 to be fired from a tank or aircraft. It was to replace the Type 92 gun and is chambered for the 7.7mm cartridge. Its barrel length is 28" and the barrel is finned for cooling. Design is similar to the Czech VZ26. This was the first Japanese machine gun that did not require oiled ammunition. Weight is about 24 lbs. Rate of fire is

Japanese Type 97 Tank • Courtesy private NFA collection, Paul Goodwin photo

approximately 500 rounds per minute. Fed by a 30-round box magazine.

Pre-1968

Exc.	V.G.	Fair
7000	6000	5500

Pre-1986 conversions

Exc.	V.G.	Fair
N/A	N/A	N/A

Pre-1986 dealer samples

Exc.	V.G.	Fair
N/A	N/A	N/A

Japanese Type 98

This is a copy of the German MG 15-ground gun. First used in 1938. Fed by a 75-round saddle drum with a rate of fire of 900 rounds per minute.

Pre-1968

Exc.	V.G.	Fair
8500	7500	7000

Pre-1986 conversions

Exc.	V.G.	Fair
N/A	N/A	N/A

Pre-1986 dealer samples

Exc.	V.G.	Fair
N/A	N/A	N/A

Japanese Model 96 with plaque that reads, "Presented to U.S.M.A. by two former superintendents: General Douglas MacArthur and Lt. Gen. Robert L. Eichelberger captured at Buna, New Guinea, Dec. 27, 1942" • Courtesy West Point Museum, Paul Goodwin photo

Type 99 • Courtesy private NFA collection, Paul Goodwin photo

Japanese Type 99

Chambered for the 7.7x58mm Arisaka cartridge, this machine gun was first produced for the Japanese army in 1939, and is an improved version of the Type 96. Although first produced in 1939 it was not issued until 1942 and first used in combat in 1943. It is fitted with a 21.3" quick change barrel and a 30-round top feed magazine. Its rate of fire is 850 rounds per minute. It weighs about 23 lbs. The gun is marked on the right front side of the receiver with date of manufacture and maker's symbols. The gun has a bipod under the barrel and a monopod under the toe of the buttstock. Production ceased with the end of WWII.

Pre-1968
Exc.	V.G.	Fair
8000	7000	6500

Pre-1986 conversions
Exc.	V.G.	Fair
5000	4000	3000

Pre-1986 dealer samples
Exc.	V.G.	Fair
N/A	N/A	N/A

Japanese Machine Gun Trainer

These guns were built in small machine shops all over Japan in the 1930s and 1940s so that young school-age males could be taught the basic techniques and operations of machine guns. Blowback operation. This gun does in fact fire a reduced load of either 6.5mm or 7.7mm cartridges, as well as blanks and is registered as a machine gun under the NFA. These guns, as a group, are different enough so that no two will be exactly the same. **CAUTION: DO NOT FIRE THIS GUN, IT IS UNSAFE.**

Pre-1968
Exc.	V.G.	Fair
3500	2500	1500

Pre-1986 conversions
Exc.	V.G.	Fair
N/A	N/A	N/A

Pre-1986 dealer samples
Exc.	V.G.	Fair
N/A	N/A	N/A

Japanese Machine Gun Trainer • Paul Goodwin photo

MEXICO

Mexican Military Conflicts, 1870-1945

The first three quarters of the 19th century were periods of almost constant strife and civil war for Mexico. Beginning in 1876 Mexico was ruled by Porfirio Diaz. The country was relatively stable and at peace for the 35 years of his rule. Beginning in the early 20th century, a new generation of revolutionaries demanded power for the people. Such men as Emiliano Zapata and Pancho Villa threatened the stability of the government. It was Francisco Madero who overthrew Diaz in 1911. A succession of reformist governments followed with the eventual formation of the PRI party in 1929 and a stable political climate through the Second World War and beyond.

HANDGUNS

NOTE: Other than the Obregon, the Mexican military has relied on foreign purchases of its military handguns. The principal sidearm is the Colt Model 1911 in .45 ACP, purchased from the U.S. government. Mexico has also purchased pistols from Heckler & Koch, the P7M13, and numerous Smith & Wesson revolvers and pistols for its police forces.

OBREGON

Pistola Automatica Sistema Obregon

This is a .45 caliber semiautomatic pistol with a 5" barrel. Similar to the Colt M1911A1 but with a combination slide and safety latch on the left side of the frame. The breech is locked by rotating the barrel, instead of the Browning swinging link. This unusual locking system results in a tubular front end appearance to the pistol. Originally designed for the Mexican military, it was not adopted as such and only about 1,000 pistols were produced and sold commercially, mostly to Mexican military officers. The pistol is 8.5" overall and weighs about 40 ozs. The magazine holds seven cartridges. This is a rare pistol, therefore an independent appraisal is suggested prior to sale.

Exc.	V.G.	Good	Fair	Poor
4500	2750	1250	750	400

Colt Model 1911A1

This is the standard service pistol of the Mexican military in .45 ACP.

SUBMACHINE GUNS

NOTE: The Mexican military availed itself of the Thompson submachine gun in various models, from the Model 1921 to the Model M1A1. The Mexican government has also purchased directly from the U.S. government a number of M3A1 .45 ACP submachine guns. From Germany the Mexican government purchased the HK MP5 and the HK 53. The MP5 is currently made in Mexico under license from HK.

Mendoza (HM-3)

Developed by Rafael Mendoza in the 1950s, this submachine gun is produced by Productos Mendoza S.A. in Mexico City. This is a relatively small select-fire gun chambered for the .45 ACP, .38 Super, or 9mm cartridges. Barrel length is 10", although some examples are found with 16" barrels in full automatic fire only. The box magazine capacity is 20 rounds. Rate of fire is about 550 rounds per minute. Weight is about 5 lbs. Stock is tubular steel. An unknown number of these guns are used by the Mexican army.

RIFLES

NOTE: Mexico used a number of different models of the Mauser bolt action rifle. Since the end of World War II, the Mexican military has purchased a number of foreign rifles for military use. These consist of U.S. M1 and M2 carbines, Colt M16A1 rifles in the 1970s, FN-FAL rifles, some of which were assembled in Mexico beginning in 1968 with FN supplied parts. In 1979 Mexico began to produce, under license from HK, the G3 rifle (G3A3 and G3A4).

PEABODY

Spanish Rifle (1869)

Identical to the Spanish rifle. Chambered for the .43 Spanish centerfire cartridge and fitted with a 33" barrel. Full stock with two barrel bands. Blued barrel and case hardened furniture. About 8,500 rifles were produced for the Mexican government.

Exc.	V.G.	Good	Fair	Poor
—	1500	1000	500	200

WHITNEY

Model 1873 Rifle

This is a rolling block design similar to the Remington. It does not use the hammer to lock the block. Fitted with a 35" barrel and full stock with three barrel bands. Chambered for the 11.15x58T Spanish Remington cartridge. Weight is about 9.5 lbs. On the right side of the receiver is the Mexican crest. Upper tang is marked with "Whitney Arms."

Exc.	V.G.	Good	Fair	Poor
—	1500	900	500	200

Model 1873 Carbine

Similar to the rifle but with 20.5" barrel and two-piece stock. Fitted with cavalry bar sling and ring on stock. Weight is about 7.25 lbs.

Exc.	V.G.	Good	Fair	Poor
—	1500	900	500	200

REMINGTON ROLLING BLOCK

Model 1897 Rifle

Chambered for the 7x57mm Spanish Mauser cartridge. Full stocked with two barrel bands. Barrel length is 30". Weight is about 8.5 lbs. Marked Remington on upper tang. Rear sight is ladder-type marked to 2,300 yards.

Exc.	V.G.	Good	Fair	Poor
—	750	500	300	100

MAUSER

M1895 Rifle

This was the standard rifle for the Mexican army under the Diaz regime. It is similar to the Spanish Model 1893. Fitted with an almost full stock with straight grip with no finger grooves. Barrel length is 29" and chambered for the 7x57mm cartridge. Rear leaf sight graduated to 2,000 meters. Bayonet lug. Magazine capacity is 5 rounds. Weight is about 8.5 lbs. Produced by both DWM and the Spanish firm Oviedo.

Exc.	V.G.	Good	Fair	Poor
225	125	90	60	25

M1895 Carbine

Similar to the Model 1895 rifle except with 17.25" barrel, bent bolt handle, and side-mounted sling. No bayonet fittings. Weight is about 7.5 lbs. Some but not all are marked with Mexican crest on receiver ring.

Exc.	V.G.	Good	Fair	Poor
225	125	80	50	25

M1902 Rifle

This model has an improved Model 98 action. Nearly full-length stock with half-length upper handguard. This model was built by DWM and Steyr. Barrel length is 29". Caliber is 7x57mm. Straight bolt handle. Rear sight graduated to 2,000 meters. Mexican crest on receiver ring. Weight is about 8.75 lbs.

Exc.	V.G.	Good	Fair	Poor
375	250	170	100	60

M1907 Steyr Rifle

This rifle was fitted with an almost full-length stock with pistol grip. Upper barrel band has a stacking hook. Bayonet lug accepts Model 98 bayonet. Barrel length is 29". Caliber is 7x57mm. Straight bolt. Weight is about 8.75 lbs. Marked, "STEYR.MODEL 1907/DATE" on receiver ring.

Exc.	V.G.	Good	Fair	Poor
375	250	190	140	90

Mexican Mauser Model 1910 • Courtesy Paul S. Scarlata

M1910 Rifle

This was the first Mauser produced by Mexico at the *Fabrica Nacional de Cartuchos* and the *Fabrica Nacional de Armas* in Mexico City. Similar to the Model 1902 rifle. Straight grip stock. Bayonet stud for Model 1895 bayonet. Barrel length is 29" and caliber is 7x57mm. Marked on top of receiver ring.

Exc.	V.G.	Good	Fair	Poor
250	125	80	60	20

M1910 Carbine

Very similar to the Model 1895 carbine with the addition of the Model 98 action and barley corn front sights. Mexican crest on receiver ring. Weight is about 8 lbs. Barrel length is 17.5" and caliber is 7x57mm.

Exc.	V.G.	Good	Fair	Poor
175	100	80	70	25

M1912 Steyr Rifle

Mexico bought these rifles directly from Steyr. This model is fitted with a 29" barrel and large receiver ring with straight bolt. Nearly full-length stock with pistol grip. Chambered for the 7x57mm cartridge. Receiver ring marked "MODEL 1912" over "STEYR" over the date. Weight is about 8.75 lbs.

Exc.	V.G.	Good	Fair	Poor
350	250	175	100	75

M1912 Steyr Short Rifle

This short rifle is the same as the Model 1912 rifle except for turned down bolt handle and barrel length.

Exc.	V.G.	Good	Fair	Poor
350	250	175	100	75

FN M24 Short Rifle

Approximately 25,000 of these rifles were bought from FN by Mexico in 1926 and 1927. This then is the standard FN Model 1924 version with pistol grip stock without finger grooves. Barrel length is 23.5" and caliber is 7x57mm. Weight is about 8.5 lbs.

Exc.	V.G.	Good	Fair	Poor
200	150	90	70	40

FN M24 Carbine

Same as above but with 16" barrel and no bayonet fittings. The barrel length was the shortest ever used on a Mauser rifle. Weight is about 7.5 lbs. Very Rare.

Exc.	V.G.	Good	Fair	Poor
450	300	200	100	75

VZ12/33 Carbine

This is the Czech export Model 12/33 carbine. Pistol grip stock. Barrel length is 22" and caliber is 7x57mm. Weight is about 8.5 lbs. Marked with Mexican crest on receiver ring.

Exc.	V.G.	Good	Fair	Poor
300	200	170	125	90

ARISAKA

Model 1913

Identical to the Japanese service rifle of the same model but chambered for the 7x57mm cartridge. The rear sight has been modified for this cartridge. The nose cap has been modified to accept the standard Mexican bayonet. The Mexican eagle and "REPUBLICA MEXICANA" are marked on the barrel near the breech. About 40,000 rifles were ordered but only 5,000 delivered in 1913. Manufactured in Japan in Koishikawa.

Exc.	V.G.	Good	Fair	Poor
850	600	450	300	200

NOTE: A few carbines were also built. These will bring a premium of 60%.

MONDRAGON

Model 1908 & Model 1915

Firearms designed by Manuel Mondragon were produced on an experimental basis first at St. Chamond Arsenal in France and later at SIG in Neuhausen, Switzerland. The latter company was responsible for the manufacture of the two known production models: the Model 1908 and 1915.

The Model 1908 Mondragon semiautomatic rifle holds the distinction of being the first self-loading rifle to be issued to any armed forces. Only about 400 of these rifles were delivered to the Mexican army in 1911 when the revolution broke out. The rifle was chambered for the 7x57mm Mauser cartridge and featured a 24.5" barrel. It has an 8-round box magazine. Weight is about 9.5 lbs. SIG had several thousand of these rifles left after the Mexicans were unable to take delivery. When WWI got under way the Swiss firm sold the remaining stocks to Germany. These rifles were called the Model 1915 and they were all identical to the Model 1908 except for the addition of a 30-round drum magazine.

Courtesy Rock Island Auction Company

Exc.	V.G.	Good	Fair	Poor
6000	4000	2000	1000	750

FABRICA NACIONAL de ARMAS
Mexico City

Model 1936

This bolt action rifle was chambered for the 7mm cartridge and uses a short-type Mauser action. The rifle is of Mexican design and resembles the Springfield Model 1903A1 in appearance.

A Mondragoon Model 1908 rifle was sold at auction for $7,475. Condition is near mint. *Rock Island Auction Company, August 2004*

Barrel length is 22" with a 5-round non-detachable magazine. Tangent rear sight with "V" notch. Weight is about 8.25 lbs.

Exc.	V.G.	Good	Fair	Poor
400	300	250	175	110

Model 1954

This Mexican-produced and designed rifle also uses a Mauser action, but resembles a Springfield Model 1903A3 in appearance. The stock is laminated plywood. Barrel length is 24" and chambered for the .30-06 cartridge. Weight is approximately 9 lbs. Some of these rifles may still be in service.

Exc.	V.G.	Good	Fair	Poor
400	300	250	175	110

MACHINE GUNS

NOTE: The Mexican military has used a variety of foreign-built machine guns. The Madsen Model 1934, the Model 1896 Hotchkiss 7mm machine gun, and the Browning Model 1919, as well as the 5.56mm Ameli, the FN MAG, and the HK 21A1, and the Browning .50 M2HB. Mexico also produced its own excellent gun, the Mendoza C-1934 light machine gun and the RM2 gas operated machine gun issued in 1960.

Model 1936 • Courtesy private collection, Paul Goodwin photo

NETHERLANDS

Dutch Military Conflicts, 1870-Present

The period from 1870 to the beginning of War World I was one of economic prosperity and stability. The Netherlands suffered economic loss during World War I because of the Allied blockade. During World War II the country suffered heavy damage and loss of life during the German occupation. After the war, the Netherlands lost many of its colonies, beginning with a war in Indonesia, which gained its independence in 1949. The independence of New Guinea followed in 1962, and Suriname in 1975. In 2001 the Dutch military had a total of 50,430 personnel. Reserves were 32,000. The army had 23,000 total personnel.

HANDGUNS

During World War II, the Dutch also used the Enfield revolver chambered for the .38 Special cartridge, as well as the Webley Model I in .38 Special, the Webley Model VI chambered for the .455 cartridge.

Since the end of World War II, the Dutch have used the Walther P5, the HK P9S, the FN High Power (both Belgian and Canadian built), the Smith & Wesson Model 19, the Colt Python (4"), the Colt Model 1911A1, the FN Model 1910, and the FN Model 1910/22.

Model 1873 (Old Model)

This solid-frame double action revolver is based on the Chamelot Delvigne design. Chambered for the 9.4mm cartridge. Fitted with a 6.3" octagonal barrel. Gate loaded non-fluted cylinder holds 6 rounds. With no ejector rod, a separate rod was required. Smooth wooden grips with lanyard ring. Was issued in 1873 and remained in service through 1945. Built by a number of different companies such as J.F.J. Bar, DeBeaumont, P. Stevens, Hembrug, etc. Military marked. Weight is about 44 oz.

NOTE: An Officer's Model was also used but was not military issue and not military marked. Major differences are fluted cylinder, checkered wooden grips, and 5" barrel.

Courtesy Geschichte und Technik der europaischen Militarrevolver, Journal-Verlag Schwend GmbH with permission

Exc.	V.G.	Good	Fair	Poor
750	600	500	400	250

Model 1873 (New Model)

Similar to the Old Model but with 6.3" round barrel. First issued in 1909. Built by Hembrug. Military marked.

Exc.	V.G.	Good	Fair	Poor
750	550	400	300	150

Model 1873/1919

This model is based on the Model 1873 but modified to fire tear gas projectiles. Chambered for the 9.4mm cartridge but with a 12mm caliber barrel. Barrel length was only 1.9" in length with no front sight. Smooth wooden grips with lanyard ring. In service from 1919 to 1945. Built by Hembrug and military marked.

Courtesy Geschichte und Technik der europaischen Militarrevolver, Journal-Verlag Schwend GmbH with permission

A Dutch military revolver sold at auction for $632.50. Condition is 95 percent worn blue. Wood is good.
Rock Island Auction Company, August 2004

Courtesy Geschichte und Technik der europaischen Militarrevolver, Journal-Verlag Schwend GmbH with permission

Exc.	V.G.	Good	Fair	Poor
1200	850	550	—	—

Model 94 (Colonial Model)

This double action revolver was first issued to the Dutch Colonial Army in 1894 and remained in service until 1945. Chambered for the 9.4mm cartridge and fitted with a 4.3" barrel. Fluted cylinder holds 6 rounds. Checkered wooden grips with lanyard ring. Built by Hembrug. Military marked.

Courtesy Geschichte und Technik der europaischen Militarrevolver, Journal-Verlag Schwend GmbH with permission

Exc.	V.G.	Good	Fair	Poor
600	400	300	200	100

SUBMACHINE GUNS

The Dutch military uses the UZI submachine gun (IMI), and several variants of the HK MP5. During World War II, the Dutch purchased a number of American made UD submachine guns in 9mm. There were no submachine guns of Dutch design issued to its military.

RIFLES

The Dutch military has used a number of different foreign-made military rifles including: FN FAL, HK PSG 1, HK 33SG1, and the U.S. M1 rifle. During WWII the Dutch used the Johnson semiautomatic rifle in its Far East colonies.

BEAUMONT/VITALI

Model 1871 Rifle

This single shot black powder rifle, chambered for the 11.3x51R cartridge, featured a heavy internally recessed two-piece bolt handle with a V-spring to activate the striker. The bolt head included the extractor. There was no ejector. Barrel length was 32.7". One-piece stock with two barrel bands. Fitted for a socket bayonet. Original rifles were issued in the white. Rear sight graduated to 1,100 meters. Weight is about 9.75 lbs.

Courtesy Milwaukee Public Museum, Milwaukee, Wisconsin

Exc.	V.G.	Good	Fair	Poor
400	250	150	100	75

Model 1871 Carbine

Same as above but with 22" barrel. Also fitted for a socket bayonet.

Exc.	V.G.	Good	Fair	Poor
500	350	250	125	100

Model 1871/88

This model was a conversion to the Vitali magazine. It featured a bolt-mounted ejector and a magazine cut-off on the left side of the receiver. Magazine capacity is 4 rounds. All other specifications are the same as the Model 1871. Rear sight is graduated to 1,300 meters. Weight is approximately 10 lbs. This rifle was used by the Dutch army and remained in secondary service through World War II.

Exc.	V.G.	Good	Fair	Poor
375	200	150	100	75

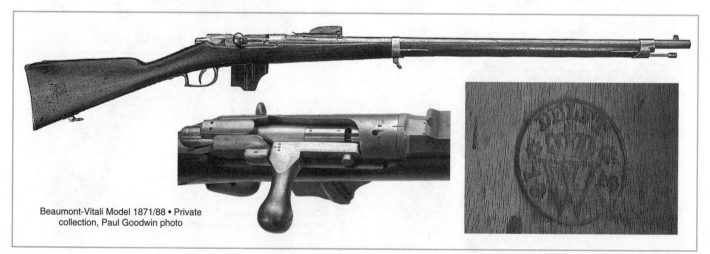

Beaumont-Vitali Model 1871/88 • Private collection, Paul Goodwin photo

MANNLICHER

NOTE: Some of these rifles have a wooden block covering the left side of the magazine. These were added after 1914 to protect the magazines from damage. Rifles without this modification are referred to as the "Old Model," while rifles with the change are called "New Models." Prices listed below are for the "Old Models."

NOTE: Many of these rifles were converted to .303 British by Indonesia. Prices remain about the same for these conversions.

Model 1895 Rifle

This 6.5x53R rifle was produced in two versions. One for the regular army and the other for the Dutch East Indies. The colonial model has two gas escape holes in the receiver ring. The rifle is full-stocked with a half-length handguard. It is fitted with a bayonet bar. Barrel length is 31". Magazine capacity is 5 rounds and is clip loaded. After World War II, many of these rifles were rebored and converted to .303 British. Built by both Steyr and Hembrug. Weight is about 9.5 lbs.

Courtesy Paul S. Scarlata from *Mannlicher Military Rifles*, Andrew Mobray Publishers

Exc.	V.G.	Good	Fair	Poor
350	200	125	75	50

Model 1895 No. 1 Cavalry Carbine

This model featured a half stock with no handguard and sling bars on the left side. Barrel length is 17.7". Weight is about 6.75 lbs. Built by both Steyr and Hembrug.

Exc.	V.G.	Good	Fair	Poor
450	300	250	125	75

Model 1985 No. 2 Gendarmerie Carbine

This model is a full-stocked version with bayonet fittings. Weight is about 7 lbs.

Exc.	V.G.	Good	Fair	Poor
450	300	250	125	75

Model 1895 No. 3 Engineer & Artillery Carbine

Similar to the No. 2 carbine but with long handguard. Weight is almost 7 lbs.

Courtesy Paul S. Scarlata from *Mannlicher Military Rifles*, Andrew Mobray Publishers

Exc.	V.G.	Good	Fair	Poor
450	300	250	125	75

Model 1895 No. 4 Bicycle Troops' Carbine

Similar to the No. 3 carbine but with handguard the same length as the stock.

Courtesy Paul S. Scarlata from *Mannlicher Military Rifles*, Andrew Mobray Publishers

Exc.	V.G.	Good	Fair	Poor
500	350	300	150	100

Model 1917

Sometimes called the "machine gunner's rifle" because ammunition was the same as the Dutch Lewis and Schwarzlose machine guns. Chambered for the 8x57 cartridge and fitted with a 31.3" barrel with quadrant sight to 2,000 meters. Similar action to the Model 1895. Weight is about 9.25 lbs. Built by Hembrug.

Exc.	V.G.	Good	Fair	Poor
400	250	200	150	100

Model 1895 No. 5 Carbine A5

This model was built by Hembrug beginning in 1930 and is a cut-down version of the Model 1895 rifle. It was issued to the Dutch Air Force. Barrel length is 17.9". Weight is about 7.75 lbs.

Exc.	V.G.	Good	Fair	Poor
600	450	300	200	100

MAUSER (FN)

M1948 Carbine

This rifle was built by FN for the Dutch police. Chambered for the 7.9x57mm cartridge and fitted with a 17.3" barrel with bayonet fittings. Full stock with pistol grip and upper handguard. Magazine capacity is 5 rounds. Marked with letter "J" or "W" with crown on receiver ring. Rear sight is V notch graduated from 200 to 1,400 meters. Weight is about 7.5 lbs.

Exc.	V.G.	Good	Fair	Poor
400	250	200	125	90

MACHINE GUNS

In 1908 the Dutch adopted the Schwarzlose machine gun in 7.92Rmm, various Madsen models chambered for the 6.5mm cartridge, the Lewis gun in 6.5mm, and the Vickers Model 1918 in 7.92mm. The Dutch military has also used the FN MAG, the Bren Mark 2 in .303, and the .50 M2 HB. During World War II the Dutch also used the Johnson LMG in .30-06 as well as the Browning Model 1919 variants.

NORWAY

Norwegian Military Conflicts, 1870-Present

In 1870 Norway was ruled by Sweden. An upsurge in Norwegian nationalism forced Sweden to dissolve its ties and grant independence as a constitutional monarchy to Norway in 1905. Norway remained neutral during World War I. However, the country was occupied by Germany from 1940 to 1945 during World War II. Since the end of the war, Norway has remained independent economically and socially from the rest of Europe, having rejected membership in the European Union on two occasions.

HANDGUNS

NAGANT

Model 1883 Revolver

Adopted in 1883, this Nagant 6-round revolver has a solid frame with loading gate and mechanical rod ejection. Double action. Chambered for the 9x23R Belgian Nagant cartridge. Barrel is part round and part hexagon and is 5.5" long. Fluted cylinder and checkered wood grips with lanyard loop. Weight is about 32 oz. This model stayed in service until 1940. It was issued to both officers and NCOs.

Courtesy Geschichte und Technik der europaischen Militarrevolver, Journal-Verlag Schwend GmbH with permission

Exc.	V.G.	Good	Fair	Poor
1250	750	400	275	150

Model 1887/93 Revolver

Similar in appearance to the Model 1883 but chambered for the 7.5x22R Norwegian Nagant cartridge. Barrel length is 4.5". Weight is about 28 oz. In service until 1940.

Courtesy Geschichte und Technik der europaischen Militarrevolver, Journal-Verlag Schwend GmbH with permission

Exc.	V.G.	Good	Fair	Poor
1250	750	400	275	150

Model 1912/14

All of the Model 1912/14 pistols were produced by the Norwegian arsenal at Kongsberg Vapenfabrikk. The official designation of the Norwegian Colt pistol was "COLT AUTOMATISK PISTOL, MODEL 1912, CAL. 11.43 M/M." In 1917 the designation changed to "11.25 M/M AUTOMATISK PISTOL MODEL 1914." The new marking began with serial number 96 (see Table 1). For a more detailed explanation of the differences in the Norwegian pistols see Clawson's, *Colt .45 Government Models, 1912 through 1970.*

Kongsberg Vapenfabrikk Model M/1914 (Norwegian) copy SN 1-96

(Rarely seen) (Condition 99-100 percent add 20-30 percent)

Exc.	V.G.	Good	Fair	Poor
3500	2200	1150	850	600

Norwegian slide legend left side • Courtesy Karl Karash

Kongsberg Vapenfabrikk Model M/1914 (Norwegian) copy SN 97-29614, and 30536-32854

(Numbers must match)

Norwegian slide markings right side • Courtesy Karl Karash

Exc.	V.G.	Good	Fair	Poor
1400	900	750	600	400

Kongsberg Vapenfabrikk Model M/1914 (Norwegian) copy SN 29,615 to 30,535

Waffenamt marked on slide and barrel. Numbers must match. Waffenamt marked M/1914s outside this range are probably FAKES. Condition 99-100 percent add 20-30 percent.

Exc.	V.G.	Good	Fair	Poor
3000	1900	1150	850	600

Kongsberg Vapenfabrikk Model M/1914 (Norwegian) copy SN 97-29614 and 30536-32854

(Numbers must match)

Notice the extended slide stop on the left side • Courtesy Karl Karash

Exc.	V.G.	Good	Fair	Poor
1400	900	750	600	400

Norwegian slide legend left side with extended slide stop • Courtesy Karl Karash

Kongsberg Vapenfabrikk Model M/1914 (Norwegian) copy SN 29615 to 30535

Waffenamt marked on slide and barrel. Numbers must match. Waffenamt marked M/1914s outside this range are probably FAKES. Condition 99-100 percent add 20-30 percent. A little over 900 were produced.

Exc.	V.G.	Good	Fair	Poor
3000	1900	1150	850	600

TABLE 1

DATE	SERIAL RANGE	DATE	SERIAL RANGE
1917	1-95	1929	20101-21400
1918	96-600	1932	21441-21940
1919	601-1150	1933	21941-22040
1920	1151-1650	1934	22041-22141
1921	1651-2200	1936	22142-22211
1922	2201-2950	1939	22212-22311
1923	2951-4610	1940	22312-22361
1924	4611-6700	1941	22362-26460
1925	6701-8940	1942	26461-29614
1926	8941-11820	1945	29615-30535
1927	11821-15900	1947	32336-32854
1928	15901-20100		

SUBMACHINE GUNS

Norway used the German MP40, designated the M40, chambered for the 9x19mm Parabellum cartridge. The Norwegian military also issued the British Sten gun, as well as the HK MP5A2 and MP5A3. The Norwegian Marines use the Suomi 37/39 submachine gun.

RIFLES

The Norwegian military also uses the HK G3 rifle, the Mauser 98K converted to 7.62x51mm, as well as now-obsolete U.S. M1 Garands and U.S. M1 and M2 carbines.

REMINGTON ROLLING BLOCK

NOTE: See also U.S. Rifles, Remington, for Remington built rolling block rifles for Norway.

Model 1867 Rifle

Built in Norway by Christiana, Husqvarna, or Kongsberg. Fitted with a 37.3" barrel with three barrel bands and full length stock. Brass buttplate. Chambered for the 12.17x42R Norwegian Remington rimfire cartridge. Weight is about 10 lbs.

Exc.	V.G.	Good	Fair	Poor
850	650	500	300	150

Model 1889 Carbine

This model was essentially a Model 1867 fitted with a 24" barrel chambered for the 8x58R Danish Krag cartridge. Built at Kongsberg. Weight is about 8.5 lbs.

Exc.	V.G.	Good	Fair	Poor
1100	800	650	425	225

JARMANN
Kongsberg

Model 1880-1882 Experimental

In 1880-1882 about 500 Jarmanns were produced in Sweden for use in trials in Norway. This experimental model used a curved 5-round box magazine mounted from the top right side of the receiver forward of the bolt handle. Chambered for the 10.15x61Rmm cartridge and fitted with a 32" barrel. Marked with Carl Gustaf markings.

Exc.	V.G.	Good	Fair	Poor
Too Rare To Price				

Model 1884 Rifle

Bolt action rifle with magazine tube under barrel with 8-round capacity. Chambered for the 10.15x61R Jarmann cartridge. Full stocked with two barrel bands. Fitted with a 32.5" barrel. Weight is about 10 lbs. These rifles made at Kongsberg and marked with a "K" on the receiver ring.

Exc.	V.G.	Good	Fair	Poor
Too Rare To Price				

NOTE: A carbine version was built but never adopted by Norway.

Model 1884/87

Similar to the Model 1884 but with recalibrated rear sight for smokeless powder.

Exc.	V.G.	Good	Fair	Poor
Too Rare To Price				

MAUSER

K98k Reissued Short Rifle (.30-06)

The only difference between this rifle and the standard issue German model is the markings. The Norwegian word "HAER" meaning "Army" is stamped on the receiver ring. A number of other stampings that denote Norwegian military organizations may also be seen, such as: HV=Home Guard; FLY=Air Force; KNM=Navy; K.ART=Coast Artillery; NSB=Government Railway; POLITI=Police.

Exc.	V.G.	Good	Fair	Poor
350	240	190	100	70

K98k Action Military Target Rifle (Model 59)

Exc.	V.G.	Good	Fair	Poor
400	300	250	200	100

Model 84S

This rifle uses a modified Mauser 98 military action with the original markings removed. Chambered for the 7.62mm NATO cartridge and first introduced in 1984. Built by Vapensmia A/S in Norway. Fitted with a heavy barrel by the German company Heym. Has a 5-round detachable magazine. Fitted with a 6x42 Schmidt & Bender scope. Adjustable trigger. Laminated birch stock. This rifle was also sold commercially.

Exc.	V.G.	Good	Fair	Poor
1500	1150	800	500	300

KRAG JORGENSEN

See also *U.S., Rifles, Krag*

NOTE: The Norwegian Krag rifles differ from the U.S. Krags primarily in that it does not have a cartridge cutoff. The Norwegian Krags were used by the Norwegian army as its principal long arm until the Germans occupied Norway in 1940. The majority of these rifles were built at Kongsberg, although some were produced at Steyr and FN Herstal. Norwegian Krags were chambered for the 6.5x55mm Swedish Mauser cartridge.

Model 1894 Rifle

This rifle is full stocked with pistol grip and full-length handguard. Barrel length is 30". Box magazine is located in horizontal position and has a capacity of 5 rounds. Tangent rear sight. Weight is approximately 9 lbs.

Courtesy Paul S. Scarlata, *Collecting Classic Bolt Action Military Rifles*

Exc.	V.G.	Good	Fair	Poor
1000	750	600	400	150

Model 1895 Carbine

This model is half stocked with short handguard and fitted with a 20.5" barrel. Magazine capacity is 5 rounds. Weight is about 7.5 lbs. Very similar in appearance to the U.S. Krag carbine.

Courtesy Paul S. Scarlata, *Collecting Classic Bolt Action Military Rifles*

Exc.	V.G.	Good	Fair	Poor
1500	850	650	400	200

Model 1897 Carbine

Similar to the Model 1895 carbine except the rear sling swivel is located near the toe of the buttstock.

Exc.	V.G.	Good	Fair	Poor
1500	850	650	400	200

Model 1904 Carbine

This model has a 20.5" barrel with full stock and upper handguard but no bayonet lug. Weight is about 8.4 lbs. Estimated production is about 2,750.

Exc.	V.G.	Good	Fair	Poor
1500	850	650	400	200

Model 1906 Boy's Training Rifle

Introduced in 1906 for use at schools and shooting clubs. Chambered for the 6.5x55mm cartridge. Barrel length is about 20.5". Weight is about 7.25 lbs. No upper handguard with shorter stock dimensions. Turned down bolt handle. One barrel band has front swivel. Estimated production is about 3,321. Rare.

Exc.	V.G.	Good	Fair	Poor
N/A	—	—	—	—

SNAP SHOT
WHAT'S IT LIKE - THE NORWEGIAN KRAG-JORGENSEN

The highest accolade that can be bestowed upon a bolt-action rifle is that is functions "...almost as smooth as a Krag."

The Krag-Jorgensen rifle was developed at the Norwegian state arsenal by Ole H. Krag, the director of Kongsberg Vapenfabrikk, and his chief designer, Erik Jorgensen. Its most distinctive feature was a magazine which lay horizontally beneath the bolt and which was loaded by means of a loading gate on the right side of the receiver. The gate cover was swung open, whereupon the magazine follower and spring were compressed. After manually loading the magazine, the cover was closed which released follower. A cutoff allowed the rifle to be used a single-loader.

The Krag's bolt had a single frontal locking lug which locked into a matching mortise in the bottom front of the receiver. To provide additional locking, the bolt handle turned down into a notch at the rear of the receiver while the bolt guide rib bore on the front of the receiver bridge to provided additional locking. This style of bolt and magazine system allowed cartridges to be fed and chambered smoothly and permitted rapid and smooth bolt manipulation.

Krags were adopted by Danish and the American armies in 1889 and 1893, respectively. It was not until 1894 that it was approved in its native country.

The Norwegian Krag-Jorgensengevaer M/1894 should be considered the best of the Krag designs. Quality of materials and manufacture were exacting, resulting in improved strength while accuracy was enhanced by chambering it for the 6.5x55 Mauser cartridge. Many different models of rifles, carbines and sniper rifles were manufactured between 1896 and 1940

Several years ago I added a Krag-Jorgensenkarabin M/1912 to my, rather extensive, Krag collection. It was manufactured 1918 and was in VG+ condition with a worn but clean bore. Test fired with Swedish surplus 6.5x55 ammunition at 100 yards it proved capable of shooting sub-3-inch groups for as long as I wanted to pull the trigger. That funky magazine was just plain fun to load and as I worked the bolt, the old axiom "Like a hot knife through butter" kept coming to mind. Damn, I love Krags!

Paul Scarlata

Model 1907 Carbine

Similar to the Model 1907 but with sling swivels located on rear barrel band and buttstock.

Exc.	V.G.	Good	Fair	Poor
1500	850	650	400	200

Model 1912 Carbine

Full stocked with 24" barrel and 5-round magazine. Fitted with a bayonet lug on nose cap. Weight is about 8.5 lbs. About 30,100 were produced.

Courtesy Paul S. Scarlata, *Collecting Classic Bolt Action Military Rifles*

Exc.	V.G.	Good	Fair	Poor
1200	650	450	300	150

Model 1923 Sniper

This model is fitted with a full stock and checkered pistol grip. Full-length handguard. Heavy barrel length is 26.2". Bayonet fittings on nose cap. Micrometer rear sight with aperture. Marked "M.1894" on receiver. Magazine capacity is 5 rounds. Weight is about 9 lbs. Scarce with total production of about 630 rifles.

Courtesy Paul S. Scarlata, *Collecting Classic Bolt Action Military Rifles*

Exc.	V.G.	Good	Fair	Poor
3750	2250	1250	650	300

Model 1925 Sniper

Fitted with a 30" heavy barrel similar to the Model 1894 rifle but with checkered pistol grip and micrometer rear peep sight. Weight is approximately 10 lbs. Scarce.

Exc.	V.G.	Good	Fair	Poor
3500	2250	1250	650	300

Model 1930 Sniper

This model has a sporter-style half stock with checkered full pistol grip. Heavy 29.5" barrel. No bayonet fittings. Micrometer rear sight. Marked "M/1894/30." Weight is approximately 11.5 lbs. Scarce.

Exc.	V.G.	Good	Fair	Poor
3500	2250	1250	650	400

MACHINE GUNS

Norway used the Hotchkiss machine gun, chambered for the 6.5mm cartridge, beginning in 1911, as well as the Model 1914 and Model 1918 Madsen guns. The Browning Model 1917 water-cooled gun was used by the Norwegians and designated the Model 29. After World War II the Norwegian military used the Browning Model 1919A4, as well as the MG 34 and MG 42. Currently Norway has adopted the MG 42/59 as its standard machine gun, designating it the LMG 3.

POLAND

Polish Military Conflicts, 1870 to Present

From 1772 to 1918 Poland was part of Prussia, Austria, and Russia, and as such it did not exist as an independent state. Following World War I Poland received its independence. In 1920-21 a border dispute led to war with Russia. Poland won some of its claims in the Treaty of Riga. In 1926 Joseph Pillsudski, Chief of State since 1918, assumed dictatorial power. After his death in 1935 a military junta assumed power. In 1939 Nazi Germany invaded Poland, precipitating World War II. After the war a government was established under Soviet auspices. In 1947 government control gave the Communists full control of the country. In 1990 the first free elections were held in Poland with the election of Lech Walesa as president.

Courtesy Richard M. Kumor Sr.

Exc.	V.G.	Good	Fair	Poor
3000	2300	1500	500	100

VIS-35

A 9mm semiautomatic pistol with a 4.5" barrel, fixed sights, and an 8-shot magazine. On this model there is no manual safety; however, a decocking lever is installed that allows the hammer to be safely lowered on a loaded chamber. Versions made prior to WWII are engraved with a Polish eagle on the slide and "FB" and "VIS" are molded into the grips. These pre-war pistols are slotted for a holster stock. German production pistols were made without the decocking lever and subsequently without the stripping catch. They also eliminated the stock slot. These pistols were stamped "P35p" and bear the Waffenamt inspector's mark "WaA77." Near the end of the war, the take-down was eliminated and the grips were replaced with crude wooden grips. The slide, barrel, and frame are all numbered to match each other.

NOTE: Prices quoted are for 1939 dated guns. Earlier years bring a significant premium.

HANDGUNS

RADOM

Fabryka Broniw Radomu

This company was established after World War I and produced military arms for Poland. During WWII the Radom factory was operated by the Nazis. Production was not recommenced after the war.

Ng 30

A copy of the Russian Nagant revolver chambered for the 7.62mm Russian cartridge. Approximately 20,000 were manufactured during 1930 and 1936.

A Polish Army issue VIS-35 was sold at auction for $4,600. Dated 1938 with no German military markings. Polish eagle acceptance stamp. Condition is 98 percent original military blue. Holster is in very good condition.

Rock Island Auction Company, August 2004

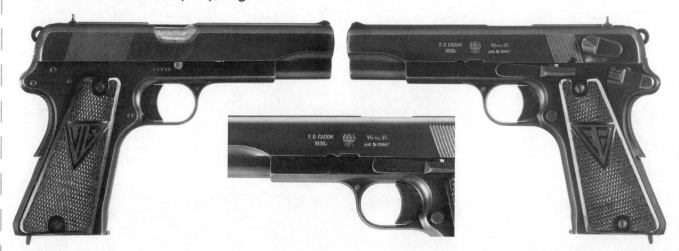

Polish Eagle Model-1936 through 1939

Courtesy Richard M. Kumor Sr.

Exc.	V.G.	Good	Fair	Poor
2200	1700	1200	350	200

Nazi Captured Polish Eagle—Waffenamt Marked

Exc.	V.G.	Good	Fair	Poor
4000	3500	1800	650	300

Nazi Polish Eagle (Navy marked)

Courtesy Richard M. Kumor Sr.

Nazi Production Model (Model 35[p])

Exc.	V.G.	Good	Fair	Poor
650	500	300	200	175

NOTE: Will command a premium price.

Nazi Production Model—"bnz" code

This is a late Nazi production with no other slide markings other than "bnz." A rare variation.

Courtesy Richard M. Kumor Sr.

Exc.	V.G.	Good	Fair	Poor
2200	1800	1200	650	500

VIS-35 Reissue

This is an exact copy of the original VIS-35 pistol. Limited to 100 pistols with less than that number imported into the U.S. The importer, "Dalvar of USA," is stamped on the barrel.

NIB	Exc.	V.G.	Good	Fair	Poor
2300	—	—	—	—	—

Model 64

A PPK size pistol chambered for the 9mm Makarov cartridge. Rare.

NIB	Exc.	V.G.	Good	Fair	Poor
250	150	100	75	50	—

Tokarev (Pistolet TT)

Polish copy with manual safety. Well made.

Exc.	V.G.	Good	Fair	Poor
400	300	250	125	100

P-83

This pistol is chambered for the 9x18 (Makarov) cartridge. It is fitted with a 3.5" barrel and has a double action trigger with decocker. Magazine capacity is 8 rounds. Weight is about 25 oz. Black oxide finish. Developed in the early 1970s, it is similar to a Makarov pistol except it is built from stampings. Used by Polish army and security forces.

NOTE: A commercial version is chambered for the 9x17 Short (.380) cartridge.

NIB	Exc.	V.G.	Good	Fair	Poor
300	200	—	—	—	—

P-93

Similar to the P-83 differing only in cosmetics but chambered for 9mm Makarov only. The decocking lever is on the frame instead of the slide. Barrel length is 3.9". Black oxide finish.

NIB	Exc.	V.G.	Good	Fair	Poor
350	250	200	150	—	—

MAG-95

This pistol is chambered for the 9mm Parabellum cartridge and fitted with a 4.5" barrel. Magazine capacity is 15 rounds. Trigger is double action with external hammer. Weight is about 38 oz. Black oxide finish. Optional 20-round magazine. In use by Polish forces on NATO duty.

NIB	Exc.	V.G.	Good	Fair	Poor
550	425	—	—	—	—

SUBMACHINE GUNS

NOTE: Poland was supplied with Soviet made PPSh M1941 and PPS M1943 submachine guns.

M1943/52

This gun is a Polish-built modification of the Soviet PPS M1943 submachine gun in 7.63mm caliber. It is select fire and is fitted with a 9.5" barrel. Magazine capacity is a 35-round box. Rate of fire is about 600 rounds per minute. Weight is approximately 8 lbs. Wooden buttstock.

Polish Model 1943/52 • Courtesy Thomas Nelson, *World's Submachine Guns, Vol. I*

Pre-1968
Exc.	V.G.	Fair
15000	13000	11000

Pre-1986 conversions
Exc.	V.G.	Fair
N/A	N/A	N/A

Pre-1986 dealer samples
Exc.	V.G.	Fair
N/A	N/A	N/A

WZ-63

Introduced in 1964, this submachine gun is a small, almost pistol-size weapon chambered for the 9x18mm Makarov cartridge. It is fitted with a 6" barrel with folding metal butt. The folding is designed to be used as a front vertical grip, if desired. A noticeable spoon-shaped muzzle compensator is used.

Magazine is a box type with 15- or 25-round capacity. Rate of fire is about 600 rounds per minute. Weight is approximately 4 lbs.

Pre-1968
Exc.	V.G.	Fair
12500	11000	10000

Pre-1986 conversions
Exc.	V.G.	Fair
N/A	N/A	N/A

Pre-1986 dealer samples
Exc.	V.G.	Fair
N/A	N/A	N/A

RIFLES

MAUSER

NOTE: Poland began producing Mauser rifles and carbines in early 1902 at the Warsaw arsenal.

M98 Rifle

This rifle is similar to the German Gew 98 with a tangent rear sight instead of the German style. Nearly full stock with pistol grip and finger grooves on the forend. Half length upper handguard.

Exc.	V.G.	Good	Fair	Poor
375	225	125	90	60

M98AZ Rifle

This rifle is the same as the German Model 98AZ. In addition to the standard placement of sling swivels, a sling bar is fitted to the left side of the stock. Polish wood is used on the stock in place of walnut.

Polish M98AZ • Courtesy Richard M. Kumor Sr.

Exc.	V.G.	Good	Fair	Poor
750	600	500	275	100

Wz 29 Short Rifle

This rifle was built at the Radom factory. Barrel length is 23.6" and caliber is 7.92x57mm. Straight bolt handle. Almost full stock with pistol grip and grasping grooves on the fore stock. A sling bar is fitted to the left side of the stock. Tangent leaf rear sight graduated to 2,000 meters. Weight is about 9 lbs.

Exc.	V.G.	Good	Fair	Poor
500	400	225	100	60

Polish 98 Mauser, Courtesy Paul S. Scarlata

Polish Wz 29 • Courtesy Richard M. Kumor Sr.

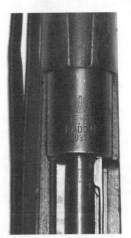

Wz 98a Rifle

Exc.	V.G.	Good	Fair	Poor
550	450	300	150	90

Wz 29 .22 Caliber Training Rifle

Exc.	V.G.	Good	Fair	Poor
2000	1500	900	—	—

Kbk 8 Wz 31 .22 Caliber Training Rifle

Exc.	V.G.	Good	Fair	Poor
2000	1500	900	—	—

Wz 48 .22 Caliber Training Rifle

Produced after World War II as a training rifle.

Polish Wz 48 Training Rifle • Private collection, Paul Goodwin photo

Exc.	V.G.	Good	Fair	Poor
350	200	100	—	—

Model 1891 Polish Nagant

A 7.62mm caliber bolt action rifle with a 28.75" barrel, 5-shot integral magazine, ladder rear sight, and a full-length stock secured by two barrel bands. Blued with a walnut stock.

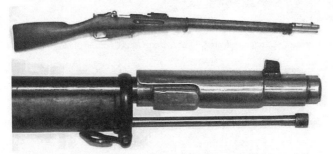

Polish Model 1891 with close-up of bayonet and fittings • Courtesy Richard M. Kumor Sr.

Exc.	V.G.	Good	Fair	Poor
150	125	100	75	50

NOTE: Add $150 to $250 for correct bayonet.

Polish Model 1891/30 Sniper Rifle

These are the Soviet rifles used by the Poles but refinished. Polish sniper rifles are identified by the serial numbered mounting rails being the same as the scope.

Exc.	V.G.	Good	Fair	Poor
1200	900	700	N/A	N/A

Model 1891/98/25 Polish Nagant

The production of these rifles started in the early 1920s at the Warsaw arsenal. Chambered for the 7.92mm cartridge but fit-

ted with a bayonet lug and stamped with a small crowned Polish Eagle on receiver and bolt. It has a 23.5" barrel with 5-round non-detachable box magazine. Leaf rear sight. Weight is approximately 8 lbs. A very rare variation. Original, unaltered examples will command a premium price. About 77,000 of these rifles were produced.

Courtesy Richard M. Kumor Sr.

Exc.	V.G.	Good	Fair	Poor
500	450	400	—	—

Polish Model 1944 Nagant

Produced in Poland after the end of World War II until about 1962. Polish markings on the receiver, stock, and barrel. Poland's East Bloc code was "11."

Exc.	V.G.	Good	Fair	Poor
1800	1500	1000	400	—

KbKg Model 1960 or PMK-DGM and PMKM

All of these rifles are copies of AK-47 variations. Both the PMK and PMKM are sometimes equipped with grenade launchers fitted to the muzzle.

Pre-1968

Exc.	V.G.	Fair
30000	27500	25000

Pre-1986 conversions

Exc.	V.G.	Fair
N/A	N/A	N/A

Pre-1986 dealer samples

Exc.	V.G.	Fair
N/A	N/A	N/A

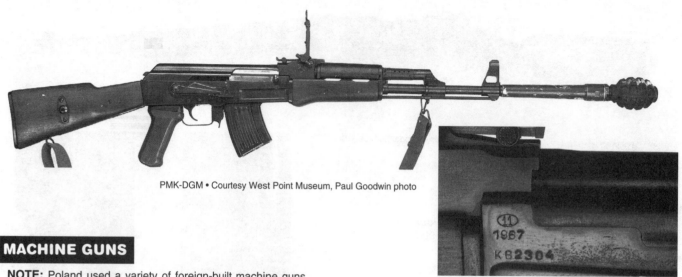

PMK-DGM • Courtesy West Point Museum, Paul Goodwin photo

MACHINE GUNS

NOTE: Poland used a variety of foreign-built machine guns prior to World War II. Some of these were the Browning Model 1917s and the BAR. Both of these guns were chambered for the 7.92mm cartridge. After the war Poland used Soviet-issued weapons.

Polish BAR (Wz 28)

This Polish BAR was chambered for the 7.92x57mm cartridge with skids on its bipod instead of spikes and a bipod attached to the gas regulator instead of the muzzle. Barrel length is 24" with AA ring sight base. Approximately 12,000 Polish-built BARs were produced between 1930 and 1939. These guns are marked "R.K.M. BROWNING WZ. 28 P.W.U.F.K. (DATE) (SERIAL NUMBER)" located on the receiver. A number of these guns (est. 500) saw service in the Spanish Civil War and were used by German military forces.

Pre-1968

Exc.	V.G.	Fair
25000	22500	20000

Pre-1986 conversions

Exc.	V.G.	Fair
N/A	N/A	N/A

Pre-1986 dealer samples

Exc.	V.G.	Fair
12000	11000	10000

Polish Wz 28 • Courtesy private NFA collection • Paul Goodwin photo

PORTUGAL

Portugal Military Conflicts, 1870-Present

From 1870 to just past the turn of the 20th century Portugal was a country torn by internal political strife. After Carlos I was assassinated in 1908 a republic was established, but an army coup in 1926 brought the republic to an end. Dictator Antonio Salazar maintained Portugal's neutrality during World War II. Close relations were developed with the U.S. in the early 1950s. Beginning in the 1960s Portugal was forced to deal with its colonies desire for independence and military action was mounted against rebels in its African colonies. By the middle of the 1970s most of Portugal's colonies achieved independence. In 2001 Portugal's active armed forces numbered about 43,000.

HANDGUNS

Portugal adopted the Walther PP in 7.65x17mm, and the Walther P1 in 9mm. FN provided the machinery to manufacture the FN 35 GP pistol. Heckler & Koch also sold its VP70M to the Portuguese military.

Model 1878 Army

This 9.1x17.5R Portuguese Abadie cartridge officer's revolver was fitted with a 4.5" octagon barrel and 6-round fluted cylinder. The revolver was double action with a solid frame and gate loaded. The most unique features is the Abadie system of linking the loading gate to the hammer to prevent accidental discharge while loading. Weight is about 27 oz. This revolver remained in service until 1919.

Courtesy Geschichte und Technik der europaischen Militarrevolver, Journal-Verlag Schwend GmbH with permission

Exc.	V.G.	Good	Fair	Poor
750	600	400	200	150

Model 1886 Army/Navy

This revolver was issued to troopers. Chambered for the 9.35x17.5R Portuguese Abadie cartridge. Double action with solid frame and gate loaded. Octagon barrel is 5.6" long. Cylinder is fluted and holds 6 rounds. Weight is about 30 oz. This revolver also employs the Abadie loading gate system. Remained in service until 1910.

Courtesy Geschichte und Technik der europaischen Militarrevolver, Journal-Verlag Schwend GmbH with permission

Exc.	V.G.	Good	Fair	Poor
750	600	400	200	150

Model 1907 Portuguese Contract

Similar to the commercial guns but with a lanyard ring like the French contract model. Chambered for the 7.65mm cartridge. Original Portuguese pistols will have the Portuguese Crest on the grips. Only about 1,150 of these pistols were produced and very few have the original Portuguese grips. Very rare. Proceed with caution.

Exc.	V.G.	Good	Fair	Poor
1500	1000	750	600	300

SUBMACHINE GUNS

The Portuguese military has used a wide variety of submachine guns over the years purchased from other countries. Some of these sub guns are: the Beretta M12, Vigneron, Uzi, Sterling MK4, Ingram M10, the Star Z-45, and the Franchi LF-57.

FBP M948

Produced in Portugal at its government arsenal in 1948. Chambered for the 9mm parabellum cartridge and fitted with a 9.8" barrel. Blowback operation. Sliding wire stock. Cycle rate is about 500 rounds per minute. Magazine capacity is 32 rounds. Weight is about 7.5 lbs. Designed by Major Goncalves Cardoso of the Portuguese Army. Combines features from the German MP40 and the American M3 grease gun.

Pre-1968

Exc.	V.G.	Fair
N/A	N/A	N/A

Pre-1986 conversions (or U.S.-manufactured receivers)

Exc.	V.G.	Fair
N/A	N/A	N/A

Pre-1986 dealer samples

Exc.	V.G.	Fair
N/A	N/A	N/A

FBP M976

This is an improved version of the above model. Cycle rate is about 65-rounds per minute. A 36-round magazine was also available along with the 32-round type. In service until the 1980s.

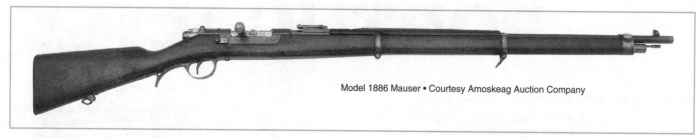

Model 1886 Mauser • Courtesy Amoskeag Auction Company

Pre-1968

Exc.	V.G.	Fair
N/A	N/A	N/A

Pre-1986 conversions (or U.S.-manufactured receivers)

Exc.	V.G.	Fair
N/A	N/A	N/A

Pre-1986 dealer samples

Exc.	V.G.	Fair
N/A	N/A	N/A

RIFLES

Portugal has used the Galil type 5.56mm rifle, the HK33, the FN FAL, small quantities of the AR-10, and the FMBP government arsenal produced G3 rifle.

STEYR

Model 1885 Rifle

Built in Austria for the Portuguese Army this is a single shot block breech action operated by the trigger guard. Full stocked. Chambered for the 8x60R Guedes cartridge. Barrel length is 33.3" and weight is about 9 lbs.

Exc.	V.G.	Good	Fair	Poor
—	1200	750	450	250

MANNLICHER

Model 1896

Produced by Steyr about 4,200 cavalry carbines were acquired by Portugal in 6.5x53Rmm. Barrel length is 17.7". Five-round clip-loaded magazine. Marked Steyr on the left side of the receiver and the Portuguese crest on the receiver ring. No bayonet attachment.

Exc.	V.G.	Good	Fair	Poor
300	200	125	100	50

MAUSER

Model 1886 (Mauser-Kropatschek)

Built by Steyr this rifle came in three configurations: carbine, short rifle, and rifle. Chambered for the 8x60R (later 8x56R) cartridge. Carbines were fitted with a 20.5" barrel, short rifle with 26" barrels, and rifles with 32.25" barrels. The short rifle

Model 1885 Rifle • Courtesy Rock Island Auction Company

and carbine did not have an upper handguard as did the rifle which was fitted with a clip-on handguard. All three variations had bayonet attachments.

Exc.	V.G.	Good	Fair	Poor
300	200	125	80	50

M1904 Mauser-Verueiro Rifle

Chambered for the 6.5x58Rmm cartridge and designed by a Portuguese officer (Vergueiro). Fitted with a 29.1" barrel, 5-round flush box magazine. Tangent rear leaf sight to 2,000 meters. Carlos I crest on the receiver ring. Weight is about 8.5 lbs. The stock has an almost superficial pistol grip and upper handguard from the receiver to upper barrel band. The rifle is fitted with a split bridge receiver and modified Mannlicher-Schoenauer bolt.

Courtesy Rock Island Auction Company

Exc.	V.G.	Good	Fair	Poor
300	200	125	80	50

M1904/M39 Rifle

This model was the result of a conversion of the Model 1904 to conform to the 1930s Model 1937-A rifle. Rifle was rechambered to 7.92x57mm, the barrel shortened to 23.6". The front sight was fitted with sight protectors. Markings are the same as the Model 1904 rifle. Weight is about 8 lbs.

Exc.	V.G.	Good	Fair	Poor
300	200	125	80	50

M1933 Standard Model Short Rifle

Portugal purchased a number of this model directly from Germany. They are standard German export models in every respect.

Exc.	V.G.	Good	Fair	Poor
350	250	200	150	90

M1933 Standard Model Carbine

As above but in carbine configuration.

Exc.	V.G.	Good	Fair	Poor
350	250	200	150	90

M1937-A Short Rifle

This rifle replaced the Model 1904 in 1937. Similar to the German K98k carbine. Chambered for the 7.92x57mm cartridge and fitted with a 23.6" barrel. Box magazine holds 5 rounds and is flush with the bottom of the stock. Rear leaf tangent sight to 2,000 meters. Front sight has sight protectors. Portuguese national crest of the receiver ring. Weight is about 8.75 lbs.

Exc.	V.G.	Good	Fair	Poor
400	300	225	150	100

M1941 Short Rifle

Exc.	V.G.	Good	Fair	Poor
425	300	225	150	100

MACHINE GUNS

The Portuguese military has used the MG42, HK21, FN MAG, M60D, M219, .50 M2 HB machine guns.

The Portuguese purchased in 1938 a number of modified Dreyse Model 1918 machine guns which the Portuguese referred to as the Model 938.

ROMANIA

Romanian Military Conflicts, 1870-Present

In 1861 the principalities of Moldavia and Wallachia (formerly under Russian control) were united to form Romania, which became independent in 1878. In 1881 Romania became the Kingdom of Romania. Romania was involved in the Second Balkan War in 1913 with Serbia, Greece, and Turkey against Bulgaria for a larger share of Macedonia. Romania and its allies defeated Bulgaria. This Balkan conflict helped to hasten the Balkan nationalism that precipitated World War I. In 1916 Romania joined forces with the Allies against Austria-Hungary and Germany. At the conclusion of World War I, Romania was ceded additional land, but its history was marked by increased domestic turmoil and violence. In the 1930s, the rise of the Iron Guard, a fascist organization, overthrew the Romanian king and established a dictatorship. Romania joined Germany against Russia in 1941. Soviet troops entered Romania in 1944 and shortly after the end of World War II a Communist government took power. While Romania was part of the Soviet empire it maintained a certain independence, especially in its foreign policy. In 1990 an election was held that ousted most of the Communists from the government but failed to find solutions to domestic unrest and strife.

HANDGUNS

Steyr Hahn Model 1911

Chambered for the 9mm Steyr cartridge, this pistol was made by Steyr for the Romanian military in 1913 and 1914, as well as other military forces. This particular model is marked with Romanian crest over 1912 on left of slide. Some of these pistols were used by Romanian military during World War II.

Exc.	V.G.	Good	Fair	Poor
500	375	300	250	150

Beretta Model 1934 Romanian Contract

This model is identical to the Beretta Model 1934 except the slide is marked "9mm Scurt" instead of "9mm Corto." Built for the Romanian military in 1941 with an estimate of approximately 20,000 manufactured in Italy.

Courtesy Orvel Reichert

Exc.	V.G.	Good	Fair	Poor
525	425	325	225	125

Model 74

A Romanian copy of the Walther PP chambered for the 7.65mm (.32 ACP) cartridge. This pistol has an aluminum frame and is similar to the FEG Hungarian R61 with the exception of a heel-type magazine release.

Exc.	V.G.	Good	Fair	Poor
250	150	125	100	80

Soviet TT33 (Copy)

This model is not fitted with a safety and has no import stamp. It is original military issue.

Exc.	V.G.	Good	Fair	Poor
850	700	600	500	300

NOTE: For pistols with safety and import stamp deduct 75 percent.

Soviet PM (Copy of Makarov)

Fitted with a safety but with no import stamp.

Exc.	V.G.	Good	Fair	Poor
450	350	300	200	100

SUBMACHINE GUNS

Before 1939 Romania acquired Beretta 9mm Model 1938A submachine guns. After 1939 the Romanian armed forces used the Beretta 38/42 in 9mm Parabellum. Then after the war Romania adopted the Czech VZ24 and VZ26 guns.

Orita M 1941

This gun was manufactured in Romania at Cugir Arsenal. It is similar to the MP 41 but uses magazines that are similar in appearance to the German model but are not interchangeable with it. Fitted with a one-piece wooden stock. Chambered for the 9mm Parabellum cartridge. Semiautomatic or full auto fire. The rear leaf and ramp sight is quite large and located well forward on the barrel. Barrel length is 11.25". Magazine capacity is 25 rounds. The gun has a cycle rate of about 600 rounds per minute. Weight is approximately 7.75 lbs.

RIFLES

PEABODY

Romanian Rifle (1867-1868)

Chambered for the .45 Romanian centerfire cartridge and fitted with a 32.25" barrel. Blued barrel with casehardened furniture. Full stock with two barrel bands. Oiled wooden stocks. A total of 25,000 rifles were made in serial range 21,000 to 52,000.

Exc.	V.G.	Good	Fair	Poor
—	1500	1000	500	200

PEABODY-MARTINI
Witten, Germany

Model 1879 Peabody-Martini Rifle

Made in Germany and based on the Turkish Model 1874 rifle. Chambered for the 11.43x60R Peabody-Martini cartridge. Fitted with a 33.25" barrel. Full stocked with two barrel bands. Weight is about 9.5 lbs.

Exc.	V.G.	Good	Fair	Poor
—	850	500	300	150

MANNLICHER

Model 1892

Introduced in 1892 and built by Steyr, this turn bolt rifle is chambered for the 6.5x53Rmm cartridge. This model is full stocked with straight grip and half-length handguard. Fitted with a cleaning rod and bayonet fittings. Barrel length is 28.5". Leaf rear sight. Clip loaded magazine has a 5-round capacity. Weight is about 9 lbs. Marked "OE" over "W.G." on receiver ring and "MD. 1892" on left side of receiver.

Exc.	V.G.	Good	Fair	Poor
250	150	100	75	50

Model 1893

This is an improved version of the Model 1892 with stacking hook added and bolt modifications to prevent faulty assembly. Other specifications are the same as the Model 1892.

Exc.	V.G.	Good	Fair	Poor
225	125	90	75	50

Model 1893 Carbine

This is a short version of the Model 1893 rifle with 17.7" barrel. No handguard and no bayonet fittings. Weight is approximately 7.25 lbs.

Exc.	V.G.	Good	Fair	Poor
300	200	150	100	75

MAUSER

VZ24 Short Rifle

This model is a copy of the Czech VZ24 Short Rifle. The only difference is the Romanian crest on the receiver ring.

Exc.	V.G.	Good	Fair	Poor
375	280	200	140	80

STATE FACTORIES

Romanian Mosin-Nagant M1944

These rifles are marked on the receiver with a small arrowhead in a triangle below a wreath with the letters "RPR." Romanian stocks are marked with a "C" in a diamond. These rifles were produced in the 1950s.

Exc.	V.G.	Good	Fair	Poor
250	150	100	75	50

PSL Sniper Rifle (misnamed FPK)

This model is chambered for the 7.62x54Rmm cartridge and fitted with a modified AKM-type receiver. Magazine capacity is 10 rounds. Buttstock is similar to the Soviet SVD but with a molded cheekpiece. The muzzle brake is of Romanian design. Equipped with a telescope sight. Weight is about 10.5 lbs.

Exc.	V.G.	Good	Fair	Poor
800	700	550	400	200

SKS

A Romanian-manufactured version of the Russian rifle.

Exc.	V.G.	Good	Fair	Poor
250	150	125	100	75

AK-47 (semiautomatic version)

Romanian copy of the Soviet AK-47.

Exc.	V.G.	Good	Fair	Poor
400	300	200	150	100

AKM

Copy of the Soviet AKM except for a noticeable curved-front vertical fore grip formed as part of the forend.

Courtesy West Point Museum, Paul Goodwin photo

Pre-1968

Exc.	V.G.	Fair
8500	8000	7500

Pre-1986 conversions

Exc.	V.G.	Fair
N/A	N/A	N/A

Pre-1986 dealer samples

Exc.	V.G.	Fair
N/A	N/A	N/A

AKM-R

This is a compact version of the Soviet AKM with an 8" barrel and side-folding metal butt. Magazine capacity is 20 rounds. Chambered for the 7.62x39mm cartridge. Rate of fire is about 600 rounds per minute. Weight is approximately 7 lbs.

Pre-1968

Exc.	V.G.	Fair
18000	16000	14000

Pre-1986 conversions

Exc.	V.G.	Fair
N/A	N/A	N/A

Pre-1986 dealer samples

Exc.	V.G.	Fair
N/A	N/A	N/A

AK-74

Similar to the Soviet 5.45x39mm version of this model but with a full-length handguard. Forend is fitted with vertical foregrip. Produced with metal or wooden buttstock. Semiautomatic version only.

Exc.	V.G.	Good	Fair	Poor
300	250	200	150	100

MACHINE GUNS

The Romanians used Soviet-built RPDs, SGMs, PK, PKB, PKS, PHTs, and the Soviet-made DShK 38/46.

RPK (Romanian Manufacture)

Copy of Soviet RPK.

Pre-1968

Exc.	V.G.	Fair
N/A	N/A	N/A

Pre-1986 conversions

Exc.	V.G.	Fair
15000	14000	13000

Pre-1986 dealer samples

Exc.	V.G.	Fair
12500	11500	10500

Romanian Schwarzlose converted to 7.62 caliber with larger waterjacket and metal belt • Courtesy Robert E. Naess

RUSSIA
Former USSR/Warsaw Pact

Russian/Soviet Military Conflicts, 1870 - 2000

After the Crimean War, 1854-1856, Russian expansion continued into Caucasus, Turkestan, and eastern Asia. Alexander II was assassinated in 1881. Oppressive imperial rule followed under Alexander III and Nicholas II. The Russo-Japanese War of 1905 led to the Revolution of 1905, the results of which forced Nicholas to grant a Parliament and constitution. World War I led to the collapse of imperial rule and the country was thrown into revolution in 1917. During World War I, Russia had a total of 12,000,000 military personnel with 5,300,000 killed or wounded.

Lenin took control, but civil war lasted until 1920 when the Soviet regime emerged victorious. In 1922 Russia became part of the USSR. Despite a non-aggression treaty with Hitler, Russia was invaded by Nazi Germany in 1941. Russian military forces fought several famous battles against the Germans throughout the war. In 1945 Russian forces entered Berlin and forced the Allies to partition Berlin and later Germany. A total of 30,000,000 people served in the Russian military during the war. Of that number, 11,000,000 were killed, but the number of wounded is unknown. Civilian casualties are estimated at 6,700,000.

From the end of World War II, military forces of the USSR and Warsaw Pact nations were engaged in numerous military adventures. Perhaps the best known was the 10-year struggle in Afghanistan. In 1991 the USSR collapsed and Russia resumed her autonomy. Since that time Russia has been engaged in trying to control rebellious ethnic areas of the country from gaining independence, namely Chechnya and Tatarstan. As of 2001 Russia had 977,100 personnel on active duty. Active duty army was 321,000 personnel. Russia has 20,000,000 reserve forces.

HANDGUNS

NOTE: Russia contracted for a number of Smith & Wesson revolvers over a period of years. The number of these revolvers purchased by Russia was about 350,000. These revolvers were made for the Russian military and are covered under *U.S., Handguns, Smith & Wesson.*

NAGANT

Model 1895 "Gas Seal" Revolver

A 7.62mm caliber single or double action revolver with a 4.35" barrel and 7-shot cylinder. Called a Gas Seal because as the hammer is cocked, the cylinder is moved forward to engage the barrel breech forming a seal between the cylinder and the barrel. Blued with either walnut or plastic grips. Weight was approximately 28 oz. In service from 1895 to approximately 1947.

Built by Nagant Brothers in Liege, Belgium. The Russians also built the gun under license at their arsenal in Tula.

Exc.	V.G.	Good	Fair	Poor
250	150	100	75	50

NOTE: Single action only versions are much less encountered and will command a 50 percent premium. Prices reflect revolvers that have original finish, and are not arsenal refinished.

Model 1895 Nagant .22 Caliber

As above but chambered for .22 caliber cartridges. Converted at the Tula arsenal from surplus 7.62mm revolvers. Used as a training revolver from 1925 to 1947.

Exc.	V.G.	Good	Fair	Poor
650	500	350	250	100

Mosin-Nagant Model 1895 • Paul Goodwin photo

Exc.	V.G.	Good	Fair	Poor
1000	700	500	300	200

A Model 1895 Nagant Training Revolver in .22 caliber sold at auction for $977.50. Condition is very good.
Rock Island Auction Company, Sept. 2002

Model 1895 Nagant (KGB)

This is a standard Nagant with the important exception of a 3.5" barrel and shorter grip frame. Used by the Russian secret police during the Stalin years. Extremely rare. Proceed with caution.

Nagant KGB Model • Courtesy Richard M. Kumor Sr.

Exc.	V.G.	Good	Fair	Poor
2000	1500	1000	—	—

FN 1900 Russian Contract

An unknown number of these FN pistols were purchased by the Russian government. Little information is known. Proceed with caution.

FN Model 1900 Russian Contract Pistol • Courtesy Richard M. Kumor Sr.

SOVIET STATE FACTORIES

Tokarev TT-30 & TT-33

Fyedor Tokarev was a Russian weapons designer who began his career at the Sestroretsk rifle factory in 1907. He was responsible for the development of machine guns, pistols, and automatic rifles. The TT series of pistols were just some of his designs.

In 1930 the TT-30 was adopted, and in 1933 a slightly modified version, the TT-33, was introduced. A 7.62mm semiautomatic pistol with a 4.5" barrel and 8-shot magazine. This model was produced in a number of communist countries. Each country had its own model designation for the pistol. In Poland and Yugoslavia it is called the M57; in Hungary it was known as the M48; in China the M51 and M54; and in North Korea the M68. The North Korean M68 differs from the other Tokarevs in the location of the magazine release and the elimination of the barrel locking link.

TT-33 • Courtesy Richard M. Kumor Sr.

Exc.	V.G.	Good	Fair	Poor
500	400	250	125	100

NOTE: In 1941 the German army captured a number of Russian pistols, namely the TT-33. It was designated the Pistol 615 (r). Add 50 percent for these examples. Add 50 percent for TT-30, for cut-aways add 200 percent.

Russian officer with TT33 Tokarev, Courtesy Paul S. Scarlata

Tokarev Model R-3

A training version of the TT Tokarev pistols chambered for the .22 caliber cartridge.

Exc.	V.G.	Good	Fair	Poor
650	550	400	300	150

Tokarev Model R-4

A long barrel target version of the TT Tokarev pistol chambered for the .22 caliber cartridge.

Exc.	V.G.	Good	Fair	Poor
650	550	400	300	150

TK TOZ (Tula Korovin)

A .25 caliber pocket pistol produced by the Soviet arsenal at Tula. Fitted with a 2.7" fixed barrel. Magazine capacity is 8 rounds. Weight is approximately 14 oz. Used by military officers and police units. Produced from 1926 to about 1935.

Courtesy Orvel Reichert

Exc.	V.G.	Good	Fair	Poor
450	350	300	200	100

Makarov

This semiautomatic pistol is similar in appearance to the Walther PP pistol and is chambered for the 9mm Makarov (9x18mm) cartridge. It has a double action trigger and is fitted with fixed sights. Barrel length is 3.6" and overall length is 6.4". Weight is approximately 25 oz. Magazine capacity is 8 rounds.

Exc.	V.G.	Good	Fair	Poor
175	100	80	60	50

SNAP SHOT
THE MAKAROV PISTOL

When non-gun owners ask me what handgun I would recommend to them for personal protection that is both GOOD and CHEAP, I almost always recommend that they take a look at one of the variations of the Mararov.

By good they mean reliable, durable, and effective. By cheap they mean $150 or less. As this is written Bulgarian-made Makarovs are available in that price range and in recent times so have been Chinese, Russian, and surplus East German Makarovs many of which are still available on the second-hand market.

The Makarov is better than just good it is quite excellent. Its biggest drawback is that the cartridge it is normally chambered for, the 9x18mm Makarov, is marginal in power for self-defense use by some standards. However, it is powerful enough to do the job, particularly when modern hollow-point ammunition is used. More importantly, a Makarov in the hand is far better than a more expensive more powerful handgun that is still in the gun shop because you can't afford it.

The Makarov is an improved spin-off of the German Walther PP. Like that pistol, it is blowback operated, has a similar take-down system, is medium sized, and has a double-action trigger mechanism. It is better than the Walther in that it has a manual safety that is easier to use, a slide release, generally has a better trigger pull, and it is more reliable particularly with hollow-point ammunition because of a more direct feeding cycle.

Introduced in the early 1950s in the Soviet Union, the Makarov has been manufactured in quite a few countries. While a few examples showed up in Vietnam, the pistol was quite uncommon in the U. S. until the fall of the Iron Curtain. Now the pistols are common and ammunition is even made in the U. S. by several manufacturers.

Charles Karwan

Stechkin

A select fire pistol chambered for the 9x18 Makarov cartridge. Fitted with a 5.5" barrel and a 20-round magazine. Rate of fire is about 750 rounds per minute. Weight is approximately 36 oz. This was the standard service pistol of the Soviet army between 1955 and 1975. A wooden stock/holster is supplied with the pistol.

NOTE: It is not known how many, if any, of these machine pistols are in the U.S. and are transferable. Prices listed below are estimates only.

Pre-1968 (Extremely Rare)

Exc.	V.G.	Fair
30000+	—	—

Pre-1986 conversions

Exc.	V.G.	Fair
N/A	N/A	N/A

Pre-1986 dealer samples

Exc.	V.G.	Fair
N/A	N/A	N/A

Stechkin with stock • Courtesy Thomas Nelson, *The World's Machine Pistols, Vol. II*

SUBMACHINE GUNS

PPD-1934/38 (Pistol Pulyemet Degtyarev)

Introduced in 1938 and based on the Bergman MP28 submachine gun. Select fire. The buttstock is wooden. Barrel is 10.5" with perforated barrel jacket and tangent sight. Chambered for the 7.62 Soviet pistol cartridge. Magazine capacity is 25-round box or 71-round drum. Rate of fire is approximately 800 rounds per minute. Weight is about 8.5 lbs.

Pre-1968

Exc.	V.G.	Fair
17000	15000	13000

Pre-1986 conversions

Exc.	V.G.	Fair
N/A	N/A	N/A

Pre-1986 dealer samples

Exc.	V.G.	Fair
N/A	N/A	N/A

PPD-1940

First produced in 1940, this Russian-built submachine gun is chambered for the 7.62 Soviet pistol cartridge. The gun was fitted with a 71-round drum magazine and 10" barrel. The rate of fire was 800 rounds per minute. The serial number and factory code are located on top of the receiver. Weight is about 8 lbs. Production ceased in 1941.

Pre-1968

Exc.	V.G.	Fair
17000	15000	13000

Pre-1986 conversions

Exc.	V.G.	Fair
N/A	5500	5000

Pre-1986 dealer samples

Exc.	V.G.	Fair
N/A	N/A	N/A

PPSh-41 (Pistol Pulyemet Shpagin)

This Russian select fire submachine gun was produced from 1941 until 1947. About five million were built and many were sold throughout the world. Some were converted from the 7.62 pistol cartridge to the 9mm cartridge by Germany. The gun

---

SNAP SHOT
THE PPSh41 SMG

The most prolific SMG of WWII and probably of all time, the 7.62x25mm Soviet PPSh41 was also one of the very best and most effective. Originally produced just in the Soviet Union, it was eventually made in Iran, China, North Korea, and several other Eastern bloc countries. Most parts are made from welded stampings so it can be made quite efficiently for a low cost.

During WWII the Soviets employed the PPSh41 almost like an assault rifle with entire infantry units armed with this weapon, putting out huge volumes of fire during an attack. It was an awesome weapon for urban house-to-house fighting and proved to be an excellent jungle warfare weapon in Indochina.

While most SMGs are only effective out to 100 yards, with the better ones effective to about double that distance, the PPSh41 is quite effective even at 300 yards in the hands of a good shooter due to its flat-shooting cartridge, good design layout, and good sights. It can also be fired quite accurately semiautomatically.

Known as the Russian "burp gun" because of its high 800+ rpm cyclic rate of automatic fire, this SMG used either 35-round stick magazines or 71-round drum magazines. They have chrome-lined barrels, are extremely simple to maintain, and utterly reliable. Field stripping to remove the bolt and gain access to the barrel and receiver for maintenance can be accomplished in seconds. Weighing about 9 pounds with a loaded stick magazine it is short and handy, though the heavier and much wider drum magazine makes the weapon much more awkward to handle.

In WWII German forces used captured PPSh41s extensively and even rebarreled them to 9mm Parabellum with a magazine well adapter to allow the use of the German MP-40 magazine. Because of its superb design, high level of performance, huge production, wide distribution, and historical significance, the PPSh41 is one of the top SMGs of all time.

Charles Karwan

PPD-1940 • Courtesy West Point Museum, Paul Goodwin photo

PPsh41/Viet Cong • Paul Goodwin photo

could use a 71-round drum magazine or a 35-round box magazine. Rate of fire was 900 rounds per minute. The barrel was 10.3" long with slotted barrel jacket and weighed almost 8 lbs. Early models had a tangent back sight while most were fitted with a two-position, flip-up rear sight. Markings are located on the receiver.

NOTE: A German conversion 9mm kit was made for this gun. The kit uses MP-40 magazines. Very rare. Too rare to price.

Courtesy Richard M. Kumor Sr.

Pre-1968

Exc.	V.G.	Fair
15000	14000	13000

Pre-1986 conversions

Exc.	V.G.	Fair
N/A	N/A	N/A

Pre-1986 dealer samples

Exc.	V.G.	Fair
N/A	N/A	N/A

PPS 1943 (Pistol Pulyemet Sudaev)

Chambered for the 7.62 pistol cartridge this full automatic only submachine gun is fitted with a 10" barrel with slotted barrel jacket and 35-round box magazine. The receiver and jacket are stamped out of one piece of sheet steel. The metal butt folds behind the ejection port. Rate of fire is about 700 rounds per minute. Weight is approximately 7.5 lbs. Introduced in 1943 as an improvement over the PPsh-41.

PPS 1943 • Courtesy Steve Hill, Spotted Dog Firearms

PPS 1943 • Paul Goodwin photo

Pre-1968

Exc.	V.G.	Fair
16000	14000	12000

Pre-1986 conversions

Exc.	V.G.	Fair
N/A	N/A	N/A

Pre-1986 dealer samples

Exc.	V.G.	Fair
N/A	N/A	N/A

RIFLES

BERDAN

Berdan Model 1870 (Berdan II)

After Colt had built and supplied the Russians with the first Berdan rifles, BSA of Birmingham, England, produced another 30,000. BSA, in 1871 and 1872, also provided the tooling and machinery so that the Russians could build their own version of the Berdan. A total of 3,500,000 Russian Berdans were built at the arsenals in Ishevsk, Sestroryetsk, and Tula. This single-shot model had an octagon receiver with a short bolt handle. Caliber was 10.66x57Rmm with a barrel length of 32.5". Marked with the Russian arsenal on top of the receiver ring flat. These rifles saw service as late as World War I. Some captured Russian rifles were issued to German units during WWI.

Exc.	V.G.	Good	Fair	Poor
850	600	400	300	100

MOSIN-NAGANT

The first Mosin-Nagant rifles were developed at Tula by Sergi Mosin. The feed system was developed by Belgian designer Leon Nagant. The Russians had inadequate production facilities to build these rifles so many of them were produced by Chatelleraut, Remington, and Westinghouse. SIG made barrels for the rifles and Valmet, Tikkakoske rebuilt and modified Russian rifles. The Mosin-Nagant was also produced in Poland, Hungary, Romania, and China. For history and technical details see Terence W. Lapin's, *The Mosin-Nagant Rifle*, North Cape Publications, 1998.

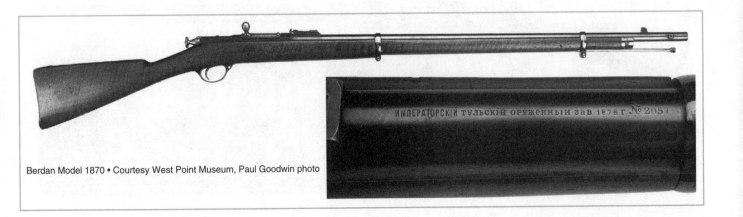

Berdan Model 1870 • Courtesy West Point Museum, Paul Goodwin photo

NOTE: During World War II the Germans captured thousands of Russian weapons. Many of these were Russian Mosin-Nagant rifles. These rifles were reissued with German code numbers to designate them as foreign equipment (*Fremdgerat*). Part of the code included the lower case (r) denoting that the rifle was Russian.

Model 1891

A 7.62x54Rmm caliber bolt action rifle with a 31.6" barrel, 5-shot integral magazine, ladder rear sight, and a full-length stock secured by two barrel bands. Blued with a walnut stock. The Model 1891, before 1918, was fitted with an octagonal receiver ring with a heavyweight rear barrel section behind the rear sight. Pre-1908 version did not have upper handguards. Post-1908 rifles had sling swivels mounted through slots in the butt and forearm. Front sight was an unhooded blade while the rear sight was a ramp and leaf affair. Weight of these rifles was about 9.5 lbs. Used extensively in the Russo-Japanese War of 1904-1905. A total of over 9,000,000 of these rifles were built between 1892 and 1922.

German military designation 252 (r).

Exc.	V.G.	Good	Fair	Poor
200	125	100	75	60

NOTE: Some Model 1891 rifles captured by Austria were converted to take the 8x50R Austrian cartridge. These examples are extremely rare and command a $300 premium.

Model 1891 Dragoon Rifle

Same as above but for a 28.75" barrel. Fitted with a short handguard with sling slots in buttstock and forend. Weight was reduced to about 8.5 lbs. Replaced the Model 1891 rifle as standard issue after 1920.

German military designation 253 (r).

Exc.	V.G.	Good	Fair	Poor
250	150	125	75	60

Model 1891 Cossack Rifle

This variant is almost identical to the Dragoon Rifle but instead is fitted with a tangent rear sight. The rifle was not issued with a bayonet.

German military designation 254 (r).

Exc.	V.G.	Good	Fair	Poor
250	150	125	75	60

Model 1891/30 Rifle

This is an improved version of the Model 1891 Dragoon rifle. The older octagon receiver is replaced with a cylindrical one. It has a 28.7" barrel with metric rear tangent sights. Front sight is hooded. The bayonet ring was changed to a spring loaded catch type. Five-round magazine. Weight is about 8.7 lbs. Introduced in 1930. Over 17,000,000 of these rifles were produced between 1930 and 1944.

Exc.	V.G.	Good	Fair	Poor
225	125	100	75	60

SNAP SHOT
THE SOVIET MOSIN M91/30

In 1891 Russian ordnance adopted its first smokeless powder repeating rifle the M91 Mosin-Nagant. It and its descendants, like the M91/30, are among the most widely distributed, most prolific, and longest-serving military rifles in history. The fact that they are strong, accurate, and reliable may have something to do with it. Remarkably its 7.62x54Rmm cartridge is still the standard medium machine gun and sniper rifle cartridge for a significant number of countries.

Shortly after the Russian Revolution the production of the M91 Mosin rifle with its 31.5-inch barrel ceased in favor of the 28.8-inch barreled Dragoon rifle. In 1930 the basic M91 Dragoon rifle was further modified for easier manufacture by changing the octagonal receiver to a round configuration, given improved sights, and an improved cartridge interrupter. It was designated the M91/30. In 1938 a 20-inch barreled carbine version was introduced designated the M38. During WWII the Soviets also adopted the M44 carbine which was basically the M38 carbine with an integral folding bayonet.

One variation or another of the M91/30 rifle remained in production until the 1960s and many remained in regular military use long after that. They were made in huge quantities by the Soviet Union, China, North Korea, Poland, Romania, and Hungary. The Czechs and the Bulgarians have also made distinctive model variations using Russian M91/30 Mosins for the base.

The Mosin M91/30 models were the primary rifles of the Soviet Army during WWII and the M91/30 sniper rifles were the most prolific sniper rifles of that war. Mosin M91/30 variations were also the primary rifles used by Chinese and North Korean forces in the Korean War and were also common arms of the Communist forces in Indochina.

As you can see the M91/30 Mosin rifle got around. It is easily one of the most historically significant bolt-action military rifles in history and second only to the M98 Mauser series in total production.

Charles Karwan

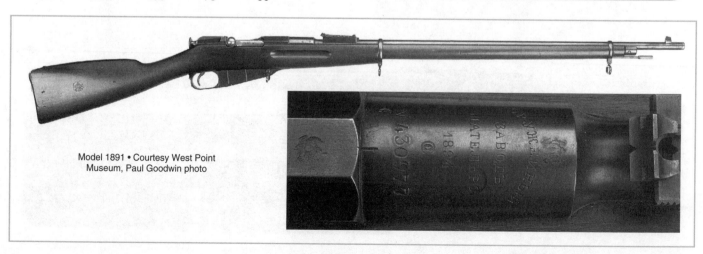

Model 1891 • Courtesy West Point
Museum, Paul Goodwin photo

Model 1944 carbine with receiver markings • Paul Goodwin photo

Model 1891/30 Sniper Rifle w/3.5 power PU scope

This is a Model 1891/30 with a scope attached to the left of the receiver, and a longer turned-down bolt handle. Fitted with iron sights.

Courtesy Richard M. Kumor Sr.

Exc.	*V.G.*	*Good*	*Fair*	*Poor*
1200	900	700	400	N/A

NOTE: There are a number of Czech CZ 54 and CZ 57 sniper rifles based on the Mosin, as well as Finnish sniper rifles based on the Mosin. All examples, if extant, are worth a minimum of 100 percent premium over the Russian Model 1891/30 PU. Deduct 50 percent for imported rifles.

Model 1891/30 Sniper Rifle w/4 power P.E. scope (Rare)

This is a Model 1891/30 with a scope attached. This scope was used until about 1940. Most, but not all, of these scopes are dated 1921 to 1935 and made by Carl Zeiss in Jena, Germany.

Close-up of P.E. scope • Courtesy Richard M. Kumor Sr.

Exc.	*V.G.*	*Good*	*Fair*	*Poor*
2250	1700	1100	850	N/A

NOTE: Deduct 50 percent for imported rifles.

Model 1907/1910 Carbine

As above, with a 20" barrel and modified sights. No bayonet fittings. Leaf sight is graduated in Russian arshins form of measurement from 400 to 2,000. Weight is 7.5 lbs.

German military designation 453 (r).

Exc.	*V.G.*	*Good*	*Fair*	*Poor*
250	150	125	100	75

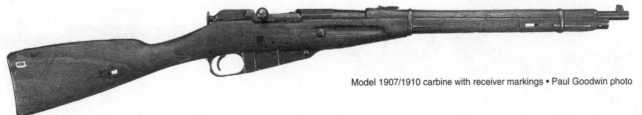

Model 1907/1910 carbine with receiver markings • Paul Goodwin photo

Model 1938 Carbine

This model replaced the Model 1907/1910 carbine. It is fitted with a 20" barrel. Rear tangent sight is in meters from 1 through 10. No bayonet fittings. Weight is about 7.5 lbs. Produced from 1939 to 1944. Very few were produced in 1945. About 2,000,000 were produced.

NOTE: Many Model 91/30 rifles were arsenal converted to M38 carbine configuration. These may be marked M91/59. Conversions done in Bulgaria, Czechoslovakia, and possibly the Soviet Union.

German military designation 454 (r).

Exc.	V.G.	Good	Fair	Poor
375	250	150	100	75

Model 1944 Carbine

This was the last Mosin-Nagant. It was fitted with a folding bayonet hinged at the barrel muzzle. The barrel was about 1/2" longer than the Model 1938 carbine. Rear tangent sight is in meters from 1 through 10. With the bayonet this carbine weighed about 9 lbs. This model was copied by the Chinese and designated the Type 53. This model was also made in Poland and Romania. The Russian Model 1944 Carbine was used in Afghanistan in the 1980s and by Palestinian guerrilla groups, also in the 1980s.

Exc.	V.G.	Good	Fair	Poor
250	150	125	75	50

NOTE: Add 15 percent for no import markings.

TOKAREV

Fyedo Vassilevich Tokarev designed not only the Tokarev rifle in 1938 and 1940, but the pistol and machine gun that bear his name as well. An experimental model, the Model 1930 was built for military trials. The Model 1935, fitted with a 17.75" barrel, was built for trials but was not successful. Only about 500 were produced.

M1938 Rifle (SVT)

A 7.62x54Rmm caliber gas-operated semiautomatic or select fire rifle with a 24" barrel with muzzle break and 10-shot magazine (15 rounds in select fire). Cleaning rod in stock. Blued with a two-piece hardwood stock extending the full-length of the rifle. Upper handguard is 3/4 length of barrel. Weight is about 8.5 lbs. Manufactured from 1938 to 1940. Approximately 150,000 of these rifles were manufactured.

M1938 Sniper • Courtesy Richard M. Kumor Sr.

Courtesy Richard M. Kumor Sr.

Exc.	V.G.	Good	Fair	Poor
1200	800	600	200	100

NOTE: Add 300 percent for Sniper variation.

SNAP SHOT
THE TOKAREV SVT40 RIFLE

The Tokarev SVT40 was second only to the M1 Garand as the most prolific semiautomatic service rifle used in WWII. Its basic bolt mechanism was so good that it was also used in the Swedish AG42 Ljungmann, the French MAS Models 44, 49, and 49/56, the Soviet SKS, as well as the Belgian SAFN M1949 and FAL rifles.

The SVT40 was an improved version of the SVT38 that saw its combat baptism in the Russo-Finnish Winter War of 1939. The SVT40 was quite an excellent rifle. It was significantly lighter than our M1 and its 10-round detachable magazine was a major improvement over the M1's 8-round en bloc clip system. Also fielded extensively as a scoped sniper rifle, its scope was mounted directly over the bore of the rifle instead of offset as with our M1.

In spite of these good features, the SVT40 never replaced the venerable Mosin-Nagant bolt-actions as the standard Soviet service rifle for several reasons. First, the poorer quality of the wartime Soviet ammunition severely compromised the rifle's reliability. This was very well demonstrated by the Finns with captured SVT40 rifles that they used very effectively with the higher quality Finnish ammunition.

The SVT40 was considerably more difficult and expensive to manufacture than the M91/30 Mosin bolt action rifle and required a special tool to properly maintain and adjust its gas system. The average Soviet peasant conscript did not have the training to properly maintain an SVT40 in good operating condition, nor was there time, personnel, and facilities available to train him. As a consequence the SVT40 was often just issued to NCOs or troops with higher levels of training than the average draftee. Regardless, the Soviets employed far more SVT40 rifles during WWII than was previously thought and the rifle gave an excellent account of itself in fierce fighting against the Nazis.

Charles Karwan

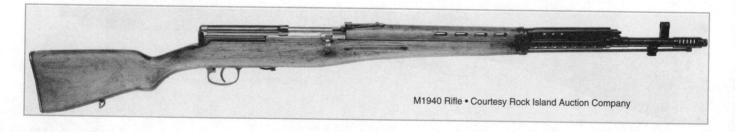

M1940 Rifle • Courtesy Rock Island Auction Company

Female Russian soldier with Tokarev rifle, Courtesy Paul S. Scarlata

M1940 Rifle (SVT)

An improved semiautomatic version of the M1938 with half stock and half-length slotted handguard with a sheet metal handguard and muzzle brake. Ten-round magazine. Weight is about 8.5 lbs. Approximately 2,000,000 were produced.

CAUTION: All Tokarev SVT carbines (18.5" barrel) encountered with "SA" (Finnish) markings were altered to carbine configuration by their importer and have little collector value. It is believed that few, perhaps 2,000, SVT 40 carbines were ever made by the USSR.

Courtesy Richard M. Kumor Sr.

Exc.	V.G.	Good	Fair	Poor
600	500	350	200	150

NOTE: Add 50 percent for no importer marking. Add 300 percent for Sniper variation.

DRAGUNOV

Yevgeni Fyordorov Dragunov was born in 1920. He was in the Soviet army from 1939 to 1945. After the war he worked in the Izhevsk rifle factory where he designed and developed the Dragunov rifle.

SVD Sniper Rifle

This model, developed as a replacement for the Mosin-Nagant Model 1891/30 Sniper rifle, was introduced in 1963. It is chambered for the 7.62x54R cartridge. It is fitted with a 24.5" barrel with prong-style flash hider and has a skeleton stock with cheek rest and slotted forearm. Semiautomatic with an action closely resembling the AK series of rifles. A PSO-1 telescope sight with illuminated reticle is supplied with the rifle from the factory. This sight is fitted to each specific rifle. Magazine capacity is 10 rounds. Weight is about 9.5 lbs.

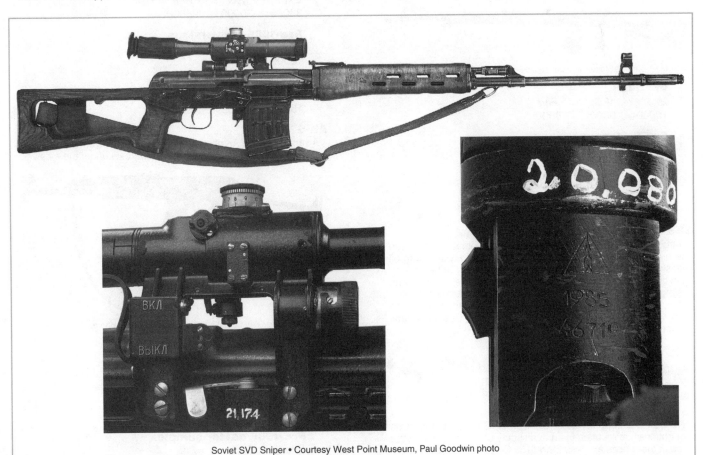

Soviet SVD Sniper • Courtesy West Point Museum, Paul Goodwin photo

A captured Soviet 7.62x54R SVD sniper rifle, Afghanistan, Courtesy Blake Stevens, *Kalashnikov, The Arms and the Man*, Collector Grade Publications.

Exc.	V.G.	Good	Fair	Poor
4000	3500	3000	—	—

SIMONOV

Sergei Simonov was born in 1894 and later became a master gunsmith. He worked in a machine gun factory in the 1920s. He designed and developed several different firearm designs including the rifle that bears his name.

Simonov AVS-36

First built in Russia in 1936, this rifle is chambered for the 7.62x54R Soviet cartridge. Fitted with a 24.3" barrel with muzzle brake and a 20-round magazine. This automatic rifle has a rate of fire of 600 rounds per minute. It weighs 9.7 lbs. Production ceased in 1938.

AVS-36 • Courtesy Steve Hill, Spotted Dog Firearms

Pre-1968
Exc.	V.G.	Fair
10000	9000	8000

Pre-1986 conversions
Exc.	V.G.	Fair
N/A	N/A	N/A

Pre-1986 dealer samples
Exc.	V.G.	Fair
N/A	N/A	N/A

SKS

Introduced in 1946 this 7.62x39mm semiautomatic rifle is fitted with a 20.5" barrel and 10-shot fixed magazine. Blued with oil finished stock and half-length upper handguard. It has a folding blade-type bayonet that folds under the barrel and forearm. Weight is about 8.5 lbs. This rifle was the standard service arm for most Eastern bloc countries prior to the adoption of the AK-47. This rifle was also made in Romania, East Germany, Yugoslavia, and China.

NOTE: The importation of Chinese SKS rifles in very large quantities has resulted in an oversupply of these rifles with the result that prices are less than $150 for guns in excellent condition. However, this situation may change and, if that occurs,

the price will adjust accordingly. Study local conditions before purchase or sale of this firearm.

KALASHNIKOV

Mikhail Kalashnikov was born in 1920. He was drafted into the Soviet army in 1939. He won the Order of the Red Star for bravery in combat during the German invasion of Russia in 1941. He became an amateur gun designer and after several unsuccessful attempts developed the AK series of rifles for the 7.62x39mm cartridge.

Avtomat Kalashnikov AK-47

Designed by Mikhail Kalashnikov and first produced in 1947, the Russian AK-47 is chambered for the 7.62x39mm cartridge and operates on a closed bolt principal. Select fire. The standard model is fitted with a 16" barrel and a fixed beech or birch stock. Early rifles have no bayonet fittings. Magazine capacity is 30 rounds. Rate of fire is 700 rounds per minute. Rear sight is graduated to 800 meters. The bolt and carrier are bright steel. Weight is 9.5 lbs. Markings are located on top rear of receiver. This model was the first line rifle for Warsaw Pact. The most widely used assault rifle in the world and still in extensive use throughout the world.

North Korean AK-47 • Photo courtesy private NFA collection

Pre-1968
Exc.	V.G.	Fair
33000	30000	28000

Pre-1986 conversions
Exc.	V.G.	Fair
15000	13000	11000

Pre-1986 dealer samples
Exc.	V.G.	Fair
15000	14000	13000

AK-S

A variation of the AK rifle is the AK-S. Introduced in 1950, this rifle features a folding steel buttstock which rests under the receiver.

AK-S • Courtesy West Point Museum, Paul Goodwin photo

Pre-1968
Exc.	V.G.	Fair
33000	30000	28000

Pre-1986 conversions
Exc.	V.G.	Fair
15000	13000	11000

Pre-1986 dealer samples
Exc.	V.G.	Fair
15000	14000	13000

Four AKs from top to bottom: Soviet first model with fabricated sheet steel receiver; Soviet second model with machined receiver; Chinese Type 56 with 2nd type machined receiver; bottom later perfected stamped receiver • Courtesy Blake Stevens, *Kalashnikov: Arms and the Man*, Ezell

AKM

This variation of the AK-47, introduced in 1959, can be characterized by a small indentation on the receiver above the magazine. Pressed steel receiver with a parkerized bolt and carrier. Laminated wood furniture and plastic grips. The forend on the AKM is a beavertail-style. The rear sight is graduated to 1,000 meters. Barrel length and rate of fire was the same as the AK-47 rifle. Several other internal production changes were made as well. Model number is located on the top rear of the receiver. Weight is approximately 8.5 lbs.

Photo courtesy private NFA collection

Pre-1968
Exc.	V.G.	Fair
38000	36000	34000

Pre-1986 conversions
Exc.	V.G.	Fair
15000	13000	11000

Pre-1986 dealer samples
Exc.	V.G.	Fair
15000	14000	13000

AKM-S

In 1960 the AKM-S was introduced which featured a steel folding buttstock as seen on the AK-S. Weight is approximately 8 lbs.

AKM-S • Courtesy West Point Museum, Paul Goodwin photo

Pre-1968
Exc.	V.G.	Fair
38000	36000	34000

Pre-1986 conversions
Exc.	V.G.	Fair
15000	13000	11000

Pre-1986 dealer samples (Rare)
Exc.	V.G.	Fair
15000	14000	13000

AK-74 Assault Rifle

Similar to the AK-47 but chambered for the 5.45x39mm cartridge. Magazine capacity is 30 rounds. Barrel length is 16.35". Select fire with semiauto, full auto, and 3-shot burst. Weight is about 8.9 lbs. Rate of fire is approximately 650 to 700 rounds per minute.

NOTE: There are no known original Soviet transferable examples in the U.S. Prices below are for pre-1986 conversions only using AKM receiver and original parts.

Courtesy Steve Hill and Doug McBeth, A.S.D. Firearms

Pre-1968
Exc.	V.G.	Fair
N/A	N/A	N/A

Pre-1986 conversions
Exc.	V.G.	Fair
15000	13000	11000

Pre-1986 dealer samples
Exc.	V.G.	Fair
N/A	N/A	N/A

AK-74 (Semiautomatic only)

Introduced in 1974, this rifle is chambered for a smaller caliber, the 5.45x39.5mm, than the original AK-47 series. It is fitted with a 16" barrel with muzzle brake and has a 30-round plastic magazine. The buttstock is wooden. Weight is approximately 8.5 lbs.

In 1974 a folding stock version was called the AKS-74, and in 1980 a reduced caliber version of the AKM-SU called the AK-74-SU was introduced. No original military AK-74s are known to exist in this country.

Exc.	V.G.	Good	Fair	Poor
N/A	—	—	—	—

AK-47 COPIES

NOTE: These are copies of the Kalashnikov designs with only minor alterations. Because original military select fire AK assault rifles are so rare this list includes *semiautomatic rifles only* unless otherwise noted. These rifles listed below are built in their country of origin and contain no U.S.-made parts, i.e. receivers, etc. Some of these rifles may not be available to the collector and are listed for reference purposes only.

BULGARIA

AK-47

This is an exact copy of the Russian AK-47.

Exc.	V.G.	Good	Fair	Poor
700	600	500	400	300

AKN-47

This is an exact copy of the Russian AKS.

Exc.	V.G.	Good	Fair	Poor
800	700	600	500	400

AK-47-MI

This is a copy of an AK-47 fitted with a 40mm grenade launcher.

AK-47-MI • Courtesy West Point Museum, Paul Goodwin photo

Exc.	V.G.	Good	Fair	Poor
N/A	N/A	N/A	N/A	N/A

AK-74/AKS-74

These are copies of the Russian models. They were also exported in 5.56x45mm caliber.

AKN-74 • Courtesy West Point Museum, Paul Goodwin photo

Exc.	V.G.	Good	Fair	Poor
N/A	N/A	N/A	N/A	N/A

CHINA

See *China, Rifles.*

EGYPT

MISR (Maadi)

A copy of the AKM with insignificant dimensional differences. Sometimes seen with single brace folding metal buttstock.

Pre-Ban

Exc.	V.G.	Good	Fair	Poor
1500	1200	950	750	500

ARM

This model is a MISR modified to semiautomatic only. It is fitted with a thumbhole stock. It is usually seen with a 10-round magazine.

Exc.	V.G.	Good	Fair	Poor
350	250	200	150	100

EAST GERMANY

MPiK

A copy of the AK-47 without a cleaning rod.

Exc.	V.G.	Good	Fair	Poor
N/A	N/A	N/A	N/A	N/A

MpiKS

A copy of the AKS without cleaning rod.

Exc.	V.G.	Good	Fair	Poor
N/A	N/A	N/A	N/A	N/A

MPiKM

A copy of the AKM with a cleaning rod. Early models used wooden stocks while later ones used plastic. Not fitted with a muzzle compensator.

Courtesy Blake Stevens, *Kalashnikov, The Arms and the Man*, Collector Grade Publications.

Exc.	V.G.	Good	Fair	Poor
N/A	N/A	N/A	N/A	N/A

MPiKMS

Copy of a AKMS without shaped muzzle.

Exc.	V.G.	Good	Fair	Poor
N/A	N/A	N/A	N/A	N/A

KKMPi69

A version of the MPiKM without the gas cylinder. Chambered for the .22 caliber Long Rifle cartridge and used as a training rifle.

Exc.	V.G.	Good	Fair	Poor
N/A	N/A	N/A	N/A	N/A

HUNGARY

See *Hungary, Rifles.*

IRAQ

Tabuk

This model is a copy of the Soviet AKM. An export version was built in 5.56mm.

Exc.	V.G.	Good	Fair	Poor
N/A	N/A	N/A	N/A	N/A

NORTH KOREA

Type 58

This model is a copy of the Soviet AK-47 solid receiver without the finger grooves on the forearm.

Type 58 • Courtesy West Point Museum, Paul Goodwin photo

Pre-1968

Exc.	V.G.	Fair
20000	11000	8500

Pre-1986 conversions

Exc.	V.G.	Fair
5500	5000	4500

Pre-1986 dealer samples

Exc.	V.G.	Fair
5000	4000	3750

Type 68

This is a copy of the Soviet AKM-S with lightening holes drilled into the folding butt.

Exc.	V.G.	Good	Fair	Poor
N/A	N/A	N/A	N/A	N/A

POLAND
See *Poland, Rifles.*

ROMANIA
See *Romania, Rifles.*

YUGOSLAVIA
See *Yugoslavia, Rifles.*

MACHINE GUNS

NOTE: Russia used early Maxim guns against the Japanese during the Russo-Japanese War of 1904-1905. The Russian military also used the Madsen Model 1902 and the Colt Model 1914 during World War I, as well as the Lewis gun.

World War I Russian machine gun crew with M1905 • Robert G. Segel collection

Model 1905 Maxim
The first machine gun built in Russia at the Tula arsenal. Based on the Belgian Model 1900 Maxim with 28" barrel with smooth bronze water jacket. Fed by a 250-round belt with a 450 rounds per minute rate of fire. Gun weighs about 40 lbs.

Pre-1968

Exc.	V.G.	Fair
20000	18000	16000

Pre-1986 conversions (side-plate)

Exc.	V.G.	Fair
15000	13000	11000

Pre-1986 dealer samples (Rare)

Exc.	V.G.	Fair
N/A	N/A	N/A

NOTE: For matching numbers add a 10 percent premium.

Model 1910 Maxim (SPM)
This is a Russian-built water-cooled machine gun chambered for the 7.62x54R cartridge. Early guns use a smooth water jacket while later ones used corrugated type. In 1941 these guns were given a large water-filling cap so that ice and snow could be used in extreme conditions. Barrel length is 28". Fed by a 250-round cloth belt. Rate of fire is approximately 550 rounds per minute. Gun weighs about 52 lbs. and the tripod weighs about 70 lbs.

Pre-1968

Exc.	V.G.	Fair
20000	18000	16000

Pre-1986 conversions (side-plate)

Exc.	V.G.	Fair
15000	13000	11000

Pre-1986 dealer samples

Exc.	V.G.	Fair
N/A	N/A	N/A

NOTE: For matching numbers add a 10 percent premium.

Model DP 28 (Degtyarev Pulyemet)
This was the first original Russian-designed light machine gun. Developed in 1926 by Vasily Degtyarev at the Tula Arms Factory this gun was chambered for the 7.62x54R Russian cartridge. It was an air-cooled gun with 24" finned barrel. It was fitted with a rifle-style stock and bipod. It was fed with a 47-round flat drum. Rate of fire is approximately 550 rounds per minute. Weight is about 20 lbs. Designed as a light infantry machine gun. Used by all Warsaw Pact countries.

This was the first in a series of DP variants. The DA is an aircraft mounted machine gun. The DT is a tank mounted weapon with a 60-round drum. Others are the DPM, the DTM, and the RP46.

Russian Model 1905 in caliber 7.62mm produced at Tula Arsenal •
Courtesy private NFA collection, Paul Goodwin photo

Maxim M1910 • Courtesy private NFA collection,
Paul Goodwin photo

Private NFA collection • Gary Gelson photo

Pre-1968

Exc.	V.G.	Fair
18000	16000	14000

**Pre-1986 conversions
(or remanufactured guns)**

Exc.	V.G.	Fair
18000	16000	14000

Pre-1986 dealer samples (Rare)

Exc.	V.G.	Fair
N/A	N/A	N/A

DP • Paul Goodwin photo

Model 1939 DS Gun

A medium machine version of the DP 28. Two rates for fire: 550 rounds per minute and 1100 rounds per minute. Fed by a 250-round cloth belt. Weight is about 26 lbs. Limited production. No known examples in the U.S.

Pre-1968

Exc.	V.G.	Fair
N/A	N/A	N/A

Pre-1986 conversions (or remanufactured guns)

Exc.	V.G.	Fair
N/A	N/A	N/A

Pre-1986 dealer samples (Rare)

Exc.	V.G.	Fair
N/A	N/A	N/A

Model DPM

Introduced in 1944, this is a modification of the DP machine gun by placing the return spring in a tube at the rear of the receiver, sticking out over the butt. A pistol grip was added to facilitate firing. The bipod was attached to the barrel casing. No grip safety but a safety lever in its place. Barrel length is 24" and the drum capacity is 47 rounds. Rate of fire is 550 rounds per minute. Weight is approximately 27 lbs.

Pre-1968

Exc.	V.G.	Fair
15000	13000	11000

Pre-1986 conversions

Exc.	V.G.	Fair
10000	8000	6000

Pre-1986 dealer samples

Exc.	V.G.	Fair
7500	6500	5500

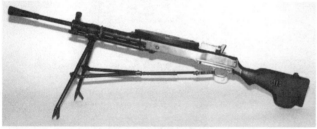

Russian DP with unusual bipod triangulation • Courtesy Robert E. Naess

Model RP-46

This gun is a version of the DP series of machine guns and is a metallic belt or magazine fed 7.62mm caliber. It was de-signed to be used as a company-size machine gun and is fitted with a 24" quick change heavy barrel. Introduced in 1946. Weight is about 29 lbs. Rate of fire is approximately 650 rounds per minute. The North Koreans use this same gun designated as the Type 64.

NOTE: Many RP-46s were fitted with DP or DPM components by the Soviets. These components are dated prior to 1946. The prices listed are for RP-46 guns with RP-46 (1946) components.

Pre-1968

Exc.	V.G.	Fair
22000	20000	18000

Pre-1986 conversions (or remanufactured guns)

Exc.	V.G.	Fair
19000	17000	16000

Pre-1986 dealer samples (Rare)

Exc.	V.G.	Fair
N/A	N/A	N/A

Model RPK

Introduced around 1960 this model is the light machine gun equivalent to the AKM assault rifle. It is fitted with a 23" non-quick change barrel. It uses either a 75-round drum magazine or a 40-round box magazine. It is also capable of using the 30-round magazine of the AK and AKM rifles. This model replaced the RPD as the squad automatic weapon (SAW) of the Soviet army.

Pre-1968

Exc.	V.G.	Fair
25000	23000	21000

Pre-1986 conversions

Exc.	V.G.	Fair
18000	16000	14000

Pre-1986 dealer samples (Rare)

Exc.	V.G.	Fair
N/A	N/A	N/A

Model RPKS

This is the Model RPK with a side folding stock. All other dimensions and specifications are the same.

Pre-1968

Exc.	V.G.	Fair
25000	23000	21000

Pre-1986 conversions

Exc.	V.G.	Fair
18000	16000	14000

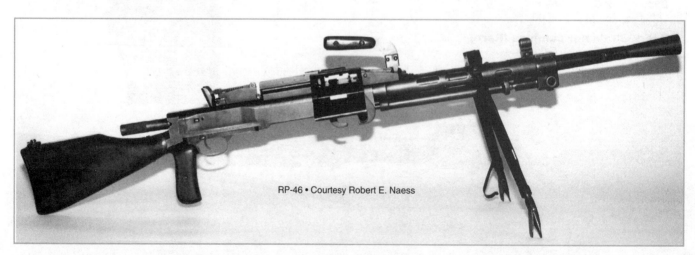

RP-46 • Courtesy Robert E. Naess

Model RPK • Courtesy West Point Museum, Paul Goodwin photo

Pre-1986 dealer samples (Rare)

Exc.	V.G.	Fair
N/A	N/A	N/A

Model RPK-74

Similar to the RPK but chambered for the 5.45x39mm cartridge. Select fire with 4 positions: safe, semi-auto, full auto, and 3-shot burst. Barrel length is 23.6". Magazine capacity is 45-round box magazine. Also uses a 30-round magazine. Weight is about 12 lbs. and rate of fire is approximately 650 to 700 rounds per minute.

NOTE: There are no known original Soviet transferable examples in this country. Prices listed are for conversion using Russian AKM receiver and Russian parts.

Courtesy Steve Hill and Doug McBeth, A.S.D. Firearms

Pre-1968

Exc.	V.G.	Fair
N/A	N/A	N/A

Pre-1986 conversions (A.S.D. Firearms)

Exc.	V.G.	Fair
17500	15000	13000

Pre-1986 dealer samples (Rare)

Exc.	V.G.	Fair
N/A	N/A	N/A

Model PK/PKS (Pulemet Kalashnikova/Stankovy)

This is a general purpose air-cooled machine gun that is chambered for the 7.62mm Soviet cartridge. When this gun is mounted on a bipod it is designated the Model PK; when mounted on a tripod it is called a Model PKS. The operating system of this gun is the same as the AK series except turned upside down. It is fitted with a 26" quick change barrel and can be fed by a 100-, 200-, or 250-round metal belt. The rate of fire is about 700 rounds per minute. Weight is approximately 20 lbs. Introduced in 1963.

The PK, when mounted on tanks, is designated the PKT. The PKM is an improved version of the PK with lighter components. The PKMS is a PKM mounted on a tripod. The PKB is a PKM without butt, bipod, pistol grip, or trigger. Instead, a spade grip with trigger is fitted to the receiver.

Pre-1968

Exc.	V.G.	Fair
N/A	N/A	N/A

Pre-1986 conversions (only 1 known)

Exc.	V.G.	Fair
—	38000	—

Pre-1986 dealer samples (Rare)

Exc.	V.G.	Fair
N/A	N/A	N/A

Model DShK M38-M1938/46

Introduced in 1938 this is a heavy air-cooled gas operated machine gun chambered for the 12.7x108mm cartridge. The feed system on the early guns (M1938) uses a rotary mechanism while the later versions (M1939/46) use a conventional lever system. The barrel is 42" and finned with muzzle brake. Fed by a 50-round metal belt either from the right or left side. The rate of fire is about 550 rounds per minute. Weight of the gun is approximately 75 lbs. The mount can weigh 250 lbs. This was the primary heavy machine gun in Korea in 1950-1953, and it was used both as a ground gun and as an anti-aircraft gun. The gun is mounted on a wheeled carriage or a heavy tripod.

NOTE: Many M1938/46 guns were converted from M1938 models. It is extremely difficult to determine when the conversion was done and by whom. Proceed with caution.

Courtesy Steve Hill, Spotted Dog Firearms

Russian RPD • Courtesy private NFA collection, Paul Goodwin photo

Pre-1968 (Very Rare)
Exc.	V.G.	Fair
—	45000	42500

Pre-1986 conversions reweld
Exc.	V.G.	Fair
—	40000	—

Pre-1986 dealer samples (Rare)
Exc.	V.G.	Fair
—	20000	19000

Degtyarev RPD
This is a belt-fed machine gun chambered for the 7.62x39mm cartridge. It has a rate of fire of 700 rounds per minute and is fitted with a 100-round disintegrating belt carried in a drum. It has a 20.5" barrel and weighs about 15.6 lbs. This weapon was at one time the standard squad automatic weapon in the Soviet bloc. It was produced in large numbers and is still in use today in Southeast Asia and Africa.

Pre-1968 (Very Rare)
Exc.	V.G.	Fair
36000	35000	34000

Pre-1986 conversions
Exc.	V.G.	Fair
35000	33000	31500

Pre-1986 dealer samples
Exc.	V.G.	Fair
N/A	N/A	N/A

Goryunov SG43
This model was the standard Soviet machine gun during WWII. Chambered for the 7.62x54R Soviet cartridge, it is fitted with a 28" smooth barrel and is fed with a 250-round metal link belt. Rate of fire is 650 rounds per minute. Its weight is about 30 lbs. Marked on the top of the receiver. In production from 1943 to 1955.

Pre-1968
Exc.	V.G.	Fair
25000	23000	21000

Pre-1986 conversions (reweld)
Exc.	V.G.	Fair
20000	18000	16000

Pre-1986 dealer samples
Exc.	V.G.	Fair
N/A	N/A	N/A

Model SGM
A modified version of the SG43 with fluted barrel and cocking handle on right side of receiver. Dust covers on both feed and ejection ports. Barrel length is 28". Weight is approximately 30 lbs. Fed by 250-round metal link belt.

There are variants of the SG43 which are the SGMT, a tank mounted version with electric solenoid. The SGMB is similar to the SGM but with dust covers over feed and ejection ports.

Pre-1968 (Very Rare)
Exc.	V.G.	Fair
25000	23000	21000

Pre-1986 conversions
Exc.	V.G.	Fair
N/A	N/A	N/A

Pre-1986 dealer samples
Exc.	V.G.	Fair
N/A	N/A	N/A

SG 43 • Courtesy private NFA collection, Paul Goodwin photo

SPAIN

Spanish Military Conflicts, 1870-Present

During the middle of the 19th century Spain was occupied with domestic power struggles. In 1868 a constitutional monarchy was established, followed by a republic from 1873 to 1874. Spain lost its last colony, Cuba, with its defeat by the United States in the Spanish-American War of 1898. In 1928 a military dictatorship was established and a second republic was created. Spanish separatists weakened the republic with the result that a Communist government came to power. This helped to create an internal struggle that led to the Spanish Civil War, 1936 to 1939. During this conflict the Germans supported Franco with men and weapons. During World War II Spain sided with the Axis powers, but did not enter the war. Franco died in 1975. Spain joined the European Union in 1986. Spain is also a member of NATO.

HANDGUNS

NOTE: Officers in the Spanish military provided their own sidearms during the later half of the 19th century and into the early 20th century. The Spanish government provided guidelines for purchase and many Spanish officers purchased Smith & Wesson and Merwin & Hulbert revolvers. In 1884 the Spanish government directed its military officers corps to purchase the Smith & Wesson .44 Double Action Top Break built by Orbea y Compania of Eibar, Spain. It was designated the Model 1884. There were a number of Spanish gun makers building revolvers during the late 19th century, and many of these handguns were used by the Spanish military but were not marked as such. During WWI Spain provided a number of handguns to Britain, France, and other countries due to the shortage of military sidearms in those countries. We only touch on the more significant models.

It is also important to note that various Spanish manufacturers sold almost one million copies of the FN/Browning Model 1903 to the French during World War I.

Bibliographical Note: For additional historical information, technical data, and photos see Leonardo Antaris, *Astra Automatic Pistols*, Colorado, 1998.

Bergmann-Bayard Model 1908

Built by the Belgium firm of Pieper SA from 1908 to about 1914. Caliber is 9x23mm Bergman-Bayard with 4" barrel. Many foreign contracts were built in this model with Spain being one of the largest. See also *Denmark*.

Courtesy Rock Island Auction Company

Exc.	V.G.	Good	Fair	Poor
1250	950	700	400	200

CAMPO GIRO

Model 1910

Similar to the above, in 9mm Largo. Tested, but not adopted, by the Spanish army.

Exc.	V.G.	Good	Fair	Poor
1200	800	650	500	450

Model 1913

An improved version of the above.

Model 1913 • Courtesy James Rankin

Exc.	V.G.	Good	Fair	Poor
950	750	650	500	450

Model 1913/16

An improved version of the above.

Courtesy James Rankin

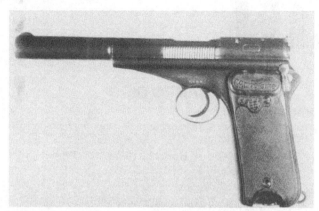

Courtesy James Rankin

Exc.	V.G.	Good	Fair	Poor
650	450	375	300	200

ASTRA-UNCETA SA

During World War II the German army and air force purchased a number of Astra 400 and 600 pistols. They were of excellent quality.

Astra 400 or Model 1921

A 9x23 Bergmann caliber semiautomatic pistol with a 6" barrel. Blued with black plastic grips. This model was adopted for use by the Spanish army. Approximately 106,000 were made prior to 1946. Recent importation has depressed the price of these guns.

NOTE: Any with Nazi proofmarks are worth a 100 percent premium, but caution is advised because there are no known examples, even though about 6,000 pistols were delivered to the German army in 1941.

Courtesy Orvel Reichert

Exc.	V.G.	Good	Fair	Poor
450	300	150	75	40

Astra 400 Copies (Ascaso, R.E.)

During the Spanish Civil War, the Republican forces were unable to procure enough handguns from established weapons factories as these were in Nationalists' hands. The Republicans built their own factories to produce copies of the Spanish army's Model 1921 Astra 400. These are exact copies except for the markings.

Exc.	V.G.	Good	Fair	Poor
500	350	200	100	75

Astra 300

As above, in 7.65mm or 9mm short. A few used during World War II by German forces may bear Waffenamt marks. Between 1941 and 1944 some 63,000 were produced in 9mm Kurz, and about 22,000 were produced in 7.65mm. Approximately 171,000 were manufactured prior to 1947.

Top to bottom: Ascaso left side, R.E. right side, close-up of Ascaso barrel marking • Courtesy Orvel Reichert

Exc.	V.G.	Good	Fair	Poor
500	300	200	150	100

NOTE: Nazi Proofed add 25 percent.

Astra 600

Similar to the Model 400, but in 9mm Parabellum. In 1943 and 1944 approximately 10,500 were manufactured. Some of these World War II guns will often have Nazi proof stamp and bring a premium. An additional 49,000 were made in 1946 and commercially sold.

Exc.	V.G.	Good	Fair	Poor
450	300	200	150	100

ASTRA 900 SERIES

The Astra 900 series of pistols were copied from the Mauser Model 1896, but while similar in appearance to the Mauser, the Astra 900 series is mechanically quite different. Many consider the Astra 900 series as good as, or better than, its German equivalent.

NOTE: The prices listed include original Astra matching wooden stock/holster numbered to the pistol. For pistols with detachable magazines numbered to the gun add a small premium. For non-matching stock/holster deduct $300 to $500. For Chinese stock/holsters deduct $500. Original Astra stocks are difficult to locate.

Astra Model 900

Introduced in 1928 this is similar in appearance to the Mauser C96 pistol. Fitted with a 5.5" barrel chambered for the 7.63mm cartridge and fitted with a ring hammer. Ten-round box magazine with charger loading. Weight is about 40 oz. Production discontinued in 1955. Between 1928 and 1944 almost 21,000 were manufactured. Some of these pistols (about 1,000) were purchased by the German military in France in 1943. No military acceptance marks but can be identified by serial number (see Still, *Axis Pistols*). Serial numbers 32788 through 33774 were used by the German army during WWII. These examples will bring a 50 percent premium.

NOTE: A large number of Astras exported to China are frequently found in fair to poor condition. Some of these are marked with Chinese characters. During the late 1950s a number of Chinese Astras were brought into the U.S. These pistols appear to be in much better condition.

Photo courtesy Tom Nelson, *The World's Machine Pistol and Submachine Guns, Vol. IIA*, Ironside International Publishers

Exc.	V.G.	Good	Fair	Poor
2500	1750	1000	600	300

Astra Model 901

Introduced in 1928, this is similar to the Model 900 (5.5" barrel) but with select fire capability. Fixed 10-round magazine. Many of these pistols were sold to China in the 1930s. Rate of fire is about 900 rounds per minute. Weight is about 44 oz. Only about 1,600 of these pistols were produced. Exceedingly rare. Only a tiny number of these pistols are transferable, perhaps fewer than five.

Photo courtesy Tom Nelson, *The World's Machine Pistol and Submachine Guns, Vol. IIA*, Ironside International Publishers

Pre-1968

Exc.	V.G.	Fair
9500	8000	7500

Pre-1986 conversions

Exc.	V.G.	Fair
N/A	N/A	N/A

Pre-1986 dealer samples

Exc.	V.G.	Fair
N/A	N/A	N/A

Astra Model 902

Same as above but with 7" barrel. Some went to China with various military units in the 1930s, but most remained in Spain. Weight is approximately 53 oz. About 7,000 of these pistols were built. Very rare in this country for transferable examples. Perhaps fewer than 10 known.

Photo courtesy Tom Nelson, *The World's Machine Pistol and Submachine Guns, Vol. IIA*, Ironside International Publishers

Pre-1968

Exc.	V.G.	Fair
9500	8000	7500

Pre-1986 conversions

Exc.	V.G.	Fair
N/A	N/A	N/A

Pre-1986 dealer samples

Exc.	V.G.	Fair
N/A	N/A	N/A

Astra 903/903E

This is a detachable 10- or 20-round magazine pistol developed in 1932. Fitted with a 6.25" barrel. Select fire. Some of these pistols were sold to China and others went to the German army in France in 1941 and 1942. No German acceptance proofs, but can be identified by serial number (see *Still*). Some 3,000 of this model were produced. It is estimated that fewer than 15 of these pistols are transferable in the U.S.

Photo courtesy Tom Nelson, *The World's Machine Pistol and Submachine Guns, Vol. IIA*, Ironside International Publishers

Pre-1968

Exc.	V.G.	Fair
10000	9000	8500

Pre-1986 conversions

Exc.	V.G.	Fair
N/A	N/A	N/A

Pre-1986 dealer samples

Exc.	V.G.	Fair
5000	4500	4000

Astra Model 904 (Model F)

Similar to the other 900 series machine pistols but chambered for the 9mm Largo cartridge and fitted with a rate reducer that reduces the rate of fire from 900 rounds per minute to approximately 350 rounds per minute. Magazine is 10- or 20-round detachable design. The Model 904 was first produced in 1933 and was the prototype of the Model F. Only 9 Model 904s were built. About 1,100 Model F pistols were issued, most of which went to the Spanish Guardia Civil. Perhaps fewer than 10 of these pistols are known to exist on a transferable basis in the U.S.

Pre-1968

Exc.	V.G.	Fair
12500	11000	10000

Astra Model F • Courtesy Chuck Karwan

Pre-1986 conversions

Exc.	V.G.	Fair
N/A	N/A	N/A

Pre-1986 dealer samples

Exc.	V.G.	Fair
6000	5500	5000

Astra A-80

A .38 Super, 9mm, or .45 caliber double action semiautomatic pistol with a 3.75" barrel and either a 9- or 15-shot magazine depending upon the caliber. Blued or chrome-plated with plastic grips. Introduced in 1982.

NIB	Exc.	V.G.	Good	Fair	Poor
500	350	300	250	200	100

Astra A-90

As above, in 9mm or .45 caliber only. Introduced in 1986.

NIB	Exc.	V.G.	Good	Fair	Poor
450	350	300	250	200	100

ROYAL

Royal machine pistols were manufactured by Beistegui Hermanos in Eibar, Spain. These were the first machine pistols made in Spain, starting in 1927. These pistols were used extensively by the Chinese during their civil wars in the 1930s and against the Japanese during World War II.

Royal MM31 (1st Model)

First produced in 1927. Chambered for the 7.63mm cartridge. The pistol was capable of selective fire and semiautomatic fire, as well as full automatic fire. Magazine capacity was 10 or 20 rounds in a fixed box magazine. Barrel lengths were 5.5" with some made in 6.3" and 7". Rear tangent sight. Rate of fire was about 850 rounds per minute. Production stopped on the first model in 1929 with approximately 23,000 pistols built. Extremely rare.

Pre-1968

Exc.	V.G.	Fair
20000	20000	20000

Pre-1986 conversions

Exc.	V.G.	Fair
N/A	N/A	N/A

Pre-1986 dealer samples

Exc.	V.G.	Fair
N/A	N/A	N/A

Royal MM31 (2nd Model)

This model has three variations. All were chambered for the 7.63mm cartridge and all were select fire models. All had a cycle rate of fire of about 850 rounds per minute. Early versions had either a 5.5" or 7" barrel. The last version was fitted with a 5.5" barrel only. The 1st variation had a fixed 10-round magazine while the 2nd variation had a 20-round fixed magazine. The 3rd version had a detachable 10-, 20-, or 30-round magazine. All variations were marked "MM31" or "ROYAL." Very rare.

Photo courtesy Tom Nelson, *The World's Machine Pistol and Submachine Guns, Vol. IIA*, Ironside International Publishers

Pre-1968

Exc.	V.G.	Fair
9500	8500	8000

Pre-1986 conversions

Exc.	V.G.	Fair
N/A	N/A	N/A

Pre-1986 dealer samples

Exc.	V.G.	Fair
N/A	N/A	N/A

Super Azul

This was the 4th variation of the MM31, introduced in 1931, often referred to as the Super Azul or New Model. Chambered for the 7.63mm cartridge, it was also offered in 9mm Bergmann and .38 Colt Super Automatic. Select fire. Fitted with a 5.5" barrel and a detachable magazine with a capacity of 10, 20, or 30 rounds. Magazine will interchange with German Mauser Schnellfeuer pistol. Rate of fire of about 850 rounds per minute. Production ceased in 1936 with the outbreak of the Spanish Civil War.

Pre-1968

Exc.	V.G.	Fair
9500	8500	8000

Pre-1986 conversions

Exc.	V.G.	Fair
N/A	N/A	N/A

Pre-1986 dealer samples

Exc.	V.G.	Fair
N/A	N/A	N/A

Royal MM34

Chambered for the 7.63mm cartridge and fitted with a 7" barrel. Fixed magazine capacity of 10 or 20 rounds. Fitted with a rate reducer in the grip. Select fire with full auto fire at various adjustable rates. Marked "MM34"on right side of frame. Extremely rare.

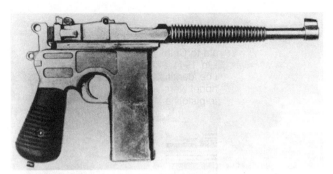

Photo courtesy Tom Nelson, *The World's Machine Pistol and Submachine Guns, Vol. IIA*, Ironside International Publishers

Pre-1968

Exc.	V.G.	Fair
9500	8500	8000

Pre-1986 conversions

Exc.	V.G.	Fair
N/A	N/A	N/A

Pre-1986 dealer samples

Exc.	V.G.	Fair
N/A	N/A	N/A

LLAMA

Model IX

Chambered for the 7.65mm Para, 9mm Largo, or .45 ACP, this model has a locked breech with no grip safety. Built from 1936 to 1954.

Exc.	V.G.	Good	Fair	Poor
400	275	200	150	100

Model IX-A

This version of the Model IX is fitted with a grip safety. Current production models are chambered for the .45 ACP only. Weighs about 30 oz. with 5" barrel.

Exc.	V.G.	Good	Fair	Poor
325	225	150	125	100

ECHEVERRIA, STAR-BONIFACIO SA

NOTE: These pistols are stamped with a letter code to denote year built: For 1938 the letter "N," up to 1945 the letter "P."

Bibliographical Note: For photos, production data, and in-depth history, see *Star Firearms* by Leonardo M. Antaris. This book is a must for the Spanish handgun collector. The book can be obtained from Firac Publications, 1230 East Rusholme St. #107, Davenport, IA 52803.

Model 1914

Similar to the Model 1908, with a 5" barrel and larger grips that have the Star name molded into them. This model was the first to have the six-pointed star surrounded by rays of light (that became the Star trademark) stamped on its slide.

The French Army purchased approximately 20,000 Model 1914s for use during World War I. These pistols had coarse checkering and no name inset into the grips. Later pistols were fitted with 5.5" barrels. Many French army magazines were stamped with "BE" in a circle. All French military pistols were finished with a highly dark blue finish. Small parts were fire blue.

Exc.	V.G.	Good	Fair	Poor
350	250	200	150	100

Model CO

First produced in 1929 and later dropped from production during the Spanish Civil War, this model was produced again in 1941. About 600 of these pistols were sold to the German military during 1941 and 1942. Chambered for the 6.35mm cartridge and fitted with a 3.3" barrel. This model stayed in production until 1956. Prices are for military examples.

Exc.	V.G.	Good	Fair	Poor
600	500	400	300	150

Star Model A

A modification of the Model 1919, chambered for the 7.63 Mauser, 9mm Largo, and 9mm Luger (scarce), as well as the rarely seen 9mm Steyr. Barrel length is 5". The slide is similar in appearance to the 1911 Colt, and the spur hammer has a small hole in it. Early models had no grip safety, but later production added this feature. Some models are slotted for addition of a shoulder stock. This model was popular with the Spanish Civil Guard as well as the Spanish Air Force (stamped with air force logo).

Exc.	V.G.	Good	Fair	Poor
400	300	200	150	100

Star Model A Super

An improved version of the Model A with a new takedown lever on the right side of the frame and a loaded chamber indicator.

Exc.	V.G.	Good	Fair	Poor
450	325	225	175	125

Star Model M (MD)

A select fire version of the Model A. Most were chambered for 9x23mm cartridge while some were chambered for the .45 ACP cartridge. This pistol was built during the 1930s. Some examples were sold to Nicaragua and Argentina. Rate of fire is about 800 rounds per minute. The selector switch is located on the right side of the slide. Several thousand were produced.

Star Model M • Courtesy Chuck Karwan

Pre-1968

Exc.	V.G.	Fair
7500	7000	6500

Pre-1986 conversions

Exc.	V.G.	Fair
N/A	N/A	N/A

Pre-1986 dealer samples

Exc.	V.G.	Fair
4000	3500	3000

Star Model B

Similar to the Model A. It is chambered for 9mm Parabellum and has a spur hammer with no hole. This model was introduced in 1928. Approximately 20,000 pistols were sold to the German army and about 6,000 to the German navy. These military pistols are stamped with German military acceptance stamps. About 15,000 Model Bs were sold to Bulgaria during 1943 and 1944. Also used by the German Police and the Republic of South Africa.

Courtesy Leonardo M. Antaris, *Star Firearms*, with permission

Courtesy Leonardo M. Antaris, *Star Firearms*, with permission

Exc.	V.G.	Good	Fair	Poor
400	250	200	175	125

Star Model B Super

Introduced in 1946, this model features a new takedown system with the lever on the right side of the frame. A loaded chamber indicator was also added. Production ended in 1983. Adopted by the Spanish army in 1946.

Courtesy Leonardo M. Antaris, *Star Firearms*, with permission

Exc.	V.G.	Good	Fair	Poor
450	325	250	200	100

Star Model 1941 S

This model was purchased by the Spanish air force and is stamped on the right side of the frame with the air force seal. Most of these air force pistols were produced between 1945 and 1947, with a total production of about 9,100 pistols. A large number of Model S pistols were also sold to police agencies in Spain and elsewhere. The balance of production was sold commercially. Prices listed below are for air force examples. Deduct 50 percent for commercial pistols.

Courtesy Richard M. Kumor Sr.

Exc.	V.G.	Good	Fair	Poor
600	400	300	200	100

Star Model SI

Chambered for the 7.65mm cartridge, this pistol was ordered by the Portuguese navy beginning in 1946. Between 1946 and 1948 a total of about 4,900 pistols were ordered for the Portuguese. Also, about 300 pistols were sold to the Chilean navy in 1964. A number of these pistols were also sold to police agencies in Spain and Europe. The balance of the Model SI production was commercial.

Exc.	V.G.	Good	Fair	Poor
500	375	300	200	100

Star Model BM

A steel-framed 9mm that is styled after the Colt 1911. It has an 8-shot magazine and a 4" barrel. It is available either blued or chrome-plated.

NIB	Exc.	V.G.	Good	Fair	Poor
450	300	250	200	150	125

Star Model 28

The first of Star's high-capacity 9s. It is a double action semi-automatic chambered for the 9mm Parabellum cartridge. It has a 4.25" barrel and a steel frame. The magazine holds 15 shots. The construction of this pistol was totally modular, and it has no screws at all in its design. It is blued with checkered synthetic grips and was manufactured from 1981 to 1983. Only some 16,000 pistols were built.

NIB	Exc.	V.G.	Good	Fair	Poor
600	475	350	250	200	125

Star Model 30M

An improved version of the Model 28 that is quite similar in appearance. It was introduced in 1982 and built until 1989. About 100,000 were manufactured.

NIB	Exc.	V.G.	Good	Fair	Poor
500	350	300	250	200	125

Star Model 30/PK

Similar to the Models 28 and 30M, with a lightweight alloy frame.

Courtesy Leonardo M. Antaris, *Star Firearms*, with permission

NIB	Exc.	V.G.	Good	Fair	Poor
500	350	300	250	200	125

SUBMACHINE GUNS

The Spanish made a number of submachine guns, both domestic designs and copies of foreign guns. The Spanish MP28 II was a copy of the Bergmann MP28 II in 9mm Bergmann caliber. The Model 1941/44 was a copy of the German Erma. Star made a number of submachine guns in the 1930s that were used on a limited basis in the Spanish Civil War. These were the S135, the RU35, and the TN35, all chambered for the 9x23 Largo cartridge. The first two of these models had adjustable rates of fire and the last, the TN35, had a rate of fire of about 700 rounds per minute. However, these guns were never standard issue in the Spanish army.

Star Z-45

This design is based on the German MP40 but with the cocking handle on the left side. It was fitted with an 8" barrel that was easily removable and covered by a perforated barrel jacket. The gun has a two-stage trigger: pull slightly for single shots and pull more for full automatic fire. Magazine is a 30-round box type. Gun has a rate of fire of about 450 rounds per minute. Weight is approximately 8.5 lbs. Introduced into service in 1944. This weapon is supplied with either a fixed wood stock or folding metal one. The Z-45 was the standard submachine gun of the Spanish army and was sold to Chile, Cuba, Portugal, and Saudi Arabia.

Photo courtesy Tom Nelson, *The World's Machine Pistol and Submachine Guns, Vol. IIA*, Ironside International Publishers

Pre-1968
Exc.	V.G.	Fair
17500	15500	14000

Pre-1986 conversions
Exc.	V.G.	Fair
N/A	N/A	N/A

Pre-1986 dealer samples
Exc.	V.G.	Fair
N/A	N/A	N/A

Star Z-62

This select-fire submachine gun was introduced in 1960 and is chambered for the 9mm Largo or 9mm Parabellum cartridge. It has an 8" barrel with perforated barrel jacket. Folding metal buttstock. The box magazine has a 20-, 30-, or 40-round capacity. Rate of fire is about 550 rounds per minute. Weight is approximately 6.5 lbs. This gun was issued both to the Spanish army and the *Guardia Civil*. Marked "STAR EIBAR ESPANA MODEL Z-62" with the serial number on the left side of the magazine housing. Produced until about 1970.

Pre-1968
Exc.	V.G.	Fair
17000	15000	13000

Pre-1986 conversions
Exc.	V.G.	Fair
N/A	N/A	N/A

Pre-1986 dealer samples
Exc.	V.G.	Fair
8500	7500	6500

Star Z-70

Introduced into the Spanish army in 1971, this select-fire submachine gun is chambered for the 9x19mm cartridge, and is considered an improved version of the Z-62 with new trigger mechanism. It is fitted with an 8" barrel and has a rate of fire of 550 rounds per minute. Choice of 20-, 30-, or 40-round magazines. Folding metal stock. Weight is about 6.3 lbs. Built by Star Banifacio Echeverria in Eibar, Spain. No longer in production. Used mainly by the Spanish armed forces.

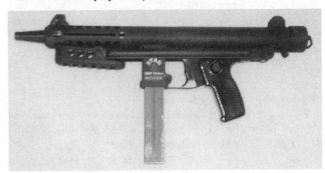

Photo courtesy private NFA collection

Pre-1968
Exc.	V.G.	Fair
N/A	N/A	N/A

Pre-1986 conversions
Exc.	V.G.	Fair
N/A	N/A	N/A

Pre-1986 dealer samples
Exc.	V.G.	Fair
7500	6500	6000

RIFLES

PEABODY

Spanish Rifle (1869)

Chambered for the .43 Spanish centerfire cartridge and fitted with a 33" barrel. Full stock with two barrel bands. Blued barrel and case hardened furniture. About 10,000 rifles were produced for the Spanish government.

Exc.	V.G.	Good	Fair	Poor
—	1750	1250	600	200

REMINGTON ROLLING BLOCK

Model 1870 Rifle

This is the standard Remington rolling block single-shot rifle with a 35" barrel. Chambered for the 11.15x57R Spanish Remington cartridge. Full stocked with three barrel bands. Weight is about 9.25 lbs. Upper tang marked Remington.

Exc.	V.G.	Good	Fair	Poor
—	—	750	400	100

Model 1870 Carbine

Same as the rifle but with 27" barrel and full stock with two barrel bands. Weight is about 8.75 lbs. Made at Oviedo Armoury from 1871 to about 1889.

Exc.	V.G.	Good	Fair	Poor
—	—	1150	600	200

Model 1870 Short Rifle

Similar to the Model 1870 pattern but with 32" barrel. Weight is about 8.75 lbs. Manufactured at Oviedo.

Exc.	V.G.	Good	Fair	Poor
—	—	900	500	150

Model 1871 Infantry Rifle

Fitted with a 37" barrel and chambered for the 11.15x57R Spanish Remington cartridge. Full stock with three barrel bands. Bayonet fittings. Weight is about 9 lbs. Built at Oviedo and Placencia armories.

Exc.	V.G.	Good	Fair	Poor
—	—	750	400	100

Model 1871 Short Rifle

As above but with 28" barrel with full stock and two barrel bands. Weight is about 8.75 lbs. Produced at Placencia Armoury.

Exc.	V.G.	Good	Fair	Poor
—	—	900	500	150

Model 1871 Cavalry Carbine

As above but with 23" barrel and half stock with sling swivels and sling bar on left side of stock. Weight is about 7.25 lbs.

Exc.	V.G.	Good	Fair	Poor
—	—	1150	600	200

Model 1871 Artillery Carbine

As above but full stocked with two barrel bands and bayonet fitting.

Exc.	V.G.	Good	Fair	Poor
—	—	1150	600	200

Model 1889 Dragoon Carbine

This model was a short version of the Model 1871 rifle with full stock, two barrel bands, and no bayonet fittings. Barrel length is 31.5". Weight is about 8.75 lbs.

Exc.	V.G.	Good	Fair	Poor
—	—	1150	600	200

MAUSER

M1891 Rifle

Based on the Turkish Model 1890 rifle with full stock and no handguard. Chambered for 7.65x53mm cartridge with barrel length of 29". Exposed 5-round box magazine. Weight is about 9 lbs.

Exc.	V.G.	Good	Fair	Poor
350	225	180	130	90

M1892 Rifle

Similar to the Model 1891 but with internal charger loaded magazine, improved extractor, and removable magazine floor plate. Chambered for 7.65x53mm cartridge. Half-length handguard. Barrel length is 29". Weight is about 9 lbs.

Exc.	V.G.	Good	Fair	Poor
400	260	190	130	90

M1892 Carbine

Same action as the Model 1891 rifle but full stock with nose cap, bent bolt handle, sling bar, and saddle ring. Chambered for 7.65x53mm cartridge. Barrel length is 17.5". Weight is about 7.5 lbs. Built by Loewe.

Exc.	V.G.	Good	Fair	Poor
350	225	180	120	80

M1893 Rifle

Built by Loewe and Oviedo this model is considered to be the "Spanish Mauser." Chambered for the 7x57mm cartridge and fitted with a 29" barrel. Buttstock has straight grip. A charger loading magazine is concealed in the buttstock. The receiver has a charger loading guide in the receiver bridge. Weight is about 8.5 lbs.

Spanish Mauser Model 1893 • Paul Goodwin photo

Exc.	V.G.	Good	Fair	Poor
250	140	100	80	40

M1893 Short Rifle

This is a short version of the Model 1893 rifle with a 21.5" barrel. Fitted with bent bolt and half-length handguard. Weight is about 8 lbs.

Exc.	V.G.	Good	Fair	Poor
325	210	180	110	50

M1895 Carbine

As above but with 17.5" barrel. Weight is about 7 lbs.

Exc.	V.G.	Good	Fair	Poor
350	250	185	110	80

M/G 98 Modified Rifle

Identical to the German G 98 but chambered for the 7x57mm cartridge and fitted with a tangent rear sight. Spanish markings on receiver ring.

Exc.	V.G.	Good	Fair	Poor
325	225	175	120	90

M1916 Short Rifle

This model was built by Fabrica de Armas in Oviedo, Spain, from 1916 to 1951. A shortened version of the Model 1893 rifle with 21.75" barrel and chambered for the 7x57mm cartridge. Rear sight graduated to 2,000 meters. Almost full stock with upper handguard. Sight protectors on front sight. Spanish crest on receiver ring. Weight is about 8 lbs.

NOTE: Many of these rifles were converted to the 7.62mm NATO cartridge. Prices will remain about the same for these converted examples.

Exc.	V.G.	Good	Fair	Poor
250	150	100	75	40

M1916 Carbine

Produced at the Oviedo arsenal. Fitted with a 17" barrel chambered for the 7x57mm cartridge. Straight grip stock with 3/4-length stock and upper handguard. No bayonet fittings. Bent bolt handle. Weight is about 6.75 lbs.

Exc.	V.G.	Good	Fair	Poor
275	160	110	85	50

M1933 Standard Model Short Rifle

This rifle is chambered for the 7x57mm cartridge and fitted with a 22" barrel. Straight grip stock with upper handguard. Tangent leaf rear sight graduated to 2,000 meters. Marked with Mauser banner over the date of manufacture on receiver. Weight is about 8.2 lbs.

Exc.	V.G.	Good	Fair	Poor
400	280	220	180	110

M1943 Short Rifle

This model replaced the Model 1916 Short Rifle. Chambered for the 7.92x57mm cartridge and fitted with a 23.6" barrel. Stock is 3/4-length with pistol grip. Straight bolt handle. Tangent leaf rear sight graduated to 2,000 meters. Weight is about 8.5 lbs. Marked with Spanish crest on receiver ring.

Model 1943 Short Rifle • Courtesy Cherry's Fine Guns

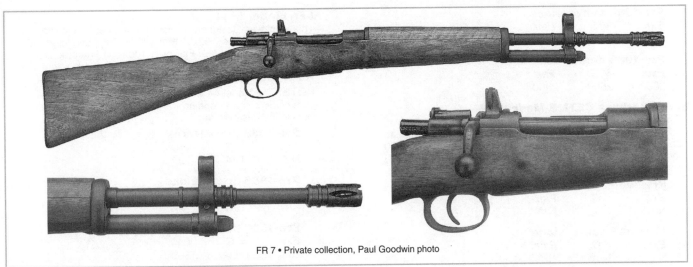

FR 7 • Private collection, Paul Goodwin photo

NOTE: This model was made for the Spanish army and air force. The army model has a bayonet lug while the air force model does not.

Exc.	V.G.	Good	Fair	Poor
325	200	140	90	40

FR 7 Special Purpose Rifle (Training/Reserve)

An arsenal-converted (1950s) Model 1916 short rifle with 18.5" CETME barrel. Upper wooden handguard. Chambered for the 7.62x51 CETME cartridge. Weight is about 7.5 lbs.

Exc.	V.G.	Good	Fair	Poor
275	150	100	70	50

FR 8 Special Purpose Rifle (Training/Reserve)

Arsenal-converted Model 43 in the same configuration as the FR 7.

Exc.	V.G.	Good	Fair	Poor
275	150	100	70	50

CETME

CETME Autoloading Rifle (Sport)

A .308 caliber semiautomatic rifle with a fluted chamber, a 17.74" barrel, an aperture rear sight, and a 20-round detachable magazine. Black with a military-style wood stock. It is identical in appearance to the H&K 91 assault rifle.

NIB	Exc.	V.G.	Good	Fair	Poor
2500	2000	1500	900	—	—

Model 58

Introduced in 1958 and manufactured by Centro de Estudios de Materials Especiales (CETME), this Spanish-made rifle is similar to the HK G3 rifle and is chambered for the 7.62x51mm cartridge. This is a select-fire weapon with a rate of fire of about 600 rounds per minute. The bipod, when retracted, acts as a metal forend. Barrel length is 17". Tangent rear sight. Weight is approximately 11 lbs.

CETME Model 58 • Courtesy Thomas Nelson, *The World's Assault Rifles*

Pre-1968

Exc.	V.G.	Fair
6000	5000	4500

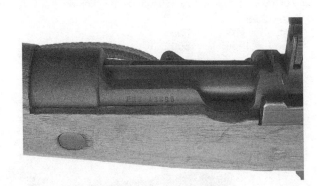

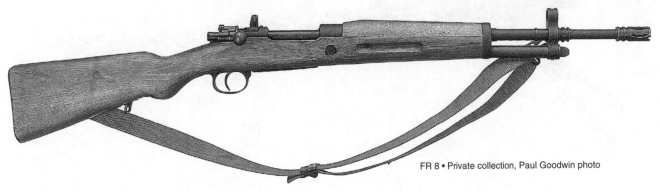

FR 8 • Private collection, Paul Goodwin photo

Pre-1986 conversions

Exc.	V.G.	Fair
N/A	N/A	N/A

Pre-1986 dealer samples

Exc.	V.G.	Fair
3000	2500	2000

Santa Barbara CETME Model L

First produced in 1984, this 5.56x45mm select fire rifle was adopted by the Spanish army. It is fitted with a 15.6" barrel and 30-round magazine. It also has a fixed stock. Rate of fire is 650 rounds per minute. Weight is about 7.5 lbs. A short barrel (12.5") carbine version is known as the Model LC. Still in service.

Pre-1968

Exc.	V.G.	Fair
N/A	N/A	N/A

Pre-1986 conversions

Exc.	V.G.	Fair
N/A	N/A	N/A

Pre-1986 dealer samples

Exc.	V.G.	Fair
5000	5000	5000

MACHINE GUNS

In 1907, the Spanish used the 7mm Hotchkiss machine gun and later the Model 1914, also in 7mm. The Spanish armed forces also adopted the Madsen Model 1902 and Model 1922 guns. During the Spanish Civil War, large numbers of foreign machine guns were sent to Spain, including the Soviet Maxim Tokarev, Soviet DP guns, Czech VZ26, VZ30, and ZB53 as well as other German and Italian machine guns. At the present time the Spanish army uses the MG 42/59 machine gun.

FAO Model 59

This is a Spanish-built gun designed on the Czech ZB26. It is chambered for the 7.62mm cartridge and is belt-fed with 50-round metallic links in a drum. Full automatic fire only. Barrel length is 22" with attached bipod. Gun weighs about 20 lbs. Rate of fire is approximately 650 rounds per minute.

Pre-1968

Exc.	V.G.	Fair
16500	15500	15000

Pre-1986 conversions

Exc.	V.G.	Fair
14000	13000	11000

Pre-1986 dealer samples

Exc.	V.G.	Fair
N/A	N/A	N/A

ALFA Model 1944

This gun was designed for use as a heavy machine gun. Chambered for the 7.92x57 Mauser cartridge and fitted with a 29.5" barrel. Select fire. Fed by a 100-round metallic link belt loaded in a drum. Rate of fire is about 800 rounds per minute. Weight is approximately 28 lbs.

NOTE: The Model 44 was also supplied to Egypt with aluminum cooling fins extending the length of the barrel and large slots in the gas cylinder.

Pre-1968 (Very Rare)

Exc.	V.G.	Fair
N/A	N/A	N/A

Pre-1986 conversions

Exc.	V.G.	Fair
N/A	N/A	N/A

Pre-1986 dealer samples (10 known)

Exc.	V.G.	Fair
20000	18000	16000

ALFA Model 55

Introduced in 1955, this is an updated version of the Model 44 chambered for the 7.62mm cartridge and fitted with a shorter 24" ribbed barrel with a lighter tripod. Rate of fire is about 800 rounds per minute. Weight is approximately 28 lbs.

Pre-1968

Exc.	V.G.	Fair
N/A	N/A	N/A

Pre-1986 conversions

Exc.	V.G.	Fair
N/A	N/A	N/A

Pre-1986 dealer samples

Exc.	V.G.	Fair
N/A	N/A	N/A

Ameli

Introduced in 1980, this is a light air-cooled machine gun chambered for the 5.56x45mm cartridge. It is fitted with a 15.75" barrel with slotted jacket, carry handle, and bipod. Barrel is quick change with flash hider. Belt-fed with 100- or 200-round belts. Plastic stock with pistol grip. Rate of fire is about 900 rounds per minute. Weight is approximately 11.5 lbs. Similar in appearance to the MG42 but smaller in size.

Pre-1968

Exc.	V.G.	Fair
N/A	N/A	N/A

Pre-1986 conversions

Exc.	V.G.	Fair
N/A	N/A	N/A

Pre-1986 dealer samples

Exc.	V.G.	Fair
20000	18000	16000

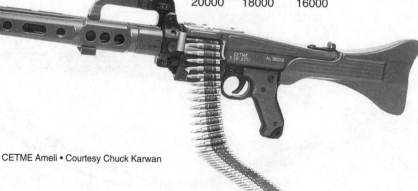

CETME Ameli • Courtesy Chuck Karwan

SWEDEN

Swedish Military Conflicts, 1870-Present

As an outcome of the Swedish defeat against France in 1808, Sweden lost Finland to Russia but gained Norway. This union with Norway remained until 1905, when Norway was granted its independence. During the 20th century, Sweden avoided involvement in both world wars and maintained its neutrality during the Cold War. Sweden joined the European Union in 1995.

HANDGUNS

Sweden purchased a small number, about 10,000, of Walther P-38 pistols in 1939, designated the Model 39. Also, a limited number of Walther PP pistols were used by the army as well.

Model 1871

The Swedish military issued the Lefaucheux-Francotte 6-shot revolver built by Auguste Francotte in Liege, Belgium, and also by Husqvarna. The frame was solid with fixed cylinder and no mechanical ejection. Chambered for the 11mm cartridge and fitted with a 5.9" round barrel. Checkered wooden grips with lanyard loop. Six-round cylinder is non-fluted. Weight is about 41 oz. First adopted by the cavalry and then included other units as well. In use between 1871 and 1890.

Courtesy Geschichte und Technik der europaischen Militarrevolver, Journal-Verlag Schwend GmbH with permission

Exc.	V.G.	Good	Fair	Poor
1250	750	500	350	200

Model 1863/79

This revolver is a converted pinfire to 11mm centerfire. Octagon barrel is 6.2". Smooth wooden grips with lanyard loop. Built by Lefaucheux in Paris. In use between 1879 and 1890.

Courtesy Geschichte und Technik der europaischen Militarrevolver, Journal-Verlag Schwend GmbH with permission

Exc.	V.G.	Good	Fair	Poor
800	500	300	175	100

Model 1884

In 1884 the Swedish Navy chose the French Model 1873 revolver as its issue sidearm. It was designated the Model 1884. It was chambered for the 11mm cartridge and fitted with a 4.4" half-round half-octagon barrel. Checkered wood grips with lanyard loop. It was built in St. Etienne. Used by the navy from 1884 to 1887.

Courtesy Geschichte und Technik der europaischen Militarrevolver, Journal-Verlag Schwend GmbH with permission

Exc.	V.G.	Good	Fair	Poor
650	400	250	175	125

HUSQVARNA

Model 1887 Officer's Model

This double action revolver was chosen by the Swedish army as its official sidearm. It was a 6-shot double action Nagant design chambered for the 7.5mm cartridge with fluted cylinder. It was fitted with a 4.5" half-round half-octagon barrel. Checkered wood grips with lanyard loop. Weight is about 24 oz. The first of these revolvers were built by the Nagant brothers in Liege beginning in 1887, and starting in 1897 these guns were built at Husqvarna as well. Issued until 1947.

NOTE: Between 1897 and 1905 Husqvarna produced about 13,000 of these revolvers. They were delivered with a holster, spare cylinder, cleaning rod, and screwdriver. Many of these revolvers were also sold on the commercial market as well.

Left side of Model 1887 Swedish revolver • Courtesy Daniel Rewers collection, Paul Goodwind photo

Courtesy Rock Island Auction Company

Exc.	V.G.	Good	Fair	Poor
500	300	150	100	75

Model 1907 (Browning Model 1903)

This pistol is a copy of the FN Browning Model 1903 made for the Swedish army beginning in 1907. Built by Husqvarna. It is chambered for the 9x20 Browning Long cartridge. It is identical in every way to the FN model. This pistol remained in service until 1940. Many were converted to the .380 caliber and imported into the U.S.

Courtesy Orvel Reichert

Exc.	V.G.	Good	Fair	Poor
350	250	200	150	100

NOTE: If converted to .380 caliber reduce values by 50 percent.

Lahti Model 40

A 9mm caliber semiautomatic pistol with a 5.5" barrel and 8-shot magazine. The grip is cut for a shoulder stock. Designed by Aimo Johannes Lahti, built with some alterations to the original design by Husqvarna and adopted as the standard Swedish sidearm in 1942. It differs from the Finnish version in that it does not have a loaded chamber indicator. The front sight is also higher. Production stopped in 1946 with some 84,000 pistols produced.

Exc.	V.G.	Good	Fair	Poor
550	400	275	225	150

SUBMACHINE GUNS

The Swedes used the Thompson submachine gun designated the 11mm Model 40 in limited numbers. They also used the Finnish Suomi (Model 37-39) and the Bergmann Model 34, designated the Swedish Model 39.

Carl Gustav 45

This 9mm weapon was first produced in 1945 in Sweden. This submachine gun is still in use. Models built between 1945 and 1948 are fitted with a 50-round Suomi magazine, while after 1948 guns have a 36-round two column magazine. It is used by the Swedish and Indonesian armies. Some integral silencer versions were used by Special Forces in Vietnam. Barrel is

Swedish "K" (M45/B) with integral suppressor •
Courtesy West Point Museum, Paul Goodwin photo

8.25" in length. Fitted with retractable stock. Rate of fire is about 600 rounds per minute. Weight is about 8 lbs. This is the principal submachine gun in use by the Swedish army today.

Courtesy Richard M. Kumor Sr.

Carl Gustav M45/B • Photo courtesy private NFA collection

Pre-1968

Exc.	V.G.	Fair
15000	13000	12000

Pre-1986 conversions

Exc.	V.G.	Fair
7500	6500	5500

Pre-1986 dealer samples

Exc.	V.G.	Fair
7500	6500	5500

NOTE: Add 33 percent for M45/B model, which features a different non-removable magazine well, green finish, and improved bolt retention. There is also an M45/C that is fitted with a bayonet lug and a M45/E that is select fire.

RIFLES

REMINGTON

Sweden utilized the Remington rolling block rifles. Some of these were produced by Remington and others by Carl Gustav and Husqvarna.

Model 1867 Rifle

Chambered for the 12.17x42mm rimfire cartridge and fitted with a 35.5" barrel. Full stock with three barrel bands, cleaning rod, and bayonet lug on right side. Weight is about 9.25 lbs.

Exc.	V.G.	Good	Fair	Poor
—	—	600	400	100

Model 1864/68/85 Carbine

Chambered for the 12.7x42mm rimfire cartridge and fitted with a 16.5" barrel. Rear sight graduated from 250 to 800 meters. Full stock with cleaning rod and one barrel band. Built by Carl Gustav.

Exc.	V.G.	Good	Fair	Poor
—	1050	850	550	200

Model 1870

Built by Carl Gustav and Husqvarna, this model is chambered for the 12.7x42mm rimfire cartridge. Fitted with a 16.5" barrel with rear sight graduated from 250 to 900 meters. Full stock with one barrel band at the muzzle. Weight is about 6 lbs.

NOTE: Many of these rifles were later converted to centerfire.

Exc.	V.G.	Good	Fair	Poor
—	1050	850	550	200

Model 1884 Rifle

Chambered for the 10.15x61Rmm cartridge and fitted with a 31" barrel.

Exc.	V.G.	Good	Fair	Poor
—	750	600	400	100

Model 1884 Carbine

As above but with 16.5" barrel.

Exc.	V.G.	Good	Fair	Poor
—	1050	850	550	200

Model 1889

Chambered for the 8x58Rmm Danish Krag cartridge and fitted with a 33" barrel with rear sight graduated from 300 to 2,400 meters. Full stock with two barrel bands. Sling swivel on first barrel band and in front of triggerguard. Finger grooves in stock ahead of breech and below rear sight. Bayonet lug.

Exc.	V.G.	Good	Fair	Poor
950	750	600	400	100

MAUSER

NOTE: These Mauser rifles were built either by Mauser, Carl Gustav, or Husqvarna. On the right side of the buttstock is frequently seen a tin disk with the unit number and sometimes a capital letter. The letter "I" stands for infantry, "A" for artillery, "T" for reserves, and "K.FL." for marines.

M1894 Carbine

Chambered for the 6.5x55mm cartridge and fitted with a 17.5" barrel. Full stocked in European carbine-style with half-length handguard with finger grooves. Turned down bolt. Magazine capacity is 5 rounds. Leaf rear sight graduated from 300 to 1,600 meters. Weight is about 7.5 lbs. About 12,000 of these rifles were built by Mauser, the rest by the Swedish firms mentioned above.

Exc.	V.G.	Good	Fair	Poor
950	700	500	400	200

M1896 Rifle

Action similar to the Model 1894 but with a 29" barrel, full-length stock, half-length upper handguard, and bayonet lug. Rear sight graduated from 300 to 2,000 meters on Mauser and Gustav-built rifles and 100 to 800 meters on Husqvarna built rifles. Swedish crown over maker and date stamped on receiver ring. Magazine capacity is 5 rounds. Weight is about 9 lbs.

NOTE: A number of these rifles were sent to Finland during the early days of World War II to fight the Soviets. A number were also sent to Denmark as well. These Danish rifles have a Danish silver coin in the right side of the buttstock in place of the Swedish marking disk.

Courtesy Rock Island Auction Company

Exc.	V.G.	Good	Fair	Poor
300	175	100	80	60

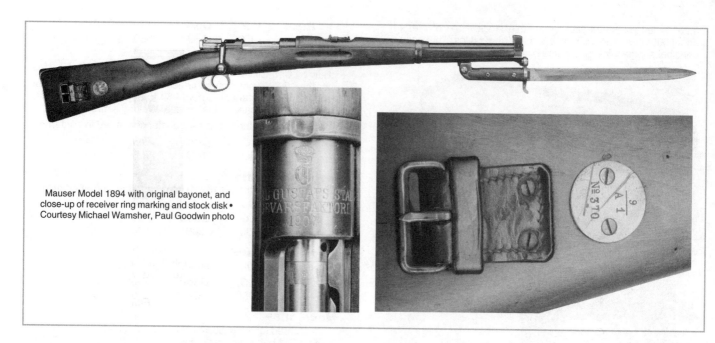

Mauser Model 1894 with original bayonet, and close-up of receiver ring marking and stock disk • Courtesy Michael Wamsher, Paul Goodwin photo

Model 1896 Sniper Rifle with M44 Scope • Courtesy Rock Island Auction Company

Model 1896 with AGA42 Scope. close-up of scope and markings • Courtesy Stoddard Martial collection, Paul Goodwin photo

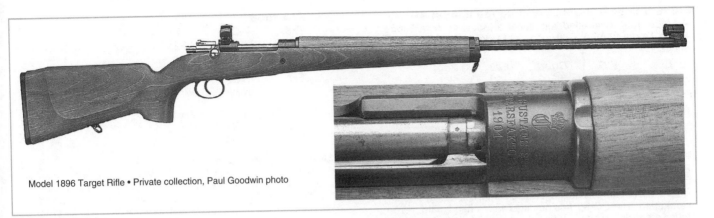

Model 1896 Target Rifle • Private collection, Paul Goodwin photo

M1896 Sniper Rifle/M41 AGA scope
This is a Model 1896 rifle with Model 41 AGA scope mounted.

Exc.	V.G.	Good	Fair	Poor
1500	1200	850	650	500

M1896 Sniper Rifle/M42 AGA scope
This is a Model 1896 rifle with Model 42 AGA scope mounted.

Exc.	V.G.	Good	Fair	Poor
1500	1200	850	650	500

Swedish mountain troops with M1896 Mausers • Courtesy Paul S. Scarlata

Model 96-38
About 30,000 Model 1896 rifles were shortened to the same overall length as the Model 1938 Short Rifle. The straight bolt handle of the Model 1896 was retained. Weight is about 8.375 lbs.

Exc.	V.G.	Good	Fair	Poor
300	175	125	75	50

Model 38 Short Rifle
Similar to the Model 1896 but with turned-down bolt handle and barrel length of 23.5". Designed for mounted troops. Magazine capacity is 5 rounds. Rear sight graduated from 100 to 600 meters. Weight is approximately 9 lbs. Built by Husqvarna.

Exc.	V.G.	Good	Fair	Poor
400	275	200	150	100

Model 38/22 Training Rifle
Similar to the Model 38 Short Rifle but chambered for the .22 caliber rimfire cartridge.

Exc.	V.G.	Good	Fair	Poor
500	350	250	200	150

M1938/40 Short Rifle (Model 40)
This model is a Swedish modified German Kar. 98k converted to the 8x63mm machine gun cartridge. The rifle was fitted with a muzzle brake to soften recoil but the cartridge was too powerful for the gun. Four-round magazine. Weight is about 9.5 lbs.

Exc.	V.G.	Good	Fair	Poor
300	150	100	80	50

Model CG 63 Match Rifle with close-ups of front and rear sights • Courtesy Stoddard Martial collection, Paul Goodwin photo

M1896 Sniper Rifle/M44 AGA scope (Model 41)

A Model 1896 Rifle fitted with either a Model 44 AGA 3x65 scope, Model 42 AGA 3x65 scope, or Model 41 4x90 ZF Ajack scope.

Exc.	V.G.	Good	Fair	Poor
1500	1200	850	650	500

M1896 Military Target Rifles

A Model 1896 rifle with special micrometer target sights.

Exc.	V.G.	Good	Fair	Poor
400	250	200	150	110

Model CG-63 and CG-80 Target Rifle

Built by Carl Gustav, this rifle was chambered for the .22 rim-fire, 6.5x55mm, or 7.62mm cartridge. Fitted with a medium weight 29.1" barrel. Half-length stock with half-length upper handguard. The CG-80 was not fitted with a handguard. Five round magazine. It has a turned-down bolt handle flattened on top. Generally fitted with aperture rear sight mounted on receiver bridge. Many minor variations are encountered in this rifle. Weight is approximately 9.5 lbs.

Exc.	V.G.	Good	Fair	Poor
850	700	500	300	200

Ljungman AG-42B

Designed by Eril Eklund and placed in service with the Swedish military in 1942—less than one year after it was designed. The rifle is a direct gas-operated design with no piston or rod. It is chambered for the 6.5mm cartridge and has a 24.5" barrel with a 10-round detachable magazine. This rifle has military-type sights and a full-length stock and handguard held on by barrel bands. Rear sight is graduated from 100 to 700 meters. There are provisions for a bayonet. There is also an Egyptian version of this rifle known as the "Hakim" and a Danish version that was manufactured by Madsen. The U.S. AR-15 rifles use the same type of gas system.

AG-42B action • Courtesy Chuck Karwan

Exc.	V.G.	Good	Fair	Poor
500	325	250	150	100

MACHINE GUNS

The Swedish armed forces have utilized a wide variety of machine guns from several countries. Sweden adopted the Schwarzlose Model 14 in 6.5mm caliber, the Browning Model 1917A1 water-cooled gun (Model 36), the Browning Model 1919A6 (Model 42), the Czech VZ26 in 6.5mm caliber (Model 39), and more currently the FN MAG in 7.62mm (Model 58). These early FN MAG guns were chambered for the 6.5x55mm Mauser cartridge.

Swedish Model 36

This is the Swedish version of the Browning Model 1917 water-cooled gun. The gun shown is in a twin anti-aircraft configuration, and is too rare to price.

Pre-1968

Exc.	V.G.	Fair
28000	26000	24000

Pre-1986 conversions

Exc.	V.G.	Fair
N/A	N/A	N/A

Pre-1986 dealer samples

Exc.	V.G.	Fair
15000	14000	13000

Swedish BAR Model 21

Designated the Swedish Kg. (*Kulsprutegevar*, light machine gun) these guns were built in Sweden under license from Colt between 1923 and 1935. Chambered for the Swedish 6.5x55mm cartridge. This model does not have a quick change barrel as originally built. A little over 8,000 of these BARs were built in Sweden during its production life.

Pre-1968

Exc.	V.G.	Fair
25000	23000	21000

Pre-1986 conversions

Exc.	V.G.	Fair
N/A	N/A	N/A

Pre-1986 dealer samples

Exc.	V.G.	Fair
12000	11000	10000

Swedish Model 1936 Twin • Courtesy private NFA collection, Paul Goodwin photo

Model 21 Swedish BAR • Private NFA collection, Gary Gelson photo

Swedish BAR Model 37

The Model 37 Swedish BAR is an improved version of the Model 21 with a screw-on receiver extension that allowed the adoption of a quick change barrel. A total of about 15,000 Model 37s were produced between 1937 and 1944.

NOTE: A number of Model 21s were refitted with quick change barrels and designated the Model 21/37.

Pre-1968 (Very Rare)

Exc.	V.G.	Fair
12000	10000	9000

Pre-1986 conversions

Exc.	V.G.	Fair
N/A	N/A	N/A

Pre-1986 dealer samples

Exc.	V.G.	Fair
6000	5000	4500

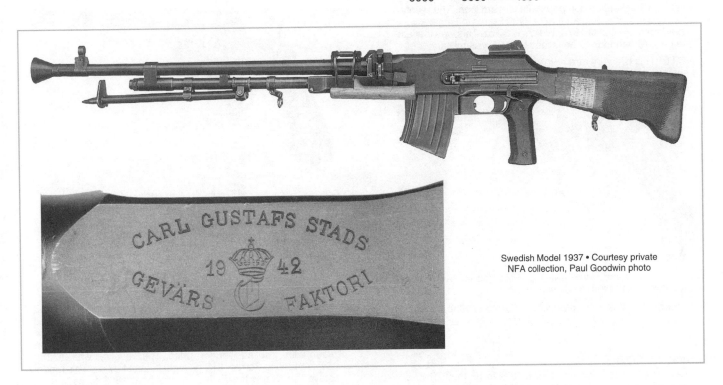

Swedish Model 1937 • Courtesy private NFA collection, Paul Goodwin photo

SWITZERLAND

Swiss Military Conflicts, 1870-Present

In 1815 Switzerland was guaranteed perpetual neutrality by the Treaty of Vienna, thus it remained neutral in both World Wars. Switzerland was not a member of the United Nations until 2002 and is not a member of the EU.

National defense is based on a system of universal conscription by which every Swiss male is liable for military duty between the ages of 20 and 50. The Swiss soldier is the only soldier in the world who keeps his equipment, including arms and ammunition, at home, and who performs his obligatory duty each year in civilian clothes. Once his military rifle is issued, the Swiss soldier keeps it at home for life. In 2001, Switzerland had a total active duty military force of 3,600 personnel. Reserve forces were 351,000, of those 320,000 were in the army.

Courtesy Geschichte und Technik der europaischen Militarrevolver, Journal-Verlag Schwend GmbH with permission

Exc.	V.G.	Good	Fair	Poor
1500	—	—	—	—

HANDGUNS

Model 1872

This Swiss Model 1872 is a 10.4mm rimfire revolver with a 6-shot fluted cylinder. It is fitted with a 5.9" octagon barrel. The frame is solid with fixed fluted cylinder and mechanical rod ejection. Checkered wood grips with lanyard loop. The revolver was built by the Belgian firm of Pirlot Freres in Liege. It was issued from 1872 until 1878. Weight is 37 oz. This was the last foreign-built handgun to be issued to the Swiss military.

NOTE: This is a very rare revolver as most were converted to centerfire with the Model 1872/78 in 1878.

Courtesy Geschichte und Technik der europaischen Militarrevolver, Journal-Verlag Schwend GmbH with permission

Exc.	V.G.	Good	Fair	Poor
N/A	—	—	—	—

Model 1872/78

This is a centerfire converted Model 1872 in 10.4mm. This revolver was rarely used by the Swiss military.

Model 1878

This was the first Swiss-made revolver used by the Swiss military. Made in Bern, this Schmidt-Galand-type revolver was chambered for the 10.4mm cartridge. The frame was solid with fixed cylinder and mechanical rod ejection. 4.5" octagon barrel. Checkered grips with the Swiss cross on the left side. Weight was about 35 oz. This revolver was issued to cavalry units with about 6,000 in service.

Courtesy Geschichte und Technik der europaischen Militarrevolver, Journal-Verlag Schwend GmbH with permission

Exc.	V.G.	Good	Fair	Poor
1750	1000	600	350	250

Model 1882

This revolver was similar in appearance to the Model 1878 but was chambered for the smaller 7.5mm cartridge. It was fitted with a 4.5" octagon barrel. Early Model 1882 revolvers were fitted with hard rubber checkered grips while later guns will be seen with grooved wooden grips. This revolver was built in Switzerland at Bern or SIG. Weight is about 27 oz. This model stayed in use in the Swiss military from 1882 to as late as 1950.

Right side of the Model 1882 Swiss revolver • Courtesy Rock Island Auction Company

Left side of Model 1882 Swiss revolver with details • Courtesy Daniel Rewers collection, Paul Goodwin photo

Model 1929 Swiss revolver • Courtesy Daniel Rewers collection, Paul Goodwin photo

Exc.	V.G.	Good	Fair	Poor
1250	850	500	300	200

Exc.	V.G.	Good	Fair	Poor
1250	850	500	300	200

Model 1929

This is a solid frame double action revolver that is gate loaded. The round barrel is 4.5". Chambered for the 7.5x23R Swiss revolver cartridge. The fluted cylinder holds 6 rounds. Checkered bakelite grips. Weight is about 28 ozs. The grip on the Model 1929 is of a different shape than the Model 1882.

SNAP SHOT
THE 1906 SWISS LUGER PISTOL

The German-made Luger pistol is certainly a "Classic" design and will forever rank with the most notable of military service sidearms used during the past century, but the truth is the Swiss adopted the Luger before the German military did. The difference, however, is the 1906 Swiss Luger was chambered for the 7.65mm Parabellum cartridge and as such soon established a terrible reputation for stopping enemy antagonists. None-the-less the Swiss continued with the 1906 Luger for a long number of years after adopting it two years before the Germans did.

The Swiss didn't like the idea the sole source of this new service pistol was Germany, so in 1917 they were able to secure the tooling necessary to manufacture the gun in Switzerland. The 1906 Swiss Luger is often referred as the 'new' Luger as opposed to all previous models because the 1906 Swiss Luger was the first model employing the coil spring recoil spring. Earlier models had used a leaf spring which developed the nasty habit of breaking during various governmental trials held around the world.

The main distinguishing feature of the 1906 Swiss Luger versus later models of the same pistol is the prominent grip safety and the fact the grip frame remains somewhat straight at the bottom. Subsequent models starting with the German military 1908 model all feature a prominent widening or bulge at the very bottom of the grip frame.

The 1906 Swiss was first purchased with a 6-inch barrel but later versions featured a 100mm barrel or one close to 4 inches in length. The 1906 Swiss Luger featured an eight-round magazine and remains a historic pistol and one often sought by small arms collectors around the world.

Frank W. James

LUGER

WAFFENFABRIK BERN

Switzerland was the first country to adopt the Luger as a military sidearm with its contract purchase of the Model 1900 from DWM. Another contract for the Model 1906 soon followed. Because DWM could no longer supply Switzerland with Lugers during World War I, the Swiss firm of Waffenfabrik Bern (W+F Bern) produced its own version based on the Model 1906.

Bibliographical Note: For additional historical information, technical data, and photos, see Vittorio Bobba, *Parabellum; A Technical History of Swiss Lugers*, Italy, 1996.

NOTE: There are a number of sub-variations of Swiss Lugers that may affect value. It is strongly suggested that thorough research of this model be undertaken prior to a sale.

Model 1906 Bern

A Swiss-made copy of the German Model 1906 Luger. Made in caliber 7.65mm, fitted with a 4.75" barrel, and marked "WAFFENFABRIK BERN" under the Geneva cross on top of the toggle. The grips on this pistol are unique in that most are checkered walnut with a plain border on the front and rear edges. About 17,000 of these pistols were manufactured. This model was most likely produced between 1918 and 1933, and was built for the Swiss military.

Courtesy James Rankin

Exc.	V.G.	Good	Fair	Poor
4500	3000	2000	1400	1000

Model 1929

Similar to the above, with the exception that the toggle finger pieces are smooth, the grip frame is uncurved, safety lever is a flat configuration, and the grip safety is of inordinate size. Fitted with plastic grips. Chambered for caliber 7.65mm. About 30,000 of these pistols were produced. Sold both for military and commercial use.

Courtesy James Rankin

Exc.	V.G.	Good	Fair	Poor
3250	2000	1500	1200	900

SIG

Schweizerische Industrie Gesellschaft, Neuhausen am Rheinfalls, Switzerland

Biographical Note: For historical background, technical data, and photos, see Lorenz Vetter, *Das grosse Buch der SIG-Pistolen*, Verlag Stocker-Schmid AG, 1995.

NOTE: The P210 pistol was designated the SP47/8 prior to 1957, when it was renamed the P210. There are a number of production changes on this pistol that follow a chronological order.

P210

A 7.65mm or 9mm semiautomatic pistol with a 4.75" barrel and 8-shot magazine. Fixed rear sight. Blued with plastic grips. In 1996 the 9mm version was the only one imported. Weight is about 32 oz. This model was also used by the Danish army (Model 49).

NIB	Exc.	V.G.	Good	Fair	Poor
2500	1500	1300	1100	800	500

NOTE: For 1996, a .22 caliber conversion unit serialized to the gun was available. Add $600 for this option.

P210-1

As above, with an adjustable rear sight, polished finish, and walnut grips. Imported prior to 1987. Weight is about 31 oz.

NIB	Exc.	V.G.	Good	Fair	Poor
2750	2250	1500	1150	800	—

P210-2 (Swiss Army Model 49-SP47/8)

This model is similar to the P210-1 with the exception that it has a sandblasted matte finish and black plastic grips with fixed sights. Adopted by the Swiss army in 1947 and still in service.

A Swiss P 49 military version of the P210. Note the Letter prefix on the serial number; a military designation • Courtesy Simon Stoddard collection, Paul Goodwin photo

NIB	Exc.	V.G.	Good	Fair	Poor
2250	1750	1350	1000	750	300

P210-3

Introduced in 1950, this model was issued to the Swiss police in Lausanne and Basel. Early examples are polished blue and later examples are sandblasted matte blue. Fixed sights. Production ceased in 1983. Very few of these pistols were sold on a commercial basis. Very scarce.

NIB	Exc.	V.G.	Good	Fair	Poor
N/A	—	—	—	—	—

P210-4

Special model produced for the West German Border Police. Fixed rear sight. Walnut grips on early models and black plastic grips on later models. Early models have blued finish while later models have sandblasted matte finish.

NIB	Exc.	V.G.	Good	Fair	Poor
2250	1750	1350	1000	750	300

P210-5

A commercial version as above, with an extended length barrel of 5.9" (150mm) or 7.1" (180mm), adjustable rear sight, target trigger, and walnut grips. Front sight is fitted to front of extended barrel, not the slide. Offered in a standard and heavy frame weight. Polished blue finish. Weight is about 35 oz. for standard weight frame.

NIB	Exc.	V.G.	Good	Fair	Poor
3750	2750	1750	1200	800	400

P210-6

A commercial version as above, with a 4.75" barrel. Front sight is fitted to slide. Adjustable rear sight on some of these variations, fixed sight on others. Polished blue finish.

SIG P210-6 Commercial Version • Courtesy SIG Arms

NIB	Exc.	V.G.	Good	Fair	Poor
2750	2250	1500	1250	800	400

P210-7

This model is chambered for the .22 rimfire cartridge and fitted with a 4.75" barrel. Most of the variations of this model are built for commercial and export sales except one variation, which was built for the West German Border Guards as a practice pistol. Fixed sights. Checkered plastic grips.

NIB	Exc.	V.G.	Good	Fair	Poor
N/A	—	—	—	—	—

P220-P225 (Swiss Army Model P-75)

Swiss army military sidearm. This is a high-quality, double action semiautomatic pistol chambered for .38 Super, .45 ACP, and 9mm Parabellum. It has a 4.41" barrel and fixed sights and features the decocking lever that was found originally on the Sauer Model 38H. There are two versions of this pistol: one with a bottom magazine release (commonly referred to as the European model) and the other with the release on the side (commonly referred to as the American model), as on the Model 1911 Colt. The frame is a lightweight alloy that is matte finished and is available in either blue, nickel, or K-Kote finish with black plastic grips. The .45 ACP magazine capacity is 7 rounds and the pistol weighs 25.7 oz.; the .38 Super magazine capacity is 9 rounds and the pistol weighs 26.5 oz.; the 9mm magazine holds 9 rounds and the overall weight is 26.5 oz. This model was manufactured from 1976 and is still in production. The 9mm version in this model is no longer in production. The prices listed below are for guns with a standard blue finish.

Swiss issue P225 with close-up of markings • Courtesy Danile Rewers collection, Paul Goodwin photo

NIB	Exc.	V.G.	Good	Fair	Poor
750	550	400	300	200	150

NOTE: For the K-Kote finish add $40, for nickel slide add $40.

SUBMACHINE GUNS

Steyr-Solothurn (Solothurn SI-100 or MP34[o])

See *Austria, Submachine Guns, Steyr.*

MP41/44

This model was developed by Furrer and built by W+F Bern arsenal between 1936 and 1942. Chambered for the 9mm Luger cartridge. Recoil operated with a toggle system similar to the Luger pistol but turned on its side. Slotted barrel jacket with 10" barrel with forward vertical handgrip and pistol grip wooden stock. Rate of fire is about 900 rounds per minute. Magazine capacity is 40 rounds. Very expensive to produce with the result that less than 5,000 guns were manufactured. Weight is about 11.5 lbs.

Swiss MP41 • Courtesy private NFA collection, Paul Goodwin photo

Pre-1968 (Rare)

Exc.	V.G.	Fair
19500	18500	18000

Pre-1986 conversions

Exc.	V.G.	Fair
N/A	N/A	N/A

Pre-1986 dealer samples

Exc.	V.G.	Fair
N/A	N/A	N/A

MP43/44

The Swiss version of the Suomi with a bayonet lug and flip over rear sight. Built by Hispano Suiza under license from Finland. Rate of fire is about 800 rounds per minute and weight is approximately 10.5 lbs. Magazine capacity is 50-round box type.

Swiss M43/44 • Courtesy private NFA collection, Paul Goodwin photo

Pre-1968 (Rare)

Exc.	V.G.	Fair
19500	19000	18000

Pre-1986 conversions

Exc.	V.G.	Fair
N/A	N/A	N/A

Pre-1986 dealer samples

Exc.	V.G.	Fair
N/A	N/A	N/A

RIFLES

PEABODY

Swiss Rifle (1867)

Chambered for the .41 Swiss rimfire cartridge, this rifle was fitted with a 31.625" barrel. Full stock with two barrel bands. The barrel is blued and the furniture casehardened. On the left side of the receiver are a cross and "W" inside an oval. "Peabody" stamped on left side of receiver. About 15,000 rifles were sold to the Swiss. Serial number range: 5500 to 21000.

Exc.	V.G.	Good	Fair	Poor
—	1250	750	500	200

VETTERLI

Bern, SIG, Pfenninger

This rifle was invented by Friderich Vetterli at Neuhausen, Switzerland, in 1867. This was the first bolt action repeating rifle to be used as a military service weapon. It was adopted on January 8, 1869, and predated the Fruwirth by three years. It is chambered for the .41 Swiss rimfire cartridge (10.4mm). It has a 12-round tubular magazine that is loaded through a side gate similar to a Winchester lever action. There is a swinging cover on the loading gate. The finish is blue, with a full-length walnut stock secured by one barrel band and an endcap. There is a full-length cleaning rod located under the barrel. The receiver has a round configuration and the triggerguard has a rear spur. The rifle and its variations were built between 1869 and 1881.

Model 1869 Infantry Rifle

This model has a turn bolt action with two lugs locking into the receiver body. Full stock with no hand guard. Barrel length is 33". Cleaning rod. A swing-down loading gate is on the right side of the receiver. Magazine capacity is 12 rounds. Weight is about 10.25 lbs.

Exc.	V.G.	Good	Fair	Poor
—	950	600	300	100

Model 1870 Cadet Rifle

Same action as the Model 1869 but single shot only. Barrel length is 26.75". Weight about 7 lbs.

Exc.	V.G.	Good	Fair	Poor
—	750	400	200	100

Model 1871 Rifle

This rifle is fitted with a 33" barrel. Sights calibrated from 200 to 1,000 meters. Magazine capacity is 11 rounds. Weight is about 10.25 lbs.

Paul Goodwin photo

Exc.	V.G.	Good	Fair	Poor
—	750	400	200	100

Model 1871 Stuzer (Short Rifle) (Sharpshooter)

This short rifle was fitted with two barrel bands on its 30" barrel. 9-round magazine. Fitted with a curved buttplate. Double set trigger. Weight is about 10 lbs.

Exc.	V.G.	Good	Fair	Poor
1000	700	550	400	150

Model 1871 Carbine

The carbine has an 18.5" barrel with no bayonet fittings. Full stock with 6-round tube magazine. Rear sling swivel behind triggerguard. Weight is about 7 lbs.

Exc.	V.G.	Good	Fair	Poor
—	1500	800	400	200

Model 1878 Rifle

This model was a modified version of the Model 1878. Fitted with a full-length stock with curved buttplate and chambered for the 10.4x42R rimfire cartridge. The rear sight is graduated to 1,200 meters. Barrel length is 33" with an 11-round tube

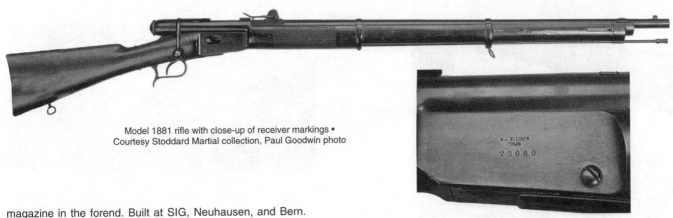

Model 1881 rifle with close-up of receiver markings •
Courtesy Stoddard Martial collection, Paul Goodwin photo

magazine in the forend. Built at SIG, Neuhausen, and Bern. Weight is about 10 lbs.

Exc.	V.G.	Good	Fair	Poor
450	300	250	200	100

NOTE: There is some disagreement as to production of a Model 1878 Carbine. As a rule it is thought that some M1878 rifle barrels were cut to 18.5". These are thought to be arsenal conversions. These cut-down "carbines" are worth less than original rifles.

Model 1878 Sharpshooter

Similar to the Model 1878 rifle but fitted with double set triggers and crescent butt.

Exc.	V.G.	Good	Fair	Poor
750	500	350	225	100

Model 1881 Rifle

This model is the same as the Model 1878 above with the exception of a 1,600 meter graduated rear sight. Weight is about 10 lbs.

Exc.	V.G.	Good	Fair	Poor
600	400	250	200	100

Model 1881 Sharpshooter

Similar to the Model 1881 but fitted with double set triggers.

Exc.	V.G.	Good	Fair	Poor
750	500	350	225	100

SCHMIDT RUBIN
Eidgenossische Waffenfabrik Bern
Bern, Switzerland (1875-1993)

BOLT NOTE: The bolts on this series were made stronger by shortening the overall length of the bolt and the length from the locking lug to the bolt face. These distances measure:

Model 1889: 8 3/4" overall bolt length, 7" from back of locking lug to bolt face.

Model 1889/11 and Model 1911: 8" overall bolt length, 4 1/2" from back of locking lug to bolt face.

Model 1931: 5 3/8" overall bolt length, 1/2" from back of locking lug to bolt face.

[*The above information was supplied by Simeon Stoddard.*]

Model 1889

A 7.5mm straight pull bolt action rifle with a 30.75" barrel and 12-shot magazine. Blued with a full-length walnut stock secured by two barrel bands. Approximately 212,000 were manufactured.

Exc.	V.G.	Good	Fair	Poor
350	200	175	125	90

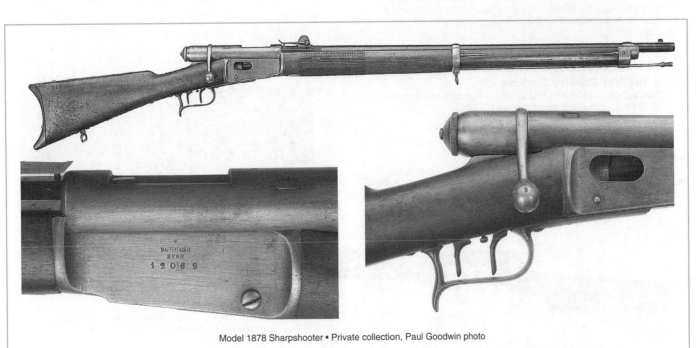

Model 1878 Sharpshooter • Private collection, Paul Goodwin photo

Schmidt Rubin, Model 1889 • Paul Goodwin photo

Model 1889/96

Similar to the Model 1889 with a shortened action. The locking lug is moved forward 2 1/2" on the bolt sleeve. There were approximately 127,000 made between 1897 and 1912.

Exc.	V.G.	Good	Fair	Poor
450	325	250	180	125

Model 1897 Cadet Rifle

A single shot Cadet Rifle with reduced overall size. Barrel length is 23.3". These rifles were sighted for a reduced charge cartridge for target use and to reduce recoil. Sights calibrated for 200 to 400 meters. Weight is about 7.75 lbs. Approximately 7,900 were manufactured between 1898 and 1927.

Exc.	V.G.	Good	Fair	Poor
1200	1000	700	500	350

Model 1900 Short Rifle

A shortened version of the Model 1896, with a 6-shot magazine and 23.3" barrel. Weight is about 8.25 lbs. Approximately 18,750 were manufactured between 1901 and 1911.

Exc.	V.G.	Good	Fair	Poor
650	400	250	175	125

Model 1900/11 Short Rifle

Modified between 1911 and 1920 to more closely resemble the Model 1911 Carbine with new barrel and sights.

Exc.	V.G.	Good	Fair	Poor
400	250	175	125	75

Model 1905 Carbine

Adopted in 1905 as a replacement for the Mannlicher 1893. Barrel length is 21.5". Weight is about 8 lbs. Magazine capacity is 6 rounds. Approximately 7,900 were manufactured between 1906 and 1911.

Exc.	V.G.	Good	Fair	Poor
650	400	250	175	125

Model 1905/11 Cavalry Carbine

Modified between 1911 and 1920 to more closely resemble the Model 1911 Carbine with new barrel and sights.

Exc.	V.G.	Good	Fair	Poor
400	250	175	125	75

Model 1896/11

Updated version of the 1896 rifle to more closely resemble the Model 1911 rifle. Changes included new barrel and sight, and an inlet pistol grip into the straight 1896 stock. Modification program took place between 1911 and 1920.

Exc.	V.G.	Good	Fair	Poor
350	200	150	100	75

Model 1911 Rifle

Straightened and redesigned bolt to better handle the higher performance 1911 cartridge. Barrel length is 30.7". Magazine capacity was reduced from 12 to 6 rounds in the Model 1911. Other changes included a pistol grip and flat buttplate on the stock. Approximately 133,000 were manufactured between 1913 and 1919.

Exc.	V.G.	Good	Fair	Poor
300	175	125	75	50

Model 1911 Carbine

Same action as the Model 1911 rifle with a 23.25" barrel. Approximately 185,000 were manufactured between 1914 and 1933.

Exc.	V.G.	Good	Fair	Poor
350	200	100	80	60

NOTE: Although produced in larger numbers than the Model 1911 rifle, the carbine will command a higher price.

Model 1931 Short Rifle

Similar to the above, with a redesigned lock work, 25.7" barrel, and 6-shot magazine. This was the final version of the

Model 1896/11 with barrel and receiver markings • Courtesy Stoddard Martial collection, Paul Goodwin photo

Model 1911 • Courtesy West Point Museum, Paul Goodwin photo

Model 1911 rifle • Courtesy Paul S. Scarlata

standard K31. Fitted with a highly modified bolt for the .22 caliber rimfire cartridge.

Exc.	V.G.	Good	Fair	Poor
950	750	600	350	250

Hammerili Match K31

This rifle is produced by Hammerili and is so marked on the receiver ring. These rifles have rear military sight omitted and a target sight installed at the rear of the receiver. Very limited production.

Exc.	V.G.	Good	Fair	Poor
4500	3750	3000	2000	1200

Schmidt-Rubin design. Instead of locking lugs into the receiver, the lugs were repositioned to lock into the receiver ring thereby greatly increasing the strength of the rifle. This change also increased the length of the barrel without increasing the overall length of the rifle. Approximately 528,180 were manufactured between 1933 and 1958.

Exc.	V.G.	Good	Fair	Poor
300	175	125	75	50

Model 1931 Short Rifle with shooter added target sights

Many shooters in Switzerland have modified Model 1931s with target sights. These can range in price due to the quality of the sights added.

Prices range from $550 to $350.

Model 1931 .22 Target Rifle

This is the single-shot training version of the K31 with sights set for 50 meters. The rifle is the same overall length as the

Model 1911 Carbine with close-up of receiver markings • Courtesy Daniel Rewers collection, Paul Goodwin photo

Model K-31 with shooter added sights • Courtesy Daniel Rewers collection, Paul Goodwin photo

Model K-31 with close-up of receiver markings • Courtesy
Stoddard Martial collection, Paul Goodwin photo

Hammerli Match K-31 with close-ups of receiver markings, and front and rear sights • Courtesy Daniel Rewers collection, Paul Goodwin photo

Modelo 1931 .22 training rifle. Close-up bolt shows it in the open and closed position • Courtesy Stoddard Martial collection, Paul Goodwin photo

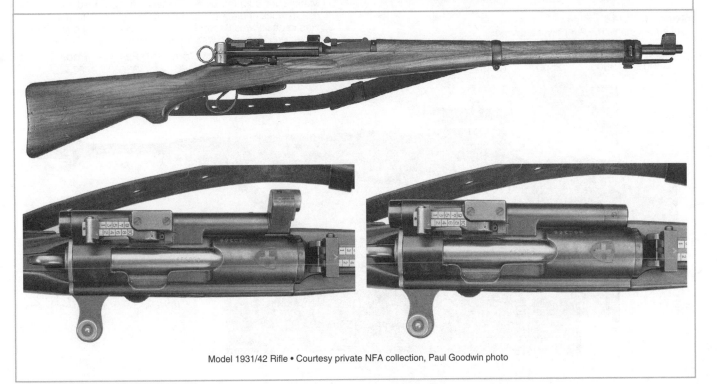

Model 1931/42 Rifle • Courtesy private NFA collection, Paul Goodwin photo

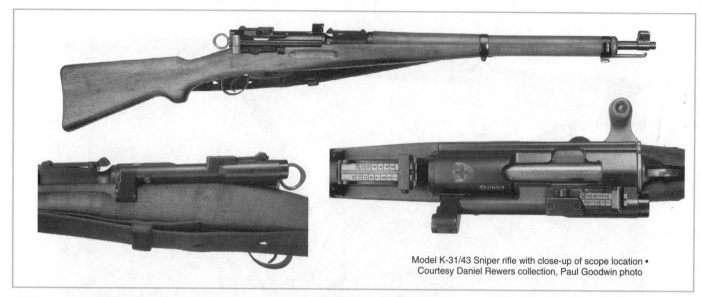

Model K-31/43 Sniper rifle with close-up of scope location •
Courtesy Daniel Rewers collection, Paul Goodwin photo

MODEL 1931 SNIPER VARIANTS

There are a number of different sniper variants to the Model 1931 rifle. The first attempt was an experimental model, the Model 1940, fitted with a Wild & Gerber scope, which was positioned high above the receiver by means of an odd looking scope mount with a forehead protector attached to it. The second experimental model was the Model 1942 with a small detachable scope fitted to the left side of the receiver. All of these rifles were manufactured in small quantities.

Model 1931/42

Built by Waffenfabrik Bern on the Model 31 action and stock. Barrel length is 25.7" with 6-shot magazine. Walnut stock with handguard. This variant is fitted with a 1.8 power integral telescope attached to the left side of the receiver. It has a unique periscope type rotating objective. This rifle is also fitted with open sights to 1,500 meters.

Exc.	V.G.	Good	Fair	Poor
4500	3500	2500	1000	—

Model 1931/43

As above but with a 2.8 power telescope.

Exc.	V.G.	Good	Fair	Poor
4500	3500	2500	1000	—

Model 1955

This model, introduced in 1955, is built on a Model 1931 action. Barrel length is 25.7". A muzzle brake is fitted. This model is fitted with a 3.5 power Kern Aarau telescope mounted on the receiver bridge. Beechwood stock is 2/3 length with handguard and checkered pistol grip. Integral bipod built into midpoint of stock. Weight is about 12 lbs.

Exc.	V.G.	Good	Fair	Poor
4500	3500	2500	1000	—

MANNLICHER

Model 1893 Carbine

This is a Mannlicher straight pull design carbine with a 21.5" barrel chambered for the 7.5x53.5mm cartridge. It was the only Mannlicher adopted by Switzerland. It was fitted with a full-length stock and upper handguard. No bayonet fittings. Magazine capacity was 6 rounds and it was charger loaded. The receiver ring is marked with a small Swiss cross.

Exc.	V.G.	Good	Fair	Poor
1000	800	650	350	225

Model 1955 Rifle • Courtesy private NFA collection, Paul Goodwin photo

Mannlicher Model 1893 Carbine • Courtesy
West Point Museum, Paul Goodwin photo

SIG
Schweizerische Industrie Gesellschaft,
Neuhausen am Rheinfalls, Switzerland

SSG 2000

This is a high-grade, bolt action, sniping-type rifle chambered for .223, 7.5mm Swiss, .300 Weatherby Magnum, and .308 Winchester. It has a 24" barrel and was furnished without sights. It has a 4-round box magazine. The finish is matte blued with a thumbhole-style stippled walnut stock with an adjustable cheekpiece. This model was discontinued in 1986.

NIB	Exc.	V.G.	Good	Fair	Poor
8000	6000	3500	1500	—	—

SSG 3000

Chambered for the .308 Win. cartridge, this model is fitted with a 23.4" barrel and ambidextrous McMillian Tactical stock. Magazine capacity is 5 rounds. Overall length is 46.5", and approximate weight is 12 lbs. This model comes in three different packages. They are listed below.

Level I

Base model with no bipod or scope, but with carrying case.

NIB	Exc.	V.G.	Good	Fair	Poor
2600	2000	—	—	—	—

Level II

At this level a Leupold Vari-X III 3.5-10x40mm Duplex scope and Harris bipod with carrying case.

NIB	Exc.	V.G.	Good	Fair	Poor
3500	2750	—	—	—	—

Level III

Rifle is supplied with a Leupold Mark 4 M1-10x40mm Mil-Dot Scope with Harris bipod and carrying case.

NIB	Exc.	V.G.	Good	Fair	Poor
4500	3500	—	—	—	—

SIG AMT

This is a semiautomatic rifle chambered for the .308 cartridge. Fitted with a 19" barrel and wooden buttstock and forearm. Folding bipod standard. Box magazine capacity is 5, 10, or 20 rounds. Weight is about 10 lbs. Built from 1960 to 1974.

NIB	Exc.	V.G.	Good	Fair	Poor
4500	3850	3250	2500	1500	1000

SIG PE57

Similar to the above but chambered for the 7.5x55 Swiss cartridge.

NIB	Exc.	V.G.	Good	Fair	Poor
4500	4100	3500	2700	1700	1300

Bern Stg 51 Assault Rifle

Developed after the end of World War II; the Swiss wanted their own version of a true assault rifle. Waffenfabrik Bern was one of the companies involved in this project. The result was the Stg 51 first built in 1951. This rifle was chambered for the 7.5mm short cartridge, a special cartridge made specifically for this rifle and no longer produced. The rifle is select fire and does so in both models in closed-bolt position. A 30-round box magazine supplies the gun that has a rate of fire of about 800 rounds per minute. The barrel is 22.5" in length and is fitted with a muzzle brake/flash suppressor. A mid-barrel bipod is fitted just ahead of the forend. Weight is approximately 10.5 lbs.

PE57 Assault Rifle • Courtesy Chuck Karwan

Swiss Stg Model 51 (2nd Model) • Courtesy private NFA collection, Paul Goodwin photo

A second model of this rifle was also produced with internal modifications and some small external differences. Both models were issued to the Swiss army, most likely on a trial basis. Extremely rare.

NOTE: The first model of this rifle will interchange some parts with the German FG 42. The second model will interchange all of its parts with the German FG 42.

Bern Stg 51 (First Model)

Pre-1968

Exc.	V.G.	Fair
75000+	—	—

Pre-1986 conversions

Exc.	V.G.	Fair
N/A	N/A	N/A

Pre-1986 dealer samples

Exc.	V.G.	Fair
N/A	N/A	N/A

Bern Stg 51 (Second Model)

Pre-1968

Exc.	V.G.	Fair
75000+	—	—

Pre-1986 conversions

Exc.	V.G.	Fair
N/A	N/A	N/A

Pre-1986 dealer samples

Exc.	V.G.	Fair
N/A	N/A	N/A

Bern Stg 54 (Sturmgewehr W+F 1954)

Introduced in 1954 and chambered for the 7.5mm cartridge, this assault rifle is fitted with a 28.4" barrel including muzzle brake. Weight is approximately 11 lbs. Rate of fire is about 800 rounds per minute. Select fire. Magazine capacity is 30 rounds. Fitted with a bipod. This was an experimental model

Swiss SIG Model 51 (2nd Model) • Courtesy private NFA collection, Paul Goodwin photo

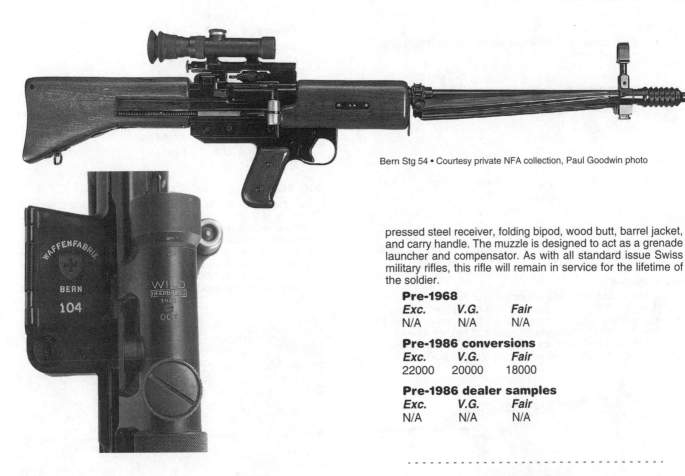

Bern Stg 54 • Courtesy private NFA collection, Paul Goodwin photo

pressed steel receiver, folding bipod, wood butt, barrel jacket, and carry handle. The muzzle is designed to act as a grenade launcher and compensator. As with all standard issue Swiss military rifles, this rifle will remain in service for the lifetime of the soldier.

Pre-1968

Exc.	V.G.	Fair
N/A	N/A	N/A

Pre-1986 conversions

Exc.	V.G.	Fair
22000	20000	18000

Pre-1986 dealer samples

Exc.	V.G.	Fair
N/A	N/A	N/A

- -

and it was produced in a number of different variants. Extremely rare.

Pre-1968

Exc.	V.G.	Fair
Too Rare to Price		

Pre-1986 conversions

Exc.	V.G.	Fair
N/A	N/A	N/A

Pre-1986 dealer samples

Exc.	V.G.	Fair
N/A	N/A	N/A

SIG Stgw 57 Assault Rifle

This rifle is a select fire chambered for the 7.5x55mm Swiss cartridge. Barrel length is 23". Box magazine capacity is 24 rounds. Weight is about 12.25 lbs. Adopted by the Swiss army with about 600,000 of these rifles produced between 1957 and 1983. It is based on the German StG 45. The rifle has a

SIG Stgw 57 rifle with close-up of receiver markings •
Courtesy Stoddard Martial collection, Paul Goodwin photo

SIG 550

This semiautomatic rifle is chambered for .223 cartridge and fitted with an 18" barrel.

Courtesy Rock Island Auction Company

NIB	Exc.	V.G.	Good	Fair	Poor
9000	7000	5500	3000	—	—

SIG 551

Same as above but fitted with a 16" barrel.

NIB	Exc.	V.G.	Good	Fair	Poor
9500	7500	6500	4000	—	—

SIG SG510-4

There are actually four different versions of this rifle. This version fires the 7.62x51mm cartridge and is fitted with a 19.7" barrel. A military version, adopted by the Swiss army, is called the Stgw 57(510-1). Magazine capacity is 20 rounds. Weight is 9.3 lbs. Rate of fire is 600 rounds per minute. Produced from 1957 to 1983. Markings are on left rear of receiver.

SIG SG 510-4 • Courtesy Thomas Nelson, *World's Assault Rifles*

Pre-1968 (Rare)

Exc.	V.G.	Fair
N/A	N/A	N/A

Pre-1986 conversions

Exc.	V.G.	Fair
20000	18000	16000

Pre-1986 dealer samples

Exc.	V.G.	Fair
15000	14000	13000

SIG 530-1

This rifle is a scaled-down version of the Stgw 57 assault rifle chambered for the 5.56x45mm cartridge. Operated by a gas piston system instead of a delayed blowback operation. Receiver is pressed steel with synthetic butt and forend. Barrel is 18" in length with compensator and grenade launcher rings. Magazine capacity is 30 rounds. Weight is about 7.5 lbs. Rate of fire is 600 rounds per minute. There is also a folding stock version of this rifle.

SIG 530-1 • Courtesy Thomas Nelson, *World's Assault Rifles*

Pre-1968

Exc.	V.G.	Fair
N/A	N/A	N/A

Pre-1986 conversions

Exc.	V.G.	Fair
N/A	N/A	N/A

Pre-1986 dealer samples

Exc.	V.G.	Fair
N/A	N/A	N/A

SIG SG540

Designed by the Swiss (SIG) and built in Switzerland, and also built in France by Manurhin beginning in 1977. This 5.56x45mm rifle is in service by a number of African and South American countries. It is fitted with an 18" barrel, 20- or 30-round magazine and has a rate of fire of 800 rounds per minute. It is fitted with a fixed stock. Its weight is 7.8 lbs. Marked "MANURHIN FRANCE SG54X" on right side of receiver. This rifle is still in production. There are also two other variants called the SG542 and SG543.

Swiss troops with Swiss Maxim. Gun is fitted with muzzle booster or blank fire adaptor • Courtesy John M. Miller

Pre-1968

Exc.	V.G.	Fair
N/A	N/A	N/A

Pre-1986 conversions

Exc.	V.G.	Fair
N/A	N/A	N/A

Pre-1986 dealer samples (Rare)

Exc.	V.G.	Fair
17500	16500	15000

MACHINE GUNS

The Swiss adopted the Maxim machine gun in 1894. The Swiss military also used the Maxim Model 1900. More recently the Swiss have used the FN MAG in addition to its own Swiss-built guns.

Model 1911 Maxim (MG11)

Built by W+F Bern and chambered for the 7.5x55mm Swiss cartridge. Fitted with a plain steel water jacket, otherwise identical to the German MG 08. This was the standard Swiss heavy machine gun and remained in service until 1951.

Swiss Model 1911 Maxim • Courtesy private NFA collection, Paul Goodwin photo

Swiss Maxim markings • Courtesy private NFA collection, Paul Goodwin photo

Pre-1968

Exc.	V.G.	Fair
35000+	32500	30000

Pre-1986 conversions

Exc.	V.G.	Fair
20000	18000	16000

Pre-1986 dealer samples (Rare)

Exc.	V.G.	Fair
N/A	N/A	N/A

Model Flab MG29

Developed by Adolph Furrer and built in 1929 by W+F Bern, this machine gun was chambered for the 7.5mm Swiss cartridge. Fed by metal belts. It was designed for use on armored vehicles and for anti-aircraft applications. The gun has a high rate of fire of about 1,100 rounds per minute. Weight is about 20 lbs. Rare.

Swiss Flab MG29 with close-up of markings • Courtesy private NFA collection, Paul Goodwin photo

Pre-1968

Exc.	V.G.	Fair
35000+	32500	—

Pre-1986 conversions

Exc.	V.G.	Fair
N/A	N/A	N/A

Pre-1986 dealer samples

Exc.	V.G.	Fair
N/A	N/A	N/A

Model 25 Light

Introduced in 1926, this gun was designed as a light air-cooled gun chambered for the 7.5x55mm Swiss cartridge. The gun uses a toggle action that opens sideways. It is fitted with a 23" barrel with slotted barrel jacket, flash hider, and bipod. The buttstock is wooden. The magazine is mounted on the right side of the gun and has a capacity of 30 rounds. Rate of fire is about 450 rounds per minute. Weight is approximately 24 lbs.

Pre-1968

Exc.	V.G.	Fair
35000+	—	—

Pre-1986 conversions

Exc.	V.G.	Fair
N/A	N/A	N/A

Pre-1986 dealer samples (Rare)

Exc.	V.G.	Fair
20000	18000	16000

Furrer M25 Light • Courtesy private NFA collection, Paul Goodwin photo

TURKEY & OTTOMAN EMPIRE

Ottoman Empire and Turkish Military Conflicts, 1870-Present

Russia and the Ottoman Empire went to war in 1877, and the Ottomans lost valuable lands and influence. These losses continued when, in 1881, Tunisia was lost to the French, and Eastern Rumelia to Bulgaria in 1885. A revolt occurred in 1909 and the Sultan was deposed, but a group of army officers known as the Young Turks were actually in control of what was left of the Empire. Pressure continued on the Ottomans with the loss of Tripoli to the Italians in 1911, and the two Balkan Wars in 1912 and 1913. With the start of World War I the Ottomans aligned with the Central Powers of Germany, Austria-Hungary, and Bulgaria. The results of World War I were a disaster for the Ottoman Empire, with the only bright spot being the Ottoman victory over Allied forces at the Battle of Gallipoli. In 1922 the Republic of Turkey was formed, ending the Ottoman Empire. Turkey remained neutral during most of World War II, until February 1945, when it declared war on Germany and Japan. After the end of the war, Turkey remained aligned with the United States and joined NATO in 1952. Beginning in 1960 and lasting almost 30 years, Turkey suffered through a number of weak governments. Turkey did not participate in the Persian Gulf War.

HANDGUNS

The Ottoman Empire purchased a number of Smith and Wesson Number 3 revolvers (see *U.S. Handguns, Smith & Wesson*). Handguns were not favored by Turkish military officers. Turkey also purchased Mauser C96 pistols (see *Germany, Handguns, Mauser*). Turkey also ordered about 70,000 Smith & Wesson Model 10 revolvers in 1980. The Turkish military also uses the Colt Model 1911A1 pistol.

Kirrikale (MKE)
Made in Ankara and Istanbul, this .380 caliber pistol is a close copy of the Walther Model PP.

Exc.	V.G.	Good	Fair	Poor
750	500	400	300	200

SUBMACHINE GUNS

Turkey uses the U.S. M3A1 submachine gun as well as the HK MP5.

RIFLES

During World War I, Turkey captured large numbers of Russian Mosin-Nagant rifles and carbines. These weapons were used by the Turks during World War I and subsequent conflicts. The Turkish crescent moon is frequently found stamped on various parts.

Over the past 40 years, Turkey has used a number of foreign-built rifles including the HK G3, the FN FAL, the M16A2, and the M1 rifle, as well as the M1 carbine.

MARTINI

Model 1874 Peabody-Martini Rifle
Chambered for the .45 Turkish centerfire cartridge and fitted with a 32.5" barrel. Blued barrel and furniture with case hardened or blued receiver. Numbered in Arabic script. About 630,000 built for Turkey for use in the Russo-Turkish wars.

Exc.	V.G.	Good	Fair	Poor
—	950	600	300	150

MAUSER

M1887 Rifle
This model is a variation of the German Model 71/84. Differences are a smaller triggerguard, a double locking bolt handle, higher comb, and 9.5x60mm Turkish blackpowder caliber. Rear sight graduated to 1,600 meters. Markings in Turkish on the receiver ring, left side rail, and rear sight. Barrel length is 30". Weight about 9.25 lbs. Tubular magazine has an 8-round capacity. About 220,000 were delivered to Turkey.

Exc.	V.G.	Good	Fair	Poor
450	350	300	200	150

M1890 Rifle
Chambered for the smokeless powder 7.65x53mm cartridge and fitted with a 29" barrel. Rear sight graduated to 2,000 meters. Weight is approximately 8.75 lbs. Markings in Turkish. Full length stock with short upper handguard. Box magazine has a 5-round capacity. About 280,000 rifles were produced for the Turkish government.

Exc.	V.G.	Good	Fair	Poor
375	280	225	180	110

M1890 Carbine
As above but with 19.5" barrel. Weight is approximately 7.75 lbs.

Exc.	V.G.	Good	Fair	Poor
450	350	300	200	150

M1893 Rifle
Similar to the Spanish Model 1893 but built with a magazine cutoff. Chambered for the 7.65x53mm cartridge and fitted with a 29" barrel. Weight is about 9 lbs. Rear sight graduated to 2,000 meters. Markings in Turkish. Full length stock with half length upper handguard. Approximately 200,000 delivered to Turkey.

Exc.	V.G.	Good	Fair	Poor
350	250	150	100	70

M1903 Rifle
Chambered for the 7.65x53mm cartridge and fitted with a 29" barrel, this model features a pistol grip full-length stock with half-length upper handguard. Magazine capacity is 5 rounds. Tangent rear sight graduated to 2,000 meters. Turkish crescent and star on the receiver. Weight is about 9 lbs. This model was the standard infantry rifle for the Turkish army from World War I to World War II.

Exc.	V.G.	Good	Fair	Poor
400	275	200	150	70

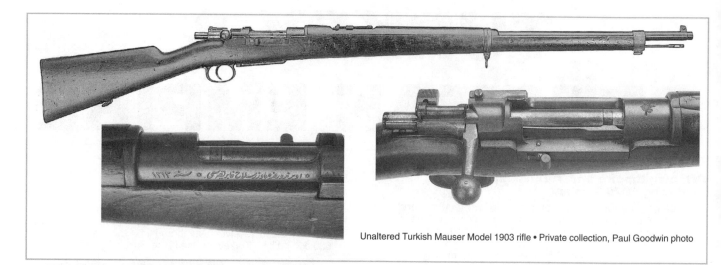

Unaltered Turkish Mauser Model 1903 rifle • Private collection, Paul Goodwin photo

SNAP SHOT
WHAT'S IT LIKE - TURKISH TUFEK 1903 MAUSER

There is no debate that Paul Mauser was one of the greatest firearm designers in history and it can be fairly stated that ALL of his bolt-action rifles were unqualified successes. Germany's first smokeless powder rifle, the Gewehr 88, had proven a disappointment leading the army to approach Mauser for a replacement. Mauser was ready for them because, by 1896 he had, for all practical purposes, perfected the genre. His Gewehr 98 used a one-piece, cock-on-opening bolt with dual frontal lugs which locked into the receiver ring and a third lug on the rear of the bolt body, while a long, non-rotating extractor insured smooth feeding and extraction. The charger-loaded, stagged-column box magazine was fast to load and fed rounds smoothly.

Within a decade the "98 Mauser" was the most popular military rifle in the world, a position it would maintain until 1945 - and beyond. The Ottoman Empire had been one of Mauser's biggest customers, buying hundreds of thousands of rifles from 1887 onwards.

I recently had the opportunity to test fire a Turkish Tufek 1903, a 98-type Mauser made shortly before the Great War. While originally chambered for the 7.65x53 cartridge, in the 1930s most were rebarreled for the 7.9x57. Years of hard service had left little of the original finish but pre-war German quality was still obvious in the rugged construction and smoothly operating bolt. Test firing was done with Turkish-made 7.9x57 ammo from the 1950s. Loading the five-round magazine with chargers was fast and fumble free and the rifle had a decent trigger. While the traditional V notch/inverted V blade sights are not my favorite set up, its 29-inch barrel provided a long sighting radius and it proved pleasingly accurate. At 100 yards my best attempt had five holes inside of 3 inches.

These rifles saw service with the Turks from 1903 through the late 1970s. I can think of no better testimonial to the genius of Paul Mauser.

Paul Scarlata

Turkish Mauser Model 1903 • Courtesy Paul S. Scarlata

M1903/38 (converted to 8mm)

Exc.	V.G.	Good	Fair	Poor
300	200	100	75	40

M1905 Carbine

Fitted with a full length stock with half length upper handguard and fitted with a 21.5" barrel chambered for the 7.65x53mm cartridge. Rear sight graduated to 1,600 meters. Magazine capacity is 5 rounds. Weight is approximately 8.25 lbs. Markings in Turkish. Only about 20,000 of these carbines were produced.

Exc.	V.G.	Good	Fair	Poor
500	350	200	110	60

M98/22 Rifle

This model is a Czech Model 98/22 with Turkish or Czech markings.

Courtesy Rock Island Auction Company

Exc.	V.G.	Good	Fair	Poor
150	100	70	50	30

M38 Short Rifle

This model is an arsenal-reworked rifle with 24" barrel chambered for the 7.92x37mm cartridge. Tangent rear sight graduated to 2,000 meters. Magazine capacity is 5 rounds. Marked with the Turkish crescent and star. Weight is about 9 lbs.

Exc.	V.G.	Good	Fair	Poor
150	100	70	50	30

M38 Short Rifle with Folding Bayonet

As above but with bayonet folding under the barrel.

Exc.	V.G.	Good	Fair	Poor
175	125	80	60	30

MACHINE GUNS

During World War I Turkey acquired the German Maxim Model 08/15 in 7.92mm caliber.

The Turkish military relies on the Turkish-built, under license, German MG3, the M1918A2, the M1919 A6, and the .50 M2 HB.

UNITED STATES

U.S. Military Conflicts, 1870-Present

After the end of the American Civil War in 1865, America turned its attention back to westward expansion. The period from 1870 to 1890 was marked by a series of Indian wars that finally ended, for the most part, in 1890. The country turned its attention overseas with the annexation of Hawaii in 1898, and Puerto Rico, Guam, and the Philippines in the Spanish-American War of 1898. A brief excursion into Mexico in 1915-1916 combated the Mexican forces of Pancho Villa. In 1917 the U.S. entered World War I on the side of the Allies and withdrew from European involvement at war's end, November 11, 1918. During World War I, the U.S. had a total of 4,350,000 military personnel, and by the end of the conflict had suffered 255,896 killed and wounded. With the Japanese attack on Pearl Harbor December 7, 1941, America once again fought against foreign aggression in the Pacific and Europe. The U.S. had 16,354,000 military personnel during World War II and suffered 1,076,200 killed or wounded during that conflict. As a world power at the end of the war in August 1945, the United States found itself taking a leading role in combating the Communist invasion of Korea in 1950. A cease fire was signed July 27, 1953. After the French defeat in the Indochina War (1946-1954), the U.S. began to increase its presence in South Vietnam and with the Tonkin Gulf Resolution of 1964 the war rapidly escalated. A cease fire in 1973 ended U.S. involvement in Vietnam with the loss of over 55,000 troops. A number of military actions took place in such places as Panama (1989) and in 1991 with the Persian Gulf War, Somalia, and later in the Balkans. In 2001, total military personnel was 1,367,700. Of these, 477,800 were in the Army and 171,300 in the Marine Corp. Special Operations forces in 2001 were: Army 15,300; Navy 4,000; and Air Force 9,320.

Bibliographical Note: There are a number of excellent books on general U.S. military firearms. Some of them are Bruce Canfield's *U.S. Infantry Weapons of World War I*, Mowbray, 2000, and *U.S. Infantry Weapons of World War II*, Mowbray, 1992. Norm Flayderman's *Flayderman's Guide to Antique American Firearms and Their Values*, 7th edition, Krause Publications, 1998. Thomas Batha, *U.S. Martial .22RF Rifles*, Excalibur Publications, 2000.

The famous flaming bomb ordnance mark with "U.S." stamp.

HANDGUNS

Bibliographical Note: There are a number of comprehensive publications on U.S. military handguns, some of which are: *U.S. Handguns of World War II, The Secondary Pistols and Revolvers*, Charles W. Pate, Mowbray, 1999. *U.S. Military Automatic Pistols, 1894-1920*, Scott Meadows, Ellis Publications, 1993.

COLT

Bibliographical Note: There are a number of excellent books on Colt firearms, many of which cover Colt's military models. A few of these books are: John W. Brunner, *The Colt Pocket Hammerless Automatic Pistols*, Phillips Publications, 1996. Keith Cochrane, *Colt Cavalry, Artillery and Militia Revolvers*, South Dakota, 1987. Kopec, Graham, and Moore, *A Study of the Colt Single Action Army Revolver*, California, 1976. For the Colt Model 1911 references see *Colt Model 1911* section.

NOTE: It should be pointed out that the U.S. military purchased and used a number of different Colt pistols and revolvers over the years. In some cases these handguns will be marked with military acceptance stamps or inspector's stamps. In other cases there may be no markings. The following models are some of the most often encountered military marked Colt handguns.

Early Military Model 1873-1877

The serial number range on this first run of military contract revolvers extends to #24000. The barrel address is in the early script style with the # symbol preceding and following. The frame bears the martial marking "US," and the walnut grips have the inspector's cartouche stamped on them. The front sight is steel as on all military models; the barrel length, 7.5". The caliber is .45 Colt, and the ejector rod head is the bull's-eye or donut style with a hole in the center of it. The finish features the military polish and case colored frame, with the remainder blued. Authenticate any potential purchase; many spurious examples have been noted. The Sioux Indian Campaign of 1876 saw its first use in a major military

Paul Goodwin photo

operation. In the Battle of the Little Bighorn, 1976, Custer's troops were armed with the Model 1873 revolver.

Exc.	V.G.	Good	Fair	Poor
55000	45000	35000	17000	6000

NOTE: Certain 3-digit and 4-digit serial numbers will command a substantial premium. Seek an expert appraisal prior to sale.

Late Military Model 1878-1891

The later Military Models are serial numbered to approximately #136000. They bear the block-style barrel address without the # prefix and suffix. The frames are marked "US," and the grips have the inspector's cartouche. The finish is the military-style polish, case colored frame, and the remainder, blued. Grips are oil-stained walnut. On the military marked Colts, it is imperative that potential purchases be authenticated, as many fakes have been noted. This was the standard sidearm during the Indian campaigns up to 1890.

Exc.	V.G.	Good	Fair	Poor
30000	22000	12000	8000	5000

NOTE: Revolvers produced from 1878 to 1885 will command a premium. Seek an expert appraisal prior to sale.

SNAP SHOT
COLT MODEL P SINGLE ACTION ARMY - CAVALRY MODEL

Seldom has the simultaneous introduction of a new firearm and a new cartridge had such an impact on the future of handguns as did the 1873 Colt Model P and the .45 Colt cartridge. Its predecessor of 1847, the mighty Walker Colt was the only revolver to equal the power of this new cartridge; so powerful that the powder charge was reduced when soldiers complained of the heavy recoil. The Model P, equipped with a 7 1/2-inch barrel, was Colt's first solid-frame revolver. In the hands of a skilled marksman it was only slightly less effective than a carbine. The new Colt was so much more advanced than were the revolver conversions of cap-and-ball models and the Colt 1872 "Open Top" that the former six guns were immediately reduced to obsolescence. However, the baby was not thrown out with that bathwater, because the new Colt retained the same familiar balance and feel of the 1851 Navy and 1860 Army models but with a solid frame. The U.S. Army's first contract with Colt for the new revolver was for 8,000 of the models. By 1891 over 37,000 Model P revolvers had been ordered by the Army.

Without a doubt, my most enduring recollection of the Model P is when Matt Dillon drew his Colt and fired with blazing speed to open the Television show "Gunsmoke" every Saturday night. The civilian name for the legendary Colt is the Peacemaker. My own favorite 7 1/2 Colt Peacemaker is a 3rd Generation Single Action Army in .44 Special. It is fully engraved and bears a gold bust of one of my heroes. A cowboy who carried a 7 1/2 Colt, served in the U.S. Army, and was President of the U.S. when the .44 Special cartridge was introduced in 1907. His name was Theodore Roosevelt. He too appreciated the balance and feel of the Cavalry Model P; the Single Action Army.

Kenny Durham

Artillery Model 1895-1903

A number of "US" marked SAAs were returned either to the Colt factory or to the Springfield Armory, where they were altered and refinished. These revolvers have 5.5" barrels and any combination of mixed serial numbers. They were remarked by the inspectors of the era and have a case colored frame and a blued cylinder and barrel. Some have been noted all blued within this variation. This model, as with the other military marked Colts, should definitely be authenticated before purchase. Some of these revolvers fall outside the 1898 antique cutoff date that has been established by the government and, in our experience, are not quite as desirable to investors. They are generally worth approximately 20 percent less.

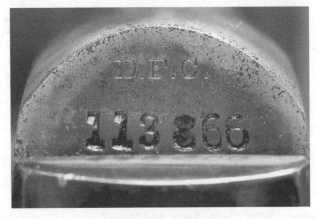

Courtesy Rock Island Auction Company

Exc.	V.G.	Good	Fair	Poor
18000	12500	8000	4000	3000

Model 1902 (Philippine/Alaskan)

This is a U.S. Ordnance contract Model 1878. It has a 6" barrel and is chambered for .45 Colt. The finish is blued, and there is a lanyard swivel on the butt. This model bears the U.S. inspector's marks. It is sometimes referred to as the Philippine or the Alaskan model. The triggerguard is quite a bit larger than standard. About 4,600 produced in serial number range 43401 to 48097.

Courtesy Butterfield & Butterfield

Exc.	V.G.	Good	Fair	Poor
5500	3500	1800	1000	600

Model 1889 Navy

The 1889 Navy is an important model from a historical standpoint, as it was the first double-action revolver Colt manufactured with a swing-out cylinder. They produced 31,000 of them between 1889 and 1894. The Model 1889 is chambered for the .38 Colt and the .41 Colt cartridges. The cylinder holds 6 shots. It is offered with a 3", 4.5", or 6" barrel, and the finish was either blued or nickel-plated. The grips are checkered hard rubber with the "Rampant Colt" in an oval molded into them. The patent dates 1884 and 1888 appear in the barrel marking, and the serial numbers are stamped on the butt.

Exc.	V.G.	Good	Fair	Poor
3000	1500	1000	600	300

NOTE: For 3" barrel add 20 percent. Add a premium for blued models.

Model 1889 U.S. Navy-Martial Model

This variation has a 6" barrel, is chambered for .38 Colt, and is offered in blued finish only. "U.S.N." is stamped on the butt. Most of the Navy models were altered at the Colt factory to add the Model 1895 improvements. An original unaltered specimen would be worth as much as 50 percent premium over the altered values shown.

Courtesy Butterfield & Butterfield, San Francisco, California

Exc.	V.G.	Good	Fair	Poor
9000	5000	2500	1000	500

Model 1892 "New Army and Navy"

This model is similar in appearance to the 1889 Navy. The main differences are improvements to the lockwork function. It has double bolt stop notches, a double cylinder locking bolt, and shorter flutes on the cylinder. The .38 Smith & Wesson and the .32-20 were added to the .38 Colt and .41 Colt chamberings. The checkered hard rubber grips are standard, with plain walnut grips found on some contract series guns. Barrel lengths and finishes are the same as described for the Model 1889. The patent dates 1895 and 1901 appear stamped on later models. Colt manufactured 291,000 of these revolvers between 1892 and 1907. Antiques before 1898 are more desirable from an investment standpoint.

Exc.	V.G.	Good	Fair	Poor
2000	1200	500	300	100

NOTE: For 3" barrel add 20 percent.

U.S. Navy Model

Exc.	V.G.	Good	Fair	Poor
3500	2750	1500	1000	750

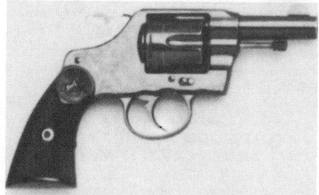

Courtesy Butterfield & Butterfield, San Francisco, California

U.S. Army Model

The initial Army purchase was for 8,000 Model 1892 revolvers, almost all of which were altered to add "Model 1894" improvements. Unaltered examples will bring a premium.

Exc.	V.G.	Good	Fair	Poor
3500	2000	800	600	400

Model 1894/96 Army Model

This model is an improved Model 1892 with a better locking mechanism for the cylinder. Many Model 1892 models were converted in this manner. By the middle of 1897, all U.S. troops were issued the Model 1894 revolver, which was the first military handgun to use smokeless powder cartridges. Marked "U.S ARMY MODEL 1894" on the bottom of the butt. The Model 1896 was identical to the Model 1894. The Model 1901 was the same as the Model 1894 with the addition of a lanyard swivel. The Model 1903 was identical to the Model 1894 with a smaller bore diameter (9.068mm) and a modified grip.

Colt Model 1896 Army with cartouche • Paul Goodwin photo

Paul Goodwin photo

Exc.	V.G.	Good	Fair	Poor
3500	2000	800	600	400

Model 1905 Marine Corps

This model is a variation of the Model 1894. It was derived from the late production with its own serial range #10001-10926. With only 926 produced between 1905 and 1909, it is quite rare on today's market and is eagerly sought after by Colt Double Action collectors. This model is chambered for the .38 Colt and the .38 Smith & Wesson Special cartridges. It holds 6 shots, has a 6" barrel, and is offered in a blued finish only. The grips are checkered walnut and are quite different than those found on previous models. "U.S.M.C." is stamped on the butt; patent dates of 1884, 1888, and 1895 are stamped on the barrel. One hundred-twenty-five of these revolvers were earmarked for civilian sales and do not have the Marine Corps markings; these will generally be found in better condition. Values are similar.

Courtesy Faintich Auction Services, Inc., Paul Goodwin photo

Exc.	V.G.	Good	Fair	Poor
4500	3500	2000	1500	750

Military Model of 1909 (New Service)

Made both in a commercial and military version, this revolver was chambered for the .45 Colt cartridge, fitted with a 5.5" barrel and walnut grips with lanyard swivel. Total military procurement was approximately 20,000 revolvers.

U.S. Army Model 1909, #30000-#50000

Marked "U.S. ARMY MODEL 1909" on butt. A total of about 18,000 were produced for the U.S. Army.

Courtesy Faintich Auction Services, Inc., Paul Goodwin photo

Exc.	V.G.	Good	Fair	Poor
3000	1500	800	300	200

U.S. Navy Model 1909, #30000-#50000

Same as above with "U.S.N." on butt. About 1,000 were produced for the U.S. Navy.

Exc.	V.G.	Good	Fair	Poor
3500	2000	1000	350	250

U.S. Marine Corps Model 1909, #30000-#50000

Checkered walnut grips. "U.S.M.C." on butt. About 1,200 were built for the Marine Corps.

Exc.	V.G.	Good	Fair	Poor
4500	2750	1350	650	450

U.S. Army Model 1917, #150000-#301000

Smooth walnut grips, 5.5" barrel, .45 ACP, model designation stamped on butt and barrel. The Model 1917 differed from the Model 1909 in that it had a shorter cylinder for half-moon clips for the .45 ACP cartridge, a wider cylinder stop lug on the sideplate, and a tapered barrel instead of a straight barrel. Blued, unpolished finish. Approximately 150,000 were purchased by the U.S. military.

Exc.	V.G.	Good	Fair	Poor
1250	850	500	300	225

Official Police (Martially marked)

This model was purchased by the military during World War II in barrel lengths of 4", 5", and 6". It has a polished blue finish. Chambered for the .38 Special cartridge. Checkered walnut grips. About 5,000 were purchased by the U.S. Army during WWII. The Defense Supply Corporation also purchased about 5,000 revolvers from Colt as well.

Exc.	V.G.	Good	Fair	Poor
750	600	400	300	150

Commando Model (Martially marked)

This model, for all intents and purposes, is an Official Police chambered for .38 Special, with 2" and 4" barrels. This model has a matte blue finish, no checkering on the cylinder latch or trigger and matte finish on top of the frame. Checkered plastic grips. Stamped "Colt Commando" on the barrel. There were approximately 50,000 manufactured from 1942 to 1945 for use in World War II.

Courtesy Richard M. Kumor Sr.

Exc.	V.G.	Good	Fair	Poor
850	750	400	200	100

NOTE: Add 100 percent for 2" barrel.

Detective Special (Martially marked)

Chambered for the .38 Special cartridge and fitted with a 2" barrel. Blued finish with checkered cylinder latch and trigger. Checkered walnut grips. Approximately 5,000 were purchased by armed forces, mostly for military intelligence and police units.

Exc.	V.G.	Good	Fair	Poor
650	500	300	150	100

Air Crewman Special (Martially marked)

This model was especially fabricated for the Air Force to be carried by their pilots for protection. It is extremely lightweight at 11 oz. The frame and the cylinder are made of aluminum alloy. It has a 2" barrel and is chambered for a distinctive .38 Special "M41" military cartridge with a chamber pressure of 16,000 pounds per square inch. The finish was blued, with checkered walnut grips. There were approximately 1,200 manufactured in 1951 with special serial numbers A.F. 1 through A.F. 1189.

Air Crewman • Courtesy Little John's Auction Service, Paul Goodwin photo

Exc.	V.G.	Good	Fair	Poor
4000	2500	1500	800	250

COLT SEMIAUTOMATIC PISTOLS

The Colt Firearms Co. was the first of the American gun manufacturers to take the advent of the semiautomatic pistol seriously. This pistol design was becoming popular among European gun makers in the late 1880s and early 1900s. In the United States, however, the revolver was firmly ensconced as the accepted design. Colt realized that if the semiauto could be made to function reliably, it would soon catch on. The powers that be at Colt were able to negotiate with some of the noted inventors of the day, including Browning, and to secure or lease the rights to manufacture their designs. Colt also encouraged the creativity of their employees with bonuses and incentives and, through this innovative thinking, soon became the leader in semiauto pistol sales—a position that they have never really relinquished to any other American gun maker. The Colt semiautomatic pistols represent an interesting field for the collector of Colt handguns. There were many variations with high enough production to make it worthwhile to seek them out.

Model 1900

This was the first of the Colt automatic pistols. It was actually a developmental model with only 3,500 being produced. The Model 1900 was not really a successful design. It was quite clumsy and out of balance in the hand and was not as reliable in function as it should have been. This model is chambered for the .38 rimless smokeless cartridge. It has a detachable magazine that holds seven cartridges. The barrel is 6" in length. The finish is blued, with a case-colored hammer and safety/sight combination. The grips are either plain walnut, checkered walnut, or hard rubber. This pistol is a Browning design, and the left side of the slide is stamped "Browning's Patent" with the 1897 patent date. Colt sold 250 pistols to the navy and 300 to the army for field trials and evaluation. The remaining 3,300 were sold on the civilian market. This model was manufactured from 1900-1903.

Standard Civilian Production

Exc.	V.G.	Good	Fair	Poor
7500	5000	3000	1250	750

NOTE: Civilian model with sight/safety combination add 40 percent.

U.S. Navy Military Model

Colt serial numbers 1001 to 1250 with navy numbers, "U.S.N. 1 TO U.S.N. 250" on the left side of frame. 250 built.

Model 1900 Navy model with sight safety • Paul Goodwin photo

Exc.	V.G.	Good	Fair	Poor
7500	6000	5000	2500	1000

U.S. Army Military Model

1st contract
100 built.

Exc.	V.G.	Good	Fair	Poor
22000	18000	10000	4000	2000

2nd contract
200 built.

Exc.	V.G.	Good	Fair	Poor
20000	16000	8000	3000	1500

Model 1902 Military Pistol

This model is a somewhat larger, heavier pistol than the 1902 Sporting Pistol. It has the same .38 ACP chambering and 6" barrel, detachable magazine holding 8 rounds. The grip of this model is larger and squared off to accommodate the larger magazine, and it has a lanyard swivel on the butt. There were

A Colt Model 1900 2nd Army contract pistol sold at auction for $5,462.50. Factory alteration and reblue. Sight safety altered by factory. Stamped "US."
Amoskeag Auction Company, Nov. 2004

approximately 18,000 manufactured between 1902 and 1929. The vast majority of these pistols were commercial models.

Early Model with Front of Slide Serrated

Model 1902 U.S. military with early front slide serrations • Paul Goodwin photo

Exc.	V.G.	Good	Fair	Poor
3500	2250	1250	750	450

SNAP SHOT
THE COLT 1902 DOUBLE ACTION REVOLVER

As everyone knows the Philippine Insurrection following the Spanish-American war clearly established the need for a .45 caliber handgun to replace the .38 caliber Model 1892 revolver. A number of stopgap measures were taken including re-issuing the Colt Single Action Army revolvers that were in deep storage. Another short-term fix was the purchase by the United States military of 5,006 Colt Double Action Revolvers, caliber .45, Model of 1902.

Commonly called the "Philippine Model" or "Alaskan Model", the latter due to the large triggerguard, these guns were not seen as a long-term solution to the handgun stopping power dilemma experienced with the previous .38 caliber revolvers.

The 1902 .45 caliber double-action revolver bore than a passing resemblance to the original Colt Single Action Army. The main reason being the size of the cylinder and the presence of the ejector rod fastened to the lower right side of the barrel. The cylinder loaded via a loading gate, but in this instance it was more of a steel flap as opposed to the curved 'gate' of the original Single Action Army.

The frame, however, on the Model 1902 double-action revolver was much different than the Colt SAA in that it featured a 'bird'shead' style of grip, complete with lanyard ring at its bottom. At the top of the grip was a prominent 'hook' to aid the shooter when firing the gun with a double-action trigger pull. The size and length of the double-action trigger was the gun's most distinguishing feature and as it was overly long it required a large triggerguard. This led some to believe it was made for use with a gloved hand; hence the 'Alaskan' moniker.

Although the Colt Model 1902 double-action revolver was never a great success, it didn't need to be because it was always viewed as a short-term solution to the failure of the .38 caliber double-action revolver.

Frank W. James

Standard Model with Rear of Slide Serrated

Model 1902 military with rear slide serrations • Paul Goodwin photo

Exc.	V.G.	Good	Fair	Poor
2500	1750	1000	500	400

U.S. Army Marked
#15001-#15200 with front serrations, 200 built.

Exc.	V.G.	Good	Fair	Poor
15000	12500	5000	2000	600

Model 1903 Hammerless, .32 Pocket Pistol

Courtesy Orvel Reichert

SNAP SHOT
THE COLT 1903 MODEL M .32 ACP PISTOL

If a self-defense pistol should have as many sharp corners as a well worn bar of soap, then the 1903 Colt Model 'M' in .32 ACP caliber is probably the best example to ever come from a major firearms manufacturer. Introduced in 1903, the Colt Model M is a blowback-operated semi-automatic pistol that was manufactured by Colt Firearms until shortly after the close of World War II. It was purchased by the United States Government in significant numbers during the war to supply general officers and agents of the OSS.

Often referred to as a 'pocket' pistol, the Colt 1903 is a little on the large size to be considered a true pocket pistol, but it is an exceptional pistol that is both thin and relatively light considering its all-steel construction. It weighs 24 ounces and the magazine holds eight rounds of .32 ACP ammo. The 1903 Colt has a frame-mounted manual safety and a grip-safety at the back of the frame. The workings and design of this grip-safety are different than that found on the 1911 pistol, but it actually works extremely well and very reliably in all examples I've encountered during my life. The magazine in held in place by a heel clip, but that isn't a bad thing for a pistol carried in a pocket or close to the body. The sights are miniscule and require good lighting for truly effective employment, but the pistol is capable of surprising accuracy when the light is sufficient.

Even though many view its chambering as anemic, the 1903 Colt is a true "classic" self-defense pistol and if you are a devotee of old movies can often be seen in the hands of Humphrey Bogart. That has to count for something in terms of charisma.

Frank W. James

A Model 1903 General Officer's pistol issued to Brigadier General Steve Chappius sold at auction for $17,250. General Chappius was awarded the DSC for his role in the defense of Bastogne. Condition is 98 percent original finish.
Rock Island Auction Company, August 2004

Model 1903 Hammerless with 4" barrel • Courtesy Richard M. Kumor Sr.

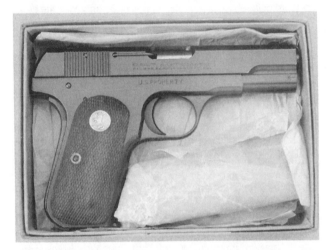

This was the second pocket automatic Colt manufactured. It was another of John Browning's designs, and it developed into one of Colt's most successful pistols. This pistol is chambered for the .32 ACP cartridge. Initially the barrel length was 4"; this was shortened to 3.75". The detachable magazine holds 8 rounds. The standard finish is blue, with quite a few nickel plated. The early model grips are checkered hard rubber with the "Rampant Colt" molded into them. Many of the nickel-plated pistols had pearl grips. In 1924 the grips were changed to checkered walnut with the Colt medallions. The name of this model can be misleading as it is not a true hammerless but a concealed hammer design. It features a slide stop and a grip safety. Colt manufactured 572,215 civilian versions of this pistol and approximately 200,000 more for military contracts. This model was manufactured between 1903 and 1945.

NOTE: A number of these pistols were shipped to the Philippine army as well as other foreign military forces, but no clear record of these shipments exist. However, about 24,000 Colt Hammerless pistols were sold to Belgium between 1915 and 1917. Serial numbers for these pistols are available (see Brunner, *The Colt Pocket Hammerless Automatic Pistols*). In addition, several thousand Colt .32 pocket pistols, as well as Colt .25 and .380 pocket models, were shipped to England during World War I. During World War II, Colt supplied about 8,000 Colt pocket pistols in various calibers to England in blued and parkerized finish marked "U.S. PROPERTY." (See Brunner.)

NOTE: Early Model 1897 patent date add 40 percent. Nickel plated with pearl grips add $100. 4" barrel to #72000 add 20 percent.

U.S. Military Model

Chambered for .32 caliber only and some of them marked "U.S. Property" on frame. Blue or parkerized finish.

NOTE: Pistols issued to General Officers will command a premium. Also, blued pistols will command a premium.

NOTE: See also *Belgium, Handguns, FN.*

Model 1903, U.S. marked, issued to Gen. Ahee • Courtesy Richard M. Kumor Sr.

Exc.	V.G.	Good	Fair	Poor
1500	950	500	300	250

Model 1908 Hammerless .380 Pocket Pistol

This model is essentially the same as the .32 Pocket Pistol, chambered for the more potent .380 ACP, also known as the 9mm Browning Short. Other specifications are the same. Colt manufactured approximately 138,000 in this caliber for civilian sales. An unknown number were sold to the military.

Standard Civilian Model

Exc.	V.G.	Good	Fair	Poor
800	650	475	350	250

NOTE: Nickel with pearl grips add $100.

Military Model M

Some have serial prefix "M," marked "U.S. Property" on frame, blued finish.

NOTE: None of these pistols were originally parkerized.

Exc.	V.G.	Good	Fair	Poor
2500	1750	750	500	300

Model 1908 Hammerless .25 Pocket Pistol

This was the smallest automatic Colt made. It is chambered for the .25 ACP cartridge, has a 2" barrel, and is 4.5" long overall. It weighs a mere 13 oz. This is a true pocket pistol. The detachable magazine holds 6 shots. This model was offered in blue or nickel-plate, with grips of checkered hard rubber and checkered walnut on later versions. This model has a grip safety, slide lock, and a magazine disconnector safety. This was another Browning design, and Fabrique Nationale manufactured this pistol in Belgium before Colt picked up the rights to make it in the U.S. This was a commercial success by Colt's standards, with approximately 409,000 manufactured between 1908 and 1941.

NOTE: A small number of these pistols were bought by the OSS during World War II from retailers or distributors. These pistols are probably not martially marked. Beware of fakes that are marked by an engraving tool.

Courtesy Orvel Reichert

Civilian Model

Exc.	V.G.	Good	Fair	Poor
600	400	300	200	100

Military Model

"U.S. Property" stamped on right frame. Very rare.

Exc.	V.G.	Good	Fair	Poor
3750	3000	1000	450	300

Model 1905 .45 Automatic Pistol

The Spanish American War and the experiences with the Moros in the Philippine campaign taught a lesson about stopping power or the lack of it. The United States Army was convinced that they needed a more powerful handgun cartridge. This led Colt to the development of a .45-caliber cartridge suitable for the semiautomatic pistol. The Model 1905 and the .45 rimless round were the result. In actuality, this cartridge was not nearly powerful enough to satisfy the need, but it led to the development of the .45 ACP. Colt believed that this pistol/cartridge combination would be a success and was geared up for mass production. The Army actually bought only 200 of them, and the total production was approximately 6,300 from 1905 to 1911. The pistol has a 5" barrel and detachable 7-shot magazine and is blued, with a case-colored hammer. The grips are checkered walnut. The hammer was rounded on the first 3,600 pistols and was changed to a spur hammer on the later models. The right side of the slide is stamped "Automatic Colt/Calibre 45 Rimless Smokeless." This model was not a commercial success for Colt—possibly because it has no safety whatsoever except for the floating inertia firing pin. The 200 military models have grip safeties only. A small number (believed to be less

than 500) of these pistols were grooved to accept a shoulder stock. The stocks were made of leather and steel and made to double as a holster. These pistols have been classified "Curios and Relics" under the provisions of the Gun Control Act of 1968.

Civilian Model

Exc.	V.G.	Good	Fair	Poor
6000	4500	2750	950	400

Military Model, Serial #1-201

Known as the 1907 Contract Pistol, it has a lanyard loop, a loaded chamber indicator, spur hammer, and a grip safety and bears the inspector's initials "K.M."

Exc.	V.G.	Good	Fair	Poor
18000	16000	8500	2500	950

COLT 1911
Model designations and prices by Karl Karash

The popularity of the Military Colt 1911/1911A1 and its commercial Government Model sisters has recently skyrocketed to unheard of levels. The reasons for this popularity, despite general economic woes that have left the stock market in tatters, are many including the recent release of such superb movies as *Saving Private Ryan*, *We Were Soldiers*, *Band of Brothers*, and *The Lost Battalion*; the availability of massive amounts of WWII historical features on The History Channel; the widespread use of the Internet and Internet auctions as a tool for buying and selling collectable pistols; and probably a general realization that the heroes of WWII are dying at a geometric rate. Every 1911/1911A1 collector has his own reasons for trying to accumulate the best, the most comprehensive, and the most complete collection. Some collectors want to have one GI (Government Issue) but not necessarily original pistol that they can shoot. Others want a collection of completely original pistols in as pristine condition as is possible that they will probably never shoot, let alone touch without wearing white gloves. The vast majority of collectors want pistols in original condition and in as good of condition as they can afford. This general tendency has recently driven up the selling prices of collectible (original) Military 1911/1911A1 pistols to unheard-of levels. Prices realized on Internet auctions seem to break new records daily. These Internet auctions are especially troubling to the older collectors who are used to one-on-one buying and selling at gun shows and gun stores. Pistols sold through the Internet auctions usually have one or more pictures that can range from seemingly crystal clear (but perhaps digitally enhanced) to very fuzzy. The pictures are often of poor quality, and hide as much as they reveal. The conventional hands-on transaction, where the buyer uses his knowledge and examines the pistol live, has been replaced by an electronic process

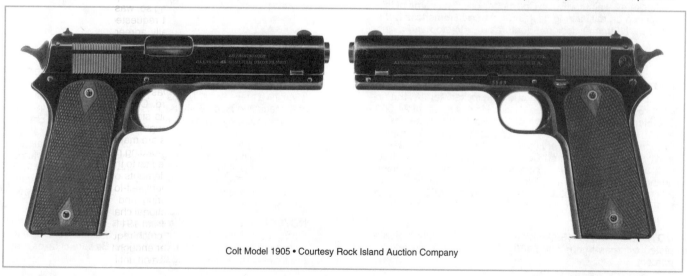

Colt Model 1905 • Courtesy Rock Island Auction Company

that almost completely isolates the buyer from the seller. Nonetheless, the popularity of these auctions seems to be increasing, and the final selling prices continue to set new records. Live auctions, too, are still popular and they too are realizing record prices, but there are big changes in the way live auctions are doing business. The most successful live auctions (the ones that attract the best guns and get the highest prices), have changed with the times and are listing their entire catalog "online" so that it can be viewed freely by millions of prospective buyers. Most smaller auction houses continue to list their sale items only in a hard copy catalog that must be purchased before even getting an idea of what is in the auction. Hopefully these latter auctions houses will realize that they must make use of information technology and list their entire catalog online or they may go the way of the DoDo bird. The dramatic increase in collecting has been largely from new inexperienced collectors. (We were all inexperienced once.) The new (and often young) collectors are usually computer savvy and have no trouble finding sites specific to 1911/1911A1 pistols, as well as a number of online gun auction sites. They are however, probably not prepared for the minefield that awaits them when they attempt to purchase a pistol based on fuzzy low resolution pictures from a person known only by a screen name. Experienced collectors know that there are a large number of refinished, restored, cold blued, altered, faked, or just plain messed-with pistols that will be represented as original. Often these undesirables can only be distinguished by a "hands on" inspection. Indeed, the army of new collectors has attracted its own group of camp followers and jackals who trail behind hoping to pick off an especially inexperienced straggler. This unsavory lot hopes to pass off a non-collectible, often messed-with pistol as if it was an original item. Usually the seller will attempt to take advantage of the inexperienced buyer by "spinning a yarn," as well as claiming knowledge of what an original should be. Greed has NOT gone out of fashion. The selling of collectibles is usually treated as "buyer beware," and legal redress is often impractical. In-depth knowledge and experience are the only weapons collectors have to protect themselves from the predators who are waiting to pounce. Before buying a pistol, read the books. Go to the auctions. Attend the gun shows. Talk to and get to know other collectors. Above all, look at original pistols, as many of them as you can get to see and hold in your hands (white gloved of course) and learn what they look like. Carrying around a pair of white cotton gloves in a plastic bag is a good way to show collectors that you are serious and will not leave fingerprints on their pistols. Never pass up the opportunity to look at a collection. Never forget that an original pistol may be worth many thousands of dollars, while a similar refinished pistol would be worth only a utility shooter price. Also remember that the widespread collector interest has generated greatly inflated prices, as well as widespread counterfeiting and fakery. Only by education in depth can the collector "hold his own" with these predators and avoid costly mistakes.

There are four reference books on the Colt .45 Auto Pistol so indispensable to collecting .45s that they will be mentioned by name: *Colt .45 Service Pistols, Models of 1911 and 1911A1*, *Colt .45 Government Models (Commercial Series)*, and *Collectors Guide to Colt .45 Service Pistols, Models of 1911 and 1911A1* all by Charles Clawson. And *U.S. Military Automatic Pistols 1894-1920* by Edward S. Meadows. Of the four books, only the "*Collectors Guide to Colt .45 Service Pistols*" third edition, by Charles Clawson is available and collectors new and old alike are urged to obtain a copy before the supply dries up. It contains the latest information as well as serial number data. One book reviewer who should probable confine his efforts to the rompings of the Royal Family has labeled Mr. Clawson's monumental work as "required reading for beginning collectors and those who need to refresh themselves on the most rudimentarly details fo the subject." This is total nonsense. Few collectors expect to be spoon fed. Some beginners who initially expect that the overlap of features between variations and exceptions should be expicitly detailed in a book, will eventually realize that most variations have overlap and that no one will

ever examine more than a smattering of examples. Consequently, no textbook will ever list all exceptions and overlaps. Most collectors who have experience in other fields of manufactured items take it for granted that "there is often the exception to the rule, and that overlap is a part of collecting." 1911/1911A1 pistols are remarkably free of the overlap and exceptions seen in other areas of collecting. To seek out and examine the overlap and the exceptions is what makes this field especially interesting for new and experienced collectors alike.

Note that since these pistols are primarily collector's items, and since originality and condition are the two factors that determine a pistol's value, the condition categories here differ from the stated categories in the front of this book. All prices are for pistols having all original parts and all finish present is factory-original finish. Broken parts, replaced parts, gun-smithing, and cold blue touch-ups will require appropriate deductions from all categories. Refinished pistols can be considered to be in or below POOR condition or as non-collectible shootable pistols. This is because once refinished, all traces of originality disappear and it becomes impossible to differentiate between a refinished pistol and a complete fake. Arsenal reworks are generally refinished, and while they are considered collectible pistols, they have their own categories that have values much lower than original pistols. The few cases of Arsenal marked but original finish pistols should probably be considered similar to original pistols but with British markings applied, and an appropriate deduction taken because the markings make the pistol less desirable than a plain pistol.

We define the condition categories in terms of the percentage of original finish remaining: Excellent = 96 percent to 98 percent original finish, VG = 90 percent to 95 percent original finish, Good = 70 percent to 89 percent original finish, Fair = 45 percent to 69 percent original finish, and Poor condition = less than 45 percent original finish.

The amount of original finish can be accurately estimated by comparing the amount and thickness of the remaining finish on each part of the pistol's surface with its portion (in percent) of the total surface area. Then, add up the percents remaining. Thinning finish only counts for a portion of area covered. For example, if the finish on the front strap covers the entire surface, but the finish is only half as dense or thick as new finish, the contribution to the total is half of 7.6 percent, or 3.8 percent, and if the remainder of the pistol was as new, the pistol would have 96.2 percent finish.

The U.S. Military Model of 1911 was developed by a combination of the genius of John Browning plus a lot of interaction and feedback from the Ordnance Department. John T. Thompson, Lt. Colonel of the Ordnance Department, informed Colt's Patented Firearms Manufacturing Company on March 29, 1911, that the (M1911) self loading pistol had passed all prescribed tests [Editor's note: And by doing so, was adopted by The Department.] and the Department requested a quote on 30,262 pistols. The price that was finally agreed on was $14.25 per pistol and one magazine. Additional magazines were to be 50 cents each. The first 40 pistols were assembled on December 28, 1911, with an additional 11 pistols assembled the next day. The first shipment, a single wooden case of M1911 pistols serial numbered from 1 to 50, was made on January 4, 1912, from the Colt factory in Hartford, Conn., to the Commanding Officer, Springfield Armory. This single crate, marked on the outside "Serial Numbers 1 Through 50," has become "the stuff that (M1911 collectors') dreams are made of." The M1911 pistol was the most advanced self loading pistol of its time and in the eyes of many, it has remained so to this date. Yet while this is probably an exaggeration, elements of its design have become adopted in most subsequent self-loading designs. While hundreds of minor manufacturing and ergonomic changes have been made, only one functional change was made to the M1911 during its manufacture from 1911 to 1945. Removal of the original dimpled magazine catch required pushing the entire catch body into the frame far enough that the fingers could grasp and turn the protruding portion until the tooth of the catch lock left its groove in the receiver. Upon coming free, the catch lock and spring (propelled by the energy stored in the spring), often flew out of sight and landed in a mud puddle. At about serial number 3190, the design was changed and a slot was cut in the magazine catch body as well as in the head of the magazine catch lock. This greatly facilitated the disassembly of the pistol, as well as reduced the chances of losing a part. Yet Colt's manufacturing changes, Ordnance Department mandated changes (including 1911/1911A1 improvements), marking, commercial derivatives, and part variations used during manufacture by the various suppliers, amounted to over 200 variations; enough to keep even the most ardent collector in pursuit for decades.

SNAP SHOT
THE ORIGINAL COLT 1911 PISTOL

The original Colt 1911 pistol was revolutionary in a number of ways, but it was NOT the gun most shooters recognize today as *"their"* beloved 1911 .45 caliber semi-auto pistol. John Browning may be given his due as a genius for designing the great 1911 pistol, but the original 1911 pistol had a number of admittedly minor, though annoying, shortcomings. These small details kept the gun from attaining what some would refer to as 'perfection', even though it remains one of the best self-defense fighting pistols ever created.

To begin with the original had the tiniest, I mean absolutely miniscule, of openings in the rear blade. This small notch in the rear blade combined with the thin front sight would have made eagles squint while trying to achieve a good sight picture.

Those who have only shot a 1911 pistol equipped with an IPSC-inspired beavertail grip safety have no idea of the degree of discomfort one can experience when shooting an original 1911 loaded with .45 caliber hardball ammo. In a short phrase, you will experience the loss of flesh. It occurs between the thumb and forefinger and is the direct result of the hammer digging a hole in the top of your hand. The U.S. Army-mandated improvements of 1926 helped to a small degree, but for most it remained a serious problem even with the 'A1' modifications.

The cut-outs in the frame behind the trigger were also part of the 1926 'A1' improvement program and these were made strictly for improved shooter comfort.

The original 1911 pistol had a flat mainspring housing and a 'long' trigger. These two features were also changed during the 1926 upgrade and are probably the two most challenged changes ever performed on the 1911 pistol. Many shooters today, myself included, prefer the flat mainspring housing, but the Army felt it was needed to improve the natural aiming of the pistol by the average soldier and thus resulted the 'arched' mainspring housing. As for the 'long' trigger, until I suffered the loss of the end of my trigger finger I preferred these as well, but now I'm forced to seek the shortest trigger available on any 1911 pistol, original or otherwise.

The best thing about the original 1911 pistol is it was created in the first place and multitudes of shooters have been eternally grateful to John Browning for it.

Frank W. James

COLT FOREIGN CONTRACT 1911 PISTOLS

NOTE: These foreign contract pistols are included as military pistols despite their commercial serial numbers. The majority of these pistols were used by foreign governments as military, police, or other government agency sidearms.

First Argentine Contract C6201-C6400
These pistols were delivered to the two Argentine battleships under construction at two U.S. shipyards. Rarely seen better than Good. Many of these pistols have been reblued and parts changed. Reblue = Fair/Poor.

Courtesy Karl Karash collection

Exc.	V.G.	Good	Fair	Poor
N/A	1200	700	525	350

Second Argentine Contract C20001-C21000
Most of these pistols have been reblued and had parts changed. Reblue = Fair/Poor.

Exc.	V.G.	Good	Fair	Poor
1800	1200	750	450	300

Subsequent Argentine 1911 Contracts after C21000
Many of these pistols have been reblued and parts changed. Reblue = Fair/Poor.

Courtesy Karl Karash collection

Exc.	V.G.	Good	Fair	Poor
1500	1000	750	450	275

Canadian Contract (About 5,000 pistols from C3000 to C14000)

Many pistols have owner's markings applied. (Condition 99-100 percent add 20-30 percent)

Exc.	V.G.	Good	Fair	Poor
2500	1800	950	550	400

First and Second British .455 Contract (200 pistols from W19000 to W19200) and 400 from W29001 to W29444

All "JJ" marked. Many pistols have owner's markings applied. (Condition 99-100 percent add 20-30 percent)

Exc.	V.G.	Good	Fair	Poor
3400	2100	1000	750	600

NOTE: Many of the .455 caliber pistols have been converted to .45 caliber by replacing their barrels. Converted pistols are usually considered no better than Good condition.

WWI British Contracts

This series is chambered for the British .455 cartridge and is so marked on the right side of the slide. The British "Broad Arrow" property mark will often be found. These pistols were made from 1915 to 1918. Some pistols are RAF marked on the left side of the frame (add 30 percent for RAF.) RAF pistols normally have an endless welded steel ring through the lanyard loop. Many of these pistols have been reblued. Reblued=Fair/Poor. (Condition 99-100 percent add 20-30 percent)

Left side of frame stamped "RAF" • Courtesy Karl Karash collection

Right side of slide stamped "CALIBER .455" • Courtesy Karl Karash collection

Exc.	V.G.	Good	Fair	Poor
2500	1700	1200	900	700

French Contract (5,000 pistols between C17800 and C28000)

Very seldom seen. (Condition 99-100 percent add 20-30 percent)

Exc.	V.G.	Good	Fair	Poor
4500	3000	1500	900	700

1911 Russian Order

This variation is chambered for .45ACP and has the Russian version of "Anglo Zakazivat" stamped on the frame (English Order). There were about 51,100 pistols between serial C21000 and C89000 shipped. This variation is occasionally encountered today, and a few have been recently imported from Russia. At least one example is known that bears the Finnish arsenal mark "SA." This pistol may have been captured by the Finns as Russia invaded Finland prior to WWII. There could be thousands of these in warehouses ready to be released on the market. A precipitous drop in value might result. One should be extra cautious if contemplating a purchase, as fakes have been noted. However, original pistols in V.G. or better condition are in high demand despite the market uncertainties. (Condition 99-100 percent add 20-30 percent)

Courtesy Karl Karash collection

Exc.	V.G.	Good	Fair	Poor
5500	4225	3100	2000	1400

Kongsberg Vapenfabrikk Model M/1912 (Norwegian) Contract SN 1-96

(Rarely seen) (Condition 99-100 percent add 20-30 percent)

Exc.	V.G.	Good	Fair	Poor
7500	4600	2800	2000	1500

Norwegian-Kongsberg Vapenfabrikk Pistol Model 1914

Serial number 97-32854 (99-100 percent add 20-50 percent)

Exc.	V.G.	Good	Fair	Poor
1500	1200	900	700	600

Kongsberg Vapenfabrikk Model 1914 (Norwegian) Waffenamt Marked

Serial number 29615-30535 Waffenamt marked on slide and barrel (99-100 percent) add 20-30 percent) CAUTION: Fakes have been reported. Any waffenamt marked pistol outside this serial range is probably counterfeit.

Exc.	V.G.	Good	Fair	Poor
4500	3500	2500	2000	1500

MODEL 1911 AUTOMATIC PISTOL, U.S. MILITARY SERIES

Colt Manufacture

Marked "MODEL OF 1911 U.S. ARMY" or "MODEL OF 1911 U.S. NAVY" on right slide, "UNITED STATES PROPERTY" on left front frame until about Serial Number 510000, then above trigger right. Serial number located on right front frame until Serial Number 7500, then above trigger right. Pistols have high polish and fire blue small parts until Serial Number 2400, then finish changed to non-reflective dull blue. Double diamond grips throughout. Dimpled mag catch from 1-3189, dimpled/slotted mag catch from Serial Number 3190 to about 6500, and slotted thereafter. Lanyard loop magazine (3 types) until about Serial Number 127000. Type 1 (stepped base until about Serial Number 4500, Type 2 (keyhole until about Serial Number 35000), and Type 3 (plain). Thereafter, two-tone non-looped magazine used through end of 1911 production. Add 5 percent if type I (Step Base) magazine is present (up to SN 4500). NOTE: as there were many variations in the early pistols which affect their rarity and value, several valuation groups follow.

Model 1911 U.S. Army marked • Paul Goodwin photo

Serial Number 43 was shipped in first case of 50 pistols on January 4, 1912 • Courtesy Karl Karash collection

Below SN 101 "LARGE" "UNITED STATES PROPERTY" and other unique features

High polish mirror finish with brilliant fire blue parts. Unmarked fully blued barrel. (Condition 99-100 percent add 20-70 percent)

Mag catches • Courtesy Karl Karash collection

Courtesy Karl Karash collection

Exc.	V.G.	Good	Fair	Poor
37500	20000	15000	10000	6000

Courtesy Karl Karash collection

Three Digit "MODEL OF 1911 U.S. ARMY" marked slide. SN 100 through SN 500

High polish mirror finish with brilliant fire blue parts. Unmarked fully blued barrel until SN 400. H (with serifs) marked on back of the barrel hood (sometimes called "barrel overhang" or "barrel extension") until SN 500. (Condition 99-100 percent add 20-70 percent)

Exc.	V.G.	Good	Fair	Poor
16500	11000	6500	4000	3000

Three-Digit "MODEL OF 1911 U.S. NAVY" marked slide. SN 501 through SN 1000

Extremely rare in original condition. High polish mirror finish with brilliant fire blue parts. H (with serifs) marked on back of the barrel hood (sometimes called "barrel overhang" or "barrel extension") (fully blued). Some seemingly original early NAVY pistols have been observed with the later dull finish. Note that below SN 2400, pistols with the later "Fine" finish are likely to have been refinished. Buyers should be very wary. However, most (or all) of the small number of observed NAVY pistols in this first batch are reported to have the later dull (fine) finish and do not have fire blue parts. (Later dull finish in this range where mirror and fire blue is expected, equal to Poor condition. (Condition 99-100 percent add 30-100 percent)

Exc.	V.G.	Good	Fair	Poor
20000	15000	10000	6000	4500

Model 1911 U.S. Navy marked • Paul Goodwin photo

Four Digit "MODEL OF 1911 U.S. ARMY" marked slide with fire blue parts

Very rare in original condition. SN 1001 to 1500 and 2001 to 2400 only. High polish mirror finish with brilliant fire blue parts. Barrel is H marked (with serifs) on rear of barrel hood. The only documented original early pistols (below SN 2400) with the later dull ("fine") finish are a very small group of test pistols in the SN 1201 to about SN 1600 range. Pistols below SN 2400 with the later "fine" finish are likely to have been refinished. Buyers should be exceptionally wary. (Later dull finish in this range less 65 percent. Unless documented test pistol then less 25 percent.) (Condition 99-100 percent add 20-70 percent)

Exc.	V.G.	Good	Fair	Poor
12000	8000	5000	3000	2000

Four-Digit "MODEL OF 1911 U.S. ARMY" marked slide without fire blue parts

Five groups SN 2401 to 2500, SN 3801 to 4500, SN 5501 to 6500, SN 7501 to 8500, SN 9501 to 9999. Dull (fine) no fire blue small parts. An H with serifs was marked on the rear of the

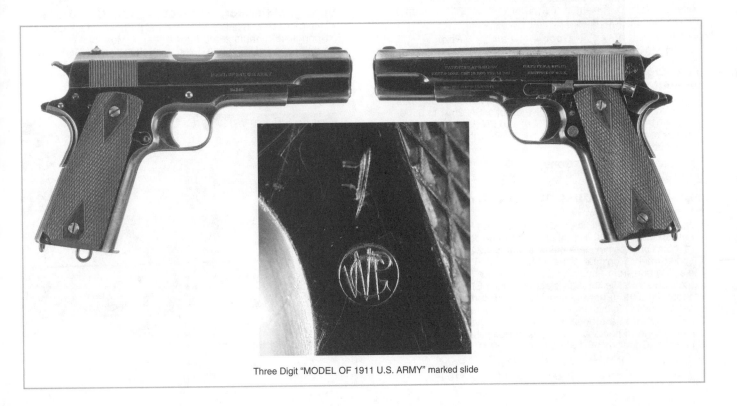

Three Digit "MODEL OF 1911 U.S. ARMY" marked slide

barrel hood until SN 7500. After 7500 no serifs. Condition 99-100 percent add 20-50 percent)

Exc.	V.G.	Good	Fair	Poor
6000	4550	3400	2450	1675

1913 production USMC SN 3501 to 3800

Rarely seen and often well used. (Condition 99-100 percent add 20-50 percent)

Courtesy Karl Karash collection

Exc.	V.G.	Good	Fair	Poor
12000	8000	6000	3500	3000

Four-Digit "MODEL OF 1911 U.S. NAVY" marked slide with fire blue parts

Extremely rare in original condition. Fire blue parts and high polish from SN 1501 to SN 2000 only. Barrel is fully blued and H with serifs marked on rear of hood. The only documented original pistols (below SN 2400) with the later dull ("fine") finish are a very small group of test pistols in the SN 1201 to about SN 1600 range. However most or all of the reported pistols of this second NAVY batch (SN 1501 to SN 2000) have the high polish and fire blue parts. Below SN 2400, pistols with the later dull ("fine") finish are likely to have been refinished. Buyers should be exceptionally wary. Later dull finish in this range where mirror and fire blue are expected equal to Poor condition. (Unless documented test pistol then less 25 percent.) (Condition 99-100 percent add 20-100 percent)

Exc.	V.G.	Good	Fair	Poor
21000	15000	8000	5000	3500

Four-Digit "Model of 1911 U.S. NAVY" marked slide without fire blue parts

Barrel is fully blued and H marked on rear of hood (H has serifs until SN 7500, then no serifs). Five groups: SN 2501 to 3500, SN 4501 to 5500, SN 6501 to 7500, and SN 8501 to 9500. All pistols should have the later dull finish. (Condition 99-100 percent add 20-30 percent)

Exc.	V.G.	Good	Fair	Poor
10200	5700	3900	2325	1675

Five-Digit Colt "MODEL OF 1911 U.S. ARMY" marked slide

No fire blue, and dull finish. Circled horse on left rear of slide until about SN 20000. H (without serifs) marked on rear of barrel hood until somewhere below about SN 24xxx. P (without serifs) marked on rear of barrel hood and H visible through ejection port from about SN 24200 to about SN 24900. H P (horizontal) visible through eject port from SN 24900 to SN about 110,000. (There is considerable uncertainty as to the barrel marking in the SN 19xxx to SN 242xx range as too few original pistols have been examined.) H on back of hood add serial range 15 percent. P on back of hood serial range add 30 percent. (Condition 99-100 percent add 20-30 percent)

Exc.	V.G.	Good	Fair	Poor
4500	3500	2500	2000	1150

1913 production SN 36401 to 37650 USMC shipment

Slide marked "MODEL OF 1911 U.S. ARMY" on ALL ORIGINAL USMC shipped pistols. (Any "USMC" marked 1911 pistol should be considered a FAKE. Rarely seen and often well used. Extremely rare in high condition. (Condition 99-100 percent add 20-100 percent)

Courtesy Karl Karash collection

Exc.	V.G.	Good	Fair	Poor
6100	4700	3350	2300	1600

Five-Digit "MODEL OF 1911 U.S. NAVY" marked slide

4 groups: SN (10501-11500, 12501-13500, 38001-44000, 96001-97537) (Condition 99-100 percent add 20-30 percent)

Exc.	V.G.	Good	Fair	Poor
6800	5300	3300	2400	1500

Six-Digit "MODEL OF 1911 U.S. NAVY" marked slide

SN (109501-110000). These 500 NAVY marked pistols were shipped to the Brooklyn Navy Yard for the Naval Militia and are more often found than most other batches. These are the only NAVY marked pistols to bear the JMG cartouche. (Condition 99-100 percent add 20-30 percent)

Exc.	V.G.	Good	Fair	Poor
7000	4800	3000	2400	1550

Springfield Armory "MODEL OF 1911 U.S. ARMY"

Dull (Rust Blued) finish, ALL external parts are identifiable as Springfield manufactured by the shape. Most pistols have a combination of "S" marked and unmarked parts. Made in four SN groups: 72571-83855, 102597-107596, 113497-120566. Springfield Armory SN 72571 to about 75000 with short stubby hammer add 15 percent. (Condition 99-100 percent add 20-30 percent)

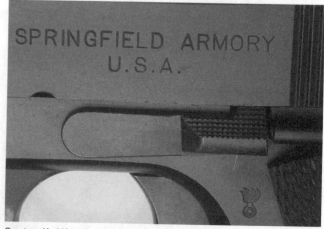

Courtesy Karl Karash collection

Exc.	V.G.	Good	Fair	Poor
7250	5000	3500	2500	1500

SERIAL NUMBERS ASSIGNED TO M1911 AND 1911A1 CONTRACTORS

Year	Serial No.	Manufacturer	Year	Serial No.	Manufacturer
1912	1-500	Colt	1917	216187-216586	Colt
	501-1000	Colt USN		216587-216986	Colt USMC
	1001-1500	Colt	1918	216987-217386	Colt USMC
	1501-2000	Colt USN		217387-232000	Colt
	2001-2500	Colt		232001-233600	Colt USN
	2501-3500	Colt USN		233601-594000	Colt
	3501-3800	Colt USMC		1-13152	Rem-UMC
	3801-4500	Colt	1919	13153-21676	Rem-UMC
	4501-5500	Colt USN		594001-629500	Colt
	5501-6500	Colt		629501-700000	Winchester
	6501-7500	Colt USN			(Assigned)
	7501-8500	Colt	1924	700001-710000	Colt
	8501-9500	Colt USN	1937	710001-711605	Colt
	9501-10500	Colt		711606-712349	Colt USN
	10501-11500	Colt USN	1938	712350-713645	Colt
	11501-12500	Colt	1939	713646-717281	Colt USN
	12501-13500	Colt USN	1940	717282-721977	Colt
	13501-17250	Colt	1941	721978-756733	Colt
1913	17251-36400	Colt	1942	756734-793657	Colt
	36401-37650	Colt USMC		793658-797639	Colt USN
	37651-38000	Colt		797640-800000	Colt
	38001-44000	Colt USN		S800001-S800500	Singer
	44001-60400	Colt		H800501-H801000	H&R (Assigned,
1914	60401-72570	Colt			none delivered)
	72571-83855	Springfield		801001-856100	Colt
	83856-83900	Colt	1943	*856405-916404	Ithaca
	83901-84400	Colt USMC		*916405-1041404	Remington-Rand
	84401-96000	Colt		*1041405-1096404	Union Switch
	96001-97537	Colt		1088726-1092896	Colt
	97538-102596	Colt		1096405-1208673	Colt
	102597-107596	Springfield		1208674-1279673	Ithaca
1915	107597-109500	Colt		1279674-1279698	Replacement
	109501-110000	Colt USN			numbers
	110001-113496	Colt		1279699-1441430	Remington-Rand
	113497-120566	Springfield	1944	1441431-1471430	Ithaca
	120567-125566	Colt		1471431-1609528	Remington-Rand
	125567-133186	Springfield		1609529-1743846	Colt
1916	133187-137400	Colt		1743847-1816641	Remington-Rand
1917	137401-151186	Colt		1816642-1890503	Ithaca
	151187-151986	Colt USMC		1890504-2075103	Remington-Rand
	151987-185800	Colt		2075104-2134403	Ithaca
	185801-186200	Colt USMC	1945	2134404-2244803	Remington-Rand
	186201-209586	Colt		2244804-2380013	Colt
	209587-210386	Colt USMC		2380014-2619013	Remington-Rand
	210387-215386	Colt Frames		2619014-2693613	Ithaca
	215387-216186	Colt USMC			

* Colt duplicated other manufacturers' serial numbers

Remington UMC "MODEL OF 1911 U.S. ARMY"

Dull finish, ALL parts MUST be Remington made. Most examples seem to have a deteriorated finish, probably due to poor surface preparation. EEC accepted and marked. Mainspring housing "E" marked, barrels "P" marked. Most pistols show thinning finish as well as flaking with little apparent wear. Pistols numbered in their own block of numbers from 1 to 21676 in large gothic letters. Almost never seen in better than Excellent condition. Beware of refinished pistols masquerading as original. Very late pistols show a one-line right side marking (add 15 percent). (Condition 99-100 percent add 20-30 percent)

Courtesy Karl Karash collection

Remington U.S. Model 1911, marked "Remington/UMC" • Paul Goodwin photo

Exc.	V.G.	Good	Fair	Poor
6200	4000	3000	2100	1600

1911 Colt "NRA" marked pistol

An unknown number of shipped Colt 1911 pistols were taken from stores and sold to NRA members. These pistols ranged from about SN 70000 to the high 150000 range. Pistols were marked N.R.A. under the serial or at the right front of the frame. The number is unknown, perhaps 300. Both crude and clever fakes abound. (Condition 99-100 percent add 20-30 percent) So few of these rare pistols have been sold publicly that these prices are intended as a rough guide only.

Courtesy Karl Karash collection

Exc.	V.G.	Good	Fair	Poor
6600	4200	2700	1800	1400

1911 Springfield "NRA" marked pistol

An unknown number of shipped Colt 1911 pistols were taken from stores and sold to NRA members. These pistols ranged from about SN 70000 to the high 129000 range. Pistols were marked N.R.A. under the serial or at the right front of the frame. The number of N.R.A. marked Springfields is unknown, but based on observed pistols, it is perhaps 600. Both crude and clever fakes abound. (Condition 99-100 percent add 20-30 percent) Note that at one time these NRA marked pistols sold for about twice what a normal Springfield sold for, but lately, the very few examples sold seem to have sold for about the same price as a normal Springfield. This trend may reflect the undocumentability of the NRA marking as well as the ease with which the mark can be counterfeited.

Courtesy Karl Karash collection

Exc.	V.G.	Good	Fair	Poor
7250	6100	3600	2500	1500

1915-1918 Springfield Suspended Serial Numbers Reassigned to Colt

These receiver were apparently shipped as replacement parts (incomplete pistols) because they lack an Ordnance acceptance mark. Springfield's unused assigned serial numbers (SN 128617 to SN 133186) were re-assigned to Colt when Springfield ceased production of 1911 pistols. These receivers were apparently numbered and used as needed until late 1917 when a new series of serial numbers were assigned (SN 210387 through SN 215386) These receivers are found with most any post 1911 slide. (Condition 99-100 percent add 20-30 percent)

Exc.	V.G.	Good	Fair	Poor
4600	3400	2500	1700	1200

Six-Digit Colt 1915 - 1918 "MODEL OF 1911 U.S. ARMY" marked slide.

Dull blue finish. Vertically oriented "P H" or "H P" marked on barrel, visible through eject port from about SN 110000 to SN 425000. Slides marked "MODEL OF 1911 U.S. ARMY" on ALL ORIGINAL USMC shipped pistols. Any "USMC" marked 1911 pistol should be considered a FAKE. (Condition 99-100 percent add 20-30 percent)

Exc.	V.G.	Good	Fair	Poor
3800	2500	1800	1500	1100

The following categories are listed relative to the pricing of the previous "Six-Digit" SN Colt 1915-1918 "MODEL OF 1911 U.S. ARMY" marked slide:

1916 production with "S" marked frame, slide, and barrel add 60 percent

1916 production with partial "S" marked frame, slide, or barrel add 35 percent

1916 production with normally marked frame, slide, and barrel add 20 percent

1916 production 151187 to 151986 USMC shipment add 45 percent (Often well used)

1917 production 185801 to 186200 USMC shipment add 45 percent (Often well used)

1917 production 209587 to 210386 USMC shipment add 45 percent (Often well used)

1917 production 210387 to 215386 replacement frames add 45 percent (Rarely seen)

1917 production 215387 to 216186 USMC shipment add 45 percent (Rarely seen)

1917 production 216187 to 216586 ARMY transferred from USMC add 15 percent (Rarely seen)

1917 production 216587 to 217386 USMC shipment add 45 percent (Rarely seen)

1917 production 223953 to 223990 NAVY (ARMY marked) add 15 percent

1917 production 232001 to 233600 NAVY (ARMY marked) add 15 percent

1918-1919 production with eagle over number acceptance mark

Often called the Black Army because the coarse wartime finish appeared almost black. The black finish started about SN 375000. No inspector's cartouche from about serial number 302000 to end of 1911 production (SN 625000). Barrel marked with letters H and P through about SN 425000. "HP" with a common leg, horizontal orientation visible through ejection port from about SN 425000 to end of 1911 production. (If flaking present deduct 25 percent, watch out for reblue if no flaking present.) (Condition 99-100 percent add 20-30 percent)

Courtesy Karl Karash collection

Exc.	V.G.	Good	Fair	Poor
3900	2500	1700	1250	900

North American Arms of Montreal QB "1911"

Made for U.S. but none delivered to Army. Less than 100 pistols assembled from parts. Rarely seen. Numbered on trigger under left grip and on left rear slide. Similar to five-digit Colt "ARMY" marked slide, but add 500 percent. (Condition 99-100 percent add 20-30 percent) So few of these pistols have been sold publicly that these prices are intended as a rough guide only.

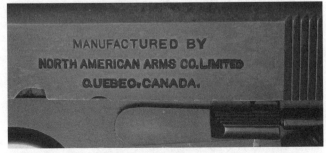

1911 North American Arms of Montreal • Courtesy Karl Karash collection

Exc.	V.G.	Good	Fair	Poor
26000	20000	16000	10000	7300

A Model 1911 North American Arms Co. of Quebec, Canada, sold at auction for $16,800. Documented. Condition is 15 to 30 percent blue with light scratches, dings, and minor nicks. Grips are very good.
Little John's Auction Service, Inc., Jan. 2005

Paul Goodwin photo

Four-Digit X Numbered Rework

These pistols were renumbered when their original serial numbers were either defaced, obliterated, or became too light to read during rebuilding or refinishing. The four-digit X prefix serial numbers (X1000 through X4385) were assigned after WWI (1924) and were used by Springfield through 1953. All are considered "Arsenal Refinished."

Exc.	V.G.	Good	Fair	Poor
1350	1100	800	750	600

"Military to Commercial Conversions"

Some 1911 military pistols that were brought home by GIs were subsequently returned to the Colt factory by their owners for repair or refinishing. If the repair included a new barrel, the pistol would have been proof fired and a normal verified proof-mark affixed to the triggerguard bow in the normal commercial practice. If the pistol was refinished between 1920 and 1942, the slide would probably be numbered to the frame again in the normal commercial practice. Slides were numbered on the bottom disconnector rail during part of 1920, and after that they were numbered under the firing pin stop plate. These pistols are really a re-manufactured Colt pistol of limited production and should be valued at least that of a contemporary 1911A1 commercial pistol. (Pistols without VP or numbered slide usually cannot be authenticated, deduct 60 percent). Very seldom seen. (Condition 99-100 percent add 30 percent).

Exc.	V.G.	Good	Fair	Poor
2100	1500	1200	950	750

MODEL 1911A1 AUTOMATIC PISTOL MILITARY MODEL

COLT FOREIGN CONTRACT 1911A1 PISTOLS

These foreign contract pistols are included as military pistols despite their commercial serial numbers. These pistols were supplied by Colt to foreign governments as military, police, or other government agency sidearms. Many of these pistols have recently been imported into the USA, but only a few have been in "collectible, original" condition. Most have been refinished and sold at utility prices. The prices that the handful of original pistols sell for have been kept down by their poorer brothers and sisters. These original finish pistols, when found, may be some of the few remaining bargains out there. Pistols were shipped to Mexico, Philippines, Shanghai, Haiti, etc. but specific prices for these variations are not practical because they are seldom seen.

Argentine Army Modello 1927

Serial numbered 1 through 10000. Marked "EJERCITO AR-GENTINO. Colts Cal.45 MOD.1927" on the right slide, and "Colts Pt. F.A. MFG. Co....etc." on the left slide. VP marked under left stock. Serial numbered on top of slide, under mainspring housing. Most of these pistols have been reblued and original finish pistols are very rare. Prices shown are for original pistols and the common reblued pistols would be equal to the Fair/Poor categories, depending on appearance.

Exc.	V.G.	Good	Fair	Poor
1000	700	500	400	300

Argentine Army "SIST.COLT CAL. 11.25mm MOD 1927"

Serial numbers extend to over 112000. Made in Argentina under Colt license. This is a high quality 1911A1 copy with parts that generally interchange with Colt's 1911A1s. Marked "SIST.COLT CAL.11.25mm MOD 1927" on the right slide, and "D.G.F.M.-(F.M.A.P.)." on the left slide. Serial numbered on top of slide, frame, and barrel. Many of these pistols have been reblued, although original finish pistols are often seen. Prices shown are for original pistols and the more common reblued pistols would be equal to the Fair/Poor categories, depending on appearance.

Exc.	V.G.	Good	Fair	Poor
700	600	500	400	325

Argentine Navy, Coast Guard, Air Force, or Army Contract "Government Model"

Pistols serial numbered from about C130000 to about C190000. Marked "Armada Nacional," "Marina Argentina," "Aeronautica Argentina" or "Ejercito Argentina" on the right slide, and "Colts Pt. F.A. MFG. Co....etc." on the left slide. VP marked on left triggerguard bow. Serial numbered and marked as were normal commercial pistols. Most of these pistols have been reblued and original finish pistols are seldom seen. Prices shown are for original pistols and the common reblued pistols would be equal to the Fair/Poor categories, depending on appearance.

Exc.	V.G.	Good	Fair	Poor
750	600	500	400	300

Argentine Navy, Coast Guard, Air Force, or Army Pistols

Serial numbered through about 112000. Marked "Armada Nacional," "Marina Argentina," "Aeronautica Argentina," or "Ejercito Argentina" on the right slide, and "D.G.F.M.-(F.M.A.P.)." on the left slide. Most of the recent imports of these pistols have been reblued and collectable original finish pistols are seldom seen except when from older collections. Prices shown are for original pistols, and the common reblued pistols would be equal to the Fair/Poor categories, depending on appearance.

Argentine Seal • Courtesy Karl Karash collection

Exc.	V.G.	Good	Fair	Poor
550	450	350	270	225

Argentine Navy "Government Model" With Swartz Safety

Serial numbered from about C199000 to about C2010001. Marked "Republica Argentina, Armada Nacional-1941" on the right slide, and "Colts Pt. F.A. MFG. Co....etc." on the left slide. VP marked on left triggerguard bow. Serial numbered and marked as were normal 1941 commercial pistols. Most or all of these pistols have the Swartz safeties. Most of these pistols have been reblued or parkerized when imported, and original finish collectable pistols are very rare. Prices shown are for original pistols, and the common reblued pistols would be equal to the Fair/Poor categories, depending on appearance. The very rare Swartz safeties (only a few thousand total were produced) in these pistols are under-appreciated by most collectors, and make this variation highly undervalued, especially for the few original finish pistols. The Swartz firing pin block safety can be observed by pulling the slide back all the way and looking at the top of the frame. A Swartz safety equipped 1911A1 pistol will have a second pin protruding up, next to the conventional disconnector pin. This second pin pushes a spring-loaded piston in the rear part of the slide that is visible when the slide is pulled back and the slide is viewed from underneath. This piston, in turn, blocks the firing pin when relaxed. A second Swartz safety (the Swartz Sear Safety) is usually built into pistols equipped with the Swartz firing pin block safety. The sear safety can sometimes be detected by the drag marks of the notched sear on the round portion of the hammer that the sear rides on. Pulling the hammer all the way back will expose these drag marks if they are visible. Presence of the drag marks however, does not insure that the Swartz modified sear safety parts are all present.

Exc.	V.G.	Good	Fair	Poor
1700	1200	900	700	500

Brazilian Army Contract "Government Model"

Pistols serial numbered from about C190000 to about C214000. Marked "Ejercito Brazilia" on the right slide, and "Colts Pt. F.A. MFG. Co....etc." on the left slide. VP marked on left triggerguard bow. Serial numbered and marked as were normal commercial pistols. Only a few of these complete pistols have made it to the USA, but many slides were sold as surplus parts when Brazil converted from .45 Cal to 9mm. Most or all of these slides have been reblued and original finish pistols are very rarely seen. Prices shown are for original pistols, and the common reblued pistols would be equal to the Poor category or below, depending on appearance. Separate slides would have the value of a high quality "after market" part.

Exc.	V.G.	Good	Fair	Poor
1500	1100	900	700	500

COLT MANUFACTURE

Service Model Ace

In 1937 Colt introduced this improved version of the Ace pistol. It utilizes a floating chamber invented by David "Carbine" Williams, the firearms designer who invented short stroke piston that is the basis of the M1 carbine while serving time on a southern chain gang. Colt advertised that this floating chamber gave the Service Model Ace the reliability and feel that the Ordnance Department wanted. However the floating chamber probably reduced the long term reliability of the pistol since it tends to lead-up with most ammunition. The serial number is prefixed by the letters "SM." The external configuration is the same as the Ace, and the slide is marked "COLT SERVICE MODEL ACE .22 LONG RIFLE." Colt sold most to the Army and a few on a commercial basis. There were a total of 13,803 manufactured before production ceased in 1945. (99-100 percent finish add 33 percent) Original boxes usually bring a healthy premium of 10 percent to 20 percent.

Blued Pistols (before serial #SM3840)

Exc.	V.G.	Good	Fair	Poor
6000	3000	2000	1600	1350

Parkerized Pistols (after about serial # SM3840)

Exc.	V.G.	Good	Fair	Poor
3000	2000	1500	1000	700

Transition Model of 1924

SN 700001 to 710000. Some very early Transition pistols (SN 700004 and SN 700009) have been observed to have matching numbered slides. The number of pistols so numbered is not known, but if enough pistols surface, the serial number range may eventually be deduced. A pistol with a matching numbered slide will probably bring a premium. Made in 1924. All were accepted by Walter T. Gordon and marked with the "G" forms the outer circle is seen through about SN 7022000. The second type has an outer circle around the "G." Brushed blue finish, all 1911A1 features (arched mainspring housing, short checkered trigger, long tang on grip safety, trigger finger cut-outs, full checkered walnut grips, etc.). However, they retained the "MODEL OF 1911 U.S. ARMY" slide marking. No verified proof or final inspector's mark on triggerguard bow, interlaced "H P" and "K" marked barrel, and serifed "H" over firing pin stop plate. (Add 20-30 percent for 99-100 percent finish.)

Courtesy Karl Karash collection

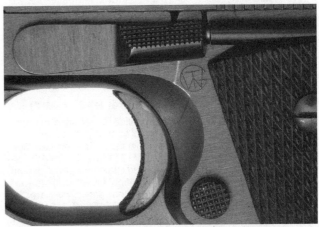

First Type acceptance markings • Courtesy Karl Karash collection

Exc.	V.G.	Good	Fair	Poor
6200	4500	3200	2000	1300

First Transition Model of 1937

SN 710001 to about 711001. Numbered slide under firing pin stop plate. No "P" marking on frame or slide. Brushed blue finish, all 1911A1 features (arched mainspring housing, short checkered trigger, long tang on grip safety, trigger finger cut-outs, full checkered walnut grips, etc.). However, they retained the "MODEL OF 1911 U.S. ARMY" slide marking. Verified proof and final inspector's mark on triggerguard bow. "COLT .45 AUTO" marked magazine floorplate with flattened letters and "COLT .45 AUTO" marked barrel. Extremely rare. Pistols with mis-matched number (but still second type 1937 slide) deduct 40 percent. (Add 30-40 percent for 99-100 percent finish.) So few of these pistols have sold publicly that these prices are intended as a rough guide only.

Exc.	V.G.	Good	Fair	Poor
8000	6500	5000	4000	2200

SNAP SHOT
THE COLT ACE (EARLY VERSION)

Work on a .22 caliber version of the Government Model .45 caliber pistol began almost as soon as the 1911 pistol was adopted by the United States military. The reason was simple. The government wanted a 'gallery' pistol chambered for .22 rimfire ammo to enable an easy means of teaching soldiers how to shoot a pistol. The early efforts with the full size Government Model came to nothing, but John Browning did create a pistol that most recognize today as the Woodsman.

The work continued, however, in trying to build a Government Model sized pistol in .22 rimfire. In mid-1925, Colt submitted for trial a blowback version of the .45 service pistol that was rejected and returned for modification. Colt continued on the project and by 1930 Colt introduced the "ACE" which was marketed to the civilian sporting arms market. It featured an operating system which was simplified for a .22 rimfire chambering. The locking lugs on top of the barrel and the link under the barrel were eliminated. A solid cross block was substituted for the link and a much smaller recoil spring replaced the original spring meant for use with the .45 ACP cartridge. The gun then became a pure blowback design.

The Colt ACE employed a 10-round magazine and featured a fully adjustable target rear sight and a standard front sight blade. The NRA reviewed the new ACE in 1931 and discovered the .22 cartridge did not possess sufficient power to consistently operate the heavy .45 style slide. Colt sold 13 ACE pistols to the army in 1931 with a total of 206 being delivered by 1936 when the U.S. Army stopped purchase in favor of another design.

In 1938, the "Service ACE" was introduced which utilized the Carbine Williams 'floating chamber' that improved the performance of the design with .22 rimfire ammunition and the Colt ACE was relegated to the annuals of firearms trivia.

Frank W. James

Second Transition Model of 1937

About SN 711001 to 712349. Numbered slide under firing pin stop plate. "P" marking on frame and top of slide. Brushed blue finish, all 1911A1 features (arched mainspring housing, short checkered trigger, long tang on grip safety, trigger finger cutouts, full checkered walnut grips, etc.). However, they retained the "MODEL OF 1911 U.S. ARMY" slide marking. Verified proof and final inspector's mark on triggerguard bow. "COLT .45 AUTO" marked magazine floorplate with flattened letters and "COLT .45 AUTO" marked barrel. Extremely rare. Pistols with mis-matched number (but still second type 1937 slide) deduct 40 percent. (Add 30-40 percent for 99-100 percent finish.) So few of these rare pistols have sold publicly that these prices are intended as a rough guide only.

Exc.	V.G.	Good	Fair	Poor
8000	6500	5000	4000	2200

Model of 1911A1, 1938 Production

SN 712350 to 713645. Numbered slide under firing pin stop plate. "P" marking on frame and top of slide. No markings on right side of slide. Brushed blue finish, all 1911A1 features (arched mainspring housing, short checkered trigger, long tang on grip safety, trigger finger cutouts, full checkered walnut grips, etc.). Right side of receiver is marked "M1911A1 U.S. ARMY" forward of the slide stop pin, and "United States Property" behind the slide stop pin. Verified proof and final inspector's mark on triggerguard bow. Most are "H" marked on left side by magazine catch. "COLT .45 AUTO" marked magazine floorplate with flattened letters and "COLT .45 AUTO" marked barrel. Extremely rare. Pistols with mis-matched number (but still second type 1937 slide) deduct 40 percent. (Add 50 percent to 100 percent for 99-100 percent finish.) So few of these rare pistols have been sold publicly that these prices are intended as a rough guide only.

NOTE: All Military .45 cal. pistols after 710000 were officially M1911A1, although they were first called Improved M1911.

Exc.	V.G.	Good	Fair	Poor
20000	15000	10000	6000	4500

Model of 1911A1, 1939 Production (1939 NAVY)

SN 713646 to 717281. Numbered slide under firing pin stop plate. "P" marking on frame and top of slide. No markings on right side of slide. Brushed blue finish. Shortened hammer. Right side of receiver is marked "M1911A1 U.S. ARMY" forward of the slide stop pin, and "United States Property" behind the slide stop pin. Verified proof and final inspector's mark on triggerguard bow. Full checkered walnut grips. Most are "H" marked on left side by magazine catch. "COLT .45 AUTO" marked magazine floorplate with flattened letters, and "COLT .45 AUTO" marked barrel. Extremely rare. Pistols with mis-matched number (but still second type 1937 slide) deduct 25 percent. (Add 20-30 percent for 99-100 percent finish.)

Exc.	V.G.	Good	Fair	Poor
5000	3500	2500	2000	1400

Model of 1911A1, 1940 Production (CSR)

SN 717282 to 721977. Numbered slide under firing pin stop plate. "P" marking on frame and top of slide. No markings on right side of slide. Brushed blue finish. Shortened hammer. Right side of frame is marked "M1911A1 U.S. ARMY" forward of the slide stop pin, and "United States Property" behind the slide stop pin. Verified proof and final inspector's mark on triggerguard bow. "CSR" (Charles S. Reed) marked on left side below slide stop. "COLT .45 AUTO" marked magazine floorplate with flattened letters, and "COLT .45 AUTO" marked barrel. Full checkered walnut grips but some pistols may have early brittle plastic grips. Extremely rare. Pistols with mis-matched number (but still second type 1937 slide) deduct 25 percent. (Add 20-30 percent for 99-100 percent finish.)

Courtesy Karl Karash collection

Exc.	V.G.	Good	Fair	Poor
5100	3500	2500	1800	1350

Model of 1911A1, 1941 Production (RS and early WB)

SN 721978 to 756733. Numbered slide under firing pin stop plate. "P" marking on frame and top of slide. No markings on right side of slide. Brushed blue finish through about SN 736000. Parkerizing was used thereafter until the end of Colt production. Any Colt pistol after about SN 737000 with a blued finish is likely to be a FAKE. Shortened hammer. Right side of frame is marked "M1911A1 U.S. ARMY" forward of the slide stop pin, and "United States Property" behind the slide stop pin. Verified proof and final inspector's mark on triggerguard bow. "RS" (Robert Sears) marked on left side below slide stop starting at about SN 723000, ending about 750500. After about SN 750500, pistols were marked "WB" (Waldemar S. Broberg). "COLT .45 AUTO" marked magazine floorplate with flattened letters, and "COLT .45 AUTO" marked barrel. Early pistols may have wood grips, later pistols have hollow back (without ribs) plastic grips. Prices are for blued finish. (Parkerized finish less 25 percent.) Extremely rare. Pistols with mis-matched number (but still second type 1937 slide) deduct 20 percent. (Subtract 5 percent to 10 percent for British proofs, most collectors prefer virgin pistols. Add 20-50 percent for 99-100 percent finish.)

Exc.	V.G.	Good	Fair	Poor
4250	2950	2000	1500	1200

Model of 1911A1, 1942 Production (WB)

SN 756733 to about 856100. Numbered slide under firing pin stop plate. All subsequent Colt made 1911A1 pistols have a "P" marking on frame and top of slide. No markings on right side of slide. Parkerized finish. Shortened hammer. Right side of frame is marked "M1911A1 U.S. ARMY" forward of the slide stop pin, and "United States Property" behind the slide stop pin. Colt plastic stocks with narrow concave rings and hollow backs with no ribs through SN 803000, wide rings around screws and hollow backs with ribs thereafter. A number of original in the SN 820000 range have been observed with 1911 type slide stops. This is a good example of a seemingly out of sequence part that would often be changed by someone with a hair trigger trying to make his pistol "Like the Book" when in reality they would be messing up an original rare variation. Verified proof and final inspector's mark on triggerguard bow, and "COLT .45 AUTO" marked barrel. "WB" (Waldemar S. Broberg) marked on left side below slide stop. "COLT .45 AUTO" marked magazine floorplate with flattened letters, sand blasted bottom. (Subtract 5 percent to 10 percent for British proofs, most collectors seem to prefer virgin pistols. Add 20-30 percent for 99-100 percent finish.)

Exc.	V.G.	Good	Fair	Poor
2600	1900	1500	1200	875

Model of 1911A1, 1942 NAVY

3982 pistols shipped to Naval supply depots, Oakland, Calif., and Sewalls Point, Va. Numbered SN 793658 to SN 797639. Numbered slide under firing pin stop plate. "P" marking on frame and top of slide. No markings on right side of slide. Parkerized finish. Shortened hammer. Right side of frame is marked "M1911A1 U.S. ARMY" forward of the slide stop pin, and "United States Property" behind the slide stop pin. Verified proof and final inspector's mark on triggerguard bow. "WB" (Waldemar S. Broberg) marked on left side below slide stop. "COLT .45 AUTO" marked magazine floorplate with flattened letters, sand blasted bottom, and "COLT .45 AUTO" marked barrel. (Subtract 5 percent to 10 percent for British proofs, most collectors seem to prefer virgin pistols. Add 20-30 percent for 99-100 percent finish.)

Exc.	V.G.	Good	Fair	Poor
3100	2000	1700	1400	1000

Model of 1911A1, Singer Manufacturing Co., Educational Order 1941

Exactly 500 pistols accepted and shipped. "J.K.C." (John K. Clement) marked on left side below slide stop. At least two un-numbered (and not marked United States Property) pistols were made and retained by employees. Slightly dull blue finish, brown plastic hollow-back grips, unmarked blue magazine, wide spur hammer, checkered slide stop, thumb safety, trigger, and mainspring housing. About 100 of the original 500 are known. Very Rare and most highly desired. Exercise caution when contemplating a purchase as fakes, improved, and re-blued models abound. Be extra cautious with an example that is 98 percent or better. (Add 50 percent for 99-100 percent finish. Original pistols un-numbered or numbered with out-of-sequence numbers subtract 50 percent to 70 percent. Subtract 5 percent to 10 percent for British proofs, most collectors seem to prefer virgin pistols. Reblued, restored subtract 90 percent to 95 percent.)

Singer Legend • Courtesy Karl Karash collection

Exc.	V.G.	Good	Fair	Poor
36000	25000	17500	14000	9000

Rock Island Arsenal Replacement numbers

SN 856101 to 856404. Replacement numbers issued to allow a pistol whose number had been defaced or worn away during refinishing to be numbered again. Very rare; only one known.

Exc.	V.G.	Good	Fair	Poor
1500	1200	900	750	600

Model of 1911A1, Military. 1943 Production (GHD marked)

SN 867000 to about 1155000. Colt had its own serial numbers assigned within this range, but in addition, Colt duplicated Ithaca's serial numbers between 865404, and 916404 as well as Remington Rand's between 916405 and 958100, and US&S's between 1088726 and 1092896. Numbered slide under firing pin stop plate until about SN 1140000. "P" marking on frame and top of slide. Parkerized. Right side of frame is marked

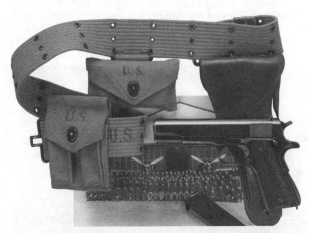

"M1911A1 U.S. ARMY" forward of the slide stop pin, and "United States Property" behind the slide stop pin. Verified proof and final inspector's mark on triggerguard bow. "GHD" (Guy H. Drewry) marked on left side below slide stop. Plain blued or contract magazine, and "COLT .45 AUTO" marked barrel. Colt plastic stocks with wide rings around screws. (Subtract 5 percent to 10 percent for British proofs, most collectors prefer virgin pistols. Add 20-30 percent for 99-100 percent finish.) Colt in Ithaca or Remington Rand range add 10 percent, Colt in U.S.& S range add 20 percent.

Pre (Approx.) SN 114000 with matching slide

Exc.	V.G.	Good	Fair	Poor
2350	1650	1200	900	750

Post (Approx.) SN 114000 with matching slide

Exc.	V.G.	Good	Fair	Poor
2000	1550	1225	1000	875

Model of 1911A1, Commercial to Military Conversions. 1943 Production

(A few were WB marked, most were GHD marked.) SN 860003 to about 867000. Numbered slide under firing pin stop plate. "P" marking on frame and top of slide. Commercial markings on right side of slide. Parkerized finish over previously blued finish. Original Commercial SN peened and restamped with military numbers. Most have the Swartz grip safety cutouts in slide and frame but not the Swartz parts. None of the Commercial to military conversions have the Swartz "sear safety." No slides marked "NATIONAL MATCH" have been reported. If any exist, a NM slide pistol would command a premium. Shortened hammer. Right side of frame is marked "M1911A1 U.S. ARMY" forward of the slide stop pin, and "United States Property" behind the slide stop pin. Verified proof and final inspector's mark on triggerguard bow. "GHD" (Guy H. Drewry) marked on left side below slide stop. "COLT .45 AUTO" marked magazine floorplate with flattened letters, sand blasted bottom. Colt plastic stocks with wide rings around screws. (Subtract 5 percent to 10 percent for British proofs, most collectors seem to prefer virgin pistols. Add 20-30 percent for 99-100 percent finish. Add 10-30 percent for NM marked slide.)

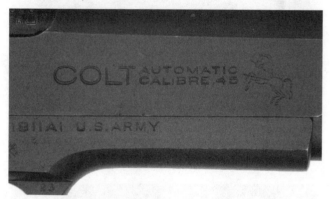

Courtesy Karl Karash collection

Exc.	V.G.	Good	Fair	Poor
3100	2150	1750	1500	1000

Model of 1911A1, Military with Commercial Slide. 1943 Production (GHD marked)

SN 867000 to about 936000. Perhaps a few hundred total. Numbered slide under firing pin stop plate. "P" marking on frame and top of slide. Commercial markings on right side of slide. Parkerized finish over previously blued finish (slide only). Most have the Swartz grip safety cutouts in slide but not in frame. None have the Swartz parts. Frames are generally new military manufacture. Shortened hammer. Right side of frame is marked "M1911A1 U.S. ARMY" forward of the slide stop pin, and "United States Property" behind the slide stop pin. Verified proof and final inspector's mark on triggerguard bow. "GHD" (Guy H. Drewry) marked on left side below slide stop. May have "COLT .45 AUTO" marked magazine floorplate with flattened letters with sand blasted bottom or plain blued magazine. Colt plastic stocks with wide rings around screws. Barrels marked "COLT .45 AUTO." (Subject 5-10 percent for British proofs, most collectors seem to prefer virgin pistols) (Add 20-30 percent for 99-100 percent finish.)

Exc.	V.G.	Good	Fair	Poor
3000	2400	1900	1400	900

Model of 1911A1, Canadian Broad Arrow/C marked 1943 Production

Marked with the "C" broad arrow Canadian Property mark on the left rear of the slide and left of the receiver above the magazine catch. 1515 pistols (GHD marked) SN 930000 to about 939000. Numbered slide under firing pin stop plate. "P" marking on frame and top of slide. Commercial markings on right side of slide on a few, otherwise blank. Parkerized finish. Right side of frame is marked "M1911A1 U.S. ARMY" forward of the slide stop pin, and "United States Property" behind the slide stop pin. Verified proof and final inspector's mark on triggerguard bow. "GHD" (Guy H. Drewry) marked on left side below slide stop. All appear to have British proofs except a few pistols in "Fair" condition that were recently sold at auction. These pistols without British proofs were apparently used in Canadian prisons and recently released. Beware non-British marked Canadian pistols in better than "Good" condition, as at least one of these same former prison pistols has appeared for sale in "New" condition. Barrels marked "COLT .45 AUTO." Most have

plain blued magazine. Colt plastic stocks with wide rings around screws. (Add 30 percent for 99-100 percent finish. Add 25 percent for numbered commercial marked slide.)

Courtesy Karl Karash collection

Exc.	V.G.	Good	Fair	Poor
2500	1900	1500	1200	900

Model of 1911A1, Military. 1944 Production (GHD marked)

SN 1,155,000 to about SN 1208673, and 1609529 to 1720000. Un-numbered slide. "P" marking on frame and top of slide. Parkerized. Right side of frame is marked "M1911A1 U.S. ARMY" forward of the slide stop pin, and "United States Property" behind the slide stop pin. Verified proof and final inspector's mark on triggerguard bow. "GHD" (Guy H. Drewry) marked on left side below slide stop. Barrels marked "COLT .45 AUTO." Plain blued or contract magazine. Colt plastic stocks with wide rings around screws. (Subtract 5 percent to 10 percent for British proofs, most collectors seem to prefer virgin pistols. Add 20-30 percent for 99-100 percent finish.)

Exc.	V.G.	Good	Fair	Poor
2000	1550	1225	1000	875

Model of 1911A1, Military. 1945 GHD Acceptance Mark

GHD marked SN 1720000 to 1743846, and 2244804 to 2368781. Un-numbered slide. "P" marking on frame and top of slide. Parkerized. Right side of frame is marked "M1911A1 U.S. ARMY" forward of the slide stop pin, and "United States Property" behind the slide stop pin. Verified proof and final inspector's mark on triggerguard bow. "GHD" (Guy H. Drewry) marked on left side below slide stop. Early barrels marked "COLT .45 AUTO," later examples marked with a "C" in a square. Colt plastic grips with wide rings around screws. (Subtract 5 percent to 10 percent for British proofs, most collectors seem to prefer virgin pistols. Add 20-30 percent for 99-100 percent finish.)

Exc.	V.G.	Good	Fair	Poor
2000	1550	1225	1000	875

Model of 1911A1, Military. 1945 JSB Acceptance Mark

Around SN 2360600 a small number (perhaps a few thousand pistols) were acceptance marked under the authority of John S. Begley, a civilian employee of the Ordnance Department who had the title "Army Inspector of Ordnance". Un-numbered slide. "P" marking on frame and top of slide. Parkerized. Right side of frame is marked "M1911A1 U.S. ARMY" forward of the slide stop pin, and "United States Property" behind the slide stop pin. Verified proof and final inspector's mark on triggerguard bow. "JSB" (John S. Begley) acceptance mark on left side below slide stop. Plain blued or contract magazine. Barrels marked with a "C" in a square. Colt plastic grips with wide rings around screws. Extremely rare! Subtract 5 percent to 10 percent for British proofs, most collectors seem to prefer virgin pistols. Add 30-50 percent for 99-100 percent finish.)

Exc.	V.G.	Good	Fair	Poor
5900	4200	3000	2200	1600

Colt, Model of 1911A1, Military. 1945 No Acceptance Mark

(Un-inspected and usually no ordnance wheel.) Very rare and are usually found around SN 2354000. Un-numbered slide. "P" marking on frame and top of slide. Parkerized. Right side of frame is marked "M1911A1 U.S. ARMY" forward of the slide stop pin, and "United States Property" behind the slide stop pin. Verified proof and final inspector's mark on triggerguard bow. Plain blued or contract magazine. Barrels marked with a "C" in a square. Colt plastic grips with wide rings around screws. Very rare. These pistols may not have been delivered but they may have been sold commercially. Add 20-30 percent for 99-100 percent finish.)

Exc.	V.G.	Good	Fair	Poor
1750	1400	950	650	450

Ithaca Gun Co. 1943-1945 Production

FJA inspected, un-numbered slide. Right side of frame is marked "M1911A1 U.S. ARMY" forward of the slide stop pin, and "United States Property" behind the slide stop pin. Plastic Keyes Fibre grips, stamped trigger, flat sided hammer, late pistols had serrated flat sided hammer, HS marked barrel, contract magazine. A few early pistols had an I prefix Serial Number. A few into the 1.28 million range had the "M1911A1 U.S. ARMY" on the right side of the slide. A few thousand early pistols were made with reclaimed WWI Colt frames ("H" marked on top of frame, and heart shaped cutouts). Add 50 percent for Colt frame. (Subtract 5 percent to 10 percent for British proofs, most collectors prefer virgin pistols.) (Add 30-40 percent for 99-100 percent finish. Add 20 percent for "M1911A1 U.S. ARMY" marked slide, but only in the proper SN range. Add 15 percent for DU-LITE finish, below about SN 905000. Add 150 percent for I prefix.) Recent discovered shipping documents show certain pistols going to Navy units and Airfield orders, however it is still too early to determine the associated premium for these shipments.

Exc.	V.G.	Good	Fair	Poor
1700	1300	1000	800	600

Remington Rand Co. 1942-1943 Production

"NEW YORK" (Type I) marked slide. FJA inspected, un-numbered slide. Right side of frame is marked "M1911A1 U.S. ARMY" forward of the slide stop pin, and "United States Property" behind the slide stop pin. DU-LITE (blued over sand blasting) finish. Plastic Keyes Fibre grips with no rings around screws. Milled trigger, flat sided hammer, "COLT .45 AUTO" marked barrel, contract magazine. Fine checkered mainspring housing. (Subtract 5 percent to 10 percent for British proofs, most collectors seem to prefer virgin pistols. Add 30-50 percent for 99-100 percent finish.) (Pistols shipped after 1942 (after SN 921699) seem to be less desirable. Subtract 15 percent.

Courtesy Karl Karash collection

Exc.	V.G.	Good	Fair	Poor
3000	2000	1500	1200	900

Remington Rand Co. 1943 Production

Large "N.Y." (Type II) marked slide. FJA inspected, un-numbered slide. Right side of frame is marked "M1911A1 U.S. ARMY" forward of the slide stop pin, and "United States Property" behind the slide stop pin. DU-LITE (blued over sand blasting) finish. Plastic Keyes Fibre grips with small rings around screws. Stamped trigger, flat sided hammer, "HS" marked barrel, contract magazine. Fine checkered mainspring housing. Note that there appears to be considerable overlap of features near the 1 million serial range. (Subtract 5 percent to 10 percent for British proofs, most collectors seem to prefer virgin pistols. Add 30-50 percent for 99-100 percent finish.)

Courtesy Karl Karash collection

Exc.	V.G.	Good	Fair	Poor
2100	1500	1150	950	750

Remington Rand Co. 1943-1945 Production

Small "N. Y." (Type III) marked slide. FJA inspected, un-numbered slide. Right side of frame is marked "M1911A1 U.S. ARMY" forward of the slide stop pin, and "United States Property" behind the slide stop pin. Parkerized (phosphate over sand blasting) finish. Plastic Keyes Fibre grips with small rings around screws. Stamped trigger, flat-sided hammer, "HS" marked barrel, contract magazine. Serrated mainspring housing. (Subtract 5 percent to 10 percent for British proofs, most collectors prefer virgin pistols. Add 40 percent for 99-100 percent finish.)

Courtesy Karl Karash collection

Exc.	V.G.	Good	Fair	Poor
1400	1100	900	825	750

Remington Rand Co. 1942-1945 Production

Numbered Presentation pistol (all observed are Type III) marked slide. They were usually disposed of as giveaways to contracting personnel and employees, however several remained in the company safe long after WWII until they were eventually sold. No inspector, un-numbered slide. The only frame marking is a two- or three-digit number above trigger right. Parkerized (phosphate over sand blasting) finish. Plastic

Keyes Fibre grips with small rings around screws. Stamped trigger, flat-sided hammer, "HS" marked barrel, contract magazine. Serrated mainspring housing. (Add 30 percent for 99-100 percent finish.) Add 10 percent to 20 percent for original box.

Exc.	V.G.	Good	Fair	Poor
3500	2500	1800	1400	1200

Remington Rand Co. 1942-1945 Production

ERRS prefix Presentation pistol (all observed are Type III) marked slide. They were usually disposed of as giveaways to contracting personnel and employees, however several remained in the company safe long after WWII until they were eventually sold. No inspector, un-numbered slide. The only frame marking is a two- or three-digit number with the "ERRS" prefix above trigger right. Parkerized (phosphate over sand blasting) finish. Plastic Keyes Fibre grips with small rings around screws. Stamped trigger, flat-sided hammer, "HS" marked barrel, contract magazine. Serrated mainspring housing. Popular wisdom seems to be that "ERRS" meant "Experimental Remington Rand"; however, there seems to be no evidence to support that notion. The true meaning of ERRS may never be known. (Add 30 percent for 99-100 percent finish.) Add 10 percent to 20 percent for original numbered box. Some ERRS pistols were DU-LITE blued and some were "P" proofed, too few to establish an accurate premium.

Exc.	V.G.	Good	Fair	Poor
3500	2800	2200	1800	1250

Union Switch Signal Co.

Swissvale, Pennsylvania. 55,000 pistols total delivered in 1943. US&S pistols have become one of the most sought after of all the 1911/1911A1 pistols.

Courtesy Karl Karash collection

Union Switch Signal Co. 1943 Production. Type I

(No "P" on frame or slide. From SN 1041405 to about 1060000 with probable overlap. RCD inspected, un-numbered slide.

Right side of frame is marked "M1911A1 U.S. ARMY" forward of the slide stop pin, and "United States Property" behind the slide stop pin. DU-LITE (blued over sand blasting) finish. Plastic Keyes Fibre grips with or without rings around screws. Stamped, blued trigger, flat-sided hammer, "HS" marked barrel, contract magazine. Checkered mainspring housing. (Add 30-40 percent for 99-100 percent finish.)

Courtesy Karl Karash collection

Exc.	V.G.	Good	Fair	Poor
4000	3000	2400	1800	1400

Union Switch Signal Co. 1943 Production. Type II

("P" on top edge of slide.) From about SN 1060000 to about 1080000 with probable overlap. RCD inspected, un-numbered slide. Right side of frame is marked "M1911A1 U.S. ARMY" forward of the slide stop pin, and "United States Property" behind the slide stop pin. DU-LITE (blued over sand blasting) finish. Plastic Keyes Fibre grips with or without rings around screws. Stamped, blued trigger, flat sided hammer, "HS" marked barrel, contract magazine. Checkered mainspring housing. (Add 30-40 percent for 99-100 percent finish.)

Courtesy Karl Karash collection

Exc.	V.G.	Good	Fair	Poor
4000	3000	2400	1800	1400

Union Switch Signal Co. 1943 Production. Type III

"P" on frame and slide in the normal locations. From about SN 1080000 to 1096404 with probable overlap. RCD inspected, un-numbered slide. Right side of frame is marked "M1911A1 U.S. ARMY" forward of the slide stop pin, and "United States Property" behind the slide stop pin. DU-LITE (blued over sand blasting) finish. Plastic Keyes Fibre grips with or without rings around screws. Stamped, blued trigger, flat-sided hammer, "HS" marked barrel, contract magazine. Checkered mainspring housing. (Add 30-40 percent for 99-100 percent finish.)

Courtesy Karl Karash collection

Exc.	V.G.	Good	Fair	Poor
4000	3000	2400	1800	1400

Union Switch Signal Co. 1943 Production. Exp.

About 100 Pistols. ("EXP" followed by a one- or two-digit number on receiver partially under right grip.) These pistols usually have some apparent defect about them which may have caused them to be rejected and written off. They were believed to have been disposed of as giveaways to contracting personnel and employees. No inspector, no Ordnance mark un-numbered slide. Some pistols were finished with the DU-LITE process (blued over sand blasting) that closely resembled the finish of the delivered military pistols. The "EXP" and serial number marking was hand applied and is partially obscured by the right stock panel. Other EXP marked pistols were blued over such heavy buffing that the pistols have an amateur look about them. This, along with the crudeness of the markings, might lead one to question the authenticity of the blued EXPs. However, most evidence indicates that they are indeed genuine US&S made pistols. Popular wisdom seems to be that "EXP" meant "Experimental"; however, there seems to be no evidence to support that notion. Plastic Keyes Fibre grips with or without rings around screws. Stamped, blued trigger, flat-sided hammer, "HS" marked barrel, contract magazine. Checkered mainspring housing. (Add 30-40 percent for 99-100 percent finish. Subtract 50 percent for blued or buffed.) Most observed have type II slides.

Courtesy Karl Karash collection

Exc.	V.G.	Good	Fair	Poor
5200	3750	2800	2200	1700

Seven-Digit X Numbered Rework

These pistols were renumbered when their original serial numbers were either defaced, obliterated, or became too light to read during rebuilding or refinishing. The seven-digit X prefix serial numbers (X2693614 through X2695212) were assigned to various arsenals from 1949 to 1957. Some of the reworks are done in small batches and are more distinctive and collectable than the 4 digit X numbers. Each batch of pistols may have unique characteristics as they are done at different times by various arsenals. All are considered "Arsenal Refinished."

Courtesy Karl Karash collection

Exc.	V.G.	Good	Fair	Poor
1100	850	700	500	350

Military Arsenal Rework

Many 1011/1011A1 pistols were reworked/refurbished at government arsenals such as Augusta Arsenal (AA), Rock Island Arsenal (RIA), Springfield Armory (SA), Raritan Arsenal (no mark), and others. Some arsenals applied an identification/inspection mark to each pistol rebuilt, but others did not mark them in any way. Some of the reworks were sold through the NRA and has sales/shipping papers that identified the serial number of the pistol Most of these same pistols also had shipping boxes. An original shipping box and papers may increase the price by $200. (A fake box is worth about $2.00, and most of the boxes seen and advertised as originals are fakes.) solme reworked pistols appear to have most or all original parts but have been refinished with a Parkerized finish. A few pistols went through a rebuild facility and carry the rebuild facility's mark, but appear to be original pistols and were not refinished or rebuilt. Most rebuilt pistols have new plastic stocks as well as a new barrel. Each batch of rebuilt pistols may have unique characteristics as they are done at different times by various arsenals. Therefore it is often impossible to determine when a pistol was reworked, if it has been altered since it left the rebuild facility, or even if it was reworked in a government facility. Consequently, although reworked pistols are considered collectable, they are likely to remain at the bottom of the collectable price structure for the foreseeable future. (Add up to $100 for ORIGINAL box, add up to $100 for numbered shipping papers.) Prices shown are for government facility marked (AA, RIA, SA, etc.) reworks, equivalent to Poor condition if no Government facility markings, unless with original numbered box and papers. Add $2.00 for fake box. Completely original pistols with rework marks on them, like their original pistol category but less 20 percent.

Exc.	V.G.	Good	Fair	Poor
850	700	575	500	400

State of New York Government Model

250 pistols in the serial number range of about 255000-C to about 258000-C with factory roll mark "PROPERTY OF THE STATE OF NEW YORK" with a verified proof and "Government Model" marking. A few of the parts were leftover military. This is a state militia pistol. (99 percent to 100 percent finish add 33 percent. For the few consecutive pairs known add 15 percent premium. A few match pistols were made by Al Dinan in the early 1960s; add 15 percent.)

Courtesy Karl Karash collection

Exc.	V.G.	Good	Fair	Poor
2300	1500	1100	800	500

Military National Match

These are .45 caliber pistols rebuilt from service pistols at Springfield Armory between 1955 and about 1967. In 1968 the last year of the program, all rebuilding took place at Rock Island Arsenal. These pistols were built and rebuilt each year with a portion being sold to competitors by the NRA. Each year improvements were added to the rebuild program. Four articles in the *American Rifleman* document these pistols well: August, 1959; April, 1963; June, 1966; and July, 1966. Many parts for these pistols have been available and many "look-alike" pistols have been built by basement armorers. Pistols generally came with a numbered box or papers. Add 40 percent for numbered box and papers. When well worn these pistols offer little advantage over a standard well worn pistol. Pistols must be in original match condition to qualify as Military National Match pistols.

Courtesy Karl Karash collection

Exc.	V.G.	Good	Fair	Poor
1400	1000	875	750	550

COLT WOODSMAN

By Major Robert Rayburn, USAF retired, photos by Paul Goodwin

NOTE: Colt Woodsman pistols with military markings are seldom seen. The total number used by the U.S. military is relatively small, and many of those never received any government markings. Often the only way to determine a military connection is by requesting a historical letter by serial number from Colt Firearms.

This Woodsman was cut up by the government and sold as scrap metal. The threaded section at the muzzle is probably for the Maxim type silencer, and suggest that not all of the WWII contract Match Target pistols were used exclusively for marksmanship training.

Military Woodsman Match Target–6-5/8 inch barrel

After the United States entered World War II at the end of 1941, civilian production at Colt was stopped and the total effort was devoted to the U.S. military. Slightly more than 4000 First Series Match Target Woodsmans were delivered on U.S. Government contract from 1942-1944. Most of them, but not all, had serial numbers above MT12000. With possible rare exceptions they all had U.S. Property or U.S. military markings, standard blue finish, and extended length plastic stocks. The plastic stocks are sometimes erroneously called elephant ear stocks. The military plastic stocks are still relatively easy to find and inexpensive and, since they will fit any First Series Colt Woodsman, they are often used as replacement grips on non-military guns. Since the military guns had plastic grips, rather than the costly and desirable "Elephant Ear" grips, the salvage value in the Fair and Poor condition range is less than that for the civilian model.

Colt Match Target Woodsman, serial number MT13970, was 1 of 300 shipped to the Naval Supply Depot, Norfolk, VA on 4 October, 1943. On the left side is the crossed cannon mark of the Ordnance Department, and on the right are the GHD initials of Major Guy H. Drury, the in-house government inspector at Colt Firearms during World War II. Other than the military markings and the plastic stocks, the pistol is identical to the prewar commercial model.

Exc.	V.G.	Good	Fair	Poor
2800	1600	750	450	350

U.S. Marine Corps Match Target

On December 10, 1947 Colt shipped 50 Woodsmans to the Depot Quartermaster, U.S. Marine Corp. in Philadelphia, PA. Another 50 were shipped to the same destination five days later. The 100 pistols in these two shipments were among the very first of the postwar, second series Woodsmans, and all were 6-inch Match Target models. Some bore single digit serial numbers, and all serial numbers in these shipments were under 400.

Colt Match Target Woodsman, serial number 98-S. Marked USMC PROPERTY on the right side of the receiver just below the serial number. Area has been enhanced for identification purposes.

Exc.	V.G.	Good	Fair	Poor
Too Rare To Price				

U.S. Marine Corps Sport

In 1953 2,500 Woodsman Sport Models were sold to the USMC, 1250 were shipped to the Marine Corps Supply Annex, Barstow, CA on June 30th, and the other 1250 to the Marine Corps Supply Depot at Camp Lejeune, NC on July 17th. Serial numbers in both shipments were around 130000-S. This version is seldom found intact, although many have turned up that have been destroyed by the government prior to being sold as scrap metal.

USMC Woodsman Sport model, serial number 130003-S.

Exc.	V.G.	Good	Fair	Poor
Too Rare To Price				

U.S. Air Force Target

In June, 1949 Colt contracted with the U.S. government to deliver 950 Woodsman Target pistols. These were to be the standard commercial model, modified with a fixed 1/10 inch front sight blade integral with the ramp base, and a semi-fixed rear sight. In addition the following components were to be omitted: slide stop, magazine safety, lanyard loop, grip adapters, and screwdriver. 925 of these pistols were shipped to the Transportation Officer, Ogden Air Material Area, Ogden, Utah. In those cold war days the USAF was flying nuclear armed bombers over the arctic regions to provide a response should an attack come from the Soviet Union. The Colt packing list indicates that the pistols were for use in Arctic Survival Kits. The other 25 pistols in the contract were sent to the Springfield Ordnance Depot. Serial numbers of all 950 pistols were in the 64000-S and 65000-S range. Many of these were later declared surplus and sold to U.S. citizens via the DCM program. They had no military markings of any type. Almost all of these pistols are in near new condition.

Air Force Target without markings • Courtesy Bob Rayburn

Air Force Target without markings • Courtesy Bob Rayburn

Exc.	V.G.	Good	Fair	Poor
1900	1500	—	—	—

NOTE: For pistols in DCM box with papers in excellent condition add 25 percent.

U.S. Coast Guard Match Target

There were at least three post-WWII Woodsman shipments to the U.S. Coast Guard: 25 pistols on June 23, 1955, 30 on December 21, 1955, and 50 on February 5, 1958. All were Match Target models with 6-inch barrels.

Colt Match Target Woodsman, serial number MT3658, was one of eight guns of the same type shipped to the US Coast Guard Academy on December 21, 1938. Colt shipping records indicate that U.S. COAST GUARD was factory engraved (NOT roll marked) on the right hand side of the receiver. It is otherwise standard in all respects.

Exc.	V.G.	Good	Fair	Poor
Too Rare To Price				

REMINGTON

Model 1865 Navy Rolling Block Pistol

A spur trigger single-shot rolling block .50 caliber rimfire cartridge pistol with an 8.5" round barrel. Blued, case hardened with walnut grips and forend. The barrel marked "Remingtons, Ilion N.Y. U.S.A. Pat. May 3d Nov. 15th, 1864 April 17th, 1866." Examples bearing military inspection marks are worth approximately 30 percent more than the values listed below. Examples are also to be found altered to centerfire cartridge and these are worth approximately 10 percent less than the values listed below. Approximately 6,500 were manufactured between 1866 and 1870.

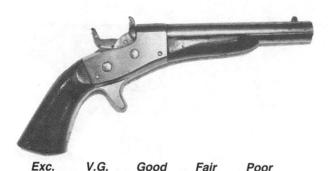

Exc.	V.G.	Good	Fair	Poor
—	—	3250	1500	600

Model 1867 Navy Rolling Block Pistol

A .50 caliber single-shot rolling block pistol with a 7" round barrel. Blued, case hardened with walnut grips and forend. The majority of these pistols were purchased by the United States government and civilian examples without inspection marks are worth approximately 30 percent more than the values listed.

Exc.	V.G.	Good	Fair	Poor
—	—	2750	1100	600

Model 1871 Army Rolling Block Pistol

A .50 caliber rolling block single-shot pistol with an 8" round barrel. Blued, case hardened with walnut grips and forend. The distinguishing feature of this model is that it has a rearward extension at the top of the grip and a squared butt. Approximately 6,000 were made between 1872 and 1888. Of these 6,000 approximately 5,000 were purchased by the U.S. government and are marked with inspector cartouche. Engraved ivory-stocked versions, as pictured below, will bring considerable premiums.

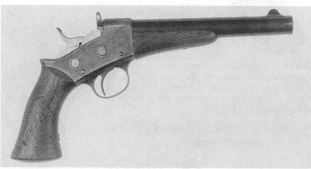

Exc.	V.G.	Good	Fair	Poor
—	—	2000	900	400

Model 1875 Single-Action Army

A .44 Remington or .44-40 or .45 caliber single-action revolver with a 7.5" barrel. Blued or nickel-plated, case hardened with walnut grips. Some examples are to be found fitted with a lanyard ring at the butt. The barrel marked "E. Remington & Sons Ilion, N.Y. U.S.A." Approximately 25,000 were manufactured between 1875 and 1889.

No known U.S. contracts but some revolvers may have been sold and delivered to Egypt. Mexican government purchased about 1,000 revolvers during the 1880s. Mexican examples are rare and worth a premium.

Courtesy Milwaukee Public Museum, Milwaukee, Wisconsin

Exc.	V.G.	Good	Fair	Poor
—	—	4250	1750	600

NOTE: Blued version add 40 percent.

SMITH & WESSON

NOTE: For historical information, photos, and technical data, see Jim Supica and Richard Nahas, *Standard Catalog of Smith & Wesson 2nd Ed.*, Krause Publications.

Model 2 Army or Old Model

Similar in appearance to the Model 1 2nd Issue, this revolver was extremely successful from a commercial standpoint. It was released just in time for the commencement of hostilities in the Civil War. Smith & Wesson had, in this revolver, the only weapon able to fire self-contained cartridges and be easily carried as a backup by soldiers going off to war. This resulted in a backlog of more than three years before the company finally stopped taking orders. This model is chambered for .32 rimfire long and has a 6-shot nonfluted cylinder and 4", 5", or 6" barrel lengths. It has a square butt with rosewood grips and is either blued or nickel-plated. There were approximately 77,155 manufactured between 1861 and 1874.

A number of Model 2 revolvers with 6" barrels were sold to the state of Kentucky between 1862 and 1863 for the 7th Kentucky Cavalry. Most Model 2 revolvers used in the Civil War were purchased privately by individual soldiers.

NOTE: A slight premium for early two-pin model.

Courtesy Chester Krause

Courtesy Mike Stuckslager

5" or 6" Barrel—Standard Barrel

Exc.	V.G.	Good	Fair	Poor
—	1500	950	450	—

4" Barrel—Rare! Use Caution

Exc.	V.G.	Good	Fair	Poor
—	5000	3000	1500	—

.38 Safety Hammerless Army Test Revolver

There were 100 sold to the U.S. government in 1890. They have 3rd Model features but are in the 2nd Model serial number range, 41333-41470. Fitted with 6" barrels and marked "US."

CAUTION: Be very wary of fakes. Seek an expert appraisal prior to a sale.

Exc.	V.G.	Good	Fair	Poor
10000	7000	5000	3000	2000

Model 3 American 1st Model

This model represented a number of firsts for the Smith & Wesson Company. It was the first of the top break, automatic ejection revolvers. It was also the first Smith & Wesson in a large caliber (it is chambered for the .44 S&W American cartridge as well as the .44 Henry rimfire on rare occasions). It was also known as the 1st Model American. This large revolver is offered with an 8" round barrel with a raised rib as standard. Barrel lengths of 6" and 7" were also available. It has a 6-shot fluted cylinder and a square butt with walnut grips. It is blued or nickel-plated. It is interesting to note that this model appeared three years before Colt's Single Action Army and perhaps, more than any other model, was associated with the historic American West. There were only 8,000 manufactured between 1870 and 1872.

U.S. Army Order—Serial Number Range 125-2199

One thousand (1,000) produced with "U.S." stamped on top of barrel; "OWA" on left grip.

Exc.	V.G.	Good	Fair	Poor
15000	9500	7500	3250	2500

NOTE: Add 10 percent premium for original nickel finish.

Model 3 Russian 1st Model—Cyrillic

This model is quite similar in appearance to the American 1st and 2nd Model revolvers. S&W made several internal changes to this model to satisfy the Russian government. The markings on this revolver are distinct, and the caliber for which it is chambered, .44 S&W Russian, is different. There were approximately 20,000 Russian-contract revolvers. The serial number range is 1-20000. They are marked in Russian Cyrillic letters. The Russian double-headed eagle is stamped on the rear portion of the barrel with inspector's marks underneath it. All of the contract guns have 8" barrels and lanyard swivels on the butt. These are rarely encountered, as most were shipped to Russia. The commercial run of this model numbered approximately 4,655. The barrels are stamped in English and include the words "Russian Model." Some are found with 6" and 7" barrels, as well as the standard 8". There were also 500 revolvers that were rejected from the Russian contract series and sold on the commercial market. Some of these are marked in English, some Cyrillic. Some have the Cyrillic markings ground off and the English restamped. This model was manufactured from 1871 to 1874.

Russian Contract Model—Cyrillic Barrel Address

Exc.	V.G.	Good	Fair	Poor
—	8500	6000	2000	—

Model 3 Russian 2nd Model—Foreign Contracts

This revolver was known as the "Old Model Russian." This is a complicated model to understand as there are many variations within the model designation. The serial numbering is quite complex as well, and values vary greatly due to relatively minor model differences. Before purchasing this model, it would be advisable to secure competent appraisal as well as to read reference materials solely devoted to this firearm. This model is chambered for the .44 S&W Russian, as well as the .44 rimfire Henry cartridge. It has a 7" barrel and a round butt featuring a projection on the frame that fits into the thumb web. The grips are walnut, and the finish is blue or nickel-plated. The trigger-

guard has a reverse curved spur on the bottom. There were approximately 85,200 manufactured between 1873 and 1878.

Courtesy Jim Supica, Old Town Station

Russian Contract Model

70,000 made; rare, as most were shipped to Russia. Cyrillic markings; lanyard swivel on butt.

Exc.	V.G.	Good	Fair	Poor
—	5000	3750	1500	—

1st Model Turkish Contract

.44 rimfire Henry, special rimfire frames, serial-numbered in own serial number range 1-1000.

Exc.	V.G.	Good	Fair	Poor
—	6750	4750	1750	—

2nd Model Turkish Contract

Made from altered centerfire frames from the regular commercial serial number range. 1,000 made. Use caution with this model.

Exc.	V.G.	Good	Fair	Poor
—	6500	4500	1500	—

Japanese Govt. Contract

Five thousand made between the 1-9000 serial number range. The Japanese naval insignia, an anchor over two wavy lines, found on the butt. The barrel is Japanese proofed, and the words "Jan.19, 75 REISSUE July 25, 1871" are stamped on the barrel, as well.

Exc.	V.G.	Good	Fair	Poor
—	4000	3250	1200	—

Model 3 Russian 3rd Model—Foreign Contracts

This revolver is also known as the "New Model Russian." The factory referred to this model as the Model of 1874 or the Cavalry Model. It is chambered for the .44 S&W Russian and the .44 Henry rimfire cartridge. The barrel is 6.5", and the round butt is the same humped-back affair as the 2nd Model. The grips are walnut and the finish is blue or nickel-plated. The most notable differences in appearance between this model and the 2nd Model are the shorter extractor housing under the barrel and the integral front sight blade instead of the pinned-on one found on the previous models. This is another model that bears careful research before attempting to evaluate. Minor variances can greatly affect values. Secure detailed reference materials and qualified appraisal. There were approximately 60,638 manufactured between 1874 and 1878.

Turkish Model

Five thousand made of altered centerfire frames, made to fire .44 rimfire Henry. "W" inspector's mark on butt and "CW" cartouche on grip. Fakes have been noted; be aware.

Exc.	V.G.	Good	Fair	Poor
—	4750	3000	1200	—

Japanese Contract Model

One thousand made; has the Japanese naval insignia, an anchor over two wavy lines, stamped on the bottom of the frame strap.

Exc.	V.G.	Good	Fair	Poor
—	3500	2250	1000	—

Russian Contract Model

Barrel markings are in Russian Cyrillic. Approximately 41,100 were produced.

Exc.	V.G.	Good	Fair	Poor
—	4500	3750	1500	—

Model 3 Russian 3rd Model (Loewe & Tula Copies)

The German firm of Ludwig Loewe produced a copy of this model that is nearly identical to the S&W. This German revolver was made under Russian contract, as well as for commercial sales. The contract model has different Cyrillic markings than the S&W and the letters "HK" as inspector's marks. The commercial model has the markings in English. The Russian arsenal at Tula also produced a copy of this revolver with a different Cyrillic dated stamping on the barrel.

Courtesy Mike Stuckslager

Loewe

Exc.	V.G.	Good	Fair	Poor
—	3750	2500	1000	—

Tula

Exc.	V.G.	Good	Fair	Poor
—	4000	2750	1100	—

Model 3 Schofield

In 1870 Major George W. Schofield heard about the new S&W Model 3 revolver and wrote to the company expressing a desire to be an exclusive sales representative for them. At that time S&W was earnestly attempting to interest the government in this revolver and obviously felt that the Major could be of help in this endeavor, perhaps because his brother, General John Schofield, was president of the Small Arms Board. Major Schofield was sent one Model 3 revolver and 500 rounds of ammunition free of charge. After testing the revolver, Schofield felt that it needed a few changes to make it the ideal cavalry sidearm. With the company's approval, Schofield made these changes and secured patents. The company eventually began production of what became known as the Model 3 Schofield 1st Model. The Major was paid a 50-cent royalty per revolver. The eventual production of this model ran to a total of 8,969, with the last one sold in 1878. What was hoped to be the adopted government-issue sidearm never materialized—for a number of reasons. First, the Colt Single Action Army being used by the cavalry had a longer chamber than the S&W and could fire the Schofield ammunition. The Schofield could not fire the longer Colt .45 cartridges. This resulted in disastrous mix-ups on more than one occasion, when Colt ammunition was issued to troops armed with the Schofields. The company was not happy about paying the 50-cent royalty to Major Schofield. Sales of their other models were high and they simply did not care about this model, so they eventually ceased its

production. It was a popular model on the American frontier and is quite historically significant.

Model 3 Schofield 1st Model

The modifications that made this model differ from the other Model 3 revolvers were quite extensive. The Schofield is chambered for the .45 S&W Schofield cartridge. The top break latch was moved from the barrel assembly to the frame. It was modified so that the action could be opened by simply pulling back on the latch with the thumb. This made it much easier to reload on horseback, as the reins would not have to be released. A groove was milled in the top of the raised barrel rib to improve the sighting plain. The extractor was changed to a cam-operated rather than rack-and-gear system. The removal of the cylinder was simplified. There were 3,000 contract Schofields and 35 commercial models. The contract revolvers were delivered to the Springfield Armory in July of 1875. These guns are stamped "US" on the butt and have the initials "L" and "P" marking various other parts. The grips have an inspector's cartouche with the initials "JFEC." There were 35 1st Models made for and sold to the civilian market; these revolvers do not have the "US" markings. The Schofield has a 7" barrel, 6-shot fluted cylinder, and walnut grips. The 1st Model is blued, with a nickel-plated original finish gun being extremely rare.

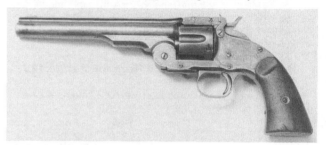

Courtesy Mike Stuckslager

"US" Contract–3,000 Issued

Exc.	V.G.	Good	Fair	Poor
12000	7500	4250	1750	1000

Civilian Model, No "US" markings

Very rare, 35 made, use caution. **UNABLE TO PRICE.** At least double the military model values. Expert appraisal needed.

Model 3 Schofield 2nd Model

The difference between the 1st and 2nd Model Schofield revolvers is in the barrel latch system. The 2nd Model latch is rounded and knurled to afford an easier and more positive grip when opening the revolver. A group of 3,000 of these revolvers was delivered to the Springfield Armory in October of 1876, and another 2,000 were delivered in 1877. These 2nd Model contract revolvers were all blued. There were an additional 649 civilian guns sold as well. The civilian models were not "US" marked and were offered either blued or nickel-plated. A total of 8,969 Model 3 Schofield 2nd Models were manufactured. The last sale was recorded in 1878.

Courtesy Jim Supica, Old Town Station

"US" Contract—4,000 Issued

Exc.	V.G.	Good	Fair	Poor
—	8500	3750	1750	950

Civilian Model—646 Made

Exc.	V.G.	Good	Fair	Poor
—	8500	3750	1750	950

Model 3 Schofield—Surplus Models

Many Schofields were issued to various states under the Militia Act, some of which were used in the Spanish American War. After the government dropped the Schofield as an issue cavalry sidearm, the remaining U.S. inventory of these revolvers was sold off as military surplus. Many were sold to dealers such as Bannerman's or Schuyler, Hartley & Graham, two large gun dealers who then resold the guns to supply the growing need for guns on the Western frontier. Schuyler, Hartley & Graham sold a number of guns to the Wells Fargo Express Co. Almost all of these weapons had the barrels shortened to 5", as were many others sold during this period. Some were nickel plated. Beware of fakes when contemplating purchase of the Wells Fargo revolvers.

SNAP SHOT
SMITH & WESSON MODEL NO. 3 SCHOFIELD

If there is one attribute of Smith & Wesson that is universally accepted it is the quality of their revolvers. Another would have to be their innovative ideas such as the bored-through cylinder that forced their competitors out of the cartridge-firing revolvers until the patent expired. The Model No. 3 was Smith & Wesson's first model that could handle the power of the .44 Henry rimfire cartridge. When submitted to the U.S. Army in 1870 the Ordnance Board found the revolver to be much to their liking with one exception. They wanted a centerfire cartridge. S&W obliged by creating a .44 centerfire cartridge that would eventually become the .44 Russian. Thus began a very successful relationship with the Russian Army but a smaller one with the U.S. Army that would sputter and die within a few years.

When the U.S. Army adopted the .45 Colt cartridge, Smith & Wesson sought and got approval of a .45 cal cartridge of their own design (the .45 S&W) having a larger rim for extraction but of shorter length than the .45 Colt. Cavalry officer Maj. George Schofield, a fan of the Smith & Wesson No. 3, designed an improved latch system that allowed a mounted soldier to open the revolver with one hand and eject the spent cartridges with a quick flip of the wrist or by sweeping the barrel against his leg to trip the ejector. When loaded, the action could be closed with equal dexterity, no longer requiring two hands to reload the revolver. Thus modified the No. 3 became simply known as the Schofield Army Revolver. Over 8,000 were made and the troops preferred the Schofield. But, the .45 Colt cartridge was too long for shorter Schofield cylinder. And, when mix ups in ammunition supplies occurred, the Schofield was rendered useless. For that single reason the Schofield fell into disapproval and all were removed from service.

The S&W Schofield with its 7-inch barrel is a pleasure to shoot. Certainly the linage of the Smith & Wesson target models can be traced to the No. 3. It is one of America's great single-action revolvers.

Kenny Durham

Wells Fargo & Co. Model

Exc.	V.G.	Good	Fair	Poor
—	5500	2500	1500	900

Surplus Cut Barrel—Not Wells Fargo

Exc.	V.G.	Good	Fair	Poor
3000	1800	1400	1100	800

New Model No. 3 Single Action

Always interested in perfecting the Model 3 revolver, D.B. Wesson redesigned and improved the old Model 3 in the hopes of attracting more sales. The Russian contracts were almost filled so the company decided to devote the effort necessary to improve on this design. In 1877 this project was undertaken. The extractor housing was shortened, the cylinder retention system was improved, and the shape of the grip was changed to a more streamlined and attractive configuration. This New Model has a 3.5", 4", 5", 6", 6.5", 7", 7.5", or 8" barrel length with a 6-shot fluted cylinder. The 6.5" barrel and .44 S&W Russian chambering is the most often encountered variation of this model, but the factory considered the 8" barrels as standard and these were kept in stock as well. The New Model No. 3 was also chambered for .32 S&W, .32-44 S&W, .320 S&W Rev. Rifle, .38 S&W, .38-40, .38-44 S&W, .41 S&W, .44 Henry rimfire, .44 S&W American, .44-40, .45 S&W Schofield, .450 Rev., .45 Webley, .455 MkI and .455 MkII. They are either blued or nickel-plated and have checkered hard rubber grips with the S&W logo molded into them or walnut grips. There are many sub-variations within this model designation, and the potential collector should secure detailed reference material that deals with this model. There were approximately 35,796 of these revolvers manufactured between 1878 and 1912. Nearly 40 percent were exported to fill contracts with Japan, Australia, Argentina, England, Spain, and Cuba. There were some sent to Asia, as well. The proofmarks of these countries will establish their provenance but will not add appreciably to standard values.

Standard Model—6.5" barrel, .44 S&W Russian

Courtesy Mike Stuckslager

Exc.	V.G.	Good	Fair	Poor
—	3700	2000	1000	—

Japanese Naval Contract

This was the largest foreign purchaser of this model. There were over 1,500 produced with the anchor insignia stamped on the frame.

Courtesy Mike Stuckslager

Courtesy Mike Stuckslager

Exc.	V.G.	Good	Fair	Poor
—	3700	2500	1000	—

Japanese Artillery Contract

This variation is numbered in the 25,000 serial range. They are blued, with a 7" barrel and a lanyard swivel on the butt. Japanese characters are stamped on the extractor housing.

Exc.	V.G.	Good	Fair	Poor
—	6000	2500	1250	—

Maryland Militia Model

This variation is nickel-plated, has a 6.5" barrel, and is chambered for the .44 S&W Russian cartridge. The butt is stamped "U.S.," and the inspector's marks "HN" and "DAL" under the 1878 date appear on the revolver. There were 280 manufactured between serial numbers 7126 and 7405.

Exc.	V.G.	Good	Fair	Poor
—	12500	6000	3000	—

NOTE: Rarity makes valuation speculative.

Australian Contract

This variation is nickel-plated, is chambered for the .44 S&W Russian cartridge, and is marked with the Australian Colonial Police Broad Arrow on the butt. There were 250 manufactured with 7" barrels and detachable shoulder stocks. The stock has the Broad Arrow stamped on the lower tang. There were also 30 manufactured with 6.5" barrels without the stocks. They all are numbered in the 12,000-13,000 serial number range.

NOTE: The total number of the revolvers made is greater than the number mentioned, but no exact number can be given.

Courtesy Mike Stuckslager

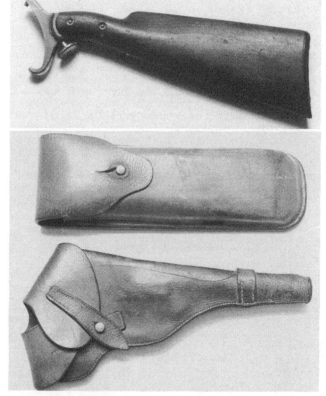

Courtesy Mike Stuckslager

Revolver with stock and holsters

Exc.	V.G.	Good	Fair	Poor
—	8000	4750	2750	—

NOTE: Deduct 40 percent for no stock.

Argentine Model

This was essentially not a factory contract but a sale through Schuyler, Hartley & Graham. They are stamped "Ejercito/Argentino" in front of the triggerguard. The order amounted to some 2,000 revolvers between the serial numbers 50 and 3400.

Exc.	V.G.	Good	Fair	Poor
—	7000	3500	1750	—

Turkish Model

This is essentially the New Model No. 3 chambered for the .44 rimfire Henry cartridge. It is stamped with the letters "P," "U" and "AFC" on various parts of the revolver. The barrels are all 6.5"; the finish, blued with walnut grips. Lanyard swivels are found on the butt. There were 5,461 manufactured and serial numbered in their own range, starting at 1 through 5461 between 1879 and 1883.

Courtesy Mike Stuckslager

Exc.	V.G.	Good	Fair	Poor
—	6500	3500	1750	—

U.S. Revenue Cutter Service (U.S. Coast Guard)

This model was issued to the U.S. Revenue Cutter Service as a standard issue sidearm. Fitted with 5", 6", or 6.5" barrels. The revolver is not marked but there are known serial numbers that identify this as a military variation. Consult an expert prior to sale, or see *Standard Catalog of Smith & Wesson* for a list of known serial numbers.

Exc.	V.G.	Good	Fair	Poor
—	8000	5000	2750	—

New Model No. 3 Frontier Single Action

This is another model similar in appearance to the standard New Model No. 3. It has a 4", 5", or 6.5" barrel and is chambered for the .44-40 Winchester Centerfire cartridge. Because the original New Model No. 3 cylinder was 1-7/16" in length this would not accommodate the longer .44-40 cartridge. The cylinder on the No. 3 Frontier was changed to 1-9/16" in length. Later, the company converted 786 revolvers to .44 S&W Russian and sold them to Japan. This model is either blued or nickel-plated and has checkered grips of walnut or hard rubber. They are serial numbered in their own range from 1 through 2072 and were manufactured from 1885 until 1908. This model was designed to compete with the Colt Single Action Army but was not successful.

Courtesy Mike Stuckslager

.44-40—Commercial Model

Exc.	V.G.	Good	Fair	Poor
—	5000	2500	1250	—

Japanese Purchase Converted to .44 S&W Russian

Exc.	V.G.	Good	Fair	Poor
—	4000	2000	1000	—

.38 Hand Ejector Military & Police 1st Model or Model of 1899

This was an early swing-out cylinder revolver, and it has no front lockup for the action. The release is on the left side of the frame. This model is chambered for the .38 S&W Special cartridge and the .32 Winchester centerfire cartridge (.32-20), has a 6-shot fluted cylinder, and was offered with a 4", 5", 6", 6.5", or 8" barrel in .38 caliber, and 4", 5", and 6-1/2" in .32-20 caliber. The finish is blued or nickel-plated; the grips, checkered walnut or hard rubber. There were approximately 20,975 manufactured between 1899 and 1902 in .38 caliber; serial number range 1 to 20975. In the .32-20 caliber, 5,311 were sold between 1899 and 1902; serial number range 1 to 5311.

Courtesy Mike Stuckslager

Commercial Model

Exc.	V.G.	Good	Fair	Poor
750	650	600	450	350

U.S. Navy Model

One thousand produced in 1900, .38 S&W, 6" barrel, blued with checkered walnut grips, "U.S.N." stamped on butt, serial number range 5000 to 6000.

Courtesy Rock Island Auction Company

Exc.	V.G.	Good	Fair	Poor
2500	1750	800	500	300

U.S. Army Model

One thousand produced in 1901, same as Navy Model except that it is marked "U.S.Army/Model 1899" on butt, "K.S.M." and "J.T.T." on grips, serial number range 13001 to 14000.

Exc.	V.G.	Good	Fair	Poor
2750	2000	950	600	300

.38 Hand Ejector Military & Police 2nd Model or Model of 1902—U.S. Navy Model

Chambered for .38 Long Colt cartridge with Navy serial number range 1001 to 2000. Marked "u.s.n." with anchor stamped on butt. Smith & Wesson serial number stamped on front tang in the 25001 to 26000 serial range. Some 1025 revolvers were produced.

Courtesy Rock Island Auction Company

Exc.	V.G.	Good	Fair	Poor
2500	2000	900	500	300

.45 Hand Ejector U.S. Service Model of 1917

WWI was on the horizon, and it seemed certain that the United States would become involved. The S&W people began to work with the Springfield Armory to develop a hand-ejector model that would fire the .45-caliber Government cartridge. This was accomplished in 1916 by the use of half-moon clips. The new revolver is quite similar to the .44 Hand Ejector in appearance. It has a 5.5" barrel, blued finish with smooth walnut grips, and a lanyard ring on the butt. The designation "U.S.Army Model 1917" is stamped on the butt. After the war broke out, the government was not satisfied with S&W's production and actually took control of the company for the duration of the war. This was the first time that the company was not controlled by a Wesson. The factory records indicate that there were 163,476 Model 1917s manufactured between 1917 and 1919, the WWI years. After the war, the sale of these revolvers continued on a commercial and contract basis until 1949, when this model was finally dropped from the S&W product line.

Paul Goodwin photo

Military Model

Exc.	V.G.	Good	Fair	Poor
1000	700	300	200	150

Commercial Model
High gloss blue and checkered walnut grips.

Exc.	V.G.	Good	Fair	Poor
600	450	300	200	150

.455 Mark II Hand Ejector 1st Model

This model was designed the same as the .44 Hand Ejector 1st Model with no caliber stamping on the barrel. It has a barrel length of 6.4". Of the 5,000 revolvers produced and sold, only 100 were commercial guns, the rest were military. Produced between 1914 and 1915. The commercial model is worth a premium.

Exc.	V.G.	Good	Fair	Poor
1100	750	400	300	200

.455 Mark II Hand Ejector 2nd Model

Similar to the first model without an extractor shroud. Barrel length was also 6.5". Serial number range was 5000 to 74755. Manufactured from 1915 to 1917.

Exc.	V.G.	Good	Fair	Poor
650	450	300	200	150

Model 10 (.38 Military & Police)—Military Marked

This model has been in production in one configuration or another since 1899. It was always the mainstay of the S&W line and was originally known as the .38 Military and Police Model. The Model 10 is built on the K, or medium frame, and was always meant as a duty gun. It was offered with a 2", 3", 4", 5", or 6" barrel. Currently only the 4" and 6" are available. A round or square butt is offered. It is chambered for the .38 Special, .38 S&W, and .22 rimfire and is offered in blue or nickel-plate, with checkered walnut grips. The Model designation is stamped on the yoke on all S&W revolvers. This model, with many other modern S&W pistols, underwent several engineering changes. These changes may affect the value of the pistol and an expert should be consulted. The dates of these changes are as follows:

10-None-1957	10-3-1961	10-5-1962
10-1-1959	10-4-1962	10-6-1962
10-2-1961		

NIB	Exc.	V.G.	Good	Fair	Poor
550	350	250	150	125	90

Victory Model

Manufactured during WWII, this is a Model 10 with a sand-blasted and parkerized finish, a lanyard swivel, and smooth walnut grips. The serial number has a V prefix. This model was available in only 2" and 4" barrel lengths. The Victory Model was discontinued on April 27, 1945, with serial number VS811119.

Victory Model marked "N.Y.M.I." • Courtesy Richard M. Kumor Sr.

Navy marked Smith & Wesson Victory model • Courtesy Amoskeag Auction, Co., Inc.

Exc.	V.G.	Good	Fair	Poor
450	300	150	100	75

NOTE: Top strap marked Navy will bring a 75 percent premium. Navy variation with both top strap and side plate marked will bring a 100 percent premium. Navy variation marked "N.Y.M.I." will bring a 125 percent premium. Revolvers marked "U.S.G.C." or "U.S.M.C." will bring a premium of unknown amount. Exercise caution.

Model 11 (.38/200 British Service Revolver)

First produced in 1938, S&W manufactured these revolvers for the British Commonwealth in 4", 5", or 6" barrels. Early models are bright blue, later models are parkerized. Square butt with checkered walnut grips. Lend Lease guns marked "UNITED STATES PROPERTY." Production ended in 1945 with 568,204 built. Nicknamed the .38/200 British Service Revolver. Smith & Wesson began producing this model again in 1947 and sold many of these throughout the 1950s and 1960s when production ceased again in 1965. There are several rare variations of this model that will greatly affect its value. Consult an expert if special markings and barrel lengths are encountered.

Exc.	V.G.	Good	Fair	Poor
400	300	200	100	75

USAF M-13 (Aircrewman)

From 1952 to about 1957 the Air Force purchased a large quantity of Model 12s with alloy frames and cylinders. They were intended for use by flight crews as survival weapons in emergencies. This model was not officially designated "13" by S&W, but the Air Force requested these revolvers be stamped "M13" on the top strap. This model was rejected by the Air Force in 1960 because of trouble with the alloy cylinder.

NOTE: Beware of fakes. Seek expert advice before purchase.

Exc.	V.G.	Good	Fair	Poor
1200	850	600	350	200

Model 39 Steel Frame

Semiautomatic pistol chambered for the 9mm cartridge. Fitted with a 4" barrel, walnut stocks, blue finish, and adjustable rear sight. Military version of this pistol has a dull blue finish, no walnut grips, with double action trigger. Manufactured from 1954 to 1966. Some of these military models are found without serial numbers. A special variation was used with a suppressor in Vietnam, and modified with a slide lock for single shot. Named the "Hush Puppy."

Exc.	V.G.	Good	Fair	Poor
1200	900	700	500	300

NOTE: Pricing does not include the suppressor.

Model 56 (KXT-38 USAF)

Introduced in 1962, this is a 2" heavy barrel built on the K frame. It is chambered for the .38 Special. There were approx-

imately 15,000 of these revolvers built when it was discontinued in 1964. It was marked "US" on the backstrap. A total of 15,205 were produced, but most were destroyed.

NIB	Exc.	V.G.	Good	Fair	Poor
Too Rare To Price					

HIGH STANDARD

Model B-US

A .22 Long Rifle caliber semiautomatic pistol with a 4.5" round tapered barrel and a 10-shot magazine. A version of the Model B with slight modifications to the frame. U.S. marked Model Bs will be found in both original Model B frame and Model B-US frame. An estimated 14,000 made for the U.S. government 1942-1943. Black, monogrammed hard rubber grips. Blued finish. Black checkered hard rubber grips. Type II takedown only. Most are marked "PROPERTY OF U.S." on the top of the barrel and on the right side of the frame. Crossed cannon ordnance stamp usually found on the right side of the frame. Box with papers add premium of 20 percent. Most guns are found in serial number range from about 92344 to about 111631.

Courtesy Rock Island Auction Company

Exc.	V.G.	Good	Fair	Poor
725	475	275	180	150

Model USA—Model HD

Similar to the Model HD with 4.5" barrel and fixed sights, checkered black hard rubber grips and an external safety. Early models blued; later model parkerized. Introduced 1943; approximately 44,000 produced for the U.S. government. Most are marked "PROPERTY OF U.S." on the top of the barrel and on the right side of the frame. Crossed cannon ordnance stamp usually found on the right side of the frame. Box with papers add 20 percent premium. Most pistols are found in serial number range from about 103863 to about 145700.

Exc.	V.G.	Good	Fair	Poor
750	550	400	250	175

Model USA—Model HD-MS

A silenced variation of the USA Model HD. Approximately 2500 produced for the OSS during 1944 and 1945. 6.75" shrouded barrel. Early pistols blued; later pistols parkerized. Only a few registered with BATF for civilian ownership. All NFA rules apply. Box with papers will bring a 10 percent premium. Most guns are found in serial number range from about 110074 to about 130040.

Model HD-MS • Courtesy Chuck Karwan

Exc.	V.G.	Good	Fair	Poor
6000	5000	—	—	—

Supermatic S-101

A .22 Long Rifle caliber semiautomatic pistol with 10-round magazine. Medium weight round barrel with blued finish, adjustable sights, brown plastic thumb rest grips. Grooved front and back straps on frame. The 6.75" barrel incorporates a muzzle brake with one slot on either side of the front sight. Marked "U.S." on the left side of the frame, above and in front of the triggerguard with characters approximately .150" high. Box with papers will bring a 13 percent premium. Most guns found in serial number range beginning at about 446,511.

Catalog # 9119—1954 to 1957.

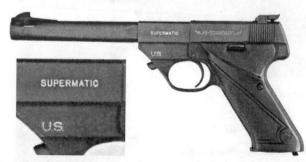

Supermatic "US" marked • Courtesy John J. Stimson Jr.

Exc.	V.G.	Good	Fair	Poor
700	400	275	195	150

Supermatic Citation Model 102 & 103

As above but with tapered barrel with an enlarged register at the muzzle end to hold a removable muzzle brake; adjustable sights; 2 and 3 oz. adjustable weights; checkered plastic grips, and blued finish. Grooved front and rear straps on frame. Marked "U.S." on left side of frame, above and in front of the triggerguard in characters approximately .150" high. Box with papers add 13 percent premium.

Catalog # 9260—1958 to 1963.

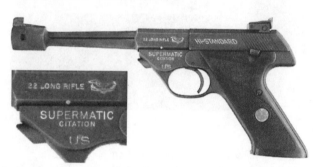

Supermatic Citation "US" marked • Courtesy John J. Stimson Jr.

Exc.	V.G.	Good	Fair	Poor
700	500	400	325	200

Supermatic Tournament 102 & 103

As above but with round tapered barrel. Blued finish, adjustable sights, checkered plastic grips. Smooth front and back straps on frame. Marked "U.S." on left side of frame, above and in front of the triggerguard in characters approximately .150" high.

Two different models catalog numbers 9271 and 9274. A contract in 1964 had mostly 9271 with some 9274. A contract in 1965 was all #9274. Catalog #9271 has a 6.75" barrel. Specifics of the #9274 are presently unknown.

Box with papers add 13 percent premium.

Catalog # 9271—1958 to 1963.

Supermatic Tournament "US" marked • Courtesy John J. Stimson Jr.

Exc.	V.G.	Good	Fair	Poor
575	400	290	200	175

T-3

A semiautomatic double action pistol made under contract to the U.S. government on a development contract. All types are blowback design. A preliminary model gun exists in the white in a private collection. No serial number and no folding triggerguard. The other pistols all have folding triggerguards for use with gloved hands. These guns are also blowback design and have barrels with angular grooves in the chamber to reduce recoil. Fitted with a 4" barrel. Made in three distinct types.

Type 1 pistols were probably made in a lot of four pistols each with a 7-round single column magazine. Serial number 1 does not include the plunge to increase the trigger pull when the trigger guard is folded. The magazine release for the Type 1 is like other High Standard pistols. Grips are checkered black plastic. Serial number 2 is in the Springfield Museum. Serial numbers 1, 3, and 4 are in private collections.

T-3 Type 1 • Courtesy John J. Stimson Jr.

Type 2 pistols were probably built in a lot of four pistols with a 7-round single column magazine. The magazine release on Type 2 pistols is located in the frame where the triggerguard meets the front grip strap. The 2nd type incorporated a thicker triggerguard and a wider frame and slide. Serial numbers 1, 2, and 3 are in the Springfield Museum, while serial number 4 is in a private collection.

T-3-Type 2 • Courtesy John J. Stimson Jr.

Type 3 pistols have a 13-round double-column magazine with a Type 2 triggerguard and magazine release. The magazine is similar to the Browning High Power. The frame and slide are wider than Type 2. One is known to exist in the Rock Island Arsenal Museum and the other is in a private collection. There are two others believed to exist.

Exc.	V.G.	Good	Fair	Poor
8500	7750	—	—	—

HECKLER & KOCH
See also-Germany

H&K Mark 23 Model O (SOCOM)
Very similar to H&K's U.S. government contract pistol developed for U.S. military special operation units. Chambered for the .45 ACP and fitted with a 5.87" barrel, this pistol has a polymer frame with steel slide. Magazine capacity is 10 rounds on civilian models and 12 rounds on military models. Barrel is threaded for noise suppressor. Weight is about 42 oz. Limited availability in fall 1996 to about 2,000 pistols.

NIB	Exc.	V.G.	Good	Fair	Poor
2250	1750	1250	—	—	—

Mark 23 Suppressor
This is the same suppressor as sold to the U.S. military for use on the Mark 23 pistol. This unit can be fitted to the threaded barrel of the Mark 23 and be adjusted for point of aim. With water the dB sound reduction is 33-35dB. Produced by Knight Armament Corp. of Vero Beach, Fla. This suppressor, with a different piston assembly, can be fitted to the USP Tactical.

NOTE: Suppressors require a Class III transfer tax. All NFA rules apply to the sale or purchase of these suppressors.

NIB	Exc.	V.G.	Good	Fair	Poor
1500	—	—	—	—	—

BERETTA
See also Italy

Model M9 Limited Edition
Introduced in 1995 to commemorate the 10th anniversary of the U.S. military's official sidearm, this 9mm pistol is limited to 10,000 units. Special engraving on the slide with special serial numbers. Slide stamped "U.S. 9MM M9-BERETTA U.S.A.-65490."

Standard Model

NIB	Exc.	V.G.	Good	Fair	Poor
750	600	400	300	200	100

U.S. Beretta Model M9 • Paul Goodwin photos

Deluxe Model

Walnut grips with gold plated hammer and grip screws.

NIB	Exc.	V.G.	Good	Fair	Poor
850	700	450	350	200	100

SAVAGE

Model 1907/10/11

Manufactured in 1905 in .45 ACP, this pistol was tested in the U.S. Army trials. A few were sold commercially. It weighs 32 oz., and has an overall length of 9". Magazine capacity is 8 rounds. Checkered two-piece walnut grips. Blued finish. An improved version was built in 1910 and another version was built in 1911. This last version was a completely redesigned pistol: the Model 1911. Some 288 pistols were built in three different versions. Once the Army trials were over, Savage refinished the pistols with a matte blue finish and sold some of them commercially.

Courtesy James Rankin

Model 1907 Test Pistol

Manufactured in 1907 in .45 ACP, this pistol was tested in the U.S. Army trials. About 290 pistols were produced for these trials. Double stack magazine held 8 rounds.

Photo courtesy Bailey Brower, Jr.

Exc.	V.G.	Good	Fair	Poor
12500	10000	9500	6000	2000

Model 1910 Test Pistol

This was a modified Model 1907 with a heavier slide, which was not concave like the Model 1907. There were a total of nine Model 1910s built.

Exc.	V.G.	Good	Fair	Poor
Too Rare To Price				

Model 1911 Test Pistol

This example was completely modified with a longer and thinner grip. Checkered wood grips were attached by friction instead of screws, the slide release was modified, a full grip safety was added, and a heavier serrated hammer (cocking

A Model 1907 Test pistol, .45 ACP, sold at auction for $12,650. Condition is 98 percent finish. Grips are mint.
Rock Island Auction Company, August 2004

lever) was added. Four of these pistols were built. Serial #1 has never been located.

Exc.	V.G.	Good	Fair	Poor
Too Rare To Price				

Model 1917

This semiautomatic pistol is chambered for the 7.65mm cartridge. It is fitted with an external hammer and without the grip safety. The form of the grip frame has been widened. Manufactured between 1917 and 1928. This pistol was sold to the French government during World War I and used by the French military. Approximately 27,000 of these pistols were sold to France. See also *France, Handguns, Savage*.

Exc.	V.G.	Good	Fair	Poor
300	225	175	100	75

STURM, RUGER & CO.

Mark I Target Pistol (U.S. marked)

This is a semiautomatic target pistol with 6.88" barrel and target sights. Stamped "U.S." on top of receiver. First produced in 1956. Blued finish. Rebuilt or refinished pistols may be parkerized and stamped with arsenal stamp.

Exc.	V.G.	Good	Fair	Poor
800	600	400	250	150

GUIDE LAMP
Division of General Motors

Liberator

A .45 ACP caliber single shot pistol with a 3.5" smooth bore barrel and overall length of 5.5". This pistol is made primarily of stampings and was intended to be air dropped to partisans in Europe during WWII. The hollow grip is designed to hold a packet of four extra cartridges. Originally packaged in unmarked cardboard boxes with an illustrated instruction sheet.

Courtesy Richard M. Kumor Sr.

NIB	Exc.	V.G.	Good	Fair	Poor
4000	2500	1500	650	300	175

SUBMACHINE GUNS

Bibliographical Note: For historical information, technical data, and photos, see Tracie Hill, *Thompson: The American Legend*, Collector Grade Publications, 1996.

Colt 9mm (Model 635)

Based on the M16, this submachine gun is chambered for the 9mm cartridge. It was first produced in 1990. It has the capability of semi-automatic or full automatic fire. The barrel length is 10.125" with a 20- or 32-round magazine. The gun is fitted with a retractable stock. As with the M16, this gun fires from a closed bolt. Weight is about 6.5 lbs. Rate of fire is about 900 rounds per minute. "SMG" and serial number are marked on left side of magazine housing. Used by the U.S. military, although not in any official capacity, and other countries' military forces.

This model has several other variants:

Model 634—As above but with semi-automatic fire only.
Model 639—Same as the M635 but with 3-round burst.
Model 633HB—Fitted with 7" barrel and hydraulic buffer. (Manufactured after 1986)

NOTE: See also *U.S., Rifles, M16.*

Photo courtesy private NFA collection

Pre-1968

Exc.	V.G.	Fair
N/A	N/A	N/A

Pre-1986 conversions, for OEM add 20 percent

Exc.	V.G.	Fair
20000	18500	17500

Pre-1986 dealer samples

Exc.	V.G.	Fair
N/A	N/A	N/A

Ingram Model 10

Chambered for the 9mm or .45 ACP cartridge, this submachine gun is fitted with a 5.7" barrel and a 30-round magazine. It has a rate of fire of 1,100 rounds per minute. The empty weight is approximately 6.3 lbs. This submachine gun was used by various government agencies in Vietnam. A version chambered for the .380 cartridge is known as the Model 11.

Photo courtesy private NFA collection

Pre-1968

Exc.	V.G.	Fair
3000	2500	1500

Pre-1986 conversions

Exc.	V.G.	Fair
N/A	N/A	N/A

Pre-1986 dealer samples

Exc.	V.G.	Fair
N/A	N/A	N/A

Reising 50/55

First built in 1941, the gun was chambered for the .45 ACP cartridge. It was first used by Marines in the Pacific but failed to be combat reliable. The Model 50 was fitted with a wooden buttstock and 10.8" barrel. Magazine capacity was 12 or 20 rounds. Rate of fire was 550 rounds per minute. The gun has a select fire mechanism for single round operation. Marked "HARRINGTON & RICHARDSON WORCESTER MASS USA" on the top of the receiver. Weight was about 6.75 lbs.

The Model 55 is the same mechanism but with a wire folding stock and no muzzle compensator. The weight of the Model 55 was 6.25 lbs. About 100,000 Reising Model 50s and 55s were built between 1941 and 1945 when production ceased.

NOTE: Commercial guns will bring less than military marked guns. Add about 25 percent for U.S. martially marked guns.

Courtesy Richard M. Kumor Sr.

Pre-1968

Exc.	V.G.	Fair
4500	4000	3500

SNAP SHOT
REISING MODEL 50

The US Harrington & Richardson .45 caliber Model 50 submachine gun has had a bad rap for many years. Until rather recently, it was a stepchild in the collector community with prices quite low in comparison with other World War II-era submachine guns. The main complaint was that it was not widely used by our armed forces and that the gun suffered malfunctions due to an incompatibility of switching parts and parts failure (in particular the firing pin breaking near the tip, action bar cracking, fragile one-piece bumper plug, radial cracks on the muzzle compensator and burring of the top portion of the bolt). While these issues were addressed in later production runs, the cloud of doubt still remained. Nevertheless, the gun enjoyed widespread popularity with police departments and when properly maintained is quite reliable.

Unlike most submachine guns from that era that operated as direct open-bolt blow-back; the Reising is distinctive in that it fires from a delayed blow-back closed bolt. This allows for greater accuracy with the first shot in full-automatic fire and well aimed shots in semiautomatic mode.

One of the first things one notices when firing the Reising for the very first time is that the rate of fire is quite a bit higher than the 450-500 rounds per minute as is listed in their catalogues and manuals. Actual rate of fire is 750-850 rounds per minute. Since the weapon fires from a closed bolt, the bolt is very light. The high rate of fire using the .45 ACP round causes a lot of muzzle climb even with the compensator, resulting in controllability issues when firing full automatic; though the 20-round capacity magazines do encourage self discipline in fire management.

However, with an adequate supply of spare parts and religiously keeping the gun clean and well oiled, it will provide hours of fun at the range. This is a perfect entry-level classic submachine gun.

Robert G. Segel

Pre-1986 conversions

Exc.	V.G.	Fair
N/A	N/A	N/A

Pre-1986 dealer samples

Exc.	V.G.	Fair
2500	2000	1500

THOMPSON SUBMACHINE GUNS
Text and prices by Nick Tilotta

Thompson Model 1921AC/21A, 1921/28 Navy

The first Thompsons to come to market were the Model 1921s, manufactured by Colt Patent Firearms for Auto Ordnance Corporation in New York, New York. Between March 1921 and April 1922 15,000 guns were built. Of those 15,000 manufactured, only about 2,400 weapons exist in a transferable state today. Transferable, meaning weapons that can be bought, sold, or traded legally within the U.S. Three models of the Model 1921 were produced. The Model 1921A had a fixed front sight and a rate of fire of 800 rounds per minute. The Model 1921AC has a Cutts compensator instead of a fixed front sight and an 800-rounds-per-minute rate of fire. The Model 1928 Navy was fitted with a Cutts compensator and a heavier actuator that reduced the rate of fire to 600 rounds per minute. All of these Navy models had the number "8" stamped crudely over the number "1" on the left side of the receiver. Of the 15,000 Colt Model 1921s produced, approximately 25 percent were Model 1921As, 33 percent were Model 1921ACs, and 41 percent were 1928 Navys. A handful of Model 1927s were manufactured by Colt and left the factory as semiautomatics. However, the ATF considers these guns machine guns and requires that all NFA rules apply. These Model 1927s are quite rare and represent only about 1 percent of total production. They do not seem to sell for the same dollar figures that the machine guns do.

All Colt-manufactured Thompsons were bright blued; none were parkerized. All had walnut stocks, grips, and forearms manufactured by Remington. With the exception of a few prototypes, all Colt Thompsons were chambered for the .45 ACP cartridge. All internal parts were nickel plated and all barrels were finned. All weapons had a Lyman rear sight assembly. A removable rear stock was standard. All weapons were marked with a "NEW YORK, USA" address on the right side of the receiver. "COLT PATENT FIREARMS" was marked on the left side of the receiver. These Colt Thompsons would accept a 20- or 30-round box magazine as well as a 50-round "L" drum or 100 round "C" drum. Weight is about 10.75 lbs. Prices below are for original Colt guns with original parts and finish.

NOTE: Model 1921As, early serial numbers, previous ownership, and documentation can dramatically add to the prices below. In addition, missing components, re-barreled weapons, etc, will see a substantial reduction in price, as these original components are almost extinct. Re-finishing or re-bluing will result in a substantial reduction in value by as much as 50 percent.

Pre-1968

Exc.	V.G.	Fair
35000	25000	20000

Pre-1986 conversions

Exc.	V.G.	Fair
N/A	N/A	N/A

Pre-1986 dealer samples

Exc.	V.G.	Fair
N/A	N/A	N/A

PRICING NOTE: For Thompsons with historical background such as Texas Ranger or gangster guns prices can exceed 50 percent to 100 percent of above with documentation.

THOMPSON: ON THE SIDE OF LAW & ORDER

Robert M. Hausman

An outstanding exhibit telling the story of the Thompson Submachine Gun was on exhibit during the latter half of 2004 in the William B. Ruger Gallery of the National Firearms Museum at the NRA headquarters in Fairfax, Virginia.

The Thompson is one of the most easily recognized firearms in modern history. Hollywood black-and-white classics, such as "Little Caesar", early lurid tabloid newspaper stories, as well as the more recent film, "Dillinger," have made the profile of the Thompson gun a familiar image to the general public. However, the gun also has a very interesting history and once played a vital role in America's national defense.

This exhibit translated for the viewer the many models and types of Thompsons produced from 1919 through the present day. Examples of models produced by such manufacturers as Colt, Savage, Auto-Ordnance and others were on display, as well as modern versions produced by Auto-Ordnance/Kahr Arms. The Thompson Submachine Gun is currently more popular with collectors and shooters today than it has ever been.

Thompson Submachine Gun, Model of 1919. It is believed that only 40 Model of 1919 prototypes were constructed by Auto-Ordnance. This is an Annihilator III, Model G and has no factory-stamped serial number. This is the only unmodified Annihilator III, Model G known to exist.

Thompson Submachine Gun, Model of 1921AC, serial number 147. This Thompson was shipped from Colt's on May 24, 1921, to R.J. Coach & Co., of Cleveland, Ohio, a private detective/security firm, as a Model of 1921A. The Thompson later became owned by the Cleveland Ohio City Police Department and was modified to have the Cutts Compensator added to the barrel. It is shown with its FBI-style hard case, which carried the gun, one Type L (50-round) drum magazine, and four 20-round box magazines.

THOMPSON *(CONT.)*

Thompson Submachine Gun, Model of 1923. These models of the Thompson were converted Model of 1921s which had a longer barrel chambered for the .45 Remington-Thompson cartridge added. This cartridge had a 1/10" longer case than a standard .45 ACP round. This allowed a larger powder charge to propel a 250-grain bullet. The idea was to give the Thompson a greater range and hitting power. Several variations were produced with bipod, bayonet, Maxim Suppressor or Cutts Compensator. The cartridge and firearm never were a successful combination.

Perhaps one of the best action photos of WWII, this United States Marine provides covering fire with his Thompson M1 for his squad's BAR gunner in the South Pacific.

THOMPSON (CONT.)

Thompson Submachine Gun, Model of 1928, serial number 1195TF. In 1980, Auto-Ordnance, West Hurley, N.Y., produced a fully automatic .22 caliber Thompson. Due to various production problems and reliability issues, the production was ended in 1981, with a total of 220 produced. However, 62 of these receivers were later converted back to .45 ACP.

Motorcycle couriers were well-equipped during World War II with Thompson guns carried in scabbards.

THOMPSON (CONT.)

Thompson Submachine Gun, Model M1, serial number M220A. In 1986, a single production run of fully automatic Thompsons was made by Auto-Ordnance, West Hurley, N.Y. Only 609 of these were produced prior to the Firearms Owners Protection Act of 1986, which prohibited the new manufacture of full automatics for civilian ownership.

The All Thompson Shoot & Show is an annual event of the Thompson Collectors Association (POB 8710, Newark, OH 43055) since 1991. Members compete in two separate matches for numerous awards.

The opportunity to fire a Thompson submachine gun was offered as an inducement for recruits into the Navy Seabees during WWII.

THOMPSON (CONT.)

Thompson Semi-Auto, Model of 1927A1, serial number KA 1093. In January of 1999, the name Auto-Ordnance Corporation was transferred from Numrich Arms to Kahr Arms, headquartered in Blauvelt, N.Y. Auto-Ordnance/Kahr has continued the production of the Model of 1927A1 Thompson semi-automatic carbines in several configurations. The first model produced is this M1927A1 with a blued finish and steel receiver.

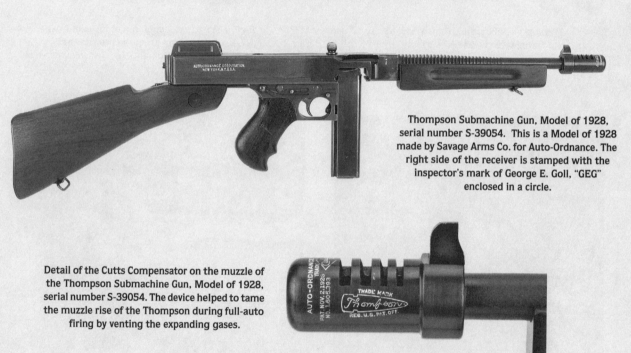

Thompson Submachine Gun, Model of 1928, serial number S-39054. This is a Model of 1928 made by Savage Arms Co. for Auto-Ordnance. The right side of the receiver is stamped with the inspector's mark of George E. Goll, "GEG" enclosed in a circle.

Detail of the Cutts Compensator on the muzzle of the Thompson Submachine Gun, Model of 1928, serial number S-39054. The device helped to tame the muzzle rise of the Thompson during full-auto firing by venting the expanding gases.

Thompson Submachine Gun, Model M1, serial number 90025. Made by Auto-Ordnance in Bridgeport, CT, this military M1 has inspectors and acceptance cartouches from Frank J. Atwood. This gun was a veteran "bring-back" from WWII. Note the early style rear sight configuration.

THOMPSON *(CONT.)*

Thompson Submachine Gun, Model of 1921AC, serial number 5672.   This Thompson is a "Reel Hero's Gun."
It starred in several movies and was once owned by Ellis Props and Graphics in Hollywood, California.
The last movie this gun appeared in was "The Untouchables" with Kevin Costner and Sean Connery.
This Thompson has had its appearance altered several times since it left the factory in January 1922.

Half-scale Thompson Model of 1928. This miniature was made by Edmond H. de la Garrigue in 1966 as a non-firing version.
It is complete with a Type L drum body and miniature copies of ammo boxes and manual.

THOMPSON (CONT.)

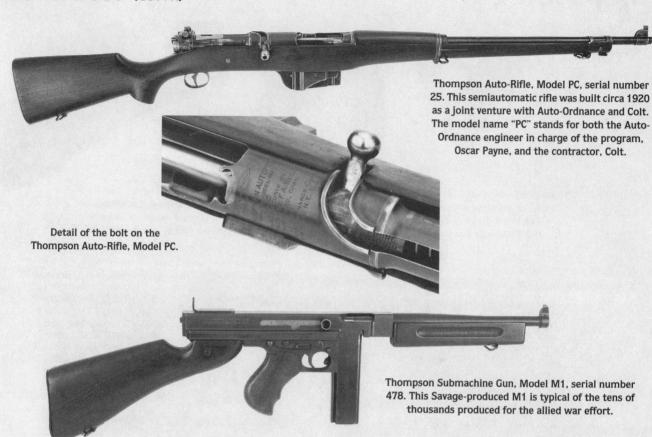

Thompson Auto-Rifle, Model PC, serial number 25. This semiautomatic rifle was built circa 1920 as a joint venture with Auto-Ordnance and Colt. The model name "PC" stands for both the Auto-Ordnance engineer in charge of the program, Oscar Payne, and the contractor, Colt.

Detail of the bolt on the Thompson Auto-Rifle, Model PC.

Thompson Submachine Gun, Model M1, serial number 478. This Savage-produced M1 is typical of the tens of thousands produced for the allied war effort.

A period photograph depicting a soldier firing the Thompson Submachine Gun, Model of 1923 chambered for the .45 Remington-Thompson cartridge.

Thompson Model 1921 with close-up of receiver stamping • Paul Goodwin photo

Thompson Model 1928 Commercial/1928A1 Military

The next limited run of Thompsons came just before and right at the beginning of WWII. This version is called the Model 1928AC or Commercial model. These weapons were assembled by Savage Arms in Utica, New York, using original Colt internal components. The receivers were still marked with the New York address but void of any "Colt" markings. Most weapons were simply marked "MODEL 1928." The first of these guns have blued receivers and blued barrels. The second run had parkerized receivers and blued barrels. These guns are quite rare and command premium prices.

At the outbreak of WWII, the demand for the Thompson gun soared. A brake lining facility in Bridgeport, Conn., was acquired to accommodate the increased demand for production. Three models of Thompsons were born in this WWII era. The first was the Model 1928A1 Thompson. This version was a copy of the Model 1928 Navy Colt Thompson. Most were parkerized with much less detail paid to fine machining. This gun was assembled in two locations: Utica, N.Y., and Bridgeport,

Conn. Receivers produced in Utica were marked with an "S" prefix in front of the serial number. Receivers marked with an "AO" prefix were produced in Bridgeport. Receivers were marked on the right side "AUTO ORDNANCE CORPORATION, BRIDGEPORT, CT," no matter where the receiver was manufactured. The Utica, N.Y., plant concentrated its efforts on manufacturing components while the Bridgeport facility concentrated on assemblies. As production increased, the Model 1928A1 lost many of its "unnecessary" components such as the finned barrel, the costly Lyman sight, and finely checkered selector switches. Approximately 562,000 Thompsons were produced in the Model 1928A1 configuration. All of the weapons were parkerized, and some have finned barrels and some have smooth barrels. Some of these guns were also fitted with Lyman sights, some have a stamped "L" type sight that may or may not have protective ears. As a general rule of thumb, most Model 1928 Commercial guns were fitted with a vertical foregrip while most Model 1928A1 guns were fitted with a horizontal forearm, and all had removable butt stocks. Used by Allied forces during WWII. Used both 20- or 30-round box magazines and 50- or 100-round drum magazines.

A Thompson Model 1921A DEWAT sold at auction for $23,000. Condition is 96 percent original blue. *Amoskeag Auction Company, May 2004*

Thompson Model 1928 Commercial

Pre-1968

Exc.	V.G.	Fair
35000	25000	20000

Pre-1986 conversions

Exc.	V.G.	Fair
N/A	N/A	N/A

Pre-1986 dealer samples

Exc.	V.G.	Fair
18000	12000	10000

Thompson Model 1928A1 Military

Pre-1968

Exc.	V.G.	Fair
22000	18000	16000

Pre-1986 conversions

Exc.	V.G.	Fair
N/A	N/A	N/A

Pre-1986 dealer samples

Exc.	V.G.	Fair
12000	10000	8000

Thompson M1/M1A1

In April 1942, the M1 Thompson was introduced. It was a simplified version of the Model 1928 with a smooth barrel, stamped rear "L" sight, and a fixed rear stock. The expensive Model 1928-type bolt assembly was modified to simplified machining procedures. The result was a repositioned cocking knob on the right side of the receiver. Some 285,000 M1s were produced before being replaced by an improved version, the "M1A1," in April 1942. This version of the Thompson has a fixed firing pin machined into the bolt face, and had protective ears added to the rear sight assembly. All M1 Thompsons were fitted with a horizontal forearm and fixed butt stock. Approximately 540,000 M1A1 Thompsons were produced before the end of WWII. All M1 and M1A1 Thompsons used stick or box magazines only.

NOTE: Many of these weapons were reworked by a military arsenal during the war and may have been refinished; however, it does not significantly reduce the value of the gun. In addition to the rework, many of the serial numbered lower assemblies were not assembled with the correct serial numbered receiver. Although this may disturb some collectors, it should not significantly devalue the weapon. A very small percentage of these weapons were marked "US PROPERTY" behind the rear sight and this increases the value by as much as $1,000.

Courtesy Richard M. Kumor, Sr.

Pre-1968

Exc.	V.G.	Fair
18000	16000	14000

Pre-1986 conversions

Exc.	V.G.	Fair
N/A	N/A	N/A

Pre-1986 dealer samples

Exc.	V.G.	Fair
10000	8000	6000

Third Generation Thompsons

In 1975, the Auto Ordnance Corp., West Hurley, New York, began production of the new Model 1928 Thompson. It was an attempt to produce a version of the Thompson for the civilian collector as well as a limited number of law enforcement sales. The early weapons were manufactured from surplus WWII components and were quite acceptable in quality. As time wore on, however, many of the components were of new manufacture and lesser quality. Between 1975 and 1986, approximately 3,200 models of the 1928 were produced. Some of these guns were commemorative models. The weapons had finned barrels, flip-up rear leaf sights, removable stocks, and blued finish. In 1985 and 1986, approximately 600 versions of the M1 Thompson were built. These were actually a version of the M1A1 military Thompson with blued finish. With the exception of a short production run for export in 1992, production of these weapons was banned in May 1986 by Federal law. All receivers were marked "AUTO-ORDNANCE WEST HURLEY, NEW YORK" on the right side of the receiver and "THOMPSON SUB-MACHINE GUN, CALIBER .45 M1" on the left side. All serial numbers carried the letter "A" suffix. A very limited number of .22 caliber models were produced in the Model 1928 configuration, but had limited success in the market.

Thompson Model 1928—West Hurley

Pre-1968

Exc.	V.G.	Fair
15000	12000	8000

Pre-1986 conversions

Exc.	V.G.	Fair
N/A	N/A	N/A

Pre-1986 dealer samples

Exc.	V.G.	Fair
7500	6000	4000

Thompson Model M1—West Hurley

Pre-1968

Exc.	V.G.	Fair
14000	11000	7000

Pre-1986 conversions

Exc.	V.G.	Fair
N/A	N/A	N/A

Pre-1986 dealer samples

Exc.	V.G.	Fair
7000	5500	3500

Thompson Model 1928 .22 caliber—West Hurley

Pre-1968

Exc.	V.G.	Fair
10000	8000	6000

Pre-1986 conversions

Exc.	V.G.	Fair
N/A	N/A	N/A

Pre-1986 dealer samples

Exc.	V.G.	Fair
5000	4000	3000

UD (United Defense) M42

Built by Marlin for U.S. military forces beginning in 1942. Designed by Carl Swebilius, founder of High Standard. Well constructed of excellent materials. Chambered for the 9mm Parabellum cartridge. Select fire with rate of fire of 700 rounds per minute. Barrel length was 10.8". Weight is about 9 lbs. Markings on left side of receiver are "UNITED DEFENSE SUPPLY CORP/US MODEL 42/MARLIN FA CO NEW HAVEN." Magazine capacity is 20 rounds. Limited quantities produced with an estimate of about 15,000 produced. It seems that the majority were built to be sold to the Netherlands during WWII but, because of the war, they could not be delivered, so most were

U.S. M3 with silencer • Courtesy Chuck Karwan

US M3

First produced in the U.S. in 1942, this submachine gun was chambered for the .45 ACP or 9mm cartridge (special conversion kit). It is similar in concept to the British Sten gun. It was fitted with an 8" barrel and folding metal stock. The box magazine capacity was 30 rounds. The rate of fire was 400 rounds per minute. Weight of the M3 was about 8 lbs. It was produced until 1944. Marked "GUIDE LAMP DIV OF GENERAL MOTORS/US MODEL M3" on top of the receiver. Approximately 600,000 M3s were produced. Built by the Guide Lamp Division of General Motors.

NOTE: A suppressed version of this gun was built for the OSS in World War II, and used for covert operations in Vietnam as well. Too rare to price.

US M3 • Courtesy Richard M. Kumor Sr.

Pre-1968

Exc.	V.G.	Fair
18000	16000	14000

Pre-1986 conversions (or current U.S. manufacture)

Exc.	V.G.	Fair
8000	7000	6500

Pre-1986 dealer samples

Exc.	V.G.	Fair
9000	8000	7000

US M3A1

Similar to the M3 but with significant changes and improvements. This model has a larger ejection port, the retracting handle has been eliminated, a finger hole is used for cocking, disassembly grooves were added, a stronger cover spring was installed, a larger oil can is in the grip, a stock plate and magazine filler were added to the stock, and a guard was added for the magazine catch. First produced in 1944. Approximately 50,000 M3A1s were built. This version was built by Guide Lamp and Ithaca.

shipped to the American OSS for use in Europe and the Far East. These guns saw a lot of action during the war.

Private NFA collection, Gary Gelson photo

Pre-1968

Exc.	V.G.	Fair
15000	13000	12000

Pre-1986 conversions

Exc.	V.G.	Fair
12000	10000	9000

Pre-1986 dealer samples

Exc.	V.G.	Fair
9000	8000	7000

An M-3 submachine gun registered as a DEWAT sold at auction for $10,925. Condition is 95 percent overall finish. A single 30-round magazine included.
Amoskeag Auction Company, May 2004

US M3A1 • Photo courtesy private NFA collection

A Peabody military rifle in .43 Spanish with 33-inch barrel sold at auction for $3,162.50. Complete with bayonet. Inspector's cartouche. Condition is 95 percent overall.
Rock Island Auction Company, August 2004

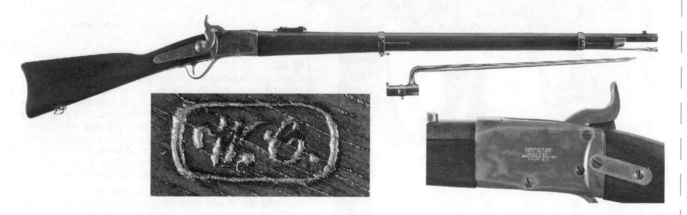

Pre-1968

Exc.	V.G.	Fair
18000	16000	14000

Pre-1986 conversions (or current U.S. manufacture)

Exc.	V.G.	Fair
N/A	N/A	N/A

Pre-1986 dealer samples

Exc.	V.G.	Fair
9000	8000	7000

RIFLES

PEABODY
Providence, Rhode Island

These rifles were made by the Providence Tool Company from 1866 to 1871. Total production for all models was approximately 112,000. These rifles were produced in a wide variety of calibers and used by military forces in Canada, Spain, Switzerland, and others. They were also issued to three state militias: Connecticut, Massachusetts, and South Carolina.

NOTE: U.S. and Canadian marked will bring a premium over foreign marked rifles of about 20 percent.

Rifle

This is a lever-action, top-loading rifle with side hammer. Full stocked with two barrel bands. The front sight also serves as a bayonet fitting. Weight is about 10 lbs. The .45-70 caliber is the most sought after chambering. Also chambered for the .50-60 Peabody Musket rimfire. In general, European calibers denote foreign military contracts.

NOTE: Canada acquired 3,000 rifles in .50-60 caliber in 1865. Switzerland acquired 15,000 rifles in .41 Swiss rimfire in 1867. Romania acquired 25,000 rifles in .45 Romanian centerfire. France acquired 39,000 rifles during the Franco-Prussian War. Some rifles were chambered for the .43 Spanish centerfire cartridge and some were chambered for the .50-79 cartridge.

Exc.	V.G.	Good	Fair	Poor
—	2000	1150	500	200

Carbine

This version has the same action but is half stocked with a single barrel band. Chambered for the .45 Peabody rimfire cartridge. Fitted with a 20" barrel. Weight is about 8.5 lbs.

Exc.	V.G.	Good	Fair	Poor
—	2750	1500	750	300

Model 1874 Peabody-Martini Rifle

This rifle was almost identical to the British Martini-Henry Mark I rifle (.45 Martini Henry cartridge). Built by the Providence Tool Company, it was not adopted by any U.S. military. About

A Peabody Carbine sold at auction for $2,875. Condition is excellent with 90 percent case colors. "WO" cartouche. Blue is 80 percent. Wood is near mint.
Rock Island Auction Company, August 2004

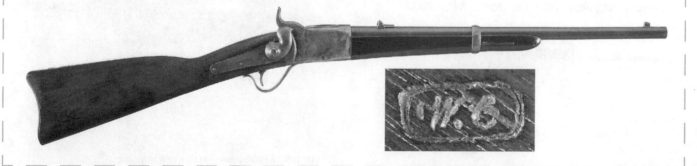

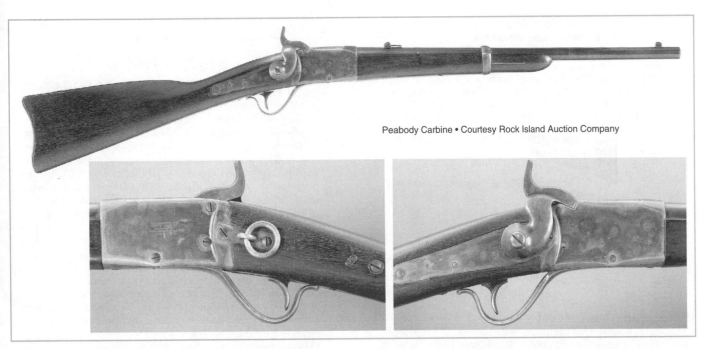

Peabody Carbine • Courtesy Rock Island Auction Company

600,000 were sold to the Turkish military and used in the Russo-Turkish War, 1877-1878. Marked "PEABODY-MARTINI PATENTS." Rifle chambered for the .45 Turkish caliber and fitted with a 32.5" barrel with two barrel bands. Full stock. Weight is about 8.75 lbs.

NOTE: A few rifles were chambered for the .50-70 Gov't. cartridge.

Exc.	V.G.	Good	Fair	Poor
—	1200	600	300	150

Model 1874 Peabody-Martini Carbine

As above but with 21.5" barrel and one barrel band. Half stocked. Fitted with a saddle ring.

NOTE: Some of the rifles and carbines were sold to the Japanese Navy and exhibit both Turkish and Japanese markings.

Exc.	V.G.	Good	Fair	Poor
—	1500	800	400	200

Model 1879 Peabody-Martini Rifle

See *Romania, Rifle, Peabody-Martini.*

SNAP SHOT
PEABODY-MARTINI RIFLE

If there is one military arm by which the name designations are thoroughly confusing it has to be the **Peabody Rifle**; or is it the **Peabody-Martini**? No, it has to be the **Martini-Henry** or does it? See what I mean?

The rifle developed by Henry O. Peabody should have been a resounding success with the U.S. Army. It was not. In late 1864, by the time Peabody had his side-hammer rifle, utilizing a pivoting breach block, ready for production the war was practically over. With a glut of arms at war's end, the Ordinance Dept. was more focused on modernizing the existing stockpile than acquiring new designs. However, a few National Guard units and several foreign countries adopted the **Peabody Rifle**.

A Swiss gunsmith by the name of Frederich von Martini improved the design by eliminating the side lock and incorporating a spring-loaded firing pin that was cocked upon opening the action. Martini was able to sell the design to the British who after much testing added to the rifle the Alexander Henry system of rifling. The now hammerless, self cocking rifle became what we know as the **Martini-Henry** chambered for the British .577/450 cartridge. The rifle through several model designations (Mark I – IV) took its place in the long line of Enfield-produced rifles having served the British Empire for over three decades. But, the same rifles were also produced in the United States and designated as **Peabody-Martini** rifles.

Back at the Providence Tool Company in Rhode Island, the very factory that had produced the original **Peabody rifle**, production of the Martini-Henry rifles was in full swing for the Turkish Army. The company had tried to sell the side-hammer Peabody design to the Turks but they chose the Martini improved hammerless design. Through some bizarre arrangements which even included Oliver Winchester, the Providence Tool Company produced over 600,000 exact copies of the British Martini-Henry rifles but were stamped as being **Peabody-Martini** rifles.

Now, one last tidbit of trivia to further muddy the water. Some of the original Peabody (side-hammer) rifles for the Connecticut Militia were refurbished with .45-70 barrels having Alexander Henry rifling. Were these **Peabody-Henry** rifles or what? Time for a Martini!

Kenny Durham

SPENCER
Boston, Massachusetts

Spencer Model 1860 Carbine

This was one of the most popular firearms used by Union forces during the Civil War. It is chambered for a metallic rimfire cartridge known as the "No. 56." It is actually a .52 caliber and was made with a copper case. The barrel is 22" in length. The finish is blued, with a carbine-length walnut stock held on by one barrel band. There is a sling swivel at the butt. There were approximately 45,733 manufactured between 1863 and 1865. Cartouche marked.

Courtesy Butterfield & Butterfield, San Francisco, California

Exc.	V.G.	Good	Fair	Poor
—	—	4750	2000	500

Military Rifle–Navy Model

This model is similar to the carbine, with a 30" round barrel and a full-length walnut stock held on by three barrel bands. It features an iron forend tip and sling swivels. The Civil War production consisted of two models. A Navy model was manufactured between 1862 and 1864 (there were approximately 803 of these so marked).

Exc.	V.G.	Good	Fair	Poor
—	—	5000	2250	600

Military Rifle–Army Model

There were approximately 11,471 produced for the army during the Civil War. They are similar to the navy model except that the front sight doubles as a bayonet lug. They were manufactured in 1863 and 1864. There were also, according to Marcot, about 200 built for the navy. Cartouche marked, "MMJ or DAP" or both.

Courtesy Milwaukee Public Museum, Milwaukee, Wisconsin

Exc.	V.G.	Good	Fair	Poor
—	—	4000	1750	600

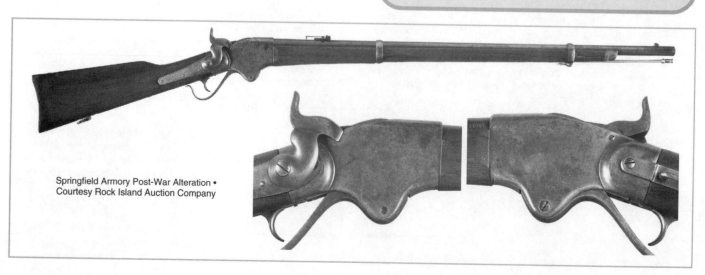

Springfield Armory Post-War Alteration •
Courtesy Rock Island Auction Company

Springfield Armory Post-War Alteration

After the conclusion of the Civil War, approximately 11,000 carbines were refurbished and rechambered for .50 caliber rimfire. The barrels were sleeved, and a device known as the "Stabler cut-off" was added to convert the arm to single-shot function. Often they were refinished and restocked. The inspector's marks "ESA" will be found in an oval cartouche on the left side of the stock. These alterations took place in 1867 and 1868.

Exc.	V.G.	Good	Fair	Poor
—	—	3750	1500	500

Burnside Model 1865 Spencer Carbine Contract

This model was manufactured by the Burnside Rifle Company in 1865. They are similar to the Civil War-type carbine and are marked "By Burnside Rifle Co./Model 1865". Cartouche marked "HEV and GC" or "LH and GC". There were approximately 30,502 manufactured for the U.S. Army, and 19,000 of these had the Stabler cut-off device.

NOTE: There were a number of other variations in the Spencer line. It would behoove anyone interested in collecting this fine Civil War firearm to educate oneself on these variances and to secure individual appraisal if transactions are contemplated. This is a complex model with many subtle variations. The best place to begin is with Roy Marcot's book, *Spencer Repeating Firearms*, 1983.

Exc.	V.G.	Good	Fair	Poor
—	—	3750	1500	500

SHARPS RIFLE MANUFACTURING COMPANY

Metallic Cartridge Conversions (1867)

In 1867 approximately 32,000 Model 1859, 1863 and 1865 Sharps were altered to .52-70 rimfire and centerfire caliber. These conversions are cartouche marked in the middle of the left side of the butt stock.

Carbines (.52-70 CF—27,000 converted)

Exc.	V.G.	Good	Fair	Poor
—	—	3500	2000	600

Rifles (.50-70 centerfire—1,086 converted)

Exc.	V.G.	Good	Fair	Poor
—	—	4500	2500	600

Model 1869

A .40-50 to .50-70 caliber model produced in a military form with 26", 28", or 30" barrels; as a carbine with 21" or 24" barrels and in a sporting version with various barrel lengths and a forend stock fitted with a pewter tip. Approximately 650 were made.

SNAP SHOT
THE SHARPS CONVERSION RIFLES & CARBINES

At the end of the Civil War the U.S. Arsenals were filled with a quantity of muzzle-loading and breech-loading arms in numbers too significant to ignore as surplus. An economic solution was to convert the arms to that of metallic cartridge firing breechloaders. Some designs were impractical to convert and thus sold as surplus. But the Sharps New Models 1859, 1863, and 1865 were ideally suited for metallic cartridges. On October 26, 1867, the Sharps Rifle Manufacturing Company received a contract to convert Sharps percussion carbines to fire the .50 Govt. (.50-70) cartridge. Thus set in place the development of what was to eventually become one of the most renowned single-shot rifles of all time, the Model 1874 Sharps.

The Sharps conversion consisted of reinforcing (relining) the .52 cal. barrel to .50 cal., modifying or replacing the breech block and hammer, plus other less significant changes. On those that I have examined, the Lawrence priming system has been left intact. Interestingly, if the existing .52 caliber barrels were found to be in good repair and not oversized, they were modified only chambering the arm for the .50 caliber cartridge, relying on the soft lead bullets to expand to the greater diameter. By 1869 most of the suitable surplus Civil War Sharps had been converted. Additionally, the Sharps Company and private gunsmiths converted civilian-owned Sharps to .50-70 and other calibers. In the movie Quigley Down Under, Matthew Quigley (Tom Selleck) states that his rifle is a conversion, meaning that it was once a military percussion carbine. The carbines were used effectively by cavalry units on several fronts during the ensuing years. When the .50 cal cartridge was replaced by the .45 Govt. (.45-70) the Sharps were gradually withdrawn from regular service, issued to State Militia units, and ultimately sold as surplus when the transition to .45 cal was accomplished. The conversion of the Sharps straight-breech percussion carbines to that of chambering centerfire metallic cartridges signaled the end of one era and the beginning of a new age in firearms.

Kenny Durham

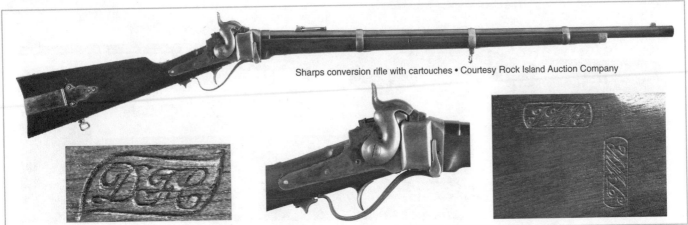

Sharps conversion rifle with cartouches • Courtesy Rock Island Auction Company

Carbine

.50-70, saddle ring on frame.

Exc.	V.G.	Good	Fair	Poor
—	—	4750	2000	500

Military Rifle

.50-70, 30" barrel with three barrel bands.

Exc.	V.G.	Good	Fair	Poor
—	—	5500	2250	800

Model 1870 Springfield Altered

Chambered for .50-70 caliber and fitted with a 35.5" barrel with two barrel bands, walnut stock, case hardened lock and breechlock. Buttplate stamped "US". Also built for Army trials with 22" barrel converted to centerfire.

First Type

Most common, straight breech.

Courtesy Butterfield & Butterfield

Exc.	V.G.	Good	Fair	Poor
—	—	4000	1750	500

Second Type

Model 1874 action, serial #1 to 300.

Exc.	V.G.	Good	Fair	Poor
—	—	6750	3000	750

Carbine

22" barrel converted to centerfire.

Exc.	V.G.	Good	Fair	Poor
—	—	8250	5000	1250

PEDERSEN, JOHN D.
Denver, CO & Jackson, WY

NOTE: Thanks to Jim Supica for his research into the Pedersen rifle and carbine that appeared for sale in his Old Town Station Dispatch.

John D. Pedersen was the inventor and designer of the Pedersen device that consisted of a conversion unit to be installed in a modified Springfield .30-06 bolt action rifle. This device allowed the rifle to function as a semiautomatic. At the end of World War I the idea was discarded. During the 1920s, Pedersen and John Garand began working on a new semiautomatic military rifle for U.S. forces. Pedersen's design was chambered for the .276 caliber and his rifle eventually lost out to Garand's rifle, the M1. The Pedersen rifles and carbines appear to be part of a test group for military trials. Total number built is unknown.

NOTE: Most Springfield-manufactured Pedersen rifles are so rare as not to be available to the collector. Therefore, only those rifles made by Vickers are listed.

Pedersen Rifle

Chambered for .276 Pedersen cartridge. Marked "PEDERSEN SELF LOADER PA/VICKERS-ARMSTRONG LTD." on the left side of the receiver. In oval over chamber marked "C/2." Rare.

Exc.	V.G.	Good	Fair	Poor
12500	7500	—	—	—

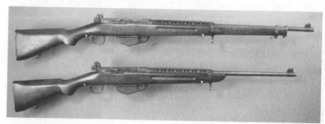

Pedersen rifle at top, carbine at bottom • Courtesy Jim Supica, Old Town Station

Pedersen Carbine

Same caliber and markings as rifle, but with 23" barrel. Rare.

Exc.	V.G.	Good	Fair	Poor
15000	8500	—	—	—

SPRINGFIELD ARMORY

This was America's first federal armory. It began producing military weapons in 1795 with the Springfield Model 1795 musket. The armory has supplied famous and well-known military weapons to the United States military forces throughout its history. The armory was phased out in 1968. The buildings and its collections are now part of the National Park Service.

Bibliographical Note: For further information, technical data, and photos, see the following: Robert W.D. Ball, *Springfield Armory Shoulder Weapons, 1795-1968*, Antique Trader Books, 1997. Blake Stevens, *U.S. Rifle M14 From John Garand to the M21*, Collector Grade Publications. William S. Brophy, *The Springfield 1903 Rifles*, Stackpole Books, 1985. Bruce Canfield, *A Collector's Guide to the '03 Springfield*, Andrew Mowbray Publishers, 1991.

Joslyn Breech-Loading Rifle

Until recently, this rifle was considered a post-Civil War breechloading conversion of a muzzleloading musket, but information developed since the 1970s indicates that this was the first true breechloading cartridge rifle to be made in quantity by a national armory, circa 1864. Actions were supplied to the Springfield Armory by the Joslyn Firearms Co. where they

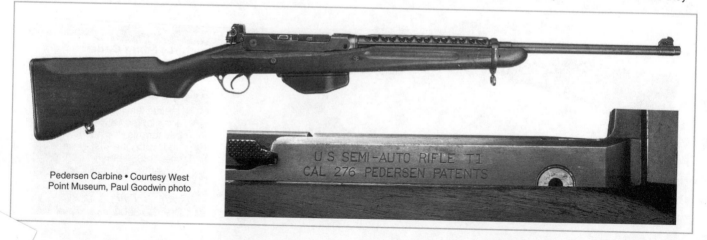

Pedersen Carbine • Courtesy West Point Museum, Paul Goodwin photo

U S SEMI-AUTO RIFLE T1
CAL 276 PEDERSEN PATENTS

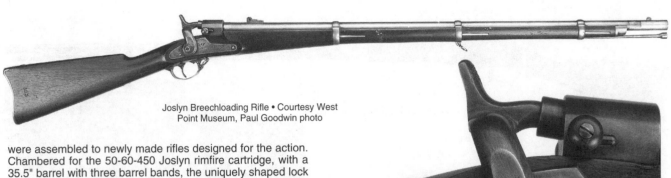

Joslyn Breechloading Rifle • Courtesy West
Point Museum, Paul Goodwin photo

were assembled to newly made rifles designed for the action. Chambered for the 50-60-450 Joslyn rimfire cartridge, with a 35.5" barrel with three barrel bands, the uniquely shaped lock with eagle ahead of the hammer, "U.S./Springfield" on the front of the lock, with "1864" at the rear. Walnut stock specially made for the barreled action and lock. Converted to 50-70 centerfire will command approximately $100 more.

SNAP SHOT
SPRINGFIELD MODEL 1866 – 2ND ALLIN CONVERTSION

A milestone in firearms development has always been an introduction of a new rifle firing a newly developed cartridge. Such was the case when the .50 Govt. cartridge (.50-70) was chambered for the new Springfield Model 1866 centerfire rifle. The rifle and the companion cartridge were an immediate success with the troops and civilians lucky enough to get their hands on one. In its short span as the primary U.S. Service Rifle, the 2nd Allin racked up a number of impressive showings. Within a year after being issued to the troops the 1866 accounted two notable successes; the Hayfield Fight near Ft. Smith and the Wagon Fight near Ft. Kearney. Hundreds of buffalo were felled by William F. "Buffalo Bill" Cody with his 2nd Allin Conversion to which he referred as "Lucretia Borgia" because of her lethality. In 1871, over 26,000 Model 1866s were sold to arms suppliers for France for use in the Franco-Prussian War.

The Model 1866 was called the 2nd Allin Conversion because of how the rifle was transformed from a .58 cal muzzle-loading rifled musket into a .50 cal breech-loading metallic cartridge centerfire rifle. Springfield 1863 muskets were converted by milling out about 3 inches of the upper half of the barrel from the breech plug forward. The barrel was bored to .64 cal, a .50 cal liner soldered in place, and a hinged breech block attached to the barrel. Given the model designation of "1866" the converted rifle was the first U.S. Service rifle to use the central fire priming system or centerfire primers as we know it today. The new .50 cal centerfire cartridge propelling a 450-gr. bullet over 1200 fps from the transformed rifle was an awesome leap forward at the time. So much so that 27 soldiers and 9 civilians held off 1000 Sioux warriors for 3 hours until help arrived during the Wagon Box Fight.

My 1866 has a bore that shows almost no wear; a testament to those who have cared for her over the last century and one quarter. Some day, it is my goal to take her to the lands of the Lakota to respectfully harvest a buffalo as did her sister Lucretia long ago.

Kenny Durham

Exc.	V.G.	Good	Fair	Poor
—	2500	1200	700	400

Model 1865 U.S. Breech-Loading Rifle, Allin Conversion, aka First Model Allin

Designed in .58 caliber rimfire, with a 40" barrel with three flat barrel bands. The breechlock is released by a thumb latch on the right side, pivoted upward, with the firing pin contained within the breechblock. 5,000 Model 1861 percussion muskets were altered using this method at the Springfield Armory circa 1865. The breechblock is unmarked, while the lock is marked with the eagle ahead of the hammer, as well as "U.S./Springfield," with all specimens dated 1865 at the rear.

Exc.	V.G.	Good	Fair	Poor
—	5000	3000	1500	1200

Model 1866 U.S. Breech-Loading Rifle, Allin Conversion, aka Second Model Allin

Produced in .50 caliber centerfire, with a 40" barrel with a .50 caliber liner tube inserted and brazed, walnut stock with three barrel bands with band springs. Differences between the First and Second Model Allin include a lengthened bolt, a firing pin spring, and a stronger internal extraction system. The breechblock is marked with "1866" over an eagle, while the lock bears standard Springfield markings with either an 1863 or 1864 date. A total of 25,000 Model 1863 percussion muskets were thus altered at the Springfield Armory around 1866.

Exc.	V.G.	Good	Fair	Poor
—	4000	2200	800	500

Model 1867 U.S. Breech-Loading Cadet Rifle

This model is a .50 caliber centerfire, 33" barrel, two band, scaled down version of the Model 1866 Second Model Allin "trapdoor." No sling swivels; a narrow triggerguard. The breechblock has a blackened finish, with deeply arched cutouts on both sides of the underside, leaving a narrow flat ridge in the center. The breechblock is marked 1866/eaglehead. The lock plate was made especially for this rifle and is noticeably thinner. The plate is marked with the usual eagle and "US/Springfield," with the date "1866" behind the hammer. About 424 rifles were produced at the Springfield Armory between 1876 and 1868.

Exc.	V.G.	Good	Fair	Poor
—	10000	7500	3000	800

Model 1866 Breechloading rifle with lock • Paul Goodwin photo

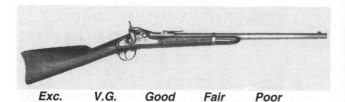

Model 1868 Rifle

This is a single shot Trapdoor rifle chambered for the .50 caliber centerfire cartridge. It features a breechblock that pivots forward when a thumblatch at its rear is depressed. It has a 32.5" barrel and a full-length stock held on by two barrel bands. It has iron mountings and a cleaning rod mounted under the barrel. It features an oil-finished walnut stock. The lock is marked "US Springfield." It is dated either 1863 or 1864. The breechblock features either the date 1869 or 1870. There were approximately 51,000 manufactured between 1868 and 1872.

Courtesy Little John's Auction Service, Inc., Paul Goodwin photo

Exc.	V.G.	Good	Fair	Poor
—	2500	1250	500	350

Model 1869 Cadet Rifle

This is a single shot trapdoor rifle chambered for .50 caliber centerfire. It is similar to the Model 1868 with a 29.5" barrel. There were approximately 3,500 manufactured between 1869 and 1876.

Courtesy Little John's Auction Service, Inc., Paul Goodwin photo

Exc.	V.G.	Good	Fair	Poor
—	3250	1500	500	200

Model 1870

There are two versions of this Trapdoor breechloader—a rifle with a 32.5" barrel and a carbine that features a 22" barrel and a half-stock held on by one barrel band. They are both chambered for .50 caliber centerfire and feature the standard Springfield lock markings and a breechblock marked "1870" or "Model 1870." There were a total of 11,500 manufactured between 1870 and 1873. Only 340 are carbines; they are extremely rare.

Rifle

Courtesy Milwaukee Public Museum, Milwaukee, Wisconsin

Exc.	V.G.	Good	Fair	Poor
—	3750	1750	800	500

Carbine
Very Rare.

Exc.	V.G.	Good	Fair	Poor
—	16500	9500	3500	1500

Model 1871 Rolling Block U.S. Army Rifle

This model is a .50 caliber centerfire, 36" barrel, with two barrel bands, and rolling block action. Sights, sling-swivels, and most other details as for the Model 1870 Remington U.S. Navy rifle. Case-hardened frame, bright finished iron mountings. Two piece walnut stock. Known as the "locking action" as the hammer went to half cock when the breechblock was closed. No serial numbers. Left side of frame marked "Model 1871." Right side marked with eagle over "U.S./Springfield/1872." On the tang, marked "REMINGTON'S PATENT. PAT.MAY 3D, NOV. 15TH, 1864, APRIL 17TH, 1868." About 10,000 rifles were produced between 1871 and 1872 under a royalty agreement with Remington Arms Co.

Exc.	V.G.	Good	Fair	Poor
—	4500	2000	750	500

Model 1871 Ward-Burton U.S. Rifle

A .50 caliber centerfire, 32.63" barrel secured by two barrel bands. This is an early bolt action, single shot rifle, with the cartridge loaded directly into the open action, with cocking on the closing of the bolt. Walnut stock, sling swivels on the forward barrel band and the front of the triggerguard. Not serially numbered. The top of the bolt marked, "WARD BURTON PATENT DEC. 20, 1859-FEB. 21, 1871." Left side of the action marked with American eagle motif and "US/SPRINGFIELD." 1,011 rifles (32.625" barrel) and 316 carbines (22" barrel) produced at the Springfield Armory basically as a trial weapon.

Courtesy Greg Martin Auctions

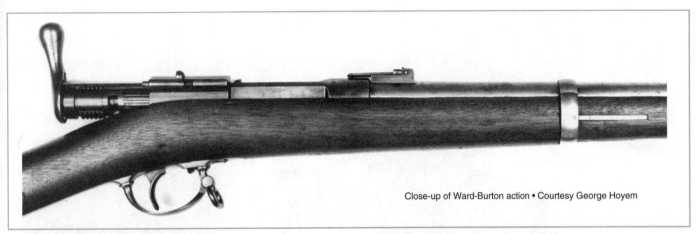

Close-up of Ward-Burton action • Courtesy George Hoyem

A Ward Burton Saddle Ring Carbine was sold at auction for $4,600. Chambered for the .50-70 cartridge and fitted with a 22-inch round barrel. Condition is brown patina with gray receiver. Wood very good.
Rock Island Auction Company, August 2004

Rifle

Exc.	V.G.	Good	Fair	Poor
—	4250	2000	750	400

Carbine

Exc.	V.G.	Good	Fair	Poor
—	6500	3000	950	450

Model 1873

This is a Trapdoor breechloading rifle chambered for the .45-70 cartridge. The rifle version has a 32.5" barrel with a full-length stock held on by two barrel bands. The carbine features a 22" barrel with a half-stock held on by a single barrel band, and the cadet rifle features a 29.5" barrel with a full length stock and two barrel bands. The finish of all three variations is blued and case-colored, with a walnut stock. The lock is marked "US Springfield 1873." The breechblock is either marked "Model 1873" or "US Model 1873." There were approximately 73,000 total manufactured between 1873 and 1877.

NOTE: Prices listed are for rifles in original configuration.

Rifle
50,000 manufactured.

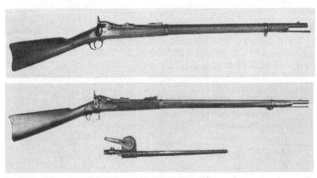

Courtesy Milwaukee Public Museum, Milwaukee, Wisconsin

Exc.	V.G.	Good	Fair	Poor
—	2750	1000	400	200

Carbine
20,000 manufactured.

Exc.	V.G.	Good	Fair	Poor
—	9000	4000	1750	700

Cadet Rifle
3,000 manufactured.

Exc.	V.G.	Good	Fair	Poor
—	1750	750	600	300

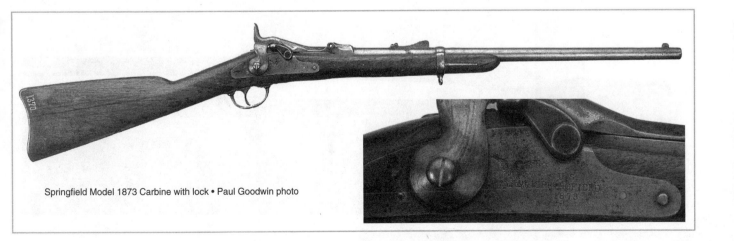

Springfield Model 1873 Carbine with lock • Paul Goodwin photo

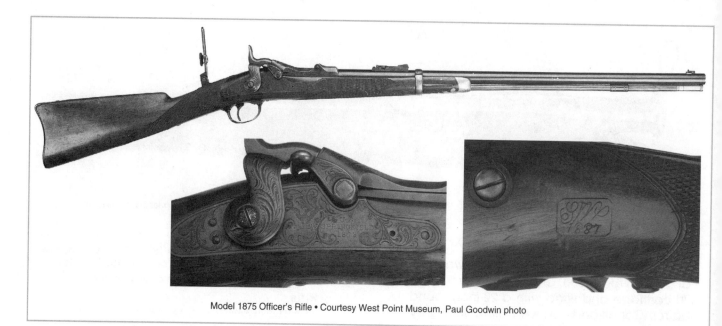

Model 1875 Officer's Rifle • Courtesy West Point Museum, Paul Goodwin photo

Model 1875 Officer's Rifle

This is a high-grade Trapdoor breechloader chambered for the .45-70 cartridge. It has a 26" barrel and a half-stock fastened by one barrel band. It is blued and case-colored, with a scroll engraved lock. It has a checkered walnut pistol grip stock with a pewter forend tip. There is a cleaning rod mounting beneath the barrel. This rifle was not issued but was sold to army officers for personal sporting purposes. There were only 477 manufactured between 1875 and 1885.

Exc.	V.G.	Good	Fair	Poor
35000	25000	10000	7000	3500

Model 1875 Lee Vertical Action Rifle

A .45-70 centerfire, 32.63" barrel secured by two barrel bands. Martini-style dropping block action, with a unique, centrally mounted hammer with an exceptionally long spur. In order to open the breech, the hammer must be given a sharp blow with the heal of the hand; the insertion of a cartridge will automatically close the breech, while the hammer is cocked by hand. All blued finish. Stacking and sling swivel on upper band, with sling swivel on triggerguard. Serially numbered 1 through 143 on the internal parts only. Upper tang marked, "U.S. PAT. MAR 16, 1875," no barrel proofmarks; inspector's initials "ESA" in an oval on the stock. 143 rifles produced in 1875 at the Springfield Armory, basically as a trials weapon.

Exc.	V.G.	Good	Fair	Poor
8500	5500	2500	1500	1000

A Model 1875 1st Model Officer's Rifle sold at auction for $23,625. Condition is near mint. *Greg Martin Auctions, November 2004*

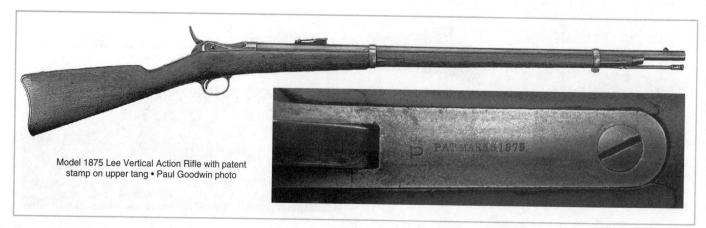

Model 1875 Lee Vertical Action Rifle with patent stamp on upper tang • Paul Goodwin photo

Model 1877 Cadet Rifle • Paul Goodwin photo

A Springfield Model 1877 Carbine sold at auction for $7,312.50. Saddle ring with ESA/1977 cartouche. Condition is 85 percent plumb brown with 85 percent blue. Wood excellent. Excellent bore.
Greg Martin Auctions, November 2004

Model 1877

This is a Trapdoor breechloading rifle chambered for the .45-70 cartridge. It was issued as a rifle with a 32" barrel and a full-length stock held on by two barrel bands, a cadet rifle with a 29.5" barrel, and a carbine with a 22" barrel, half-stock, and single barrel band. This version is similar to the Model 1873. In fact, the breechblock retained the Model 1873 marking. The basic differences are that the stock is thicker at the wrist and the breechblock was thickened and lowered. This is basically a mechanically improved version. There were approximately 12,000 manufactured in 1877 and 1878.

Rifle
3,900 manufactured.

Exc.	V.G.	Good	Fair	Poor
—	3500	1750	1250	650

Cadet Rifle
1,000 manufactured.

Exc.	V.G.	Good	Fair	Poor
—	3500	1750	1250	650

Carbine
4,500 manufactured.

Courtesy Milwaukee Public Museum, Milwaukee, Wisconsin

Exc.	V.G.	Good	Fair	Poor
—	7000	3000	1250	850

Model 1879 (Model 1873/1879)

This is essentially a Model 1873 with 1879 improvements. The most noticeable improvement is that the receiver is wider and thicker so that it is no longer flush with the barrel, which results in a two-step junction between barrel and receiver. These guns are found in the 100,000 to 280,000 serial number range.

Exc.	V.G.	Good	Fair	Poor
—	3000	1200	500	200

SNAP SHOT
SPRINGFIELD MODEL 1879 LONG RANGE RIFLE

Military marksmanship has waxed and waned over the years between times of crisis. In 1874 the first Creedmoor match was held in New York generating an immense interest in long-range target shooting. By 1879, the U.S. Army began to focus on marksmanship; capitalizing on the prestige of the Creedmoor matches by establishing rifle teams. Special long-range Trapdoor rifles were built just for this purpose. The standard .45-70 ammunition at the time was loaded with 405-grain bullet which was ballistically ineffective at 1000 yards for target shooting. The Long Range target rifles were equipped with barrels 32 inches long, having Ballard rifling of 6 lands and grooves at a rate of one turn in 18 inches. Additionally, these rifles were chambered for the .45-80-500 Winchester cartridge using a paper patched bullet. The .45-80 cartridge measured 2.4 inches long similar to the Sharps 2- 4/10 case factory loaded with 100 grains of powder. It could be that the Arsenals felt that the additional 20 grains of powder might be too much for the Springfield action. Two of the rifles were reported to have had their breechblocks blown off presumably by .45-80 ammunition. Approximately 182 of the special rifles were built. The introduction of the M1881, 500-grain bullet and the model 1884 rifle with the Buffington sight eliminated the need for the long-range rifles firing special ammunition. From then on standard-issue rifles and ammunition were used for military target competition.

Today, original Long Range Springfield rifles are some of the most sought after collectable Trapdoor models. I know of one original rifle that as of about 3 years ago was still being used in the NRA National Long Range Creedmoor Championships. The owner was fully intent on passing the grand old rifle on to his grandson. The Davide Pedersoli Co. produces a close reproduction of the Long Range Springfield rifle however it is chambered for the .45-70. It is as close as most of us will come to owning one.

Kenny Durham

Model 1880

This version features a sliding combination cleaning rod/bayonet that is fitted in the forearm under the barrel. It retained the 1873 breechblock markings. There were approximately 1,000 manufactured for trial purposes in 1880.

Courtesy Milwaukee Public Museum, Milwaukee, Wisconsin

Exc.	V.G.	Good	Fair	Poor
—	4750	2200	1000	500

Model 1881 Marksman Rifle

This is an extremely high-grade Trapdoor breechloading rifle chambered for the .45-70 cartridge. It has a 28" round barrel and is similar to the Model 1875 Officer's Rifle in appearance. It features a full-length, high grade, checkered walnut stock held on by one barrel band. It has a horn Schnabel forend tip. The metal parts are engraved, blued, and case-colored. It has a vernier aperture sight as well as a buckhorn rear sight on the barrel and a globe front sight with a spirit level. There were only 11 manufactured to be awarded as prizes at shooting matches.

CAUTION: This is perhaps the supreme rarity among the Trapdoor Springfields, and one should be extremely cognizant of fakes.

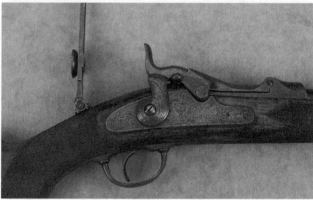

Exc.	V.G.	Good	Fair	Poor
—	75000	60000	20000	5000

Model 1881 Long Range Rifle

This model is a Model 1879 chambered for the .45-80 cartridge. The barrel has six groove rifling. The stock has a shotgun butt with Hotchkiss buttplate. Some of these rifles had uncheckered walnut stock with detachable pistol grip and Sharps peep and globe sights. According to Flayderman, this rifle falls between serial numbers 162000 and 162500. It is estimated that less than 200 were produced between 1897 and 1880.

Exc.	V.G.	Good	Fair	Poor
—	27500	12500	5000	2000

Model 1882 U.S. Magazine Rifle, Chaffee-Reese

A .45-70 caliber centerfire, 27.78" barrel secured by two barrel bands. One of the early bolt action repeaters, with the cartridges carried in a tubular feed in the butt. Iron mountings, with a blued finish, walnut stock, stacking swivel and sling swivel on the upper barrel band, and a sling swivel on the front of the triggerguard. Not serially numbered. Left side of breech marked "US SPRINGFIELD, 1884," the barrel marked "V.P." with eagle head proof. Unfortunately, most rifles found are lacking the feed mechanism in the butt, which lowers the value approximately 15 percent. 753 rifles were produced at the Springfield Armory in 1884.

A Model 1882 Chaffe-Reese Magazine rifle sold at auction for $4,218.75. Stock stamped with SWP/1884 cartouche. Condition is near mint.
Greg Martin Auctions, November 2004

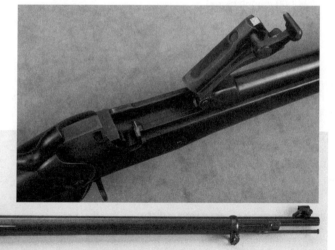

Model 1881 Long Range Rifle • Courtesy Little John's Auction Service, Inc., Paul Goodwin photo

Model 1882 U.S. Magazine rifle, Chaffee-Reese • Paul Goodwin photo

Courtesy Rock Island Auction Company

Exc.	V.G.	Good	Fair	Poor
4250	2500	2000	900	750

Model 1884

This is also a breechloading Trapdoor single shot rifle chambered for the .45-70 cartridge. It was issued as a standard rifle with a 32.75" barrel, a cadet rifle with a 29.5" barrel, and a military carbine with a 22" barrel. The finish is blued and case-colored. This model features the improved Buffington rear sight. It features the socket bayonet and a walnut stock. There were approximately 232,000 manufactured between 1885 and 1890.

Courtesy Bob Ball

Rifle
200,000 manufactured.

Exc.	V.G.	Good	Fair	Poor
—	2000	750	500	200

Cadet Rifle
12,000 manufactured.

Exc.	V.G.	Good	Fair	Poor
—	1500	600	400	200

Carbine
20,000 manufactured.

Exc.	V.G.	Good	Fair	Poor
—	3500	1500	700	250

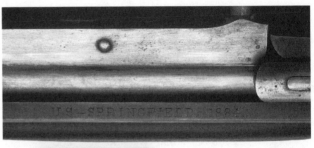

Springfield Model 1884 •
Paul Goodwin photo

Model 1886 Experimental "Trapdoor" Carbine, aka Experimental Model 1882 third/fourth type

Apparently both of these designations are misnomers, as the weapon was officially referred to as the "24" Barrel Carbine. Collectors now call it the Model 1886 to conform to the year of manufacture. The most outstanding feature is the almost full length stock with uncapped, tapered forend. The single upper barrel band is fitted with a bent, or wraparound swivel to facilitate insertion in a saddle scabbard. Lower swivel on butt, with a sling ring and bar on the left side. Cleaning rod compartment in the butt. Buffington-type Model 1884 rear sight marked XC on leaf. About 1,000 produced during 1886.

Exc.	V.G.	Good	Fair	Poor
—	7500	3000	1100	500

Model 1888 Rifle with ramrod
bayonet • Courtesy Rock
Island Auction Company

Springfield Fencing Musket, Type I • Paul Goodwin photo

Model 1888

This version is similar to its predecessors except that it features a sliding, ramrod-type bayonet that was improved so that it stays securely locked when in its extended position. The breechblock was still marked "Model 1884." This was the last Springfield Trapdoor rifle produced. There were approximately 65,000 manufactured between 1889 and 1893.

Exc.	V.G.	Good	Fair	Poor
—	2250	1000	450	200

Trapdoor Fencing Musket

This is a non-gun that was used by the army in teaching bayonet drills. They had no desire to damage serviceable rifles during practice, so they produced this version to fill the bill. There were basically four types produced.

Type I

This version is similar to the Model 1873 rifle without a breech or lock. The finish is rough, and it is unmarked. It was designed to accept a socket bayonet. One should secure a qualified appraisal if a transaction is contemplated. There were 170 manufactured in 1876 and 1877.

Exc.	V.G.	Good	Fair	Poor
—	1500	750	400	300

Type II

This version is basically a Model 1884 with the hammer removed and the front sight blade ground off. It accepted a socket bayonet that was covered with leather and had a pad on its point.

Exc.	V.G.	Good	Fair	Poor
—	850	300	250	200

Type III

This version is similar to the Type II except that it is shortened to 43.5" in length. There were approximately 1,500 manufactured between 1905 and 1906.

Exc.	V.G.	Good	Fair	Poor
—	1150	450	350	300

Type IV

This version is similar to the Type III except that the barrel was filled with lead. There were approximately 11,000 manufactured between 1907 and 1916.

Exc.	V.G.	Good	Fair	Poor
—	650	300	250	200

Model 1870 Rolling Block

This is a single shot breechloading rifle with a rolling-block action. It is chambered for .50 caliber centerfire and has a 32.75" barrel. It has a full-length forend held on by two barrel bands. The finish is blued and case-colored, with a cleaning rod mounted under the barrel. The stock and forend are walnut. The frame is marked "USN Springfield 1870." There is an anchor motif marked on the top of the barrel. It also features government inspector's marks on the frame. This rifle was manufactured by Springfield Armory under license from Remington Arms Company for the United States Navy. The first 10,000 produced were rejected by our navy and were sent to France and used in the Franco-Prussian War. For that reason,

this variation is quite scarce and would bring a 20 percent premium. There was also a group of approximately 100 rifles that were converted to the .22 rimfire cartridge and used for target practice aboard ships. This version is extremely rare. There were approximately 22,000 manufactured in 1870 and 1871.

Courtesy Milwaukee Public Museum, Milwaukee, Wisconsin

Standard Navy Rifle

Exc.	V.G.	Good	Fair	Poor
—	2500	950	500	250

Rejected Navy Rifle

Exc.	V.G.	Good	Fair	Poor
—	2000	700	400	200

.22 Caliber

Exc.	V.G.	Good	Fair	Poor
—	6000	2500	900	600

U.S. Krag Jorgensen Rifle

NOTE: This firearm will be found listed in its own section of this text.

SPRINGFIELD MODEL 1903 & VARIATIONS

These rifles were built by Springfield, Remington, Rock Island Arsenal, and Smith-Corona.

Model 1903

This rifle was a successor to the Krag Jorgensen and was also produced by the Rock Island Arsenal. It was initially chambered for the .30-03 Government cartridge and very shortly changed to the .30-06 cartridge. Its original chambering consisted of a 220-grain, metal jacket soft-point bullet. The German army introduced its spitzer bullet so our government quickly followed suit with a 150-grain, pointed bullet designated the .30-06. This model has a 24" barrel and was built on what was basically a modified Mauser action. It features a 5-round integral box magazine. The finish is blued, with a full length, straight-grip walnut stock with full handguards held on by two barrel bands. The initial version was issued with a rod-type bayonet that was quickly discontinued when President Theodore Roosevelt personally disapproved it. There were approximately 74,000 produced with this rod bayonet; and if in an unaltered condition, these would be worth a great deal more than the standard variation. **It is important to note that the early models with serial numbers under 800,000 were not**

Model 1903 with rod bayonet • Courtesy Little
John's Auction Service, Inc., Paul Goodwin photo

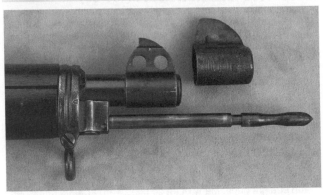

heat treated sufficiently to be safe to fire with modern ammunition. There were a great many produced between 1903 and 1930. The values represented reflect original specimens; WWII alterations would be worth approximately 15 percent less.

Rod Bayonet Version (Original & Unaltered)

Exc.	V.G.	Good	Fair	Poor
35000	20000	15000	12500	10000

NOTE: For rifles restored to Rod Bayonet configuration but in original condition deduct 85 percent.

Rod Bayonet Model 1903 (Altered to Model 1905 in .30-03)

Exc.	V.G.	Good	Fair	Poor
25000	15000	7500	4000	1500

Rod Bayonet Model 1903 (Altered to Model 1905 in .30-06)

Exc.	V.G.	Good	Fair	Poor
4750	3000	1500	850	500

Model 1903 Rifle with 1905 Modifications

This model was built in Springfield between 1905 to 1906. Chambered for .30-03 cartridge. Overall barrel length is 24.206" (chamber & bore length is 23.949"). These rifles were newly manufactured and therefore are unaltered. No ramrod bayonet. Model 1905 front and rear sight. Front barrel band is a double strap with bayonet stud and stacking swivel. There is

A Model 1903 Rod Bayonet rifle sold at auction for $19,125. Condition is 80 percent blue. Rifle has not been converted.
Greg Martin Auctions, November 2004

Model 1903 with Model 1905 Modifications • Courtesy Little John's Auction Service, Inc., Paul Goodwin photo

a Model 1905 knife bayonet designed for this model. Rear sight graduated to 2,400 yards with a silver line above and below peep sight aperture. Very Rare.

Original & Unaltered Examples

Exc.	V.G.	Good	Fair	Poor
22500	15000	8000	3000	1000

Altered to .30-06

Exc.	V.G.	Good	Fair	Poor
4000	2500	1200	800	400

Model 1903 Rifle
(Altered from Model 1905 in .30-06)

This model was altered to accept a new pointed bullet that required a shortened cartridge case. This required a shorter chamber. The barrel was shortened by setting it deeper into the receiver by .200" therefore making the overall barrel length 24.006" in length (chamber & bore length is 23.749"). This new cartridge was adopted in 1906 and called the "Cartridge, Ball, Caliber 30, Model Of 1906." or more commonly known as the .30-06. The rear sight base was also moved forward .200" of an inch and a new graduated rear sight up to 2,700 yards was installed. According to Flayderman the easiest way to determine a Model 1905 altered rifle "... is to remove the upper barrel band to see if a plugged hole appears 1/4" forward of the present upper band screw hole."

Model 1903 altered from Model 1905 • Courtesy Little John's Auction Service, Inc., Paul Goodwin photo

Exc.	V.G.	Good	Fair	Poor
3750	2750	1000	700	500

Model 1903 Rifle (1907-1910 in .30-06)

This variation was built both by Springfield and Rock Island. It features a stock with a square corner beside the receiver ring on the right side, a smooth and pointed trigger, smooth buttplate, the bolt handle is not bent back, blued metal. The receiver has a black or mottled finish. Early examples do not have a cross bolt in the stock while rifles built after 1908 have a single cross bolt. About 130,000 were produced in serial number range 269000 to 400000. Original examples are rare as most were arsenal rebuilt with parkerized finish and new features.

Model 1903 dated 1909 • Courtesy Little John's Auction Service, Paul Goodwin photo

Exc.	V.G.	Good	Fair	Poor
3750	2750	1250	750	500

Model 1903 Rifle (1910-1917 in .30-06)

This variation features a stock with tapered rather than square corner on right side of receiver ring. The trigger is serrated and not pointed. Checkered buttplate, bolt handle is not bent back, and metal is blued. Stock has a single cross bolt. Most were arsenal rebuilt. About 250,000 were manufactured between serial numbers 385000 to 635000. Between 1910 and 1913, these rifles were also built by Rock Island.

NOTE: A small number of these rifles were sold to civilians through the DCM program. They are marked "NRA" on the triggerguard. These examples are worth approximately 20 percent more.

Courtesy Little John's Auction Service, Inc. • Paul Goodwin photo

Exc.	V.G.	Good	Fair	Poor
3750	2750	1000	700	500

Model 1903 Rifle (1917-1921 in .30-06)

This variation features a parkerized finish with smooth buttplate, many have smooth triggers that have a thick contour. Two cross bolts in stock. This particular variation does not have the attention to detail and finish that peacetime rifles have. Many of these rifles were arsenal rebuilt. About 590,000 of this variation were manufactured between serial numbers 635000 to 1225000.

Exc.	V.G.	Good	Fair	Poor
3750	2700	1200	700	500

NOTE: Rifles built between 1917 and 1918 will bring a 20 percent premium.

Model 1903 Rifle (1921-1929)

This variation features parkerized metal finish with checkered buttplate and serrated triggers. Stock have grasping grooves and straight grips. Many of these rifles were arsenal refinished and reassembled with different combinations of parts. About 80,000 were manufactured between serial numbers 1200000 and 1280000.

Exc.	V.G.	Good	Fair	Poor
3500	2250	900	700	500

Model 1903 Rifle Stripped for Air Service

Special 29" stock, 5.75 upper handguard specially made for this rifle, solid lower barrel band retained by screw underneath, rear leaf sight shortened and altered to open sight with square notch. 25-round extension magazine used. Some 910 rifles produced during the first half of 1918, with serial numbers ranging between 857000 and 863000; all barrels dated in first half of 1918. A very rare and desirable rifle, with the magazine almost impossible to find. Values shown include magazine.

Model 1903 with Air Service magazine • Courtesy Richard M. Kumor Sr.

Exc.	V.G.	Good	Fair	Poor
20000	12500	7500	3500	1000

Model 1903 Mark 1

This version is similar to the original except that it was cut to accept the Pedersen device. This device allows the use of a semiautomatic bolt insert that utilizes pistol cartridges. The rifle

An NRA marked Model 1903 sold at auction for $2,250. Condition is 85 percent blue wtih excellent wood.
Greg Martin Auctions, November 2004

has a slot milled into the receiver that acts as an ejection port. The device was not successful and was scrapped. There were approximately 102,000 rifles that were produced with this millcut between 1918 and 1920.

Exc.	V.G.	Good	Fair	Poor
3000	2000	1500	1200	600

NOTE: The values given are for the rifle alone—not for the device. Rifle must contain all original Mark I parts. For rifles with the device and magazine add $35,000; for rifles with the device but no magazine add $30,000; for the metal carrying scabbard add $7,500.

Model 1903 Sniper Rifle

Selected Model 1903 rifles were fitted with telescopic sights from 1907 to 1919; apparently 25 rifles so equipped in 1906, but the type of scope has not been definitely identified. If proven original to the period, specimens would be worth more than shown in the values guide. 400 rifles were fitted with the Warner-Swasey Model 1906, 6-power telescope sight in 1911, with the sights marked Model 1908, as well as with the full Warner-Swasey markings. Scope numbers do not match the rifle numbers. Rifles fitted with this Model 1908 scope will bring approximately 30 percent more than the values shown. Approximately 5,000 rifles were fitted with the Model 1913

Pedersen Device • Paul Goodwin photo

Paul Goodwin photo

A Model 1903 A1 sniper rifle sold at auction for $10,925. Documented as U.S. Marine Corp. sniper rifle. Inspector's cartouche. Unertl scope and mounts. Condition is 98 percent arsenal parkerized finish. Scope is near mint.
Rock Island Auction Company, April 2004

A Pedersen device with magazine and metal scabbard sold at auction for $37,375. Condition is 98 percent.
Rock Island Auction Company, December 2004

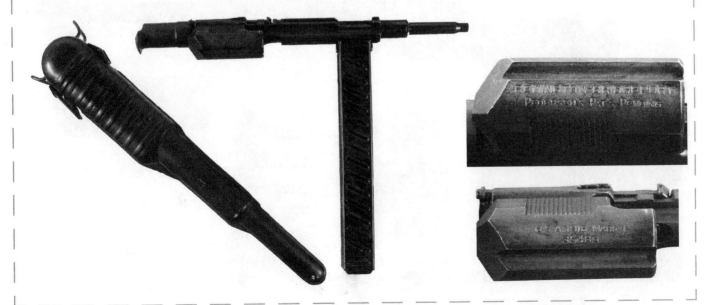

Warner-Swasey telescopic sight up to 1919; similar to the Model 1908, they were only 5.2 power. When originally fitted, the scopes were numbered to the rifles; however, scopes were sold separately from the rifles as surplus and were never numbered. These were later fitted to other weapons and the chance of finding matching numbers greatly decreases. Values shown are for original guns with original, matching telescopes.

The U.S. Marine Corps also had its own versions of the Model 1903 Sniper. Early rifles were fitted with a Winchester A5 5X scope or a Lyman 5A 5X scope. Later examples were fitted with a Unertl 8X scope marked "USMC." All Marine Corps scopes had target bases.

Courtesy Bob Ball

Exc.	V.G.	Good	Fair	Poor
7000	5500	4250	2500	1500

NOTE: A few Model 1903 and 1903A1 rifles will have barrels marked "USMC" and the date. These barrels were installed by the Sedgley Company. Add a premium of about 15 percent for these barrels.

Model 1903 A1

This version is a standard Model 1903 rifle that was fitted with a Type C, semi-pistol grip stock. All other specifications were the same except for a checkered butt and serrated trigger.

Exc.	V.G.	Good	Fair	Poor
2750	1250	750	500	400

WORLD WAR II MODEL 1903s

For a complete explanation, with photos and technical data see Bruce Canfield's, *U.S. Infantry Weapons of World War II.*

According to Canfield, the majority of World War II Model 1903 rifles were rebuilt. The extent varied from rifle to rifle. Look for the following alterations:

1. Refinished metal with greenish parkerizing.
2. Stock and handguard replaced or refinished. Replacement stock lacked finger grooves.
3. Replacement barrels were made by Springfield, Sedgley, and High Standard. Two-digit date stamped on new barrels.
4. A gas escape hole was added, but not to all WWII receivers.
5. Component parts were sometimes of a later vintage.

Model 1903 (Remington, WWII)

Remington began production of the Model 1903 in November 1941. These very early rifles are identical to the Rock Island Model 1903. About 1,273 of these early rifles were produced. The balance of Remington Model 1903 rifles were built using less expensive methods. Tolerances were eased and more stamped parts were employed. These rifles were stamped "Remington Model 1903," and small parts were stamped "R." These early Remington rifles will be found in serial number range 3000 to about 3050000.

Exc.	V.G.	Good	Fair	Poor
750	500	300	200	100

NOTE: Very early Remington rifles, the first 1,273, will bring a premium over the later rifles.

Model 1903 (Remington, WWII, Modified)

This version of the Model 1903 was a further attempt to reduce cost and increase production. The right gas escape hole was eliminated, and a number of machining operations were omitted. This version is known as the Model 1903 Modified. These

---

A Model 1903 Springfield sniper rifle sold at auction for $6,750. Dated 2-18 and fitted with a Warner & Swasey scope. Complete with scope case. No cartouches on rifle. Condition is about 65 percent finish. Optics are very good. Wood very good.
Greg Martin Auctions, November 2004

rifles are found in serial number range 3050000 to about 3365000.

Exc.	V.G.	Good	Fair	Poor
600	400	300	200	100

Model 1903 A3

This version was introduced in May of 1942 for use in WWII. It basically consisted of improvements to simplify mass production. It features an aperture sight and various small parts that were fabricated from stampings; this includes the triggerguard, floorplate, and barrel band. The finish is parkerized. Receiver ring is marked "03-A3." This model was manufactured by Remington and Smith-Corona.

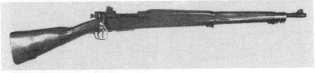

Courtesy Bob Ball

Exc.	V.G.	Good	Fair	Poor
600	475	300	200	100

SNAP SHOT
M1903 A3

World War II was barely underway when it became apparent to the U.S. Military that the need for semiautomatic M1 Garand rifles could not be met due to a lack of manufacturing capability. The M1903 was simpler and cheaper to manufacture, and used the same cartridge as the M1 Garand, so the decision was made to bring the venerable M1903 back into production, but further simplified to expedite production. The Remington Arms company was asked in 1941 to create a simplified wartime production variant of the M1903. The M1903 A3 rifle featured a number of parts made from steel stampings instead of machining, such as triggerguard and magazine assembly and barrel bands. Receiver-mounted aperture sights replaced the M1903's complex tangent sights. Some M1903 A3 rifles were also manufactured with 2-groove barrels instead of 4-groove barrels, but the former have no degradation in accuracy. Remington Arms Company and Smith-Corona Typewriters manufactured M1903 A3 rifles. The M1903 A4 sniper rifles, manufactured by the Remington Arms Company, were no more than factory 'accurized' M1903 A3s with the open sights replaced by telescopic optical sights. The M1903 A3 rifle is a manually operated, bolt-action, magazine-fed rifle, using a modified Mauser 98 action. The Mauser-type non-rotating claw type extractor is used. A magazine cut-off on the left side of the receiver is also a bolt stop switch. This switch, when engaged, limits the bolt travel so a spent case can be extracted but a new cartridge will not be fed from the magazine, thus converting the rifle to a single-shot. The safety is also of Mauser type, located at the rear of the bolt. The M1903 A3 is a striker-fired design, cocking as the bolt is opened. A knurled firing pin knob protrudes from the rear of the bolt, which makes visual or tactile checking whether the action is cocked or not simple.

Charlie Cutshaw

Model 1903 A4

Most of these rifles were marked "A3" and not "A4." The markings were rotated to the side in order not to be covered by the scope mount. This is a sniper-rifle version of the Model 1903. It is fitted with permanently mounted scope blocks and furnished with a telescopic sight known as the M73B1. This scope was manufactured by Weaver in El Paso, Texas, and was commercially known as the Model 330C. The rifle has no conventional iron sights mounted. This model was built by Remington.

NOTE: For those few rifles marked "A4" add a premium of 10 percent.

Rifle with WWII rare "French" M73B2 scope • Notice the markings and characteristics of front sight removal • Courtesy Michael Wamsher, Paul Goodwin photo

Model 82 scope circa post-Korean War • Courtesy Richard M. Kumor Sr.

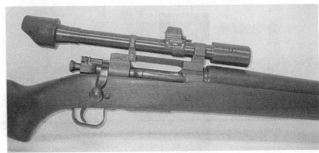

Model 84 scope circa Korea and Vietnam wars • Courtesy Richard M. Kumor Sr.

Exc.	V.G.	Good	Fair	Poor
3000	2500	1750	650	350

NOTE: For rifles with M84 scope deduct $250.

Model 1903 NRA National Match

This version was based on a standard 1903 service rifle that was selected for having excellent shooting qualities. The parts were then hand-fit, and a special rifled barrel was added that was checked for tolerance with a star gauge. The muzzle of this barrel was marked with a special star with six or eight rays

Remington Model 1903/A4 sniper with M73B1 Scope set, semi-pistol grip stock variation, boxed FJA cartouche, and correct factory original bolt handle stock clearance cutout • Courtesy Michael Wamsher, Paul Goodwin photo

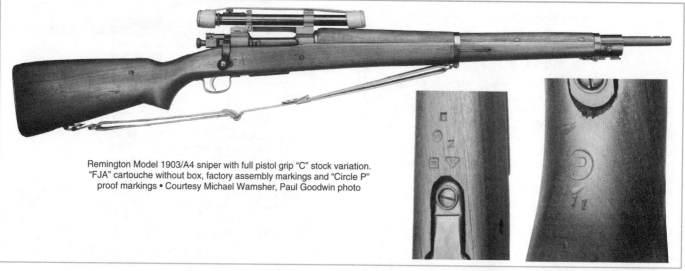

Remington Model 1903/A4 sniper with full pistol grip "C" stock variation. "FJA" cartouche without box, factory assembly markings and "Circle P" proof markings • Courtesy Michael Wamsher, Paul Goodwin photo

Examples of different scopes and their markings used on the Model 1903/A4 rifle. From right to left: Early Weaver Model 330 scope, M73B1 scope, and M82 scope • Courtesy Michael Wamsher, Paul Goodwin photo

Model 1903 "NB" National Match showing markings • Paul Goodwin photo

radiating from it. These NRA rifles were drilled and tapped to accept a Lyman No. 48 rear sight. They are marked with the letters "NRA" and have a flaming bomb proofmark on the triggerguard. There were approximately 18,000 manufactured between 1921 and 1928.

Exc.	V.G.	Good	Fair	Poor
3750	2400	2000	1400	800

NOTE: Prices are for verifiable samples.

Model 1903 A1 National Match

Basically the same as the Model 1903 National Match rifle except for the "C" type, or pistol grip stock, without grasping grooves. Bolts and stocks numbered to the receiver. "P" in a circle proof on the underside of the pistol grip, with either a "DAL" in a rectangular cartouche, or S.A./SPG in a square cartouche. Rifles will be found with either a regular or reversed safety. Approximately 11,000 produced with a serial number range from 1285000 to 1532000.

Exc.	V.G.	Good	Fair	Poor
4500	3000	2000	1200	600

NOTE: Prices are for verifiable samples.

Model 1903 Style National Match Special Rifle

This rifle is identical to the National Match, but with a completely different buttstock configuration identical to the Model 1922 NRA. Large shotgun type steel buttplate; full pistol grip. About 150 rifles produced during 1924.

Model 1903 National Match Special Rifle • Courtesy Butterfield & Butterfield

Exc.	V.G.	Good	Fair	Poor
8500	6500	5500	3500	2500

NOTE: Prices are for verifiable samples.

Model 1903 Style "NB" National Match Rifle

This rifle produced with the "B" type stock with more drop than standard, suitable only for off-hand shooting; pistol grip configured with a noticeably squared profile. Deep checkered buttplate. Circle "P" proof in underside of pistol grip. About 195 rifles built between 1925 and 1926.

Exc.	V.G.	Good	Fair	Poor
8500	6500	5500	3500	2500

NOTE: Prices are for verifiable samples.

Model 1903 NRA Sporter

This version is similar to the National Match rifle but features a half-length, Sporter-type stock with one barrel band. It also features the Lyman No. 48 receiver sight. This version was

A Springfield Model 1903 National Match rifle sold at auction for $9,000. Condition is 90 percent finish. Excellent wood and excellent bore.
Greg Martin Auctions, November 2004

Model 1903 NRA Sporter • Courtesy Little John's Auction Service, Inc., Paul Goodwin photo

produced for commercial sales. There were approximately 6,500 manufactured between 1924 and 1933.

Exc.	V.G.	Good	Fair	Poor
3000	2200	1800	1400	800

NOTE: Prices are for verifiable samples.

Model 1903 NBA Sporter Rifle

The barrel, action, and sights of this rifle are identical to the Model 1903 NRA Sporter rifle above. However it is fitted with a "B" type stock. Grasping grooves and squared pistol grip profile. Circle "P" proof in the underside of the pistol grip. 589 rifles produced at the Springfield Armory during 1925 and 1926.

NOTE: Prices are for verifiable samples.

Exc.	V.G.	Good	Fair	Poor
8500	6500	5500	3500	2500

Model 1903 Heavy Barreled Match Rifles

These rifles were made in a bewildering number of types and variations. Commonly encountered are the style "T" with NRA type stocks. Barrels, which came in three lengths, 26", 28", and 30", measured .860" at the muzzle and 1.250" at the breech. Lyman 48 rear sight; Winchester globe front sight on a modified B.A.R. front band, telescope blocks on the receiver and barrel. Some fitted with adjustable hook type buttplates, set triggers, Garand speed locks, as well as cheekpieces (all commanding premium dollars). INTERNATIONAL MATCH rifles (worth at least double the values shown) have many variant features which were changed annually at the request of the individual shooter. These features include palm rests, double set triggers, beaver-tail forends, checkered pistol grips, Swiss style buttplates, etc. Generally the Winchester 5A telescopic sight was used. These rifles are considered rare. Another variation is the 1922 MATCH SPRINGFIELD RIFLE with NRA type stock with grasping grooves, a 24" barrel with service type front sight mount and small base integral with the barrel, as well as telescopic blocks on the barrel. 566 rifles produced at the Springfield Armory between 1922 and 1930.

Exc.	V.G.	Good	Fair	Poor
7000	5500	4000	2500	1500

NOTE: Values shown are for the standard heavy barrel match rifle without any special features.

Model 1903 .22 Caliber Gallery Practice Rifle "Hoffer-Thompson"

This practice rifle differed from the standard issue '03 as follows: the barrel bored and rifled to .22 caliber, the breech chambered for the Hoffer-Thompson cartridge holder, the rear sight graduated to 240 yards, the mainspring shortened, the stocks generally found without cross bolts or the circle "P" on the underside of the pistol grip. Receivers produced after 1901 usually are marked with ".22" on the top of the bridge. About 15,525 rifles were produced at the Springfield Armory between 1907 and 1918.

Exc.	V.G.	Good	Fair	Poor
3250	2200	1400	1000	700

A Springfield Model 1903 heavy barrel match rifle sold at auction for $11,250. Fitted with scope mounts. Lyman peep sight. Condition is 95 percent.
Greg Martin Auctions, November 2004

Model 1917

In 1917, when the United States entered WWI, there was a distinct rifle shortage. There were production facilities set up for the British pattern 1914 rifle. This "Enfield" rifle was redesigned to accept the .30-06 cartridge and was pressed into service as the U.S. rifle Model 1917. This rifle appears similar to the British pattern 1914 rifle. In fact, they are so similar that in WWII, when over a million were sold to Britain for use by their Home Guard, it was necessary to paint a 2" stripe around the butt so that the caliber was immediately known. The barrel length is 26", and it has a 6-round integral box magazine. The finish is matte-blue, with a walnut stock. Towards the end of production parkerized parts were added. The breech is marked "U.S. Model 1917." This was a robust and heavy-duty rifle, and many are used in the manufacture of large-bore custom rifles to this day. There were approximately 2,200,000 manufactured by Remington, Winchester, and Eddystone between 1917 and 1918. The majority were produced at Eddystone, Pennsylvania.

During World War II all parts were parkerized, and barrels were supplied by the Johnson Automatics Company as a result of the rebuild.

NOTE: Add 30 percent for Winchester and Remington models.

Model 1917 Rifle (Winchester) • Courtesy Rock Island Auction Company

Remington Model 1917 Receiver Markings • Courtesy Karl Karash

Exc.	V.G.	Good	Fair	Poor
800	600	400	200	150

French troops with the Model 1917 • Courtesy Paul S. Scarlata

Model 1922

This is a bolt-action training rifle chambered for the .22 rimfire cartridge. It appears similar to the Model 1903 but has a 24.5" barrel and a half-length stock without hand guards, held on by a single barrel band. It has a 5-round detachable box magazine. The finish is blued, with a walnut stock. The receiver is marked "U.S. Springfield Armory Model of 1922 Cal. 22." It also has the flaming bomb ordnance mark. There were three basic types of the Model 1922: the standard issue type, the NRA commercial type, and the models that were altered to M1 or M2. There were a total of approximately 2,000 manufactured between 1922 and 1924. The survival rate of the original-issue types is not large as most were converted.

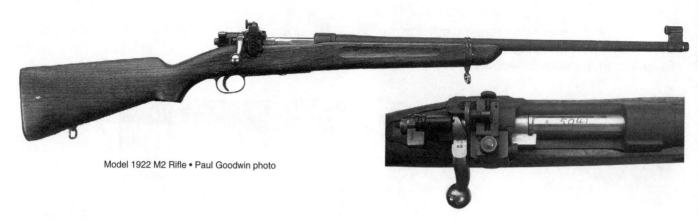

Model 1922 M2 Rifle • Paul Goodwin photo

Issue Type

Exc.	V.G.	Good	Fair	Poor
1250	750	450	250	200

Altered Type

Exc.	V.G.	Good	Fair	Poor
600	400	250	200	150

NRA Type—Drilled and Tapped for Scope

Courtesy Greg Martin Auctions

Exc.	V.G.	Good	Fair	Poor
1200	850	550	300	150

Model 1922 M1

This version is quite similar to the Model 1922, with a single-point striker system and a detachable box magazine that does not protrude from the bottom of the stock. The finish is parkerized and the stock is made of walnut. There were approximately 20,000 manufactured between 1924 and 1933.

Courtesy Little John's Auction Service, Inc., Paul Goodwin photo

Unaltered Type

Exc.	V.G.	Good	Fair	Poor
1250	850	550	300	200

Altered to M2

Courtesy Greg Martin Auctions

Exc.	V.G.	Good	Fair	Poor
600	400	250	200	150

Unaltered NRA Type

Exc.	V.G.	Good	Fair	Poor
950	750	500	300	250

NRA Type Altered to M2

Exc.	V.G.	Good	Fair	Poor
700	500	400	300	250

Model M2

This is an improved version of the Model 1922 M1 that features an altered firing mechanism with a faster lock time. It has a knurled cocking knob added to the bolt and a flush-fitting detachable magazine with improved feeding. There were approximately 12,000 manufactured.

Exc.	V.G.	Good	Fair	Poor
800	600	400	300	200

U.S. Rifle M1 (Garand)

Springfield Armory was one of the manufacturers of this WWII service rifle. It is listed in the Garand section of this text.

A Model 1922M1 NRA target rifle sold at auction for $3,375. Ordnance bomb over 11-29 on top of barrel. Original sales record. Condition is 95 percent blue.
Greg Martin Auctions, November 2004

Springfield M21 Sniper Rifle

This is the sniper rifle version of the M14 rifle with ART II scope. Early models were fitted with an M84 scope and Griffin & Howe mounts. This scope was followed by the ART I and finally the ART II scope in the early 1970s.

M21 with ART II scope and case • Courtesy Richard M. Kumor Sr.

Exc.	V.G.	Good	Fair	Poor
7000	5500	4000	—	—

NOTE: Prices are for verifiable and registered samples.

KRAG JORGENSEN

The first small bore, bolt action repeating rifle that used smokeless powder that was adopted by the U.S. government as a service rifle. It was adopted as the Model 1892 and was similar to the rifle being used by Denmark as a service rifle. All of the Krag-Jorgensens were manufactured at the Springfield Armory. There are 11 basic variations of Krag Rifles, and all except one are chambered for the .30-40 Govt. cartridge. They are bolt actions that hold 5 rounds in the unique side-mounted hinged magazine. All of the Krags have walnut stocks and handguards that are oil-finished. They all have dark gray case-hardened receivers and blued barrels. See also *Denmark, Rifles, Krag Jorgensen.*

Bibliographical Note: For historical information, technical data, and photos, see Lt. Col. William Brophy's, *The Krag Rifle,* Gun Room Press, 1985.

NOTE: One should be aware that there have been many alterations based on the Krag rifle by many gunsmiths through the years, and the one consistency is that all of these conversions lowered the value of the rifle and rendered it un-collectible. Proceed with caution. Prices listed are for original rifles as they left the factory.

Model 1892

Approximately 24,500 of these rifles produced, dated 1894, 1895, and 1896. They have 30" barrels and are serial numbered from 1-24562. Nearly all were converted to the latter Model 1896, and the original 1st Type is extremely scarce.

1st Type

Serial numbered from 1-1500 and is dated 1894 only. It features a wide upper barrel band and a brass tipped one-piece cleaning rod mounted under the barrel. There is no compartment in the butt, and the muzzle is not crowned and appears flat. The upper handguard does not extend over the receiver, and the buttplate is flat, without a compartment. One should be wary of fakes and secure

expert appraisal if a transaction is contemplated. Unaltered specimens are extremely rare.

Exc.	V.G.	Good	Fair	Poor
—	30000	20000	6500	3000

2nd Type

Similar to the 1st Type, with a front barrel band that is cut out in the center and does not appear solid. The cleaning rod is a one piece steel type. The serial number range is 1500-24562, and the dates 1894 or 1895 are stamped on the receiver and the stock. Again be wary of fakes. This is a rare rifle.

Exc.	V.G.	Good	Fair	Poor
—	10000	7500	4000	1500

Model 1892 Altered to 1896 Model

Encompassed nearly the entire production run of the Model 1892 Krag rifle. They still bear the dates 1894, 1895, and 1896 on the receiver; but they do not have a one piece cleaning rod under the barrel, but instead a three-piece type inserted into the buttstock, and the hole in the stock has been plugged. The front barrel band was changed. The top handguard covers the receiver, and the buttplate is curved at the bottom. The muzzle is crowned.

Exc.	V.G.	Good	Fair	Poor
—	850	400	250	150

Model 1895 Carbine (Variation)

Marked "1895" and "1896" on the receiver—without the word "Model." They were produced before the Model 1896 was officially adopted, and they are serial numbered from 25000 to 35000. They are similar to the Model 1896 Carbine, with a smaller safety and no oiler bottle in the butt.

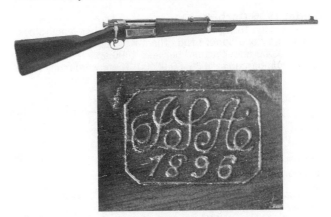

Model 1895 Carbine • Courtesy Rock Island Auction Company

Exc.	V.G.	Good	Fair	Poor
—	3000	1250	650	300

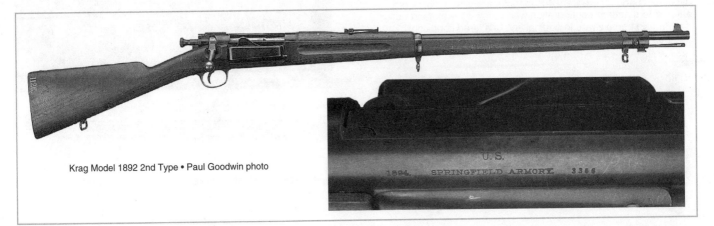

Krag Model 1892 2nd Type • Paul Goodwin photo

Altered Model 1896 • Paul Goodwin photo

Model 1896 Rifle

Similar to the altered Model 1892 and has a 30" barrel with the cleaning kit in the butt. The rear sight was improved, and the receiver is marked "U.S. Model 1896" and "Springfield Armory." Lightening cuts were made in the barrel channel to reduce weight. A total of about 62,000 Model 96 rifles were produced in the same serial number range as the Model 1896 carbine of 37240 to 108471. The stock is dated 1896, 1897, and 1898. There were many of these altered to the later stock configurations—in the field or at the Springfield Armory. These changes would lower the value, and one should secure expert appraisal on this model.

Courtesy Richard M. Kumor Sr.

Exc.	V.G.	Good	Fair	Poor
—	1750	750	400	250

Model 1896 Carbine

Similar to the 1896 Rifle, with a 22" barrel and half-length stock held on by one barrel band. There were approximately less than 20,000 manufactured between 1896 and 1898, and the serial number range is 35000-90000. There were many rifles cut to carbine dimensions—be wary of these alterations!

Courtesy Jim Supica, Old Town Station

Exc.	V.G.	Good	Fair	Poor
—	3000	1250	650	300

Model 1896 Cadet Rifle

A rare variation produced for use by the Military Academy at West Point. The dimensions are the same as the 1896 Rifle with a one-piece cleaning rod under the barrel and the 1896-type front band. There were 400 manufactured, and most were altered to standard configuration when they were phased out in 1898. Extremely rare in original and unaltered condition.

Exc.	V.G.	Good	Fair	Poor
—	—	37500	15000	—

Krag Rifle • Courtesy Paul S. Scarlata

Model 1898 Rifle

This model is similar to the Model 1896 in appearance except that the receiver is marked "U.S./Model 1898." The bolt handle was modified, and the sights and handguards were improved. There were 330,000 manufactured between 1898 and 1903, and the serial number range is 110000-480000.

Exc.	V.G.	Good	Fair	Poor
—	1750	750	300	150

Model 1896 Cadet Rifle • Courtesy West Point Museum, Paul Goodwin photo

Model 1898 Carbine

Similar to the rifle, with a 22" barrel and a bar and ring on the left side of the receiver. There were approximately 5,000 manufactured in 1898 and 1899. The serial range is 118000-134000. Again, be aware that many of the rifles have been converted to carbine dimensions over the years. When in doubt, secure an independent appraisal.

Courtesy Little John's Auction Service, Inc., Paul Goodwin photo

Exc.	V.G.	Good	Fair	Poor
—	3000	1500	750	400

Model 1898 Carbine 26" Barrel

An attempt to satisfy both the infantry and the cavalry. There were 100 manufactured for trial, and the serial number range is between 387000-389000. Be wary of fakes.

Courtesy Little John's Auction Service, Inc., Paul Goodwin photo

Exc.	V.G.	Good	Fair	Poor
—	17500	7500	2500	900

Model 1898 Practice Rifle

The only Krag not chambered for the .30-40 cartridge. It is chambered for the .22 rimfire and was designed as a target-practice rifle. It has a 30" barrel and is identical in exterior appearance to the Model 1898 Rifle. The receiver is marked the same as the standard model—with "Cal .22" added. There were approximately 840 manufactured in 1906 and 1907. Serial numbers are above 475,000.

Exc.	V.G.	Good	Fair	Poor
—	4500	2000	850	300

Krag Carbine • Courtesy Paul S. Scarlata

Model 1899 Carbine

The last of the Krags. It is similar to the 1898, with the "Model 1899" stamped on the receiver and a 2" longer stock. There were approximately 36,000 manufactured between 1900 and 1903. Serial numbers observed are between 222609 and 362256. These numbers are part of the Model 1898 rifle series.

Courtesy Milwaukee Public Museum, Milwaukee, Wisconsin

Exc.	V.G.	Good	Fair	Poor
—	2000	850	600	350

Model 1899 Philippine Constabulary Carbine

Approximately 8,000 modified to accept the knife bayonet at the Springfield Armory and the Rock Island Arsenal. The Springfield pieces are marked "J.F.C." on the stock. This model has a 22" barrel with the full, but shortened, stock of the rifle held on with two barrel bands. One must exercise extreme care as many rifles were altered in a similar manner at later dates.

Exc.	V.G.	Good	Fair	Poor
—	2500	1250	600	300

NOTE: Prices are for verifiable samples.

Arsenal Conversions

In the 1920s, the Department of Civilian Marksmanship had a number of Krag rifles converted for their use. These are Model 1898 rifles shortened to 24" and fitted with Model 1899 Carbine stocks. Some of these rifles were also fitted with rifle stocks shortened to carbine length. These conversions are beginning to be regarded as legitimate variations by some collectors of Krag rifles.

Exc.	V.G.	Good	Fair	Poor
—	450	250	175	100

Model 1899 Philippine Constabulary Carbine • Courtesy Rock Island Auction Company

COLT

NOTE: For historical information, technical details, and photos, see Blake Stevens' and Edward Ezell's, *The Black Rifle: M16 Retrospective*, Collector Grade Publications, 1994.

Berdan Single Shot Rifle (M.1870)

This is a scarce rifle on today's market. There were approximately 30,200 manufactured, but nearly 30,000 of them were sent to Russia. This rifle was produced from 1866-1870. It is a trapdoor-type action chambered for .42 centerfire. The standard model has a 32.5" barrel; the carbine, 18.25". The finish is blued, with a walnut stock. This rifle was designed and the patent held by Hiram Berdan, Commander of the Civil War "Sharpshooters" Regiment. This was actually Colt's first cartridge arm. The 30,000 rifles and 25 half-stocked carbines that were sent to Russia were in Russian Cyrillic letters. The few examples made for American sales have Colt's name and Hartford address on the barrel.

NOTE: For information on Russian-built Berdan rifles, see *Russia, Rifles, Berdan.*

Courtesy Milwaukee Public Museum, Milwaukee, Wisconsin

Rifle Russian Order
30,000 manufactured.

Exc.	V.G.	Good	Fair	Poor
—	2500	1000	450	—

Carbine Russian Order
25 manufactured.

Exc.	V.G.	Good	Fair	Poor
—	6000	3000	1250	—

Rifle U.S. Sales
100 manufactured.

Exc.	V.G.	Good	Fair	Poor
—	5000	2250	1250	—

Carbine U.S. Sales
25 manufactured.

Exc.	V.G.	Good	Fair	Poor
—	9500	4500	2000	—

Colt-Franklin Military Rifle

This is a rifle that was not a successful venture for Colt. The patents were held by William B. Franklin, a vice-president of the company. This was a bolt-action rifle with a primitive, gravity-fed box magazine. It is chambered for the .45-70 government cartridge, has a 32.5" barrel, and is blued, with a walnut stock. The rifle has the Colt Hartford barrel address and is stamped with an eagle's head and U.S. inspector's marks. There were only 50 of these rifles produced, and it is believed that they were prototypes intended for government sales. This was not to be, and production ceased after approximately 50 were manufactured in 1887 and 1888.

Exc.	V.G.	Good	Fair	Poor
—	8500	4500	2000	—

Lightning Slide Action, Medium Frame

This was the first slide action rifle Colt produced. It is chambered for .32-20, .38-40, and .44-40, and was intended to be a companion piece to the SAAs in the same calibers. The rifle has a 26" barrel with 15-shot tube magazine; the carbine, a 20" barrel with 12-shot magazine. The finish is blued, with case-colored hammer; the walnut stock is oil-finished; and the forend is usually checkered. The Colt name and Hartford address are stamped on the barrel along with the patent dates. There were approximately 89,777 manufactured between 1884 and 1902. The military variant is listed below.

Military Rifle or Carbine

Chambered for .44-40 caliber, fitted with short magazine tube, bayonet lug, and sling swivels. These guns are fitted with various barrel lengths.

Exc.	V.G.	Good	Fair	Poor
—	4500	2000	1000	600

U.S. M14/M14E2

Based on the famous M1 Garand design this select fire rifle is chambered for the 7.62x51mm cartridge. It has a 21.8" barrel and a 20-round magazine. It weighs approximately 11.2 lbs. Rate of fire is about 750 rounds per minute. Marked "US RIFLE 7.62MM M14" on the rear top of the receiver. Production began in 1957 and ceased in 1963. Produced by Harrington & Richardson (537,512 total production) stamped "HRA," Springfield (167,172 total production) stamped "SA," Winchester (356,510 total production) stamped "66118" or "OM," and TRW (319,163 total production) stamped "TRW." The M14E2 version is a light machine gun variant with bipod, folding forward hand grip, and muzzle compensator.

NOTE: A sniper version of this rifle was designated the M21 and fitted with a Leatherwood telescope sight. *See that listing.*

Courtesy Richard M. Kumor Sr.

Pre-1968

Exc.	V.G.	Fair
8500	8000	7500

A demilled Springfield M14 reweld by Hahn Machine sold at auction for $6,900. Semiauto only. Cartouche and bayonet. Condition is 98 percent original finish.
Rock Island Auction Company, April 2004

M16A2 MODIFICATIONS:

1. Flash suppressor is now a muzzle brake.
2. Barrel is heavier with rifle twist changed from 1 in 12 to 1 in 7.
3. Front sight is a square post adjustable for elevation.
4. Handguards are interchangeable ribbed top and bottom halves.
5. The circumference of the slip ring is now canted for a better grip.
6. Upper receiver is strengthened at the front attachment point to the lower receiver, as well as a fired case deflector behind the ejection port.
7. Completely redesigned fully adjustable rear sight.
8. Forward assist is now a round button type.
9. Pistol grip has a thumb swell and is made from stronger nylon with checkering on both sides.
10. Change lever is now, SAFE, SEMI, and BURST on most but not all A2 models.
11. The stock is stronger and 5/8" longer.
12. Buttplate is squared and checkered with internal storage cavity.

The M14 in Vietnam

Pre-1986 conversions
(or U.S. manufacture/M1A Springfield Armory)

Exc.	V.G.	Fair
4500	4250	4000

Pre-1986 dealer samples

Exc.	V.G.	Fair
N/A	N/A	N/A

M16 ASSAULT RIFLE

The M16 rifle has a great many variations and configurations. Some of these variations are available to the collector and others are so rare as to be, for practical purposes, unavailable to the collector. Nevertheless, we think it important to include as many variations as may be encountered by the collector. Some of the more common ones will be priced while others, because of their rarity, will not show a value. Keep in mind that the M16 series of rifles is comprised of two main parts: the upper receiver and lower receiver. The upper receiver is not considered a firearm by the ATF and is not registered. Nor is the upper receiver marked or serial numbered to the lower receiver. Conversely, the lower receiver is serial numbered and marked with its model designation. It is therefore quite possible for upper receivers to be matched to lower receivers that are not in an original factory configuration. In order to be factory original, both upper and lower receivers must be configured at the factory prior to shipment. This is sometimes impossible to determine. It is therefore highly recommended that an expert be consulted prior to a sale to help determine originality.

MODEL NOTE: On early models, the "A" suffix usually means it has a forward assist and the "B" suffix usually means it has a burst mechanism. Model numbers began with the 600 series,

M16A1 with Colt AR-15 markings with M203 grenade launcher • Paul Goodwin photo

then the 700 series, which are based on the M16A2. The 800 series models are grenade launchers (M203). The 900 series models have flat top upper receivers and removable carry handles. The following are model designations with Colt nomenclature:

XM16 became the M16
XM16E1 became the M16A1
M16A1E1 became the M16A2
M16A2E4 became the M16A4

GRENADE LAUNCHER NOTE: M203 launchers will retail for about $4,500 NIB, Launchers made by AAI will bring $15,000 because of their rarity.

NOTE: As a general rule of thumb, "U.S. Property" marked guns will bring a premium, in some cases a substantial one, depending on model and configuration. These premiums will be so stated where applicable. The M16 was also produced by GM's Hydramatic division and Harrington & Richardson, Inc. Production began in late 1968. M16s from either manufacturer are rarely encountered. Rifles made by H&R will bring about 85 percent of a comparable Colt M16, while the Hydramatic rifles will bring almost double that of a Colt M16. This premium does not apply to rifles that have been re-welded.

Colt M16 NOTE: The Colt M16 comes in a variety of configurations (upper receivers), some of which are mentioned here. It is important to note that these configurations are based on the same lower receiver. In the case of civilian ownership, the lower receiver is the registered part of the firearm as far as the BATF is concerned. Therefore, it is possible, with a registered lower receiver, to interchange upper receiver components to a wide variety of different configurations from 9mm to .223 LMG uppers. Be aware that this interchangeability works best with Colt parts.

Bibliographical Note: For a full and complete description with photos, see Dan Shea's *Machine Gun Dealers Bible*, 4th edition, Moose Lake Publishing. See Blake Stevens and Edward Ezell, *The Black Rifle, M16 Retrospective*, Collector Grade Publications, for an in-depth examination of the history and development of the M16. Since the 2nd edition of this book a new publication by Christopher R. Bartocci, *Black Rifle II:The M16 into the 21st Century*, Collector Grade Publications, 2004 is highly recommended.

600 Series

Colt/Armalite AR-15/M16 Model 601

This rifle was first produced in 1960 with many variants following. Chambered for the 5.56x45mm cartridge it has a 20.8" barrel with flash hider. Magazine capacity is 20 or 30 rounds. Weight is 7 lbs. Rate of fire is 800 rounds per minute. Used extensively in Vietnam and now throughout the world. Some were marked "COLT AR-15 PROPERTY OF US GOVT.M16 CAL 5.56MM" on left side of magazine housing, but early guns were not marked "US Property." There is a wide variation in prices and models. Prices listed below are for the standard Colt/Armalite rifle.

NOTE: For Armalite only marked rifles no price given because of rarity. For Colt only marked rifles deduct $2,000.

AR-15 markings • Courtesy James Alley

Pre-1968

Exc.	V.G.	Fair
20000	18500	17500

Pre-1986 conversions, for OEM A1 add 40 percent

Exc.	V.G.	Fair
N/A	N/A	N/A

Pre-1986 dealer samples

Exc.	V.G.	Fair
N/A	N/A	N/A

Colt Model 602

This U.S. ("US Property") model was fitted with a 20" barrel. It has no forward assist. Select fire in full or semiauto.

SNAP SHOT
M16A1

The U.S. Army began testing small arms effectiveness in the late 1940s, and by the early 1950s, had concluded that infantry small arms should be of approximately .22 caliber, high-velocity, select-fire and effective out to 300 meters. This began the process that led up to the adoption of the M16A1 on 28 February 1967. Eugene Stoner, working for Armalite Division of Fairchild Aircraft Corporation in 1957, developed the rifle that would eventually become the M16A1. The M16A1 rifle is a gas-operated, select-fire, magazine-fed weapon, with a 20-inch barrel and a 1 in 12 twist rate. The M16A1 rifle was fitted with the forward assist device used on all military and most civilian AR-15 type rifles since then. This device consists of the spring-loaded button with internal claw, that engages the serrations on the right side of the bolt carrier to push it forward if the pressure of the return spring is insufficient to do so (for example, due to the fouling inside the receiver or chamber). The rifle will not fire unless the bolt is locked and the bolt carrier is in its forward-most position. The trigger/hammer group consists of a hammer, a trigger, a disconnector, a full-auto sear and springs. The fire selector / safety switch has 3 positions: "safe", "semi" (single shots), and "auto" (full automatic). The flash hiders on the earliest M16A1s were prong-type, with three slots, but were replaced with "bird-cage" flash hiders with four closed slots on the M16A1 because the earlier type caught in vegetation. The M16A1 can be equipped with under barrel 40mm M203 grenade launcher. Standard sights of the M16A1 consist of a protected front post, adjustable for elevation and an aperture flip-up rear, with two range settings. Rear sights are mounted within the carrying handle and are adjustable for windage. The M16A1 remained in service until replaced by the M16A2 in 1982.

Charlie Cutshaw

Early AR-15 Model 01 • Paul Goodwin photo

CAR-15 • Courtesy James Alley

Colt Model 603 (M16A1)
This U.S. ("US Property") model has a 20" barrel with forward assist. Barrel has a 1 in 12 twist rate. Select fire in full or semi-auto.

Pre-1968
Exc.	V.G.	Fair
18000	17000	16500

Pre-1986 conversions, for OEM A1 add 40 percent
Exc.	V.G.	Fair
N/A	N/A	N/A

Pre-1986 dealer samples
Exc.	V.G.	Fair
N/A	N/A	N/A

Colt Model 604 (M16)
This U.S. ("US Property") Air Force model has a 20" barrel with a 1 in 12 twist. No forward assist. Select fire in full and semiauto.

Pre-1968
Exc.	V.G.	Fair
18000	17000	16500

Pre-1986 conversions, for OEM A1 add 40 percent
Exc.	V.G.	Fair
N/A	N/A	N/A

Pre-1986 dealer samples
Exc.	V.G.	Fair
N/A	N/A	N/A

Colt Model 605A CAR-15 Carbine
This U.S. ("US Property") version is the short barrel (10") version of the rifle with a forward assist. A select fire in full and semiauto.

Pre-1968
Exc.	V.G.	Fair
22000	20000	18500

Pre-1986 OEM/Colt
Exc.	V.G.	Fair
N/A	N/A	N/A

Pre-1986 dealer samples
Exc.	V.G.	Fair
N/A	N/A	N/A

Colt Model 605B
This U.S. ("US Property") version is the same as above but with semiauto, full auto, and burst (3-round) select fire. No forward assist.

Pre-1968
Exc.	V.G.	Fair
22000	20000	18500

Pre-1986 conversions, for OEM A1 add 40 percent
Exc.	V.G.	Fair
N/A	N/A	N/A

Pre-1986 dealer samples
Exc.	V.G.	Fair
N/A	N/A	N/A

Colt Model 606
This is the export version of the Model 616.

Pre-1968
Exc.	V.G.	Fair
18000	17000	16500

Pre-1986 conversions, for OEM A1 add 40 percent
Exc.	V.G.	Fair
N/A	N/A	N/A

Pre-1986 dealer samples
Exc.	V.G.	Fair
N/A	N/A	N/A

Colt Model 606B
As above, but with burst version.

Pre-1968
Exc.	V.G.	Fair
18000	17000	16500

Pre-1986 conversions, for OEM A1 add 40 percent
Exc.	V.G.	Fair
N/A	N/A	N/A

Pre-1986 dealer samples
Exc.	V.G.	Fair
N/A	N/A	N/A

Colt Model 607
This U.S. ("US Property") version is an SMG with sliding buttstock and 10" barrel. Designed for use by tank, helicopter, and APC crews. Length with stock closed is 26", with stock extended about 28.7". Weight is about 5.3 lbs.

Pre-1968
Exc.	V.G.	Fair
20000	18000	17500

Pre-1986 conversions, for OEM A1 add 40 percent
Exc.	V.G.	Fair
N/A	N/A	N/A

Pre-1986 dealer samples
Exc.	V.G.	Fair
N/A	N/A	N/A

Colt Model 608 Survival Rifle
This rifle was built in prototype only and its design was for use by aviation personnel. Fitted with a 10" barrel, cone shaped flash suppressor, short fixed buttstock, round handguard, no forward assist, no bayonet lug, and short pistol grip. Overall length is 29". Weight was slightly more than 4.7 lbs. Designed to be broken down to fit the standard USAF seat pack. Fewer than 10 manufactured.

Colt Survival Rifle Model 608 • Courtesy James Alley

Pre-1968
Exc.	V.G.	Fair
30000	29000	28500

Pre-1986 OEM/Colt
Exc.	V.G.	Fair
N/A	N/A	N/A

Pre-1986 dealer samples
Exc.	V.G.	Fair
N/A	N/A	N/A

Colt Model 609 (XM177E1)
This is a U.S. Army version of the Commando with an 11.5" barrel with a 1 in 12 twist rate. This model has a forward assist. Select fire in full auto or semiauto.

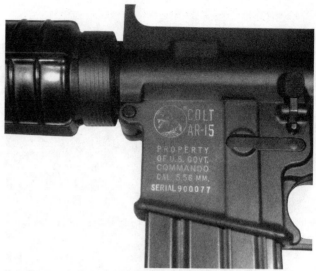

Markings for U.S. property for Commando model • Courtesy James Alley

Pre-1968
Exc.	V.G.	Fair
25000	22500	21500

Pre-1986 OEM/Colt
Exc.	V.G.	Fair
N/A	N/A	N/A

Pre-1986 dealer samples
Exc.	V.G.	Fair
N/A	N/A	N/A

Colt Model 610 (GAU-5/A)
This is the U.S. Air Force version of the XM177 Commando with 10" barrel with 1 in 12 twist and no forward assist. Select fire in full auto or semiauto.

Pre-1968
Exc.	V.G.	Fair
25000	22500	21500

Pre-1986 OEM/Colt
Exc.	V.G.	Fair
N/A	N/A	N/A

Pre-1986 dealer samples
Exc.	V.G.	Fair
N/A	N/A	N/A

Colt Model 613
This is export version of the 603.

Pre-1968
Exc.	V.G.	Fair
12500	11500	10500

Pre-1986 conversions, for OEM A1 add 40 percent
Exc.	V.G.	Fair
N/A	N/A	N/A

Pre-1986 dealer samples
Exc.	V.G.	Fair
N/A	N/A	N/A

Colt Model 614
This is the export version of the Model 604.

Pre-1968
Exc.	V.G.	Fair
12500	11500	10500

An M16A1 sold at auction for $13,800. Fitted with a 16" barrel with forward assist. Collapsible buttstock. Condition is excellent. *Amoskeag Auction Company, May 2004*

Pre-1986 conversions, for OEM A1 add 40 percent

Exc.	V.G.	Fair
N/A	N/A	N/A

Pre-1986 dealer samples

Exc.	V.G.	Fair
N/A	N/A	N/A

Colt Model 616

This U.S. ("US Property") version is fitted with a 20" heavy barrel with 1 in 12 twist rate. No forward assist. Select fire in full auto or semiauto.

Pre-1968

Exc.	V.G.	Fair
20000	18500	17500

Pre-1986 conversions, for OEM A1 add 40 percent

Exc.	V.G.	Fair
N/A	N/A	N/A

Pre-1986 dealer samples

Exc.	V.G.	Fair
N/A	N/A	N/A

Colt Model 619

This is the export version of the 609.

Pre-1968

Exc.	V.G.	Fair
20000	18500	17500

Pre-1986 conversions, for OEM A1 add 40 percent

Exc.	V.G.	Fair
N/A	N/A	N/A

Pre-1986 dealer samples

Exc.	V.G.	Fair
N/A	N/A	N/A

Colt Model 621

This U.S. ("US Property") version is fitted with a 20" heavy barrel with 1 in 12 twist. It is fitted with a forward assist. Select fire in full auto or semiauto.

Pre-1968

Exc.	V.G.	Fair
20000	18500	17500

Pre-1986 conversions, for OEM A1 add 40 percent

Exc.	V.G.	Fair
N/A	N/A	N/A

Pre-1986 dealer samples

Exc.	V.G.	Fair
N/A	N/A	N/A

Colt Model 629 (XM177E2)

This is the U.S. Army version of the Commando with 11.5" barrel with 1 in 12 twist. Sliding butt stock. Fitted with a forward

Colt Model 629 (XM177E2) • Courtesy James Alley

assist. Select fire in full auto or semiauto. Equipped with a 4.5"
flash suppressor. Weight is about 6.2 lbs without magazine.

Pre-1968

Exc.	V.G.	Fair
25000	22500	21000

Pre-1986 OEM/Colt

Exc.	V.G.	Fair
N/A	N/A	N/A

Pre-1986 dealer samples

Exc.	V.G.	Fair
N/A	N/A	N/A

Colt Model 630 (GAU-5/A/B)

This is the U.S. Air Force version of the XM177E1 with 11.5"
barrel with 1 in 12 twist. No forward assist. Select fire in full
auto or semiauto.

Pre-1968

Exc.	V.G.	Fair
25000	22500	21000

Pre-1986 OEM/Colt

Exc.	V.G.	Fair
N/A	N/A	N/A

Pre-1986 dealer samples

Exc.	V.G.	Fair
N/A	N/A	N/A

Colt Model 639

This is the export version of the Model 629.

Pre-1968

Exc.	V.G.	Fair
20000	18500	17500

Pre-1986 OEM/Colt

Exc.	V.G.	Fair
N/A	N/A	N/A

Pre-1986 dealer samples

Exc.	V.G.	Fair
N/A	N/A	N/A

Colt Model 645 (M16A2)

This model is an improved variation of the M16A1 Standard rifle with a 1 in 7 barrel twist and a heavier 20" barrel. A case
deflector is mounted on the right side. Sights are an improved
version of the standard M16 type. Forward assist. Improved
flash suppressor, buttstock, and pistol grip. First produced in
1982. *See list of M16A2 modifications on prior page.*

Pre-1968

Exc.	V.G.	Fair
N/A	N/A	N/A

Pre-1986 OEM/Colt

Exc.	V.G.	Fair
16000	15000	14000

Pre-1986 dealer samples

Exc.	V.G.	Fair
N/A	N/A	N/A

Colt Model 646 (M16A3)

This is the U.S. ("US Property") version of the M16A3 except
that there is no 3-round burst but full auto and semiauto.

Colt Model 649 (GAU-5/A/A)

This is the U.S. Air Force version of the XM177E2 with 11.5"
barrel with 1 in 12 twist rate and no forward assist. Select fire
with full auto and semiauto. Equipped with a 4.5" flash suppressor.

Pre-1968

Exc.	V.G.	Fair
25000	22500	21500

Pre-1986 OEM/Colt

Exc.	V.G.	Fair
N/A	N/A	N/A

Pre-1986 dealer samples

Exc.	V.G.	Fair
N/A	N/A	N/A

Colt Model 651

This is the export version of the rifle with 14.5" barrel.

Pre-1968

Exc.	V.G.	Fair
20000	18500	17500

Pre-1986 conversions

For OEM A1 add 40 percent.

Exc.	V.G.	Fair
N/A	N/A	N/A

Pre-1986 dealer samples

Exc.	V.G.	Fair
N/A	N/A	N/A

Colt Model 652

This is the export version of the rifle with 14.5" barrel and no
forward assist.

Pre-1968

Exc.	V.G.	Fair
15000	14000	13000

**Pre-1986 conversions, for OEM A1 add 40
percent**

Exc.	V.G.	Fair
N/A	N/A	N/A

Pre-1986 dealer samples

Exc.	V.G.	Fair
N/A	N/A	N/A

Colt Model 653

This is the export version of the rifle with 14.5" barrel and sliding buttstock.

Pre-1968

Exc.	V.G.	Fair
15000	14000	13000

**Pre-1986 conversions, for OEM A1 add 40
percent**

Exc.	V.G.	Fair
N/A	N/A	N/A

Pre-1986 dealer samples

Exc.	V.G.	Fair
N/A	N/A	N/A

Colt Model 655 (Sniper)

This was a U.S. ("US Property") prototype version with a 20"
barrel with a 1 in 9 twist rate. It has a forward assist. The upper
receiver has a high profile scope mount and was to have been
fitted with a Leatherwood Realist scope and Sionics suppressor. Select fire with full auto or semiauto.

Colt Model 656 (Sniper)

Same as above but with a special low profile upper receiver
with no carry handle and low profile scope mount.

700 Series-Export Versions of the M16A2

NOTE: A2 Military serial number are in the 6000000 range and
A2 Civilian models are in the 8000000.

Model 711 • Courtesy James Alley

Colt Model 701 Export Rifle

This is the M16A2 with 20" barrel and all the A2 features. Weight is about 7.5 lbs.

Colt Model 703 Test Model

This is a test model with a gas piston designated the M703/16A2. Test model used an AK type bolt and carrier. Test model is not priced.

Colt Model 703 Export Rifle

[There are two different types of 703s. Colt used the same model designation twice. See above.] Select fire with semi, 3-round burst, and full auto. The Export Model is an M16A2 style rifle.

Pre-1968

Exc.	V.G.	Fair
N/A	N/A	N/A

Pre-1986 OEM/Colt

Exc.	V.G.	Fair
18500	17500	16500

Pre-1986 dealer samples

Exc.	V.G.	Fair
N/A	N/A	N/A

Colt Model 707 Export rifle

This is a M16A2 with 20" A1 style barrel with 1 in 7 twist rate. Select fire with semi, 3-round burst. Weight is about 7.5 lbs.

Pre-1968

Exc.	V.G.	Fair
N/A	N/A	N/A

Pre-1986 conversions, for OEM A1 add 40 percent

Exc.	V.G.	Fair
18500	17500	16500

Pre-1986 dealer samples

Exc.	V.G.	Fair
N/A	N/A	N/A

Colt Model 711 Export Rifle

This model is the same as the M16A2 but fitted with M16A1 sights and standard weight M16A1 barrel.

Pre-1968

Exc.	V.G.	Fair
N/A	N/A	N/A

Pre-1986 conversions, for OEM A1 add 40 percent

Exc.	V.G.	Fair
16500	15500	15000

Pre-1986 dealer samples

Exc.	V.G.	Fair
N/A	N/A	N/A

Colt Model 713 Export Rifle

This model is fitted with an M16A1 upper receiver with case deflector 20" A1 barrel with 1 in 7 twist. Buttstock is A2 type. The compensator is A2 type with A2 lower receiver with select fire in semi and 3-round burst. Weight is about 7 lbs.

Pre-1968

Exc.	V.G.	Fair
N/A	N/A	N/A

Pre-1986 conversions, for OEM A1 add 40 percent

Exc.	V.G.	Fair
16500	15500	15000

Pre-1986 dealer samples

Exc.	V.G.	Fair
N/A	N/A	N/A

Colt Model 723 Export Carbine

This model is an M16A2 carbine with lightweight 14.5" barrel, M16A1 sights, and telescoping stock. Select fire in semiauto and full auto.

Pre-1968

Exc.	V.G.	Fair
N/A	N/A	N/A

Pre-1986 conversions, for OEM A1 add 40 percent

Exc.	V.G.	Fair
18500	17500	16500

Pre-1986 dealer samples

Exc.	V.G.	Fair
N/A	N/A	N/A

Colt Model 725 Export Carbine

Same as the Model 723 but with semiauto and three-round burst select fire.

Pre-1968

Exc.	V.G.	Fair
N/A	N/A	N/A

Pre-1986 conversions, for OEM A1 add 40 percent

Exc.	V.G.	Fair
17500	16500	15500

Pre-1986 dealer samples

Exc.	V.G.	Fair
N/A	N/A	N/A

M16A2 Model 723 and Model 733 • Courtesy James Alley

Colt Model 727 Carbine

This is the M16A2 version of the M4 Carbine. Fitted with a 14.5" barrel capable of accepting the M203 grenade launcher. Rifling twist is 1 in 7. Sliding buttstock. Rate of fire is 700 to 950 rounds per minute. Select fire in semiauto and full auto. Weight is about 5.65 lbs without magazine.

Pre-1968

Exc.	V.G.	Fair
N/A	N/A	N/A

Pre-1986 conversions, for OEM A1 add 40 percent

Exc.	V.G.	Fair
18500	17500	16500

Pre-1986 dealer samples

Exc.	V.G.	Fair
N/A	N/A	N/A

Colt Model 733 Export Commando

This model is the M16A2 Commando with an 11.5" barrel, M16A1 sight, telescoping butt.

Pre-1968

Exc.	V.G.	Fair
N/A	N/A	N/A

Pre-1986 OEM/Colt

Exc.	V.G.	Fair
20000	18500	17500

M16A2 Model 727 • Courtesy James Alley

Pre-1986 dealer samples

Exc.	V.G.	Fair
N/A	N/A	N/A

Colt Model 741 Export Heavy Barrel

This is an M16A2 with 20" heavy barrel that is magazine fed. Designed as a SAW (Squad Automatic Weapon). Weight is about 10 lbs.

Pre-1968

Exc.	V.G.	Fair
N/A	N/A	N/A

Pre-1986 conversions, for OEM A1 add 40 percent

Exc.	V.G.	Fair
18500	17500	16500

Pre-1986 dealer samples

Exc.	V.G.	Fair
N/A	N/A	N/A

Colt Model 750 LMG (See *U.S., Machine Guns*)

Colt Model 720 M4 (Original Version)

This is a short barrel version of the M16 with collapsible stock. Chambered for 5.56x45mm cartridge. It is fitted with a 14.5" barrel and has a magazine capacity of 20 or 30 rounds. Its rate of fire is 800 rounds per minute. Weight is about 5.6 lbs. Marked "COLT FIREARMS DIVISION COLT INDUSTRIES HARTFORD CONN USA" on the left side of the receiver, with "COLT M4 CAL 5.56MM" on the left side of the magazine housing. In use with

---

SNAP SHOT
M16A4

The M16A4 is a refinement of the original AR-15/M16 designed by Eugene Stoner. It evolved from the AR-15 into the M16, then the M16A1, then the M16A2 and finally into the M16A3 and M16A4. A list of all the improvements and additions to these weapons would fill several pages. The M16A4 is a flat-topped version of the M16A2, with a MIL-STD-1913 (Picatinny) rail to mount optics (scopes, night vision, laser or red dot) or a detachable carry handle that also houses a rear sight assembly. It also has the step-down in the barrel to mount the M203 under-barrel grenade launcher. A 1 in 7 rifling twist, with six lands and grooves, stabilizes heavier bullets. Weight is 5.65 pounds, without magazine, and the 5.56 x 45 mm cartridge is standard. The U.S. Military adopted the M16A4 in 1994, at the same time as the M16A3. These two very similar weapons differ only in that the M16A3 is capable of semiauto and full auto, while the M16A4 has semiauto, three-round burst and full auto. The retention of the 20-inch barrel is seen by some as an advantage over the current M4 and M4A1, with their shorter barrels, as it maintains the same muzzle velocity as the M16A2. The modified handguards on the M16A3 and M16A4 are capable of attaching Knight's Armament RAS (rail adapter system), which allows the weapon to be configured with high-intensity flashlights, laser sighting devices, night vision optics and other accessories. The M16A4 has a cyclic rate of 700 to 950 rounds per minute.

Charlie Cutshaw

American military forces as well as several South American countries.

Photo courtesy private NFA collection

Pre-1968

Exc.	V.G.	Fair
N/A	N/A	N/A

Pre-1986 conversions or OEM/Colt (Rare)

Exc.	V.G.	Fair
25000	22500	21500

Pre-1986 dealer samples

Exc.	V.G.	Fair
N/A	N/A	N/A

900 Series

Colt Model 920—M4

This model is the current U.S. ("US Property") version of the flat top carbine with 14.5" barrel with a 1 in 7 twist rate, forward assist, sliding buttstock, and A2 improvements. Select fire with 3-round burst and semiauto.

Colt Model 921—M4A1

This U.S. ("US Property") model is the same as the Model 920, except it is full auto with no burst feature.

Colt Model 945—M16A4

This U.S. ("US Property") version is the flat top version of the M16A2.

Close-up of left and right side of M16A4 receiver, Copyright by Colt Defense LLC. used with permission, all rights reserved, Courtesy Blake Stevens, *Black Rifle II*, Collector Grade Publications.

Specialty Series

Colt CAR-15 Model M1 Heavy Assault Rifle

This was a prototype with a heavy AR-15 20" barrel. Fires from a closed bolt. Uses standard M16 magazines. Weight without magazine is about 7.6 lbs. Semi or full auto fire. Rate of fire is approximately 800 to 850 rounds per minute.

Colt CAR-15 Model M2 Belt-fed Heavy Assault Rifle

Similar to the M1 version with the addition of a removable belt feeding mechanism designed by Rob Roy. Weight is about 8.3 lbs. Also feeds from standard M16 magazines. Less than 20 M2s were built.

SNAP SHOT
M4 AND M4A1 CARBINES

The M4 and M4A1 are carbine-length versions of the M16A3 and M16A4. Though carbine versions of the M16 had been used since the 1960's (the XM177, and the CAR-15), demand for these was limited to select groups. However, during and after the Cold War, Special Operations Groups needed more compact, versatile weapons. In 1994, the U.S. Army adopted the Colt model 720 selective-fire carbine as the M4. It was intended to replace some M9 pistols and MP5 submachine guns, as well as give a more easily carried, shoulder-fired weapon to troops that were not regularly in harm's way, and a compact, interchangeable platform for Special Operations. It is more comfortable to carry than the full-size M16A2 series due to its lighter weight and smaller size. The M4 and M4A1 are equipped with a 14.5" barrel and a four-position sliding butt stock, and in the collapsed position, the entire unit is under 30 inches in length. They have a MIL-STD-1913 rail under the detachable carry handle for mounting specialized optics, such as laser, night vision optics and optical sights. The four position sliding butt stock allows the weapon to go from an almost machine pistol size to a carbine with full butt stock. Both the M4 and M4A1 have a cut down in the barrel for the M203 grenade launcher. The M4 has semiautomatic fire and three-round burst capability, and the M4A1 is semiautomatic and full auto. Effective range of the M4 is stated as being 600 meters. Data from field use does not support this claim. Loss of velocity from the shorter barrel affects the effectiveness of the 5.56 x 45 cartridge. The shorter gas system produces more stress on the moving parts, resulting in premature failure, or the requirement for more strict maintenance. Although the M4-M4A1 are and will continue to be good personal defense weapons for non-frontline troops, their use as battle rifles for Special Operations may be short-lived due to the development of new small arms for special operations.

Charlie Cutshaw

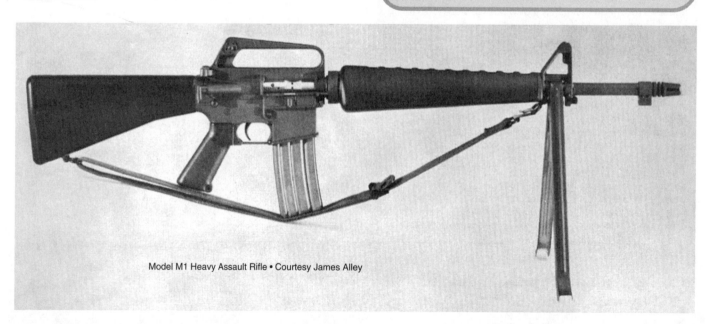

Model M1 Heavy Assault Rifle • Courtesy James Alley

M2 Belt fed with close-up • Courtesy James Alley

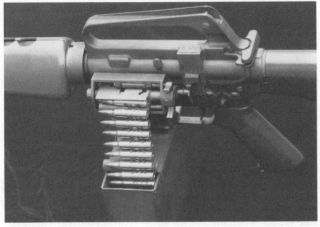

Pre-1968

Exc.	V.G.	Fair
N/A	N/A	N/A

Pre-1986 OEM/Colt

Exc.	V.G.	Fair
35000+	—	—

Pre-1986 dealer samples

Exc.	V.G.	Fair
N/A	N/A	N/A

Colt M231 Firing Port Weapon

This gun was never assigned a Colt model number but was fitted with a 15.6" barrel and a 1 in 12 twist rate. It fired from an open bolt in full auto only. It had no sights or buttstock. All original Colt firing port guns have an "F" prefix as part of the serial number and are marked "US PROPERTY."

Pre-1968

Exc.	V.G.	Fair
N/A	N/A	N/A

Pre-1986 OEM/Colt

Exc.	V.G.	Fair
22000	20000	18500

Pre-1986 dealer samples

Exc.	V.G.	Fair
N/A	N/A	N/A

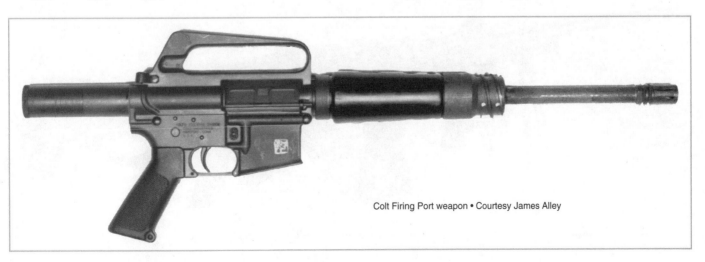

Colt Firing Port weapon • Courtesy James Alley

Colt ACR Advanced Combat rifle

This model was built in prototype only and was designed to fire special duplex cartridges. It was fitted with a 20" barrel, flattop receiver with special rib designed by Aberdeen Human Engineering Labs. It has a sliding buttstock with a hydraulic buffer. Select fire in full auto or semiauto.

Pre-1968

Exc.	V.G.	Fair
N/A	N/A	N/A

Pre-1986 OEM/Colt

Exc.	V.G.	Fair
Too Rare To Price		

Pre-1986 dealer samples

Exc.	V.G.	Fair
N/A	N/A	N/A

Colt CMG-1

One prototype was built of this model. It was a belt-fed light machine gun designed by Rob Roy and fitted with a 20" barrel with a 1-in-12 twist. Rate of fire of 650 rounds per minute. Weight is about 12.5 lbs. Fires from an open bolt. Designed to be used as a tripod mount, bipod mount, vehicle mount, or solenoid fixed machine gun.

Colt CMG1 • Courtesy James Alley

Colt CMG-2

This was an improved version of the CMG-1 designed by George Curtis and Henry Tatro. Approximately 6 were produced, 5 in 5.56 NATO and 1-in-7.62 NATO. It was fitted with a 20" quick change barrel with a 1 in 8.87" twist for the 68 grain GX-6235 bullet. Hydraulic buffer in buttstock. Bipod. Weight was about 15 lbs. Cycle rate is about 650 rounds per minute. It is fed by a 150-round belt fed drum magazine. These prototypes were built by Colt between 1967 and 1969.

Pre-1968

Exc.	V.G.	Fair
N/A	N/A	N/A

Pre-1986 OEM/Colt

Exc.	V.G.	Fair
40000+	—	—

Pre-1986 dealer samples

Exc.	V.G.	Fair
N/A	N/A	N/A

NOTE: There is little in the way of sales history, though there have been guns offered for sale in the $40,000 to $75,000 range on rare occasions.

M16 Rimfire Conversion Kits

There are several different conversion kits featuring different designs both adapted by the U.S. military. Both of these kits use a 10-round magazine but are not interchangeable with each other. The first is the Rodman design, known as the Air Force Model, built by OK Industries, New Britain, CT and the second is the M261 built by the Maremont Corp., Saco, ME. TM 9-6920-363-12 was issued with the M261 conversion kit. The Atchisson Mark I and Mark II kits and the Atchisson Mark III made by Jonathan Ciener, Inc., are also used by military forces in the U.S. as well as by foreign governments. The Ciener kit was introduced about 1988 and is designed to be used in both the M16 and AR15 rifles, both semiautomatic fire and full auto fire. Rate of fire is between 700 and 800 rounds per minute in the M16.

NOTE: Colt built a conversion kit produced for commercial sale but this kit was not adopted by the military.

Ciener Kit Mark III

Exc.	V.G.	Good	Fair	Poor
200	150	—	—	—

AR-15 SERIES

AR-15 Sporter (Model #6000)

A semiautomatic rifle firing from a closed bolt was introduced into the Colt product line in 1964. Similar in appearance and function to the military version, the M-16. Chambered for the .223 cartridge. It is fitted with a standard 20" barrel with no forward assist, no case deflector, but with a bayonet lug. Weighs about 7.5 lbs. Dropped from production in 1985.

NIB	Exc.	V.G.	Good	Fair	Poor
2100	1500	1100	700	600	400

AR-15 Sporter w/Collapsible Stock (Model #6001)

Same as above but fitted with a 16" barrel and sliding stock. Weighs approximately 5.8 lbs. Introduced in 1978 and discontinued in 1985.

Colt CMG 2 • Courtesy James Alley

NIB	Exc.	V.G.	Good	Fair	Poor
2150	1600	1200	800	600	400

NOTE: PRICES FOR AR-15 RIFLES AND CARBINES ARE SUSPENDED DUE TO AN UNSETTLED MARKET. BOTH BUYER AND SELLER ARE STRONGLY ADVISED TO SEEK EXPERT ASSISTANCE PRIOR TO A SALE.

AR-15 Carbine (Model #6420)

Introduced in 1985 this model has a 16" standard weight barrel. All other features are the same as the previous discontinued AR-15 models. This version was dropped from the Colt product line in 1987.

NIB	Exc.	V.G.	Good	Fair	Poor
—	—	—	—	—	—

AR-15 9mm Carbine (Model #6450)

Same as above but chambered for 9mm cartridge. Weighs 6.3 lbs.

NIB	Exc.	V.G.	Good	Fair	Poor
—	—	—	—	—	—

AR-15A2 (Model #6500)

Introduced in 1984, this was an updated version with a heavier barrel and forward assist. The AR sight was still utilized. Weighs approximately 7.8 lbs.

NIB	Exc.	V.G.	Good	Fair	Poor

AR-15A2 Govt. Model Carbine (Model #6520)

Added to the Colt line in 1988, this 16" standard barrel carbine featured for the first time a case deflector, forward assist, and the improved A2 rear sight. This model is fitted with a 4-position telescoping buttstock. Weighs about 5.8 lbs.

NIB	Exc.	V.G.	Good	Fair	Poor

AR-15A2 Gov't. Model (Model #6550)

This model was introduced in 1988; it is the rifle equivalent to the Carbine. It features a 20" A2 barrel, forward assist, case deflector, but still retains the bayonet lug. Weighs about 7.5 lbs. Discontinued in 1990.

NIB	Exc.	V.G.	Good	Fair	Poor

AR-15A2 H-Bar (Model #6600)

Introduced in 1986, this version features a special 20" heavy barrel. All other features are the same as the A2 series of AR15s. Discontinued in 1991. Weighs about 8 lbs.

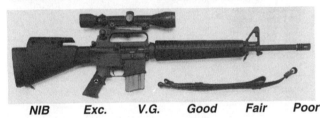

NIB	Exc.	V.G.	Good	Fair	Poor
—	—	—	—	—	—

AR- 15A2 Delta H-Bar (Model #6600DH)

Same as above but fitted with a 3x9 Tasco scope and detachable cheekpiece. Dropped from the Colt line in 1990. Weighs about 10 lbs. Equipped with a metal carrying case.

NIB	Exc.	V.G.	Good	Fair	Poor
—	—	—	—	—	—

Sporter Lightweight Rifle

This lightweight model has a 16" barrel and is finished in a matte black. It is available in either a .223 Rem. caliber (Model #6530) that weighs 6.7 lbs., a Model #6430 w/A1 sights, 9mm caliber weighing 7.1 lbs., or a Model #6830 7.65x39mm that weighs 7.3 lbs. The .223 is furnished with two five-round box magazines as is the 9mm and 7.65x39mm. A cleaning kit and sling are also supplied with each new rifle. The buttstock and pistol grip are made of durable nylon and the handguard is reinforced fiberglass and aluminum lined. The rear sight is adjustable for windage and elevation. These newer models are referred to simply as Sporters and are not fitted with a bayonet lug and the receiver block has different size pins.

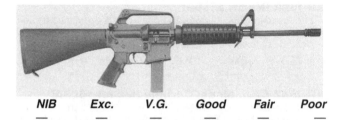

NIB	Exc.	V.G.	Good	Fair	Poor
—	—	—	—	—	—

Sporter Target Model Rifle (Model #6551)

This 1991 model is a full size version of the Lightweight Rifle. The Target Rifle weighs 7.5 lbs. and has a 20" barrel. Offered in .223 Rem. caliber only with target sights adjustable to 800 meters. New rifles are furnished with two 5-round box magazines, sling, and cleaning kit. Same as the Model 6550 except for a rib around the magazine release.

Copyright by Colt Defense LLC. used with permission, all rights reserved, Courtesy Blake Stevens, *Black Rifle II*, Collector Grade Publications

NIB	Exc.	V.G.	Good	Fair	Poor
—	—	—	—	—	—

Sporter Match H-Bar (Model #6601)

This 1991 variation of the AR-15 is similar to the Target Model but has a 20" heavy barrel chambered for the .223 caliber. This model weighs 8 lbs. and has A2 sights adjustable out to 800 meters. Supplied with two 5-round box magazines, sling, and cleaning kit.

NIB	Exc.	V.G.	Good	Fair	Poor
—	—	—	—	—	—

Sporter Match Delta H-Bar (Model #6601 DH)

Same as above but supplied with a 3x9 Tasco scope. Has a black detachable cheekpiece and metal carrying case. Weighs about 10 lbs. Discontinued in 1992.

NIB	Exc.	V.G.	Good	Fair	Poor
—	—	—	—	—	—

Match Target H-BAR Compensated (Model MT6601C)

Same as the regular Sporter H-BAR with the addition of a compensator.

NIB	Exc.	V.G.	Good	Fair	Poor
—	—	—	—	—	—

Colt AR-15 and Colt Sporter Terminology

There are three different and distinct manufacturing cycles that not only affect the value of these rifles but also the legal consequences of their modifications.

Pre-Ban Colt AR-15 rifles (Pre-1989): Fitted with bayonet lug, flash hider, and stamped AR-15 on lower receiver. Rifles that are NIB have a green label. It is legal to modify this rifle with any AR-15 upper receiver. These are the most desirable models because of their pre-ban features.

Colt Sporters (Post-1989-pre-September, 1994): This transition model may or may not have a bayonet lug, but it does have a flash hider. There is no AR-15 designation stamped on the lower receiver. Rifles that are NIB have a blue label. It is legal to modify this rifle with upper receivers made after 1989, i.e., pre-ban. These rifles are less desirable than pre-ban AR-15s.

Colt Sporters (Post-September, 1994): This rifle has no bayonet lug, no flash hider, and does not have the AR-15 designation stamped on the lower receiver. Rifles that are NIB have a blue label. It is legal to modify this rifle only with upper receivers manufactured after September 1994. These rifles are the least desirable of the three manufacturing periods because of their lack of pre-ban military features and current manufacture status.

Sporter Competition H-Bar (Model #6700)

Introduced in 1992, the Competition H-Bar is available in .223 caliber with a 20" heavy barrel counterbored for accuracy. The carry handle is detachable with A2 sights. With the carry handle removed the upper receiver is dovetailed and grooved for Weaver-style scope rings. This model weighs approximately 8.5 lbs. New rifles are furnished with two 5-round box magazines, sling, and cleaning kit.

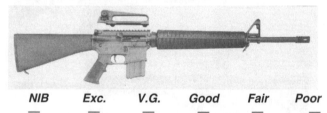

NIB	Exc.	V.G.	Good	Fair	Poor
—	—	—	—	—	—

Sporter Competition H-Bar Select w/scope (Model #6700CH)

This variation, also new in 1992, is identical to the Sporter Competition with the addition of a factory mounted scope. The rifle has also been selected for accuracy and comes complete with a 3-9X Tasco rubber armored variable scope, scope mount, carry handle with iron sights, and nylon carrying case.

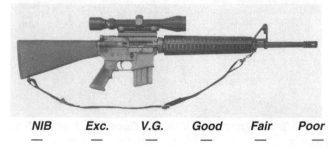

NIB	Exc.	V.G.	Good	Fair	Poor
—	—	—	—	—	—

Match Target Competition H-BAR Compensated (Model MT6700C)

Same as the Match Target with a compensator.

NIB	Exc.	V.G.	Good	Fair	Poor
—					

AR-15 Carbine Flat-top Heavyweight/Match Target Competition (Model #6731)

This variation in the Sporter series features a heavyweight 16" barrel with flat-top receiver chambered for the .223 cartridge. It is equipped with a fixed buttstock. Weight is about 7.1 lbs.

NIB	Exc.	V.G.	Good	Fair	Poor
—	—	—	—	—	—

AR-15 Tactical Carbine (Model #6721)

This version is similar to the above model with the exception of the buttstock which is telescoping and adjusts to 4 positions. Chambered for the .223 cartridge with a weight of about 7 lbs. A majority of these guns were for law enforcement only.

NIB	Exc.	V.G.	Good	Fair	Poor
—	—	—	—	—	—

Colt Accurized Rifle CAR-A3 (Model CR6724)

This variation was introduced in 1996 and features a free floating 24" stainless steel match barrel with an 11-degree target crown and special Teflon coated trigger group. The handguard is all-aluminum with twin swivel studs. Weight is approximately 9.26 lbs.

NIB	Exc.	V.G.	Good	Fair	Poor
—	—	—	—	—	—

U.S. CALIBER .30 CARBINE

Bibliographical Note: There are a number of variations, sights, stock configurations, etc., that are too numerous to cover in this publication. It is strongly recommended that for additional historical information, technical data, and photos see Larry L. Ruth's, *War Baby!, The U.S. Caliber .30 Carbine*, Collector Grade Publications, 1992.

This carbine was designed by William Roemer, Edwin Pugsley, and others at the Winchester Repeating Arms Company in late 1940 and early 1941. The only feature that can be credited to David Marsh "Carbine" Williams is the short stroke piston design. The U.S. M1 Carbine was produced by a number of manufacturers as listed below. The M1 A1 version was produced by Inland. The selective fire version is known as the Model M2. The exact number of carbines produced is unknown but approximately 6,000,000 carbines were built during World War II.

NOTE: Deduct 50 percent for imports.

U.S. M3 Carbine

This model is identical to the select fire M2 carbine with the exception of no rear sight and the scope mount to support a variety of scopes for specific uses.

U.S. M3 Carbine • Paul Goodwin photo

M3 Carbine with scope • Courtesy Richard M. Kumor Sr.

NOTE: For M3 Carbines with infra red scope add $1,000.

Pre-1986

Exc.	V.G.	Fair
4000	3500	3000

Pre-1986 conversions

Exc.	V.G.	Fair
3000	2750	2500

Pre-1986 dealer samples

Exc.	V.G.	Fair
2500	2750	2500

U.S. M2 Carbine

First produced in 1944 this select fire rifle is the automatic version of the famous M1 carbine. It has a 17.8" barrel and a 15- or 30-round magazine. It is chambered for the .30 Carbine cartridge (7.62x33mm). Its rate of fire is 750 rounds per minute. Weight is about 5.25 lbs. Marked "U.S.CARBINE CAL .30 M2" on top of chamber. Saw limited use in World War II but was widely used by American forces during Korea.

Pre-1968

Exc.	V.G.	Fair
6000	5500	5000

Pre-1986 conversions

Exc.	V.G.	Fair
3000	2750	2500

Pre-1986 dealer samples

Exc.	V.G.	Fair
2500	2750	2500

U.S. M1 Carbine

Introduced in 1941, this is a semiautomatic, gas operated carbine with a 18" barrel and a magazine capacity of 15 or 30 rounds. Half stocked with upper handguard and single barrel band. Bayonet bar located on barrel. Flip up rear sight. Chambered for the .30 U.S. Carbine cartridge. Weight is about 5.25 lbs. Widely used by U.S. military forces during World War II.

NOTE: Prices are for carbines in World War II factory original configuration. Any M1 Carbine with the earliest features sucha as "I" oiler cut stock, high wood, flip rear sight, and narrow barrel band will bring more than the later variations.

U.S. M2 Carbine, with selector switch and cartouche • Paul Goodwin photo

German infantry during Battle of the Bulge, the rear man is carrying a U.S. M1 carbine • Courtesy John M. Miller

Inland

Exc.	V.G.	Good	Fair	Poor
1500	1200	600	425	350

Underwood

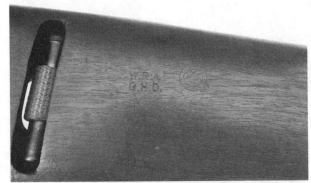

Early Underwood cartouche with large square box with WRA over GHD • Courtesy Michael Wamsher, Paul Goodwin photo

---

SNAP SHOT
M1 CARBINE

In 1938, the U.S. Army issued a request for a lightweight shoulder arm to provide to personnel whose duties did not involve front-line combat. The theory was that it would be easier to train support troops with a carbine than a sidearm and the carbine would have more power and a greater range. This request was shelved until 1940, when World War II was imminent. By this time, the specifications included a new cartridge of .30 caliber but far less powerful than the U.S. .30-06 cartridge. The cartridge, officially named the "Cartridge, ball, .30 caliber, M1", was developed by the Winchester company. It was a straight-case, rimless design with round-nose bullet weighing 110 grains and muzzle velocity of 1860 fps. Muzzle energy was about twice that of .45ACP pistol cartridge but still almost three times less that of .30-06 rifle cartridge. Winchester's design won the U.S. Army trials. David "Carbine" Williams developed the gas system, but Winchester employees developed the rest of the carbine in-house. First delivered to the U.S. Army in 1942, the M1 Carbine is a gas-operated, semiautomatic, with an 18-inch barrel, a half stock, an upper hand guard and a single barrel band. A flip up, diopter rear sight was standard. It uses a 15-round, detachable box magazine. Early carbines had no provision for a bayonet, but later versions have a lug mated to the barrel. The M1A1 is essentially the same, but came with a folding stock and a pistol grip for paratroop use. The M2 and M3 were later variations, with select fire capability, and came with a 30-round magazine. From 1942 to 1945, more than 6 million of these weapons were produced. It was made by no less than 11 different manufacturers, and was used in WWII, Korea and throughout the VietNam War by Vietnamese and some U.S. troops in an advisory role. It remains a popular small arm in the civilian community.

Charlie Cutshaw

Exc.	V.G.	Good	Fair	Poor
1600	1250	600	425	350

S.G. Saginaw

Exc.	V.G.	Good	Fair	Poor
1800	1300	600	425	350

IBM

Exc.	V.G.	Good	Fair	Poor
1800	1100	600	425	350

Quality Hardware

Exc.	V.G.	Good	Fair	Poor
1700	1100	600	425	350

National Postal Meter

Early National Postal Meter cartouche with NPM over FJA in large square box • Courtesy Michael Wamsher, Paul Goodwin photo

Exc.	V.G.	Good	Fair	Poor
1800	1100	600	425	350

Standard Products

Exc.	V.G.	Good	Fair	Poor
1900	1200	650	450	375

Rockola

Exc.	V.G.	Good	Fair	Poor
2000	1400	700	450	375

SG Saginaw (Grand Rapids)

Exc.	V.G.	Good	Fair	Poor
2000	1400	700	450	375

Winchester

Early Winchester cartouche • Courtesy Michael Wamsher, Paul Goodwin photo

Exc.	V.G.	Good	Fair	Poor
2000	1400	700	450	375

M1 Carbine manufacturer's stampings • Courtesy Karl Karash

Irwin Pedersen-Rare

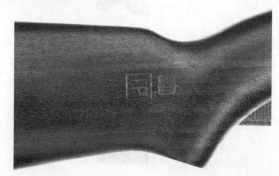

Irwin Pedersen cartouche with boxed IP and Ordnance Wheel Crossed Cannons • Courtesy Michael Wamsher, Paul Goodwin photo

Exc.	V.G.	Good	Fair	Poor
4000	2200	950	650	500

M1 Carbine Cutaway

Used by factories and military armorers to facilitate training. Examples with documentation will bring a substantial premium.

M1 Carbine cutaway • Courtesy Richard M. Kumor Sr.

Exc.	V.G.	Good	Fair	Poor
2500	1500	900	600	500

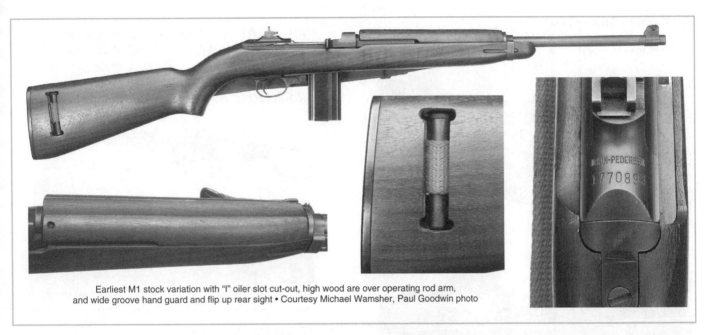

Earliest M1 stock variation with "I" oiler slot cut-out, high wood are over operating rod arm,
and wide groove hand guard and flip up rear sight • Courtesy Michael Wamsher, Paul Goodwin photo

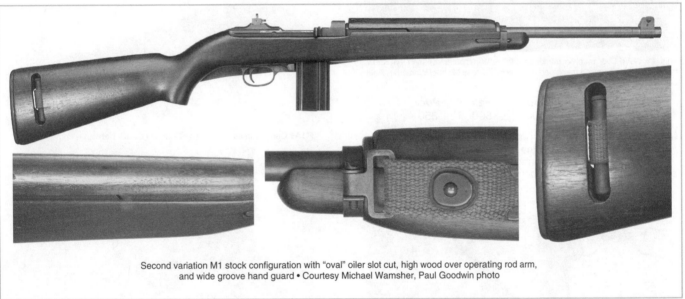

Second variation M1 stock configuration with "oval" oiler slot cut, high wood over operating rod arm,
and wide groove hand guard • Courtesy Michael Wamsher, Paul Goodwin photo

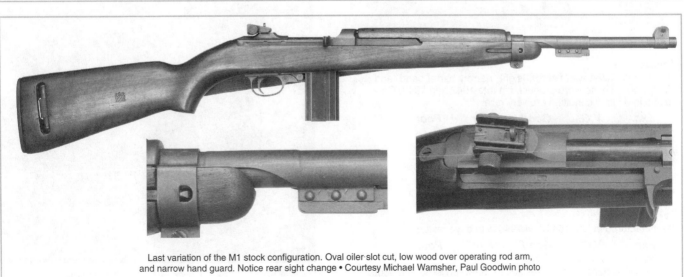

Last variation of the M1 stock configuration. Oval oiler slot cut, low wood over operating rod arm,
and narrow hand guard. Notice rear sight change • Courtesy Michael Wamsher, Paul Goodwin photo

M1 Carbine Sniper (T-3)

This is an M1 carbine with a M84 scope mounted with forward vertical grip. Used in Korea.

This is a WWII "T-3" receiver markings with the Winchester variation that show the style of the one piece machined receiver • Courtesy Michael Wamsher, Paul Goodwin photo

Exc.	V.G.	Good	Fair	Poor
1500	1000	800	500	350

U.S. M1A1 Paratrooper Model

The standard U.S. M1 Carbine fitted with a folding stock. Approximately 110,000 were manufactured by Inland between 1942 and 1945. Weight is about 5.8 lbs. There are three variations of this carbine.

Courtesy Richard M. Kumor Sr.

Variation I

Earliest variation with flip rear sight, narrow barrel band, and high wood. These were produced in late 1942 and 1943. Carbines in original condition are very rare.

Exc.	V.G.	Good	Fair	Poor
4500	3500	2250	—	—

Variation II

Manufactured in 1944 with no bayonet lug and low wood.

Exc.	V.G.	Good	Fair	Poor
3500	2500	1250	—	—

Variation III

Manufactured in late 1944 and 1945 with bayonet lug.

Exc.	V.G.	Good	Fair	Poor
3000	2400	1200	—	—

NOTE: Original jump cases sell for between $150 and $300.

An M1A1 paratrooper carbine sold at auction for $4,600. Produced October-November, 1944. Sling. Condition is 95 percent original black.
Rock Island Auction Company, April 2004

An example of a U.S. M1 Presentation Carbine • Courtesy Richard M. Kumor Sr.

M1A1 Carbine in its jump case • Courtesy Chuck Karwan

Courtesy Blake Stevens, *War Baby*, Collector Grade Publications.

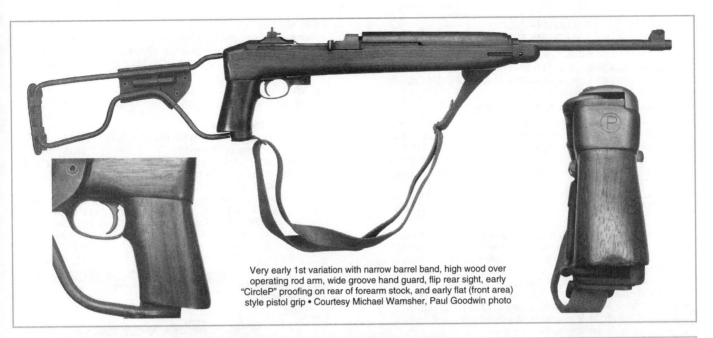

Very early 1st variation with narrow barrel band, high wood over operating rod arm, wide groove hand guard, flip rear sight, early "CircleP" proofing on rear of forearm stock, and early flat (front area) style pistol grip • Courtesy Michael Wamsher, Paul Goodwin photo

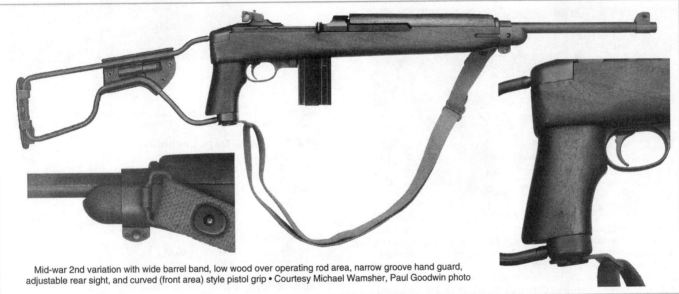

Mid-war 2nd variation with wide barrel band, low wood over operating rod area, narrow groove hand guard, adjustable rear sight, and curved (front area) style pistol grip • Courtesy Michael Wamsher, Paul Goodwin photo

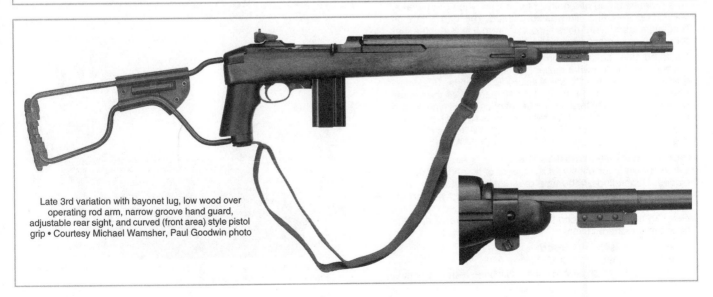

Late 3rd variation with bayonet lug, low wood over operating rod arm, narrow groove hand guard, adjustable rear sight, and curved (front area) style pistol grip • Courtesy Michael Wamsher, Paul Goodwin photo

GARAND
(U.S. M1 Rifle)
U.S. Rifle, CAL. M1 (Garand)

Bibliographical Note: For further information, technical, and photos see Bruce Canfield, *Complete Guide to the M1 Garand and the M1 Carbine.* Andrew Mowbray, Inc.

An Introduction to the U.S. M1 Rifle by Simeon Stoddard

Adopted in 1936, the M1 remained the standard issue rifle of the United States until it was replaced by the M14 in 1957. It was designed by John C. Garand, who worked for Springfield Armory from 1919 until his retirement in 1953. During this time, Garand concentrated his efforts on the development of a semi-automatic shoulder weapon for general issue to the U.S. armed forces. The M14 rifle, the replacement for the M1, was a compilation of his design work as well.

With the exceptions noted, all values given are for rifles which are in original, as produced condition. Development of the M1 was an ongoing project until it was replaced, as Garand never finished perfecting his basic design. Over 5,400,000 M1 rifles were built, with the majority of them going through a rebuilding process at least once during their service life. During rebuilding, rifles were inspected and unserviceable parts replaced. Parts used for replacement were usually of the latest revision available or what was on hand.

Major assemblies and parts were marked with a government drawing size/part number. This number is often followed with the revision number (see photo above). Barrels were marked, with the exception of early Springfield Armory and all Winchester production, with the month and year of manufacture. It must be remembered that this date only refers to when the barrel was produced, and has nothing to do with when the receiver was produced or the rifle was assembled. This barrel date on "original as produced" rifles should be from 0 to 3 months, before the receiver was produced.

Restored rifles, defined as ones with parts added/replaced, to more closely match what they might have been originally, are worth less money than "original as produced" rifles. This difference should be on the order of 30-40 percent of the values shown, and is due to the low number of rifles of this type. When in doubt, get an appraisal. To tell what parts should be correct, study chapters 5 & 6 of *"The M1 Garand: WWII"* and chapters 7 & 8 of *"The M1 Garand: Post WWII"* by Scott A. Duff.

Rebuilt Rifle, any manufacture

Value shown is for rifles with a majority of its parts mixed/replaced. Depending on the type of rebuilding that a rifle went through, rifles could be completely disassembled with no attempt to put parts together for the same rifle. Valued mainly for shooting merits. Bore condition, gauging and overall appearance are important factors.

Exc.	V.G.	Good
900	550	425

NOTE: Rifles built by Winchester will bring a small premium.

DCM Rifles

These rifles should have the correct paperwork and shipping boxes to receive the prices listed. Prices should be considered to be the base price as some DCM M1's fall into the following categories:

Exc.	V.G.	Good
850	575	450

Navy Trophy Rifles

The Navy continued to use the M1 rifle as its main rifle far into the 1960s. They were modified to shoot the 7.62x51 NATO (Winchester) round. This was accomplished at first with a chamber insert, and later with new replacement barrels in the NATO caliber. The Navy modified rifles can be found of any manufacture, and in any serial number range. As a general rule, Navy rifles with new barrels are worth more due to their better shooting capabilities. Paperwork and original boxes must accompany these rifles to obtain the values listed.

U.S. Navy Rifle modified to .308 caliber. Close-up shows polished or chrome plated bolt lugs • Courtesy Stoddard Martial collection, Paul Goodwin photo

U.S.N. Crane Depot rebuild

Exc.	V.G.	Good
1800	1000	900

AMF rebuild

Exc.	V.G.	Good
1150	1000	900

H&R rebuild

Exc.	V.G.	Good
1000	900	800

Springfield Armory Production

Exc.	V.G.	Good
1250	1000	900

Springfield Armory M1 with front sight without protective screw cap • Courtesy Michael Wamsher, Paul Goodwin photo

Springfield Armory M1 later style rear sight with bar type rear sight knob • Courtesy Michael Wamsher, Paul Goodwin photo

Gas Trap sn: ca 81-52000

Values shown for original rifles. Most all were updated to gas port configuration. Look out for reproductions being offered as original rifles! Get a professional appraisal before purchasing.

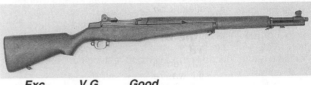

Exc.	V.G.	Good
40000	35000	25000

M1 Garand Gas Trap close-up • Courtesy Chuck Karwan

Gas Trap/modified to gas port

These rifles should have many of their early parts. Must be original modifications and not restored.

Exc.	V.G.	Good
5000	3500	2500

Pre-Dec. 7, 1941 gas port production sn: ca 50000-Appx. 410000

Exc.	V.G.	Good	Fair	Poor
4000	2200	1300	750	650

NOTE: Rifles built in 1940 in excellent and original condition will bring a premium of $1,500+.

WWII Production sn: ca 410000-3880000

SA/GHS Cartouche

Exc.	V.G.	Good	Fair	Poor
3500	1500	900	750	500

SA/EMF Cartouche

Exc.	V.G.	Good	Fair	Poor
3200	1500	900	750	500

SA/GAW Cartouche

Exc.	V.G.	Good	Fair	Poor
3100	1500	900	750	500

SA/NFR Cartouche

Exc.	V.G.	Good	Fair	Poor
2900	1200	900	750	500

POST WWII Production sn: ca 4200000-6099361

SA/GHS Cartouche

Exc.	V.G.	Good	Fair	Poor
2800	1200	650	500	400

National Defense Stamp

Exc.	V.G.	Good	Fair	Poor
2500	1000	650	500	400

Very Late 6000000 sn

Exc.	V.G.	Good	Fair	Poor
2500	1000	650	500	400

Winchester Production

Winchester produced around 513,000 M1 rifles during WWII. Their first contract was an educational order in 1939. This contract was for 500 rifles and the gauges and fixtures to produce the rifles. Winchester's second contract was awarded during 1939 for up to 65,000 rifles. Winchester M1's are typified by noticeable machine marks on their parts, and did not have the higher grade finish that is found on Springfield Armory production. Watch for fake barrels, and barrels marked "Winchester" which were produced in the 1960s as replacement barrels.

Winchester Educational Contract sn: 100000-100500

Exc.	V.G.	Good	Fair	Poor
10000	6000	4500	3000	2000

Winchester sn: 100501-165000

Rifles of this serial number range were produced from Jan. 1941 until May 1942.

Exc.	V.G.	Good	Fair	Poor
6500	4500	2000	1500	750

Winchester sn: 1200000-1380000

Rifles in this serial number range were produced from May 1942 until Aug. 1943.

Exc.	V.G.	Good	Fair	Poor
4500	2500	1800	1000	750

NOTE: Add a premium of $1,000 for earlier rifles.

A Winchester factory display M1 Garand sold at auction for $11,500. Nickel finish and nickel bayonet. Condition is 99 percent.
Rock Island Auction Company, April 2004

Winchester sn: 2305850-2536493

Rifles in this serial number range were produced from Aug. 1943 until Jan. 1945.

Exc.	V.G.	Good	Fair	Poor
3000	2000	1250	900	550

NOTE: Add a premium of $500 for earlier rifles.

Winchester sn: 1601150-1640000

Rifles in this serial number range were produced from Jan. 1945, until June 1945. These are often referred to as **"Win-13's"** because of the revision number of the right front receiver leg.

Exc.	V.G.	Good	Fair	Poor
3500	2500	2000	1500	850

Springfield Armory post-war M1 Garand. Note later style rear sight knobs • Courtesy Michael Wamsher, Paul Goodwin photo

Harrington & Richardson Production

Between 1953 and 1956, Harrington & Richardson produced around 428,000 M1 rifles.

Exc.	V.G.	Good	Fair	Poor
1800	1200	900	500	350

International Harvester Corp. Production

Between 1953 and 1956, International Harvester produced around 337,000 M1 rifles. International at several different times during their production purchased receivers from both Harrington & Richardson and Springfield Armory. Always check for Springfield Armory heat lots on the right front receiver leg.

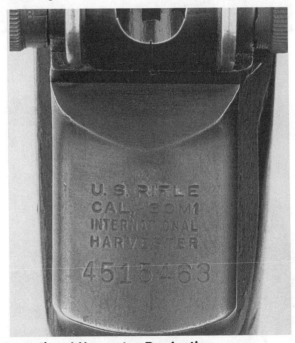

International Harvester Production

Exc.	V.G.	Good	Fair	Poor
2200	1500	800	450	350

International Harvester/with Springfield Receiver (postage stamp)

Exc.	V.G.	Good
2800	1500	900

International Harvester/with Springfield Receiver (arrow head)

Exc.	V.G.	Good
2800	1500	1000

International Harvester/with Springfield Receiver (Gap letter)

Exc.	V.G.	Good
2500	1300	900

International Harvester/with Harrington & Richardson Receiver

Exc.	V.G.	Good
1900	1200	850

M1 Experimental with one-piece upper handguard made of fiberglass • Courtesy Richard M. Kumor Sr.

British Garands (Lend Lease)

In 1941 and 1942, the U.S. sent a total of 38,000 M1 Garands to England under the Lend Lease program. These rifles were painted with a red band around the front of the handguard with the numerals "30" or "300" in black. The buttstock is stamped with a U.S. Ordnance cartouche and the initials "GHS" under "SA." Most known examples are found in the serial number range 3000000 to 600000. When these rifles were sold and imported back into the U.S., they were stamped with either London or Birmingham proof stamps.

Exc.	V.G.	Good	Fair	Poor
2250	2000	1500	1000	750

M1 Garand Cutaway

Used by factories and military armorers to facilitate training.

M1 Garand cutaway • Courtesy Richard M. Kumor Sr.

Exc.	V.G.	Good	Fair	Poor
3000	2500	1000	600	500

NOTE: For examples with documentation add 300 percent.

An M1 Garand Lend Lease rifle sold at auction for $1,840. Built December 1941. British proofs. Correct stamps. Condition is 95 percent finish. Green canvas sling.
Amoskeag Auction Company, Sept. 2003

U.S. Springfield M1 Garand Lend Lease.
Barrel date SA 9-41. Notice British proof
marks on left rear barrel, early gas
cylinder end plug, front sight with early
protective cap over front sight screw, and
1st variation rear sight knob • Courtesy
Michael Wamsher, Paul Goodwing photo

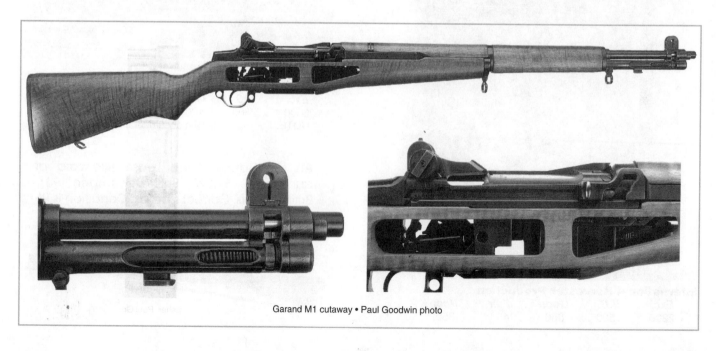

Garand M1 cutaway • Paul Goodwin photo

SCOPE VARIANTS (SNIPER RIFLES)

M1C

Springfield Armory production only. Serial number range is between ca 3200000 and 3800000. This variant is very rare with only around 7,900 produced. Should be mounted with M81, M82 or M84 scope with 7/8" scope rings. The scopes alone are worth $700 to $800 alone. Ask for government relicense paperwork, and have a serial number check run before purchase is made. If provenance cannot be established, then rifles are worth the value of their individual parts, under $2000.

NOTE: Prices listed are for the usual re-arsenaled examples with documentation. Rifles with all matching numbers and factory original condition are *extremely* rare, and would bring a substantial premium.

Exc.	V.G.	Good
10000	8000	5000

MC 1952 (USMC Issue) (sn. 10000-15000)

Same production range as above. Should be equipped with 1" scope mount and Kollmorgen scope. These rifles will command a premium. This is the rarest of the M-1 Snipers.

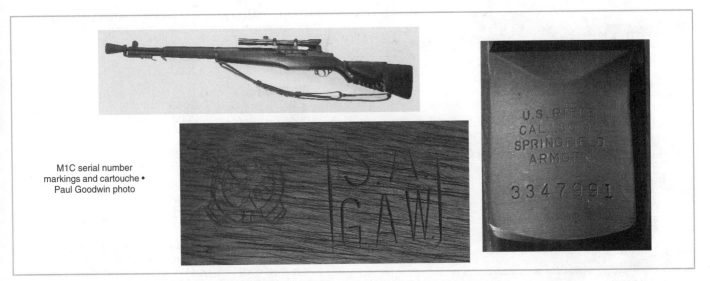

M1C serial number markings and cartouche • Paul Goodwin photo

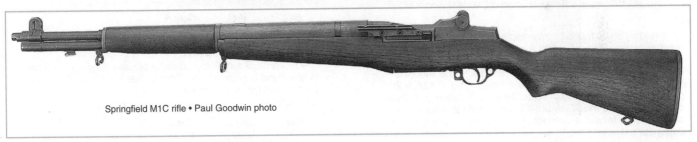

Springfield M1C rifle • Paul Goodwin photo

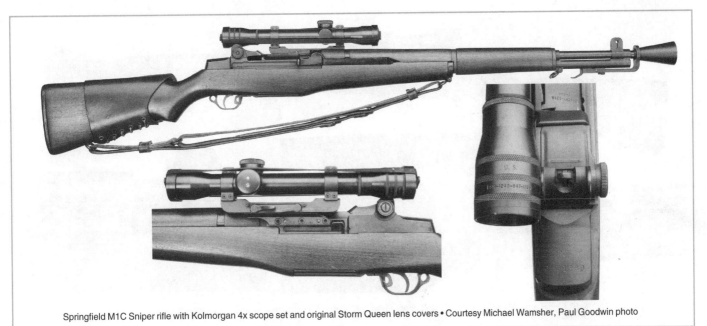

Springfield M1C Sniper rifle with Kolmorgan 4x scope set and original Storm Queen lens covers • Courtesy Michael Wamsher, Paul Goodwin photo

M1 Grand National Match • Paul Goodwin photo

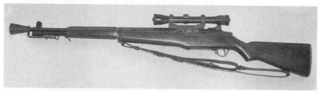

Courtesy Richard M. Kumor Sr.

Close-up of MC 1952 scope and mount • Courtesy Richard M. Kumor Sr.

M1D

This model can be found by any manufacturer and in any serial number range. This mounting system was designed by John Garand, and consists of a mounting block on the rear of the barrel. The rear hand guard is shortened and the mount attaches with a large single screw system. The modification could be made on the field repair level. It is not known how many rifles were modified, but it is very likely that they numbered into the tens of thousands. If the rifle does not come with paperwork, it is only worth the value of its parts alone, under

$1200. The Model 82 scope is worth between $500 and $700. With Kolmorgan scope set prices may bring up to $15,000.

SA mfg.

Exc.	V.G.	Good
3800	3000	2000

WRA mfg.

Exc.	V.G.	Good
4000	3000	2000

IHC mfg.

Exc.	V.G.	Good
4200	3000	2000

HRA mfg.

Exc.	V.G.	Good
4000	3000	2000

National Match Type I

Produced on Springfield Armory receivers and in serial number ranges from ca 5800000 to around 6090000. All parts are available to reproduce both types of national match rifles. To obtain values listed these rifles must come with original paperwork.

Exc.	V.G.	Good
4500	3000	1800

National Match Type II

Produced on Springfield Armory receivers, they can be found in any serial number range. These rifles should come with papers to receive values listed.

NOTE: Type I rifles are more rare than Type II.

Exc.	V.G.	Good
3200	2200	1500

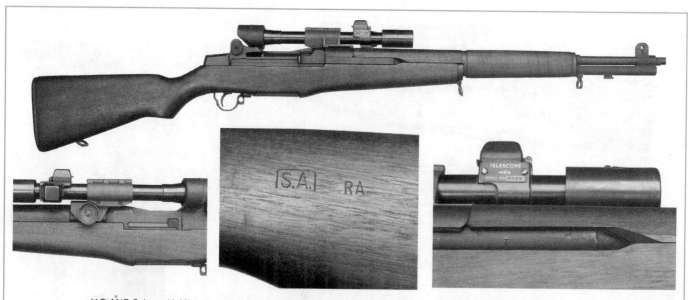

U.S. M1D Sniper with M84 scope and "RA" and open boxed "SA" cartouche • Courtesy Michael Wamsher, Paul Goodwin photo

KNIGHT'S MANUFACTURING CO.

SR-25 Lightweight Match (U.S. Navy, Mark 11 Model O)

This .308 rifle is fitted with a 20" free floating barrel. No sights. Weight is about 9.5 lbs. Adopted by U.S. Navy. Commercial version is the same except for the markings on the receiver.

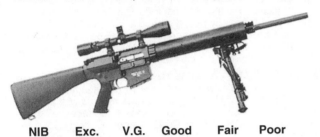

NIB	Exc.	V.G.	Good	Fair	Poor
3250	2250	1500	900	—	—

JOHNSON AUTOMATICS MFG. CO.

Model 1941

This is a recoil-operated semiautomatic rifle chambered for the .30-06 cartridge and fitted with a rotary 10-round magazine. It has a half stock with perforated handguard. Used by the U.S. Marines, Dutch Colonial forces, and U.S. special forces during World War II. Fitted with a 22" barrel and chambered for the .30-06 cartridge. Right side of the receiver is marked "CRANSTON ARMS CO." Parkerized finish. Checkered metal buttplate. Adjustable rear sight is graduated in meters. Bayonet fitted to barrel. Barrel is easily removed which was a plus for airborne Marine units. Weight is about 9.5 lbs.

NOTE: Rifles with a verifiable U.S. Marine Corp provenance will bring a premium.

Exc.	V.G.	Good	Fair	Poor
4500	3500	2000	1000	500

REMINGTON ARMS COMPANY, INC.

Split-Breech Cavalry Carbine

A .46 or .50 rimfire single-shot rolling block carbine with a 20" barrel. Blued, case hardened with a walnut stock. The tang marked "Remington's Ilion, N.Y. Pat. Dec. 23, 1863 May 3 & Nov. 16, 1864." The .50 caliber version is worth approximately 15 percent more than the .46 caliber. Approximately 15,000 .50-caliber variations were made, most of which were sold to France. Approximately 5,000 carbines were made in .46 caliber. Manufactured from 1864 to 1866.

Paul Goodwin photo

Exc.	V.G.	Good	Fair	Poor
—	—	4250	2000	500

U.S. Navy Rolling Block Carbine

A .50-70 caliber single shot rolling block carbine with a 23.25" round barrel. A sling ring is normally fitted to the left side of the frame and sling swivels are mounted on the barrel band and the bottom of the butt. Inspector's markings are to be found on the right side of the frame as well as the stock. Blued, case hardened with a walnut stock. The barrel is marked "Remington's Ilion, N.Y. U.S.A." along with the patent dates. Approximately 5,000 were manufactured in 1868 and 1869.

Exc.	V.G.	Good	Fair	Poor
—	—	3500	1250	350

Model 1867 Navy Cadet Rifle

A .50-45 caliber single shot rolling block rifle with a 32.5" barrel and full length forend secured by two barrel bands. Markings identical to the above with the exception that "U.S." is stamped on the buttplate tang. Blued, case hardened with a walnut stock. Approximately 500 were made in 1868.

Exc.	V.G.	Good	Fair	Poor
—	—	2750	1200	400

Rolling Block Military Rifles

Between 1867 and 1902 over 1,000,000 rolling block military rifles and carbines were manufactured by the Remington Company. Offered in a variety of calibers and barrel lengths, the

A Model 1941 Johnson rifle was sold at auction for $5,462. Bayonet. Condition is 95 percent. *Rock Island Auction Company, April 2004*

values listed below are for full length rifles. Foreign contract models are listed under country.

NOTE: Carbines are worth approximately 40 percent more.

Courtesy Milwaukee Public Museum, Milwaukee, Wisconsin

Exc.	V.G.	Good	Fair	Poor
—	—	750	400	100

Remington-Keene Magazine Rifle

A bolt-action rifle chambered for the .40, .43, and .45-70 centerfire cartridges with 22", 24.5", 29.25", or 32.5" barrels. It is readily identifiable by the exposed hammer at the end of the bolt. Blued, case hardened hammer and furniture, with a walnut stock. The receiver marked "E. Remington & Sons, Ilion, N.Y." together with the patent dates 1874, 1876, and 1877. The magazine on this rifle was located beneath the barrel and the receiver is fitted with a cut-off so that the rifle could be used as a single shot. Approximately 5,000 rifles were made between 1880 and 1888 in the following variations:

Sporting Rifle
24.5" barrel.

Exc.	V.G.	Good	Fair	Poor
—	2250	1200	500	200

Army Rifle
Barrel length 32.5" with a full-length stock secured by two barrel bands. Prices are for martially marked examples.

Courtesy Milwaukee Public Museum, Milwaukee, Wisconsin

Exc.	V.G.	Good	Fair	Poor
—	3500	2000	850	300

Navy Rifle
As above, with a 29.25" barrel. Prices are for martially marked examples.

Paul Goodwin photo

Exc.	V.G.	Good	Fair	Poor
—	4750	3000	1500	750

Carbine
As above, with a 22" barrel and a half-length forend secured by one barrel band.

Courtesy Milwaukee Public Museum, Milwaukee, Wisconsin

Exc.	V.G.	Good	Fair	Poor
—	3250	1500	750	350

Frontier Model
As above, with a 24" barrel and half-length forend secured by one barrel band. Those purchased by the United States

Department of the Interior for arming the Indian Police are marked "U.S.I.D." on the receiver.

Exc.	V.G.	Good	Fair	Poor
—	—	5500	3000	850

Remington-Lee Magazine Rifle

Designed by James Paris Lee, rifles of this type were originally manufactured by the Sharps Rifle Company in 1880. The Remington Company began production of this model in 1881 after the Sharps Company ceased operations. Approximately 100,000 Lee magazine rifles were made between 1880 and 1907. Their variations are as follows:

Model 1879 U.S. Navy Model
Barrel length 28", .45-70 caliber with a full-length stock secured by two barrel bands. The barrel is marked with the U.S. Navy inspector's marks and an anchor at the breech. The receiver is marked "Lee Arms Co. Bridgeport, Conn. U.S.A." and "Patented Nov. 4, 1879." Approximately 1300 were made.

Paul Goodwin photo

Exc.	V.G.	Good	Fair	Poor
—	4500	2000	750	250

Model 1882 Army Contract
This model is identifiable by the two grooves pressed into the side of the magazine. The receiver is marked "Lee Arms Co. Bridgeport Conn., U.S.A." and on some examples it is also marked "E. Remington & Sons, Ilion, N.Y. U.S.A. Sole Manufactured & Agents." Barrel length 32", caliber .45-70, full-length stock secured by two barrel bands. U.S. Inspector's marks are stamped on the barrel breech and the stock. Approximately 750 were made.

Paul Goodwin photo

Exc.	V.G.	Good	Fair	Poor
—	4500	2000	750	300

Model 1885 Navy Contract
As above, with the inspection markings (including an anchor) on the receiver ring and the left side of the stock. Approximately 1,500 were made.

Exc.	V.G.	Good	Fair	Poor
—	4500	2000	750	300

Model 1882 & 1885 Military Rifles
Barrel length 32", full-length stock secured by two barrel bands, chambered for .42 Russian, .43 Spanish, .45 Gardner or .45-70 cartridges. The values for those rifles not in .45-70 caliber would be approximately 25 percent less than those shown below. Approximately 10,000 Model 1882 rifles were made and 60,000 Model 1885 rifles. The two models can be differentiated by the fact that the cocking piece on the bolt of the Model 1885 is larger. The majority of these rifles were made for foreign contracts and commercial sales.

Exc.	V.G.	Good	Fair	Poor
—	3000	1200	550	150

Model 1899
Designed for use with smokeless and rimless cartridges, this model is marked on the receiver "Remington Arms Co. Ilion, N.Y. Patented Aug. 26th 1884 Sept. 9th 1884 March 17th 1885 Jan 18th 1887." Produced from 1889 to 1907 in the following variations:

A Remington-Lee Model 1885 Navy rifle sold at auction for $2,587.50. Complete with bayonet. Condition is 85 percent original blue turning brown. Bore is excellent.
Rock Island Auction Company, April 2004

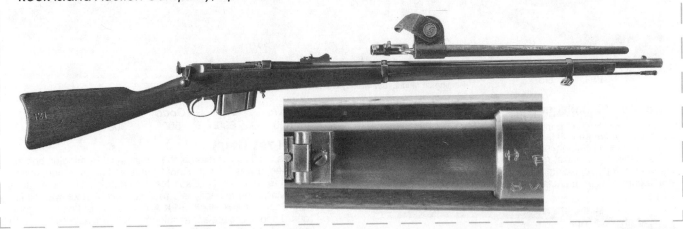

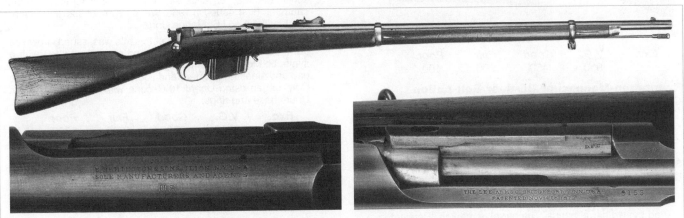

Model 1882 Military Rifle • Courtesy West Point Museum, Paul Goodwin photo

Military Rifle

Barrel length 29", 6mm USN, .30-40, .303, 7x57mm or 7.65mm caliber with a full-length stock secured by two barrel bands.

Paul Goodwin photo

Exc.	V.G.	Good	Fair	Poor
—	1250	500	200	100

NOTE: Add $250 if U.S. marked.

Military Carbine

As above, with a 20" barrel and a 3/4 length carbine stock secured by one barrel band.

Exc.	V.G.	Good	Fair	Poor
—	1750	800	300	100

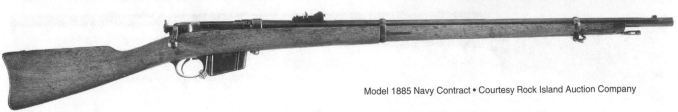

Model 1885 Navy Contract • Courtesy Rock Island Auction Company

Remington Model 1899 Military Carbine • Paul Goodwin photo

Remington-Mannlicher Berthier Bolt-Action Rifle (Model 1907/1915)

Produced for the French government, this rifle has a 31.5" barrel of 8mm Lebel caliber and a full-length stock secured by two barrel bands. The barrel marked "RAC 1907-15" and the left side of the receiver marked "Remington M'LE 1907-15." Several thousand were manufactured between 1907 and 1915.

Paul Goodwin photo

Exc.	V.G.	Good	Fair	Poor
—	950	450	200	100

Remington-Mannlicher Berthier Bolt-Action Carbine (Model 1907/1915)

As above but 24.5" barrel. Half stock with one barrel band.

Exc.	V.G.	Good	Fair	Poor
—	1100	500	200	125

Remington/Westinghouse Mosin-Nagant Bolt-Action Rifle

Produced for the Imperial Russian government, this rifle has a 32" barrel of 7.62x54mm R caliber with a full-length stock secured by two barrel bands. The barrel is marked "Remington Armory" with the date of manufacture and the receiver ring is stamped with the Russian coat-of-arms. Approximately 3,000,000 were made between 1916 and 1918.

Paul Goodwin photo

Exc.	V.G.	Good	Fair	Poor
500	400	300	100	75

Model 513-T

This is a bolt action .22 caliber training rifle with oil finished walnut stock and checkered steel butt. Barrel length is 26.75" and detachable magazine capacity is 6 rounds. Rear sight is an adjustable Redfield Model 75 RT. Most, but not all, of these rifles are drilled and tapped for telescope mounting blocks. Receiver is stamped "us property". Some of these rifles will have the arsenal rebuilder stamped on the barrel. About 70,000 of these rifles were produced under government contract from 1942 to 1944.

Exc.	V.G.	Good	Fair	Poor
800	600	500	300	200

Model 700 (M40)

This is a military version of the commercial Remington bolt action rifle. It was issued without sights and a 10x scope, chambered for the .308 (7.62x51 NATO) cartridge. Barrel length is 24". Magazine capacity is 5 rounds. Walnut stock with oil finish. Scope is a Redfield 3-9X Accu-Range. Buttplate, triggerguard and floorplate are aluminum. Weight is about 14 lbs with scope. Marked, "US RIFLE M40" with the serial number over the chamber. First issued in 1966. Weight is about 9.25 lbs. Primarily used by the U.S. Marine Corp.

In 1977, an improved version of this rifle was issued known as the M40A1. Same barrel length and scope butt-fitted with a synthetic McMillan camouflage stock, Pachmayr brown recoil pad and steel triggerguard and floorplate. In 1980, the Marine Corp began using Unertl 10X scope with mil-dot reticle with Unertl base and rings.

Exc.	V.G.	Good	Fair	Poor
5000	3500	2500	1500	1000

NOTE: Prices listed are for verifiable samples.

Remington Model 700P Rifles

Remington's line of law enforcement rifles are also used by a variety of military forces. Rifles purchased under contract will be marked for the country and service of origin. Models purchased by commercial means will not be marked.

Model 700 Police LTR (Lightweight Tactical Rifle)

Fitted with a fluted 20" barrel and chambered for the .308 or .223 cartridge this rifle weighs about 7.5 lbs. Synthetic stock.

NIB	Exc.	V.G.	Good	Fair	Poor
700	550	—	—	—	—

Model 700 Police

This model is fitted with a 26" barrel and chambered for the .308 and .223 cartridges in a short action or 7mm Rem. Mag., .300 Win. Mag., or .300 Rem. Ultra Mag. in a long action. Weight is about 9 lbs. Synthetic stock.

NIB	Exc.	V.G.	Good	Fair	Poor
630	500	—	—	—	—

Model 700 TWS (Tactical Weapons System)

Chambered for the .308 cartridge and fitted with a 26" barrel this model also features a Leupold Vari-X II 3.5x10 scope, a

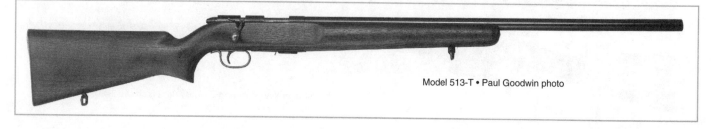

Model 513-T • Paul Goodwin photo

Harris bipod, quick adjustable sling, and a Pelican hard case. Weight of rifle is about 10.5 lbs.

Courtesy Remington Arms

NIB	Exc.	V.G.	Good	Fair	Poor
N/A	—	—	—	—	—

Model 700 VS LH

This model is a left hand version of the Model 700m Police.

NIB	Exc.	V.G.	Good	Fair	Poor
650	500	—	—	—	—

Model 40-XB KS

Two versions of this rifle are offered. In the single shot version it is chambered for the .223, .308, and .300 Win. Mag calibers. In the repeating version it is chambered in the .223 or .308 calibers. All versions are fitted with a 27.25" barrel. Weight is about 10.25 lbs. Martially marked rifles will command a premium over retail prices.

NOTE: Retail prices range from $1,200 to $1,500 depending on configuration and finish.

PARKER-HALE

Model 85 Sniper

Built by the Gibbs Rifle Co. in Martinsburg, West Virginia, this Parker-Hale designed bolt-action rifle is chambered for the .308 cartridge and fitted with a 27.5" barrel with a telescope and bipod. Box magazine capacity is 10 rounds. Weight is about 12.5 lbs. First produced in 1986.

NIB	Exc.	V.G.	Good	Fair	Poor
4000	3000	2500	—	—	—

SAVAGE

Model 1899-D Military Musket

Chambered for .303 Savage only with 28" barrel. Fitted with full military stocks. Produced from 1899 to 1915. Several hundred produced for Canadian Home Guard during WWI. These will have rack numbers on the buttplate.

Photo courtesy Amoskeag Auction Company

Exc.	V.G.	Good	Fair	Poor
3250	2000	1500	700	300

WINCHESTER REPEATING ARMS COMPANY

NOTE: The U.S. government purchased many different Winchester rifles over the years for a wide variety of purposes. During World War I, the Model 1894 carbine was purchased by the government as well as small numbers of the Model 1907 and the Model 1910 self loading rifles. There is evidence that the U.S. Coast Guard purchased several thousand of Model 1906 .22 caliber rifles for use during World War I. The Model 52 bolt action rifle was first designed by Winchester in hopes of a government contract as a military training rifle, but the end of World War I precluded that goal. During World War II, the U.S. government purchased the Winchester Model 74 .22 caliber rifles from 1941 to 1943. It is possible that many Winchester rifles were purchased by the U.S. military for assorted purposes from guard duty to pest control. Many of these rifles will be martially marked and their value has increased over the standard civilian rifle.

Bibliographical Note: For more historical information, technical data, and photos see Bruce Canfield's, *A Collector's Guide to Winchester's in the Service*. Also Thomas Henshaw, *The History of Winchester Firearms*, 1866-1992, Winchester Press, 1995. George Madis, *The Winchester Book*, 1985.

A Remington 40-X-M12 target rifle sold at auction for $1,840. Roll marked "US." Condition is 98 percent. *Rock Island Auction Company, April 2004*

Martially Inspected Henry Rifles

Beginning in 1863 the Federal Government ordered 1,730 Henry Rifles for use in the Civil War. Most of these government-inspected rifles fall into serial number range 3000 to 4000 while the balance are close to this serial-number range. They are marked "C.G.C." for Charles G. Chapman, the government inspector. These Henry rifles were used under actual combat conditions and for that reason it is doubtful that there are any rifles that would fall into the excellent condition category. Therefore no price is given.

NOTE: There are many counterfeit examples of these rifles. It is strongly advised that an expert in this field be consulted prior to a sale.

Exc.	V.G.	Good	Fair	Poor
—	—	60000	25000	12000

Model 1866

In 1866 the New Haven Arms Company changed its name to the Winchester Repeating Arms Company. The first firearm to be built under the Winchester name was the Model 1866. This first Winchester was a much-improved version of the Henry. A new magazine tube developed by Nelson King, Winchester's plant superintendent, was a vast improvement over the slotted magazine tube used on the Henry and its predecessor. The old tube allowed dirt to enter through the slots and was weakened because of it. King's patent, assigned to Winchester, featured a solid tube that was much stronger and reliable. His patent also dealt with an improved loading system for the rifle. The rifle now featured a loading port on the right side of the receiver with a spring-loaded cover. The frame continued to be made from brass. The Model 1866 was chambered for the .44 caliber Flat Rimfire or the .44 caliber Pointed Rimfire. Both cartridges could be used interchangeably.

The barrel on the Model 1866 was marked with two different markings. The first, which is seen on early guns up to serial number 23000, reads "HENRY'S PATENT-OCT. 16, 1860 KING'S PATENT-MARCH 29, 1866." The second marking reads, "WINCHESTER'S-REPEATING-ARMS.NEW HAVEN, CT. KING'S-IMPROVEMENT-PATENTED MARCH 29, 1866 OCTOBER 16, 1860." There are three basic variations of the Model 1866:

Courtesy Milwaukee Public Museum, Milwaukee, Wisconsin

1. Sporting Rifle round or octagon barrel. Approximately 28,000 were produced.

2. Carbine round barrel. Approximately 127,000 were produced.

3. Musket round barrel. Approximately 14,000 were produced.

The rifle and musket held 17 cartridges, and the carbine had a capacity of 13 cartridges. Unlike the Henry, Model 1866s were fitted with a walnut forearm. The Model 1866 was discontinued in 1898 with approximately 170,000 guns produced. The Model 1866 was sold in various special order configurations, such as barrels longer or shorter than standard, including engraved guns. The prices listed below represent only standard-model 1866s. For guns with special-order features, an independent appraisal from an expert is highly recommended.

NOTE: The Model 1866 Musket was not adopted by the U.S. military. It was sold to Mexico and Prussia. A large order of 46,000 muskets was delivered to the Turkisk governemnt in 1870 and 1871. A few muskets, about 3,000, were sold to France.

Courtesy Butterfield & Butterfield, San Francisco, California

Third Model

The third style's most noticeable characteristic is the more moderately curved receiver shape at the rear of the frame. The serial number is now stamped in block numerals behind the trigger, thus allowing the numbers to be seen for the first time without removing the stock. The barrel marking is stamped with the Winchester address. The Third Model is found between serial numbers 25000 and 149000. For the first time, a musket version was produced in this serial-number range.

Musket

Exc.	V.G.	Good	Fair	Poor
—	11000	8000	3500	2500

Fourth Model

The fourth style has an even less pronounced drop at the top rear of the frame, and the serial number is stamped in script on the lower tang under the lever. The Fourth Model is seen between serial number 149000 and 170100 with the late guns having an iron buttplate instead of brass.

Musket

Exc.	V.G.	Good	Fair	Poor
—	12000	9000	3500	2500

Model 1866 Iron Frame Rifle Musket

Overall length 54-1/2"; barrel length 33-1/4"; caliber .45 c.f. Walnut stock with case hardened furniture, barrel burnished bright, the receiver case hardened. The finger lever catch mounted within a large bolster at the rear of the lever. Unmarked except for serial numbers that appear externally on the receiver and often the buttplate tang. Approximately 25 made during the early autumn of 1866. Prospective purchasers are strongly advised to secure an expert appraisal prior to acquisition. Due to the recent identification of this model pricing schedules have yet to be established.

Exc.	V.G.	Good	Fair	Poor
N/A	—	—	—	—

Model 1866 Iron Frame Swiss Sharpshooters Rifle

As above, but in .41 Swiss caliber and fitted with a Scheutzen style stock supplied by the firm of Weber Ruesch in Zurich. Marked Weber Ruesch, Zurich on the barrel and serial numbered externally. Approximately 400 to 450 manufactured in 1866 and 1867. This musket was most likely built for Swiss military trials. Prospective purchasers are strongly advised to secure an expert appraisal prior to acquisition. Due to the recent identification of this model pricing schedules have yet to be established.

Exc.	V.G.	Good	Fair	Poor
N/A	—	—	—	—

Model 1873 Musket

This rifle was fitted with a 30" round barrel and chambered for a variety of calibers at the customer's request. Nominal calibers are: .44-40, .38-40, and .32-20. Magazine capacity was 17 rounds. Muskets were fitted with almost full length wooden stocks with cleaning rod and bayonet fittings. Many of these muskets were sold under contract to foreign governments. Survival rate is very low.

1st Model

Exc.	V.G.	Good	Fair	Poor
—	—	8500	4000	1000

2nd Model

The dust cover on the Second Model operates on one central guide secured to the receiver with two screws. The checkered oval finger grip is still used, but on later Second Models this is changed to a serrated finger grip on the rear of the dust cover. Second Models are found in the 31000 to 90000 serial number range.

Courtesy Rock Island Auction Company

Exc.	V.G.	Good	Fair	Poor
7500	4000	2000	1250	9000

3rd Model

The central guide rail is still present on the Third Model, but it is now integrally machined as part of the receiver. The serrated rear edges of the dust cover are still present on the Third Model.

Exc.	V.G.	Good	Fair	Poor
6000	3500	1250	850	500

Model 1876

Musket, 32" round barrel with full-length forearm secured by one barrel band and straight grip stock. Stamped on the barrel is the Winchester address with King's patent date. The caliber marking is stamped on the bottom of the receiver near the magazine tube and the breech end of the barrel.

First Model

As with the Model 1873, the primary difference in model types lies in the dust cover. The First Model has no dust cover and is seen between serial number 1 and 3000.

Musket

Exc.	V.G.	Good	Fair	Poor
15000	12000	6500	3000	1500

Second Model

The Second Model has a dust cover with guide rail attached to the receiver with two screws. On the early Second Model an oval finger guide is stamped on top of the dust cover while later models have a serrated finger guide along the rear edge of the dust cover. Second Models range from serial numbers 3000 to 30000.

Musket

Exc.	V.G.	Good	Fair	Poor
—	—	9500	4000	1500

Northwest Mounted Police Carbine

The folding rear sight is graduated in meters instead of yards.

Courtesy Little John's Auction Service, Inc., Paul Goodwin photo

Exc.	V.G.	Good	Fair	Poor
15000	9000	4500	2000	1250

NOTE: Deduct 50 percent from prices if factory records do not confirm NWP use. A Model 1876 NWP in excellent condition is very rare. Proceed with caution.

Musket

Exc.	V.G.	Good	Fair	Poor
18000	9000	5000	1750	1000

Third Model

The dust cover guide rail on Third Model 76s is integrally machined as part of the receiver with a serrated rear edge on the dust cover. Third Model will be seen from serial numbers 30000 to 64000.

Musket

Exc.	V.G.	Good	Fair	Poor
9500	4750	3000	1250	1000

Model 1886

Based on a John Browning patent, the Model 1886 was one of the finest and strongest lever actions ever utilized in a Winchester rifle. Winchester introduced the Model 1886 in order to take advantage of the more powerful centerfire cartridges of the time.

Musket, 30" round barrel, musket style forearm with one barrel band. Military style sights. About 350 Model 1886 Muskets were produced. This is the most rare variation of all Winchester lever action rifles.

Musket

Exc.	V.G.	Good	Fair	Poor
—	18000	9000	3500	1500

SNAP SHOT
WINCHESTER MODEL 1895 MILITARY RIFLE

The Winchester Model 1895 was the first lever-action rifle to have a box magazine and designed strictly for shooting high-velocity jacketed bullets. Chambered for the .30 U.S. (.30-40 Krag) cartridge that replaced the .45 Govt. (.45-70), the Model 1895 would seemingly have made a great military rifle. However, the qualities that make a fine sporting rifle do not necessarily make for a good military rifle. Such is the case with the Winchester Model 1895. Although the lever-action 1895 can fire five aimed shots as fast as one can work the action, the time required to replenish the magazine with fresh ammunition nullifies the rate of fire. When used for hunting, rarely does one need to reload the magazine in a speedy manner. But, in the chaos of battle a soldier must not only be able to fire rapidly, he must be able to quickly and correctly reload his rifle to continue the battle. The Model 1895 can only be reloaded by inserting the cartridges one-at-a-time into the magazine and in such a manner that the rim of each cartridge is forward of the one below otherwise the rifle will jam.

Winchester no doubt touted the repeater's quick handling action while discounting the time spent on reloading the magazine. The bolt-action Springfield Krag Rifle suffered somewhat the same problem but was faster to reload than the Model 1895. Only 10,000 Model 1895 Military rifles were built. One thousand were shipped to the Philippines and of those only 100 saw service in combat. Although the 1895 proved to be reliable and accurate the troops in the field preferred the bolt-action Krag over the lever-action 1895. The 1895s were returned to the arsenals and later sold to Cuba. Many wound up in Mexico and undoubtedly found their way back to the U.S.

Today, Military Model 1895s are sought out by collectors and command high prices. They are a small but important piece of U.S. Military and Winchester history.

Kenny Durham

> A Winchester Model 1895 carbine sold at auction for $10,125. U.S. and Ordnance marked. Complete with unmarked bayonet and leather frog. Condition is 65 percent blue.
>
> *Greg Martin Auctions, November 2004*

Model 1895 U.S. Army Musket

U.S. Army Musket, 28" round barrel chambered for the .30-40 Krag. Came equipped with or without knife bayonet. These muskets were furnished to the U.S. Army for use during the Spanish-American War and are "US" marked on the receiver.

Exc.	V.G.	Good	Fair	Poor
—	3000	1500	850	450

Model 1895 Russian Musket

Russian Musket, similar to standard musket but fitted with clip guides in the top of the receiver and with bayonet. Chambered for the 7.62x54mm R cartridge. Approximately 294,000 Model 1895 Muskets were sold to the Imperial Russian Government between 1915 and 1916. The first 15,000 Russian Muskets had 8" knife bayonets, and the rest were fitted with 16" bayonets. Some of these rifles went to Spain in its Civil War in 1936-1939.

Exc.	V.G.	Good	Fair	Poor
4000	2500	1000	500	250

Russian soldier with Winchester Model 1895, Courtesy Paul S. Scarlata

Model 1885 (Single Shot)

The High Wall musket most often had a 26" round barrel chambered for the .22 caliber cartridge. Larger calibers were available as were different barrel lengths. The High Wall Musket featured an almost full length forearm fastened to the barrel with a single barrel band and rounded buttplate.

The Low Wall musket is most often referred to as the Winder Musket named after the distinguished marksman, Colonel C.B. Winder. This model features a Lyman receiver sight and was made in .22 caliber.

U.S. and Ordnance markings will appear on rifles purchased by the government.

High Wall Musket

Exc.	V.G.	Good	Fair	Poor
4000	3000	2000	1500	900

Low Wall Musket (Winder Musket)

Courtesy Buffalo Bill Historical Center, Cody, Wyoming

Exc.	V.G.	Good	Fair	Poor
3500	2000	1200	750	400

Winchester Hotchkiss Bolt Action Rifle

This model is also known as the Hotchkiss Magazine Gun or the Model 1883. This rifle was designed by Benjamin Hotchkiss in 1876, and Winchester acquired the manufacturing rights to the rifle in 1877. In 1879, the first guns were delivered for sale. The Hotchkiss rifle was a bolt-action firearm designed for military and sporting use. It was the first bolt-action rifle made by Winchester. The rifle was furnished in .45-70 Government, and although the 1884 Winchester catalog lists a .40-65 Hotchkiss as being available, no evidence exists that such a chamber was ever actually furnished. Two different types of military configurations will be seen:

1. Carbine, 24" round or 22-1/2" round barrel with military style straight grip stock. Chambered for the 45-55 cartridge.

2. Musket, 32" or 28" round barrel with almost full length military-style straight grip stock. Winchester produced the Model 1883 until 1899, having built about 85,000 guns. Chambered for the 45-70 cartridge.

First Model

This model has the safety and a turn button magazine cut-off located above the triggerguard on the right side. The carbine has a 24" round barrel with a saddle ring on the left side of the stock. The musket has a 32" round barrel with two barrel bands, a steel forearm tip, and bayonet attachment under the barrel. The serial number range for the First Model is between 1 and about 6419.

Army Rifle

These Army models are marked with the inspector stamping of "ESA/1878" on the left side of the stock. Production total of 513 rifles.

Courtesy Butterfield & Butterfield, San Francisco, California

Exc.	V.G.	Good	Fair	Poor
—	6000	3500	900	500

Carbine

501 carbines produced.

Exc.	V.G.	Good	Fair	Poor
—	5000	2750	900	500

Navy Rifle

1,474 produced.

Exc.	V.G.	Good	Fair	Poor
—	4500	2250	900	500

Musket

Exc.	V.G.	Good	Fair	Poor
—	3000	1500	700	300

Second Model

On this model the safety is located on the top left side of the receiver, and the magazine cutoff is located on the top right side of the receiver to the rear of the bolt handle. The carbine has a 22-1/2" round barrel with a nickeled forearm cap. The musket now has a 28" barrel. Serial number range for the Second Model runs from 6420 to 22521.

Carbine

400 produced.

Exc.	V.G.	Good	Fair	Poor
—	6000	3000	900	500

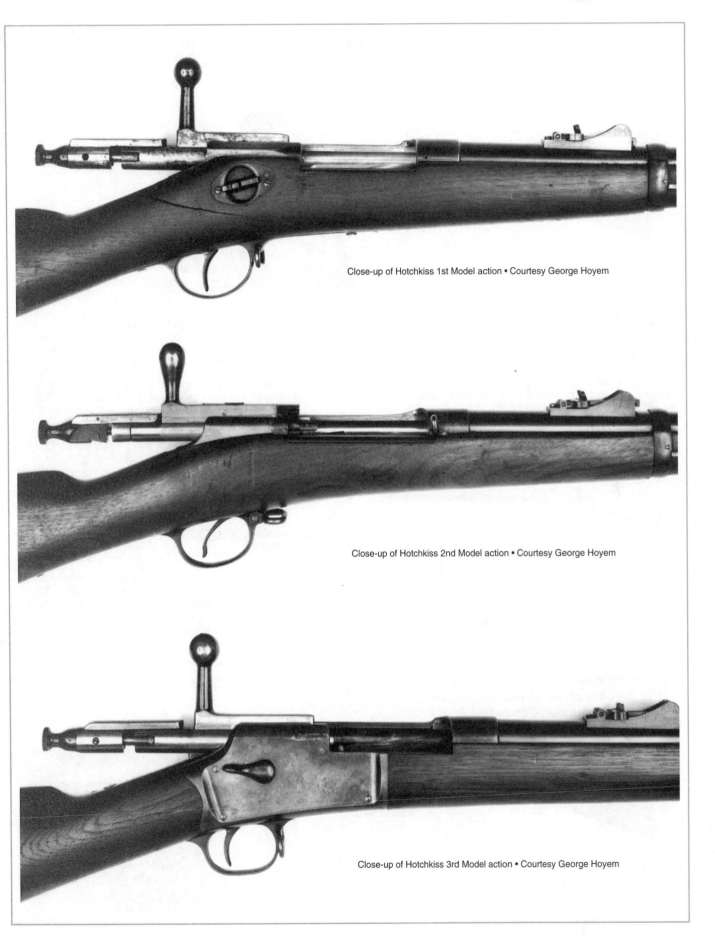

Close-up of Hotchkiss 1st Model action • Courtesy George Hoyem

Close-up of Hotchkiss 2nd Model action • Courtesy George Hoyem

Close-up of Hotchkiss 3rd Model action • Courtesy George Hoyem

A Winchester-Lee straight pull rifle was sold at auction for $17,250. Receiver is dated 1896 and "USS MAINE" is stenciled on right side of butt stock. Condition is good to very good. Salvaged from battleship Maine.
Rock Island Auction Company, April 2004

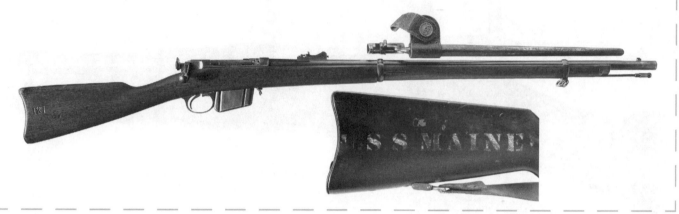

Musket

Exc.	V.G.	Good	Fair	Poor
—	3500	1750	750	350

Third Model

The Third Model is easily identified by the two-piece stock separated by the receiver. The carbine is now fitted with a 20" barrel with saddle ring and bar on the left side of the frame. The musket remains unchanged from the Second Model with the exception of the two-piece stock. Serial numbers of the Third Model range from 22552 to 84555.

Army Rifle

Courtesy Butterfield & Butterfield, San Francisco, California

Exc.	V.G.	Good	Fair	Poor
—	3500	1750	750	350

Musket

Exc.	V.G.	Good	Fair	Poor
—	3500	1750	750	350

Winchester-Lee Straight Pull Rifle

This rifle was a military firearm that Winchester built for the U.S. Navy in 1895. The Navy version was a musket type with a 28" round barrel and musket style forearm and plain walnut pistol grip stock. In 1897, Winchester offered a commercial musket version for public sale as well as a Sporting Rifle. All of these guns were chambered for the 6mm Lee (.236 Caliber) cartridge. The Sporting Rifle featured a 24" round barrel with plain walnut pistol grip stock and finger grooves in the forearm. Built from 1895 to 1905, Winchester sold about 20,000 Lee rifles; 15,000 were sold to the U.S. Navy, 3,000 were sold in the commercial version, and 1,700 were Sporting Rifles.

NOTE: Commercial and Sporting rifles will not have martial markings, inspector markings, or bayonet fittings.

U.S. Navy Musket

Exc.	V.G.	Good	Fair	Poor
—	3000	1500	700	500

NOTE: Some of these muskets were stored on the U.S. battleship Maine. Records of serial numbers exist to authenicate these muskets. Add a premium of 50 percent for these examples.

A Winchester-Lee straight pull Navy rifle sold at auction for $3,737.50. Complete with bayonet. condition is 90 percent original blue. Bore is good.
Rock Island Auction Company, April 2004

A Winchester Model 70 sold at auction for $7,720. U.S. Marine corps issue snipe rifle chambered for 30-06. Fitted with a Lyman 5A target scope. Original shipping crate. Circa 1940. Documentation. Condition is 95-98 percent blue. U.S. Property mark. Scope has 90 percent blue.
Little John's Auction Service, Inc., January 2005

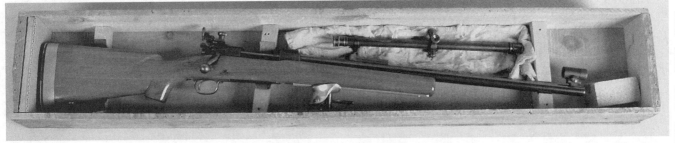

Paul Goodwin photo

HARRINGTON & RICHARDSON, INC.

Reising Model 60

A .45 ACP caliber semiautomatic rifle with an 18.25" barrel and a 12- or 20-round detachable magazine. Blued, with a walnut stock. It operates on a retarded blowback system and was developed to be used as a police weapon. Manufactured between 1944 and 1946.

Courtesy Richard M. Kumor Sr.

Reising receiver markings • Courtesy Stoddard Martial collection, Paul Goodwin photo

Exc.	V.G.	Good	Fair	Poor
1800	1450	800	450	200

Model 65 Military

A .22 l.r. caliber semiautomatic rifle with a 23" barrel and Redfield peep sights. Blued, with a walnut stock. Manufactured between 1944 and 1956.

NOTE: Add 100 percent if USMC marked.

Exc.	V.G.	Good	Fair	Poor
500	300	200	125	90

BARRETT F.A. MFG. CO.

Model 95 (M 107 Sniper Weapon System)

Introduced in 1995, this .50 caliber BMG bolt action model features a 29" barrel and a 5-round magazine. Scope optional. Weight is 22 lbs. Adopted by the U.S. Army in 2000 as an anti-material weapon out to 1,500 plus meters. This model differs from the commercial version in that it breaks down into two smaller sections; it is fitted with an 11.5" optical rail, has one takedown pin, detachable bipod with spiked feet, is fitted with front and rear iron sights, and has adjustable scope rings.

NIB	Exc.	V.G.	Good	Fair	Poor
4500	4000	3000	2000	—	—

Model 82A1 (SASR)

The US Marine Corp. traded to Barrett 112 Model 82A1 .50 caliber rifles, 100 of which were used in Desert Storm. Of the 112 rifles only 34 are in private hands. Barrett offers these rifles in very good condition with "US" stamped receivers and USMC camo finish. Serial number verification certificate.

NIB	Exc.	V.G.	Good	Fair	Poor
—	—	19900	—	—	—

Model 65 with USMC markings • Courtesy private collection, Paul Goodwin phot

SNAP SHOT
M107 (M82A3)

When EOD personnel need a method of remotely detonating unexploded ordinance, or when a light truck or grounded aircraft must be destroyed by Special Forces, the M107 (M82A3) is called on. A short recoil operated, semiautomatic firearm, the M107 is chambered for the potent .50 Browning Machine Gun (12.7 x 99 mm) cartridge. It has a very efficient muzzle brake, which reduces perceived recoil by approximately 65 percent and a bipod with spiked feet to prevent movement under recoil. The M107 has both a 10-power telescopic sight, with a ballistic reticle that incorporates a bullet drop compensator for standard ammunition, and open sights. 19-inch MIL-STD-1913 rail mounts increase the accessories that can be attached to the weapon. The M107 weighs 31 pounds, has an overall length of 45 inches, and a barrel length of 29 inches. A barrel-retaining key may be removed to allow the barrel to telescope into the upper receiver for shorter overall length for transportation. The M82A1M is the factory designation for this weapon. The US Army has adopted it as the M107, and the US Marine Corps calls the same weapon the M82A3. The M107/M82A3 is fed from a 10-round detachable box magazine. All standard .50 BMG ammunition may be fired in the weapon, with the exception of SLAP (saboted light armor piercing). The sabot from this round will not reliably pass through the muzzle brake. Military users, because of the excellent accuracy obtained with this round, recommend the MK211 Raufoss cartridge. Factory specifications state a maximum effective range of 2000 yards with match ammunition; however, successful longer shots have been recorded.

Charlie Cutshaw

SHOTGUNS

For a more detailed historical and technical account of U.S. military shotguns see Bruce Canfield's, *A Collectors Guide to United States Combat Shotguns*, Andrew Mobray, 1999. Also Thomas F. Swearengen, *The World's Fighting Shotguns*, Vol. IV, Ironside International Publishers, 1978.

WINCHESTER

Model 1897 Trench Gun (Model 1917)
Slide action hammer gun 12 gauge, 20" barrel bored to shoot buckshot, plain walnut modified pistol grip stock with grooved

SNAP SHOT
THE 1897 WINCHESTER TRENCH GUN

It's hard to imagine the German military crying 'foul', but that's exactly what they did after confronting American doughboys equipped with the first truly successful pump-action 12-gauge fighting shotgun in the trenches of eastern France.

Designed by the legendary John Browning, the 1897 Trench Gun was a variation of the standard 1897 pump-action shotgun manufactured for the sporting arms market. Its chief distinguishing characteristic besides the shorter length barrel was a ventilated handguard surrounding the barrel and the bayonet attachment point just under the muzzle. The magazine held six shells, but due to the wet and humid environment of trench warfare the shells were most often complete brass shells and not made of paper. The pump-action Model 1897 Trench gun featured an outside hammer, a side ejection pattern and the ability to 'slam-fire' when the trigger was held back and the pump-action was worked rapidly. With a cylinder bore and a 20.1 inch barrel length the Winchester Model 1897 Trench gun was just the ticket when a team of American soldiers crossed No-Man's Land and raided the German trenches. The usual tactic employed was for the Americans to line up in a straight line with the first man engaging the enemy with a continuous stream of buckshot pellets as he 'slam-fired' his Model 1897 to empty in under five seconds. As soon as he was empty, he would duck down and the second man in line would step up and unload on the Germans in the same fashion, to be followed by a third, then a fourth and finally a fifth man in line doing the same thing. By this time the first man had his Winchester Trench gun reloaded and the process repeated itself. The Germans didn't find any of this amusing due to their terrible losses and protested through the Swiss Ambassador, but General Pershing ignored their complaints and requested more Winchester Model 1897 Trench guns for the troops.

Popular today in Cowboy Action Shooting contests, the short barreled Winchester Model 1897 shotgun is still effective and every bit the equal to newer and more advanced fighting shotguns when used by a well-trained shooter.

Frank W. James

Winchester Model 1897 Trench Gun • Courtesy Rock Island Auction Company

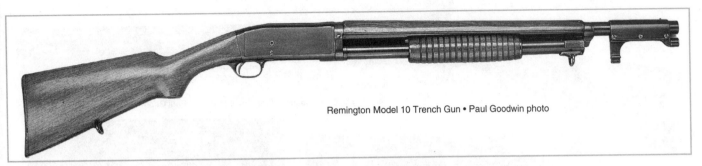

Remington Model 10 Trench Gun • Paul Goodwin photo

slide handle. Solid frame (WWI) or takedown (WWII). Fitted with barrel hand guard and bayonet. This model was furnished to the U.S. Army for trench work in World War I. It was not listed in Winchester catalogs until 1920. This model was also used in large numbers in WWII, Korea, and Vietnam. Prices below are for U.S. marked guns.

Model 97 Solid Frame-World War I

Exc.	V.G.	Good	Fair	Poor
5000	3500	2000	1000	700

Model 97 Take Down-World War II

Exc.	V.G.	Good	Fair	Poor
4500	3000	1800	800	650

NOTE: Add about $200 for Winchester marked bayonet.

A Winchester Model 1897 WWI Trench Gun sold at auction for $6,325. Bayonet and sling. Condition is 98 percent original finish.
Rock Island Auction Company, April 2004

Model 12 Trench Gun

Slide action hammerless gun 12 gauge, 20" barrel bored to shoot buckshot, plain walnut modified pistol grip stock with grooved slide handle. Solid frame or takedown. Fitted with barrel hand guard and bayonet. Finish is blued. This model was furnished to the U.S. Army for trench work in World War I and World War II. Prices below are for U.S. marked guns.

Exc.	V.G.	Good	Fair	Poor
5000	3500	2000	800	650

NOTE: Add about $200 for Winchester marked bayonet.

Model 1200

In 1968 and 1969 the U.S. military purchased a quantity of Model 1200 shotguns with 20" cylinder bored barrels, Type W bayonet adapter for the Model 1917 bayonet. Stocks were plain and uncheckered with oil finish.

Exc.	V.G.	Good	Fair	Poor
2500	1750	1200	600	300

Model 1400

The U.S. military purchased a small quantity of Model 1400 semiautomatic shotguns. these were fitted with a plain 20" barrel and choked cylinder. Scarce.

Exc.	V.G.	Good	Fair	Poor
N/A	—	—	—	—

REMINGTON

Model 10 Trench Gun

Slide action 12 gauge shotgun with 23" round barrel. No checkering on buttstock. Wooden handguard and bayonet lug. Prices below for shotgun only with military markings.

Exc.	V.G.	Good	Fair	Poor
15000	12500	10000	7500	5000

Model 11 Military Riot Gun

This is a 12 gauge 20" barrel shotgun used during WWI. Most were blued, some were Parkerized when rebuilt. Military markings with stock cartouche. Many thousands were sold to the military and are often encountered.

Exc.	V.G.	Good	Fair	Poor
1050	750	500	400	150

NOTE: A long barrel version of the Model 11 was used by the military for aerial gunnery practice. These examples will bring less.

Model 31 Military Riot Gun

This model was to replace the Model 10. Built in a short barrel (20") riot configuration, there were about 15,000 of these shotguns bought by the military but most were in the longer barrel

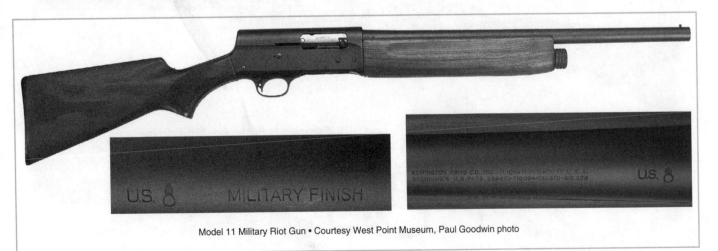

Model 11 Military Riot Gun • Courtesy West Point Museum, Paul Goodwin photo

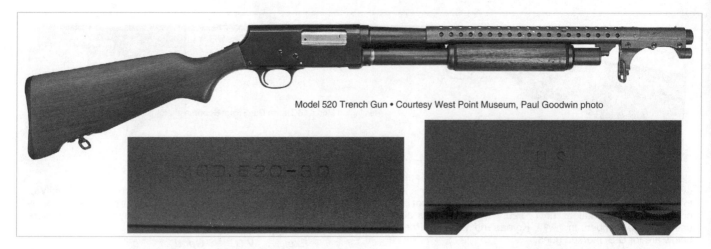

Model 520 Trench Gun • Courtesy West Point Museum, Paul Goodwin photo

lengths used for training. Stocks were not checkered. Martially marked.

Exc.	V.G.	Good	Fair	Poor
1500	1000	750	500	350

Model 870 Mark I

This is a slide action 12 gauge shotgun with Parkerized finish. Fitted with an 18" round barrel. Prices are for military marked guns.

Exc.	V.G.	Good	Fair	Poor
5000	3500	2000	1250	850

NOTE: The Model 870 is still purchased by the U.S. military in a number of different configurations. The key to the correct designation of these more current shotguns lies with the military markings.

Model 11-87P

This is a semiautomatic 12 gauge shotgun with an 18" barrel and 7-round magazine extension. Fitted with synthetic stock. Purchased by various branches of the U.S. military, this shotgun may be found in a number of different configurations. All will be military marked.

Exc.	V.G.	Good	Fair	Poor
750	600	400	300	150

SAVAGE

Model 720 Military Riot Gun

A semiautomatic 12 gauge shotgun similar in design to the Remington 11 and the Browning A-5. Some 15,000 of these shotguns were sold to the military during WWII. Martially marked. One of the more rare WWII shotguns.

Exc.	V.G.	Good	Fair	Poor
2500	1850	1500	850	500

STEVENS

Model 520 U.S. Marked Trench Gun

A slide action shotgun manufactured from 1930 to 1949. Chambered for the 12 gauge shell and fitted with a 20" barrel with cylinder choke. Fitted with a metal handguard and Stevens designed bayonet adapter. Used extensively in WWII. About 35,000 of these guns were purchased by the government during the war. Blued finish. Trench guns were fitted with metal handguards and bayonet adapters. There is also a military version without handguard called a Riot Gun. These models will also have military markings. Riot guns will bring less than Trench Guns.

Exc.	V.G.	Good	Fair	Poor
2500	1500	850	500	350

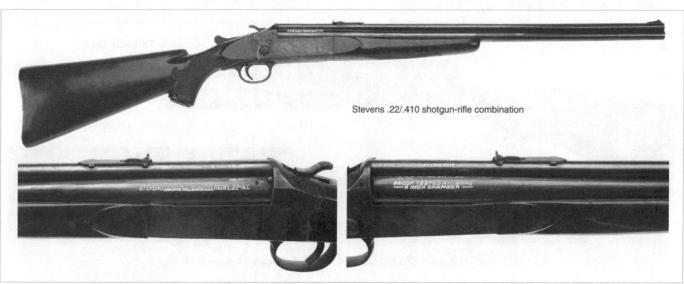

Stevens .22/.410 shotgun-rifle combination

Model 620 U.S. Marked Trench Gun

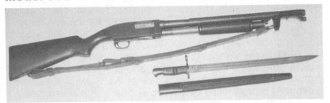

Courtesy Richard M. Kumor Sr.

Exc.	V.G.	Good	Fair	Poor
2000	1600	1100	600	300

NOTE: Add $150 for bayonet.

Stevens .22/.410 Shotgun-Rifle Combination

This was the precursor to the Model 24. First made in 1940 with a Tenite stock, this combination gun was used by some bomber crews during WWII. According to Savage records the U.S. government purchased about 10,000 of these guns during the war as well as some years after as some of these guns were marked "USAF."

Exc.	V.G.	Good	Fair	Poor
N/A	—	—	—	—

MOSSBERG

Model 590 Special Purpose (ATP8)

Fitted with a 20" shrouded barrel, bayonet lug, parkerized or blued finish. Speed feed stock and ghost ring sights. Introduced in 1987. Weight is about 7.25 lbs. Military marked. This gun is also offered in a commercial version.

NIB	Exc.	V.G.	Good	Fair	Poor
400	275	200	175	125	100

Model 590A1

A 12 gauge slide action shotgun fitted with an 18" barrel. This model differs from the commercial one by having an aluminum trigger housing instead of plastic, an aluminum safety instead of plastic, and a heavy walled barrel. The finish is Parkerized and military marked.

Exc.	V.G.	Good	Fair	Poor
450	300	250	200	100

Model RI 96

Essentially a modified Mossberg Model 9200 semiauto gas operated 12 gauge shotgun with 3" chamber fitted with an 18" barrel thicker than standard. Five round magazine. Military contract number on barrel and receiver with "US" suffix to serial number. Black phosphate finish. Issued to army special operations units in South America.

Courtesy Charlie Cutshaw

Courtesy Charlie Cutshaw

Exc.	V.G.	Good	Fair	Poor
N/A	—	—	—	—

ITHACA

For a more detailed description of Ithaca military shotguns see Walter Snyder's book, *Ithaca Featherlight Repeaters...the Best Gun Going: A Complete History of the Ithaca Model 37 and the Model 87*, Cook and Uline Publishing, 1998.

Model 37 Military Marked Trench Gun (WWII)

This is one of the scarcest military shotguns. It was built in three different configurations; 30" barrel, 20" barrel, and 20" barrel with handguard and bayonet lug (Trench Gun). A scarce shotgun, proceed with caution.

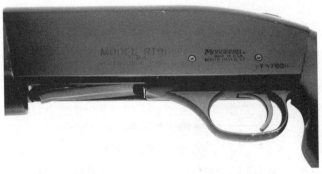

Model 37 with 20" barrel and release papers • Courtesy Richard M. Kumor Sr.

Exc.	V.G.	Good	Fair	Poor
10000	7500	5000	2500	1500

NOTE: Add $200 for government release papers and 150 percent for Trench Gun configuration.

Model 37 Military Marked Trench Gun (Vietnam)

Same as above but built from 1962 to 1963. Fitted with 20" barrel. Stock was not checkered and had oil finish. Receiver had "US" stamped. Highest serial number reported is S23710.

Exc.	V.G.	Good	Fair	Poor
3500	2500	1800	900	750

Model 37 Military Marked Trench Gun (Navy Contract)

Similar to the Model 37 Trench gun but built in 1966-1967 for the U.S. Navy Ammunition Depot. About 3,000 were built. Based on the Model 37 M&P model.

Exc.	V.G.	Good	Fair	Poor
5000	3500	2500	1250	900

BENELLI

M4 Super 90 (M1014)

Adopted by the U.S. Marine Corps this 12-gauge shotgun features a choice of three modular buttstock and two barrel configurations. Action is semiauto or slide action. Top mounted Picatinny rail. Barrel length is 18.5". Magazine capacity is 6 rounds. Ghost-ring sights. Black MILSPEC finish. Weight is about 8.4 lbs. Matte black finish. Deliveries in 2000. This model will be available in a modified form for commercial sale after military and law enforcement contracts are filled.

NIB	Exc.	V.G.	Good	Fair	Poor
1450	1150	—	—	—	—

SNAP SHOT
M1014 (BENELLI M4 TACTICAL)

The US AARDEC (Army Armament Research Development Command) in early 1999 awarded the contract for a joint service combat shotgun, XM1014, to Heckler & Koch, USA, which represented the Italian firm Benelli for the contract award. Delivery of these weapons began in 2000. Technically, the M1014 is a gas-operated, smoothbore, magazine-fed semiauto shotgun. Barrel locking is achieved by rotating bolt with two lugs. The M1014 has dual stainless steel gas cylinders, self-cleaning gas pistons and action rods for increased reliability. The gun is field stripped without any tools other than the charging handle. The telescopic stock may be replaced by pistol grip or hunting-style stock without use of tools. The barrel has an internal screw-in choke system for increased versatility. Standard sights for the M1014 are ghost-ring rear and blade front. The rear sight is adjustable with the rim of a shot shell. An accessory MIL-STD-1913 (Picatinny) rail is installed on top of the receiver, to facilitate mounting scopes, night vision devices, or other optics. The M1014 has an 18.5-inch barrel, six-round magazine capacity and weighs 8.4 pounds. The gun is so designed that it can fire 3" and 2 3/4" (76 and 70 mm) shot shells of different power without any adjustments and in any combination. Low-power rounds, such as less-than-lethal rubber slugs, must be cycled manually. All surfaces are covered by non-reflective, black MILSPEC wear and corrosion-resistant finish. The gun is very reliable in any weather conditions. The M1014 (Benelli M4 Tactical) is manufactured in Italy by Benelli Armi Spa, and is available to law enforcement and civilians. A limitation of this and any other semiautomatic shotgun is its inability to fire the full range of shotgun ammunition, which includes less-lethal and other specialized ammunition that will not cycle a semiautomatic shotgun of any type. The military, however, had no stated requirement for its combat shotgun to fire less lethal ammunition and so adopted the semiautomatic M1014.

Charlie Cutshaw

MACHINE GUNS

Bibliographical Note: For historical information, technical data, and photos see James Ballou, *Rock in a Hard Place; The Browning Automatic Rifle*, Collector Grade Publications, 2000. Wahl and Toppel, *The Gatling Gun*, New York, 1965.

Colt Gatling Gun

First invented by American Dr. Richard J. Gatling in 1861, this is a multi-barrel (6 to 10 barrels) hand-cranked machine gun. Several different models were developed and built in the 1860s with some were used in the American Civil War. Some of these early guns were chambered for the .58 caliber, while a few others were chambered for the 1" shell. The classic Gatling gun is the Model 1874 chambered for the .45-70 cartridge. There are several other models such as the Model 1879, Model 1881, the Model 1892, Model 1895, and the Model 1903. Some of these guns were tripod-mounted while others were mounted on gun carriages, and still others were deck-mounted for ship-board use. Some of the Gatling guns have exposed barrels while others are enclosed in a brass jacket. The Model 1877 bulldog is fitted with five 18" barrels enclosed in a brass jacket. The Model 1893 Police has six 12" barrels in .45-70 and weighs about 75 lbs. These guns are marked with a brass plate on top of the receiver, "GATLING'S/BATTERY/GUN 9 (PATENT DATES) MADE BY COLT'S/ PT. FIRE ARMS MFG. CO./HARTFORD, CONN.U.S.A."

NOTE: As an interesting aside, Gatling guns are still in use by military forces but are now electrically powered (GEC M134/GAU-2B Minigun) and capable of a rate of fire of 6,000 rounds per minute using the 7.62x51 cartridge.

Values for these guns are difficult to establish. Gatling guns in excellent condition in .45-70 caliber can bring between $75,000 to $200,000 and even more.

Colt Gatling Model 1883 • Photo courtesy Butterfield & Butterfield

Colt Model 1895

Designed by John Browning and built by Colt, this is a gas operated air-cooled belt-fed gun chambered for the .30-03, 6mm U.S.N., and .30-40 cartridges as well as the .30-06 (called the Model 1906 cartridge) in later applications. Rate of fire is about 450 rounds per minute. Called the "potato digger" because of its back and forth motion and proximity to the ground. This was the first non-mechanical firing machine issued to the U.S. military. It saw limited use during the Spanish-American War, the Boxer Rebellion, and as a training gun during World War I.

NOTE: See also *Colt/Marlin Model 1914/1915*

NOTE: The .30-03 cartridge was the original and earlier version of the .30-06 cartridge. Guns chambered for the older .30-03 cartridge will function and fire the .30-06 cartridge (accuracy suffers) *but the reverse is not true*. Sometimes the .30-03 cartridge is referred to as the .30-45. Both of these cartridges replaced the older .30-40 Krag as the official military round.

Pre-1968 (rare)

Exc.	V.G.	Fair
25000	23000	21000

Colt Model 1895 • Courtesy Butterfield & Butterfield

Colt Maxim 1904

This belt-fed machine gun was originally chambered for the .30-03 cartridge and then altered to the .30-06. Built on the standard Maxim M1900 pattern. Barrel length is 28.5". Rate of fire is about 500 rounds per minute. Fed by a 250-round cloth belt. Primarily used as a training gun during World War I. A total of 287 of these guns were produced. Weight is approximately 75 lbs.

Maxim Model 1904 • Robert G. Segel collection

SNAP SHOT
COLT AUTOMATIC GUN (POTATO DIGGER)

Firing the Model 1895 (and Model 1914) belt-fed, air cooled Colt Automatic Gun is an experience to enjoy and relish. Invented by John Moses Browning, it is the first practical gas-actuated machine gun not relying on any of Hiram Maxim's patents. Its distinctive feature is the external gas-impinged operating lever that swings in an arc of 170 degrees underneath the gun (resulting in the nickname of "Potato Digger"). This gun must be mounted on a tripod with adequate clearance above the ground as prone firing is prohibited due to the operating lever swinging back and forth. Any impediment to its movement will cause a stoppage.

Typical of Browning's designs, the "Digger" is relatively straightforward in its operating principles and operation. Full automatic only and fed from a 250-round cloth belt, the rate of fire is a very comfortable 400-450 rounds per minute. This allows fire control of single shots by quick trigger manipulation with a little practice. Extremely accurate, the Colt Automatic Gun was documented in many instances in World War I as being used as a single-shot sniper weapon.

Firing the "Digger" is a step back in time to an era when machine guns were *the* new technology; still being refined and no clue as to its tactical importance. Sitting high behind the gun on the bicycle-type seat mounted on the rear leg of the tripod, one goes through the unique steps of preparing to fire. Reaching far forward to grasp the operating lever near the muzzle and drawing rearward the full 170 degrees of its arc to initiate a round into the chamber and then grasping the pistol grip at the rear with the exposed trigger, firing it produces a satisfactory feeling of power well under control in a smooth operation. And, the swinging external operating lever is a sight to behold usually causing much comment from bystanders on the range. Spare parts acquisition can be a source of problems. Nevertheless, it is a great turn-of-the-century gun to own and operate.

Robert G. Segel

Maxim Model 1904 name plate • Robert G. Segel collection

Pre-1968 (very rare)

Exc.	V.G.	Fair
40000	35000	30000

Pre-1986 conversions

Exc.	V.G.	Fair
30000	27500	25000

Pre-1986 dealer samples

Exc.	V.G.	Fair
N/A	N/A	N/A

Model 1909 Benet-Mercie Machine Rifle

Developed by the French firm Hotchkiss and built in the U.S. by Colt's and Springfield Armory, this air-cooled gas-operated automatic rifle is fed by a 30-round metal strip. Chambered for the .30-06 cartridge. Rate of fire was about 400 rounds per minute. Weight of gun was approximately 27 lbs. This gun was equipped with a Model 1908 Warner & Swasey telescope. This model was used against Mexican bandits in 1915 and 1916 by the U.S. Army and in France during the early stages of World

War I. However, it did not prove to be reliable and was soon replaced by the Hotchkiss and Vickers guns. About 670 were produced by both Colt and Springfield.

Model 1909 Benet-Mercie • Robert G. Segel collection

Model 1909 Benet-Mercie Warner & Swasey telescope sight • Robert G. Segel collection

Pre-1968 (Rare)

Exc.	V.G.	Fair
15000	13000	11000

Pre-1986 conversions

Exc.	V.G.	Fair
N/A	N/A	N/A

Pre-1986 dealer samples

Exc.	V.G.	Fair
N/A	N/A	N/A

Browning M1917 & M1917A1

Based on John M. Browning's original automatic weapon design it was chambered for the .30-06 cartridge. This water-cooled gun is fitted with a 23.8" barrel and has a rate of fire of 500 rounds per minute using a cloth belt. Its empty weight for the gun only is 33 lbs. The M1917A1 tripod weighs about 53 lbs. Marked "US INSP BROWNING MACHINE GUN US CAL 30 MODEL OF 1917." This gun was produced by various manufacturers from 1917 to 1945.

About 56,000 were built prior to the end of WWI although a few saw actual combat service. In the mid 1930s, a few minor modifications were made to the gun and it became known as the Model 1917A1. These modifications follow.

The most important legacy of the Model 1917 Browning is that it led to the use of this gun as the air-cooled Model 1919. During its production life the gun was built by Colt, Remington, and Westinghouse.

Pre-1968

Exc.	V.G.	Fair
35000	32500	30000

SNAP SHOT
BROWNING M1917A1

The .30-06 US Browning M1917A1 water-cooled machine gun is one of my favorite belt-feds to shoot. With its classic lines and amazingly simple and reliable operation, the venerable Browning water-cooled runs and runs like the Energizer Bunny. It is versatile too, as it can be converted to other calibers such as .308 or 8mm making it economical to shoot and tracers are available.

With its moderate rate of fire in the 450 rounds per minute range, trigger control for single shots is easily attainable with just a little practice. The superb M1917A1 tripod is rock-steady and allows a wide range of traverse and elevation in its "free-wheeling" mode or accurate aiming with minute adjustments using the fine-tuning adjustment knobs on the T&E mechanism.

Belts are easy to load with the use of a Browning 1918 cloth belt loader. Hand-loading belts, while tedious, is not as difficult as hand-loading Maxim type belts. The Browning can be used with cloth belts or disintegrating links. I personally prefer the cloth belts as they do not cause wear on the trunion and you don't have a large mess of empty brass casings and links to sort through upon range clean-up.

The key to proper Browning function is head space and timing. This seems to intimidate a number of users but is really quite simple to learn. It is also necessary so as not to have the gun fire out of battery, usually resulting in a blown top cover. But with head space and timing gauges readily available and simple instructions in the field manuals on adjusting without the use of the gauges, there is really no excuse to be frightened by this key adjustment.

All in all, the Browning M1917A1 is as dependable as it gets and is relatively maintenance free. The feed mechanism rarely has any feeding problems and if a feed problem does occur, it is easily remedied. Spare parts are readily available. A day at the range with this classic Browning is a day of guaranteed fun.

Robert G. Segel

A gunner's view of the Browning Model 1917 during
World War II in Germany • Courtesy John M. Miller

**Pre-1986 conversions
(Non-martial current U.S. manufacture)**

Exc.	V.G.	Fair
18000	16000	14000

Pre-1986 dealer samples

Exc.	V.G.	Fair
N/A	N/A	N/A

Browning .30 Aircraft M1918

This was a modified M1917 water-cooled gun to air-cooled for
aircraft use. The water jacket was removed and replaced with
a slotted barrel jacket and spade grips. This model is referred
to as the M1918M1.

Browning Model 1917A1 • Robert G. Segel collection

Browning Model 1917 (Westinghouse) (The ID number on the side plate is a
Numrich Arms registered serial number, not an original factory Model 1917
number) • Courtesy private NFA collection, Paul Goodwin photo

Browning .30 Aircraft M1918 Fixed

As above but made as new in the same configuration with spade grips.

Browning .30 Aircraft M1919 Flexible

Same as M1918 but newly made with spade grips.

Browning M1919 A1

First utilized in 1931, this gun was a M1919 tank gun modified for ground use. It was fitted with a removable butt with a hand grip under the receiver. The barrel jacket was slotted. The front sight was mounted on the front of the receiver. Chambered for the .30-06 cartridge. Barrel length is 18". Fed with a 250-round cloth belt. Cycle rate of about 600 rounds per minute. Weight is about 40 lbs. with tripod.

Browning M1919 A2

Introduced in 1931, this gun was intended for cavalry use. The front sight was mounted on the barrel jacket. There was no butt stock. The gun was issued with the M2 tripod. Otherwise, this model is an improved M1919A1.

Browning M1919 A3

There were 72 trial samples built. This gun was essentially a M1919A2 with the front sight moved back to the receiver.

Browning M1919 A4

This air-cooled gun is chambered for the .30-06 cartridge and fitted with a 23.8" barrel. It has a rate of fire of 500 rounds per minute and is fed with a cloth belt. Weight is about 31 lbs. Marked "BROWNING M1919A4 US CAL .30" on the left side of the receiver. First produced in 1934, it is still in use today. There were a number of earlier variations of this model beginning with the M1919 aircraft gun and several improvements leading to the A4 version.

The Model 1919 was used in WWII as an infantry weapon, tank gun, and even in aircraft (M2). It has seen service all over the world in untold conflicts. Many arms experts think of the A4 version as the definitive .30 caliber machine gun.

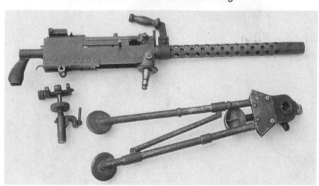

Courtesy Richard M. Kumor, Sr.

Pre-1968
Exc.	V.G.	Fair
25000	22500	20000

Pre-1986 conversions
(Non-martial current U.S. manufacture)
Exc.	V.G.	Fair
15000	12500	11000

Pre-1986 dealer samples
Exc.	V.G.	Fair
12000	11000	10000

Browning M1919 A5

This gun is an modified version of the M1919A4 for use with the M3 light tank. It was fitted with a special bolt retracting slide. Weight is about 30 lbs.

Browning M1919 A6

This model is a M1919 A4 fitted with a shoulder stock, flash hider, and bipod. Its weight is 32 lbs. Produced from 1943 to

1954. Marked "US INSP BROWNING MACHINE GUN US CAL 30" on the left side of the receiver.

Browning Model 1919A6 • Robert G. Segel collection

Pre-1968
Exc.	V.G.	Fair
25000	22500	20000

Pre-1986 conversions
(Non-martial current U.S. manufacture)
Exc.	V.G.	Fair
15000	12500	10000

Pre-1986 dealer samples
Exc.	V.G.	Fair
12000	11000	9000

Browning .30 Aircraft M2

This gun was designed for airplane use in 1931. Its rate of fire is higher than the ground gun version: 1,000 to 1,200 rounds per minute. Chambered primarily for the .30-06 cartridge but some were chambered for the .303 British round for that country's use. The gun is fed from either the left or right side as determined by the situation. It was originally designed in two configurations; as a flexible gun (for an observer) with hand grips and hand trigger or as a fixed or wing type with a back plate without hand grips. The recoil buffer in the flexible type is horizontal while the fixed gun has a vertical type buffer. Weight is about 21 lbs. Barrel length is 23.9".

Browning M2 machine gun (tripod used for photo purposes) • Courtesy Robert G. Segel

Pre-1968
Exc.	V.G.	Fair
22000	20000	18500

Pre-1986 conversions
(Non-martial current U.S. manufacture)
Exc.	V.G.	Fair
17000	15000	12500

Pre-1986 dealer samples
Exc.	V.G.	Fair
10000	8000	7000

Browning Tank M37

This gun is a version of the M1919A4 adopted for tank use. Feed mechanism was designed to be used from either side.

Pre-1968
Exc.	V.G.	Fair
25000	22500	20000

Pre-1986 conversions
(Non-martial current U.S. manufacture)

Exc.	V.G.	Fair
17000	15000	12500

Pre-1986 dealer samples

Exc.	V.G.	Fair
10000	8000	7000

MG 38

Similar in appearance to the Model 1917 (water cooled) but with several modifications such as an improved bolt handle. The MG 38 is fitted with a pistol grip back plate while the MG 38B has a double grip (spade type) black plate. Fed from a 250-round belt. Weight of MG 38 is about 35 lbs, while the MG 38B weighs about 36.5 lbs. Barrel length is 24". This gun was utilized for several different purposes and therefore has different tripods depending on the application. Rate of fire is between 400 and 650 rounds per minute.

Courtesy Robert E. Naess

Model 1924

A commercial version of the Model 1917. Some interior modifications.

Model 1928

A commercial version of the Model 1917 with interior modifications.

Pre-1968

Exc.	V.G.	Fair
35000	32500	30000

Pre-1986 conversions
(Non-martial current U.S. manufacture)

Exc.	V.G.	Fair
16000	14000	12000

Pre-1986 dealer samples

Exc.	V.G.	Fair
12000	11000	10000

MG 40

This is the commercial version of the M2 .30 caliber aircraft gun.

Pre-1968

Exc.	V.G.	Fair
22000	20000	18500

Pre-1986 conversions
(Non-martial current U.S. manufacture)

Exc.	V.G.	Fair
17000	15000	12500

A Browning M2HB by Ramo Manufacturing sold at auction for $23,000. Complete with T&E, tripod, tools, and manual. Condition is 98 percent original finish.
Greg Martin Auctions, November 2004

Pre-1986 dealer samples

Exc.	V.G.	Fair
10000	8000	7000

Browning .50 M1921

Introduced in 1925, this heavy machine gun is water cooled and recoil operated. Chambered for the .50 Browning cartridge. Rate of fire is about 450 rounds per minute. Barrel length is 36". Fed by a cloth belt. Weight of gun is 66 lbs.

Browning .50 M1921 A1

An improved version of the M1921 with a compound leverage cocking handle.

Browning .50 M2

Introduced in 1933, this gun is an improved version of the M1921 with a water jacket that extends past the muzzle. Fitted with spade grips and fed from either side. Early guns had a 36" barrels later guns were fitted with a 45" barrel. Intended for anti-aircraft use with a special mount for that purpose. Weight of gun was 100 lbs. while the tripod weighed about 375 lbs. Cycle rate is about 650 rounds per minute. Fed by a 110-round metal link belt.

Browning M2/M2HB .50

This is an air-cooled .50 caliber machine first produced in 1933. It has a 44.5" barrel and weighs about 84 lbs. Its rate of fire is 500 rounds per minute. It is belt fed. Marked "BROWNING MACHINE GUN CAL 50 M2" on the left side of the receiver. Approximately three million were produced. The gun was produced by Colt, FN, Ramo, Saco, and Winchester.

It is one of the most widely used and successful heavy machines ever produced. Besides being utilized as an aircraft, ground and vehicle weapon, the M2 is also used as an antiaircraft gun in single, twin, and four-barrel configurations. The M2 was additionally configured as a water-cooled gun for sustained fire. The commercial designation for this model was the MG 52A. Widely used throughout the world and is still in use today and still in production in the UK, USA, and Belgium.

The .50 caliber cartridge was first adopted in 1923 after extensive research by John M. Browning, Winchester, and Colt. The cartridge, like many with military applications, has a wide variety of variations.

Pre-1968

Exc.	V.G.	Fair
30000	27500	25000

Pre-1986 conversions
(Non-martial current U.S. manufacture)

Exc.	V.G.	Fair
25000	22500	20000

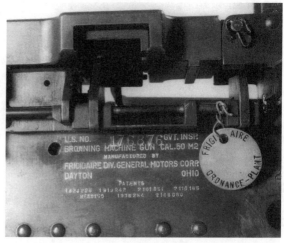

Browning M2 water-cooled anti-aircraft gun • Robert G. Segel collection

Pre-1986 dealer samples

Exc.	V.G.	Fair
N/A	N/A	N/A

NOTE: For original M2 water-cooled guns add $10,000 to pre-1968 prices.

Browning Automatic Rifle (BAR)

This is gas-operated machine gun chambered for the .30-06 cartridge. Fitted with a 23.8" barrel and a 20-round magazine, it weighs about 16 lbs. Its rate of fire is 500 rounds per minute. Marked "BROWNING BAR M1918 CAL 30" on receiver it was produced from 1917 until 1945, but saw service in the Korean War.

This Browning-designed rifle was built by Colt, Marlin, and Winchester. It has several variations from the original M1918 design. About 50,000 Model 1918 BARs saw service in Europe during World War I. The M1918A1 was first built in 1927 and has the buttplate hinged shoulder support. The bipod has spiked feet and is attached to the gas cylinder. It too is select fire. Weight for the M1918A1 is 18.5 lbs. The M1918 A2 was first built in 1932 and is fitted with a bipod with skid feet attached to the flash hider. There is a monopod beneath the buttstock. The rear sight is from a Browning M1919A4 machine gun and is adjustable for windage. This version has a rate of fire regulator that sets the rate between 450 and 650 rounds per minute. Weight for this variation is 19.5 lbs. During World War II approximately 188,000 Model 1918A2 BARs were produced. The last version is called the M1922 and was built in limited numbers. It is similar to the M1918 but with a heavy finned barrel. The bipod is attached to the barrel. Barrel length is 18" with rate of fire of 550 rounds per minute.

Photo courtesy Jim Thompson

SNAP SHOT
BAR (BROWNING AUTOMATIC RIFLE)

The Browning Automatic Rifle was developed by John Moses Browning in 1917. Designated the M1918 Caliber 30, it was intended for use in the World War I. It is a gas-operated machine gun, chambered for the same .30-06 cartridge that was used in both the 1903 Springfield and US Model 1917 rifles. It has a 24-inch barrel, uses a 20-round detachable magazine, and the 1918 weighs 16 pounds. It has a cyclic rate of approximately 500 rounds per minute. In 1927, the 1918A1 was brought out with a hinged shoulder support added to the buttplate and a bipod with spiked feet attached to the gas cylinder, and was capable of selective fire. These additions brought the 1918A1 up to 18.5 pounds. In 1932, the BAR was reconfigured to the 1918A2. A bipod with skid type feet, attached to the flash hider, replaced the first bipod. A monopod was added under the buttstock, and the rear sight from a 1919A4 Browning machine gun, adjustable for windage, was added. Weight of this variation was 19.5 pounds, and it was full automatic only, with a rate of fire selector for slow (300-450 rpm) or fast (500-650 rpm) fire. The last version built was the M1922. It had a finned, 18-inch barrel, with a bipod attached to the barrel and a cyclic rate of 550 rounds per minute. This variation was produced in very limited numbers. The BAR served in both the Army and the Marines, but was used differently. The U.S. Army assigned one BAR to each 9-man squad, whereas the Marines had three BAR rifles in each squad, with three men detailed to each weapon. A bandoleer of ammunition consisted of 12 20-round box magazines of ammunition for the BAR. Usually a robust, dependable member of the squad was picked to carry the BAR, due to its weight as well as the psychological advantage in a fire fight.

Charlie Cutshaw

Browning Automatic Rifle cutaway with markings • Paul Goodwin photo

Marine Raider with his BAR, 1942 • Courtesy Blake Stevens, *Rock in a Hard Place*, Collector Grade Publications

Pre-1968

Exc.	V.G.	Fair
30000	28000	26000

Pre-1986 conversions

Exc.	V.G.	Fair
22500	20000	18000

Pre-1986 Dealer samples

Exc.	V.G.	Fair
17500	15000	12000

Browning BAR in action, January 30, 1951, Korean front • U.S. Army photograph

Johnson M1941 & 1944

Chambered for the .30-06 cartridge, the Model 1941 was fitted with a wooden buttstock while the Model 1944 had a metal stock. Barrel length was 21.8". The M1941 had a rate of fire of 600 rounds while the M1944 had an adjustable rate of fire between 200 and 900 rounds per minute. Fed by a side mounted 20-box magazine. Weight is about 14 lbs. Produced for the Marine Corps until 1945. Marked "LIGHT MACHINE GUN JOHNSON AUTOMATICS MODEL OF 1941" above the magazine housing. About 10,000 Model 1941 guns were built.

This is an interesting model because it fires from an open bolt for full auto fire and a closed bolt for single shots. The M1941 was built by Cranston & Johnson and the M1944 was built by Johnson.

Johnson Model 1941

Pre-1968

Exc.	V.G.	Fair
25000	22500	20000

Pre-1986 conversions

Exc.	V.G.	Fair
N/A	N/A	N/A

Pre-1986 dealer samples

Exc.	V.G.	Fair
N/A	N/A	N/A

Stoner Model 63/63A

Developed in 1963 as a further evolution to the Model 63 with an improved stainless steel gas system and different style safety per U.S. Marine Corp specifications. This machine gun is chambered for the 5.56x45mm cartridge. It has an overall length of 40.24", a barrel length of 21", and a weight of approximately 11 lbs. Its rate of fire is 700 rounds per minute. It can function as a belt feed gun or can be fed by a top mounted magazine. It was used by both the U.S. Navy and Marine Corps during the Vietnam conflict. Production stopped in the early 1970s. The gun was produced by Cadillac Gage Co.

NOTE: This model is really a weapons system that is capable of a number of different configurations from carbine to machine gun. Also note that Model 63 components will not always interchange with Model 63A guns.

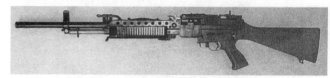

Stoner Model 63A • Photo courtesy private NFA collection

Pre-1968 (Very rare, less than 6 known)

Exc.	V.G.	Fair
65000	60000	55000

Pre-1986 conversions (Non-martial current U.S. manufacture)

Exc.	V.G.	Fair
50000	45000	40000

Pre-1986 dealer samples

Exc.	V.G.	Fair
35000	30000	25000

NOTE: Deduct 33 percent for Stoner Model 63. There are more Model 63s availabe (transferable) than Model 63As.

U.S. M60

Chambered for the 7.62x51mm cartridge, this machine gun entered U.S. service in the late 1950s. It was fitted with a 22" barrel and a rate of fire of 550 rounds per minute using a

Johnson Model 1944 • Courtesy private NFA collection, Paul Goodwin photo

Stoner Model 63 Carbine • Courtesy West Point Museum,
Paul Goodwin photo

disintegrating link belt system. The weight of the gun is 24.4 lbs. Used extensively by U.S. forces in Vietnam. Still in production and still in service with U.S. forces (Marine Corp) and many others around the world. The early M60 guns were built by Bridge & Inland.

Pre-1986 OEM/Maremont manufacture

Exc.	V.G.	Fair
35000	32500	30000

U.S. Marines with M60 in Vietnam

Pre-1986 conversions

Exc.	V.G.	Fair
25000	22500	20000

Pre-1986 dealer samples

Exc.	V.G.	Fair
18000	16500	15000

U.S. M60E3

This is an improved version of the M60 with a lightweight shorter 17" barrel. The forearm is replaced with a forward pistol grip with heat shield. The feed system has been modified to allow the cover to be closed when the bolt is forward. The gas system has been modified as well. Weight has been reduced to about 18 lbs. This model was in service with the U.S. Marine Corp, Navy, and Air Force. Built by both Maremont and Saco.

M60-E3 • Photo courtesy private NFA collection

Armalite AR-10 • Courtesy West Point Museum,
Paul Goodwin photo

Pre-1986 OEM/Maremont manufacture

Exc.	V.G.	Fair
40000	35000	32500

Armalite AR-10

Chambered for the 7.62x51mm cartridge, this select fire machine gun was fitted with a 19.8" barrel and had a 20-round magazine. Rate of fire is 700 rounds per minute. Weight is 9 lbs. Marked "ARMALITE AR10 MANUFACTURED BY AL NEDERLAND" on left side of magazine housing. Produced from 1958 to 1961. This gun was adopted by Burma, Portugal, Nicaragua, and Sudan. It was produced in limited numbers.

Pre-1968 (Very rare)

Exc.	V.G.	Fair
20000	17500	15000

Pre-1986 conversions

Exc.	V.G.	Fair
18000	16000	14000

Pre-1986 dealer samples

Exc.	V.G.	Fair
8000	7000	6000

Armalite AR-15

Introduced in 1957, this select fire rifle was fitted with a plastic butt and handguard. The rear sight also acted as a carry handle. The cocking handle was located at the rear of the receiver. The 20" barrel was fitted with a flash hider. It was a gas operated mechanism with rotating bolt. This design eventually became the U.S. military M16 rifle. Weight is about 6.25 lbs. Rate of fire was about 800 rounds per minute.

Pre-1968

Exc.	V.G.	Fair
20000	18000	16000

Pre-1986 conversions

Exc.	V.G.	Fair
18000	16000	14000

Pre-1986 dealer samples

Exc.	V.G.	Fair
N/A	N/A	N/A

Armalite AR-18

First produced in 1964 and chambered for the 5.56x45mm cartridge. Side-hinged plastic butt stock. Gas operated and select fire. Rate of fire is about 800 rounds per minute. Barrel length is 18.25". Weight is about 7 lbs. Magazine capacity is 20, 30, or 40 round detachable magazines. Designed to be a less expensive alternative to the AR-15. Built by ArmaLite. Rare.

Pre-1968 (Very rare)

Exc.	V.G.	Fair
20000	17500	15000

Pre-1986 conversions

Exc.	V.G.	Fair
15000	12500	11000

Pre-1986 dealer samples

Exc.	V.G.	Fair
12000	11000	10000

Colt/Marlin Model 1914/1915

This was a Browning design that was first produced in 1895. Nicknamed the "Potato Digger" because of its swinging arm bolt driver. It was air cooled and fired a variety of calibers both for the military and commercial sales. The Model 1914 was converted to fire the .30-06 cartridge. Rate of fire was about 450 rounds per minute. Barrel length was 28". Belt-fed by 250-round cloth belt. The Model 1915 had cooling fins added to the barrel. The gun was built from 1916 to 1919.

Canadian soldiers on the firing line with the "Potato Digger" • Robert G. Segel collection

Marlin Model 1914 • Paul Goodwin photo

Pre-1968

Exc.	V.G.	Fair
25000	22500	20000

Pre-1986 conversions

Exc.	V.G.	Fair
18000	16000	14000

Pre-1986 dealer samples

Exc.	V.G.	Fair
N/A	N/A	N/A

Robert G. Segel collection

Marlin Model 1917

This model is an improved Potato Digger with a gas pistol and cylinder fitted underneath the barrel. Chambered for the .30-06 cartridge. Designed for use in aircraft with long finned aluminum radiator around the barrel, and in tanks with a heavy armored barrel jacket. Barrel length is 28". Fed by a 250-round cloth belt with a rate of fire of approximately 600-rounds per minute. Weight is about 22 lbs.

Pre-1968

Exc.	V.G.	Fair
15000	12500	11000

Pre-1986 conversions

Exc.	V.G.	Fair
12000	10000	9000

Pre-1986 dealer samples

Exc.	V.G.	Fair
N/A	N/A	N/A

Savage-Lewis Model 1917

This a .30-06 caliber Lewis gun made by Savage during World War I. About 6,000 of these guns were chambered for the .30-06 caliber cartridge and used by the U.S. Marines and Navy until World War II. The U.S. Army purchased 2,500 of the guns but most of these Army guns were used for training purposes. See *Great Britain, Machine Guns, Lewis 0.303 in., Mark I.*

Pre-1968

Exc.	V.G.	Fair
30000	27500	25000

Pre-1986 conversions

Exc.	V.G.	Fair
18000	16000	14000

Pre-1986 dealer samples

Exc.	V.G.	Fair
N/A	N/A	N/A

Colt-Vickers Model 1915

This gun is similar to the British Vickers but built by Colt in Hartford, CT. Many of these Colt Model 1915 guns were rebuilt aircraft guns. About 12,000 were produced by Colt during the period 1915 to 1918 but few of these were original Colt-built ground guns and many of those were destroyed after the war. Therefore, original Colt-Vickers ground guns are very rare and quite desirable. See also *Great Britain, Machine Guns, Vickers.*

Pre-1968 (original Colt ground gun)

Exc.	V.G.	Fair
27000	25000	22000

Pre-1968 (Colt rebuilt aircraft gun)

Exc.	V.G.	Fair
17000	15000	13000

Marlin Model 1917 Tank Gun • Courtesy private NFA collection, Paul Goodwin photo

Pre-1986 conversions

Exc.	V.G.	Fair
17000	15000	13000

Savage-Lewis Gun • Robert G. Segel collection

Colt LMG (RO-750)

Colt Vickers Model 1915 • Robert G. Segel collection

Pre-1986 dealer samples
Exc.	V.G.	Fair
N/A	N/A	N/A

Colt LMG (RO-750)

First introduced in early 1986, this M16A2 light machine gun was designed as a squad automatic weapon (SAW). SAWs are designed to provide a more sustained fire capability than the standard M16 rifle. Similar in appearance to the M16A2 rifle, this model features a 20" heavy hammer forged barrel upper made by Diemaco with square handguard and vertical handgrip. The lower receiver fires from an open bolt full auto

only and is marked, "SAFE AND FIRE." The fixed stock houses a hydraulic buffer and special spring to reduce the rate of fire to about 650 rounds per minute. Weight is 12.75 lbs. Fed by a standard 30-round M16 magazine or other high capacity devices such as the 100 round Beta C magazine. In use by the U.S. Marine Corp. and other military forces in Central and South America and the Middle East. The Colt LMG was also utilized by the Canadian forces supplied by Colt licensee Diemaco of Canada. Still in production, but under the reintroduced name of Colt Automatic Rifle with changes to the bipod, removal of the front carry handle, and improvements in the handguard heat shield as well as a flat top upper. It is estimated by knowledgeable sources that there are less than 20 transferable examples in this country.

Pre-1968
Exc.	V.G.	Fair
N/A	N/A	N/A

Pre-1986 OEM (Very rare)
Exc.	V.G.	Fair
22500	20000	18000

Pre-1986 dealer samples
Exc.	V.G.	Fair
N/A	N/A	N/A

Colt Vickers Model 1915 with markings • Paul Goodwin photo

YUGOSLAVIA-SERBIA

Yugoslavian-Serbian Military Conflicts, 1870-Present

Once part of Turkey, then an autonomous state, Serbia became a kingdom in 1882. After the Balkan Wars of 1912 and 1913, Serbia emerged as a Balkan power. The assassination of Austrian Archduke Francis Ferdinand by a Serbian nationalist precipitated World War I when Austria declared war on Serbia. After the war, Serbia became part of what is now Yugoslavia. During World War II, Serbia allied itself with the Germans. After the war, Serbia became a republic of Yugoslavia in 1946. In the early 1990s Serbia wanted greater independence from Yugoslavia with the result of war in that region between Bosnia, Croatia, and Yugoslavia. The area is still unsettled.

Yugoslavia's existence began after World War I when it officially became identified as Yugoslavia in 1929. This period was marked by regional tensions and border disputes. In 1939, Yugoslavia aligned itself with the axis powers. The country was invaded by Germany in 1941 and partisan forces led by Marshal Tito battled the Germans and then each other in a civil war to determine control of the country after the Germans were driven out in 1944. In 1945, Tito came to power and ruled until his death in 1980. In 1990, the communist party ceded control with Serbian president Milosevic eventually coming to power. In 1995, Serbia, Croatia, and Bosnia signed a treaty ending its conflict.

NOTE: In the 1870s, military arms were produced at Kragushevat, the national arsenal in Serbia. In the 1920s, it was often referred to as Voini Techiki Zavod. This factory was destroyed during World War II. Production of weapons since World War II is at the state arms factory of Zavodi Crena Zastava, Kragujevac, often shortened to "ZCZ." After 1990, the name was changed to Zastava Arms.

HANDGUNS

At the end of World War I, Yugoslavia acquired a large number of Austrian Model 12 Steyr pistols in 9mm. The Yugoslavians have also used the FN-built M1935 pistol in 9x19 caliber.

Model 1875

This is a double action solid frame with fixed cylinder and mechanical rod ejection. Cylinder holds 6 rounds and is chambered for the 11mm cartridge. Checkered wood grips with lanyard loop. Octagon barrel is 6.2" long. Built by Auguste Francotte in Liege, Belgium. In use from 1875 to 1919.

Courtesy Geschichte und Technik der europaischen Militarrevolver, Journal-Verlag Schwend GmbH with permission

Exc.	V.G.	Good	Fair	Poor
1100	700	450	250	125

Model 1876

This model is built on a modified Lefaucheux-Chaineux solid frame with swing-out cylinder. The non-fluted cylinder is chambered for the 11mm cartridge. The half-round half-octagon barrel is 4.4". Checkered wood grips with lanyard loop. Built by Manufacture d'Ares, St. Etienne, France. In service with the Serbian army from 1876 to 1919.

Courtesy Geschichte und Technik der europaischen Militarrevolver, Journal-Verlag Schwend GmbH with permission

Exc.	V.G.	Good	Fair	Poor
950	600	425	250	125

Model 1891

Built on the Nagant-Model 1887 frame, this double action model is chambered for the 7.5mm cartridge. Fluted cylinder. The 4.5" barrel is 3/4 octagon and 1/4 round. Checkered grips with lanyard loop. Built by the Nagant brothers in Liege, Belgium. The Serbian army used this revolver from 1891 to 1945. Revolver has cyrillic markings on the frame.

Courtesy Geschichte und Technik der europaischen Militarrevolver, Journal-Verlag Schwend GmbH with permission

Exc.	V.G.	Good	Fair	Poor
2000	1000	500	350	225

Model 1898

This revolver is the same as the Austrian Model 1898, built by Rast & Gasser in Wien (Vienna), Austria. This model was built on the Schmidt-Galand double action solid frame with swing-out 8-round cylinder with multiple ejection. Chambered for the 8mm cartridge and fitted with a 4.5" round barrel. Checkered wooden grips with lanyard loop. Weight is about 33 oz.

Courtesy Geschichte und Technik der europaischen Militarrevolver, Journal-Verlag Schwend GmbH with permission

Exc.	V.G.	Good	Fair	Poor
750	500	300	150	100

Model 1910 FN Browning

Adopted by Serbia and used in World War I. Chambered for 7.65mm cartridge and fitted with a 3.5" barrel. Magazine capacity is 7 rounds. Weight about 21 oz. The principal difference between this model and its predecessors is that the recoil spring on the Model 1910 is wrapped around the barrel. This gives the slide a more graceful tubular appearance instead of the old slab-sided look. This model has the triple safety features of the 1906 Model 2nd variation and is blued with molded plastic grips. The pistol has the Yugoslavian crest on the slide and cyrillic lettering on the slide. This model was adopted by police forces and some military units around the world. It was manufactured between 1912 and 1954.

Courtesy Orvel Reichert

Exc.	V.G.	Good	Fair	Poor
450	300	200	150	125

Model 1922 FN Browning

Adopted by Yugoslavia in the 1930s in 9mm short (.380). Fitted with a 4.5" barrel and a magazine capacity of 9 rounds. Fitted with a grip safety. Yugoslavian crest on top of slide. Weight is about 25 oz. Approximately 60,000 of these pistols were produced for the Yugoslavian military between 1922 and 1925. These pistols were also used by the German occupation forces, but are not marked with German acceptance or proof stamps.

Exc.	V.G.	Good	Fair	Poor
650	500	400	300	150

Tokarev copy (Model 70)

This is a Yugoslavian copy of the Soviet TT33 in 9x19mm.

Exc.	V.G.	Good	Fair	Poor
550	400	300	200	100

Tokarev copy (Model 57)

This is a Yugoslavian copy of the Soviet Tokarev, but with a 9-round magazine in 7.62x25mm.

Exc.	V.G.	Good	Fair	Poor
1200	850	700	500	200

Tokarev copy (Model 65 for export)

This is a copy of the Tokarev in 9mm Parabellum.

Exc.	V.G.	Good	Fair	Poor
550	400	300	200	100

SUBMACHINE GUNS

Prior to World War II, Yugoslavia adopted the Erma submachine gun. After the war, Yugoslavia used the German Mp38 and Mp40. The Yugoslavian army also used British Sten guns and Beretta submachine guns as well. As a communist state, the Yugoslavians were supplied with Soviet PPDs and PPSh41 guns.

Yugoslav Model 49

Similar in appearance to the Soviet PPSh41 this gun is chambered for the 7.62 Soviet cartridge. Barrel is 10.5" and the rate of fire is 700 rounds per minute. It is fitted with a wooden stock. Weight is approximately 9.4 lbs.

Photo courtesy private NFA collection

Pre-1968

Exc.	V.G.	Fair
7500	7000	6500

Pre-1986 conversions

Exc.	V.G.	Fair
5500	4500	4000

Pre-1986 dealer samples

Exc.	V.G.	Fair
5500	4500	4000

Yugoslav Model 56

The Model 56 is chambered for the 7.62 cartridge, and is fitted with a metal folding stock and 9.8" barrel. Magazine capacity is 35 rounds. Weight is about 6.6 lbs. Rate of fire is 600 rounds per minute.

Photo courtesy private NFA collection

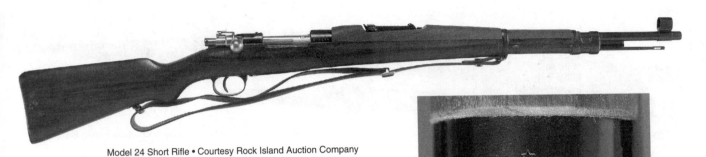

Model 24 Short Rifle • Courtesy Rock Island Auction Company

Pre-1968

Exc.	V.G.	Fair
8500	7500	6000

Pre-1986 conversions

Exc.	V.G.	Fair
6500	5500	5000

Pre-1986 dealer samples

Exc.	V.G.	Fair
3500	3200	3000

RIFLES

MAUSER

NOTE: Most of these early Mauser rifles were used by the Serbian armed forces through World War I. The Model 24 was adopted by Yugoslavia.

M78/80 Rifle

A modified G 71 rifle with 30.7" barrel with two barrel bands. Turn bolt action. Single shot in 10.15x62.8mm caliber. Weight is about 10 lbs. Fitted with a long receiver tang to support rearward bolt travel. Marked in cyrillic or German on left side rail.

Exc.	V.G.	Good	Fair	Poor
500	350	300	200	—

M1884 Koka Carbine

Chambered for 10.15mm black powder cartridge and fitted with an 18.375" barrel with turn bolt action. Tubular magazine holds 5 rounds. Full-length stock with front sling swivel on left side of barrel band and real swivel on bottom on buttstock near wrist. Weight is about 8 lbs. Marked "MODEL 1884" on right side of butt. About 4,000 were built by Mauser at its Oberndorf factory.

Exc.	V.G.	Good	Fair	Poor
500	350	300	250	200

M1899 Rifle

Produced by DWM with a full-length stock with straight grip. Barrel length is 29". Chambered for 7x57mm cartridge. Adjustable rear sight graduated to 2000 meters. Serbian crest marked on receiver ring. Magazine capacity is 5 rounds. Weight is about 9 lbs.

Exc.	V.G.	Good	Fair	Poor
450	300	250	200	100

M1899c Rifle

Chambered for either the 7.92x57mm cartridge or the 7.65x53mm cartridge and fitted with a 23.25" barrel with full-length stock with pistol grip with finger grooves. Magazine capacity is 5 rounds. Weight is about 8.5 lbs. Straight bolt handle. Marked with Serbian crest on receiver ring.

Exc.	V.G.	Good	Fair	Poor
425	275	225	150	90

M1908 Carbine

This 7x57mm caliber model is fitted with a full-length pistol grip with finger grooves. Barrel length is 17". Upper handguard extends to the lower barrel band. Bolt handle is bent. No bayonet fittings. Weight is about 6.8 lbs.

Exc.	V.G.	Good	Fair	Poor
475	325	280	210	90

M1910 Rifle

This is the standard export German Model 1910 rifle. Fitted with a 29.13" barrel and full-length stock with pistol grip. The nose cap has a bayonet lug on its bottom. Chambered for the 7x57mm cartridge. Weight is about 9 lbs. Marked with Serbian crest on receiver ring.

Exc.	V.G.	Good	Fair	Poor
425	275	200	130	80

M90 (t) Short Rifle

A Yugoslavian model that was received from the Turks following WWI. Rebarreled for 7.92x57mm and cut to 23.25". Magazine capacity is 5 rounds. Tangent rear sight graduated to 2000 meters. Weight is about 8.5 lbs.

Exc.	V.G.	Good	Fair	Poor
425	250	200	130	80

M03 (t) Short Rifle

Turkish Model 1903 converted to 7.92x57 caliber.

Exc.	V.G.	Good	Fair	Poor
400	250	200	110	70

M24 Short Rifle

This model has a full-length stock with pistol grip. Upper handguard goes from the receiver to upper barrel band. Fitted with 23.25" barrel and chambered for the 7.92x57mm cartridge. Tangent rear sight graduated to 2,000 meters. Weight is about 8.5 lbs. Yugoslavian crest over model designation on left side of receiver.

Exc.	V.G.	Good	Fair	Poor
425	275	225	100	60

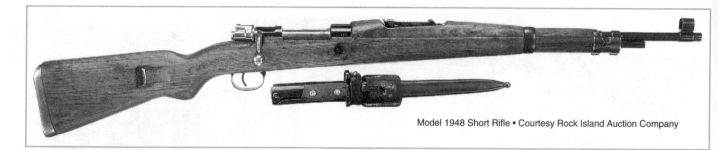

Model 1948 Short Rifle • Courtesy Rock Island Auction Company

M24 Carbine

Similar to the above model but with 16.75" barrel. Bayonet fittings are on nose cap. Weight is about 7.25 lbs.

Exc.	V.G.	Good	Fair	Poor
450	300	250	150	100

FN M30 Short Rifle

This model has a full-length stock with pistol grip. Straight bolt handle. This model is the standard FN Model 1930 configuration.

Exc.	V.G.	Good	Fair	Poor
400	225	125	70	40

FN M24 Carbine

Full stock with pistol grip and 17.5" barrel. Caliber is 7.92x57mm. Turn bolt action. Tangent leaf sight graduated to 1,400 meters. Yugoslavian crest of top of receiver ring. Weight is about 8 lbs.

Exc.	V.G.	Good	Fair	Poor
350	200	150	100	75

M1948 98k Short Rifle

This model is similar to the German 98k carbine. Almost full-length stock with pistol grip and short upper handguard. Hooded front sight with tangent leaf sight to 2000 meters. Chambered for 7.92x57mm with 5-round magazine. Weight is about 10 lbs. Communist Yugoslavian crest on receiver ring.

Exc.	V.G.	Good	Fair	Poor
350	200	100	80	50

M24/52C Short Rifle

This is an arsenal reconditioned Model 24 short rifle with communist Yugoslavian crest on the receiver ring.

Exc.	V.G.	Good	Fair	Poor
300	175	100	70	40

Model 59

This is an exact copy of the Russian SKS made under licence in Yugoslavia by Zastava. Only the markings are different.

Exc.	V.G.	Good	Fair	Poor
300	175	100	70	40

Model 59/66

This is a Yugoslavian copy of the Soviet SKS rifle. The major difference between the two is a gas shut-off valve on the gas cylinder and an integral grenade launcher fitted to the barrel.

Exc.	V.G.	Good	Fair	Poor
1500	1200	850	400	150

NOTE: Recent imports are selling in unissued condition for $200.

Model 64

This is a Yugoslavian copy of the Soviet AK-47, but with a 19.7" barrel with built-in grenade launcher sights that pivots on the barrel.

Pre-1968

Exc.	V.G.	Fair
16000	14000	12000

Pre-1986 conversions

Exc.	V.G.	Fair
N/A	N/A	N/A

Pre-1986 dealer samples

Exc.	V.G.	Fair
N/A	N/A	N/A

NOTE: Add 20 percent for folding stock.

Zastava M70B1

This Yugoslavian copy of the AK-47 rifle was first produced in 1974. It is chambered for the 7.62x39mm cartridge and is fitted with a 16.2" barrel. Its rate of fire is 650 rounds per minute. Weight is about 8 lbs. This model features a folding grenade sight behind the front sight. When raised, it cuts off the gas supply to the cylinder redirecting it to the launcher. This is the standard Yugoslav service rifle. Still in production.

Pre-1968

Exc.	V.G.	Fair
N/A	N/A	N/A

Pre-1986 conversions

Exc.	V.G.	Fair
N/A	N/A	N/A

Pre-1986 dealer samples

Exc.	V.G.	Fair
7500	6500	5500

M70B1 (Semiautomatic version)

Exc.	V.G.	Good	Fair	Poor
2350	2150	1850	900	500

M70AB2

Copy of the Soviet AKM-S. *See Russia, Rifles.*

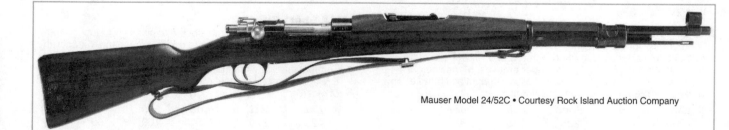

Mauser Model 24/52C • Courtesy Rock Island Auction Company

M76 Sniping Rifle

This is a copy of a Soviet AKM with a 21.5" barrel and wooden butt. The rifle is fitted with iron sights and a telescope mount. Semiautomatic operation. Chambered for the 8x57mm cartridge. Weight is about 9.5 lbs. Prices listed below are for rifles with correct matching military scope.

M76 with correct military scope • Courtesy Chuck Karwan

Exc.	V.G.	Good	Fair	Poor
2500	2000	1500	—	—

NOTE: For rifles without scope deduct $1,500. For rifles with commercial scopes but marked M76B deduct $1,000. For rifles in .308 caliber without scope deduct 70 percent.

M77B1 (Semiautomatic)

Copy of the Soviet AKM with a fixed wooden butt, straight 20-round magazine, and 16.4" barrel. Weight is about 8.5 lbs. Prices listed are for semiautomatic version.

Exc.	V.G.	Good	Fair	Poor
2250	1650	1100	800	300

M77 B1 Assault Rifle

Copy of the Soviet AKM with a fixed wooden butt, straight 20-round magazine, and 16.4" barrel. Rate of fire is about 700 rounds per minute. There are examples in this country chambered for .308 and .223. Weight is about 8.5 lbs.

NOTE: For rifles chambered for .223 add 75 percent premium.

Pre-1968

Exc.	V.G.	Fair
N/A	N/A	N/A

Pre-1986 conversions

Exc.	V.G.	Fair
N/A	N/A	N/A

Pre-1986 dealer samples

Exc.	V.G.	Fair
4500	4000	3500

MACHINE GUNS

Between the two world wars, Yugoslavia used the Schwarzlose M07/12, the Maxim 08, and the Madsen. After World War II, Yugoslavia used the MG34 and MG42 as well as some Soviet machine guns. The principal Yugoslavian machine is its own produced MG 42 designated the Model 53.

Yugoslavia also acquired several thousand U.S.-made Browning Model 1919 machine guns prior to 1964 as well as the .50 M2HB Browning heavy machine gun.

ZB30J

This was the primary light machine gun used by Yugoslavian forces prior to World War II. It is a modified copy of the Czech ZB30 gun chambered for the 7.92mm cartridge. The primary difference between the ZB30 and ZB30J is the knurled barrel ring in front of the receiver on the ZB30J.

Pre-1968

Exc.	V.G.	Fair
20000	18500	17000

Pre-1986 conversions

Exc.	V.G.	Fair
16500	15500	14000

Pre-1986 dealer samples

Exc.	V.G.	Fair
N/A	N/A	N/A

INDEX